2021

MW00848665

Greenberg's GUIDES

GORDON

LIONEL®
TRAINS® POCKET PRICE GUIDE
1901-2021

Edited by Roger Carp

Kalmbach
Media

Kalmbach Media
21027 Crossroads Circle
Waukesha, Wisconsin 53186
www.KalmbachHobbyStore.com

© 2020 Kalmbach Media
All rights reserved. This book may not be reproduced in part or in whole by
any means whether electronic or otherwise without written permission of the
publisher except for brief excerpts for review.

Published in 2020
Fortieth Edition

Manufactured in the United States of America

ISBN: 9781627008051
EISBN: 9781627008068

Front cover photo: Lionel no. 2055 small Hudson steam engine and tender,
courtesy Jack Sommerfeld, Sommerfeld's Trains & Hobbies, Butler, Wis.

Back cover photo: Lionel no. 192 operating control tower, courtesy Jack
Sommerfeld, Sommerfeld's Trains & Hobbies, Butler, Wis.

Lionel® brand name and logo used with permission.
Lionel does not set prices and valuations; these are developed independently
as third party estimates.

We constantly strive to improve Greenberg's Pocket Price Guides. If you find
missing items or detect misinformation, please contact us.
Send your comments, new information, or corrections via e-mail to books@
kalmbach.com or by mail to Lionel Pocket Price Guide Editor at the address
above.

CONTENTS

INTRODUCTION

Whether you are a longtime Lionel enthusiast or a newcomer to the toy train hobby, this guide contains the information you need to identify and evaluate thousands of items made by Lionel since 1901. Most of all, you'll have at your fingertips the most up-to-date prices for locomotives, freight cars, passenger cars, stations, tunnels, signals, track sections, transformers, and other items.

What is listed

Almost every Lionel O gauge toy train produced over the years is listed in the pages that follow.

This edition of the *Lionel Pocket Price Guide* contains information about new additions to the product line as described in Lionel catalogs, press releases, and other sources. Any additions that Lionel makes to its line after this book is printed will be reported in the next edition.

In addition, the *Lionel Pocket Price Guide* provides information about items associated with Lionel yet not mentioned in its catalogs. These uncataloged or promotional items include unique models and specially decorated locomotives and cars that Lionel produces for national and regional toy train collecting and operating groups, museums, local railroad clubs, and other customers.

When to consult this guide

Many readers of the *Lionel Pocket Price Guide* use it after the fact. They already have some trains and accessories and now want to identify and evaluate those items. Maybe someone lucked upon a bridge at a garage sale and wants to know whether it's a 300 Hellgate or a 314 deck girder type. Somebody else needs to provide his or her insurance agent with a complete list of O gauge locomotives that includes their conditions and current values. This guide contains the information needed to identify that bridge as well as determining present values for that engine roster.

In addition, the *Lionel Pocket Price Guide* can help you think about what to acquire in the future. That's really when the fun begins! You just have to spend some time considering how you want to approach the hobby. Collect, operate, or both? Prewar, postwar, or modern? Particular types of locomotives or cars? Favorite railroads? Promotional items?

Once you have a general idea of how to enjoy this hobby, you can make informed decisions about which trains you want.

UNDERSTANDING VALUES

The values presented here are an averaged reflection of prices for items bought and sold across the country during the year prior to the publication of this edition. These values are offered as guidelines and should be viewed as starting points that buyers and sellers can use to begin informed and reasonable negotiations.

In a listing for a steam locomotive, the value includes a tender, even if the tender is not listed in the description. The value of steam locomotives, particularly prewar items, may be affected significantly by the type of tender included.

Values for individual items may differ from what is listed in this price guide due to a few key factors. Where collectible trains are scarce and demand outruns supply, actual values may exceed what is shown. Values may also rise where certain items are especially popular, often because of their road names. And as with all collectibles, national and local economic conditions will impact values, which tend to drop when times are tough and demand falls.

Original packaging

Items in Like New or better condition require their original packaging to maintain their high level of value. The values given for items in Good and Excellent condition are not based on the expectation that a box and other associated items are present.

Items that do have their original packaging, especially if it is complete and undamaged, command a premium among collectors of prewar and postwar trains. No hard-and-fast rules can be stated as to how much higher their value is over the same items in Excellent condition. Generally speaking, though, boxed items in Like New condition are valued about 50 percent above the same item without a box.

Using the values

The values listed are what a consumer would pay—more or less—to get a particular item in a specific condition. One collector selling that item to another would probably ask the stated value and expect to get something close to it.

However, someone selling that same item to a person or business that intends to resell it (a train dealer) is unlikely to receive the stated value. Experience shows that sellers get about half the amount. Dealers offer less so they can earn a profit when reselling an item.

When buying or selling a toy train, you should learn more about it. Start by consulting this price guide and then look for more about it in a reference guide or website on toy trains. You can also ask more experienced hobbyists for their opinion about the item's condition and value.

FINDING A PRODUCT

The Lionel Pocket Price Guide has been divided into seven major sections.

Section 1: Prewar 1901–1942

Section 1 of the *Lionel Pocket Price Guide* is devoted to the prewar period. The entries cover just about every train, accessory, and transformer associated with Lionel's line during its first 42 years.

The only outfits (sets) listed are those of articulated streamlined trains that consist of a powered unit and attached unpowered cars.

In an item's listing, the basic description specifies its gauge (the distance between the inside of the outermost rails). During this time, Lionel catalogued models in four sizes. It is noted in parentheses whether an item is 2 7/8-inch, Standard (2 1/8 inches), O (1¼ inches), or OO (¾ inches). O gauge models intended to run on tighter 27-inch-diameter track belong to Lionel's O27 gauge line and are identified as such.

Transformers, rheostats, and many accessories were not limited to a single gauge, so their descriptions do not specify a gauge.

Section 2: Postwar 1945–1969

Section 2 concentrates on the postwar period. Nearly every train and accessory (except outfits) that Lionel cataloged between 1945 and 1969 has its own listing. By this time, Lionel no longer made trains in 2 7/8-inch, Standard, or OO gauge. Instead, it offered trains that ran on track that had a diameter of either 31 inches (O gauge) or 27 inches (O27 gauge). However, the entries in this section do not distinguish between O and O27 since only a handful of locomotives and cars could operate solely on the wider curves.

Section 3: Modern Era 1970–2019

Section 3 shows the trains, accessories, transformers, and other items that Lionel has cataloged since 1970. The modern era encompasses the products of three companies: Model Products Corp. (MPC, a division of General Mills), 1970–85; Lionel Trains Inc. (LTI), 1986–95; and Lionel LLC (LLC), 1996–2020.

These incarnations of Lionel are responsible for an enormous inventory of trains, rolling stock, transformers, and accessories. Cataloged and uncataloged O gauge items (ranging from the near-scale Standard O to the toy-like O27) can be found within the pages of this section. All items in Section 3 are arranged according to their Lionel catalog number (omitting the numeral 6 used as a prefix). The descriptions of products made during the modern era may include information that relates to where in the product line a particular item belongs. Models derived from MPC designs have been described as traditional. Rolling stock whose dimensions and features approach scale realism may be designated as Standard O (abbreviated as std O). Locomotives equipped with TrainMaster Command Control or its successor, Legacy, are identified with the abbreviation CC.

Section 4: Lionel Corporation Tinplate

Section 4 features 800 products developed jointly by Lionel and
MTH Electric Trains since 2009. These Lionel Corporation trains and
accessories are reproductions of Lionel (and some American Flyer)
tinplate items from the prewar era. You'll find trains here that operate as
tinplate trains did prior to 1942 as well as others that have been updated
with modern features and technology, such as Proto-Sound. The retail
prices are listed for these products.

Section 5: Club Cars and Special Production

Section 5 gathers the various items, principally locomotives and
rolling stock, that Lionel has made or sponsored for different hobby
organizations, museums, and businesses since the 1970s. These
uncataloged club cars and special production items are arranged
according to the groups that offered them for sale. Those groups are
listed alphabetically; regional divisions of national organizations follow
the parent organization's listing. Within each subordinate section, items
are listed in numerical (not chronological) order, with a basic description
similar to that used for cataloged entries.

Section 6: Boxes

Over the past 25 years, original boxes and other forms of packaging have
assumed significance for some collectors. These hobbyists insist that the
trains they buy come in the boxes and have the paperwork and ancillary
pieces (inserts, instruction sheets, and envelopes) that the manufacturer
packed with them before offering them for sale.

Cardboard boxes, inserts, and assorted sheets of paper are more fragile
than die-cast metal or plastic trains. They were also deemed to be less
important to the children playing with toy trains long ago and so were
not treated with the same care. Instruction sheets were lost, and boxes
were discarded. As a result, fewer boxes and instruction sheets have
survived than have the trains and accessories that went with them. In
some cases, the box that a particular locomotive, car, or even set came in
is now valued more than the item itself. Boxes are evaluated according to
standards and conditions established by the Train Collectors Association,
similar to those developed for toy trains and accessories:

P-10 **Mint:** Brand new, complete, all original as manufactured, and
unused. Flaps appear to never have been opened, and edges are
crisp. No tears, fading, or wear marks. Contains original contents
and all applicable sealing tape, wrap, and staples.

P-9 **Store New:** Complete, all original, and unused. Box may have
merchant additions such as store stamps and price tags. Must have
appropriate inner liners.

P-8 **Like New:** Complete and all original. There is evidence of light use
and aging. Box may have notations (discrete) added since leaving the
manufacturer.

P-7 **Excellent:** Complete and all original. Box shows moderate signs of being opened and closed including edge and corner wear. All flaps must be intact.

P-6 **Very Good:** Complete and all original. Box shows signs of usage such as minor abrasions, small tears, color changes, and minor soiling. Inner liners may be missing, and inner flaps may require strengthening. The box can still safely store its original contents.

P-5 **Good:** Box shows substantial wear, and edges may be damaged. Box may have extensive color fading but no evident water damage or cardboard deterioration. Exterior flaps are present, but their connection to the box may require repair. Inner liners may be missing. With care, the box can still store contents. (Any box that has been repaired cannot be graded above P-5.)

P-4 **Fair:** Box shows heavy damage and may have been repaired. Inner flaps may be missing. Box cannot store its original contents. Water damage may be present.

Values for postwar boxes in this section are shown for Good (P-5) and Excellent (P-7) conditions.

Lionel used these box types during the postwar years:

Art Deco: Original postwar box with bold orange and blue design and lettering. It was used in 1946 and 1947.

Classic: More understated design than Art Deco. It was the main component box from 1948 through 1958. Boxes can be divided into Early (1948–49), Middle (1949–55), and Late (1956–58) Classic designs, which are marked by minor lettering changes.

Orange Perforated: This was a significant change from the Classic design. The solid orange box features white lettering and a tear-out perforated front panel. It was used in 1959 and 1960.

Orange Picture: Instead of a perforated panel, this version of the Orange Perforated box features an illustration of a steam locomotive and an F3 diesel on the front. It was used from 1961 to 1964.

Hillside Orange Picture: Similar to an Orange Picture box, it is labeled with Hillside, N.J., where Lionel's plant was located. It was used in 1965.

Cellophane: Used in 1966, this box features a clear cellophane window on the front.

Hagerstown Checkerboard: It has a Lionel checkerboard pattern and Hagerstown, Maryland, printed on end flap bottoms. The box was used in 1968.

Hillside Checkerboard: This 1969 box is the same as the Hagerstown Checkerboard box, but with Hillside, New Jersey, printed on it.

Lionel also used brown corrugated and plain white boxes.

Section 7: Sets

This section lists boxed train sets catalogued by Lionel during the postwar years, 1945–1969. When collecting sets, it is important that the sets, or outfits, contain all the items, including ancillary ones, that Lionel packed with them. These items include the locomotive (and tender if a steam engine) rolling stock, any accessories, track, transformer, instructions and other paper pieces, component boxes, and the set box.

The listings include the set's catalog number, a short description, and product numbers for the locomotives, rolling stock, and any major accessories. Sets came with O27 gauge, O gauge, or Super O track. O27 and Super O track are listed in the set's description. If no track is listed, the set came with O gauge.

Set values are listed for Excellent (C-7) condition. The presence and condition of original component boxes, set boxes, inserts and other packaging materials can have a significant effect on a set's value. The values reflect the inclusion of these materials. Values of individual set and component boxes can be found in Section 6.

Due to space constraints, not every item found in a set is listed in the description. You can find more complete information on a set's contents on various websites and in *Greenberg's Guide to Lionel Trains 1945–1969 Volume III: Catalogued Sets* by Paul Ambrose. (Although the book is out of print, it is available from booksellers on the internet.)

USING THE GUIDE

Number ↓	Description ↓	Condition ⟶	Good	Exc
2561	Vista Valley Observation Car, *59–61**		75	230 ___
X6454	NYC Boxcar, *48*			
	(A) Brown body		15	35 ___
	(B) Orange body		50	140 ___
	(C) Tan body		20	60 ___
6475	Libby's Crushed Pineapple Vat Car, *63 u*		35	90 ___

Identifying a catalog number

A Lionel catalog number is usually stamped, printed, or painted on
an item. However, some products do not contain a catalog number. In
these cases, you can match the product with its catalog number using a
comprehensive reference book or website, including Lionel.com, which
contains past and current catalogs.

Two-, three-, and four-digit numbers predominated during the prewar
(1901–42) and postwar (1945–69) periods. Four- and five-digit numbers,
and now seven digit numbers, have been most common during the
modern era (1970–2020).

On the models, catalog numbers often double as road numbers,
although sometimes separate road numbers were added.

Locating an item

Sections are arranged in numerical order of catalog numbers. Items
having one or more zeroes as placeholders are listed before those without
placeholders. For example, a 004 4-6-4 Locomotive is listed before a 4
Electric Locomotive.

In the prewar and postwar sections, some items such as transformers
and track pieces, are identified by a letter. These products follow the
numbered items.

Reading an entry

Every entry begins with the product's catalog number assigned by Lionel.
(Club and special production cars may have numbers that were assigned
by the group.)

A basic description of the model follows. It gives the type of product,
lists the name of any railroad identified with it, and includes identifying
characteristics, such as color or lettering. If the item has a road number
that differs from its catalog number, that number is shown in quotation
marks. (Most of these are seen in Section 3). Abbreviations used in the
descriptions, including those of railroad names, are listed at the back of
the price guide.

Next, you'll find the year or years during which that item was part of
Lionel's cataloged product line. The years are shown in italics. If a year
is followed by a u, this item is considered to be uncataloged. It was not

part of the cataloged line but a promotional item that Lionel made or sponsored for an outside business or group.

Entries that show an asterisk (*) after the year have had one or more reissues of the item made.

Many entries feature variations, each indicated by a separate letter (A, B, and so forth). Variations amount to slight yet noteworthy differences in appearance that distinguish models that otherwise seem identical. These differences can relate to color, lettering, and details that were added or deleted. For items having many variations, an entry may not include every variation.

An entry concludes with an indication of the value of the item for several common conditions.

Condition

Lionel enthusiasts should be familiar with the condition and grading standards established by the Train Collectors Association, which are used as the basis for evaluating the condition of toy trains and accessories:

C-10 Mint: Brand new—all original, unused, and unblemished.

C-9 Factory New: Same condition as Mint but with evidence of factory rubs or slight signs of handling, shipping, and being test run at the factory.

C-8 Like New: Complete and all original with no rust or no missing parts; may show effects of being displayed or signs of age and may have been run.

C-7 Excellent: All original and may have minute scratches and paint nicks; no rust, no missing parts, and no distortion of component parts.

C-6 Very Good: Has minor scratches, paint nicks, or minor spots of surface rust; is free of dents and may have minor parts replaced.

C-5 Good: Shows evidence of heavy use and signs of play wear—small dents, scratches, minor paint loss, and minor surface rust.

C-4 Fair: Shows evidence of heavy use—scratches and dents, moderate paint loss, missing parts, and surface rust.

C-3 Poor: Requires major body repair and is a candidate for restoration; major rust, missing parts, and heavily scratched.

C-2 Restoration: Needs to be restored.

C-1 Junk: Parts value only.

Values are listed for prewar and postwar trains in Good (C-5) and

Excellent (C-7) conditions. For modern-era trains, including special production and club cars, the values for Excellent (C-7) and Mint (C-10) are shown.

You may also see NRS listed as a value. NRS (No Reported Sales) refers to an item with limited pricing data since only a handful of these scarce items may have been reported.

Determining a model's condition

Look over a model carefully to see whether it has suffered serious damage, including warping and breaking. Then note whether any parts are missing. Feel for dents in metal and cracks in plastic. Check for areas marred by rust, mildew, or chipped paint.

The TCA condition standards will assist you in evaluating your model, such as deciding whether a prewar or postwar model falls below Good or above Excellent.

The assessment of a toy train's value is based on the expectations that it has not been modified and that all parts are present and original to it. Repainting or relettering a model seriously undermines a train's value, regardless of how beat-up and scratched it may have been before undergoing modification. Any model that has been altered should be labeled as a restoration; potential buyers deserve to be informed about how it has been modified, so they do not mistake it for an original.

A model that is missing some parts should be sold as is or have those parts replaced by identical originals. A tank car cataloged in 1935 that needs a brake wheel must have a part from 1935 put on it to be considered a true original. Adding a brake wheel from 1936 undermines the car's legitimacy as much as adding one from 2021 does.

The same rule applies to the ancillary items that came with various models. The value of a flatcar may depend largely on the miniature airplane or rocket packed with it; therefore, having a load that is a genuine original is essential to maintaining the value of that flatcar. Similarly, freight loaders must have whatever cargo came with them (coal, logs, trailers, and so forth). Reproductions should be identified as such.

NOTES

Section 1
PREWAR 1901–1942

		Good	Exc
___ **001**	4-6-4 Locomotive (OO), *38-42*	195	360
___ **1**	Bild-A-Motor (O), *28-31*	60	140
___ **1**	Trolley (std), *06-14*		
___	(A) Cream body, orange band and roof	1900	4750
___	(B) White body, blue band and roof	1750	4750
___	(C) Cream body, blue band and roof	1300	3150
___	(D) Cream body, blue band and roof, Curtis Bay	2150	5550
___	(E) Blue, cream band, blue roof	1450	3150
___ **1/111**	Trolley Trailer (std), *06-14*	1000	2700
___ **002**	4-6-4 Locomotive (OO), *39-42*	160	285
___ **2**	Bild-A-Motor (std), *28-31*	100	180
___ **2**	Trolley (std), *06-16**		
___	(A) Yellow, red band	1200	3575
___	(B) Red, yellow band	1200	2250
___ **2/200**	Trolley Trailer (std), *06-16*	1000	1800
___ **003**	4-6-4 Locomotive (OO), *39-42*		
___	(A) 003W whistling Tender	190	395
___	(B) 003T nonwhistling Tender	175	355
___ **3**	Trolley (std), *06-13*		
___	(A) Cream, orange band	1400	3100
___	(B) Cream, dark olive green band	1400	3100
___	(C) Orange, dark olive green band	1400	3100
___	(D) Dark green, cream windows	1400	3100
___	(E) Green, cream windows, Bay Shore	1650	3700
___ **3/300**	Trolley Trailer (std), *06-13*	1500	3500
___ **004**	4-6-4 Locomotive (OO), *39-42*		
___	(A) 004W whistling Tender	210	350
___	(B) 004T nonwhistling Tender	190	310
___ **4**	Electric Locomotive 0-4-0 (O), *28-32**		
___	(A) Orange, black frame	550	875
___	(B) Gray, apple green stripe	580	1050
___ **4**	Trolley (std), *06-12*		
___	(A) Cream, dark olive green band	3000	4950
___	(B) Green or olive green, cream roof	3000	4950
___ **4U**	No. 4 Kit Form (O), *28-29*	1150	1600
___ **5**	0-4-0 Locomotive, no tender, early (std), *06-07*		
___	(A) NYC & HRR	1000	1450
___	(B) Pennsylvania	1400	2300
___	(C) NYC & HRRR (3 Rs)	1250	2050
___	(D) B&O RR	1500	2400
___ **5**	0-4-0 Locomotive, tender, early Special (std), *06-09*	980	1300
___ **5**	0-4-0 Locomotive, no tender, later (std), *10-11*	750	1150
___ **5**	0-4-0 Locomotive, tender, later Special (std), *10-11*	920	1200

PREWAR 1901-1942		Good	Exc	
5/51	0-4-0 Locomotive, tender, latest (std), *12-23*	800	1100	___
6	4-4-0 Locomotive (std), *06-23*	860	1250	___
6	0-4-0 Locomotive Special (std), *08-09*	2050	2950	___
7	Steam 4-4-0 Locomotive (std), *10-23**	1850	2300	___
8	Electric Locomotive 0-4-0 (std), *25-32*			___
	(A) Maroon or mojave, brass windows and trim	130	250	___
	(B) Olive green, brass windows	155	205	___
	(C) Red, brass or cream windows	171	250	___
	(D) Peacock, orange windows	520	750	___
8	Trolley (std), *08-14**			___
	(A) Cream, orange band and roof	3000	5400	___
	(B) Dark green, cream windows	3000	5400	___
8E	Electric Locomotive 0-4-0 (std), *26-32*	50	100	___
	(A) Mojave, brass windows and trim	175	250	___
	(B) Red, brass or cream windows	150	225	___
	(C) Peacock, orange windows	370	590	___
	(D) Pea green, cream stripe	465	670	___
9	Electric Locomotive 0-4-0 (std), *29**	1200	2150	___
9	Motor Car (std), *09-12*		NRS	___
9	Trolley (std), *09*	3000	5400	___
9E	Electric Locomotive (std), *28-35**	300	750	___
	(A) 0-4-0, orange	700	1250	___
	(B) 2-4-2, two-tone green	880	1600	___
	(C) 2-4-2, gunmetal gray	860	1100	___
9U	Electric Locomotive 0-4-0 Kit (std), *28-29*	975	1975	___
10	Electric Locomotive 0-4-0 (std), *25-29**			___
	(A) Mojave, brass trim	145	215	___
	(B) Gray, brass trim	125	205	___
	(C) Peacock, brass inserts	145	205	___
	(D) Red, cream stripe	580	880	___
10	Interurban (std), *10-16*			___
	(A) Maroon	3000	5750	___
	(B) Dark olive green	1200	2150	___
10E	Electric Locomotive 0-4-0 (std), *26-30*	50	100	___
	(A) Olive green, black frame		NRS	___
	(B) Peacock, dark green or black frame	245	400	___
	(C) State brown, dark green frame	435	630	___
	(D) Gray, black frame	165	220	___
	(E) Red, cream stripe	620	890	___
011	Non derailing switches, *33-37*	18	38	___
11	Flatcar, early (std), *06-08*	150	360	___
11	Flatcar, later (std), *09-15*	45	90	___
11	Flatcar, latest (std), *16-18*	50	90	___
11	Flatcar, Lionel Corp. (std), *18-26*	50	80	___
012	Switches, pair (O), *27-33*	20	40	___
12	Gondola, early (std), *06-08*	150	360	___

PREWAR 1901-1942		Good	Exc
___ **12**	Gondola, later (std), *09-15*	50	100
___ **12**	Gondola, latest (std), *16-18*	33	70
___ **12**	Gondola, Lionel Corp. (std), *18-26*	50	70
___ **013**	012 Switches and 439 panel board, *27-33*	120	190
___ **13**	Cattle Car, early (std), *06-08*	300	450
___ **13**	Cattle Car, later (std), *09-15*	150	225
___ **13**	Cattle Car, latest (std), *16-18*	65	115
___ **13**	Cattle Car, Lionel Corp. (std), *18-26*	65	115
___ **0014**	Boxcar (OO), *38-42*		
___	(A) Yellow, Lionel Lines	80	155
___	(B) Tuscan, Pennsylvania	40	75
___ **14**	Boxcar, early (std), *06-08*	195	435
___ **14**	Boxcar, later (std), *09-15*	80	105
___ **14**	Boxcar, latest (std), *16-18*	75	105
___ **14**	Boxcar, Lionel Corp. (std), *18-26*	80	105
___ **0015**	Tank Car (OO), *38-42*		
___	(A) Silver, Sun Oil	40	90
___	(B) Black, Shell	50	83
___ **15**	Oil Car, early (std), *06-08*	200	360
___ **15**	Oil Car, later (std), *09-15*	75	115
___ **15**	Oil Car, latest (std), *16-18*	75	115
___ **15**	Oil Car, Lionel Corp. (std), *18-26*	75	115
___ **0016**	Hopper Car (OO), *38-42*		
___	(A) Gray	75	160
___	(B) Black	58	115
___ **16**	Ballast Dump Car, early (std), *06-11*	400	700
___ **16**	Ballast Dump Car, later (std), *09-15*	95	175
___ **16**	Ballast Dump Car, latest (std), *16-18*	95	175
___ **16**	Ballast Dump Car, Lionel Corp. (std), *18-26*	95	175
___ **0017**	Caboose (OO), *38-42*	40	90
___ **17**	Caboose, early (std), *06-08*	220	440
___ **17**	Caboose, later (std), *09-15*	70	135
___ **17**	Caboose, latest (std), *16-18*	75	135
___ **17**	Caboose, Lionel Corp. (std), *18-26*	50	90
___ **18**	Pullman Car (std), *08*		
___	(A) Dark olive green, nonremovable roof	700	2150
___	(B) Dark olive green, removable roof	88	215
___	(C) Yellow-orange, removable roof	315	870
___	(D) Orange, removable roof	90	205
___	(E) Mojave, removable roof	305	890
___ **18**	Pullman Car (std), *11-13*	600	900
___ **18**	Pullman Car (std), *13-15*	150	270
___ **18**	Pullman Car (std), *15-18*	150	270
___ **18**	Pullman Car (std), *18-22*	90	155
___ **18**	Pullman Car (std), *23-26*	270	530
___ **19**	Combine Car (std), *08*		

PREWAR 1901-1942		Good	Exc	
	(A) Dark olive green, nonremovable roof	1100	2600	___
	(B) Dark olive green, removable roof	80	145	___
	(C) Yellow-orange, removable roof	260	430	___
	(D) Orange, removable roof	115	205	___
	(E) Mojave, removable roof	305	890	___
19	Combine Car (std), *11-13*	600	900	___
19	Combine Car (std), *13-15*	200	270	___
19	Combine Car (std), *15-18*	200	270	___
19	Combine Car (std), *18-22*	90	155	___
19	Combine Car (std), *23-26*	265	520	___
020	90-degree Crossover (O), *15-42*	4	13	___
020X	45-degree Crossover (O), *17-42*	3	10	___
20	90-degree Crossover (std), *09-32*	4	10	___
20	Direct Current Reducer, *06*	95	195	___
20X	45-degree Crossover (std), *28-32*	5	10	___
021	Switches, pair (O), *15-37*	20	50	___
21	90-degree Crossover (std), *06*	10	20	___
21	Switches, pair (std), *15-25*	35	70	___
022	Remote Control Switches, pair (O), *38-42*	40	70	___
22	Manual Switches, pair (std), *06-25*	45	75	___
023	Bumper (O), *15-33*	15	35	___
23	Bumper (std), *06-23*	15	40	___
0024	Pennsylvania Boxcar (OO), *39-42*	45	75	___
24	Railway Station (std), *06*		NRS	___
025	Bumper (O), *28-42*	17	40	___
0025	Tank Car (OO), *39-42*			___
	(A) Black, *Shell*	40	90	___
	(B) Silver, *Sunoco*	40	80	___
25	Open Station (std), *06*		NRS	___
25	Bumper (std), *27-42*	25	45	___
26	Passenger Bridge (std), *06*	15	40	___
0027	Caboose (OO), *39-42*	40	70	___
27	Lighting Set, *11-23*	15	40	___
27	Station (std), *09-12*		NRS	___
28	Double Station with dome, *09-12*		NRS	___
29	Day Coach (std), *07-22*			___
	(A) Dark olive green, 9 windows	1500	3000	___
	(B) Maroon, 10 windows	1200	1500	___
	(C) Dark green, 10 windows	3000	4500	___
	(D) Dark olive green, 10 windows	680	1000	___
	(E) Dark green, 10 windows	450	900	___
0031	2-rail 13" Curve Track (OO), *39-42*	5	10	___
31	Combine Car (std), *21-25*			___
	(A) Maroon	70	90	___
	(B) Orange	125	195	___
	(C) Dark olive green	65	90	___

PREWAR 1901-1942			Good	Exc
____		(D) Brown	75	95
____ 0032		2-rail 12 Straight Track (OO), *39-42*	10	15
____ 32		Mail Car (std), *21-25*		
____		(A) Maroon	85	125
____		(B) Orange	120	185
____		(C) Dark olive green	65	85
____		(D) Brown	70	90
____ 32		Miniature Figures, *09-18*	95	250
____ 33		Electric Locomotive 0-6-0, early (std), *13*		
____		(A) Dark olive green, NYC in oval	105	188
____		(B) Black, NYC	320	950
____		(C) Dark olive green, NYC	440	950
____		(D) Pennsylvania RR	580	1250
____ 33		Electric Locomotive 0-4-0, later (std), *13-24*	40	150
____		(A) Dark olive green or black, NYC	105	170
____		(B) Black, lettered C&O	395	720
____		(C) Maroon, red, or peacock	340	620
____ 0034		2-rail 13 Curve Track, electrical connectors (OO), *39-42*	10	15
____ 34		Electric Locomotive 0-6-0, early (std), *12*	520	860
____ 34		Electric Locomotive 0-4-0 (std), *13*	200	385
____ 35		Pullman Car (std), *12-13*		
____		(A) Dark blue	470	900
____		(B) Dark olive green	170	235
____ 35		Pullman Car (std), *14-16*		
____		(A) Dark olive green, maroon windows	35	70
____		(B) Maroon, green windows	75	105
____		(C) Orange, maroon windows	125	195
____ 35		Pullman Car (std), *15-18*	40	70
____ 35		Pullman Car (std), *18-23*		
____		(A) Dark olive green, maroon windows	30	50
____		(B) Maroon, green windows	25	45
____		(C) Orange, maroon windows	120	210
____		(D) Brown, green windows	30	50
____ 35		Boulevard Street Lamp, 6 1/8" high, *40-42*	27	50
____ 35		Pullman Car (std), *24*	40	55
____ 35		Pullman Car (std), *25-26*	40	55
____ 36		Observation Car (std), *12-13*		
____		(A) Dark blue	315	810
____		(B) Dark olive green	145	205
____ 36		Observation Car (std), *14-16*		
____		(A) Dark olive green, maroon windows	60	95
____		(B) Maroon, green windows	50	70
____		(C) Orange, maroon windows	180	290
____		(D) Brown, green windows	50	75
____ 36		Observation Car (std), *15-18*	60	80
____ 36		Observation Car (std), *18-23*		

		Good	Exc	
	(A) Dark olive green, maroon windows	40	55	___
	(B) Maroon, green windows	40	55	___
	(C) Orange, maroon windows	130	215	___
	(D) Brown, green windows	40	55	___
36	Observation Car (std), *24*	40	55	___
36	Observation Car (std), *25-26*	40	55	___
38	Electric Locomotive 0-4-0 (std), *13-24*	40	300	___
	(A) Black	100	135	___
	(B) Red	475	680	___
	(C) Mojave or pea green	405	540	___
	(D) Dark green	270	360	___
	(E) Brown	270	315	___
	(F) Red, *cream trim*	405	540	___
	(G) Maroon	170	270	___
	(H) Gray	70	125	___
41	Accessory Contactor, *37-42*	3	9	___
042	Switches, pair (O), *38-42*	15	40	___
42	Electric Locomotive 0-4-4-0, square hood, early (std), *12**	760	1650	___
42	Electric Locomotive 0-4-4-0, round hood, later (std), *13-23*	200	600	___
	(A) Black or gray	300	510	___
	(B) Maroon	1250	2050	___
	(C) Dark gray	375	600	___
	(D) Dark green or mojave	500	800	___
	(E) Peacock	1100	1800	___
	(F) Olive or dark olive green	750	1200	___
043/43	Bild-A-Motor Gear Set, *29*	40	85	___
0044	Boxcar (OO), *39-42*	40	80	___
0044K	Boxcar Kit (OO), *39-42*	75	120	___
045	Gateman, *35-36*	15	35	___
0045	Tank Car (OO), *39-42*			___
	(A) Black, Shell	40	95	___
	(B) Silver, Sunoco	40	80	___
45	Gateman, 35-36	10	25	___
0045K	Tank Car Kit (OO), *39-42*	75	120	___
45N	Automatic Gateman (std O), *37-42*	40	85	___
0046	Hopper Car (OO), *39-42*	50	90	___
0046K	Hopper Car Kit (OO), *39-42*			___
	(A) Southern Pacific	75	135	___
	(B) Reading		NRS	___
46	Crossing Gate, *39-42*	75	120	___
0047	Caboose (OO), *39-42*	30	60	___
0047K	Caboose Kit (OO), *39-42*	75	135	___
47	Crossing Gate, *39-42*	70	140	___
48W	Whistle Station, *37-42*	20	65	___
50	Electric Locomotive 0-4-0 (std), *24*			___
	(A) Dark green or dark gray	133	250	___

| --- | --- | --- | --- |
___	(B) Maroon	315	600
___	(C) Mojave	175	345
___ 50	Cardboard Train, Cars, Accessory (O), 43*	200	360
___ 0051	7" Curve Track (OO), 39-42	5	15
___ 51	0-4-0 Locomotive, late, 8-wheel (std), 12-23	800	1150
___ 0052	7" Straight Track (OO), 39-42	10	15
___ 52	Lamp Post, 33-41	45	83
___ 53	Electric Locomotive 0-4-4-0, early (std), 12-14	1200	2450
___ 53	Electric Locomotive 0-4-0, later (std), 15-19		
___	(A) Maroon	550	950
___	(B) Mojave	670	1350
___	(C) Dark olive green	560	1150
___ 53	Electric Locomotive 0-4-0, latest (std), 20-21	200	450
___ 53	Electric Locomotive 0-6-6-0, early (std), 11		NRS
___ 53	Lamp Post, 31-42	30	50
___ 0054	7" Curve Track, electrical connectors (OO), 39-42	10	15
___ 54	Electric Locomotive 0-4-4-0, early (std), 12*	2500	4050
___ 54	Electric Locomotive 0-4-4-0, late (std), 13-23	1800	2700
___ 54	Lamp Post, 29-35	60	108
___ 56	Lamp Post, removable lens and cap, 24-42		
___	(A) Mojave	85	185
___	(B) Dark gray	50	110
___	(C) 45N green	25	45
___	(D) Pea green	30	50
___	(E) Aluminum	30	45
___	(F) Copper	60	160
___	(G) Dark green	30	45
___ 57	Lamp Post with street names, 22-42		
___	(A) Orange post, Main St. & Broadway	35	55
___	(B) Orange post, Fifth Ave. & 42nd St.	40	95
___	(C) Orange post, Broadway & 21st St.	45	90
___	(D) Orange post, Broadway, 42nd St., Fifth Ave. & 21st St.	70	130
___	(E) Yellow post, Main St. & Broadway	35	89
___ 58	Lamp Post, Green		19
___ 58	Lamp Post, 7 3/8" high, 22-42		
___	(A) Cream	28	60
___	(B) Peacock	30	60
___	(C) Silver	30	60
___	(D) Maroon	33	85
___	(E) Dark green	28	50
___	(F) Orange	30	60
___ 59	Lamp Post, 8 3/4" high, 20-36	40	100
___ 060	Telegraph Post (O), 29-42	10	25
___ 60	Telegraph Post (std), 20-28	10	25
___ 60	Electric Locomotive 0-4-0, FAO Schwartz (std), 15 u		NRS
___ 0061	7" Curve Track, tubular (OO), 38	3	10

PREWAR 1901-1942		Good	Exc	
61	Lamp Post, one globe, *14-36*	35	65	___
61	Electric Locomotive 0-4-4-0, FAO Schwartz (std), *15 u*		NRS	___
0062	7" Straight Track, tubular (OO), *38*	5	10	___
62	Semaphore, *20-32*	30	50	___
62	Electric Locomotive 0-4-0, FAO Schwartz (std), *24-32 u*		NRS	___
0063	Half Curve Track, tubular (OO), *38-42*	8	15	___
63	Semaphore, single arm, *15-21*	25	50	___
63	Lamp Post, two globes, *33-42*	135	265	___
0064	7" Curve Track, tubular, electrical connectors (OO), *38*	8	15	___
64	Lamp Post, *40-42*	35	70	___
64	Semaphore, double arm, *15-21*	30	60	___
0065	Half Straight Track, tubular (OO), *38-42*	10	15	___
65	Semaphore, one-arm, *15-26*	30	60	___
65	Whistle Controller, *35*	8	15	___
0066	5 5/8" Straight Track (OO), *38-42*	10	15	___
66	Semaphore, two-arm, *15-26*	35	70	___
66	Whistle Controller, *36-39*	5	10	___
67	Lamp Post, *15-32*	85	145	___
67	Whistle Controller, *36-39*	12	30	___
068	Warning Signal (O), *25-42*	10	25	___
69N	Electric Warning Signal (std O), *36-42*	35	70	___
0070	90-degree Crossing, *38-42*	5	10	___
70	Outfit: 62 (2), 59 (1), 68 (1), *21-32*	60	130	___
071	060 Telegraph Poles, 6 pieces (std), *24-42*	70	160	___
71	60 Telegraph Post Set, 6 pieces, *21-31*	70	160	___
0072	Remote Control Switches, pair (OO), *38-42*	155	290	___
0072L	Remote Control Switch, left hand (OO), *38-42*	50	95	___
0072R	Remote Control Switch, right hand *(OO)*	50	95	___
0074	Boxcar (OO), *39-42*	35	85	___
0075	Tank Car (OO), *39-42*	50	145	___
076	Block Signal (O), *23-28*	35	105	___
76	Warning Bell and Shack, *39-42*	53	180	___
0077	Caboose (OO), *39-42*	30	60	___
77/077	Automatic Crossing Gate, *23-35*	18	50	___
78/078	Train Signal, *24-32*	40	100	___
79	Flashing Signal, *28-42*	97	175	___
80/080	Semaphore, *26-35*	50	120	___
81	Controlling Rheostat, *27-33*	5	17	___
82/082	Semaphore, *27-35*	40	120	___
83	Flashing Traffic Signal, *27-42*	65	195	___
084	Semaphore, *28-32*	60	100	___
84	Semaphore, *27-32*	43	85	___
85	Telegraph Pole (std), *29-42*	18	30	___
86	Telegraph Poles, 6 pieces, *29-42*	60	120	___
87	Flashing Crossing Signal, *27-42*	85	300	___
88	Rheostat, *15-27*	3	10	___

PREWAR 1901-1942		Good	Exc
____ 88	Direction Controller, *33-42*	4	10
____ 89	Flagpole, *23-34*	40	75
____ 90	Flagpole, *27-42*	40	95
____ 91	Circuit Breaker, *30-42*	30	50
____ 092	Signal Tower, *23-27*	85	190
____ 92	Floodlight Tower, *31-42**	150	215
____ 93	Water Tower, *31-42*	60	110
____ 94	High Tension Tower, *32-42**	150	290
____ 95	Controlling Rheostat, *34-42*	5	15
____ 96	Coal Elevator, manual, *38-40*	165	220
____ 097	Telegraph Set (O)	45	75
____ 97	Coal Elevator, *38-42*	125	240
____ 98	Coal Bunker, *38-40*	160	320
____ 99N	Train Control Block Signal, *36-42*	45	180
____ 100	Wooden Gondola (2 7/8"), *01*		NRS
____ 100	Bridge Approaches, 2 ramps (std), *20-31*	20	40
____ 100	Electric Locomotive (2 7/8"), *03-05**	2900	5200
____ 100	Trolley (std), *10-16*		
____	(A) Blue, white windows	1300	2700
____	(B) Blue, cream windows	1850	3600
____	(C) Red, cream windows	1300	2700
____ 101	Bridge, span (104) and 2 approaches (100), *20-31*	65	120
____ 101	Summer Trolley (std), *10-13*	1300	2700
____ 102	Bridge, 2 spans (104) and 2 approaches (100), *20-31*	70	175
____ 103	Bridge (std), *13-16*	40	75
____ 103	Bridge, 3 spans (104) and 2 approaches (100), *20-31*	60	145
____ 104	Bridge Center Span (std), *20-31*	20	45
____ 104	Tunnel, papier mache (std), *09-14*	50	135
____ 105	Bridge (std), *11-14*	40	70
____ 105	Bridge Approaches, 2 ramps (O), *20-31*	50	70
____ 106	Bridge, span (110) and 2 approaches (105), *20-31*	30	65
____ 106	Rheostat, *11-14*	3	10
____ 107	DC Reducer, 110V, *23-32*		NRS
____ 108	Bridge, 2 spans (110) and 2 approaches (105), *20-31*	50	90
____ 109	Bridge, 3 spans, (110) and 2 approaches (105), *20-32*	50	115
____ 109	Tunnel, papier mache (std), *13-14*	30	70
____ 110	Bridge Center Span (O), *20-31*	10	25
____ 111	Box of 50 Bulbs, *20-31*	55	105
____ 112	Gondola, early (std), *10-12*	225	400
____ 112	Gondola, later (std), *12-16*	40	65
____ 112	Gondola, latest (std), *16-18*	40	65
____ 112	Gondola, Lionel Corp. (std), *18-26*	40	65
____ 112	Station, *31-35*	145	270
____ 113	Cattle Car, later (std), *12-16*	50	70
____ 113	Cattle Car, latest (std), *16-18*	50	70
____ 113	Cattle Car, Lionel Corp. (std), *18-26*	30	55

PREWAR 1901-1942		Good	Exc	
113	Station with light fixtures, *31-34*	150	310	___
114	Boxcar, later (std), *12-16*	50	90	___
114	Boxcar, latest (std), *16-18*	40	70	___
114	Boxcar, Lionel Corp. (std), *18-26*	40	70	___
114	Station with light fixtures, *31-34*	530	1200	___
115	Station with train control, *35-42**	185	370	___
116	Ballast Car, early and later (std), *10-16*	85	115	___
116	Ballast Car, latest (std), *16-18*	65	105	___
116	Ballast Car, Lionel Corp. (std), *18-26*	55	95	___
116	Station with train control, *35-42**	640	920	___
117	Caboose, early (std), *12*	40	75	___
117	Caboose, later (std), *12-16*	40	75	___
117	Caboose, latest (std), *16-18*	40	75	___
117	Caboose, Lionel Corp. (std), *18-26*	30	60	___
117	Station, *36-42*	125	235	___
118	Tunnel, metal, 8" long (O), *20-32*	23	60	___
118L	Tunnel, metal, lighted, 8" long, *27*	20	55	___
119	Tunnel, metal, 12 long, *20-42*	25	60	___
119L	Tunnel, metal, lighted, 12" long, *27-33*	20	55	___
120	Tunnel, metal, 17 long, *22-27*	30	75	___
120L	Tunnel, metal, lighted, 17" long, *27-42*	75	140	___
121	Station, lighted (std), *09-16*			___
	(A) 14" x 10" x 9"		NRS	___
	(B) 13" x 9" x 13"	150	300	___
121	Station (std), *20-26*	75	165	___
121X	Station (std), *17-19*	110	255	___
122	Station (std), *20-30*	80	190	___
123	Station (std), *20-23*	75	210	___
123	Tunnel, paperboard base, 18 1/2" long (O), *33-42*	105	235	___
124	Lionel City Station, *20-36**			___
	(A) Tan or gray base, *pea green roof*	90	240	___
	(B) Pea green base, *red roof*	200	360	___
125	Lionelville Station, *23-25*	80	185	___
125	Track Template, *38*	1	5	___
126	Lionelville Station, *23-36*	95	205	___
127	Lionel Town Station, *23-36*	80	160	___
128	115 Station and 129 Terrace, *35-42**	900	1900	___
128	124 Station and 129 Terrace, *31-34**	900	1900	___
129	Terrace, *28-42**	600	1100	___
130	Tunnel, 26" long (O), *20-36*	100	415	___
130L	Tunnel, lighted, 26" long, *27-33*	150	450	___
131	Corner Display, *24-28*	125	295	___
132	Corner Grass Plot, *24-28*	125	295	___
133	Heart-shaped Plot, *24-28*	125	295	___
134	Lionel City Station with stop, *37-42*	230	445	___
134	Oval-shaped Plot, *24-28*	125	300	___

	PREWAR 1901-1942	Good	Exc
___ 135	Circular Plot, *24-28*	125	295
___ 136	Large Elevation, *24-28*		NRS
___ 136	Lionelville Station with stop, *37-42*	85	180
___ 137	Station with stop, *37-42*	80	160
___ 140L	Tunnel, lighted, 37" long, *27-32*	460	1050
___ 150	Electric Locomotive 0-4-0, early (O), *17*	93	180
___ 150	Electric Locomotive 0-4-0, late (O), *18-25*		
___ 150	(A) Brown, brown or olive windows	95	150
___ 150	(B) Maroon, dark olive windows	90	135
___ 152	Electric Locomotive 0-4-0 (O), *17-27*		
___	(A) Dark green	90	135
___	(B) Gray	100	160
___	(C) Mojave	340	680
___	(D) Peacock	340	680
___ 152	Crossing Gate, *40-42*	20	40
___ 153	Block Signal, *40-42*	25	45
___ 153	Electric Locomotive 0-4-0 (O), *24-25*		
___	(A) Dark green	100	160
___	(B) Gray	100	160
___	(C) Mojave	100	160
___ 154	Electric Locomotive 0-4-0 (O), *17-23*	100	180
___ 154	Highway Signal, *40-42*		
___	(A) Black base	25	50
___	(B) Orange base	83	218
___ 155	Freight Shed, *30-42**		
___	(A) Cream base, terra cotta floor	180	320
___	(B) Ivory base, red floor	240	400
___ 156	Electric Locomotive 0-4-0 (O), *17-23*	400	720
___ 156	Station Platform, *39-42*	85	115
___ 156	Electric Locomotive 4-4-4 (O), *17-23*		
___	(A) Dark green	475	810
___	(B) Maroon	540	890
___	(C) Olive green	600	1050
___	(D) Gray	670	1200
___ 156X	Electric Locomotive 0-4-0 (O), *23-24*		
___	(A) Maroon	330	495
___	(B) Olive green	200	400
___	(C) Gray	530	710
___	(D) Brown	420	600
___ 157	Hand Truck, *30-32*	20	40
___ 158	Electric Locomotive 0-4-0 (O), *19-23*		
___	(A) Gray or red windows	75	205
___	(B) Black	95	250
___ 158	Station Set: 136 Station and 2 platforms (156), *40-42*	120	280
___ 159	Block Actuator, *40*	10	30
___ 161	Baggage Truck, *30-32**	40	80

PREWAR 1901-1942		Good	Exc	
162	Dump Truck, *30-32**	40	80	___
163	Freight Accessory Set: 2 hand trucks (157), baggage truck (161), and dump truck (162), *30-42**	220	360	___
164	Log Loader, *40-42*	160	225	___
165	Magnetic Crane, *40-42*	182	340	___
165-22	Scrap Steel with bag, *40-42*	50	125	___
165-83	Steel Blanks with bag, *40-42*	50	110	___
166	Whistle Controller, *40-42*	3	10	___
167	Whistle Controller, *40-42*	8	25	___
167X	Whistle Controller (OO), *40-42*	5	15	___
168	Magic Electrol Controller, *40-42*	25	50	___
169	Controller, *40-42*	4	18	___
170	DC Reducer, 220V, *14-38*	5	10	___
171	DC to AC Inverter, 110V, *36-42*	5	15	___
172	DC to AC Inverter, 229V, *39-42*	3	7	___
180	Pullman Car (std), *11-13*			___
	(A) Maroon body and roof	145	205	___
	(B) Brown body and roof	145	255	___
180	Pullman Car (std), *13-15*	80	160	___
180	Pullman Car (std), *15-18*	80	160	___
180	Pullman Car (std), *18-22*	80	135	___
181	Combine Car (std), *11-13*			___
	(A) Maroon, dark olive doors	145	205	___
	(B) Brown, dark olive doors	145	205	___
	(C) Yellow-orange, orange doors	350	495	___
181	Combine Car (std), *13-15*	80	160	___
181	Combine Car (std), *15-18*	80	160	___
181	Combine Car (std), *18-22*	80	135	___
182	Observation Car (std), *11-13*			___
	(A) Maroon, dark olive doors	145	205	___
	(B) Brown, dark olive doors	145	205	___
	(C) Yellow-orange, orange doors	300	495	___
182	Observation Car (std), *13-15*	80	160	___
182	Observation Car (std), *15-18*	80	160	___
182	Observation Car (std), *18-22*	80	135	___
184	Bungalow, illuminated, *23-32**	65	85	___
185	Bungalow, *23-24*	50	115	___
186	184 Bungalows, set of 5, *23-32*	195	610	___
186	Log Loader Outfit, *40-41*	130	340	___
187	185 Bungalows, set of 5, *23-24*	170	590	___
188	Elevator and Car Set, *38-41*	115	370	___
189	Villa, illuminated, *23-32**	133	225	___
190	Observation Car (std), *08*			___
	(A) Dark olive green, nonremovable roof	1150	2600	___
	(B) Dark olive green, removable roof	115	205	___
	(C) Yellow-orange, removable roof	320	620	___

			Good	Exc
____		(D) Orange, removable roof	115	205
____		(E) Mojave, removable roof	345	870
____	190	Observation Car (std), 11-13	600	900
____	190	Observation Car (std), 13-15	200	295
____	190	Observation Car (std), 15-18	200	295
____	190	Observation Car (std), 18-22	80	135
____	190	Observation Car (std), 23-26	230	475
____	191	Villa, illuminated, 23-32*	125	325
____	192	Illuminated Villa Set: 189, 191, 184 (2), 27-32	400	800
____	193	Automatic Accessory Set (O), 27-29	150	325
____	194	Automatic Accessory Set (std), 27-29	100	325
____	195	Terrace, 27-30	350	740
____	196	Accessory Set, 27	200	335
____	200	Electric Express (2 7/8"), 03-05*	4000	6300
____	200	Trailer, matches No. 2 Trolley (std), 11-16	1200	2400
____	200	Turntable (std), 28-33*	85	190
____	201	0-6-0 Locomotive (O), 40-42		
____		(A) 2201B Tender, bell	375	760
____		(B) 2201T Tender, no bell	345	690
____	202	Summer Trolley (std), 10-13		
____		(A) Electric Rapid Transit	1300	2700
____		(B) Preston St.	3250	4500
____	203	Armored 0-4-0 (O), 17-21	1100	1800
____	203	0-6-0 Locomotive (O), 40-42		
____		(A) 2203B Tender, bell	400	495
____		(B) 2203T Tender, no bell	375	550
____	204	2-4-2 Locomotive (O), 40-42 u		
____		(A) Black	55	105
____		(B) Gunmetal gray	80	165
____	205	Merchandise Containers, 3 pieces, 30-38*	130	320
____	206	Sack of Coal, 38-42	5	20
____	208	Tool Set: 6 assorted tools, 34-42*	65	150
____	0209	Barrels, wooden, 6 pieces (O), 34-42		
____		(A) Solid barrels	10	25
____		(B) 2-piece barrels	53	145
____	209	Barrels, wooden, 4 pieces (std), 34-42	10	25
____	210	Switches, pair (std), 26, 34-42	40	75
____	211	Flatcar (std), 26-40*	125	195
____	212	Gondola (std), 26-40*		
____		(A) Gray or light green	100	205
____		(B) Maroon	75	135
____	213	Cattle Car (std), 26-40*		
____		(A) Mojave, maroon roof	160	365
____		(B) Terra-cotta, pea green roof	130	290
____		(C) Cream, maroon roof	300	650
____	214	Boxcar (std), 26-40*		

		Good	Exc	
	(A) Terra-cotta, dark green roof	195	390	___
	(B) Cream body, orange roof	150	270	___
	(C) Yellow, brown roof	300	495	___
214R	Refrigerator Car (std), *29-40**			___
	(A) Ivory or white, peacock roof	325	495	___
	(B) White, light blue roof	435	790	___
215	Tank Car (std), *26-40**			___
	(A) Pea green	150	215	___
	(B) Ivory	220	360	___
	(C) Aluminum	315	720	___
216	Hopper Car (std), *26-38**			___
	(A) Dark green, brass plates	195	335	___
	(B) Dark green, nickel plates	445	1100	___
217	Caboose (std), *26-40**			___
	(A) Orange, maroon roof	250	510	___
	(B) Red, peacock roof	120	235	___
	(C) Red body and roof, ivory doors	150	320	___
217	Lighting Set, *14-23*		NRS	___
218	Dump Car (std), *26-38**	220	365	___
219	Crane Car (std), *26-40**			___
	(A) Peacock, red boom	135	255	___
	(B) Yellow, light green or red boom	270	440	___
	(C) Ivory, light green boom	270	520	___
220	Floodlight Car (std), *31-40**			___
220	(A) Terra-cotta base	225	385	___
220	(B) Green base	340	485	___
220	Switches, pair (std), *26**	25	90	___
222	Switches, pair (std), *26-32*	40	100	___
223	Switches, pair (std), *32-42*	35	120	___
224/224E	2-6-2 Locomotive (O), *38-42*			___
	(A) Black, die-cast 2224 Tender	140	255	___
	(B) Black, plastic 2224 Tender	110	195	___
	(C) Gunmetal, die-cast 2224 Tender	385	950	___
	(D) Gunmetal, sheet-metal 2689 Tender	120	210	___
225	222 Switches and 439 Panel, *29-32*	115	260	___
225/225E	2-6-2 Locomotive (O), *38-42*			___
	(A) Black, 2235 or 2245 Tender	210	370	___
	(B) Black, 2235 plastic Tender	185	320	___
	(C) Gunmetal, 2225 or 2265 Tender	210	360	___
	(D) Gunmetal, 2235 die-cast Tender	285	730	___
226/226E	2-6-4 Locomotive (O), *38-41*	275	630	___
227	0-6-0 Locomotive (O), *39-42*			___
	(A) 2227B Tender, bell	600	1250	___
	(B) 2227T Tender, no bell	510	1150	___
228	0-6-0 Locomotive (O), *39-42*			___
	(A) 2228B Tender, bell	600	1250	___

			Good	Exc
___		(B) 2228T Tender, no bell	600	1150
___ 229	2-4-2 Locomotive (O), *39-42*			
___		(A) Black or gunmetal, 2689W Tender	155	240
___		(B) Black or gunmetal, 2689T Tender	120	200
___		(C) Black, 2666W whistle Tender	155	280
___		(D) Black, 2666T nonwhistling Tender	120	200
___ 230	0-6-0 Locomotive (O), *39-42*		1100	2050
___ 231	0-6-0 Locomotive (O), *39*		1000	1800
___ 232	0-6-0 Locomotive (O), *40-42*		1000	1800
___ 233	0-6-0 Locomotive (O), *40-42*		1000	1800
___ 238	4-4-2 Locomotive (O), *39-40 u*		430	710
___ 238E	4-4-2 Locomotive (O), *36-38*			
___		(A) 265W or 2225W whistle Tender	280	345
___		(B) 265 or 2225T nonwhistling Tender	275	360
___ 248	Electric Locomotive 0-4-0 (O), *27-32*		150	240
___ 249/249E	2-4-2 Locomotive (O), *36-39*			
___		(A) Gunmetal, 265T or 265W Tender	100	270
___		(B) Black, 265W Tender	110	210
___ 250	Electric Locomotive 0-4-0, early (O), *26*		125	220
___ 250	Electric Locomotive 0-4-0, late (O), *34*			
___		(A) Yellow-orange body, terra-cotta frame	145	245
___		(B) Terra-cotta body, maroon frame	160	270
___ 250E	4-4-2 Hiawatha Locomotive (O), *35-42**		400	1100
___ 250W	Hiawatha Tender (O), *35-42**		125	250
___ 251	Electric Locomotive 0-4-0 (O), *25-32*			
___		(A) Gray body, red windows	190	340
___		(B) Red body, ivory stripe	215	410
___		(C) Red body, no ivory stripe	200	380
___ 251E	Electric Locomotive 0-4-0 (O), *27-32*			
		(A) Red body, ivory stripe	225	425
		(B) Red body, no ivory stripe	215	395
		(C) Gray, red trim	195	350
252	Electric Locomotive 0-4-0 (O), *26-32*			
		(A) Peacock or olive green	85	130
		(B) Terra-cotta or yellow-orange	113	220
252E	Electric Locomotive 0-4-0 (O), *33-35*			
		(A) Terra-cotta	145	250
		(B) Yellow-orange	125	205
253	Electric Locomotive 0-4-0 (O), *24-32*			
		(A) Maroon	180	430
		(B) Dark green	105	250
		(C) Mojave	105	235
		(D) Terra-cotta	180	430
		(E) Peacock	95	195
		(F) Red	210	475
253E	Electric Locomotive 0-4-0 (O), *31-36*			

	(A) Green	150	205	___
	(B) Terra-cotta	190	305	___
254	Electric Locomotive 0-4-0 (O), *24-32*	240	340	___
254E	Electric Locomotive 0-4-0 (O), *27-34*	180	270	___
255E	2-4-2 Locomotive (O), *35-36*	485	1000	___
256	Electric Locomotive 0-4-4-0 (O), *24-30**			___
	(A) Rubber-stamped lettering	470	1175	___
	(B) no outline around Lionel	425	770	___
	(C) Lionel Lines and No. 256 on brass	450	1050	___
257	2-4-0 Locomotive (O), *30-35 u*			___
	(A) Black tender	145	300	___
	(B) Black crackle-finish tender	240	435	___
258	2-4-0 Locomotive, early (O), *30-35 u*			___
	(A) 4-wheel 257 Tender	85	170	___
	(B) 8-wheel 258 Tender	100	195	___
258	2-4-2 Locomotive, late (O), *41 u*			___
	(A) Black	60	100	___
	(B) Gunmetal	85	135	___
259	2-4-2 Locomotive (O), *32*	70	135	___
259E	2-4-2 Locomotive (O), *33-42*	80	165	___
259T	Tender	15	30	___
260E	2-4-2 Locomotive (O), *30-35**			___
	(A) Black body, *green or black frame*	385	475	___
	(B) Dark gunmetal body and frame	440	640	___
261	2-4-2 Locomotive (O), *31*	125	210	___
261E	2-4-2 Locomotive (O), *35*	190	285	___
262	2-4-2 Locomotive (O), *31-32*	185	320	___
262E	2-4-2 Locomotive (O), *33-36*			
	(A) Gloss black, copper and brass trim	110	210	___
	(B) Satin black, nickel trim	125	260	___
263E	2-4-2 Locomotive (O), *36-39**			___
	(A) Gunmetal gray	315	610	___
	(B) 2-tone blue, from Blue Comet	415	950	___
263W	Tender, gunmetal	99	200	___
264E	2-4-2 Locomotive (O), *35-36*			___
	(A) Red, Red Comet	135	295	___
	(B) Black	220	380	___
265E	2-4-2 Locomotive (O), *35-40*			___
	(A) Black or gunmetal	170	330	___
	(B) Light blue, Blue Streak	460	800	___
265T	Tender	15	28	___
267E/W	Set: 616, 617 (2), 618, *35-41*	275	560	___
270	Bridge, 10" long (O), *31-42*	33	56	___
270	Lighting Set, *15-23*		NRS	___
271	270 Bridges, set of 2, *31-33, 35-40*	65	150	___
271	Lighting Set, *15-23*		NRS	___

PREWAR 1901-1942		Good	Exc
___ 272	270 Bridges, set of 3, *31-33, 35-40*	60	165
___ 280	Bridge, 14" long (std), *31-42*	50	115
___ 281	280 Bridges, set of 2, *31-33, 35-40*	90	205
___ 282	280 Bridges, set of 3, *31-33, 35-40*	105	265
___ 289E	2-4-2 Locomotive (O), *37 u*	120	305
___ 300	Electric Trolley Car (2 7/8"), *01-05*	2000	3600
___ 300	Hellgate Bridge (std), *28-42**		
___ 300	(A) Cream towers, green truss	800	1350
___ 300	(B) Ivory towers, aluminum truss	765	1600
___ 303	Summer Trolley, *10-13*	1500	3150
___ 308	Signs, *set of 5 (O), 40-42*	30	70
___ 309	Electric Trolley Trailer (2 7/8"), *01-05*	2500	4050
___ 309	Pullman Car (std), *26-39*		
___	(A) Maroon body and roof, mojave windows	100	160
___	(B) Mojave body and roof, maroon windows	100	160
___	(C) Light brown body, dark brown roof	120	190
___	(D) Medium blue body, dark blue roof	170	280
___	(E) Apple green body, dark green roof	170	280
___	(F) Pale blue body, silver roof	100	185
___	(G) Maroon body, terra-cotta roof	130	195
___ 310	Rails and Ties, complete section (2 7/8"), *01-02*	5	15
___ 310	Baggage Car (std), *26-39*		
___	(A) Maroon body and roof, mojave windows	100	160
___	(B) Mojave body and roof, maroon windows	85	160
___	(C) Light brown body, dark brown roof	115	185
___	(D) Medium blue body, dark blue roof	170	280
___	(E) Apple green body, dark green roof	170	280
___	(F) Pale blue body, silver roof	100	175
___ 312	Observation Car (std), *24-39*		
___	(A) Maroon body and roof, mojave windows	100	160
___	(B) Mojave body and roof, maroon windows	85	160
___	(C) Light brown body, dark brown roof	120	185
___	(D) Medium blue body, dark blue roof	170	280
___	(E) Apple green body, dark green roof	170	280
___	(F) Pale blue body, silver roof	100	175
___	(G) Maroon body, terra-cotta roof	130	195
___ 313	Bascule Bridge (O), *40-42*		
___	(A) Silver bridge	235	500
___	(B) Gray bridge	250	590
___ 314	Girder Bridge (O), *40-42*	20	40
___ 315	Illuminated Trestle Bridge (O), *40-42*	30	80
___ 316	Trestle Bridge (O), *40-42*	25	50
___ 318	Electric Locomotive 0-4-0 (std), *24-32*		
___	(A) Gray, dark gray, or mojave	150	250
___	(B) Pea green	150	250
___	(C) State brown	250	395

No.	Description	Good	Exc	
318E	Electric Locomotive 0-4-0, *26-35*			——
	(A) Gray, mojave, or pea green	150	250	——
	(B) State brown	275	440	——
	(C) Black	550	1275	——
319	Pullman Car (std), *24-27*	105	175	——
320	Baggage Car (std), *25-27*	100	175	——
320	Switch and Signal (2 7/8"), *02-05*		NRS	——
322	Observation Car (std), *24-27, 29-30 u*	100	175	——
330	90-degree Crossing (2 7/8"), *02-05*		NRS	——
332	Baggage Car (std), *26-33*			——
	(A) Red body and roof, cream doors	80	120	——
	(B) Peacock body and roof, orange doors	75	115	——
	(C) Gray body and roof, maroon doors	75	115	——
	(D) Olive green body and roof, red doors	90	145	——
	(E) State brown body, dark brown roof	190	430	——
337	Pullman Car (std), *25-32*			——
	(A) Red body and roof, cream doors	95	190	——
	(B) Mojave body and roof, maroon doors	95	190	——
	(C) Olive green body and roof, red doors	105	225	——
	(D) Olive green body and roof, maroon doors	95	190	——
	(E) Pea green body and roof, cream doors	210	500	——
338	Observation Car (std), *25-32*			——
	(A) Red body and roof, cream doors	95	190	——
	(B) Mojave body and roof, maroon doors	95	190	——
	(C) Olive green body and roof, red doors	105	225	——
	(D) Olive green body and roof, maroon doors	95	190	——
339	Pullman Car (std), *25-33*			——
339	(A) Peacock body and roof, orange doors	55	90	——
339	(B) Gray body and roof, maroon doors	55	100	——
339	(C) State brown body, dark brown roof	135	380	——
339	(D) Peacock body, dark green roof	75	130	——
339	(E) Mojave body, maroon roof and doors	145	230	——
340	Suspension Bridge (2 7/8"), *02-05**		NRS	——
341	Observation Car (std), *25-33*			——
	(A) Peacock body and roof, orange doors	50	70	——
	(B) Gray body and roof, maroon doors	50	70	——
	(C) State brown body, dark brown roof	75	160	——
	(D) Peacock body, dark green roof	65	95	——
	(E) Mojave body, maroon roof and doors	135	165	——
350	Track Bumper (2 7/8"), *02-05*	225	550	——
380	Elevated Pillars (2 7/8"), *04-05**	30	70	——
380	Electric Locomotive 0-4-0 (std), *23-27*	310	440	——
380E	Electric Locomotive 0-4-0 (std), *26-29*			——
	(A) Mojave	445	630	——
	(B) Maroon	295	400	——
	(C) Dark green	370	460	——

			Good	Exc
___	**381**	Electric Locomotive 4-4-4 (std), *28-29**	1600	2100
___	**381E**	Electric Locomotive 4-4-4 (std), *28-36**		
___		(A) State green, apple green subframe	1500	2500
___		(B) State green, red subframe	1900	3250
___	**381U**	Electric Locomotive 4-4-4 Kit (std), *28-29*	1600	4100
___	**384**	2-4-0 Locomotive (std), *30-32**	415	730
___	**384E**	2-4-0 Locomotive (std), *30-32**	425	650
___	**385E**	2-4-2 Locomotive (std), *33-39**	370	670
___	**390**	2-4-2 Locomotive (std), *29**	460	820
___	**390E**	2-4-2 Locomotive (std), *29-31**		
___		(A) Black, with or without orange stripe	460	690
___		(B) 2-tone blue, cream-orange stripe	650	1050
___		(C) 2-tone green, orange or green stripe	990	2050
___	**392E**	4-4-2 Locomotive (std), *32-39**		
___		(A) Black, 384 Tender	750	1250
___		(B) Black, large 12-wheel tender	1050	1850
___		(C) Gunmetal gray	1000	1800
___	**400**	Express Trail Car (2 7/8"), *03-05**	3500	5850
___	**400E**	4-4-4 Locomotive (std), *31-39**		
___		(A) Black	1400	2150
___		(B) Blue	1550	2350
___		(C) Gunmetal or light blue	1650	2800
___		(D) Black crackle finish	1600	3500
___	**402**	Electric Locomotive 0-4-4-0 (std), *23-27*	365	570
___	**402E**	Electric Locomotive 0-4-4-0 (std), *26-29*	345	550
___	**404**	Summer Trolley (std), *10*		NRS
___	**408E**	Electric Locomotive 0-4-4-0 (std), *27-36**		
___		(A) Apple green or mojave, red pilots	770	980
___		(B) State brown, brown pilots	2000	3000
		(C) State green, red pilots	2000	3800
	412	California Pullman Car (std), *29-35**		
		(A) Light green body, dark green roof	590	1750
		(B) Light brown body, dark brown roof	620	2100
	413	Colorado Pullman Car (std), *29-35**		
		(A) Light green body, dark green roof	590	1750
		(B) Light brown body, *dark brown roof*	620	2100
	414	Illinois Pullman Car (std), *29-35**		
		(A) Light green body, *dark green roof*	590	1750
		(B) Light brown body, *dark brown roof*	620	2050
	416	New York Observation Car (std), *29-35**		
		(A) Light green body, *dark green roof*	590	1750
		(B) Light brown body, *dark brown roof*	620	2100
	418	Pullman Car (std), *23-32**	225	320
	419	Combination (std), *23-32**	190	280
	420	Faye Pullman Car (std), *30-40**		
		(A) Brass trim	485	900

PREWAR 1901-1942		Good	Exc	
	(B) Nickel trim	500	1200	___
421	Westphal Pullman Car (std), *30-40**			___
	(A) Brass trim	500	900	___
	(B) Nickel trim	500	1200	___
422	Tempel Observation Car (std), *30-40**			___
422	(A) Brass trim	485	900	___
422	(B) Nickel trim	500	1200	___
424	Liberty Bell Pullman Car (std), *31-40**			___
	(A) Brass trim	350	530	___
	(B) Nickel trim	385	650	___
425	Stephen Girard Pullman Car (std), *31-40**			___
	(A) Brass trim	350	530	___
	(B) Nickel trim	385	650	___
426	Coral Isle Observation Car (std), *31-40**			___
	(A) Brass trim	350	530	___
	(B) Nickel trim	385	650	___
428	Pullman Car (std), *26-30**			___
	(A) Dark green body and roof	250	385	___
	(B) Orange body and roof, apple green windows	390	890	___
429	Combine Car (std), *26-30**			___
	(A) Dark green body and roof	250	385	___
	(B) Orange body and roof, apple green windows	390	890	___
430	Observation Car (std), *26-30**			___
	(A) Dark green body and roof	250	385	___
	(B) Orange body and roof, apple green windows	390	890	___
431	Diner (std), *27-32**			___
	(A) Mojave body, screw-mounted roof	350	540	___
	(B) Mojave body, hinged roof	465	720	___
	(C) Dark green body, orange windows	410	720	___
	(D) Orange body, apple green windows	410	720	___
	(E) Apple green body, red windows	410	720	___
435	Power Station, *26-38**	215	400	___
436	Power Station, *26-37**			___
	(A) Power Station plate	135	265	___
	(B) Edison Service plate	270	610	___
437	Switch Signal Tower, *26-37**	190	430	___
438	Signal Tower, *27-39**			___
	(A) Mojave base, orange house	185	325	___
	(B) Black base, white house	325	640	___
439	Panel Board, *28-42**	85	145	___
440/0440	Signal Bridge, *32-35**	180	470	___
440C	Panel Board, *32-42*	90	145	___
441	Weighing Station (std), *32-36*	495	1325	___
442	Landscaped Diner, *38-42*	120	215	___
444	Roundhouse (std), *32-35**	1350	2850	___
444-18	Roundhouse Clip, *33*		NRS	___

PREWAR 1901-1942		Good	Exc
___ **450**	Electric Locomotive 0-4-0, Macy's (O), *30 u*		
___	(A) Red, black frame	295	700
___	(B) Apple green, dark green frame	415	880
___ **450**	Set: 450, matching 605, 606 (2), *30 u*	750	1800
___ **490**	Observation Car (std), *23-32**	190	255
___ **500**	Electric Derrick Car (2 7/8"), *03-04**	5000	6750
___ **511**	Flatcar (std), *27-40*		
___	(A) Dark green	65	95
___	(B) Medium green	75	165
___ **512**	Gondola (std), *27-39*		
___	(A) Peacock	35	60
___	(B) Light green	50	95
___ **513**	Cattle Car (std), *27-38*		
___	(A) Olive green, orange roof	70	165
___	(B) Orange, pea green roof	60	110
___	(C) Cream, maroon roof	90	250
___ **514**	Boxcar (std), *29-40*		
___	(A) Cream, orange roof	90	155
___	(B) Yellow, brown roof	115	285
___ **514**	Refrigerator Car, ivory or white, peacock roof, (std), *27-28*	240	400
___ **514R**	Refrigerator Car (std), *29-40*		
___	(A) Ivory, peacock roof	140	190
___	(B) White, light blue roof	350	540
___ **515**	Tank Car (std), *27-40*		
___	(A) Terra-cotta	90	145
___	(B) Ivory	105	185
___	(C) Aluminum	90	175
___	(D) Orange, red Shell decal	340	750
___ **516**	Hopper Car (std), *28-40*		
___	(A) Red	170	240
___	(B) Red, rubber-stamped data	200	300
___	(C) Light red, nickel trim	200	325
___ **517**	Caboose (std), *27-40*		
___	(A) Pea green body, red roof	50	85
___	(B) Red body and roof	105	155
___	(C) Red body, black roof, orange windows	355	640
___ **520**	Floodlight Car (std), *31-40*		
___	(A) Terra-cotta base	110	210
___	(B) Green base	110	240
___ **529**	Pullman Car (O), *26-32*		
___	(A) Olive green body and roof	25	45
___	(B) Terra-cotta body and roof	25	60
___ **530**	Observation Car (O), *26-32*		
___	(A) Olive green body and roof	25	45
___	(B) Terra-cotta body and roof	25	60
___ **550**	Miniature Figures, boxed (std), *32-36**	175	455

| --- | --- | --- | --- | --- |
551	Engineer (std), *32*	25	45	___
552	Conductor (std), *32*	20	40	___
553	Porter with stool (std), *32*	25	50	___
554	Male Passenger (std), *32*	25	45	___
555	Female Passenger (std), *32*	25	45	___
556	Red Cap with suitcase (std), *32*	25	65	___
600	Derrick Trailer (2 7/8"), *03-04**	5000	8550	___
600	Pullman Car, early (O), *15-23*			___
	(A) Dark green	65	170	
	(B) Maroon or brown	45	85	
600	Pullman Car, late (O), *33-42*			
	(A) Light red or gray, red roof	50	90	
	(B) Light blue, aluminum roof	70	120	
601	Observation Car, late (O), *33-42*			___
	(A) Light red body and roof	50	85	
	(B) Light gray, red roof	50	90	___
	(C) Light blue body, aluminum roof	70	120	
601	Pullman Car, early (O), *15-23*	50	70	___
602	Lionel Lines Baggage Car, late (O), *33-42*			___
	(A) Light red or gray, red roof	60	110	___
	(B) Light blue, aluminum roof	90	150	
602	NYC Baggage Car (O), *15-23*	33	45	
602	Observation Car (O), *22 u*	30	45	
603	Pullman Car, early (O), *22 u*	40	70	___
603	Pullman Car, later (O), *20-25*	20	45	___
603	Pullman Car, latest (O), *31-36*			___
	(A) Light red body and roof	45	85	
	(B) Red body, black roof	35	60	___
	(C) Stephen Girard green body, dark green roof	35	60	
	(D) Maroon body and roof, Macy Special	60	125	___
604	Observation Car, later (O), *20-25*	35	60	
604	Observation Car, latest (O), *31-36*			
	(A) Light red body and roof	45	85	___
	(B) Red body, black roof	35	60	___
	(C) Yellow-orange body, terra-cotta roof	35	60	
	(D) Stephen Girard green body, dark green roof	35	60	___
	(E) Maroon body and roof	70	150	___
605	Pullman Car (O), *25-32*			___
	(A) Gray, Lionel Lines	85	170	___
	(B) Gray, Illinois Central	85	170	___
	(C) Red, Lionel Lines	170	255	___
	(D) Red, Illinois Central	255	340	___
	(E) Orange, Lionel Lines	170	255	___
	(F) Orange, Illinois Central	300	430	___
	(G) Olive green, Lionel Lines	255	340	___
606	Observation Car (O), *25-32*			___

			Good	Exc
____		(A) Gray, Lionel Lines	130	215
____		(B) Gray, Illinois Central	90	170
____		(C) Red, Lionel Lines	170	255
____		(D) Red, Illinois Central	255	340
____		(E) Orange, Lionel Lines	170	255
____		(F) Orange, Illinois Central	170	255
____		(G) Olive green, Lionel Lines	255	340
____	607	Pullman Car (O), 26-27		
____		(A) Peacock, Lionel Lines	50	70
____		(B) Peacock, Illinois Central	75	115
____		(C) 2-tone green, Lionel Lines	50	75
____		(D) Red, Lionel Lines	75	110
____	608	Observation Car (O), 26-37		
____		(A) Peacock, Lionel Lines	50	70
____		(B) Peacock, Illinois Central	75	115
____		(C) 2-tone green, Lionel Lines	50	75
____		(D) Red, Lionel Lines	75	110
____	609	Pullman Car (O), 37	60	85
____	610	Pullman Car, early (O), 15-25		
____		(A) Dark green body and roof	50	65
____		(B) Maroon body and roof	60	95
____		(C) Mojave body and roof	60	95
____	610	Pullman Car, late (O), 26-30		
____		(A) Olive green body and roof	65	80
____		(B) Mojave body and roof	55	80
____		(C) Terra-cotta body, maroon roof	100	155
____		(D) Pea green body and roof	70	115
____		(E) Light blue body, aluminum roof	130	260
____		(F) Light red body, aluminum-painted roof	100	155
____	611	Observation Car (O), 37	55	80
____	612	Observation Car, early (O), 15-25		
____		(A) Dark green body and roof	40	60
____		(B) Maroon body and roof	70	90
____		(C) Mojave body and roof	70	90
____	612	Observation Car, late (O), 26-30		
____		(A) Olive green body and roof	55	80
____		(B) Mojave body and roof	55	80
____		(C) Terra-cotta body, maroon roof	100	155
____		(D) Pea green body and roof	70	115
____		(E) Light blue body, aluminum roof	130	260
____		(F) Light red body, aluminum-painted roof	100	155
____	613	Pullman Car (O), 31-40*		
____		(A) Terra-cotta body, maroon/terra-cotta roof	85	195
____		(B) Light red body, light red/aluminum roof	175	350
____		(C) Blue, two-tone blue roof	115	225
____	614	Observation Car (O), 31-40*		

PREWAR 1901-1942		Good	Exc	
	(A) Terra-cotta body, maroon/terra-cotta roof	100	190	____
	(B) Light red body, light red/aluminum roof	175	350	____
	(C) Blue, two-tone blue roof	115	225	____
615	Baggage Car (O), *33-40**	150	260	____
616E/W	Diesel only (O), *35-41*	90	215	____
616E/W	Set: 616, 617 (2), *618*	225	570	____
617	Coach (O), *35-41*			____
	(A) Blue and white	55	85	____
	(B) Chrome, gunmetal skirts	55	85	____
	(C) Chrome, chrome skirts	55	85	____
	(D) Silver-painted	55	85	____
618	Observation Car (O), *35-41*			____
	(A) Blue and white	55	85	____
	(B) Chrome, gunmetal skirts	55	85	____
	(C) Chrome, chrome skirts	55	85	____
	(D) Silver-painted	55	85	____
619	Combine Car (O), *36-38*			____
	(A) Blue, white windows band	100	205	____
	(B) Chrome, chrome skirts	100	205	____
620	Floodlight Car (O), *37-42*	50	85	____
629	Pullman Car (O), *24-32*			____
	(A) Dark green body and roof	25	40	____
	(B) Orange body and roof	25	40	____
	(C) Red body and roof	20	35	____
	(D) Light red body and roof	30	55	____
630	Observation Car, *24-32*			____
	(A) Dark green body and roof	25	40	____
	(B) Orange body and roof	25	40	____
	(C) Red body and roof	20	35	____
	(D) Light red body and roof	30	55	____
636W	Diesel only (O), *36-39*	90	175	____
636W	Set: 636W, 637 (2), 638, *36-39*	375	640	____
637	Coach (O), *36-39*	70	105	____
638	Observation Car (O), *36-39*	70	105	____
651	Flatcar (O), *35-40*	30	65	____
652	Gondola (O), *35-40*	30	55	____
653	Hopper Car (O), *34-40*	35	65	____
654	Tank Car (O), *34-42*			____
	(A) Orange or aluminum	35	60	____
	(B) Gray	40	75	____
655	Boxcar (O), *34-42*			____
	(A) Cream, maroon roof	35	60	____
	(B) Cream, tuscan roof	45	75	____
656	Cattle Car (O), *35-40*			____
	(A) Light gray, vermilion roof	40	100	____
	(B) Burnt orange, tuscan roof	70	125	____

|---|---|---|---|
___ 657	Caboose (0), *34-42*		
___	(A) Red body and roof	20	35
___	(B) Red body, tuscan roof	25	40
___ 659	Dump Car (0), *35-42*	40	90
___ 700	Electric Locomotive 0-4-0 (0), *15-16*	360	690
___ 700E	4-6-4 NYC Hudson "5344," scale (0), *37-42**	1400	2950
___ 700K	4-6-4 Locomotive, unbuilt gray primer (0), *38-42*	4400	5950
___ 701	0-6-0 PRR Locomotive "8976," 41	900	2100
___ 701	Electric Locomotive 0-4-0 (0), *15-16*	390	660
___ 702	Baggage Car (0), *17-21*	115	305
___ 703	Electric Locomotive 4-4-4 (0), *15-16*	1400	2350
___ 706	Electric Locomotive 0-4-0 (0), *15-16*	375	630
___ 708	0-6-0 PRR Locomotive "8976" (0), *39-42**	1450	2850
___ 710	Pullman Car (0), *24-34*		
___	(A) Red, Lionel Lines	200	300
___	(B) Orange, Lionel Lines	150	225
___	(C) Orange, New York Central	175	225
___	(D) Orange, Illinois Central	300	450
___	(E) 2-tone blue, Lionel Lines	300	415
___	(F) Orange, New York Central	200	260
___ 711	Remote Control Switches, pair (072), *35-42*	88	190
___ 712	Observation Car (0), *24-34*		
___	(A) Red, Lionel Lines	185	355
___	(B) Orange, Lionel Lines	140	265
___	(C) Orange, New York Central	160	310
___	(D) Orange, Illinois Central	280	530
___	(E) 2-tone blue, Lionel Lines	280	485
___ 714	Boxcar (0), *40-42**	350	610
___ 714K	Boxcar, unbuilt (0), *40-42*	220	480
___ 715	Tank Car (0), *40-42**		
___	(A) SEPS 8124 decal	340	610
___	(B) SUNX 715 decal	435	880
___ 715K	Tank Car, unbuilt (0), *40-42*	250	530
___ 716	Hopper Car (0), *40-42**	290	400
___ 716K	Hopper Car, unbuilt (0), *40-42*	350	730
___ 717	Caboose (0), *40-42**	340	510
___ 717K	Caboose, unbuilt (0), *40-42*	275	590
___ 720	90-degree Crossing (072), *35-42*	20	40
___ 721	Manual Switches, pair (072), *35-42*	50	105
___ 730	90-degree Crossing (072), *35-42*	20	40
___ 731	Remote Control Switches, pair, T-rail (072), *35-42*	80	135
___ 751E/W	Set: 752, 753 (2), 754 (0), *34-41**	640	1050
___ 752E	Diesel only (0), *34-41**		
___	(A) Yellow and brown	170	355
___	(B) Aluminum	145	340
___ 753	Coach (0), *36-41*		

		Good	Exc	
	(A) Yellow and brown	85	185	___
	(B) Aluminum	75	180	___
754	Observation Car (O), *36-41*			___
	(A) Yellow and brown	80	185	___
	(B) Aluminum	75	180	___
760	Curved Track, 16 pieces, (O72), *35-42*	40	80	___
761	Curved Track (O72), *34-42*	1	2	___
762	Straight Track (O72), *34-42*	1	2	___
762S	Insulated Straight Track (O72), *34-42*	2	5	___
763E	4-6-4 Locomotive (O), *37-42*			___
	(A) Gunmetal, 263 or 2263W Tender	1000	2125	___
	(B) Gunmetal, 2226X or 2226WX Tender	1150	2950	___
	(C) Black, 2226WX Tender	965	2650	___
771	Curved Track, T-rail (O72), *35-42*	3	10	___
772	Straight Track, T-rail (O72), *35-42*	5	25	___
772S	Insulated Straight Track, T-rail (O72), *35-42*	15	30	___
773	Fishplate Set, 50 plates (O72), *36-42*	15	30	___
782	Hiawatha Combine Car (O), *35-41**	230	380	___
783	Hiawatha Coach (O), *35-41**	140	290	___
784	Hiawatha Observation Car (O), *35-41**	205	445	___
792	Rail Chief Combine Car (O), *37-41**	215	580	___
793	Rail Chief Coach (O), *37-41**	290	800	___
794	Rail Chief Observation Car (O), *37-41**	250	800	___
800	Boxcar (2 7/8"), *04-05**	2500	4050	___
800	Boxcar (O), *15-26*			___
	(A) Light orange body, brown-maroon roof	45	70	___
	(B) Orange body and roof, PRR	25	45	___
801	Caboose (O), *15-26*	30	50	___
802	Stock Car (O), *15-26*	40	60	___
803	Hopper Car, early (O), *23-28*	25	55	___
803	Hopper Car, late (O), *29-34*	30	55	___
804	Tank Car (O), *23-28*	13	45	___
805	Boxcar (O), *27-34*			___
	(A) Pea green, terra-cotta roof	35	55	___
	(B) Pea green, maroon roof	45	115	___
805	(C) Orange, maroon roof	45	95	___
806	Stock Car (O), *27-34*			___
	(A) Pea green, terra-cotta roof	40	75	___
	(B) Orange, various color roofs	35	50	___
807	Caboose (O), *27-40*			___
	(A) Peacock body, dark green roof	20	35	___
	(B) Red body, peacock roof	20	40	___
	(C) Light red body and roof	20	40	___
809	Dump Car (O), *31-41*			___
	(A) Orange bin	40	55	___
	(B) Green bin	40	85	___

			Good	Exc
____ 810	Crane Car (O), *30-42*			
____	(A) Terra-cotta cab, maroon roof		170	270
____	(B) Cream cab, vermilion roof		130	205
____ 811	Flatcar (O), *26-40*			
____	(A) Maroon		40	83
____	(B) Aluminum		50	100
____ 812	Gondola (O), *26-42*		40	70
____ 812T	Tool Set: pick, shovel, hammer, *30-41*		40	105
____ 813	Stock Car (O), *26-42*			
____	(A) Orange body, pea green roof		76	145
____	(B) Orange body, maroon roof		55	135
____	(C) Cream body, maroon roof		100	225
____	(D) Tuscan body and roof		800	1600
____ 814	Boxcar (O), *26-42*			
____	(A) Cream, orange roof		50	145
____	(B) Cream, maroon roof		115	140
____	(C) Yellow, brown roof		110	120
____ 814R	Refrigerator Car (O), *29-42*			
____	(A) Ivory, peacock roof		100	200
____	(B) White, light blue roof		103	230
____	(C) Flat white, brown roof		600	900
____ 815	Tank Car (O), *26-42*			
____	(A) Pea green, maroon frame		250	510
____	(B) Pea green, black frame		70	155
____	(C) Aluminum, black frame		50	100
____	(D) Orange-yellow, black frame		150	255
____ 816	Hopper Car (O), *27-42*			
____	(A) Olive green		85	155
____	(B) Red body		65	140
____	(C) Black body		370	680
____ 817	Caboose (O), *26-42*			
____	(A) Peacock body, dark green roof		45	70
____	(B) Red body, peacock roof		45	80
____	(C) Light red body and roof		45	80
____ 820	Boxcar (O), *15-26*			
____	(A) Orange, Illinois Central		40	80
____	(B) Orange, Union Pacific		50	105
____ 820	Floodlight Car (O), *31-42*			
____	(A) Terra-cotta		100	180
____	(B) Green		100	175
____	(C) Light green		105	180
____ 821	Stock Car (O), *15-16, 25-26*		45	85
____ 822	Caboose (O), *15-26*		35	65
____ 831	Flatcar (O), *27-34*		20	45
____ 840	Industrial Power Station, *28-40**		1200	3050
____ 900	Ammunition Car (O), *17-21*		120	340

PREWAR 1901-1942		Good	Exc	
900	Box Trail Car (2 7/8"), *04-05**	2000	3600	___
901	Gondola (O), *19-27*	25	50	___
902	Gondola (O), *27-34*	25	45	___
910	Grove of Trees, *32-42*	70	178	___
911	Country Estate, *32-42*	195	440	___
912	Suburban Home	300	620	___
913	Landscaped Bungalow, *40-42*	140	285	___
914	Park Landscape, *32-35*	90	205	___
915	Tunnel, 65" or 60" long, *32-33, 35*	160	435	___
916	Tunnel, 29" long, *35*	95	180	___
917	Scenic Hillside, 34" x 15", *32-36*	90	205	___
918	Scenic Hillside, 30" x 10", *32-36*	90	205	___
919	Park Grass, cloth bag, *32-42*	10	20	___
920	Village, *32-33*	600	1600	___
921	Scenic Park, 3 pieces, *32-33*	980	2600	___
921C	Park Center, *32-33*	400	1050	___
922	Terrace, *32-36*	90	255	___
923	Tunnel, 40" long, *33-42*	125	225	___
924	Tunnel, 30" long (O72), *35-42*	50	135	___
925	Lubricant, *35-42*	25	120	___
927	Flag Plot, *37-42*	70	135	___
1000	Passenger Car (2 7/8"), *05**	4500	6750	___
1000	Trolley Trailer (std), *10-16*	1400	2250	___
1010	Electric Locomotive 0-4-0, Winner Lines (O), *31-32*	90	160	___
1010	Interurban Trailer (std), *10-16*	1000	1800	___
1011	Pullman Car, Winner Lines (O), *31-32*	45	75	___
1012	Station, *32*	40	70	___
1015	0-4-0 Locomotive (O), *31-32*	100	205	___
1017	Winner Station, *33*	25	70	___
1019	Observation Car (O), *31-32*	50	70	___
1020	Baggage Car (O), *31-32*	65	110	___
1021	90-degree Crossover (O27), *32-42*	1	5	___
1022	Tunnel, 18" long (O), *35-42*	15	30	___
1023	Tunnel, 19" long, *34-42*	20	40	___
1024	Switches, pair (O27), *37-42*	5	15	___
1025	Bumper (O27), *40-42*	15	25	___
1027	Transformer Station, *34*	50	115	___
1028	Transformer, 40 watts, *39*	3	10	___
1029	Transformer, 25 watts, *36*	5	20	___
1030	Electric Locomotive 0-4-0 (O), *32*	75	135	___
1030	Transformer, 40 watts, *35-38*	6	25	___
1035	0-4-0 Locomotive (O), *32*	75	115	___
1037	Transformer, 40 watts, *40-42*	7	25	___
1038	Transformer, 30 watts, *40*	2	5	___
1039	Transformer, 35 watts, *37-40*	7	20	___
1040	Transformer, 60 watts, *37-39*	10	30	___

PREWAR 1901-1942			Good	Exc
___ 1041	Transformer, 60 watts, 39-42		15	30
___ 1045	Watchman, 38-42		30	65
___ 1050	Passenger Car Trailer (2 7/8"), 05*		5000	7200
___ 1100	Summer Trolley Trailer (std), 10-13			NRS
___ 1100	Mickey Mouse Handcar, 35-37*			
___	(A) Red base		425	640
___	(B) Apple green base, orange shoes		500	880
___	(C) Orange base		600	1225
___ 1103	Peter Rabbit Handcar (O), 35-37*		330	820
___ 1105	Santa Claus Handcar (O), 35-35*			
___	(A) Red base		660	1050
___	(B) Green base		720	1200
___ 1107	Transformer Station, 33		25	70
___ 1107	Donald Duck Handcar (O), 36-37*			
___ 1107W	(A) White dog house, red roof	475		
___	(B) White dog house, green roof		450	1100
___	(C) Orange dog house, green roof		640	1850
___ 1121	Switches, pair (O27), 37-42		15	35
___ 1506L	0-4-0 Locomotive (O), 33-34		95	125
___ 1506M	0-4-0 Locomotive (O), 35		250	430
___ 1508	0-4-0 Commodore Vanderbilt with 1509 Mickey Mouse stoker Tender, 35		420	690
___ 1511	0-4-0 Locomotive (O), 36-37		110	160
___ 1512	Gondola (O), 31-33, 36-37		25	50
___ 1514	Boxcar (O), 31-37		25	40
___ 1515	Tank Car (O), 33-37		25	40
___ 1517	Caboose (O), 31-37		25	40
___ 1518	Mickey Mouse Circus Dining Car (O), 35		120	260
___ 1519	Mickey Mouse Band Car (O), 35		120	260
___ 1520	Mickey Mouse Circus Car (O), 35		120	260
___ 1536	Mickey Mouse Circus Set: 1508, 1509, 1518, 1519, 1520, 35		770	1350
___ 1550	Switches, for windup trains, pair, 33-37		2	5
___ 1555	90-degree Crossover, for windup trains, 33-37		1	2
___ 1560	Station, 33-37		15	35
___ 1569	Accessory Set, 8 pieces, 33-37		35	70
___ 1588	0-4-0 Locomotive (O), 36-37		150	250
___ 1630	Pullman Car (O), 38-42			
___	(A) Aluminum windows		35	70
___	(B) Light gray windows		45	80
___ 1631	Observation Car (O), 38-42			
___	(A) Aluminum windows		35	70
___	(B) Light gray windows		45	80
___ 1651E	Electric Locomotive 0-4-0 (O), 33		130	240
___ 1661E	2-4-0 Locomotive (O), 33		75	160
___ 1662	0-4-0 Locomotive (O27), 40-42		218	420
___ 1663	0-4-0 Locomotive (O27), 40-42		200	385

		Good	Exc	
1664/E	2-4-2 Locomotive (027), *38-42*			——
	(A) Gunmetal	60	100	——
	(B) Black	60	95	——
1666/E	2-6-2 Locomotive (027), *38-42*			——
	(A) Gunmetal	115	170	——
	(B) Black	95	145	——
1668/E	2-6-2 Locomotive (027), *37-41*			——
	(A) Gunmetal	75	115	——
	(B) Black	75	130	——
1673	Coach (0), *36-37*			——
	(A) Aluminum windows	35	75	——
	(B) Light gray windows	45	90	——
1674	Pullman Car (0), *36-37*	35	75	——
1675	Observation Car (0), *36-37*	30	70	——
1677	Gondola (0), *33-35, 39-42*			——
	(A) Light blue, Ives	40	60	——
	(B) Blue or red, Lionel	20	40	——
1679	Boxcar (0), *33-42*			——
	(A) Cream, Ives	25	40	——
	(B) Cream, Lionel	25	40	——
	(C) Cream or yellow, Baby Ruth	20	40	——
1680	Tank Car (0), *33-42*			——
	(A) Aluminum, Ives Tank Lines	60	95	——
	(B) Aluminum, no Ives lettering	13	35	——
	(C) Orange, Shell Oil	15	32	——
1681	2-4-0 Locomotive (0), *34-35*			——
	(A) Black, red frame	55	120	——
	(B) Red, red frame	110	145	——
1681E	2-4-0 Locomotive (0), *34-35*			——
	(A) Black, red frame	65	130	——
	(B) Red, red frame	130	165	——
1682	Caboose (0), *33-42*			——
	(A) Vermilion, Ives	35	70	——
	(B) Red or tuscan, Lionel	9	40	——
1684	2-4-2 Locomotive (027), *41-42*			——
	(A) Black	45	70	——
	(B) Gunmetal	45	70	——
1685	Coach (0), *33-37 u*			——
	(A) Gray, maroon roof	240	495	——
	(B) Red, maroon roof	170	335	——
	(C) Blue, silver roof	170	315	——
1686	Baggage Car (0), *33-37 u*			——
	(A) Gray, maroon roof	240	495	——
	(B) Red, maroon roof	170	335	——
	(C) Blue, silver roof	170	315	——
1687	Observation Car (0), *33-37 u*			——

	PREWAR 1901-1942		Good	Exc
____		(A) Gray, maroon roof	170	315
____		(B) Red, maroon roof	180	315
____		(C) Blue, silver roof	170	315
____	1688/E	2-4-2 Locomotive (027), *36-46*	50	125
____	1689E	2-4-2 Locomotive (027), *36-37*		
____		(A) Gunmetal	75	115
____		(B) Black	60	100
____	1689T	Tender, black	15	34
____	1690	Pullman Car (O), *33-40*	35	60
____	1691	Observation Car (O), *33-40*	35	60
____	1692	Pullman Car (027), *39 u*	45	70
____	1693	Observation Car (027), *39 u*	45	70
____	1700E	Diesel, power unit only (027), *35-37*	45	70
____	1700E	Set: 1700, 1701 (2), 1702, *35-37 u*		
____		(A) Aluminum and light red	140	250
____		(B) Chrome and light red	140	250
____		(C) Orange and gray	155	285
____	1701	Coach (027), *35-37*		
____		(A) Chrome sides and roof	20	45
____		(B) Silver sides and roof	30	55
____		(C) Orange and gray	75	150
____	1702	Observation Car (027), *35-37*		
____		(A) Chrome sides and roof	20	45
____		(B) Silver sides and roof	30	55
____		(C) Orange and gray	75	150
____	1703	Observation Car, hooked coupler, *35-37 u*	50	110
____	1717	Gondola (O), *33-40 u*	30	50
____	1717X	Gondola (O), *40 u*	25	50
____	1719	Boxcar (O), *33-40 u*	30	50
____	1719X	Boxcar (O), *41-42 u*	30	50
____	1722	Caboose (O), *33-42 u*	25	50
____	1722X	Caboose (O), *39-40 u*	25	40
____	1766	Pullman Car (std), *34-40**		
____		(A) Terra-cotta, maroon roof, brass trim	300	650
____		(B) Red, maroon roof, nickel trim	300	540
____	1767	Baggage Car (std), *34-40**		
____		(A) Terra-cotta, maroon roof, brass trim	295	850
____		(B) Red, maroon roof, nickel trim	295	700
____	1768	Observation Car (std), *34-40**		
____		(A) Terra-cotta, maroon roof, brass trim	300	650
____		(B) Red, maroon roof, nickel trim	300	540
____	1811	Pullman Car (O), *33-37*	35	70
____	1812	Observation Car (O), *33-37*	30	65
____	1813	Baggage Car (O), *33-37*	60	135
____	1816/W	Diesel (O), *35-37*	100	240
____	1817	Coach (O), *35-37*	25	50

PREWAR 1901-1942		Good	Exc	
1818	Observation Car (O), *35-37*	25	50	___
1835E	2-4-2 Locomotive (std), *34-39*	470	730	___
1910	Electric Locomotive 0-6-0, early (std), *10-11*	920	1550	___
1910	Electric Locomotive 0-6-0, late (std), *12*	550	1350	___
1910	Pullman Car (std), *09-10 u*	860	1800	___
1911	Electric Locomotive 0-4-0, early (std), *10-12*	860	1700	___
1911	Electric Locomotive 0-4-0, late (std), *13*	700	1100	___
1911	Electric Locomotive 0-4-4-0 Special (std), *11-12*	860	2500	___
1912	Electric Locomotive 0-4-4-0 (std), *10-12**			
	(A) New York, New Haven & Hartford	1550	3200	___
	(B) New York Central Lines	1300	2700	___
1912	Electric Locomotive 0-4-4-0 Special (std), *11**	2500	4500	___
2200	Summer Trolley Trailer (std), *10-13*	1100	2250	___
2203B	Tender	40	99	___
2224W	Tender	55	115	___
2225W	Tender	30	60	___
2228B	Tender	140	280	___
2235W	Tender	25	50	___
2600	Pullman Car (O), *38-42*	80	155	___
2601	Observation Car (O), *38-42*	60	115	___
2602	Baggage Car (O), *38-42*	90	185	___
2613	Pullman Car (O), *38-42**			___
	(A) Blue, 2-tone blue roof	100	300	___
	(B) State green, 2-tone green roof	200	440	___
2614	Observation Car (O), *38-42**			___
	(A) Blue, 2-tone blue roof	100	300	___
	(B) State green, 2-tone green roof	200	440	___
2615	Baggage Car (O), *38-42**			___
	(A) Blue, 2-tone blue roof	115	300	___
	(B) State green, 2-tone green roof	200	420	___
2620	Floodlight Car (O), *38-42*	65	100	___
2623	Pullman Car (O), *41-42*			___
	(A) Irvington	175	335	___
	(B) Manhattan	165	310	___
2624	Pullman Car (O), *41-42*	750	1700	___
2630	Pullman Car (O), *38-42*	30	70	___
2631	Observation Car (O), *38-42*	30	70	___
2640	Pullman Car, illuminated (O), *38-42*			___
	(A) Light blue, aluminum roof	30	70	___
	(B) State green, dark green roof	30	70	___
2641	Observation Car, illuminated (O), *38-42*			___
	(A) Light blue, aluminum roof	30	70	___
	(B) State green, dark green roof	30	70	___
2642	Pullman Car (O), *41-42*	30	70	___
2643	Observation Car (O), *41-42*	30	65	___
2651	Flatcar (O), *38-42*	30	50	___

		Good	Exc
___ 2652	Gondola (O), *38-41*	25	65
___ 2653	Hopper Car (O), *38-42*		
___	(A) Stephen Girard green	35	70
___	(B) Black	60	130
___ 2654	Tank Car (O), *38-42*		
___	(A) Aluminum, Sunoco	35	60
___	(B) Orange, Shell	35	60
___	(C) Light gray, Sunoco	40	70
___ 2655	Boxcar (O), *38-42*		
___	(A) Cream, maroon roof	35	65
___	(B) Cream, tuscan roof	40	70
___ 2656	Stock Car (O), *38-41*		
___	(A) Light gray, red roof	45	75
___	(B) Burnt orange, tuscan roof	75	115
___ 2657	Caboose (O), *40-41*	30	45
___ 2657X	Caboose (O), *40-41*	25	40
___ 2659	Dump Car (O), *38-41*	40	70
___ 2660	Crane Car (O), *38-42*	85	165
___ 2672	Caboose (027), *41-42*	20	50
___ 2677	Gondola (027), *39-41*	25	40
___ 2679	Boxcar (027), *38-42*	15	30
___ 2680	Tank Car (027), *38-42*		
___	(A) Aluminum, Sunoco	15	40
___	(B) Orange, Shell	15	40
___ 2682	Caboose (027), *38-42*	10	30
___ 2682X	Caboose (027), *38-42*	20	35
___ 2689T	Tender	15	35
___ 2689W	Tender	35	50
___ 2717	Gondola (O), *38-42 u*	20	40
___ 2719	Boxcar (O), *38-42 u*	30	50
___ 2722	Caboose (O), *38-42 u*	25	50
___ 2755	Tank Car (O), *41-42*	81	130
___ 2757	Caboose (O), *41-42*	25	45
___ 2757X	Caboose (O), *41-42*	25	40
___ 2758	Automobile Boxcar (O), *41-42*	35	60
___ 2810	Crane Car (O), *38-42*	145	210
___ 2811	Flatcar (O), *38-42*	50	95
___ 2812	Gondola (O), *38-42*		
___	(A) Green	40	85
___	(B) Dark orange	45	95
___ 2813	Stock Car (O), *38-42*	120	225
___ 2814	Boxcar (O), *38-42*		
___	(A) Cream, maroon roof	85	150
___	(B) Orange, brown roof, rubber-stamped lettering	200	700
___ 2814R	Refrigerator Car (O), *38-42*		
___	(A) White, light blue roof, nickel plates	138	260

		Good	Exc	
	(B) White, brown roof, no plates	375	660	___
2815	Tank Car (0), *38-42*			___
	(A) Aluminum	85	165	___
	(B) Orange	135	215	___
2816	Hopper Car (0), *35-42*			___
	(A) Red	100	190	___
	(B) Black	110	220	___
2817	Caboose (0), *36-42*			___
	(A) Light red body and roof	78	140	___
	(B) Flat red body, tuscan roof	115	180	___
2820	Floodlight Car (0), *38-42*			___
	(A) Stamped nickel searchlights	110	205	___
	(B) Gray die-cast searchlights	120	260	___
2954	Boxcar (0), *40-42**	145	350	___
2955	Sunoco Tank Car (0), *40-42**			___
	(A) Shell decal	225	500	___
	(B) Sunoco decal	340	690	___
2956	Hopper Car (0), *40-42**	160	400	___
2957	Caboose (0), *40-42**	110	326	___
3300	Summer Trolley Trailer (std), *10-13*	1400	2250	___
3651	Operating Lumber Car (0), *39-42*	25	55	___
3652	Operating Gondola (0), *39-42*	35	75	___
3659	Operating Dump Car (0), *39-42*	20	40	___
3811	Operating Lumber Car (0), *39-42*	35	88	___
3814	Operating Merchandise Car (0), *39-42*	90	195	___
3859	Operating Dump Car (0), *38-42*	45	90	___
Other Transformers and Motors				___
A	Miniature Motor, *04*	50	95	___
A	Transformer, 40, 60 watts, *21-37*	10	23	___
B	New Departure Motor, *06-16*	75	135	___
B	Transformer, 50, 75 watts, *16-38*	7	25	___
C	New Departure Motor, *06-16*	100	180	___
D	New Departure Motor, *06-14*	100	180	___
E	New Departure Motor, *06-14*	100	180	___
F	New Departure Motor, *06-14*	100	180	___
G	Fan Motor, battery-operated, *06-14*	100	180	___
K	Transformer, 150, 200 watts, *13-38*	18	73	___
L	Transformer, 50, 75 watts, *13-16, 33-38*	10	25	___
M	Peerless Motor, battery-operated, *15-20*	30	80	___
N	Transformer, 50 watts, *41-42*	7	20	___
Q	Transformer, 50 watts, *14-15*	10	21	___
Q	Transformer, 75 watts, *38-42*	12	28	___
R	Peerless Motor, battery-operated, reversing, *15-20*	30	75	___
R	Transformer, 100 watts, *38-42*	20	45	___
S	Transformer, 50 watts, *14-17*	13	28	___
T	Transformer, 75, 100, 150 watts, *14-28*	8	30	___

PREWAR 1901-1942			Good	Exc
___ U	Transformer, Aladdin, *32-33*		5	15
___ V	Transformer, 150 watts, *39-42*		40	75
___ W	Transformer, 75 watts, *32-33*		10	35
___ Y	Peerless Motor, battery-operated, 3-speed, *15-20*		40	80
___ Z	Transformer, 250 watts, *39-42*		83	140

Track, Lockons, and Contactors

		Good	Exc
___	0 Straight		1
___	0 Curve		1
___	072 Straight	1	2
___	072 Curve	1	2
___	027 Straight		1
___	027 Curve		1
___	Standard Straight	1	3
___	Standard Curve	1	2
___	Standard Insulated Straight, *33-42*	2	4
___	Standard Insulated Curve, *33-42*	1	2
___	0 Gauge Lockon		1
___	Standard Gauge Lockon		1
___	UTC Lockon		1
___	145C Contactor	3	10
___	153C Contactor	3	7
___	Track Clips, dozen (0), *37*	5	10

Section 2
POSTWAR 1945–1969

		Good	Exc	
5C	Test Set	861	1353	___
5D	Test Set, *54*	1238	2500	___
5E	Electronic Set Tester, *46-49*	1083	2667	___
5F	Test Set	925	1840	___
011-11	Fiber Pins, dozen (O), *46-50*	1	3	___
011-43	Insulating Pins, dozen (O), *61*	1	2	___
020	90-degree Crossover (O), *45-61*	2	8	___
020X	45-degree Crossover (O), *46-59*	3	9	___
022	Remote Control Switches, pair (O), *45-69*	20	38	___
022-500	Adapter Set (O), *57-61*	2	9	___
022A	Remote Control Switches, pair (O), *47*	24	67	___
022C-1	Switch Controller	5	11	___
25	Bumper (O), *46-47*	7	20	___
	(B) Bumper, *48-50*			___
	(A) Red, *49-50*	5	13	___
	(B) Gray, *48*	16	50	___
027C-1	Track Clips, box of 12 (027), *47, 49*	4	15	___
027C-1	Track Clips, box of 50 (027)	17	48	___
30	Water Tower, *47-50*			___
	(A) Single-walled	19	60	___
	(B) Double-walled	24	83	___
31	Curved Track (Super O), *57-66*	1	4	___
31-7	Power Blade Connection, dozen (Super O), *57-60*	3	10	___
31-15	Ground Rail Pin, dozen (Super O), *57-66*	3	10	___
31-45	Power Blade Connection, dozen (Super O), *61-66*	2	9	___
32	Straight Track (Super O), *57-66*	2	5	___
32-10	Insulating Pin, dozen (Super O), *57-60*	3	11	___
32-20	Power Blade Insulator, dozen (Super O), *57-60*	2	5	___
32-25	Insulating Pin (Super O), *57-61*		1	___
32-30	Ground Pin (Super O), *57-61*		1	___
32-31	Power Pin (Super O), *57-61*		1	___
32-32	Insulating Pin (Super O), *57-61*		1	___
32-33	Ground Pin (Super O), *57-61*		1	___
32-34	Power Pin (Super O), *57-61*		1	___
32-35	Insulating Pin, dozen (Super O to 027), *57-61*	2	3	___
32-45	Power Blade Insulators, dozen (Super O), *61-66*	3	8	___
32-55	Insulating Pins, dozen (Super O), *61-66*	3	8	___
33	Half Curved Track (Super O), *57-66*	1	5	___
34	Half Straight Track (Super O), *57-66*	2	6	___
35	Boulevard Lamp, *45-49*	12	33	___
36	Operating Car Remote Control Set (Super O), *57-66*	10	26	___
37	Uncoupling Track Set (Super O), *57-66*	8	18	___
38-85	Accessory Adapter Tracks, pair (Super O), *57-61*	6	30	___

| --- | --- | --- | --- |
____ 38	Operating Water Tower, *46-47*	94	243
____ 39	Operating Set (Super O), *57*	4	8
____ 39-5	Operating Set (Super O), *57-58*	4	8
____ 39-6	Operating Set (Super O), *57-58*	4	10
____ 39-10	Operating Set (Super O), *58*	4	8
____ 39-15	Operating Set with blade (Super O), *57-58*	4	8
____ 39-20	Operating Set (Super O), *57-58*	4	8
____ 39-25	Operating Set (Super O), *61-66*	8	28
____ 39-35	Operating Set (Super O), *59*	8	28
____ 40	Hookup Wire, *50-51, 53-63*		
____	(A) Single reel, orange or gray, with tape	6	29
____	(B) 8 sealed reels in dealer box	95	344
____ 40-25	Conductor Wire with envelope, *56-59*	9	38
____ 40-50	Cable Reel with envelope, *60-61*	12	57
____ 41	U.S. Army Switcher, *55-57*		
____	(A) Unpainted black body	50	108
____	(B) Black-painted body	288	1033
____ 042/42	Manual Switches, pair (O), *46-59*	10	24
____ 42	Picatinny Arsenal Switcher, *57*	75	256
____ 43	Power Track (Super O), *59-66*	4	13
____ 44	U.S. Army Mobile Launcher, *59-62*	60	211
____ 44-80	Missiles, *59-60*	13	24
____ 45	U.S. Marines Mobile Launcher, *60-62*	75	250
____ 45	Automatic Gateman, *46-49*	12	38
____ 45N	Automatic Gateman, *45*	16	42
____ 48	Insulated Straight Track (Super O), *57-66*	4	11
____ 49	Insulated Curved Track (Super O), *57-66*	4	9
____ 50	Section Gang Car, *54-64*		
____	(A) Gray bumpers, rotating blue man and fixed olive men, center horn, *54*	230	752
____	(B) Blue bumpers, rotating olive man and fixed blue men, center horn	28	52
____	(C) Blue bumpers, rotating olive man and fixed blue men, off-center horn	27	44
____ 51	Navy Yard Switcher, *56-57*	62	139
____ 52	Fire Car, *58-61*	65	167
____ 53	Rio Grande Snowplow, *57-60*		
____	(A) Backwards "a" in Rio Grande	69	200
____	(B) Correctly printed "a"	150	543
____ 54	Ballast Tamper, *58-61, 66, 68-69*	55	149
____ 55	PRR Tie-Jector Car, *57-61*		
____	(A) Ventilation slot behind motorman	49	136
____	(B) No slot behind motorman	40	104
____ 55-150	Ties, 24 pieces, *57-60*	15	31
____ 56	Lamp Post, *46-49*	19	40
____ 56	M&StL Mine Transport, *58*	120	288
____ 57	AEC Switcher, *59-60*	162	504

		Good	Exc	
58	GN Snowplow, *59-61*	150	369	___
58	Lamp Post, *46-50*	17	39	___
59	Minuteman Switcher, *62-63*	207	578	___
60	Lionelville Rapid Transit Trolley, *55-58*			___
	(A) Metal motorman silhouettes	95	231	___
	(B) No motorman silhouettes	36	95	___
61	Ground Lockon (Super O), *57-66*	2	6	___
61-25	Super O Ground clips, dozen, with dealer envelope	5	17	___
62	Power Lockon (Super O), *57-66*	1	4	___
64	Highway Lamp Post, *45-49*	13	35	___
65	Handcar, *62-66*			___
	(A) Light yellow	80	270	___
	(B) Dark yellow	60	233	___
68	Executive Inspection Car, *58-61*	54	158	___
69	Maintenance Car, *60-62*	70	192	___
70	Yard Light, *49-50*	10	29	___
71	Lamp Post, *49-59*	7	13	___
75	Goose Neck Lamps, set of 2, *61-63*	10	27	___
76	Boulevard Street Lamps, set of 3, *59-66, 68-69*	15	30	___
80	Controller, *60*	5	20	___
88	Controller, *46-60*	7	15	___
89	Flagpole, *56-58*	17	53	___
90	Controller, *55-66*			___
	(A) Metal clip	5	16	___
	(B) No metal clip	5	9	___
91	Circuit Breaker, *57-60*	10	26	___
92	Circuit Breaker, *59-66, 68-69*	8	16	___
93	Water Tower, *46-49*	17	44	___
96C	Controller, *45-54*	4	8	___
97	Coal Elevator, *46-50*	48	129	___
108	Trestle Set, 12 black piers,	9	25	___
109	Partial Trestle Set, *61*	5	17	___
110	Graduated Trestle Set, 22 or 24 piers, *55-69*	7	15	___
110-75	Graduated Trestle Set with 110-78 envelope	10	24	___
111	Elevated Trestle Set, 10 A piers, *56-69*	7	14	___
111-100	Elevated Trestle Piers, set of 2, *60-63*	13	33	___
112	Remote Control Switches, pair (Super O), *57-66*	36	79	___
114	Newsstand with horn, *57-59*	34	80	___
115	Passenger Station, *46-49*	100	258	___
118	Newsstand with whistle, *57-58*	38	85	___
119	Landscaped Tunnel, *57-58*	200	400	___
120	90-degree Crossing (Super O), *57-66*	5	13	___
121	Landscaped Tunnel, *59-66*		NRS	
122	Lamp Assortment, *48-52*	33	173	___
123	Lamp Assortment, *55-59*	40	155	___
123-60	Lamp Assortment, *60-63*	28	180	___

		Good	Exc
____ 125	Whistle Shack, *50-55*		
____	(A) Gray base	15	35
____	(B) Green base	22	48
____ 128	Animated Newsstand, *57-60*	49	101
____ 130	60-degree Crossing (Super O), *57-66*	6	15
____ 131	Curved Tunnel, *59-66*		NRS
____ 132	Passenger Station, *49-55*	28	58
____ 133	Passenger Station, *57, 61-62, 66*	17	42
____ 138	Water Tower, *53-57*	22	53
____ 140	Automatic Banjo Signal, *54-66*	13	26
____ 142	Manual Switches, pair (Super O), *57-66*	23	47
____ 145	Automatic Gateman, *50-66*		
____	(A) Red roof	12	37
____	(B) Maroon roof	10	29
____ 145C	Contactor, *50-60*	3	7
____ 147	Whistle Controller, *61-66*	2	6
____ 148	Dwarf Trackside Signal, *57-60*		18
____ 148-100	Controller (SPDT switch), *57-60*	5	15
____ 150	Telegraph Pole Set, *47-50*	23	37
____ 151	Automatic Semaphore, *47-69*		
____	(A) Green base, yellow blade, *47*	25	53
____	(B) Black base, yellow blade, *47*	14	25
____	(C) Black base, red blade, *47*	155	362
____	(D) Green base, yellow blade with raised lenses	18	52
____ 152	Automatic Crossing Gate, *45-49*	8	19
____ 153	Automatic Block Control Signal, *45-59*	15	24
____ 153C	Contactor	3	6
____ 154	Automatic Highway Signal, *45-69*	11	22
____ 154C	Contactor	4	7
____ 155	Blinking Light Signal with bell, *55-57*	20	48
____ 156	Station Platform, *46-49*	29	85
____ 156-5	Station Platform Fence with envelope	27	57
____ 157	Station Platform, *52-59*		
____	(A) Maroon base	15	35
____	(B) Red base	28	84
____ 157-23	Station Platform Fence with envelope	17	48
____ 160	Unloading Bin, *52-57*		
____	(A) Black plastic, long	2	5
____	(B) Black metal, short	43	72
____	(C) Multicolor Bakelite, short	6	33
____	(D) Black Bakelite, short	3	8
____ 161	Mail Pickup Set, *61-63*	22	60
____ 163	Single Target Block Signal, *61-69*	15	25
____ 164	Log Loader, *46-50*	50	134
____ 164-64	Log Set, 5 pieces, *52-58*	30	62
____ 167	Whistle Controller, *45-46*	3	8

		Good	Exc	
175	Rocket Launcher, *58-60*	54	162	___
175-50	Extra Rocket, *59-60*	9	23	___
182	Magnetic Crane, *46-49*	115	224	___
182-22	Steel Scrap with bag, *46-49*	48	107	___
192	Operating Control Tower, *59-60*	107	242	___
193	Industrial Water Tower, *53-55*			___
	(A) Red	41	75	___
	(B) Black, *53*	67	198	___
195	Floodlight Tower, *57-69*			___
195	(A) Medium tan base, rubber-stamped lettering	25	63	___
195	(B) All other variations	22	50	___
195-75	Floodlight Extension, 8-bulb (with box), *58-60*	23	60	___
196	Smoke Pellets, *46-47*	39	91	___
197	Rotating Radar Antenna, *57-59*			___
	(A) Orange platform	34	89	___
	(B) Gray platform	24	59	___
197-75	Separate Sale Radar Head with box	48	143	___
199	Microwave Relay Tower, *58-59*	27	60	___
202	UP Alco Diesel A Unit, *57*	29	71	___
204	Santa Fe Alco Diesel AA Units, *57*	64	170	___
205	Missouri Pacific Alco Diesel AA Units, *57-58*			___
	(A) Pilot without support	45	114	___
	(B) Pilot with painted metal support	73	155	___
206	Artificial Coal, large bag, *46-68*	13	21	___
207	Artificial Coal, small bag, *46-48*	7	15	___
208	Santa Fe Alco Diesel AA Units, *58-59*	61	237	___
209	New Haven Alco Diesel AA Units, *58*	192	487	___
209	Wooden Barrels, set of 6, *46-50*	7	15	___
210	Texas Special Alco Diesel AA Units, *58*	50	123	___
211	Texas Special Alco Diesel AA Units, *62-66*	60	132	___
212	Santa Fe Alco Diesel AA Units, *64-66*	62	158	___
	(A) With Built Date 8-57, *64-65*	43	80	___
	(B) Without Built Date, *66*	49	125	___
212T	Santa Fe Alco Diesel Dummy A Unit, *64-66*	27	75	___
	(A) With Built Date 8-57, *64-65*	14	33	___
	(B) Without Built Date, *66*	22	49	___
212	USMC Alco Diesel A Unit, *58-59*	63	152	___
212T	USMC Diesel Dummy A Unit, *58 u*	315	994	___
213	M&StL Alco Diesel AA Units, *64*	75	190	___
214	Plate Girder Bridge, *53-69*	7	15	___
215	Santa Fe Alco Diesel Units, *65 u*			___
	(A) AB Units	66	133	___
	(B) AA Units	95	171	___
215	Santa Fe Diesel Powered A Unit	25	39	___
216	Burlington Alco Diesel A Unit, *58*	129	333	___
216	M&StL Alco Diesel AA Units (213T dummy A unit), *64 u*	63	190	___

			Good	Exc
___	217	B&M Alco Diesel AB Units, *59*	86	206
___	217C	B&M Alco Diesel B Unit, *59*	30	70
___	218	Santa Fe Alco Diesel Units, *59-63*		
___		(A) AA Units	78	239
___		(B) AB Units	67	186
___		(C) AA Units, solid nose decal	68	216
___	218C	Santa Fe Alco B Unit, *61-63*	43	99
___	219	Missouri Pacific Alco Diesel AA Units, *59 u*	68	153
___	220	Santa Fe Alco Diesel Units, *60-61*		
___	220	(A) A Unit	35	95
___	220	(B) AA Units	71	172
___	221	2-6-4 Locomotive, 221W Tender, *46-47*		
___		(A) Gray body, black drivers	60	132
___		(B) Black body, nickel-rimmed black drivers, *47*	70	155
___		(C) Gray body, cast-aluminum drivers, *46*	110	240
___	221	Rio Grande Alco Diesel A Unit, *63-64*	28	60
___	221	Santa Fe Alco Diesel A Unit, *63-64 u*	211	714
___	221	U.S. Marine Corps Alco Diesel A Unit, *63-64 u*	190	782
___	221T	Tender		
___		(A) Gray	18	37
___		(B) Black	18	41
___	221W	Whistle Tender	27	58
___	222	Rio Grande Alco Diesel A Unit, *62*	23	55
___	223	Santa Fe Alco Diesel AB Units, *63*	64	203
___	224	2-6-2 Locomotive, 2466W or 2466WX Tender, *45-46*		
___		(A) Blackened handrails, *45*	104	245
___		(B) Silver handrails	66	143
___	224	US Navy "B" Unit	43	80
___	224	U.S. Navy Alco Diesel AB Units, *60*	99	229
___	225	C&O Alco Diesel A Unit, *60*	30	65
___	226	B&M Alco Diesel AB Units, *60 u*	75	174
___	226C	B&M Alco Diesel B Unit, *60 u*	28	75
___	227	CN Alco Diesel A Unit, *60 u*	54	128
___	228	CN Alco Diesel A Unit, *61 u*	59	134
___	229	M&StL Alco Diesel Units, *61-62*		
___		(A) A Unit, *61*	46	426
___		(B) AB Units, *62*	73	170
___	229C	M&StL Alco Diesel B Unit, *61-62*	30	70
___	230	C&O Alco Diesel A Unit, *61*	35	79
___	231	Rock Island Alco Diesel A Unit, *61-63*		
___		(A) With red stripe	43	92
___		(B) Without red stripe	174	561
___	232	New Haven Alco Diesel A Unit, *62*	48	115
___	233	2-4-2 Scout Locomotive, 233W Tender, *61-62*	30	68
___	233W	Whistle Tender	18	41
___	234T	Lionel Lines Tender	8	23

		Good	Exc	
234T	Pennsylvania Tender	17	47	___
234W	Lionel Whistle Tender	23	48	___
234W	Pennsylvania Whistle Tender	33	100	___
235	2-4-2 Scout Locomotive, 1130T or 1060T Tender, *60 u*	70	259	___
236	2-4-2 Scout Locomotive, *61-62*			___
	(A) 1050T slope-back Tender	15	42	___
	(B) 1130T Tender	15	40	___
237	2-4-2 Scout Locomotive, *63-66*			___
	(A) 1060T Tender	24	57	___
	(B) 234W Tender	31	75	___
238	2-4-2 Scout Locomotive, stripe on running board, 234W Tender, *63-64*	53	127	___
239	2-4-2 Scout Locomotive, 234W Tender, *65-66*	40	88	___
240	2-4-2 Scout Locomotive, 242T Tender, *64 u*	81	246	___
241	2-4-2 Scout Locomotive, *65 u*			___
	(A) Narrow stripe, 234W Tender	31	78	___
	(B) Wide stripe, 1130T Tender	25	62	___
242	2-4-2 Scout Locomotive, 1060T or 1062T Tender, *62-66*	17	38	___
243	2-4-2 Scout Locomotive, 243W Tender, *60*	32	82	___
243W	Whistle Tender	15	45	___
244	2-4-2 Scout Locomotive, 244T or 1130T Tender, *60-61*	19	47	___
244T	Tender	7	37	___
245	2-4-2 Scout Locomotive, 1130T Tender, *59 u*	25	71	___
246	2-4-2 Scout Locomotive, 244T or 1130T Tender, *59-61*	15	33	___
247	2-4-2 Scout Locomotive, 247T Tender, *59*			___
	(A) Closed pilot	15	70	___
	(B) Open pilot	25	150	___
247T	B&O Tender	15	30	___
248	2-4-2 Scout Locomotive, 1130T Tender, *58*	25	75	___
249	2-4-2 Scout Locomotive, 250T Tender, *58*	20	54	___
250	2-4-2 Scout Locomotive, 250T Tender, *57*	20	58	___
250T	Tender	10	24	___
251	2-4-2 Scout Locomotive, *66 u*			___
	(A) 1062T slope-back Tender	67	188	___
	(B) 250T-type Tender	67	178	___
252	Crossing Gate, *50-62*	8	20	___
253	Block Control Signal, *56-59*	11	23	___
256	Illuminated Freight Station, *50-53*			___
256	(A) Standard	23	45	___
256	(B) Light green roof	47	103	___
257	Freight Station with diesel horn, *56-57*			___
	(A) Maroon base	29	73	___
	(B) Brown base	39	95	___
	(C) Maroon or brown base, light green roof	68	145	___
260	Bumper, *51-69*			___
	(A) Die-cast	7	12	___
	(B) Black plastic	15	38	___

		Good	Exc
___ 262	Highway Crossing Gate, *62-69*	15	38
___ 264	Operating Forklift Platform, *57-60*	68	217
___ 282	Portal Gantry Crane, *54-57*	73	177
___ 282R	Portal Gantry Crane, *56-57*	63	153
___ 299	Code Transmitter Beacon Set, *61-63*	35	91
___ 308	Railroad Sign Set, die-cast, *45-49*	20	35
___ 309	Yard Sign Set, plastic, *50-59*	9	24
___ 310	Billboard Set, *50-68*	9	19
___ 313	Bascule Bridge, *46-49*	85	299
___ 313-82	Fiber Pins, dozen, *46-60*	1	2
___ 313-121	Fiber Pins, dozen, *61*	1	2
___ 314	Scale Model Girder Bridge, *45-50*	10	27
___ 315	Illuminated Trestle Bridge, *46-48*	36	109
___ 316	Trestle Bridge, *49*	18	41
___ 317	Trestle Bridge, *50-56*	14	31
___ 321	Trestle Bridge, *58-64*	15	38
___ 321-100	Trestle Bridge	23	64
___ 332	Arch-Under Trestle Bridge, *59-66*	17	35
___ 334	Operating Dispatching Board, *57-60*	67	166
___ 342	Culvert Loader, *56-58*	42	164
___ 345	Culvert Unloader, *57-59*	45	174
___ 346	Culvert Unloader, manual, *65 u*	46	134
___ 347	Cannon Firing Range Set, *64 u*	277	759
___ 348	Culvert Unloader, manual, *66-69*	68	148
___ 350	Engine Transfer Table, *57-60*	99	248
___ 350-50	Transfer Table Extension, *57-60*	73	154
___ 352	Ice Depot with 6352 Ice Car, *55-57*	63	137
___ 353	Trackside Control Signal, *60-61*	11	27
___ 356	Operating Freight Station, *52-57*		
___	(A) Dark green roof, *52-57*	36	82
___	(B) Light green roof, *57*	64	161
___ 362	Barrel Loader, *52-57*		
___	(A) Gold lettering	21	59
___	(B) Red lettering	91	347
___ 362-78	Wooden Barrels, 6 pieces, *52-57*		
___	(A) Brown	6	16
___	(B) Red	74	200
___ 364	Conveyor Lumber Loader, *48-57*	25	69
___ 364C	On/Off Switch, *48-64*	7	12
___ 365	Dispatching Station, *58-59*	41	99
___ 365-35	Set of Delivery Carts, *52*		20
___ 375	Turntable, *62-64*	61	189
___ 390C	Switch, double-pole, double-throw, *60-64*	6	13
___ 394	Rotary Beacon, *49-53*		
___	(A) Steel tower, red platform	14	38
___	(B) Steel tower, green platform	37	84

|---|---|---|---|
	(C) Aluminum tower, platform, and base	16	38 ___
	(D) Aluminum tower, red steel base	29	62 ___
	(E) Steel tower, red platform, stick-on nameplate	32	77 ___
395	Floodlight Tower, *49-56*		___
	(A) Light green, silver, or unpainted aluminum	17	43 ___
	(B) Red	33	104 ___
	(C) Dark green	81	295 ___
	(D) Yellow	47	125 ___
397	Operating Coal Loader, *48-57*		
	(A) Yellow generator, *48*	108	276 ___
	(B) Blue generator, *49-57*	29	67 ___
400	B&O Passenger Rail Diesel Car, *56-58*	70	157 ___
404	B&O Baggage-Mail Rail Diesel Car, *57-58*	141	285 ___
410	Billboard Blinker, *56-58*	18	48 ___
413	Countdown Control Panel, *62*	19	52 ___
415	Diesel Fueling Station, *55-57*	48	128 ___
419	Heliport Control Tower, *62*	150	312 ___
443	Missile Launching Platform with ammo dump, *60-62*	28	63 ___
445	Switch Tower, lighted, *52-57*	23	53 ___
448	Missile Firing Range Set, *61-63*	46	143 ___
450	Operating Signal Bridge, *52-58*	22	48 ___
450L	Signal Light Head, *52-58*	12	32 ___
452	Overhead Gantry Signal, *61-63*	40	98 ___
455	Operating Oil Derrick, *50-54*		___
	(A) Dark green tower, green top	56	113 ___
	(B) Dark green tower, red top	59	159 ___
	(C) Apple green tower, red top	90	347 ___
456	Coal Ramp with 3456 Hopper, *50-55*		___
	(A) Light gray ramp	42	125 ___
	(B) Dark gray ramp	55	134 ___
456C	Coal Ramp Controller	15	29 ___
460	Piggyback Transportation Set, *55-57*		___
	(A) Metal stick-on signs on lift truck	56	110 ___
	(B) Rubber-stamped lettering on lift truck	65	132 ___
460P	Piggyback Platform, *55-57*	20	58 ___
461	Platform with truck and trailer, *66*	60	180 ___
462	Derrick Platform Set, *61-62*	109	285 ___
464	Lumber Mill, *56-60*	41	100 ___
465	Sound Dispatching Station, *56-57*	38	82 ___
470	Missile Launching Platform with target car, *59-62*	58	95 ___
479-1	Truck for 6362 Truck Car with envelope, *55-56*	23	67 ___
480-25	Conversion Magnetic Coupler, *50-60*	1	5 ___
480-32	Conversion Magnetic Coupler, *61-69*	1	5 ___
494	Rotary Beacon, *54-66*		___
	(A) Painted steel	23	43 ___
	(B) Unpainted aluminum	23	56 ___

POSTWAR 1945-1969		Good	Exc
___ **497**	Coaling Station, *53-58*	45	101
___ **520**	LL Boxcab Electric Locomotive, *56-57*		
___	(A) Black pantograph	32	72
___	(B) Copper-colored pantograph	40	89
___ **600**	MKT NW2 Switcher, *55*		
___	(A) Black frame, black end rails	49	108
___	(B) Gray frame, yellow or black end rails	78	197
___ **601**	Seaboard NW2 Switcher, *56*		
___	(A) Red stripes with square ends	70	160
___	(B) Red stripes with round ends	76	159
___ **602**	Seaboard NW2 Switcher, *57-58*	71	150
___ **610**	Erie NW2 Switcher, *55*		
___	(A) Black frame, two-axle Magnetraction	47	151
___	(B) Yellow frame	123	313
___	(C) Replacement body with nameplates	87	291
___ **611**	Jersey Central NW2 Switcher, *57-58*	60	152
___ **613**	UP NW2 Switcher, *58*	75	224
___ **614**	Alaska NW2 Switcher, *59-60*		
___ **614**	(A) Plastic bell, no brake	89	189
___ **614**	(B) No bell, yellow brake	112	220
___ **614**	(C) "Built by Lionel" outlined in yellow near nose	151	302
___ **616**	Santa Fe NW2 Switcher, *61-62*		
___	(A) Open E-unit slot and bell/horn slots	92	206
___	(B) Plugged E-unit slot and open bell/horn slots	96	233
___	(C) Plugged E-unit slot and bell/horn slots	102	234
___ **617**	Santa Fe NW2 Switcher, *63*	105	237
___ **621**	Jersey Central NW2 Switcher, *56-57*	70	147
___ **622**	Santa Fe NW2 Switcher, *49-50*		
___	(A) Large GM decal on cab	116	240
___	(B) Small GM decal on side	93	204
___ **623**	Santa Fe NW2 Switcher, *52-54*	70	131
___ **624**	C&O NW2 Switcher, *52-54*	78	175
___ **625**	LV GE 44-ton Switcher, *57-58*	40	97
___ **626**	B&O GE 44-ton Switcher, *56-57, 59*	124	296
___ **627**	LV GE 44-ton Switcher, *56-57*	31	69
___ **628**	NP GE 44-ton Switcher, *56-57*	43	92
___ **629**	Burlington GE 44-ton Switcher, *56*	134	333
___ **633**	Santa Fe NW2 Switcher, *62*	61	129
___ **634**	Santa Fe NW2 Switcher, *63, 65-66*		
___	(A) Safety stripes	73	143
___	(B) No safety stripes	55	110
___ **635**	UP NW2 Switcher, *65 u*	52	120
___ **637**	2-6-4 Locomotive, 2046 736W Tender, *59-63*		
___	(A) 2046W Lionel Lines Tender	55	153
___	(B) 736W Pennsylvania Tender	70	201
___ **638-2361**	Van Camp's Pork & Beans Boxcar, *62 u*	15	37

POSTWAR 1945-1969		Good	Exc	
645	Union Pacific NW2 Switcher, *69*	44	129	___
646	4-6-4 Locomotive, 2046W Tender, *54-58*	112	214	___
665	4-6-4 Locomotive, 2046W, 6026W, or 736W Tender, *54-59, 66*	77	203	___
671	6-8-6 Steam Turbine Locomotive, *46-49*			___
	(A) Bulb smoke unit, 671W Tender, *46*	40	99	___
	(B) E-unit slot, heater smoke unit, 671W Tender, *47*	38	95	___
	(C) Thin nickel rims, 2671W Tender with functioning backup lights, *48*	63	208	___
	(D) Thin nickel rims, 2671W Tender, nonfunctioning backup lights, *48*	56	118	___
	(E) Thin nickel rims, 2671W Tender, no backup light lenses, *48*	52	113	___
	(F) No rims on drivers, *49*	50	110	___
671-75	Smoke Lamp, *12 volt, 46*	10	18	___
671R	6-8-6 Steam Turbine Locomotive, 4424W or 4671 Tender, *46-49*	165	303	___
671RR	6-8-6 Steam Turbine Locomotive, 2046W-50 Tender, *52*	73	160	___
671S	Smoke Conversion Kit	20	90	___
671W	Whistle Tender, *46-48*	27	55	___
675	2-6-2 Locomotive, 2466WX or 6466WX Tender, *47-49*			___
	(A) Aluminum smokestack, *47*	58	212	___
	(B) Black smokestack, *48-49*	52	169	___
675	2-6-4 Locomotive, 2046W Tender, *52*	66	161	___
681	6-8-6 Steam Turbine Locomotive			
	(A) 2671W Tender, *50-51*	50	108	___
	(B) 2046W-50 Tender, *53*	48	105	___
682	6-8-6 Steam Turbine Locomotive, 2046W-50 Tender, *54-55*	132	290	___
685	4-6-4 Hudson Locomotive, 6026W Tender, *53*	75	202	___
703-10	Smoke Lamp, 18 volt, *46*	12	22	___
726	2-8-4 Berkshire, *46-49*			___
726	(A) Turned stanchions, no front coupler, bulb smoke unit, 2426W Tender, *46*	240	527	___
726	(B) Cotter pin stanchions, E-unit slot, no front coupler, heater smoke unit, 2426W Tender, *47*	213	493	___
726	(C) Simulated front coupler, 2426W Tender, *48-49*	105	244	___
726RR	2-8-4 Berkshire Locomotive, 2046W Tender, *52*	127	257	___
726S	Smoke Conversion Kit	32	101	___
736	2-8-4 Berkshire Locomotive, *50-66*			___
	(A) No headlight wedge brace, hexagonal flagstaff base, 2671WX Tender, *50-51*	120	175	___
	(B) Headlight wedge brace, round flagstaff brace, 2046W Tender, *53-54*	118	168	___
	(C) Sheet metal and plastic trailing truck, *55-56*	113	163	___
	(D) Smaller typeface on cab number, *57-60*	110	158	___
	(E) 736W Tender, *61-66*	73	146	___
736W	PRR Whistle Tender	22	65	___
746	N&W 4-8-4 Class J Northern, *57-60*			___
	(A) Tender with long stripe	409	924	___
	(B) Tender with short stripe	363	718	___

| --- | --- | --- | --- |
___ 746W	N&W Tender		
___	(A) short stripe	45	157
___	(B) Long stripe	100	190
___ 760	Curved Track, 16 sections (O72), *54-57*	32	72
___ 773	4-6-4 Hudson Locomotive		
___	(A) Valve guides cast in steam chest, 2426W Tender, *50*	338	750
___	(B) No valve guides in steam chest, 736W Pennsylvania Tender, *64*	268	465
___	(C) 773W New York Central Tender, *64-66*	335	553
___ 773T	NYC Tender	70	150
___ 773W	NYC Whistle Tender, *64-65*	129	249
___ 773W	NYC Whistle Tender, *66*	75	135
___ 902	Elevated Trestle Set, *60*	28	149
___ 909	Smoke Fluid, large or small bottle, *57-66, 68-69*		
___	(A) ½ ounce bottle	7	29
___	(B) 2 ounce bottle	10	42
___ B909	Smoke Capsules, pack of three, *57-66, 68-69*	8	28
___ 919	Artificial Grass, *46-64*	8	16
___ 920	Scenic Display Set, *57-58*	35	84
___ 920-2	Tunnel Portals, pair, *58-59*	12	27
___ 920-3	Green Grass, *57*	4	11
___ 920-4	Yellow Grass, *57*	7	15
___ 920-5	Artificial Rock, *57-58*	3	13
___ 920-6	Dry Glue, *57-58*	3	10
___ 920-8	Dyed Lichen, *57-58*	3	15
___ 925	Lubricant, 2 ounce tube, *46-69*	3	11
___ 925-1	Lubricant, 1 ounce tube, *50-69*	1	5
___ 926	Lubricant, ½ ounce tube, *55*	2	3
___ 926-5	Instruction Booklet, *46-48*	1	4
___ 927	Lubricating Kit, *50-59*	10	25
___ 927-3	Track Cleaner	4	14
___ 928	Maintenance and Lubricating Kit, *60-63*	28	58
___ 943	Ammo Dump, *59-61*	15	36
___ 950	U.S. Railroad Map, *58-66*	18	49
___ 951	Farm Set, 13 pieces, *58*	54	122
___ 952	Figure Set, 30 pieces, *58*	30	58
___ 953	Figure Set, 32 pieces, *59-62*	46	71
___ 954	Swimming Pool and Playground Set, 30 pieces, *59*	40	96
___ 955	Highway Set, 22 pieces, *58*	30	65
___ 956	Stockyard Set, 18 pieces, *59*	40	89
___ 957	Farm Building and Animal Set, 35 pieces, *58*	60	120
___ 958	Vehicle Set, 24 pieces, *58*	45	177
___ 959	Barn Set, 23 pieces, *58*	39	79
___ 960	Barnyard Set, 29 pieces, *59-61*	60	127
___ 961	School Set, 36 pieces, *59*	45	108
___ 962	Turnpike Set, 24 pieces, *58*	68	175
___ 963	Frontier Set, 18 pieces, *59-60*	66	147

POSTWAR 1945-1969		Good	Exc	
963-100	Boxed Frontier Set, *60*	125	400	___
964	Factory Site Set, 18 pieces, *59*	70	198	___
965	Farm Set, 36 pieces, *59*	57	124	___
966	Firehouse Set, 45 pieces, *58*	65	147	___
967	Post Office Set, 25 pieces, *58*	48	111	___
968	TV Transmitter Set, 28 pieces, *58*	55	118	___
969	Construction Set, 23 pieces, *60*	61	122	___
970	Ticket Booth, *58-60*	35	119	___
971	Lichen with box, *60-64*	29	70	___
972	Landscape Tree Assortment, *61-64*	25	72	___
973	Complete Landscaping Set, *60-64*	45	129	___
974	Scenery Set, *58*	70	190	___
980	Ranch Set, 14 pieces, *60*	50	117	___
981	Freight Yard Set, 10 pieces, *60*	51	131	___
982	Suburban Split Level Set, 18 pieces, *60*	42	116	___
983	Farm Set, 7 pieces, *60-61*	33	75	___
984	Railroad Set, 22 pieces, *61-62*	56	127	___
985	Freight Area Set, 32 pieces, *61*	35	165	___
986	Farm Set, 20 pieces, *62*	45	168	___
987	Town Set, 24 pieces, *62*	30	253	___
988	Railroad Structure Set, 16 pieces, *62*	40	558	___
1001	2-4-2 Scout Locomotive, plastic body, 1001T Tender, *48*			___
	(A) Silver rubber-stamped cab number	25	70	___
	(B) White heat-stamped cab number	15	38	___
1001T	Tender	6	22	___
1002	Gondola, *48-52*			___
	(A) Black, white lettering	4	10	___
	(B) Blue, white lettering	4	12	___
	(C) Silver, black lettering	150	466	___
	(D) Yellow, black lettering	140	452	___
	(E) Red, white lettering	146	443	___
X1004	PRR Baby Ruth Boxcar, *48-52*	5	10	___
1005	Sunoco 1-D Tank Car, *48-50*	3	10	___
1007	LL SP-type Caboose, *48-52*			___
	(A) Red body	2	8	___
	(B) Red body, raised board on catwalk	10	30	___
	(C) Tuscan body	196	694	___
1008	Uncoupling Unit (O27), *57-62*	2	4	___
1008-50	Uncoupling Track Section (O27), *57-62*	2	4	___
1009	Manumatic Track Section (O27), *48-52*	4	7	___
1010	Transformer, 35 watts, *61-66*	5	10	___
1011	Transformer, 25 watts, *48-49*	4	11	___
1012	Transformer, 35 watts, *50-54*	5	9	___
1013	Curved Track (O27), *45-69*		1	___
1013-17	Steel Pins, dozen (O27), *46-60*		1	___
1013-42	Steel Pins, dozen (O27), *61-68*		2	___

| --- | --- | --- | --- |
___ **1014**	Transformer, 40 watts, *55*	5	13
___ **1015**	Transformer, 45 watts, *56-60*	6	11
___ **1016**	Transformer, 35 watts, *59-60*	5	8
___ **1018**	Half Straight Track (027), *55-69*		1
___ **1018**	Straight Track (027), *45-69*		1
___ **1019**	Remote Control Track Set (027), *46-48*	2	7
___ **1020**	90-degree Crossing (027), *55-69*	2	5
___ **1021**	90-degree Crossing (027), *45-54*	2	4
___ **1022**	Manual Switches, pair (027), *53-69*	6	11
___ **1023**	45-degree Crossing (027), *56-69*	2	5
___ **1024**	Manual Switches, pair (027), *46-52*	5	14
___ **1025**	Illuminated Bumper (027), *46-47*	6	11
___ **1025**	Transformer, 45 watts, *61-69*	5	11
___ **1026**	Transformer, 25 watts, *61-64*	2	5
___ **1032**	Transformer, 75 watts, *48*	10	19
___ **1033**	Transformer, 90 watts, *48-56*	19	35
___ **1034**	Transformer, 75 watts, *48-54*	8	19
___ **1035**	Transformer, 60 watts, *47*	7	13
___ **1037**	Transformer, 40 watts, *46-47*	4	9
___ **1041**	Transformer, 60 watts, *45-46*	9	17
___ **1042**	Transformer, 75 watts, *47-48*	13	23
___ **1043**	Transformer, 50 watts, *53-57*	5	13
___ **1043-500**	Transformer, 60 watts, ivory, *57-58*	73	143
___ **1044**	Transformer, 90 watts, *57-69*	19	38
___ **1045**	Operating Watchman, *46-50*	17	45
___ **1045C**	Contactor	4	10
___ **1047**	Operating Switchman, *59-61*	21	144
___ **1050**	0-4-0 Scout Locomotive, 1050T Tender, *59 u*	37	130
___ **1050T**	Tender	5	16
___ **1053**	Transformer, 60 watts, *56-60*	7	14
___ **1055**	Texas Special Alco Diesel A Unit, *59-60*	23	58
___ **1060**	2-4-2 Locomotive, 1050T or 1060T Tender, *60-62*	10	30
___ **1060T**	Lionel Lines Tender	7	16
___ **1060T-50**	Southern Pacific Tender, *63-64 u*	12	33
___ **1061**	0-4-0 or 2-4-2 Scout Locomotive, 1061T Tender, *64, 69*	0	0
___	(A) Slope-back Lionel Lines tender	12	27
___	(B) Paper number labels	39	134
___	(C) No number stamped on cab	30	80
___ **1061T**	Tender	4	16
___ **1062**	0-4-0 or 2-4-2 Scout Locomotive, *63-64*		
___	(A) Streamlined Southern Pacific Tender	20	45
___	(B) Other tenders	18	33
___ **1063**	Transformer, 75 watts, *60-64*	12	39
___ **1065**	Union Pacific Alco Diesel A Unit, *61*	24	74
___ **1066**	Union Pacific Alco Diesel A Unit, *64 u*	29	70
___ **1073**	Transformer, 60 watts, *61-66*	7	16

POSTWAR 1945-1969		Good	Exc	
1101	Transformer, 25 watts, *48*	3	7	___
1101	2-4-2 Scout Locomotive, 1001T Tender, *48 u*			___
	(A) Cab correctly marked "1101"	15	34	___
	(B) Cab marked "1001"	92	231	___
1110	2-4-2 Locomotive, 1001T Tender, *49, 51-52*	13	28	___
1120	2-4-2 Scout Locomotive, 1001T Tender, *50*	20	33	___
1121	Remote Control Switches, pair (027), *46-51*	11	26	___
1122	Remote Control Switches, pair (027), *52-53*	12	26	___
1122-34	Remote Control Switches, pair, *52-53*	14	27	___
1122-500	Gauge Adapter (027), *57-66*	4	10	___
1122E	Remote Control Switches, pair (027), *53-69*	11	27	___
1130	2-4-2 Locomotive, 6066T or 1130T Tender, *53-54*			___
	(A) Plastic body	15	44	___
	(B) Die-cast body	31	89	___
1130T	Tender			___
	(A) Black-painted shell	28	71	___
	(B) Black plastic shell	7	21	___
1130T-500	Tender, pink, from Girls Set	97	241	___
1144	Transformer, 75 watts, *61-66*	10	24	___
1232	Transformer, 75 watts, made for export, *48*	15	38	___
1615	0-4-0 Locomotive, 1615T Tender, *55-57*			___
	(A) No grab irons	60	127	___
	(B) Grab irons on locomotive and tender	115	255	___
1615T	Tender	14	31	___
1625	0-4-0 Locomotive, 1625T Tender, *58*	155	348	___
1625T	Tender	23	46	___
1640-100	Presidential Kit, *60*	49	152	___
1654	2-4-2 Locomotive, 1654W Tender, *46-47*	35	78	___
1654T	Tender	10	20	___
1654W	Whistling Tender	15	33	___
1655	2-4-2 Locomotive, 6654W Tender, *48-49*	35	74	___
1656	0-4-0 Locomotive, 6403B Tender, *48-49*			___
	(A) Large silver cab number	115	235	___
	(B) Small silver cab number	113	266	___
1665	0-4-0 Locomotive, 2403B Tender, *46*	183	341	___
1666	2-6-2 Locomotive, 2466W or 2466WX Tender, *46-47*			___
	(A) Number plate and two-piece bell	60	125	___
	(B) Rubber-stamped number and one-piece bell	79	150	___
1666T	Tender	10	25	___
1862	4-4-0 Civil War General, 1862T Tender, *59-62*			___
	(A) Gray smokestack	82	161	___
	(B) Black smokestack	88	175	___
1862T	Tender	21	37	___
1865	Western & Atlantic Coach, *59-62*	23	46	___
1866	Western & Atlantic Mail-Baggage Car, *59-62*	24	47	___

POSTWAR 1945-1969		Good	Exc
____ **1872**	4-4-0 Civil War General, 1872T Tender, *59-62*	107	233
____ **1872T**	Tender	31	48
____ **1875**	Western & Atlantic Coach, *59-62*	76	228
____ **1875W**	Western & Atlantic Coach, whistle, *59-62*	53	120
____ **1876**	Western & Atlantic Baggage Car, *59-62*	35	83
____ **1877**	Flatcar with fence and horses, *59-62*	46	102
____ **1882**	4-4-0 Civil War General, 1882T Tender, *60 u*	245	414
____ **1882T**	Tender, *60 u*	36	104
____ **1885**	Western & Atlantic Coach, *60 u*	105	208
____ **1887**	Flatcar with fences and horses, *60 u*	65	151
____ **2001**	Track Make-up Kit (027), *63*	300	775
____ **2002**	Track Make-up Kit (027), *63*	495	1181
____ **2003**	Track Make-up Kit (027), *63*	600	1900
____ **2016**	2-6-4 Locomotive, 6026W Tender, *55-56*	40	84
____ **2018**	2-6-4 Locomotive, *56-59, 61*		
____	(A) 6026T Tender	32	64
____	(B) 6026W Tender	43	89
____	(C) 1130T Tender	35	65
____ **2020**	6-8-6 Steam Turbine Locomotive, 2020W or 2466WX Tender, smoke lamp, *46*	75	178
____ **2020**	6-8-6 Steam Turbine Locomotive, 2020W or 6020W Tender, *47-49*	66	159
____ **2020W**	Whistling Tender	32	62
____ **2023**	Union Pacific Alco Diesel AA Units, *50-51*	65	325
____ **2023**	(A) Yellow body	91	212
____ **2023**	(B) Gray nose and side frames	1140	3572
____ **2023**	(C) Silver body	65	185
____ **2024**	C&O Alco Diesel A Unit, *69*	28	75
____ **2025**	2-6-2 Locomotive, 2466WX or 6466WX Tender, *47-49*		
____	(A) Black smokestack, *48-49*	73	165
____	(B) Aluminum smokestack, *47*	83	185
____ **2025**	2-6-4 Locomotive, 6466W Tender, *52*	73	159
____ **2026**	2-6-2 Locomotive, 6466WX Tender, *48-49*	47	82
____ **2026**	2-6-4 Locomotive, 6466W, 6466T, or 6066T Tender, *51-53*	41	78
____ **2028**	Pennsylvania GP7 Diesel, *55*		
____	(A) Gold lettering	119	243
____	(B) Yellow lettering	92	210
____	(C) Tan frame	202	511
____ **2029**	2-6-4 Locomotive, *64-69*		
____	(A) 234W Lionel Lines Tender	48	104
____	(B) LL Tender with "Hagerstown" on bottom	58	128
____	(C) 234W Pennsylvania Tender	82	180
____ **2031**	Rock Island Alco Diesel AA Units, *52-54*	74	219
____ **2032**	Erie Alco Diesel AA Units, *52-54*	66	214
____ **2033**	Union Pacific Alco Diesel AA Units, *52-54*	65	190
____ **2034**	2-4-2 Scout Locomotive, 6066T Tender, *52*	28	61
____ **2035**	2-6-4 Locomotive, 6466W Tender, *50-51*	56	124

POSTWAR 1945-1969		Good	Exc	
2036	2-6-4 Locomotive, 6466W Tender, *50*	47	92	___
2037	2-6-4 Locomotive, *54-55, 57-63*			___
	(A) 6026T or 1130T Tender	35	85	___
	(B) 6026W, 233W, or 234W whistle Tender	58	107	___
2037-500	2-6-4 Locomotive, pink, 1130T-500 Tender, *57-58*	355	933	___
2041	Rock Island Alco Diesel AA Units, *69*	52	143	___
2046	4-6-4 Locomotive, 2046W Tender, *50-51, 53*	76	157	___
2046T	Tender, for export	58	221	___
2046W	Whistle Tender	28	65	___
2046W-50	PRR Whistle Tender	31	61	___
2055	4-6-4 Locomotive, 2046W or 6026W Tender, *53-55*	79	143	___
2056	4-6-4 Locomotive, 2046W Tender, *52*	74	187	___
2065	4-6-4 Locomotive, 2046W or 6026W Tender, *54-56*	67	170	___
2203B	Tender with bell	55	120	___
2203T	Tender, *45-46*	36	54	___
2224W	Whistle Tender	24	75	___
2240	Wabash F3 AB Units, *56*	162	441	___
2242	New Haven F3 AB Units, *58-59*	200	776	___
2242C	New Haven F3 B Unit, *58-59*	64	196	___
2243	Santa Fe F3 AB Units, *55-57*			___
	(A) Gray body mold, raised molded cab door ladder	103	253	___
	(B) Typical molded cab door ladder	83	194	___
2243C	Santa Fe F3 B Unit, *55-57*	52	126	___
2245	Texas Special F3 AB Units, *54-55*			___
	(A) B Unit with portholes, *54*	207	387	___
	(B) B Unit without portholes, *55*	227	693	___
2257	SP-type caboose, *47*			___
	(A) Red body, no smokestack	5	15	___
	(B) Tuscan body and smokestack	74	318	___
	(C) Red body and smokestack	110	422	___
2321	Lackawanna FM Train Master Diesel, *54-56*			___
2321	(A) Gray roof	141	363	___
2321	(B) Maroon roof	155	411	___
2322	Virginian FM Train Master Diesel, *65-66*			___
	(A) Unpainted blue body, yellow stripes	224	490	___
	(B) Blue or black body, painted blue and yellow stripes	323	627	___
2328	Burlington GP7 Diesel, *55-56*	77	195	___
2329	Virginian GE E-33 or EL-C Electric Locomotive, *58-59*	173	459	___
2330	Pennsylvania GG1 Electric Locomotive, green, *50*	336	1019	___
2331	Virginian FM Train Master Diesel, *55-58*			___
	(A) Black and yellow stripes, gray mold, *55*	352	678	___
	(B) Yellow stripes, blue mold, *56-58*	228	539	___
	(C) Blue and yellow stripes, gray mold	525	1038	___
2332	Pennsylvania GG1 Electric Locomotive, *47-49*			___
	(A) Black	469	1139	___

			Good	Exc
____		(B) Dark green	198	582
____	**2333**	NYC F3 Diesel AA Units, *48-49*		
____		(A) Rubber-stamped lettering	234	585
____		(B) Heat-stamped lettering	173	482
____	**2333**	Santa Fe F3 Diesel AA Units, *48-49*	167	390
____	**2337**	Wabash GP7 Diesel, *58*	88	207
____	**2338**	Milwaukee Road GP7 Diesel, *55-56*		
____		(A) Orange band around shell	404	1244
____		(B) Interrupted orange band	73	187
____	**2339**	Wabash GP7 Diesel, *57*	113	231
____	**2340**	Pennsylvania GG1 Electric Locomotive, *55*		
____		(A) Tuscan	430	1027
____		(B) Dark green	305	752
____	**2341**	Jersey Central FM Train Master Diesel, *56*		
____		(A) High-gloss orange	953	2447
____		(B) Dull orange	808	2231
____	**2343**	Santa Fe F3 Diesel AA Units, *50-52*	178	438
____	**2343C**	Santa Fe F3 B Unit, *50-55*		
____		(A) Screen roof vents	91	232
____		(B) Louver roof vents	72	174
____	**2344**	NYC F3 Diesel AA Units, *50-52*	176	496
____	**2344C**	NYC F3 B Unit, *50-55*	97	215
____	**2345**	Western Pacific F3 Diesel AA Units, *52*	472	1049
____	**2346**	B&M GP9 Diesel, *65-66*	130	293
____	**2347**	C&O GP7 Diesel, *65 u*	1583	3800
____	**2348**	M&StL GP9 Diesel, *58-59*	134	273
____	**2349**	Northern Pacific GP9 Diesel, *59-60*	159	380
____	**2350**	New Haven EP-5 Electric Locomotive, *56-58*		
____		(A) Painted nose trim, white N and orange H	205	505
____		(B) Decaled nose trim, white N and orange H	107	275
____		(C) Painted nose trim, orange N and black H	754	1892
____		(D) Decaled nose trim, orange N and black H	431	964
____		(E) Orange and white stripes go through doorjambs	325	1018
____	**2351**	Milwaukee Road EP-5 Electric Locomotive, *57-58*	155	383
____	**2352**	Pennsylvania EP-5 Electric Locomotive, *58-59*		
____		(A) Tuscan body	159	391
____		(B) Chocolate brown body	209	390
____	**2353**	Santa Fe F3 Diesel AA Units, *53-55*	141	385
____	**2354**	NYC F3 Diesel AA Units, *53-55*	208	357
____	**2355**	Western Pacific F3 Diesel AA Units, *53*	405	857
____	**2356**	Southern F3 Diesel AA Units, *54-56*	333	749
____	**2356C**	Southern F3 B Unit, *54-56*	127	261
____	**2357**	SP-type Caboose, *47-48*		
____		(A) Red body and smokestack	294	507
____		(B) Tuscan body and smokestack	15	36
____		(C) Tile red, no smokestack, "6357" stamped on bottom	68	153

		Good	Exc	
2358	Great Northern EP-5 Electric Locomotive, *59-60*	249	600	___
2359	Boston & Maine GP9 Diesel, *61-62*	103	268	___
2360	Pennsylvania GG1 Electric Locomotive, *56-58, 61-63*			___
	(A) Tuscan, 5 gold stripes	537	1326	___
	(B) Dark green, 5 gold stripes	360	857	___
	(C) Tuscan, gold stripe, heat-stamped letters	360	837	___
	(D) Tuscan, gold stripe, decaled lettering	344	742	___
2363	Illinois Central F3 Diesel AB Units, *55-56*			___
	(A) Black lettering	329	697	___
	(B) Brown lettering	372	756	___
2365	C&O GP7 Diesel, *62-63*	133	261	___
2367	Wabash F3 Diesel AB Units, *55*	294	583	___
2367C	Wabash F3 Diesel B Unit, *55*	80	175	___
2368	B&O F3 Diesel AB Units, *56*	443	1008	___
2373	CP F3 Diesel AA Units, *57*	706	1484	___
2378	Milwaukee Road F3 Diesel AB Units, *56*			___
	(A) Yellow roof line stripes	521	1130	___
	(B) No roof line stripes	461	979	___
2378C	Milwaukee Road F3 Diesel B Unit, yellow roof line stripe, *56*	234	474	___
2379	Rio Grande F3 Diesel AB Units, *57-58*	345	800	___
2383	Santa Fe F3 Diesel AA Units, *58-66*	168	391	___
2400	Maplewood Pullman Car, green, *48-49*	38	96	___
2401	Hillside Observation Car, green, *48-49*	32	85	___
2402	Chatham Pullman Car, green, *48-49*	39	97	___
2403B	Tender, *46*	20	47	___
2404	Santa Fe Vista Dome Car, *64-65*	30	59	___
2405	Santa Fe Pullman Car, *64-65*	27	66	___
2406	Santa Fe Observation Car, *64-65*	24	57	___
2408	Santa Fe Vista Dome Car, *66*	37	75	___
2409	Santa Fe Pullman Car, *66*	36	74	___
2410	Santa Fe Observation Car, *66*	30	68	___
2411	Lionel Lines Flatcar, *46-48*			___
	(A) With pipes, *46*	28	74	___
	(B) With logs, *47-48*	15	38	___
2412	Santa Fe Vista Dome Car, *59-63*	30	72	___
2414	Santa Fe Pullman Car, *59-63*	33	78	___
2416	Santa Fe Observation Car, *59-63*	27	65	___
2419	DL&W Work Caboose, *46-47*	17	42	___
2420	DL&W Work Caboose with searchlight, *46-48*			___
	(A) Light or dark gray, heat-stamped lettering	45	89	___
	(B) Light or dark gray, rubber-stamped lettering	55	55	___
2421	Maplewood Pullman Car, *50-53*			___
	(A) Gray roof	28	65	___
	(B) Silver roof	23	53	___
2422	Chatham Pullman Car, *50-53*			___
	(A) Gray roof	28	65	___

| --- | --- | --- | --- |
____	(B) Silver roof	23	51
____ 2423	Hillside Observation Car, *50-53*		
____	(A) Gray roof	23	61
____	(B) Silver roof	21	47
____ 2426W	Whistle Tender, *50*	114	249
____ 2429	Livingston Pullman Car, *52-53*	45	96
____ 2430	Pullman Car, blue, *46-47*	23	87
____ 2431	Observation Car, blue, *46-47*	19	89
____ 2432	Clifton Vista Dome Car, *54-58*	28	78
____ 2434	Newark Pullman Car, *54-58*	32	79
____ 2435	Elizabeth Pullman Car, *54-58*	44	113
____ 2436	Mooseheart Observation Car, *57-58*	30	75
____ 2436	Summit Observation Car, *54-56*	25	61
____ 2440	Pullman Car, green, *46-47*		
____	(A) Silver lettering	33	62
____	(B) White lettering	26	57
____ 2441	Observation Car, green, *46-47*		
____	(A) Silver lettering	33	62
____	(B) White lettering	27	56
____ 2442	Clifton Vista Dome Car, *56*	40	85
____ 2442	Pullman Car, brown, *46-48*		
____	(A) Silver lettering	37	67
____	(B) White lettering	27	57
____ 2443	Observation Car, brown, *46-48*		
____	(A) Silver lettering	34	62
____	(B) White lettering	27	57
____ 2444	Newark Pullman Car, *56*	42	93
____ 2445	Elizabeth Pullman Car, *56*	102	204
____ 2446	Summit Observation Car, *56*	39	78
____ 2452	Pennsylvania Gondola, *45-47*		
____	(A) Whirly wheels, *45*	18	42
____	(B) Regular wheels	9	18
____	(C) Early flying shoe trucks, two holes in floor, *45*	34	89
____ 2452X	Pennsylvania Gondola, *46-47*	7	16
____ X2454	Baby Ruth Boxcar, PRR logo, *46-47*	18	40
____ X2454	Pennsylvania Boxcar, *46*		
____	(A) Brown door	79	174
____	(B) Orange door	130	368
____ 2456	Lehigh Valley Hopper, *48*		
____	(A) Flat black, 2 lines of data, *48*	13	29
____	(B) Flat black, 3 lines of data, *48*	81	213
____ 2457	PRR N5-type Caboose "477618," tintype, *45-47*	0	0
____	(A) Brown body, white lettering centered, red window frames, *45*	15	45
____	(B) Brown body, white lettering not centered, *45*	88	298
____	(C) Red body, red window frames, *46-47*	10	21
____	(D) Red body, black window frames, *46-47*	9	19

		Good	Exc	
	(E) Red body, no "Eastern Division" markings, *46-47*	10	20	___
	(F) Same as E, but black smokejack, *46-47*	10	21	___
X2458	PRR Automobile Boxcar, *46-48*	25	52	___
2460	Bucyrus Erie Crane Car, 12-wheel, *46-50*			___
	(A) Gray cab	70	222	___
	(B) Black cab	32	82	___
2461	Transformer Car, die-cast, *47-48*			___
	(A) Red transformer	27	74	___
	(B) Black transformer	27	64	___
	(C) Red transformer, number rubber-stamped on bottom	44	141	___
2465	Sunoco 2-D Tank Car, *46-48*			___
	(A) "Gas, Sunoco, and Oils" in diamond, centered	172	438	___
	(B) "Sunoco" in diamond	6	17	___
	(C) "Sunoco" extends beyond diamond	7	17	___
	(D) "Sunoco" in diamond, centered	63	120	___
2466T	Tender	17	39	___
2466W	Whistle Tender, *46-48*			___
	(A) Number heat-stamped on front, *46*		151	___
	(B) Number missing from front, *47-48*	12	23	___
2466WX	Whistle Tender, *45-48*	23	53	___
2472	PRR N5-type Caboose, tintype, *46-47*	9	23	___
2481	Plainfield Pullman Car, yellow, *50*	87	234	___
2482	Westfield Pullman Car, yellow, *50*	87	236	___
2483	Livingston Observation Car, yellow, *50*	72	213	___
2521	President McKinley Observation Car, *62-66*	61	165	___
2522	President Harrison Vista Dome Car, *62-66*	71	182	___
2523	President Garfield Pullman Car, *62-66*	70	181	___
2530	REA Baggage Car, *54-60*			___
	(A) Large doors	145	287	___
	(B) Small doors	66	153	___
2531	Silver Dawn Observation Car, *52-60*			___
	(A) Ribbed channels, round rivets	32	92	___
	(B) Ribbed channels, hex rivets	39	86	___
	(C) Ribbed channels, hex rivets, red center taillight	60	137	___
	(D) Flat channels, glued nameplates	45	103	___
2532	Silver Range Vista Dome Car, *52-60*	55	115	___
	(A) Ribbed channels, or hex rivets	41	91	___
	(B) Flat channels, glued nameplates	41	128	___
2533	Silver Cloud Pullman Car, *52-59*			___
	(A) Ribbed channels, or hex rivets	36	84	___
	(B) Flat channels, glued nameplates	47	109	___
2534	Silver Bluff Pullman Car, *52-59*			___
	(A) Ribbed channels, or hex rivets	38	89	___
	(B) Flat channels, glued nameplates	41	120	___
2541	Alexander Hamilton Observation Car, *55-56**	64	163	___
2542	Betsy Ross Vista Dome Car, *55-56**	67	172	___

____	**2543**	William Penn Pullman Car, *55-56**	63	173
____	**2544**	Molly Pitcher Pullman Car, *55-56**	65	173
____	**2550**	B&O Baggage-Mail Rail Diesel Car, *57-58*	148	433
____	**2551**	Banff Park Observation Car, *57**	106	239
____	**2552**	Skyline 500 Vista Dome Car, *57**	121	251
____	**2553**	Blair Manor Pullman Car, *57**	172	381
____	**2554**	Craig Manor Pullman Car, *57**	171	381
____	**2555**	Sunoco 1-D Tank Car, *46-48*	21	54
____	**2559**	B&O Passenger Rail Diesel Car, *57-58*	122	284
____	**2560**	Lionel Lines Crane Car, 8-wheel, *46-47*		
____		(A) Black boom	21	72
____		(B) Brown boom	25	79
____		(C) Green boom	34	87
____	**2561**	Vista Valley Observation Car, *59-61**	82	220
____	**2562**	Regal Pass Vista Dome Car, *59-61**	90	239
____	**2563**	Indian Falls Pullman Car, *59-61**	94	261
____	**2625**	Irvington Pullman Car, *46-50**		
____		(A) No silhouettes	55	150
____		(B) Silhouettes	84	244
____	**2625**	Madison Pullman Car, *46-47**	65	164
____	**2625**	Manhattan Pullman Car, *46-47**	65	164
____	**2627**	Madison Pullman Car, *48-50**		
____		(A) No silhouettes	59	165
____		(B) Silhouettes	81	237
____	**2628**	Manhattan Pullman Car, *48-50**		
____	**2628**	(A) No silhouettes	60	150
____	**2628**	(B) Silhouettes	80	213
____	**2666T**	Tender	9	18
____	**2671T**	PRR Tender, for export	64	225
____	**2671W**	Whistle Tender	37	75
____	**2671WX**	Whistle Tender	41	85
____	**2755**	Sunoco 1-D Tank Car, *45*	28	70
____	**X2758**	PRR Automobile Boxcar, *45-46*	26	52
____	**2855**	Sunoco 1-D Tank Car, *46-47*		
____		(A) Black	69	217
____		(B) Black, decal without "Gas" and "Oils"	60	204
____		(C) Gray	49	160
____	**3309**	Turbo Missile Launch Car, red body, *63-64*	16	44
____	**3309-50**	Turbo Missile Launch Car, olive body, *63-64*	166	531
____	**3330**	Flatcar with submarine kit, *60-62*	59	155
____	**3330-100**	Operating Submarine Kit with box, *60-61*	92	310
____	**3349**	Turbo Missile Launch Car, red body, *62-65*	16	47
____	**3356**	Operating Horse Car and Corral Set, *56-60, 64-66*	42	115
____	**3356**	Operating Horse Car only, *56-60, 64-66*		
____		(A) Built date, bar-end trucks, *56-60*	28	62
____		(B) No built date, AAR trucks, *64-66*	45	116

		Good	Exc	
3356-100	Black Horses, 9 pieces, *56-59*	18	28	___
3356-150	Horse Car Corral, *57-60*	22	50	___
3357	Hydraulic Maintenance Car, *62-64*	20	55	___
	(A) Blue, *62-64*	10	33	___
	(B) Teal, *62-64*	40	91	___
3357-27	Trestle Components for Cop and Hobo Car, *62*	21	52	___
3359	Lionel Lines Twin-bin Coal Dump Car, *55-58*	17	39	___
3360	Operating Burro Crane, self-propelled, *56-57*	64	159	___
3361	Operating Log Dump Car, *55-58*	15	33	___
3362	Helium Tank Unloading Car, *61-63, 69*	20	45	___
3364	Operating Dump Car with 3 logs, *65-66, 68*	15	32	___
3366	Circus Car Corral Set, *59-62*	138	301	___
3366	Circus Car Corral only, *59-62*	18	95	___
3366	Circus Car only, *59-62*	52	110	___
3366-100	White Horses, 9 pieces, *59-62*	31	56	___
3370	W&A Sheriff and Outlaw Car, *61-64*			___
	(A) AAR trucks	17	44	___
	(B) Archbar trucks	23	56	___
3376	Bronx Zoo Car, *60-66, 69*			___
	(A) Blue, white lettering	20	50	___
	(B) Green, yellow lettering	32	55	___
	(C) Blue, yellow lettering	89	275	___
3386	Bronx Zoo Car, *60*	25	60	___
3409	Helicopter Car, *61*	30	91	___
3410	Helicopter Car, *61-63*			___
	(A) 2 operating couplers, gray Navy helicopter	31	83	___
	(B) Single operating coupler, yellow helicopter, *63*	51	125	___
3413	Mercury Capsule Car, *62-64*	41	140	___
3419	Helicopter Car, *59-65*	33	73	___
3424	Wabash Operating Boxcar, *56-58*	17	60	___
3424-75	Low Bridge Signal, *56-57*	65	234	___
3424-100	Low Bridge Signal Set, *56-58*	22	44	___
3428	U.S. Mail Operating Boxcar, *59-60*	33	73	___
3429	USMC Helicopter Car, *60*	170	433	___
3434	Poultry Dispatch Car, *59-60, 64-66*			___
	(A) Gray man	42	105	___
	(B) Blue man	48	111	___
3435	Traveling Aquarium Car, *59-62*			___
	(A) Gold lettering, tank designations, and circle around L	375	1053	___
	(B) Gold lettering, tank designations, no circle around L	260	664	___
	(C) Gold lettering, no tank designations, no circle around L	103	246	___
	(D) Yellow lettering, no tank designations, no circle around L	50	122	___
3444	Erie Operating Gondola, *57-59*	27	65	___
3451	Operating Log Dump Car, *46-48*			___
	(A) Heat-stamped lettering	15	38	___
	(B) Rubber-stamped lettering	23	65	___

		POSTWAR 1945-1969	Good	Exc
___	3454	PRR Operating Merchandise Car, *46-47*		
___		(A) Red lettering	840	4164
___		(B) Blue lettering	35	111
___	3456	N&W Operating Hopper, *50-55*	20	49
___	3459	LL Operating Coal Dump Car, *46-48*		
___		(A) Aluminum bin	156	268
___		(B) Black bin	18	48
___		(C) Green bin	26	74
___	3460	Flatcar with trailers, *55-57*	34	65
___	3461	LL Operating Log Car, *49-55*		
___		(A) Black car, heat-stamped lettering	20	38
___		(B) Black car, rubber-stamped lettering	186	483
___	3461-25	LL Operating Log Car, green	20	51
___	3462	Automatic Milk Car, *47-48*		
___		(A) Flat white or cream, steel base mechanism	13	40
___		(B) Flat white or cream, brass base mechanism	24	60
___		(C) Glossy cream	65	220
___	3462-70	Magnetic Milk Cans, *52-59*	8	17
___	3462P	Milk Car Platform, *47-48*	6	15
___	X3464	ATSF Operating Boxcar, *49-52*		
___		(A) Orange body, corner steps, *49*	8	14
___		(B) Orange body, no steps, *50-52*	10	22
___		(C) Tan body	375	1250
___	X3464	NYC Operating Boxcar, *49-52*	12	27
___		(A) Corner steps, *49*	8	15
___		(B) No steps, *50-52*	6	13
___	3469	LL Operating Coal Dump Car, *49-55*	15	45
___	3470	Target Launching Car, dark blue, *62-64*	22	58
___	3470-100	Target Launching Car, light blue, *63*	60	200
___	3472	Automatic Milk Car, *49-53*	18	49
___	3474	Western Pacific Operating Boxcar, *52-53*	23	57
___	3482	Automatic Milk Car, *54-55*		
___		(A) "RT3472" on right	25	69
___		(B) "RT3482" on right	17	53
___	3484	Pennsylvania Operating Boxcar, *53*	22	52
___	3484-25	ATSF Operating Boxcar, *54*		
___		(A) White lettering	23	62
___		(B) Black lettering	320	1162
___	3494-1	NYC Operating Boxcar, *55*	36	95
___	3494-150	MP Operating Boxcar, *56*	49	118
___	3494-275	State of Maine Operating Boxcar, *56-58*		
___		(A) "3494275" on side	38	90
___		(B) No number on side	57	136
___	3494-550	Monon Operating Boxcar, *57-58*	221	405
___	3494-625	Soo Operating Boxcar, *57-58*	196	462
___	3509	Satellite Launching Car, *61*		

		Good	Exc	
	(A) Chrome satellite cover	30	70	___
	(B) Gray satellite cover	86	283	___
3510	Satellite Launching Car, *62*	38	93	___
3512	Fireman and Ladder Car, *59-61*			___
	(A) Black extension ladder	49	113	___
	(B) Silver extension ladder	67	199	___
3519	Satellite Launching Car, *61-64*	23	69	___
3520	Searchlight Car, *52-53*			___
	(A) Serif lettering	16	48	___
	(B) Sans serif lettering	15	32	___
3530	GM Generator Car, *56-58*			___
	(A) Blue fuel tank	43	119	___
	(B) Black fuel tank	40	105	___
	(C) 3530 underscored	415	1829	___
3530-50	Searchlight with pole and base, *56-56*	18	48	___
3535	Security Car with searchlight, *60-61*	34	100	___
3540	Operating Radar Car, *59-60*	38	103	___
3545	Operating TV Monitor Car, *61-62*	50	134	___
3559	Operating Coal Dump Car, *46-48*			___
	(A) Black coil housing	15	42	___
	(B) Brown coil housing	38	96	___
3562-1	ATSF Operating Barrel Car, *54*			___
	(A) Black, black unloading trough	63	193	___
	(B) Black, yellow unloading trough	61	175	___
	(C) Gray, red lettering	800	2970	___
3562-25	ATSF Operating Barrel Car, gray, *54*			___
	(A) Red lettering, no bracket tab	168	423	___
	(B) Blue lettering, no bracket tab	19	48	___
	(C) Blue lettering, bracket tab	21	62	___
3562-50	ATSF Operating Barrel Car, yellow, *55-56*			___
	(A) Painted	36	84	___
	(B) Unpainted	27	57	___
3562-75	ATSF Operating Barrel Car, orange, *57-58*	34	77	___
3619	Helicopter Reconnaissance Car, *62-64*			___
	(A) Light yellow	44	119	___
	(B) Dark yellow	67	244	___
3620	Searchlight Car, orange generator, *54-56*			___
3620	(A) Unpainted gray plastic searchlight	21	38	___
	(B) Gray-painted gray plastic searchlight	28	45	___
	(C) Unpainted orange plastic searchlight	44	112	___
	(D) Gray-painted orange plastic searchlight	59	175	___
3650	Extension Searchlight Car, *56-59*			___
	(A) Light gray	29	73	___
	(B) Dark gray	47	127	___
	(C) Olive gray	103	265	___
3656	Armour Operating Cattle Car, some with an open coil, *49-55*	14	34	___

POSTWAR 1945-1969		Good	Exc
____	(A) Black letters, Armour sticker	102	242
____	(B) White letters, Armour sticker	23	52
____	(C) Black letters, no Armour sticker	74	183
____	(D) White letters, no Armour sticker	17	41
____ 3656	Stockyard with cattle, 49-55	19	41
____ 3656-34	Cattle, black, 9 pieces, 49-58		
____	(A) Rounded ridge on base, 49	55	93
____	(B) Plain base	15	30
____ 3656-150	Corral Platform, yellow tray	215	763
____ 3662	Automatic Milk Car, 55-60, 64-66	31	66
____ 3662-79	Nonmagnetic Milk Cans, 7 pieces, white envelope	19	44
____ 3662-80	Nonmagnetic Milk Cans, 7 pieces, manila envelope	17	39
____ 3665	Minuteman Operating Car, 61-64		
____	(A) Medium blue roof	60	213
____	(B) Dark blue roof	34	75
____ 3666	Minuteman Boxcar with cannon, 64 u	192	400
____ 3672	Bosco Operating Milk Car, 59-60		
____	(A) Unpainted yellow body	75	175
____	(B) Painted yellow body	130	262
____ 3672-79	Bosco Can Set, 7 pieces, 59-60	27	59
____ 3672-79	Bosco Can Set, 7 pieces, 59-60	14	96
____ 3820	USMC Operating Submarine Car, 60-62	91	208
____ 3830	Operating Submarine Car, 60-63	37	83
____ 3854	Automatic Merchandise Car, 46-47	183	467
____ 3927	Lionel Lines Track Cleaning Car, 56-60	24	39
____ 3927-38	Track Cleaning Fluid Bottle	6	15
____ 3927-50	Track Wiping Cylinders, 25 pieces, 57-60	17	30
____ 3927-75	Track-Clean Detergent, can, 56-69	5	14
____ 4357	SP-type Caboose, electronic, die-cast stack, 48-49		
____	(A) Die-cast metal smokestack	75	188
____	(B) Matching plastic smokestack	115	270
____	(C) Matching plastic smokestack, raised board on catwalk	110	265
____ 4452	PRR Gondola, electronic, 46-49	52	121
____ 4454	Baby Ruth PRR Boxcar, electronic, 46-49	76	157
____ 4457	PRR N5-type Caboose, tintype, electronic, 46-47	49	148
____ 4671W	Whistle Tender	78	164
____ 5102	Railroad and Roadway Crossing	10	45
____ 5159-50	Maintenance and Lube Kit, 66-69	25	63
____ 5160	Viewing Stand, 63	40	142
____ 5459	LL Coal Dump Car, electronic, 46-49	53	152
____ 6001T	Tender	7	14
____ 6002	NYC Gondola, 50	4	7
____ X6004	Baby Ruth PRR Boxcar, 50	4	7
____ 6007	Lionel Lines SP-type Caboose, 50	3	6
____ 6009	Remote Control Uncoupling Track, 53-54	2	6
____ 6012	Gondola, 51-56	2	6

POSTWAR 1945-1969		Good	Exc	
6014	Bosco PRR Boxcar, *58*			___
	(A) White body	19	37	___
	(B) Red body	4	12	___
	(C) Orange body	4	8	___
6014	Chun King Boxcar, *57 u*	46	153	___
6014	Frisco Boxcar, *57, 63-69*			___
	(A) White body	5	10	___
	(B) Red body	5	8	___
	(C) White body, *coin slot*	16	40	___
	(D) Orange body, *57*	17	40	___
	(E) Orange body, *69*	10	23	___
X6014	Baby Ruth PRR Boxcar, *51-56*			___
	(A) White body	5	9	___
	(B) Red body	4	9	___
6014-100	Airex Boxcar, *60 u*	14	35	___
6014-150	Wix Boxcar, *59 u*	96	202	___
6015	Sunoco 1-D Tank Car, *54-55*			___
	(A) Painted tank	63	298	___
	(B) Unpainted tank	4	11	___
6017	Lionel Lines SP-type Caboose, *51-62*			___
	(A) Common unpainted red or Tuscan-red body	4	8	___
	(B) Glossy Tuscan-painted, orange mold	22	63	___
	(C) Semi-glossy Tuscan-painted, orange mold	13	34	___
	(D) Light or dark tile red-painted, blue mold	13	34	___
	(E) Common-brown painted body	2	5	___
6017	Lionel SP-type Caboose, unpainted maroon, *56*	10	28	___
6017-50	U.S. Marine Corps SP-type Caboose, *58*	27	69	___
6017-85	Lionel Lines SP-type Caboose, gray-painted, *58*	22	56	___
6017-100	B&M SP-type Caboose, *59, 62, 65-66*			___
	(A) Dark purple-blue	118	360	___
	(B) Medium or light blue	15	37	___
6017-185	ATSF SP-type Caboose, gray-painted, *59-60*	12	33	___
6017-200	U.S. Navy SP-type Caboose, *60*	49	161	___
6017-235	ATSF SP-type Caboose, red-painted, *62*	15	40	___
6019	Remote Control Track (O27), *48-66*	2	10	___
6020W	Whistle Tender	28	56	___
6024	Nabisco Shredded Wheat Boxcar, *57*	10	28	___
6024	RCA Whirlpool Boxcar, *57 u*	20	56	___
6025	Gulf 1-D Tank Car, *56-58*			___
	(A) Gray body, blue lettering	5	12	___
	(B) Orange body, blue lettering	6	15	___
	(C) Black body, red-orange Gulf emblem	5	13	___
6026T	Tender	13	36	___
6026W	Whistle Tender	22	53	___
6027	Alaska SP-type Caboose, *59*	31	77	___
6029	Remote Control Uncoupling Track, *55-63*	2	8	___

	POSTWAR 1945-1969		Good	Exc
___	**6032**	Short Gondola, black (027), *52-54*	2	6
___	**X6034**	Baby Ruth PRR Boxcar, *53-54*		
___		(A) Orange, blue lettering	5	10
___		(B) Orange, black lettering	6	11
___	**6035**	Sunoco 1-D Tank Car, *52-53*	4	8
___	**6037**	Lionel Lines SP-type Caboose, *52-54*		
___		(A) Tuscan	3	6
___		(B) Red	4	9
___	**6042**	Short Gondola, *59-61, 62-64*	4	9
___	**6044**	Airex Boxcar, orange lettering, *59-60 u*		
___		(A) Medium blue	10	29
___		(B) Teal blue	31	87
___		(C) Purple-blue	100	261
___	**6044-1X**	Nestles/McCall‚Äôs Boxcar, *62-63 u*	380	1797
___	**6045**	Lionel Lines 2-D Tank Car, *59-64*		
___		(A) Gray	10	22
___		(B) Orange	15	31
___		(C) Beige	10	23
___	**6045**	Cities Service 2-D Tank, *60 u*	15	33
___	**6047**	Lionel Lines SP-type Caboose, *62*		
___		(A) Unpainted, medium red	2	5
___		(B) Painted, brown	168	670
___		(C) Unpainted, coral pink	15	50
___	**6050**	Lionel Savings Bank Boxcar, *61*		
___		(A) Type I body, Blt by Lionel	19	48
___		(B) Type I body, Built by Lionel	43	143
___		(C) Type IIa body, Blt by Lionel	124	275
___	**6050-110**	Swift Boxcar, *62-63*		
___		(A) Red body	8	21
___		(B) Dark red body, 2 open holes in roof walk	43	113
___	**6050-175**	Libby‚Äôs Tomato Juice Boxcar, *63 u*	0	0
___		(A) Green stems on tomatoes	15	40
___		(B) Green stems missing	20	62
___		(C) No white lines between glass and tomatoes	25	76
___	**6057**	LL SP-type Caboose, *59-62*		
___		(A) Unpainted red plastic	3	7
___		(B) Red-painted	29	81
___		(C) Unpainted coral pink plastic	19	53
___	**6057-50**	LL SP-type Caboose, orange, *62*	20	47
___	**6058**	C&O SP-type Caboose, *61*		
___		(A) Blue lettering	16	44
___		(B) Black lettering	27	72
___	**6059**	M&StL SP-type Caboose, *61-69*		
___		(A) Painted, red	13	33
___		(B) Unpainted, red	5	11

	(C) Unpainted, maroon	6	13	___
6062	NYC Gondola with 3 cable reels, *59-62*			___
	(A) No metal undercarriage	12	27	___
	(B) Metal undercarriage	21	51	___
	(C) No metal undercarriage, no paint on bottom	38	73	___
6062-50	NYC Gondola with 2 canisters, *69*	7	17	___
6066T	Tender	9	19	___
6067	SP-type Caboose, unmarked, *61-62*			
	(A) Red	3	8	___
	(B) Yellow	6	14	___
	(C) Brown	9	18	___
6076	ATSF Hopper, *63 u*	8	24	___
6076	Lehigh Valley Hopper, short, *63*			___
	(A) Gray body	8	14	___
	(B) Black body	6	13	___
	(C) Red body	7	14	___
	(D) Yellow body, painted	468	1655	___
6076-100	Hopper, gray, unmarked, *63*	8	19	___
6110	2-4-2 Locomotive, 6001T Tender, *50-51*	15	35	___
6111	Flatcar with logs, *55-57*			___
	(A) Yellow with black lettering	10	35	___
	(B) Yellow with white lettering	108	468	___
6112	Short Gondola with 4 canisters, *56-58*			___
	(A) Black body	6	18	___
	(B) Blue body	7	18	___
	(C) White body	14	40	___
6112-5	Canister, *56-58*			___
	(A) Red or white	1	3	___
	(B) Red with black letters	22	53	___
6112-25	Canister Set, 4 pieces, red or white, with box, *56-58*	28	89	___
6119	DL&W Work Caboose, red, *55-56*	12	24	___
6119-25	DL&W Work Caboose, orange, *56-59*	17	44	___
6119-50	DL&W Work Caboose, brown, *56*	23	51	___
6119-75	DL&W Work Caboose, *57*			___
	(A) Heat-stamped letters on frame	15	35	___
	(B) Closely spaced rubber-stamped letters on frame	75	285	___
	(C) Widely spaced rubber-stamped letters on frame	83	305	___
6119-100	DL&W Work Caboose, red cab, gray tool tray, *57-66, 69*			___
	(A) Black frame, white letters	10	23	___
	(B) "Built By Lionel" builders plate, *66*	24	68	___
	(C) Black frame, red-painted cab	54	179	___
	(D) Santa Fe cab, gray tool box	10	38	___
6119-125	Rescue Caboose, olive, black frame, *64*	72	178	___
6119-125	Rescue Caboose, *64*	350	618	___
6120	Work Caboose, yellow, unmarked, *61-62*	6	14	___

|---|---|---|
6121 Flatcar with pipes, *56-57*		
(A) Yellow, red, or gray	13	53
(B) Maroon	20	73
6130 ATSF Work Caboose, *61, 65-69*		
(A) Red painted, no builders plate	14	35
(B) Red unpainted, builders plate	10	28
(C) Red painted, builders plate	63	284
6139 Remote Control Uncoupling Track (O27), *63*	1	4
6142 Short Gondola, green, blue, or black, with 2 canisters, *63-66, 69*	7	15
6142-175 Short Gondola, olive drab, with 2 canisters	57	233
6149 Remote Control Uncoupling Track (O27), *64-69*	2	6
6151 Flatcar with patrol truck, *58*		
(A) Yellow frame	36	80
(B) Orange frame	25	69
(C) Cream frame	35	83
6162 NYC Gondola with 3 white canisters, *59-68*		
(A) Blue body	9	23
(B) Red body	73	301
6162-60 Alaska Gondola with 3 red canisters, *59*	37	84
6162-100 NYC Gondola		
6162-100 (A) Red body with 3 red canisters	80	160
6162-100 (B) Teal or green body with 3 white canisters	15	33
6167 LL SP-type Caboose, red, *63-64*		
(A) Unpainted	6	9
(B) Painted	32	108
6167 SP-type Caboose, unmarked, no end rails, *63-64*		
(A) Red body	4	9
(B) Brown body	7	22
6167-50 SP-type Caboose, unmarked, yellow	5	18
6167-85 Union Pacific SP-type Caboose, *69*	10	33
6167-175 SP-type Caboose, unmarked, olive	105	347
6175 Flatcar with rocket, *58-61*		
(A) Black frame	26	61
(B) Red frame	25	61
6176 Hopper, unmarked, *63-69*		
(A) Dark yellow	10	31
(B) Gray	8	15
(C) Red	10	23
(D) Bright yellow	26	58
6176-75 Lehigh Valley Hopper, *64-66, 69*		
(A) Dark yellow	5	15
(B) Gray	6	11
(C) Black	3	9
(D) Red	15	29
(E) Bright yellow	23	52

POSTWAR 1945-1969		Good	Exc	
6176-100	Olive Drab Hopper, unmarked	50	140	___
6219	C&O Work Caboose, *60*	18	43	___
6220	Santa Fe NW2 Switcher, *49-50*			___
	(A) Large GM decal on cab	115	253	___
	(B) Small GM decal on side	80	202	___
6250	Seaboard NW2 Switcher, *54-55*			___
	(A) Seaboard decal	83	215	___
	(B) Widely spaced rubber-stamped letters	103	265	___
	(C) Closely spaced rubber-stamped letters	131	403	___
6257	SP-type Caboose, *48-52*			___
	(A) Dark red, matching plastic smokestack	165	491	___
	(B) All other variations	6	15	___
6257-25	SP-type Caboose, circled-L logo, *53-55*			___
	(A) Red painted	7	16	___
	(B) Unpainted red plastic	4	11	___
6257-50	SP-type Caboose, *56*	5	11	___
6257-100	Lionel Lines SP-type Caboose, smokestack, *63-64*	10	29	___
6257X	SP-type Caboose, red, 2 couplers, with box, *48*	26	56	___
6262	Flatcar with wheel load, *56-57*			___
	(A) Black frame, *56-57*	28	70	___
	(B) Red frame, *56*	336	771	___
6264	Flatcar with lumber for 264 Fork Lift Platform, *57-60*			___
	(A) Bar-end trucks	27	66	___
	(B) Plastic trucks	32	68	___
	(C) Separate-sale box and envelope	100	436	___
6311	Flatcar with 3 pipes, *55*	20	45	___
6315	Gulf 1-D Chemical Tank Car, *56-59, 68-69*			___
	(A) Early, painted	28	72	___
	(B) Late, unpainted	22	50	___
	(C) Late, unpainted, built date	45	113	___
6315	Lionel Lines 1-D Tank Car, *63-66*			___
	(A) Unpainted orange body	15	30	___
	(B) Painted orange body	93	340	___
6342	NYC Gondola with culvert channel and 7 pipes, *56-58, 64-66*	17	38	___
6343	Barrel Ramp Car with 6 barrels, *61-62*	17	34	___
6346	Alcoa Quad Hopper, *56*	26	59	___
6352-1	PFE Ice Car from 352 Ice Depot, *55-57*			___
	(A) 3 lines of data	56	122	___
	(B) 4 lines of data	36	91	___
	(C) Separate-sale box	909	4577	___
6356	NYC Stock Car, 2-level, *54-55*			___
	(A) Heat-stamped lettering	18	40	___
	(B) Rubber-stamped lettering	25	70	___
6357	SP-type Caboose, SP logo, *48-53*			___
	(A) Tile red, tuscan, or maroon	10	28	___

		Good	Exc
___	(B) Tile red, extra board on catwalk	127	436
___ **6357**	SP-type Caboose, no logo, *57-61*		
___	(A) Number to left	10	32
___	(B) Number to right	16	48
___ **6357-25**	SP-type Caboose, circle L logo, *53-56*		
___	(A) Maroon or tuscan body, black metal smokestack	14	25
___	(B) Maroon body, maroon metal smokestack	91	340
___ **6357-50**	ATSF SP-type Caboose, lighted, *60*	472	1143
___ **6361**	Timber Transport Car, *60-61, 64-69*		
___	(A) White lettering	32	71
___	(B) No lettering	49	128
___ **6362**	Truck Car with 3 trucks, *55-56*		
___	(A) Shiny orange	20	40
___	(B) Dull orange	33	83
___ **6376**	LL Circus Stock Car, *56-57*	26	57
___ **6401**	Flatcar, no load, gray, *60*	4	10
___ **6401-25**	Gray flatcar with load, *64-67*		
___	(A) Jeep and cannon	115	244
___	(B) Tank	95	200
___	(C) Payton automobile	23	48
___	(D) Logs	11	21
___ **6402**	Flatcar with 2 Cable Reels, *62, 64-66, 69*		
___	(A) Gray car with orange reels	5	13
___	(B) Maroon car with orange reels	6	13
___	(C) Brown car with gray or orange reels	8	15
___	(D) Gray car with gray reels	8	15
___	(E) Gray car with green reels	10	25
___ **6402**	Flatcar with blue boat, *69*	27	55
___ **6402-25**	Flatcar with 2 cable reels (gray or orange), *62, 64-66*	10	25
___ **6402-150**	Maroon Flatcar with white trailer	13	35
___ **6403B**	Tender	35	79
___ **6404**	Black Flatcar with auto, *60 u*		
___	(A) Red auto	29	71
___	(B) Yellow auto	50	99
___	(C) Brown auto	75	211
___	(D) Green auto	90	234
___ **6405**	Flatcar with piggyback van, *61*	20	47
___ **6406**	Flatcar with auto, *61*		
___	(A) Maroon frame, red auto	30	58
___	(B) Maroon frame, yellow auto	60	126
___	(C) Gray frame, dark brown auto	85	286
___	(D) Gray frame, green auto	90	238
___	(E) Gray frame, yellow auto	54	107
___	(F) Gray frame, red auto	26	50
___ **6407**	Flatcar with rocket, *63*	203	472

		Good	Exc	
6408	Flatcar with pipes, *63 u*	21	57	___
6408-50	Flatcar with 2 orange cable reels, *67 u*	17	40	___
6409-25	Flatcar with pipes, *63 u*	17	67	___
6410-25	Flatcar with 2 automobiles, *63 u*			___
	(A) Yellow autos	145	423	___
	(B) Brown autos	178	520	___
6411	Flatcar with logs, *48-50*	16	36	___
6413	Mercury Capsule Carrying Car, *62-63*			___
	(A) Medium blue frame	71	146	___
	(B) Aquamarine frame	92	214	___
	(C) Teal frame	93	239	___
6414	Evans Auto Loader with 4 cars, *55-66*			___
	(A) Premium cars (chrome bumpers, windows, rubber wheels): red, yellow, blue-green, and white	42	103	___
	(B) Cheapie cars (no wheels): 2 red and 2 yellow	152	296	___
	(C) Red cars with gray bumpers	75	188	___
	(D) Yellow cars with gray bumpers	195	442	___
	(E) Brown cars with gray bumpers	248	669	___
	(F) Green cars with gray bumpers	479	1018	___
	(G) Metal trucks, number right of Lionel, premium cars with nubs on axle first run	62	148	___
6414-25	Set of 4 Automobiles, separate sale box, *55-58*	143	339	___
6415	Sunoco 3-D Tank Car, *53-55, 64-66, 69*	14	28	___
6416	Boat Transport Car, 4 boats, *61-63*	121	246	___
6417	PRR N5c Porthole Caboose, *53-57*			___
	(A) New York Zone	18	35	___
	(B) Without New York Zone	133	242	___
6417-25	Lionel Lines N5c Porthole Caboose, *54*	15	35	___
6417-50	LV N5c Porthole Caboose, *54*			___
	(A) Tuscan	427	1388	___
	(B) Gray	58	126	___
6418	Machinery Car with 2 steel girders, *55-57*			___
	(A) Black girders, "Lionel" in raised letters	56	127	___
	(B) Orange girders, "Lionel" in raised letters	49	103	___
	(C) Pinkish orange girders, U.S. Steel	65	128	___
	(D) Black girders, U.S. Steel	64	128	___
6419	DL&W Work Caboose, *48-50, 52-55*	15	33	___
6419-25	DL&W Work Caboose, one coupler, *54-55*	15	28	___
6419-50	DL&W Work Caboose, short smokestack, *56-57*	16	39	___
6419-75	DL&W Work Caboose, one coupler, *56-57*	15	35	___
6419-100	N&W Work Caboose, *57-58*	46	118	___
6420	DL&W Work Caboose with searchlight, *48-50*			___
	(A) Heat-stamped serif lettering	37	75	___
	(B) Rubber-stamped sans serif lettering	63	145	___
6424	Twin Auto Flatcar, *56-59*			___
6424	(A) Black frame, premium cars	25	56	___

			Good	Exc
____		(B) 6805 slots, no rail stops	57	121
____		(C) AAR trucks, number on right	32	73
____	**6424-110**	Twin Auto Flatcar, 6805 slots and rail stops, *58-59*	85	177
____	**6425**	Gulf 3-D Tank Car, *56-58*	14	38
____	**6427**	Lionel Lines N5c Porthole Caboose, *54-60*	15	33
____	**6427-60**	Virginian N5c Porthole Caboose, *58*	226	416
____	**6427-500**	PRR N5c Porthole Caboose, sky blue, from Girls Set, *57-58**	171	338
____	**6428**	U.S. Mail Boxcar, *60-61, 65-66*	20	46
____	**6429**	DL&W Work Caboose, AAR trucks, *63*	130	270
____	**6430**	Flatcar with 2 trailers, *56-58*		
____		(A) Gray Cooper-Jarrett trailers	28	63
____		(B) White Cooper-Jarrett trailers	29	71
____		(C) Green Fruehauf trailers	25	69
____		(D) Gray Cooper-Jarrett trailers with Fruehauf stickers	34	74
____	**6431**	Flatcar with 2 vans and Midgetoy tractor, *66*		
____	**6431**	(A) White vans, *66*	78	178
____	**6431**	(B) Yellow vans, *66*	110	339
____	**6434**	Poultry Dispatch Stock Car, *58-59*	29	65
____	**6436-1**	LV Open Quad Hopper, black, *55, 66*		
____		(A) No spreader brace holes	44	122
____		(B) Spreader brace with holes	10	35
____	**6436-25**	LV Open Quad Hopper, maroon, *55-57*		
____		(A) No spreader brace holes	143	471
____		(B) Spreader brace with holes	20	49
____	**6436-110**	LV Quad Hopper, red, *63-68*		
____		(A) No built date	20	40
____		(B) Built date "New 3-55"	36	91
____	**6436-500**	LV Open Quad Hopper, lilac, from Girls Set, *57-58**		
____		(A) No spreader brace holes	131	381
____		(B) Spreader brace with holes	95	277
____	**6437**	PRR N5c Porthole Caboose, *61-68*	16	36
____	**6440**	Flatcar with gray vans, *61-63*	33	85
____	**6440**	Green Pullman Car, *48-49*	30	80
____	**6441**	Green Observation Car, *48-49*	28	72
____	**6442**	Brown Pullman Car, *49*	34	79
____	**6443**	Brown Observation Car, *49*	32	71
____	**6445**	Fort Knox Gold Reserve Boxcar with coin slot, *61-63*	42	89
____	**6446**	N&W Covered Quad Hopper, black or gray, *54-55*	25	55
____	**6446-25**	N&W Covered Quad Hopper, *55-57*		
____		(A) Black, white lettering	26	71
____		(B) Gray, black lettering	32	73
____		(C) Gray, AAR truck, spreader brace holes	61	176
____	**6446-60**	LV Covered Quad Hopper, *63*	78	222
____	**6447**	PRR N5c Porthole Caboose, *63*	117	318
____	**6448**	Exploding Target Range Boxcar, *61-64*		

		Good	Exc	
	(A) Red sides, white roof and ends	16	39	___
	(B) White sides, red roof and ends	16	38	___
6452	Pennsylvania Gondola, *black, 48-49*			___
	(A) Numbered "6462", *48*	18	46	___
	(B) Numbered "6452", *49*	6	19	___
X6454	Baby Ruth PRR Boxcar, *48*	72	269	___
X6454	Santa Fe Boxcar, *48*	10	28	___
X6454	NYC Boxcar, *48*	31	77	___
	(A) Brown body	14	32	___
	(B) Orange body	49	139	___
	(C) Tan body	22	50	___
X6454	Erie Boxcar, *49-52*	17	56	___
	(A) Corner steps, *49*	10	25	___
	(B) No steps, *50-52*	9	24	___
X6454	PRR Boxcar, *49-52*	18	53	___
	(A) Corner steps, *49*	11	26	___
	(B) No steps, *50-52*	10	24	___
X6454	SP Boxcar, *49-52*	13	63	___
	(A) Corner steps, broken circle in herald, *49*	15	43	___
	(B) No steps, full circle in herald, *50*	9	23	___
	(C) No steps, red-brown body, *51-52*	10	23	___
	(A) Break in herald circle between R and N, *49*	26	71	___
	(B) Complete herald circle	16	39	___
6456	Lehigh Valley Short Hopper, *48-55*			___
	(A) Black	11	24	___
	(B) Maroon	12	19	___
6456-25	Lehigh Valley Short Hopper, gray, *54-55*	20	43	___
6456-50	Lehigh Valley Short Hopper, enamel red, white lettering, *54*	240	611	___
6456-75	Lehigh Valley Short Hopper, enamel red, yellow lettering, *54*	66	148	___
6457	SP-type Caboose, *49-52*	12	23	___
	(A) Tuscan body and plastic smokejack	9	15	___
	(B) Tuscan body and metal smokejack	9	15	___
	(C) Tuscan body and black metal smokejack	8	13	___
	(D) Maroon body and black metal smokejack	8	14	___
6460	Bucyrus Erie Crane Car, black cab, 8-wheel, *52-54*	20	45	___
6460-25	Bucyrus Erie Crane Car, red cab, 8-wheel, *54*	39	95	___
6461	Transformer Car, *49-50*	32	72	___
6462	NYC Gondola, black or red, with 6 barrels, *49-54*	9	19	___
6462-25	NYC Gondola, green, with 6 barrels, *54-57*			___
	(A) N in second panel, 2 lines of data	11	35	___
	(B) N in third panel, 3 lines of data	15	45	___
6462-75	NYC Gondola, red-painted, with 6 barrels, 52-55	13	29	___
6462-125	NYC Gondola, red plastic, with 6 barrels, *55-57*	9	18	___
6462-500	NYC Gondola, pink, from Girls Set, with 4 canisters, *57-58**	73	167	___
6463	Rocket Fuel 2-D Tank Car, *62-63*	19	61	___

			Good	Exc
____	**6464-1**	WP Boxcar, *53-54*		
____		(A) Blue lettering	26	55
____		(B) Red lettering	558	1545
____	**6464-25**	GN Boxcar, *53-54*	31	85
____	**6464-50**	M&StL Boxcar, *53-56*	32	67
____	**6464-75**	RI Boxcar, green, *53-54, 69*		
____		(A) Built date, *53-54*	28	77
____		(B) No built date, *69*	40	85
____	**6464-100**	Western Pacific Boxcar, *54-55*		
____		(A) Silver body, yellow feather	40	125
____		(B) Orange body, blue feather	229	722
____	**6464-125**	NYC Pacemaker Boxcar, *54-56*	39	82
____	**6464-150**	MP Boxcar, *54-55, 57*	45	108
____	**6464-175**	Rock Island Boxcar, *54-55*		
____		(A) Blue lettering	39	104
____		(B) Black lettering	375	1010
____	**6464-200**	Pennsylvania Boxcar, *54-55, 69*	62	128
____	**6464-225**	SP Boxcar, *54-56*	45	111
____	**6464-250**	WP Boxcar, *66*	73	239
____	**6464-275**	State of Maine Boxcar, *55, 57-59*		
____		(A) Striped doors	42	75
____		(B) Solid doors	55	121
____		(C) Striped doors, AAR trucks, *59*	22	46
____	**6464-300**	Rutland Boxcar, *55-56*		
____		(A) Rubber-stamped lettering	45	105
____		(B) Split door with bottom painted green	395	1144
____		(C) Rubber-stamped lettering with solid shield	1407	3915
____		(D) Heat-stamped lettering	75	160
____		(E) Painted yellow body, rubber-stamped lettering	500	1500
____		(F) Painted yellow body, heat-stamped lettering	1350	4150
____	**6464-325**	B&O Sentinel Boxcar, *56*	185	417
____	**6464-350**	MKT Boxcar, *56*	142	293
____	**6464-375**	Central of Georgia Boxcar, *56-57, 66*		
____		(A) Unpainted maroon body	43	80
____		(B) Painted red body	775	3641
____	**6464-400**	B&O Time-Saver Boxcar, *56-57, 69*		
____		(A) BLT 5-54	44	91
____		(B) BLT 2-56	112	258
____		(C) No built date	45	111
____		(D) 54 built date on one side/56 built date on other		975
____	**6464-425**	New Haven Boxcar, *56-58, 69*	27	58
____	**6464-450**	Great Northern Boxcar, *56-57, 66*	59	130
____	**6464-475**	B&M Boxcar, *57-60, 65-66, 68*		
____		(A) Medium blue-painted or unpainted plastic	37	75
____		(B) Dark purple-painted, gray or blue mold	72	250

	Good	Exc	
(C) Dark blue-painted, yellow mold	127	390	___
6464-500 Timken Boxcar, white side band and charcoal lettering, *57-59, 69*			___
(A) Unpainted yellow body	45	121	___
(B) Painted yellow body, Type II	158	409	___
(C) Painted yellow body, Type IV	59	145	___
6464-510 NYC Pacemaker Boxcar, *57-58*	286	538	___
6464-515 MKT Boxcar, *57-58*	258	565	___
6464-525 M&StL Boxcar, *57-58, 64-66*			___
(A) Red, white lettering	31	75	___
(B) Maroon, white lettering	115	380	___
6464-650 D&RGW Boxcar, *57-58, 66*			___
(A) Yellow body, silver roof, black stripe	65	130	___
(B) Yellow body, type II, silver roof, no black stripe	548	1408	___
(C) Painted yellow body and yellow roof	650	2534	___
(D) Yellow body, type IV, silver roof, black stripe on one side only	400	1100	___
6464-700 Santa Fe Boxcar, *61, 66*	48	135	___
6464-725 New Haven Boxcar, *62-66, 68*			___
(A) Orange body	24	53	___
(B) Black body	76	193	___
6464-825 Alaska Boxcar, *59-60*	110	315	___
6464-900 NYC Boxcar, *60-66*	39	88	___
(A) Green Doors, *60-66*	19	43	___
(B) Black Doors, *60-66*	30	100	___
6465 Gulf 2-D Tank Car, *58*			___
(A) Black tank	15	55	___
(B) Gray tank	11	34	___
6465 Sunoco 2-D Tank Car, *48-56*			___
(A) Silver tank, rubber-stamped "6465"	5	14	___
(B) Silver tank, rubber-stamped "6455"	17	41	___
(C) Silver tank, no number on frame	7	16	___
(D) Glossy gray tank	10	33	___
6465-85 LL 2-D Tank Car, black, *59*	18	44	___
6465-110 Cities Service 2-D Tank, *60-62*	22	64	___
6465-160 LL 2-D Tank Car, orange with black ends, *63-64*	11	47	___
6466T Tender, *49-53*	14	33	___
6466W Whistle Tender, *49-53*	19	45	___
6466WX Whistle Tender, *49-53*	23	50	___
6467 Miscellaneous Car, *56*	23	48	___
6468 B&O Auto Boxcar, blue, *53-55*	16	42	___
6468X B&O Auto Boxcar, tuscan, *53-55*	128	264	___
6468-25 NH Auto Boxcar, *56-58*			___
(A) Black N over white H, black doors	25	68	___
(B) White N over black H, black doors	81	210	___
(C) Black N over white H, painted Tuscan doors	36	93	___
6469 Liquified Gas Tank Car, *63*	38	100	___

		Good	Exc
6470	Explosives Boxcar, *59-60*	12	33
6472	Refrigerator Car, *50-53*	10	25
6473	Horse Transport Car, *62-69*	15	25
6475	Libby‚Äôs Crushed Pineapple Vat Car, *63 u*	33	308
6475	Pickles Vat Car, *60-62*	22	67
6476	LV Short Hopper, *57-63*		
	(A) Red body	6	17
	(B) Gray body	8	21
	(C) Black body	6	17
6476-75	LV Short Hopper, black, Type VI body, *63*	8	18
6476-135	LV Short Hopper, yellow, *64-66, 68*	6	17
6476-160	LV Short Hopper, black, *69*	6	16
6476-185	LV Short Hopper, yellow, *69*	6	17
6477	Miscellaneous Car with pipes, *57-58*	23	60
6480	Explosives Boxcar, red, *61*	16	37
6482	Refrigerator Car, *57*	15	42
6500	Flatcar with Bonanza airplane, *62, 65*		
	(A) Plane, red top and wings	322	661
	(B) Plane, white top and wings	413	788
6501	Flatcar with jet boat, *62-63*	53	149
6502	Flat Car with Girder, *62*	6	30
	(A) Black flatcar	22	76
	(B) Red flatcar	35	93
6502-50	Flatcar, blue or teal, no lettering, with bridge girder, *62*	10	40
6511	Flatcar with pipes, *53-56*		
	(A) Die-cast metal truck plates, *53*	19	51
	(B) Red car, stamped metal truck plates	15	38
	(C) Brown car, stamped metal truck plates	7	25
6511-24	Set of 6 pipes with box, *55-58*	46	155
6512	Cherry Picker Car, *62-63*	31	80
6517	LL Bay Window Caboose, *55-59*		
	(A) Built date underscored	27	68
	(B) Built date not underscored	22	48
	(C) Built date not underscored, lettering higher	22	50
6517-75	Erie Bay Window Caboose, *66*	175	480
6518	Transformer Car, *56-58*	21	55
6519	Allis-Chalmers Flatcar, *58-61*		
	(A) Dark or medium orange base	25	87
	(B) Dull light orange base	44	127
6520	Searchlight Car, *49-51*		
	(A) Tan generator	688	1536
	(B) Green generator	111	308
	(C) Maroon generator	19	46
	(D) Orange generator	15	38
	(E) Green generator, black searchlight housing	132	300

| --- | --- | --- |
6530 Firefighting Instruction Car, *60-61*		—
(A) Red body, white lettering	25	74 ___
(B) Black body, white lettering	137	409 ___
6536 M&StL Open Quad Hopper, *58-59, 63*		—
(A) AAR trucks, *59, 63*	26	72 ___
(B) Bar-end trucks, *58*	45	130 ___
6544 Missile Firing Car, 4 missiles, *60-64*		
(A) White-lettered console	44	142 ___
(B) Black-lettered console	119	326 ___
6555 Sunoco 1-D Tank Car, *49-50*	13	58 ___
6556 MKT Stock Car, *58*	136	305 ___
6557 SP-type Smoking Caboose, *58-59*		—
(A) Tuscan, with non-reverse lettering	102	212 ___
(B) Brown, with reverse lettering	645	2242 ___
6560 Bucyrus Erie Crane Car, smokestack, *55-58, 68-69*		—
(A) Black frame, unpainted red-orange cab	39	96 ___
(B) Black frame, painted red cab, no "6560"	45	168 ___
(C) Black frame, unpainted gray cab	14	36 ___
(D) Black frame, unpainted red cab, closed crank spokes	11	21 ___
(E) Black frame, unpainted red cab, no "6560" on frame	13	24 ___
(F) Black frame, unpainted red cab, open crank spokes	10	20 ___
(G) Black frame, black cab	53	138 ___
(H) Dark blue frame, bronze hook	19	56 ___
6560-25 Bucyrus Erie Crane Car, 8-wheel, marked "656025", *56*	32	77 ___
6561 Cable Car, 2 reels, *53-56*		—
(A) Orange reels	16	53 ___
(B) Gray reels	28	72 ___
6562 NYC Gondola with 4 red canisters, *56-58*		—
(A) Gray body, *56*	15	45 ___
(B) Red body, *56, 58*	12	30 ___
(C) Black body, *57*	10	27 ___
6572 REA Refrigerator Car, *58-59, 63*		—
(A) Passenger trucks	79	182 ___
(B) Bar-end trucks	43	97 ___
(C) AAR trucks, *63*	25	62 ___
6630 Missile Launching Car, *61*	24	64 ___
6636 Alaska Open Quad Hopper, *59-60*	36	91 ___
6640 USMC Missile Launching Car, *60*	73	220 ___
6646 Lionel Lines Stock Car, *57*	15	37 ___
6650 IRBM Rocket Launcher, *59-63*		—
(A) "6650" stamped on left	19	48 ___
(B) "6650" stamped on right	106	270 ___
6650-80 Missile, *60*	4	9 ___
6651 USMC Cannon Car, *64 u*	77	210 ___
6654W Whistle Tender	20	40 ___

			Good	Exc
___	6656	Lionel Lines Stock Car, *49-55*		
___		(A) Brown Armour decal	23	54
___		(B) No decal	9	30
___	6657	Rio Grande SP-type Caboose, *57-58*		
___		(A) With ladder slots	57	146
___		(B) Without ladder slots	145	389
___	6660	Boom Car, *58*	25	77
___	6670	Derrick Car, *59-60*		
___		(A) "6670" stamped on left	24	70
___		(B) "6670" stamped on right	72	206
___	6672	Santa Fe Refrigerator Car, *54-56*		
___		(A) Blue lettering, 2 lines of data	19	46
___		(B) Black lettering, 2 lines of data	24	57
___		(C) Blue lettering, 3 lines of data	98	319
___	6736	Detroit & Mackinac Open Quad Hopper, *60-62*	19	43
___	6800	Flatcar with airplane, *57-60*		
___		(A) Plane, black top and wings	35	87
___		(B) Plane, yellow top and wings	44	109
___	6800-60	Airplane, *57-58*	61	243
___	6801	Flatcar with boat, white hull, brown deck, *57*	27	67
___	6801-50	Flatcar with boat, yellow hull, white deck, *58-60*	39	79
___	6801-60	Boat, *57-58*	32	110
___	6801-75	Flatcar with boat, blue hull, white deck, *58-60*	34	82
___	6802	Flatcar with 2 U.S. Steel girders, *58-59*	18	40
___	6803	Flatcar with USMC tank and sound truck, *58-59*	116	221
___	6804	Flatcar with USMC antiaircraft and sound trucks, *58-59*	118	278
___	6805	Atomic Energy Disposal Flatcar, *58-59*	43	165
___	6806	Flatcar with USMC radar and medical trucks, *58-59*	111	213
___	6807	Flatcar with amphibious vehicle, *58-59*	69	174
___	6808	Flatcar with USMC tank and searchlight truck, *58-59*	122	253
___	6809	Flatcar with USMC antiaircraft and medical trucks, *58-59*	111	216
___	6810	Flatcar with trailer, *58*	23	46
___	6812	Track Maintenance Car, *59*		
___		(A) Dark yellow superstructure	17	70
___		(B) Black base, gray platform and crank handle	17	69
___		(C) Gray base, black platform and crank handle	17	69
___		(D) Cream superstructure	40	188
___		(E) Light yellow superstructure	20	73
___	6814	Rescue Caboose, *59-61*	43	149
___	6816	Flatcar with Allis-Chalmers bulldozer, *59-60*		
___		(A) Red car	170	457
___		(B) Black car	625	1171
___	6816-100	Allis-Chalmers Bulldozer, *59-60*		
___		(A) No box	83	254
___		(B) Separate-sale box	264	718

6817	Flatcar with Allis-Chalmers motor scraper, *59-60*			___
	(A) Red car	193	448	___
	(B) Black car	640	1280	___
6817-100	Allis-Chalmers Motor Scraper, *59-60*			___
	(A) No box	147	286	___
	(B) Separate-sale box	264	733	___
6818	Flatcar with transformer, *58*	10	35	___
6819	Flatcar with helicopter, *59-60*	22	59	___
6820	Aerial Missile Transport Car with helicopter, *60-61*			___
	(A) Light blue frame	94	225	___
	(B) Medium blue frame	82	190	___
6821	Flatcar with crates, *59-60*	16	37	___
6822	Searchlight Car, *61-69*			___
	(A) Black base, gray light	18	37	___
	(B) Gray base, black light	24	46	___
6823	Flatcar with 2 IRBM missiles, *59-60*	25	65	___
6824	USMC Work Caboose, *60*	107	243	___
6824-50	Rescue Caboose, white, *64*	37	119	___
6825	Flatcar with arch trestle bridge, *59-62*	17	39	___
6826	Flatcar with Christmas trees, *59-60*	31	102	___
6827	Flatcar with Harnischfeger power shovel, *60-63*	101	228	___
6827-100	Harnischfeger Power Shovel, *60*			___
	(A) No box	58	124	___
	(B) Separate-sale box	115	264	___
6828	Flatcar with Harnischfeger crane, *60-63, 66*			___
	(A) Black flatcar, light yellow crane cab	82	235	___
	(B) Black flatcar, dark yellow crane cab	89	265	___
	(C) Red flatcar, dark yellow crane cab	374	1426	___
6828-100	Harnischfeger Construction Crane, *60*			___
	(A) No box	45	110	___
	(B) Separate-sale box	109	260	___
6830	Flatcar with submarine, *60-61*	54	138	___
6844	Missile Carrying Car, 6 missiles, *59-60*			___
	(A) Black frame	28	85	___
	(B) Red frame	364	1310	___
Other Track, Transformers, and Assorted Items				
A	Transformer, 90 watts, *47-48*	13	43	___
CO-1	Track Clips, dozen, with envelope (O), *49*	5	17	___
CO-1	Track Clips, box of 50 (O), *49*	30	80	___
CO-1	Track Clips, box of 100 (O), *49*	39	119	___
CTC	Lockon (O and O27), *47-69*	1	5	___
CTC-14	Lockons, dozen, with envelope	13	35	___
ECU-1	Electronic Control Unit, *46*	30	90	___
KW	Transformer, 190 watts, *50-65*	33	83	___
LTC	Lockon (O and O27), *50-69*	2	8	___

		Good	Exc
LW	Transformer, 125 watts, *55-56*	35	65
OC	Curved Track (O), *45-61*	0	1
OC1/2	Half Section Curved Track (O), *45-66*	0	1
OCS	Curved Insulated Track (O), *46-50*	6	15
OS	Straight Track (O), *45-61*	0	2
OSS	Straight Insulated Track, *46-50*	5	18
OTC	Lockon Track (O and O27)	2	3
Q	Transformer, 75 watts, *46*	11	26
R	Transformer, 110 watts, *46-47*	17	39
RCS	Remote Control Track (O), *45-48*	4	9
RW	Transformer, 110 watts, *48-54*	11	28
RX	Transformer, 100 watts, *47-48*	13	33
S	Transformer, 80 watts, *47*	11	30
SP	Smoke Pellets, bottle, *48-69*		
	(A) Tall, light amber bottle	14	41
	(B) Tall, dark amber bottle	13	43
	(C) Short, light amber bottle	16	53
	(D) All other bottles	8	29
	(E) Bottle on blister pack, *65*	20	69
SP-12	Dealer Display Box with 12 full smoke bottles	115	300
ST-295	Nut Driver, 5/32-inch		29
ST-296	Nut Driver, 3/15-inch		43
ST-297	Nut Driver, 7/32-inch		58
ST-300	Nut Driver Set with holder, service station item	513	892
ST-301	Wheel Puller, service station item	50	152
ST-302	Spring Adjusting Tool		76
ST-303	E Unit Spreader, service station item	40	85
ST-311	Wheel Puller, service station item	73	185
ST-320	Phillips Screwdriver, service station item	143	265
ST-321	Flathead Screwdriver, short, service station item	180	390
ST-322	Flathead Screwdriver, long, service station item	40	135
ST-325	Screwdriver Set, service station item	400	1000
ST-342	Track Pliers, service station item	75	158
ST-343	O Gauge Track Pliers, service station item	239	524
ST-350	Rivet Press, service station item	446	692
ST-350-6	Rivet Press Tool Block with tools, service station item	353	556
ST-350-17	Sliding Shoe Anvil, service station item	14	27
ST-375	Wheel Cup Tool Set, service station item	318	953
ST-378	E Unit Vice, service station item	137	321
ST-384	Track Pliers, service station item	131	233
SW	Transformer, 130 watts, *61-66*	25	70
TW	Transformer, 175 watts, *53-60*	35	90
TOC	Curved Track (O), *62-66, 68-69*		1
TOC1/2	Half Section Straight Track (O), *62-66*		1
TOS	Straight Track (O), *62-69*		1

POSTWAR 1945-1969		Good	Exc	
UCS	Remote Control Track (O), *45-69*	6	13	___
UTC	Lockon (O, 027, Standard), *45*	1	2	___
V	Transformer, 150 watts, 46-47	40	77	___
VW	Transformer, 150 watts, *48-49*	41	104	___
Z	Transformer, 250 watts, *45-47*	63	111	___
ZW	Transformer, 250 watts, *48-49*	41	107	___
ZW	Transformer, 275 watts, *50-56*	72	153	___
ZW	Transformer, 275 watts, R type, *57-66*	86	208	___

Section 3
MODERN 1970–2021

			Esc	Mint
___	366	Menards C&NW 4-4-2 Locomotive with tender, *09*	45	75
___	400	Menards C&NW Chicago Combine Car, *09*	25	40
___	403	Menards C&NW Lake Superior Observation Car, *09*	25	40
___	410	Menards C&NW Lake Michigan Coach, *09*	40	65
___	0512	Toy Fair Reefer, *81*	60	70
___	550C	31" Diameter Curved Track (O), *70*	1	2
___	550S	Straight Track (O), *70*	1	2
___	665E	Johnny Cash Blue Train 4-6-4 Locomotive, *71 u*		NRS
___	1050	New Englander Set, *80-81*	155	205
___	1052	Chesapeake Flyer Set, *80*	140	150
___	1053	James Gang Set, *80-82*	155	195
___	1070	Royal Limited Set, *80*	285	350
___	1071	Mid Atlantic Limited Set, *80*	225	230
___	1072	Cross Country Express Set, *80-81*	240	385
___	1081	Wabash Cannonball Set, *70-72*	105	120
___	1082	Yard Boss Set, *70*	120	165
___	1083	Pacemaker Set, *70*	105	120
___	1084	Grand Trunk Western Freight Set, *70*	120	140
___	1085	Santa Fe Express Diesel Freight Set, *70*	175	190
___	1091	Sears Special Steam Freight Set, *70 u*	150	165
___	1092	Sears GTW Steam Freight Set, *70 u*	150	165
___	1100	Happy Huff n' Puff, *74-75 u*	55	70
___	1150	L.A.S.E.R. Train Set, *81-82*	155	195
___	1151	Union Pacific Thunder Freight Set, *81-82*	150	175
___	1153	JCPenney Thunderball Freight Set, *81 u*	165	180
___	1154	Reading Yard King Set, *81-82*	170	190
___	1155	Cannonball Freight Set, *82*	75	85
___	1157	Lionel Leisure Wabash Cannonball Set, *81 u*		250
___	1158	Maple Leaf Limited Set, *81*	405	435
___	1159	Toys "R" Us Midnight Flyer Set, *81 u*	135	145
___	1160	Great Lakes Limited Set, *81*	280	330
___	T-1171	CN Locomotive Set, *71 u*	240	275
___	1182	Yardmaster Set, *71-72*	85	105
___	T-1172	Yardmaster Set, *71 u*		200
___	1183	Silver Star Set, *71-72*	65	80
___	T-1173	Grand Trunk Western Freight Set, *71-73 u*	175	195
___	1184	Allegheny Set, *71*	120	150
___	T-1174	Canadian National Set, *71-73 u*	265	300
___	1186	Cross Country Express Set, *71-72*	210	260
___	1187	Illinois Central Set (SSS), *71*	400	485
___	1190	Sears Special #1 Set, *71 u*	88	103
___	1195	JCPenney Special Set, *71 u*	150	165
___	1198	Unnamed Set, *71 u*		175
___	1199	Ford-Autolite Allegheny Set, *71 u*	187	207
___	1200	Gravel Gus, *75 u*	75	100
___	1223	Seattle & North Coast Hi-Cube Boxcar, *86*	25	225
___	1250	New York Central Set (SSS), *72*	315	380
___	1252	Heavy Iron Set, *82-83*	90	130
___	1253	Quicksilver Express Set, *82-83*	265	340
___	1254	Black Cave Flyer Set, *82*	75	105

MODERN 1970-2021		Esc	Mint	
1260	Continental Limited Set, *82*	308	395	___
1261	Sears Black Cave Flyer Set, *82 u*	165	195	___
1262	Toys "R" Us Heavy Iron Set, *82 u*	150	165	___
1263	JCPenney Overland Freight Set, *82 u*	150	165	___
1264	NIBCO Express Set, *82 u*	190	215	___
1265	Tappan Special Set, *82 u*	130	155	___
1280	Kickapoo Valley & Northern Set, *72*	60	75	___
1284	Allegheny Set, *72*	140	165	___
1285	Santa Fe Twin Diesel Set, *72*	95	140	___
1287	Pioneer Dockside Switcher Set, *72*	95	100	___
T-1272	Yardmaster Set, *72-73 u*	150	165	___
1290	Sears Steam Freight Set, *72 u*	150	165	___
T-1273	Silver Star Set, *72-73 u*	90	115	___
1291	Sears Steam Freight Set, *72 u*	150	165	___
1300	Gravel Gus Junior, *75 u*	70	90	___
1350	Canadian Pacific Set (SSS), *73*	460	620	___
1351	Baltimore & Ohio Set, *83-84*	205	280	___
1352	Rocky Mountain Freight Set, *83-84*	75	95	___
1353	Southern Streak Set, *83-85*	75	95	___
1354	Northern Freight Flyer Set, *83-85*	230	280	___
1355	Commando Assault Train, *83-84*	175	248	___
1359	Display Case for Set 1355, *83 u*	75	95	___
1361	Gold Coast Limited Set, *83*	390	400	___
1362	Lionel Leisure BN Express Set, *83 u*	200	300	___
1380	U.S. Steel Industrial Switcher Set, *73-75*	60	75	___
1381	Cannonball Set, *73-75*	70	75	___
1382	Yardmaster Set, *73-74*	110	135	___
1383	Santa Fe Freight Set, *73-75*	100	125	___
1384	Southern Express Set, *73-76*	75	120	___
1385	Blue Streak Freight Set, *73-74*	100	120	___
1386	Rock Island Express Set, *73-74*	120	140	___
1387	Milwaukee Road Special Set, *73*	185	285	___
1388	Golden State Arrow Set, *73-75*	215	240	___
1390	Sears 7-unit Steam Freight Set, *73 u*	170	190	___
1392	Sears 8-unit Steam Freight Set, *73 u*	150	165	___
1393	Sears 6-unit Diesel Freight Set, *73 u*	150	165	___
1395	JCPenney Set, *73 u*	150	165	___
1400	Happy Huff n' Puff Junior, *75 u*	130	140	___
1402	Chessie System Set, *84-85*	125	150	___
1403	Redwood Valley Express Set, *84-85*	170	205	___
1450	D&RGW Set (SSS), *74*	335	415	___
1451	Erie-Lackawanna Limited Set, *84*	415	465	___
1460	Grand National Set, *74*	300	330	___
1461	Black Diamond Set, *74 u, 75*	100	120	___
1463	Coca-Cola Special Set, *74 u, 75*	223	273	___
1487	Broadway Limited Set, *74-75*	160	255	___
1489	Santa Fe Double Diesel Set, *74-76*	140	165	___
1492	Sears 7-unit Steam Freight Set, *74 u*	150	165	___
1493	Sears 7-unit Steam Freight Set, *74 u*	150	165	___
1499	JCPenney Great Express Set, *74 u*	150	165	___
1501	Midland Freight Set, *85-86*	75	95	___
1502	Yard Chief Set, *85-86*	205	230	___
1506	Sears Centennial Chessie System Set, *85 u*	165	195	___
1512	JCPenney Midland Freight Set, *85 u*	90	115	___

|---|---|---|---|
___	**1549** Toys "R" Us Heavy Iron Set, *85-89 u*	160	218
___	**1552** Burlington Northern Limited Set, *85*	500	570
___	**1560** North American Express Set, *75*	275	365
___	**1562** Fast Freight Flyer Set, *85 u*	120	140
___	**1577** Liberty Special Set, *75 u*	229	238
___	**1579** Milwaukee Road Set (SSS), *75*	325	410
___	**1581** Thunderball Freight Set, *75-76*	90	100
___	**1582** Yard Chief Set, *75-76*	115	155
___	**1584** N&W "Spirit of America" Set, *75*	160	180
___	**1585** 75th Anniversary Special Set, *75-77*	226	237
___	**1586** Chesapeake Flyer Set, *75-77*	160	190
___	**1587** Capitol Limited Set, *75*	270	300
___	**1593** Sears Set, *75 u*		100
___	**1595** Sears 6-unit Diesel Freight Set, *75 u*	150	165
___	**1602** Nickel Plate Special Set, *86-91*	120	125
___	**1606** Sears Centennial Nickel Plate Set, *86 u*	165	195
___	**1608** American Express General Set, *86 u*	205	320
___	**1615** Cannonball Express Set, *86-90*	65	75
___	**1632** Santa Fe Work Train (SSS), *86*	220	255
___	**1652** B&O Freight Set, *86*	140	185
___	**1658** Town House TV and Appliances Set, *86 u*	80	95
___	**1660** Yard Boss Set, *76*	100	115
___	**1661** Rock Island Line Set, *76-77*	80	100
___	**1662** Black River Freight Set, *76-78*	75	95
___	**1663** Amtrak Lake Shore Limited Set, *76-77*	215	265
___	**1664** Illinois Central Freight Set, *76-77*	265	355
___	**1665** NYC Empire State Express Set, *76*	310	435
___	**1672** Northern Pacific Set (SSS), *76*	215	280
___	**1685** True Value Freight Flyer Set, *86-87 u*	60	75
___	**1686** Kay Bee Toys Freight Flyer Set, *86 u*	150	165
___	**1687** Freight Flyer Set, *87-90*	39	47
___	**1693** Toys "R" Us Rock Island Line Set, *76 u*	110	130
___	**1694** Toys "R" Us Black River Freight Set, *76 u*	115	135
___	**1696** Sears Steam Freight Set, *76 u*	110	130
___	**1698** True Value Rock Island Line Set, *76 u*	125	145
___	**1760** Trains n' Truckin' Steel Hauler Set, *77-78*	105	110
___	**1761** Trains n' Truckin' Cargo King Set, *77-78*	95	165
___	**1762** Wabash Cannonball Set, *77*	135	190
___	**1764** Heartland Express Set, *77*	185	240
___	**1765** Rocky Mountain Special Set, *77*	210	315
___	**1766** B&O Budd Car Set (SSS), *77*	335	390
___	**1776** Seaboard U36B Diesel, *74-76*	74	120
___	**1790** Lionel Leisure Steel Hauler Set, *77 u*	150	200
___	**1791** Toys "R" Us Steel Hauler Set, *77 u*	130	175
___	**1792** True Value Rock Island Line Set, *77 u*	100	135
___	**1793** Toys "R" Us Black River Freight Set, *77 u*	120	155
___	**1796** JCPenney Cargo Master Set, *77 u*		200
___	**1860** "Workin' on the Railroad" Timberline Set, *78*	65	85
___	**1862** "Workin' on the Railroad" Logging Empire Set, *78*	85	110
___	**1864** Santa Fe Double Diesel Set, *78-79*	155	190
___	**1865** Chesapeake Flyer Set, *78-79*	155	180
___	**1866** Great Plains Express Set, *78-79*	195	285
___	**1867** Milwaukee Road Limited Set, *78*	230	275
___	**1868** M&StL Set (SSS), *78*	215	255

		Esc	Mint	
1892	JCPenney Logging Empire Set, *78 u*	95	125	___
1893	Toys "R" Us Logging Empire Set, *78 u*	175	225	___
1960	Midnight Flyer Set, *79-81*	55	75	___
1962	Wabash Cannonball Set, *79*	90	105	___
1963	Black River Freight Set, *79-81*	75	85	___
1965	Smokey Mountain Line Set, *79*	65	85	___
1970	Southern Pacific Limited Set, *79 u*	340	365	___
1971	Quaker City Limited Set, *79*	315	335	___
1990	Mystery Glow Midnight Flyer Set, *79 u*	75	90	___
1991	JCPenney Wabash Cannonball Deluxe Express Set, *79 u*	150	165	___
1993	Toys "R" Us Midnight Flyer Set, *79 u*	115	135	___
2110	Graduated Trestle Set, 22 pieces, *70-88*	9	13	___
2111	Elevated Trestle Set, 10 pieces, *70-88*	8	11	___
2113	Tunnel Portals, pair, *84-87*	11	16	___
2115	Dwarf Signal, *84-87*	9	13	___
2117	Block Target Signal, *84-87*	23	29	___
2122	Extension Bridge, rock piers, *76-87*	24	34	___
2125	Whistling Freight Shed, *71*	36	43	___
2126	Whistling Freight Shed, *76-87*	18	26	___
2127	Diesel Horn Shed, *76-87*	25	30	___
2128	Operating Switchman, *83-86*	26	29	___
2129	Illuminated Freight Station, *83-86*	30	33	___
2133	Lighted Freight Station, *72-78, 80-84*	34	38	___
2140	Automatic Banjo Signal, *70-84*	17	21	___
2145	Automatic Gateman, *72-84*	31	47	___
2151	Operating Semaphore, *78-82*	15	19	___
2152	Automatic Crossing Gate, *70-84*	21	25	___
2154	Automatic Highway Flasher, *70-87*	19	24	___
2156	Illuminated Station Platform, *70-71*	26	34	___
2162	Automatic Crossing Gate and Signal "262," *70-87, 94, 96-98, 05*	16	27	___
2163	Block Target Signal, *70-78*	14	19	___
2170	Street Lamps, set of 3, *70-87*	13	19	___
2171	Gooseneck Street Lamps, set of 2, *80-81, 83-84*	15	18	___
2175	"Sandy Andy" Gravel Loader Kit, *76-79*	34	55	___
2180	Road Signs, 16 pieces, *77-98*		6	___
2181	Telephone Pole Set "150," *77-98*		5	___
2195	Floodlight Tower, *70-71*	38	50	___
2199	Microwave Tower, *72-75*	30	39	___
2214	Girder Bridge, *70-71, 72 u, 73-87*	5	9	___
2256	Station Platform, *73-81*	12	18	___
2260	Illuminated Bumper, *70-71, 72 u, 73*	23	35	___
2280	Nonilluminated Bumpers, set of 3, *73-84*	2	4	___
2282	Die-cast Bumpers, pair, *83 u*	12	18	___
2283	Die-cast Illuminated Bumpers "260," *84-99*	10	16	___
2290	Illuminated Bumpers, *75 u, 76-86*	7	11	___
2292	Station Platform, *85-87*	5	9	___
2300	Operating Oil Drum Loader, *83-87*	80	90	___
2301	Operating Sawmill, *80-84*	60	65	___
2302	Union Pacific Manual Gantry Crane, *80-82*	24	31	___
2303	Santa Fe Manual Gantry Crane, *80-81, 83 u*	17	21	___
2305	Getty Operating Oil Derrick, *81-84*	105	115	___
2306	Operating Ice Station with 6700 Ice Car, *82-83*	90	105	___
2307	Lighted Billboard, *82-86*	12	13	___
2308	Animated Newsstand, *82-83*	105	120	___

			Esc	Mint
____	**2309**	Mechanical Crossing Gate, *82-92*	4	7
____	**2310**	Mechanical Crossing Gate, *73-77*	2	4
____	**2311**	Mechanical Semaphore, *82-92*	4	7
____	**2312**	Mechanical Semaphore, *73-77*	2	4
____	**2313**	Floodlight Tower, *75-86*	22	27
____	**2314**	Searchlight Tower, *75-84*	22	27
____	**2315**	Operating Coaling Station, *83-84*	80	83
____	**2316**	N&W Operating Gantry Crane, *83-84*	90	125
____	**2317**	Operating Drawbridge, *75 u, 76-81*	100	130
____	**2318**	Operating Control Tower, *83-86*	40	50
____	**2319**	Illuminated Watchtower, *75-78, 80*	29	56
____	**2320**	Flagpole Kit, *83-87*	10	14
____	**2321**	Operating Sawmill, *84, 86-87*	115	133
____	**2323**	Operating Freight Station, *84-87*	43	47
____	**2324**	Operating Switch Tower, *84-87*	60	65
____	**2390**	Lionel Mirror, *82 u*	93	125
____	**2494**	Rotary Beacon, *72-74*	37	44
____	**2709**	Rico Station Kit, *81-98*		42
____	**2710**	Billboards, set of 5, *70-84*	4	10
____	**2714**	Tunnel, *75 u, 76-77*	36	43
____	**2716**	Short Extension Bridge, *88-98*	3	8
____	**2717**	Short Extension Bridge, *77-87*	2	4
____	**2718**	Barrel Platform Kit, *77-84*	3	5
____	**2719**	Watchman's Shanty Kit, *77-87*	3	5
____	**2720**	Lumber Shed Kit, *77-84, 87*	3	5
____	**2721**	Operating Log Mill Kit, *78*	2	4
____	**2722**	Barrel Loader Kit, *78*	2	4
____	**2783**	Freight Station Kit, *84*	6	10
____	**2784**	Freight Platform Kit, *81-90*	5	8
____	**2785**	Engine House Kit, *73-77*	31	39
____	**2786**	Freight Platform Kit, *73-77*	4	6
____	**2787**	Freight Station Kit, *73-77, 83*	7	10
____	**2788**	Coal Station Kit, *75 u, 76-77*	18	30
____	**2789**	Water Tower Kit, *75-77, 80*	19	24
____	**2791**	Cross Country Set, *70-71*	22	30
____	**2792**	Whistle Stop Set, *70-71*	24	34
____	**2792**	Layout Starter Pack, *80-84*	9	21
____	**2793**	Alamo Junction Set, *70-71*	22	30
____	**2796**	Grain Elevator Kit, *76 u, 77*	43	47
____	**2797**	Rico Station Kit, *76-77*	23	37
____	**2900**	Lockon, *70-98*	3	8
____	**2901**	Track Clips, dozen (O27), *71-98*		8
____	**2905**	Lockon and Wire, *74-00*		3
____	**2909**	Smoke Fluid, *70-98*		8
____	**2910**	OTC Contactor, *84-86, 88*	4	7
____	**2911**	Smoke Pellets, *70-73*	18	35
____	**2925**	Lubricant, *70-71, 72 u, 73-75*		2
____	**2927**	Maintenance Kit, *70, 78-98*		11
____	**2928**	Oil, *71*		2
____	**2951**	Track Layout Book, *70-86*	1	2
____	**2952**	Train and Accessory Manual, *70-74*	1	2
____	**2953**	Train and Accessory Manual, *75-86*	1	2
____	**2960**	Lionel 75th Anniversary Book, *75 u, 76*	15	30
____	**2980**	Magnetic Conversion Coupler, *70-71*	1	2

MODERN 1970-2021		Esc	Mint	
2985	The Lionel Train Book, *86-98*		18	___
3100	Great Northern 4-8-4 (FARR 3), *81*	335	388	___
4044	Transformer, 45-watt, *70-71*	2	7	___
4045	Safety Transformer, *70-71*	2	3	___
4050	Safety Transformer, *72-79*	2	3	___
4060	Power Master Transformer, *80-93*	4	13	___
4090	Power Master Transformer, *70-84*	50	65	___
4125	Transformer, 25-watt, *72*	2	3	___
4150	Trainmaster Transformer, *72-73, 75-77*	6	15	___
4250	Trainmaster Transformer, *74*	5	10	___
4651	Trainmaster Transformer, *78-79*	1	2	___
4690	MW Transformer, *86-89*	60	80	___
4851	AC Transformer, red or black, *85-91, 94-96*	5	10	___
5012	27" Diameter Curved Track, card of 4 *(027), 70-96*		17	___
5013	27" Diameter Curved Track *(027), 70-78*		1	___
5014	Half Curved Track (027), *70-98*		1	___
5016	36" Straight Track (027), *87-88*	1	2	___
5017	Straight Track, *card of 4 (027), 70-96*		4	___
5018	Straight Track (027), *70-78*		1	___
5019	Half Straight Track (027), *70-98*		1	___
5020	90-degree Crossover (027), *70-98*		7	___
5021	27" Manual Switch, left hand (027), *70-98*		15	___
5022	27" Manual Switch, right hand (027), *70-98*		15	___
5023	45-degree Crossover (027), *70-98*		6	___
5024	35" Straight Track (027), *88-98, 05*		3	___
5025	Manumatic Uncoupler, *71-72*	1	2	___
5027	27" Manual Switches, pair (027), *74-84*	13	21	___
5030	Track Expander Set (027), *71-84*	18	26	___
5031	Ford-Autolite Layout Expander Set, *71 u*	50	65	___
5033	27" Diameter Curved Track (027), *79-98*		1	___
5038	Straight Track (027), *79-98*		1	___
5041	Insulator Pins, dozen (027), *70-98*		1	___
5042	Steel Pins, dozen (027), *70-98*		1	___
5045	54" Diameter Curved Track Ballast (027), *87-88*	1	2	___
5046	27" Diameter Curved Track Ballast (027), *87-88*	1	2	___
5047	Straight Track Ballast (027), *87-88*	1	2	___
5049	42" Diameter Curved Track (027), *88-98*	1	2	___
5090	27" Manual Switches, 3 pair (027), *78-84*	55	70	___
5113	54" Diameter Curved Track (027), *79-98*	1	2	___
5121	27" Remote Switch, left hand (027), *70-98*	18	22	___
5122	27" Remote Switch, right hand (027), *70-98*	20	22	___
5125	27" Remote Switches, pair (027), *71-83*	20	30	___
5132	31" Remote Switch, right hand (0), *80-94*	29	30	___
5133	31" Remote Switch, left hand (0), *80-94*	22	30	___
5149	Remote Uncoupling Section (027), *70-98*		15	___
5165	72" Remote Switch, right hand (0), *87-98*	23	65	___
5166	72" Remote Switch, left hand (0), *87-98*	23	75	___
5167	42" Remote Switch, right hand (027), *88-98*	25	37	___
5168	42" Remote Switch, left hand (027), *88-98*	25	37	___
5193	27" Remote Switches, 3 pair (027), *78-83*	80	95	___
5500	10" Straight Track (0), *71-98*		1	___
5501	31" Diameter Curved Track (0), *71-98*		1	___
5502	Remote Uncoupling Section (0), *71-72*	7	9	___
5504	Half Curved Track (0), *83-98*		1	___

			Esc	Mint
___	5505	Half Straight Track (0), *83-98*		1
___	5520	90-degree Crossover (0), *71-72*	6	9
___	5522	36" Straight, *87-88*		3
___	5523	40" Straight Track (0), *88-98*		4
___	5530	Remote Uncoupling Section (0), *81-98*	10	19
___	5540	90-degree Crossover (0), *81-98*		10
___	5543	Insulator Pins, dozen *(0), 70-98*		1
___	5545	45-degree Crossover (0), *83-98*		11
___	5551	Steel Pins, dozen *(0), 70-98*		1
___	5554	54" Diameter Curved Track (0), *90-98*		2
___	5560	72" Diameter Curved Track Ballast (0), *87-88*	1	2
___	5561	31" Diameter Curved Track Ballast (0), *87-88*	1	2
___	5562	Straight Track Ballast (0), *87-88*	1	2
___	5572	72" Diameter Curved Track (0), *79-98*	2	3
___	5600	Curved Track (Trutrack), *73-74*	1	2
___	5601	Curved Track, card of 4 (Trutrack), *73-74*	6	10
___	5602	Curved Track Ballast, card of 4 (Trutrack), *73-74*	5	9
___	5605	Straight Track (Trutrack), *73-74*	1	2
___	5606	Straight Track, card of 4 (Trutrack), *73-74*	5	9
___	5607	Straight Track Ballast, card of 4 (Trutrack), *73-74*	5	9
___	5620	Manual Switch, left hand (Trutrack), *73-74*	4	13
___	5625	Remote Switch, left hand (Trutrack), *73-74*	9	17
___	5630	Manual Switch, right hand (Trutrack), *73-74*	4	13
___	5635	Remote Switch, right hand (Trutrack), *73-74*	9	17
___	5640	Left Switch Ballast, card of 2 (Trutrack), *73-74*	5	9
___	5650	Right Switch Ballast, card of 2 (Trutrack), *73-74*	5	9
___	5655	Lockon (Trutrack), *73-74*	1	2
___	5660	Terminal Track with lockon (Trutrack), *74*	1	3
___	5700	Oppenheimer Reefer, *81*	30	38
___	5701	Dairymen's League Reefer, *81*	21	23
___	5702	National Dairy Despatch Reefer, *81*	16	21
___	5703	North American Despatch Reefer, *81*	22	26
___	5704	Budweiser Reefer, *81-82*	69	77
___	5705	Ball Glass Jars Reefer, *81-82*	30	35
___	5706	Lindsay Brothers Reefer, *81-82*	26	27
___	5707	American Refrigerator Transit Reefer, *81-82*	17	20
___	5708	Armour Reefer, *82-83*	16	21
___	5709	REA Reefer, *82-83*	22	26
___	5710	Canadian Pacific Reefer, *82-83*	22	25
___	5711	Commercial Express Reefer, *82-83*	13	15
___	5712	Lionel Lines Reefer, *82 u*	47	75
___	5713	Cotton Belt Reefer, *83-84*	19	22
___	5714	Michigan Central Reefer, *83-84*	17	24
___	5715	Santa Fe Reefer, *83-84*	19	26
___	5716	Vermont Central Reefer, *83-84*	20	23
___	5717	Santa Fe Bunk Car, *83*	22	30
___	5719	Canadian National Reefer, *84*	10	16
___	5720	Great Northern Reefer, *84*	75	90
___	5721	Soo Line Reefer, *84*	21	23
___	5722	NKP Reefer, *84*	16	18
___	5724	PRR Bunk Car, *84*	15	23
___	5726	Southern Bunk Car, *84 u*	22	27
___	5727	USMC Bunk Car, *84-85*	25	30
___	5728	Canadian Pacific Bunk Car, *86*	18	23

| --- | --- | --- | --- |
5730	Strasburg Reefer, *85-86*	20	27 ___
5731	L&N Reefer, *85-86*	19	24 ___
5732	Jersey Central Reefer, *85-86*		24 ___
5733	Lionel Lines Bunk Car, *86 u*	18	24 ___
5735	NYC Bunk Car, *85-86*	33	35 ___
5739	B&O Tool Car, *86*	32	37 ___
5745	Santa Fe Bunk Car (SSS), *86*	39	45 ___
5760	Santa Fe Tool Car (SSS), *86*	30	35 ___
5900	AC/DC Converter, *79-83*	3	10 ___
6076	LV Hopper (O27), *70 u*	17	21 ___
6100	Ontario Northland Covered Quad Hopper, *81-82*	30	34 ___
6101	BN Covered Quad Hopper, *81-82*	17	31 ___
6102	GN Covered Quad Hopper (FARR 3), *81*	26	28 ___
6103	Canadian National Covered Quad Hopper, *81*	35	38 ___
6104	Southern Quad Hopper with coal (FARR 4), *83*	50	60 ___
6105	Reading Operating Hopper, *82*	34	39 ___
6106	N&W Covered Quad Hopper, *82*	30	40 ___
6107	Shell Covered Quad Hopper, *82*	14	26 ___
6109	C&O Operating Hopper, *83*	29	41 ___
6110	MP Covered Quad Hopper, *83-84*	17	27 ___
6111	L&N Covered Quad Hopper, *83-84*	13	20 ___
6113	Illinois Central Hopper (O27), *83-85*	15	25 ___
6114	C&NW Covered Quad Hopper, *83*	54	80 ___
6115	Southern Hopper (O27), *83-86*	15	19 ___
6116	Soo Line Ore Car, *84*	21	27 ___
6117	Erie Operating Hopper, *84*	29	39 ___
6118	Erie Covered Quad Hopper, *84*	31	45 ___
6122	Penn Central Ore Car, *84*	20	25 ___
6123	PRR Covered Quad Hopper (FARR 5), *84-85*	55	105 ___
6124	D&H Covered Quad Hopper, *84*	19	32 ___
6126	Canadian National Ore Car, *86*	18	24 ___
6127	Northern Pacific Ore Car, *86*	20	24 ___
6131	Illinois Terminal Covered Quad Hopper, *85-86*	15	21 ___
6134	BN 2-bay ACF Hopper (std O), *86 u*	95	115 ___
6135	C&NW 2-bay ACF Hopper (std O), *86 u*	65	80 ___
6137	NKP Hopper (O27), *86-91*	13	17 ___
6138	B&O Quad Hopper with coal, *86*	21	28 ___
6142	Gondola, black, *70*	20	33 ___
6150	Santa Fe Hopper (O27), *85-86, 92 u*	10	15 ___
6177	Reading Hopper (O27), *86-90*	14	19 ___
6200	FEC Gondola with canisters, *81-82*	13	24 ___
6201	Union Pacific Animated Gondola, *82-83*	19	25 ___
6202	WM Gondola with coal, *82*	34	36 ___
6203	Black Cave Gondola (O27), *82*	2	4 ___
6205	CP Gondola with canisters, *83*	18	26 ___
6206	C&IM Gondola with canisters, *83-85*	18	26 ___
6207	Southern Gondola with canisters (O27), *83-85*	6	8 ___
6208	Chessie System Gondola with canisters, *83 u*	21	24 ___
6209	NYC Gondola with coal (std O), *84-85*	42	46 ___
6210	Erie-Lackawanna Gondola with canisters, *84*	21	30 ___
6211	C&O Gondola with canisters, *84-85*		10 ___
6214	Lionel Lines Gondola with canisters, *84 u*	38	45 ___
6230	Erie-Lackawanna Reefer (std O), *86 u*	95	120 ___
6231	Railgon Gondola with coal (std O), *86 u*	66	76 ___

			Esc	Mint
___	6232	Illinois Central Boxcar (std O), *86 u*	65	80
___	6233	CP Flatcar with stakes (std O), *86 u*	47	50
___	6234	Burlington Northern Boxcar (std O), *85*	55	75
___	6235	Burlington Northern Boxcar (std O), *85*	33	43
___	6236	Burlington Northern Boxcar (std O), *85*	33	43
___	6237	Burlington Northern Boxcar (std O), *85*	32	47
___	6238	Burlington Northern Boxcar (std O), *85*	33	43
___	6239	Burlington Northern Boxcar (std O), *86 u*	37	55
___	6251	NYC Coal Dump Car, *85*	25	42
___	6254	NKP Gondola with canisters, *86-91*	6	11
___	6258	Santa Fe Gondola with canisters (O27), *85-86, 92 u*		3
___	X6260	NYC Gondola with canisters, *85-86*	13	15
___	6272	Santa Fe Gondola with cable reels (SSS), *86*	20	25
___	6300	Corn Products 3-D Tank Car, *81-82*	19	25
___	6301	Gulf 1-D Tank Car, *81*	20	26
___	6302	Quaker State 3-D Tank Car, *81*	42	46
___	6304	GN 1-D Tank Car (FARR 3), *81*	44	55
___	6305	British Columbia 1-D Tank Car, *81*	55	76
___	6306	Southern 1-D Tank Car (FARR 4), *83*	45	50
___	6307	PRR 1-D Tank Car (FARR 5), *84-85*	70	75
___	6308	Alaska 1-D Tank Car (O27), *82-83*	27	35
___	6310	Shell 2-D Tank Car (O27), *83-84*	19	24
___	6312	C&O 2-D Tank Car (O27), *84-85*	18	26
___	6313	Lionel Lines 1-D Tank Car, *84 u*	43	50
___	6314	B&O 3-D Tank Car, *86*	31	38
___	6317	Gulf 2-D Tank Car (O27), *84-85*	18	22
___	6357	Frisco 1-D Tank Car, *83*	42	50
___	6401	Virginian Bay Window Caboose, *81*	37	47
___	6403	Amtrak Vista Dome Car (O27), *76-77*	24	31
___	6404	Amtrak Passenger Coach (O27), *76-77*	24	31
___	6405	Amtrak Passenger Coach (O27), *76-77*	24	31
___	6406	Amtrak Observation Car (O27), *76-77*	22	29
___	6410	Amtrak Passenger Coach (O27), *77*	28	48
___	6411	Amtrak Passenger Coach (O27), *77*	24	35
___	6412	Amtrak Vista Dome Car (O27), *77*	22	33
___	6420	Reading Transfer Caboose, *81-82*	20	28
___	6421	Joshua L. Cowen Bay Window Caboose, *82*	34	40
___	6422	DM&IR Bay Window Caboose, *81*	32	38
___	6425	Erie-Lackawanna Bay Window Caboose, *83-84*	35	43
___	6426	Reading Transfer Caboose, *82-83*	14	24
___	6427	BN Transfer Caboose, *83-84*	12	21
___	6428	C&NW Transfer Caboose, *83-85*	22	25
___	6430	Santa Fe SP-type Caboose, *83-89*	4	14
___	6431	Southern Bay Window Caboose (FARR 4), *83*	42	55
___	6432	Union Pacific SP-type Caboose, *81-82*	6	10
___	6433	Canadian Pacific Bay Window Caboose, *81*	60	70
___	6435	U.S. Marines Transfer Caboose, *83-84*	9	17
___	6438	GN Bay Window Caboose (FARR 3), *81*	48	65
___	6439	Reading Bay Window Caboose, *84-85*	22	30
___	6441	Alaska Bay Window Caboose, *82-83*	45	50
___	6449	Wendy's N5c Caboose, *81-82*	64	74
___	6478	Black Cave SP-type Caboose, *82*	5	9
___	6482	Nibco Express SP-type Caboose, *82 u*	26	34
___	6485	Chessie System SP-type Caboose, *84-85*	6	10

| ---: | :--- | ---: | ---: |
6486	Southern SP-type Caboose, *83-85*	5	7 ___
6490	NKP N5c Caboose, *84 u*		NRS ___
6491	Erie-Lackawanna Transfer Caboose, *85-86*	9	17 ___
6493	L&C Bay Window Caboose, *86-87*	21	36 ___
6494	Santa Fe Bobber Caboose, *85-86*	7	9 ___
6496	Santa Fe Work Caboose (SSS), *86*	21	29 ___
6504	L.A.S.E.R. Flatcar with helicopter (027), *81-82*	18	26 ___
6505	L.A.S.E.R. Radar Car, *81-82*	17	25 ___
6506	L.A.S.E.R. Security Car, *81-82*	18	26 ___
6507	L.A.S.E.R. Flatcar with cruise missile, *81-82*	21	30 ___
6508	Canadian Pacific Crane Car, *81*	50	70 ___
6509	Depressed Center Flatcar with girders, *81*	60	85 ___
6510	Union Pacific Crane Car, *82*	55	60 ___
6515	Union Pacific Flatcar (027), *83-84, 86*	5	9 ___
6521	NYC Flatcar with stakes (std O), *84-85*	29	35 ___
6522	C&NW Searchlight Car, *83-85*	27	30 ___
6524	Erie Crane Car, *84*	55	60 ___
6526	Searchlight Car, *84-85*	23	25 ___
6529	NYC Searchlight Car, *85-86*	21	27 ___
6531	Express Mail Flatcar with trailers, *85-86*	23	32 ___
6560	Bucyrus Erie Crane Car, *71*	100	130 ___
6561	Flatcar with cruise missile (027), *83-84*	13	26 ___
6562	Flatcar with fences (027), *83-84*	13	21 ___
6564	U.S. Marines Flatcar with 2 tanks (027), *83-84*	13	21 ___
6573	Redwood Valley Express Log Dump Car (027), *84-85*	8	13 ___
6574	Redwood Valley Express Crane Car (027), *84-85*	7	13 ___
6575	Redwood Valley Express Flatcar with fences (027), *84-85*	7	13 ___
6576	Santa Fe Crane Car (027), *85-86, 92 u*	7	10 ___
6579	NYC Crane Car, *85-86*	36	44 ___
6585	PRR Flatcar with fences (027), *86-90*	5	9 ___
6587	W&ARR Flatcar with horses, *86 u*	18	26 ___
6593	Santa Fe Crane Car (SSS), *86*	41	48 ___
6700	PFE Ice Car, *82-83*		70 ___
6900	N&W Extended Vision Caboose, *82*	60	65 ___
6901	Ontario Northland Extended Vision Caboose, *82 u*	44	55 ___
6903	Santa Fe Extended Vision Caboose, *83*	80	95 ___
6904	Union Pacific Extended Vision Caboose, *83*	115	135 ___
6905	NKP Extended Vision Caboose, *83 u*	50	65 ___
6906	Erie-Lack. Extended Vision Caboose, *84*	75	90 ___
6907	NYC Wood-sided Caboose (std O), *86 u*	90	92 ___
6908	PRR N5c Caboose (FARR 5), *84-85*	43	47 ___
6910	NYC Extended Vision Caboose, *84 u*	55	60 ___
6912	Redwood Valley Express SP-type Caboose, *84-85*	9	16 ___
6913	Burlington Northern Extended Vision Caboose, *85*	70	90 ___
6916	NYC Work Caboose, *85-86*	16	22 ___
6917	Jersey Central Extended Vision Caboose, *86*	36	50 ___
6918	B&O SP-type Caboose, *86*	10	15 ___
6919	Nickel Plate Road SP-type Caboose, *86-91*	5	9 ___
6920	B&A Wood-sided Caboose (std O), *86 u*	65	80 ___
6921	PRR SP-type Caboose, *86-90*	5	9 ___
7200	Quicksilver Passenger Coach (027), *82-83*	26	34 ___
7201	Quicksilver Passenger Coach (027), *82-83*	26	34 ___
7202	Quicksilver Observation Car (027), *82-83*	26	34 ___
7203	N&W Diner "491," *82 u*	130	180 ___

			Esc	Mint
____	7204	Southern Pacific Diner, *82 u*	190	235
____	7207	NYC Diner, *83 u*	70	140
____	7208	PRR Diner, *83 u*	80	90
____	7210	Union Pacific Diner, *84*	85	110
____	7211	Southern Pacific Vista Dome Car, *83 u*	145	185
____	7215	B&O Passenger Coach, *83-84*	43	50
____	7216	B&O Passenger Coach, *83-84*	43	50
____	7217	B&O Baggage Car, *83-84*	43	50
____	7220	Illinois Central Baggage Car, *85, 87*	105	135
____	7221	Illinois Central Combination Car, *85, 87*	85	105
____	7222	Illinois Central Passenger Coach, *85, 87*	85	105
____	7223	Illinois Central Passenger Coach, *85, 87*	85	105
____	7224	Illinois Central Diner, *85, 87*	75	90
____	7225	Illinois Central Observation Car, *85, 87*	95	115
____	7227	Wabash Diner (FF 1), *86-87*	115	130
____	7228	Wabash Baggage Car (FF 1), *86-87*	90	100
____	7229	Wabash Combination Car (FF 1), *86-87*	90	100
____	7230	Wabash Passenger Coach (FF 1), *86-87*	90	100
____	7231	Wabash Passenger Coach (FF 1), *86-87*	90	100
____	7232	Wabash Observation Car (FF 1), *86-87*	85	95
____	7241	W&ARR Passenger Coach, *86 u*	43	50
____	7242	W&ARR Baggage Car, *86 u*	43	50
____	7301	Norfolk & Western Stock Car, *82*	34	45
____	7302	Texas & Pacific Stock Car (O27), *83-84*	9	14
____	7303	Erie Stock Car, *84*	41	50
____	7304	Southern Stock Car (FARR 4), *83 u*	41	45
____	7309	Southern Stock Car (O27), *85-86*	12	16
____	7312	W&ARR Stock Car (O27), *86 u*	25	30
____	7401	Chessie System Stock Car (O27), *84-85*	13	17
____	7404	Jersey Central Boxcar, *86*	26	40
____	7500	Lionel 75th Anniversary U36B Diesel, *75-77*	130	155
____	7501	Lionel 75th Anniversary Boxcar, *75-77*	28	39
____	7502	Lionel 75th Anniversary Reefer, *75-77*	30	41
____	7503	Lionel 75th Anniversary Reefer, *75-77*	41	47
____	7504	Lionel 75th Anniversary Covered Quad Hopper, *75-77*	28	40
____	7505	Lionel 75th Anniversary Boxcar, *75-77*	41	50
____	7506	Lionel 75th Anniversary Boxcar, *75-77*	20	25
____	7507	Lionel 75th Anniversary Reefer, *75-77*	27	39
____	7508	Lionel 75th Anniversary N5c Caboose, *75-77*	24	29
____	7509	Kentucky Fried Chicken Reefer, *81-82*	79	89
____	7510	Red Lobster Reefer, *81-82*	72	80
____	7511	Pizza Hut Reefer, *81-82*	71	83
____	7512	Arthur Treacher's Reefer, *82*	69	76
____	7513	Bonanza Reefer, *82*	70	78
____	7514	Taco Bell Reefer, *82*	73	94
____	7515	Denver Mint Car, *81*	64	81
____	7517	Philadelphia Mint Car, *82*	38	39
____	7518	Carson City Mint Car, *83*	34	43
____	7519	Toy Fair Reefer, *82 u*	35	42
____	7520	Nibco Express Boxcar, *82 u*	265	440
____	7521	Toy Fair Reefer, *83 u*	50	65
____	7522	New Orleans Mint Car, *84 u*	33	38
____	7523	Toy Fair Reefer, *84 u*	44	49
____	7524	Toy Fair Reefer, *85 u*	55	60

No.	Description		
7525	Toy Fair Boxcar, *86 u*		
7530	Dahlonega Mint Car, *86 u*		
7600	Frisco "Spirit of ,'76" N5c Caboose, *74-76*	3.	
7601	Delaware Boxcar, *74-76*	11	
7602	Pennsylvania Boxcar, *74-76*	12	27 ___
7603	New Jersey Boxcar, *74-76*	13	24 ___
7604	Georgia Boxcar, *74 u, 75-76*	22	26 ___
7605	Connecticut Boxcar, *74 u, 75-76*	12	32 ___
7606	Massachusetts Boxcar, *74 u, 75-76*	25	29 ___
7607	Maryland Boxcar, *74 u, 75-76*	13	34 ___
7608	South Carolina Boxcar, *75 u, 76*	38	50 ___
7609	New Hampshire Boxcar, *75 u, 76*	38	46 ___
7610	Virginia Boxcar, *75 u, 76*	155	200 ___
7611	New York Boxcar, *75 u, 76*	50	65 ___
7612	North Carolina Boxcar, *75 u, 76*	35	60 ___
7613	Rhode Island Boxcar, *75 u, 76*	36	50 ___
7700	Uncle Sam Boxcar, *75 u*	44	51 ___
7701	Camel Boxcar, *76-77*	68	78 ___
7702	Prince Albert Boxcar, *76-77*	68	84 ___
7703	Beechnut Boxcar, *76-77*	39	58 ___
7704	Toy Fair Boxcar, *76 u*	110	120 ___
7705	Canadian Toy Fair Boxcar, *76 u*	130	145 ___
7706	Sir Walter Raleigh Boxcar, *77-78*	71	80 ___
7707	White Owl Boxcar, *77-78*	71	80 ___
7708	Winston Boxcar, *77-78*	70	85 ___
7709	Salem Boxcar, *78*	68	77 ___
7710	Mail Pouch Boxcar, *78*	69	79 ___
7711	El Producto Boxcar, *78*	67	78 ___
7712	Santa Fe Boxcar (FARR 1), *79*	30	50 ___
7800	Pepsi Boxcar, *76 u, 77*	81	90 ___
7801	A&W Boxcar, *76 u, 77*	52	65 ___
7802	Canada Dry Boxcar, *76 u, 77*	44	57 ___
7803	Trains n' Truckin' Boxcar, *77 u*	20	26 ___
7806	Season's Greetings Boxcar, *76 u*	70	95 ___
7807	Toy Fair Boxcar, *77 u*	70	95 ___
7808	Northern Pacific Stock Car, *77*	37	44 ___
7809	Vernors Boxcar, *77 u, 78*	50	65 ___
7810	Orange Crush Boxcar, *77 u, 78*	45	60 ___
7811	Dr Pepper Boxcar, *77 u, 78*	48	63 ___
7813	"Season's Greetings" Boxcar, *77 u*	65	90 ___
7814	"Season's Greetings" Boxcar, *78 u*	70	95 ___
7815	Toy Fair Boxcar, *78 u*	65	85 ___
7816	Toy Fair Boxcar, *79 u*	65	85 ___
7817	Toy Fair Boxcar, *80 u*	95	105 ___
7900	D&RGW Operating Cowboy Car (027), *82-83*	22	26 ___
7901	LL Cop and Hobo Car (027), *82-83*	24	27 ___
7902	Santa Fe Boxcar (027), *82-85*	5	9 ___
7903	Rock Island Boxcar (027), *83*	8	13 ___
7904	San Diego Zoo Giraffe Car (027), *83-84*	44	55 ___
7905	Black Cave Boxcar (027), *82*	6	9 ___
7908	Tappan Boxcar (027), *82 u*	39	55 ___
7909	L&N Boxcar (027), *83-84*	40	49 ___
7910	Chessie System Boxcar (027), *84-85*	18	23 ___
7912	Toys "R" Us Giraffe Car (027), *82-84 u*	70	80 ___

			Esc	Mint
___	13	Turtleback Zoo Giraffe Car (027), *85-86*	50	60
___	7914	Toys "R" Us Giraffe Car (027), *85-89 u*	70	90
___	7920	Sears Centennial Boxcar (027), *85-86 u*	39	44
___	7925	Erie-Lackawanna Boxcar (027), *86-90*	10	18
___	7926	NKP Boxcar (027), *86-91*	8	10
___	7930	True Value Boxcar (027), *86-87 u*	34	50
___	7931	Town House TV and Appliances Boxcar (027), *86 u*	31	39
___	7932	Kay Bee Toys Boxcar (027), *86-87 u*	40	49
___	8001	NKP 2-6-4 Locomotive, *80 u*	55	65
___	8002	Union Pacific 2-8-4 Locomotive (FARR 2), *80*	310	345
___	8003	Chessie System 2-8-4 Locomotive, *80*	360	540
___	8004	Rock Island 4-4-0 Locomotive, *80-82*	190	220
___	8005	Santa Fe 4-4-0 Locomotive, *80-82*	65	75
___	8006	ACL 4-6-4 Locomotive, *80 u*	245	340
___	8007	NYNH&H 2-6-4 Locomotive, *80-81*	65	75
___	8008	Chessie System 4-4-2 Locomotive, *80*	65	75
___	8010	Santa Fe NW2 Switcher, *70, 71 u*	48	79
___	8020	Santa Fe Alco Diesel A Unit, *dummy, 70*	45	60
___	8020	Santa Fe Alco Diesel A Unit, *70-72, 74-76*	65	85
___	8021	Santa Fe Alco Diesel B Unit, *71-72, 74-76*	49	67
___	8022	Santa Fe Alco Diesel A Unit, *71 u*	80	105
___	8025	CN Alco Diesel A Unit, *71-73 u*	85	105
___	8025	CN Alco Diesel A Unit, *dummy, 71-73 u*	45	65
___	8030	Illinois Central GP9 Diesel, *70-72*	103	140
___	8031	Canadian National GP7 Diesel, *71-73 u*	80	150
___	8031	Illinois Central GP9 Diesel Dummy Unit, *70*		NRS
___	8040	Canadian National 2-4-2 Locomotive, *71 u*	43	85
___	8040	NKP 2-4-2 Locomotive, *70-72*	26	34
___	8041	NYC 2-4-2 Locomotive, *70*	55	65
___	8041	PRR 2-4-2 Locomotive, *71 u*	55	65
___	8042	GTW 2-4-2 Locomotive, *70, 71-73 u*	26	34
___	8043	NKP 2-4-2 Locomotive, *70 u*	45	65
___	8050	D&H U36C Diesel, *80*	105	220
___	8051	D&H U36C Diesel Dummy Unit, *80*	95	115
___	8056	C&NW FM Train Master Diesel, *80*	175	225
___	8057	Burlington NW2 Switcher, *80*	100	115
___	8059	Pennsylvania F3 Diesel B Unit, *80 u*	190	290
___	8060	Pennsylvania F3 Diesel B Unit, *80 u*	335	420
___	8061	Chessie System U36C Diesel, *80*	110	140
___	8062	Burlington F3 Diesel B Unit, *80 u*	205	255
___	8063	Seaboard SD9 Diesel, *80*	80	100
___	8064	Florida East Coast GP9 Diesel, *80*	150	200
___	8065	Florida East Coast GP9 Diesel Dummy Unit, *80*	95	120
___	8066	TP&W GP20 Diesel, *80-81, 83 u*	65	80
___	8071	Virginian SD18 Diesel, *80 u*	135	155
___	8072	Virginian SD18 Diesel Dummy Unit, *80 u*	75	110
___	8100	Norfolk & Western 4-8-4 "611," *81*	360	402
___	8101	Chicago & Alton 4-6-4 Locomotive "659," *81*	275	445
___	8102	Union Pacific 4-4-2 Locomotive, *81-82*	49	65
___	8104	Union Pacific 4-4-0 Locomotive "3," *81 u*	180	235
___	8111	DT&I NW2 Switcher, *71-74*	55	65
___	8140	Southern 2-4-0 Locomotive, *71 u*	22	30
___	8141	PRR 2-4-2 Locomotive, *71-72*	41	43
___	8142	C&O 4-4-2 Locomotive, *71-72*		55

MODERN 1970-2021	Esc	Mint	
8150 PRR GG1 Electric Locomotive "4935," 81	330	395	___
8151 Burlington SD28 Diesel, 81	120	145	___
8152 Canadian Pacific SD24 Diesel, 81	170	180	___
8153 Reading NW2 Switcher, 81-82	100	155	___
8154 Alaska NW2 Switcher, 81-82	120	160	___
8155 Monon U36B Diesel, 81-82	110	135	___
8156 Monon U36B Diesel Dummy Unit, 81-82		65	___
8157 Santa Fe FM Train Master, 81	280	325	___
8158 DM&IR GP35 Diesel, 81-82	90	150	___
8159 DM&IR GP35 Diesel Dummy Unit, 81-82	55	75	___
8160 Burger King GP20 Diesel, 81-82	106	128	___
8161 L.A.S.E.R. Switcher, 81-82	23	55	___
8162 Ontario Northland SD18 Diesel, 81 u	150	210	___
8163 Ontario Northland SD18 Diesel Dummy Unit, 81 u	95	140	___
8164 Pennsylvania F3 Diesel B Unit, 81 u	340	370	___
8182 Nibco Express NW2 Switcher, 82 u	90	130	___
8190 Diesel Horn Kit, 81 u		30	___
8200 Kickapoo Dockside 0-4-0T, 72	28	39	___
8203 PRR 2-4-2 Locomotive, 72, 74 u, 75	26	34	___
8204 C&O 4-4-2 Locomotive, 72	55	60	___
8206 NYC 4-6-4 Locomotive, 72-75	140	155	___
8209 Pioneer Dockside 0-4-0T with tender, 72	45	65	___
8209 Pioneer Dockside 0-4-0T, no tender, 73-76	42	55	___
8210 Joshua L. Cowen 4-6-4 Locomotive, 82	245	350	___
8212 Black Cave 0-4-0 Locomotive, 82	30	49	___
8213 D&RGW 2-4-2 Locomotive, 82-83, 84-91 u	65	70	___
8214 Pennsylvania 2-4-2 Locomotive, 82-83	55	65	___
8215 Nickel Plate Road 2-8-4 Locomotive "779," 82 u	245	285	___
8250 Santa Fe GP9 Diesel, 72, 74-75	120	145	___
8252 D&H Alco Diesel A Unit, 72	85	125	___
8253 D&H Alco Diesel B Unit, 72	50	70	___
8254 Illinois Central GP9 Diesel Dummy Unit, 72	60	65	___
8255 Santa Fe GP9 Diesel Dummy Unit, 72	60	65	___
8258 Canadian National GP7 Diesel Dummy Unit, 72-73 u	65	85	___
8261 Southern Pacific F3 Diesel B Unit, 82 u	435	445	___
8263 Santa Fe GP7 Diesel, 82	65	80	___
8264 CP Vulcan Switcher Snowplow, 82	80	100	___
8265 Santa Fe SD40 Diesel, 82	205	225	___
8266 Norfolk & Western SD24 Diesel, 82	150	225	___
8268 Quicksilver Alco Diesel A Unit, 82-83	85	105	___
8269 Quicksilver Alco Diesel A Unit, dummy, 82-83	55	65	___
8272 Pennsylvania EP-5 Electric Locomotive, 82 u	205	265	___
8300 Santa Fe 2-4-0 Locomotive, 73-74	22	25	___
8302 Southern 2-4-0 Locomotive, 73-76	29	30	___
8303 Jersey Central 2-4-2 Locomotive, 73-74	55	59	___
8304 B&O 4-4-2 Locomotive, 75	75	105	___
8304 Rock Island 4-4-2 Locomotive, 73-75	85	105	___
8304 Pennsylvania 4-4-2 Locomotive, 74-75	75	105	___
8304 C&O 4-4-2 Locomotive, 75-77	75	105	___
8305 Milwaukee Road 4-4-2 Locomotive, 73	95	120	___
8307 Southern Pacific 4-8-4 Locomotive "4449," 83	490	560	___
8308 Jersey Central 2-4-2 Locomotive, 73-74 u	36	43	___
8309 Southern 2-8-2 Locomotive "4501" (FARR 4), 83	385	495	___
8310 Nickel Plate Road 2-4-0 Locomotive, 73 u	26	50	___

		Esc	Mint
8310	Santa Fe 2-4-0 Locomotive, *74-75 u*	26	34
8310	Jersey Central 2-4-0 Locomotive, *74-75 u*	26	50
8311	Southern 0-4-0 Locomotive, *73 u*	26	34
8313	Santa Fe 0-4-0 Locomotive, *83-84*	13	17
8314	Southern 2-4-0 Locomotive, *83-85*	17	21
8315	B&O 4-4-0 Locomotive, *83-84*	85	120
8341	ACL SP-type Caboose, *86 u, 87-90*	6	8
8350	U.S. Steel Switcher, *73 u*	18	26
8351	Santa Fe Alco Diesel A Unit, *73-75*	60	65
8352	Santa Fe GP20 Diesel, *73-75*	65	105
8353	Grand Trunk Western GP7 Diesel, *73-75*	90	120
8354	Erie NW2 Switcher, *73, 75*	80	105
8355	Santa Fe GP20 Diesel Dummy Unit, *73-74*	65	90
8356	Grand Trunk Western GP7 Diesel Dummy Unit, *73-75*	65	75
8357	PRR GP9 Diesel, *73-75*	100	120
8358	PRR GP9 Diesel Dummy Unit, *73-75*	55	100
8359	Chessie System GP7 Diesel "GM50," *73*	95	120
8360	Long Island GP20 Diesel, *73-74*	70	105
8361	Western Pacific Alco Diesel A Unit, *73-75*	50	70
8362	Western Pacific Alco Diesel B Unit, *73-75*	45	65
8363	B&O F3 Diesel A Unit, *73-75*	280	310
8364	B&O F3 Diesel A Unit, dummy, *73-75*	120	160
8367	Long Island GP20 Diesel Dummy Unit, *73-75*	80	100
8368	Alaska Vulcan Switcher, *83*	120	129
8369	Erie-Lackawanna GP20 Diesel, *83-85*	125	140
8371	NYC F3 Diesel B Unit, *83*	105	150
8374	Burlington Northern NW2 Switcher, *83-85*	105	110
8375	C&NW GP7 Diesel, *83-85*	135	165
8376	Union Pacific SD40 Diesel, *83*	175	200
8377	U.S. Marines Switcher, *83-84*	55	65
8378	Wabash FM Train Master Diesel "550," *83 u*	500	690
8379	PRR Fire Car, *83 u*	80	100
8380	Lionel Lines SD28 Diesel, *83 u*	235	315
8402	Reading 4-4-2 Locomotive, *84-85*	47	55
8403	Chessie System 4-4-2 Locomotive, *84-85*	55	65
8404	PRR 6-8-6 "6200" (FARR 5), *84-85*	360	460
8406	NYC 4-6-4 Locomotive "783," *84*	445	571
8410	Redwood Valley Express 4-4-0 Locomotive, *84-85*	34	50
8452	Erie Alco Diesel A Unit, *74-75*	75	95
8453	Erie Alco Diesel B Unit, *74-75*	55	75
8454	D&RGW GP7 Diesel, *74-75*	80	110
8455	D&RGW GP7 Diesel Dummy Unit, *74-75*	50	85
8458	Erie-Lackawanna SD40 Diesel, *84*	160	190
8459	D&RGW Vulcan Rotary Snowplow, *84*	125	146
8460	MKT NW2 Switcher, *74-75*	45	65
8463	Chessie System GP20 Diesel, *74 u*	130	190
8466	Amtrak F3 Diesel A Unit, *74-76*	225	250
8467	Amtrak F3 Diesel A Unit, dummy, *74-76*	80	90
8468	B&O F3 Diesel B Unit, *74-75*	95	100
8469	CP F3 Diesel B Unit (SSS), *74*	85	110
8470	Chessie System U36B Diesel, *74*	80	110
8471	Pennsylvania NW2 Switcher, *74-76*	170	195
8473	Coca-Cola NW2 Switcher, *74 u, 75*	120	130
8474	D&RGW F3 Diesel B Unit (SSS), *74*	110	125

8475	Amtrak F3 Diesel B Unit, *74*	85		
8477	NYC GP9 Diesel, *84 u*	150	205	
8481	Union Pacific F3 Diesel B Unit, *84*	150	155	
8485	USMC NW2 Switcher, *84-85*	105	135	
8500	Pennsylvania 2-4-0 Locomotive, *75-76*	17	21	
8502	Santa Fe 2-4-0 Locomotive, *75*	17	21	
8506	PRR 0-4-0 Locomotive, *75-77*	75	90	
8507	Santa Fe 2-4-0 Locomotive, *75 u*	25	30	
8512	Santa Fe 0-4-0T Locomotive, *85-86*	22	30	
8516	NYC 0-4-0 Locomotive, *85-86*	115	140	
8550	Jersey Central GP9 Diesel, *75-76*	120	155	
8551	Pennsylvania EP-5 Electric Locomotive, *75-76*	115	120	
8556	Chessie System NW2 Switcher, *75-76*	160	200	
8558	Milwaukee Road EP-5 Electric Locomotive, *76-77*	160	195	
8559	N&W GP9 Diesel "1776," *75*	115	145	
8560	Chessie System U36B Diesel Dummy Unit, *75*	85	130	
8561	Jersey Central GP9 Diesel Dummy Unit, *75-76*	70	95	
8562	Missouri Pacific GP20 Diesel, *75-76*	130	145	
8563	Rock Island Alco Diesel A Unit, *75-76 u*	65	90	
8564	Union Pacific U36B Diesel, *75*	110	155	
8565	Missouri Pacific GP20 Diesel Dummy Unit, *75-76*	55	70	
8566	Southern F3 Diesel A Unit, *75-77*	220	370	
8567	Southern F3 Diesel A Unit, dummy, *75-77*	105	135	
8568	Preamble Express F3 Diesel A Unit, *75 u*	90	115	
8569	Soo Line NW2 Switcher, *75-77*	60	65	
8570	Liberty Special Alco Diesel A Unit, *75 u*	75	90	
8571	Frisco U36B Diesel, *75-76*	75	95	
8572	Frisco U36B Diesel Dummy Unit, *75-76*		55	
8573	Union Pacific U36B Diesel Dummy Unit, *75 u*	145	190	
8575	Milwaukee Road F3 Diesel B Unit (SSS), *75*	105	160	
8576	Penn Central GP7 Diesel, *75 u, 76-77*	90	120	
8578	NYC Ballast Tamper, *85, 87*	85	90	
8581	Illinois Central F3 Diesel B Unit, *85, 87*	130	155	
8585	Burlington Northern SD40 Diesel, *85*	355	385	
8587	Wabash GP9 Diesel "484," *85 u*	250	280	
8600	NYC 4-6-4 Locomotive, *76*	175	195	
8601	Rock Island 0-4-0 Locomotive, *76-77*	17	21	
8602	D&RGW 2-4-0 Locomotive, *76-78*	22	26	
8603	C&O 4-6-4 Locomotive, *76-77*	135	190	
8604	Jersey Central 2-4-2 Locomotive, *76 u*	39	44	
8606	B&A 4-6-4 Locomotive "784," *86 u*	720	760	
8610	Wabash 4-6-2 "672" (FF 1), *86-87*	435	610	
8615	L&N 2-8-4 Locomotive "1970," *86 u*	540	630	
8616	Santa Fe 4-4-2 Locomotive, *86*	60	65	
8617	Nickel Plate Road 4-4-2 Locomotive, *86-91*	60	65	
8625	Pennsylvania 2-4-0 Locomotive, *86-90*	21	34	
8630	W&ARR 4-4-0 Locomotive "3," *86 u*	125	150	
8635	Santa Fe 0-4-0 (SSS), *86*	80	100	
8650	Burlington Northern U36B Diesel, *76-77*	120	170	
8651	Burlington Northern U36B Diesel Dummy Unit, *76-77*	70	90	
8652	Santa Fe F3 Diesel A Unit, *76-77*	260	510	
8653	Santa Fe F3 Diesel A Unit, dummy, *76-77*	135	160	
8654	Boston & Maine GP9 Diesel, *76-77*	155	195	
8655	Boston & Maine GP9 Diesel Dummy Unit, *76-77*	90	110	

		Esc	Mint
	dian National Alco Diesel A Unit, *76*	150	195
	adian National Alco Diesel B Unit, *76*	60	75
	Alco Diesel A Unit, dummy, *76*	85	170
	rginian Electric Locomotive, *76-77*	125	137
	P Rail NW2 Switcher, *76-77*	100	135
866_	Southern F3 Diesel B Unit, *76*	165	170
8662	B&O GP7 Diesel, *86*	120	130
8664	Amtrak Alco Diesel A Unit, *76-77*	85	120
8665	BAR Jeremiah O'Brien GP9 Diesel "1776," *76 u*	100	170
8666	Northern Pacific GP9 Diesel (SSS), *76*	125	175
8667	Amtrak Alco Diesel B Unit, *76-77*	60	80
8668	Northern Pacific GP9 Diesel Dummy Unit (SSS), *76*	100	130
8669	Illinois Central Gulf U36B Diesel, *76-77*	125	165
8670	Chessie System Switcher, *76*	30	55
8679	Northern Pacific GP20 Diesel, *86*	90	105
8687	Jersey Central FM Train Master Diesel, *86*	198	276
8690	Lionel Lines Trolley, *86*	105	115
8701	W&ARR 4-4-0 Locomotive "3," *77-79*	157	210
8702	Southern 4-6-4 Locomotive, *77-78*	280	398
8703	Wabash 2-4-2 Locomotive, *77*	22	30
8750	Rock Island GP7 Diesel, *77-78*	110	125
8751	Rock Island GP7 Diesel Dummy Unit, *77-78*	50	70
8753	Pennsylvania GG1 Electric Locomotive, *77 u*	290	315
8754	New Haven Electric Locomotive, *77-78*	100	115
8755	Santa Fe U36B Diesel, *77-78*	130	150
8756	Santa Fe U36B Diesel Dummy Unit, *77-78*	75	95
8757	Conrail GP9 Diesel, *76 u, 77-78*	110	140
8758	Southern GP7 Diesel Dummy Unit, *77 u, 78*	75	95
8759	Erie-Lackawanna GP9 Diesel, *77-79*	115	175
8760	Erie-Lackawanna GP9 Diesel Dummy Unit, *77-79*	95	115
8761	GTW NW2 Switcher, *77-78*	95	130
8762	Great Northern EP-5 Electric Locomotive, *77-78*	130	140
8763	Norfolk & Western GP9 Diesel, *76 u, 77-78*	110	120
8764	B&O Budd RDC Passenger (SSS), *77*	110	135
8765	B&O Budd RDC Baggage Dummy Unit (SSS), *77*	80	100
8766	B&O Budd RDC Baggage (SSS), *77*		310
8767	B&O Budd RDC Passenger Dummy Unit (SSS), *77*	85	105
8768	B&O Budd RDC Passenger Dummy Unit (SSS), *77*	85	105
8769	Republic Steel Switcher, *77-78*	22	39
8770	NW2 Switcher, *77-78*		65
8771	Great Northern U36B Diesel, *77*	110	140
8772	GM&O GP20 Diesel, *77*	85	95
8773	Mickey Mouse U36B Diesel, *77-78*	493	645
8774	Southern GP7 Diesel, *77 u, 78*	110	135
8775	Lehigh Valley GP9 Diesel, *77 u, 78*	85	105
8776	C&NW GP20 Diesel, *77 u, 78*	87	129
8777	Santa Fe F3 Diesel B Unit (SSS), *77*	160	175
8778	Lehigh Valley GP9 Diesel Dummy Unit, *77 u, 78*	90	110
8779	C&NW GP20 Diesel Dummy Unit, *77 u, 78*	73	109
8800	Lionel Lines 4-4-2 Locomotive, *78-81*	75	105
8801	Blue Comet 4-6-4 Locomotive, *78-80*	380	500
8803	Santa Fe 0-4-0 Locomotive, *78*	14	24
8850	Penn Central GG1 Electric Locomotive, *78 u, 79*	215	305
8854	CP Rail GP9 Diesel, *78-79*	100	120

MODERN 1970-2021		Esc	Mint
8855	Milwaukee Road SD18 Diesel, *78*		115
8857	Northern Pacific U36B Diesel, *78-80*	140	180
8858	Northern Pacific U36B Diesel Dummy Unit, *78-80*	55	85
8859	Conrail Electric Locomotive, *78-82*	105	150
8860	Rock Island NW2 Switcher, *78-79*	85	100
8861	Santa Fe Alco Diesel A Unit, *78-79*	65	85
8862	Santa Fe Alco Diesel B Unit, *78-79*	36	43
8864	New Haven F3 Diesel B Unit, *78*	85	105
8866	M&StL GP9 Diesel (SSS), *78*	85	120
8867	M&StL GP9 Diesel Dummy Unit (SSS), *78*	65	95
8868	Amtrak Budd RDC Baggage, *78, 80*	195	235
8869	Amtrak Budd RDC Passenger Dummy Unit, *78, 80*	75	95
8870	Amtrak Budd RDC Passenger Dummy Unit, *78, 80*	85	115
8871	Amtrak Budd RDC Baggage Dummy Unit, *78, 80*	85	105
8872	Santa Fe SD18 Diesel, *78 u*	125	155
8873	Santa Fe SD18 Diesel Dummy Unit, *78 u*	60	85
8900	Santa Fe 4-6-4 Locomotive (FARR 1), *79*	270	310
8902	ACL 2-4-0 Locomotive, *79-82, 86 u, 87-90*	13	17
8903	D&RGW 2-4-2 Locomotive, *79-81*	17	21
8904	Wabash 2-4-2 Locomotive, *79, 81 u*	30	34
8905	Smokey Mountain Dockside 0-4-0T Locomotive, *79*	9	17
8950	Virginian FM Train Master Diesel, *79*	230	285
8951	Southern Pacific FM Train Master Diesel, *79*	237	335
8955	Southern U36B Diesel, *79*	120	195
8956	Southern U36B Diesel Dummy Unit, *79*	80	125
8957	Burlington Northern GP20 Diesel, *79*	120	150
8958	Burlington Northern GP20 Diesel Dummy Unit, *79*	85	90
8960	Southern Pacific U36C Diesel, *79 u*	130	180
8961	Southern Pacific U36C Diesel Dummy Unit, *79 u*	70	80
8962	Reading U36B Diesel, *79*	115	130
9001	Conrail Boxcar (027), *86-87 u, 88-90*	5	10
9010	GN Hopper (027), *70-71*	6	8
9011	GN Hopper (027), *70 u, 75-76, 78-83*	8	10
9012	TA&G Hopper (027), *71-72*	7	8
9013	Canadian National Hopper (027), *72-76*	5	8
9015	Reading Hopper (027), *73-75*	17	21
9016	Chessie System Hopper (027), *75-79, 87-88, 89 u*	4	6
9017	Wabash Gondola with canisters (027), *78-82*	3	5
9018	DT&I Hopper (027), *78-79, 81-82*	6	7
9019	Flatcar (027), *78*	2	3
9020	Union Pacific Flatcar (027), *70-78*	3	5
9021	Santa Fe Work Caboose, *70-71, 73-75*	9	13
9022	Santa Fe Bulkhead Flatcar (027), *70-72, 75-79*	7	13
9023	MKT Bulkhead Flatcar (027), *73-74*	7	10
9024	C&O Flatcar (027), *73-75*	3	6
9025	DT&I Work Caboose, *71-74, 77-78*	8	10
9026	Republic Steel Flatcar (027), *75-82*	5	7
9027	Soo Line Work Caboose, *75-76*	7	9
9030	Kickapoo Gondola (027), *72, 79*	5	9
9031	NKP Gondola with canisters (027), *73-75, 82-83, 84-91 u*	5	8
9032	SP Gondola with canisters (027), *75-78*	1	5
9033	PC Gondola with canisters (027), *76-78, 82, 86 u, 87-90, 92 u*		3
9034	Lionel Leisure Hopper (027), *77 u*	30	34
9035	Conrail Boxcar (027), *78-82*	5	12

MODERN 1970-2021		Esc	Mint
____ 9036	Mobilgas 1-D Tank Car (027), *78-82*	7	19
____ 9037	Conrail Boxcar (027), *78 u, 80*	7	10
____ 9038	Chessie System Hopper (027), *78 u, 80*	15	19
____ 9039	Mobilgas 1-D Tank Car (027), *78 u, 80*	10	15
____ 9040	General Mills Wheaties Boxcar (027), *70-72*	9	13
____ 9041	Hershey's Boxcar (027), *70-71, 73-76*	18	28
____ 9042	Ford-Autolite Boxcar (027), *71 u, 72 74-76*	13	21
____ 9043	Erie-Lackawanna Boxcar (027), *73-75*	13	20
____ 9044	D&RGW Boxcar (027), *75-76*	5	8
____ 9045	Toys "R" Us Boxcar (027), *75 u*	35	42
____ 9046	True Value Boxcar (027), *76 u*	26	34
____ 9047	Toys "R" Us Boxcar (027), *76 u*	40	43
____ 9048	Toys "R" Us Boxcar (027), *76 u*	33	41
____ 9049	Toys "R" Us Boxcar (027), *78 u*		NRS
____ 9050	Sunoco 1-D Tank Car (027), *70-71*	17	23
____ 9051	Firestone 1-D Tank Car (027), *74-75, 78*	15	19
____ 9052	Toys "R" Us Boxcar (027), *77 u*	26	34
____ 9053	True Value Boxcar (027), *77 u*	28	40
____ 9054	JCPenney Boxcar (027), *77 u*	14	19
____ 9055	Republic Steel Gondola with canisters, *78 u*	9	10
____ 9057	CP Rail SP-type Caboose, *78-79*	10	15
____ 9058	Lionel Lines SP-type Caboose, *78-79, 83*	5	7
____ 9059	Lionel Lines SP-type Caboose, *79 u, 81 u*	7	9
____ 9060	Nickel Plate Road SP-type Caboose, *70-72*	5	7
____ 9061	Santa Fe SP-type Caboose, *70-76*	5	8
____ 9062	Penn Central SP-type Caboose, *70-72, 74-76*	7	9
____ 9063	GTW SP-type Caboose, *70, 71-73 u*	15	19
____ 9064	C&O SP-type Caboose, *71-72, 75-77*	7	10
____ 9065	Canadian National SP-type Caboose, *71-73 u*	19	24
____ 9066	Southern SP-type Caboose, *73-76*	7	9
____ 9067	Kickapoo Valley Bobber Caboose, *72*	6	9
____ 9068	Reading Bobber Caboose, *73-76*	5	7
____ 9069	Jersey Central SP-type Caboose, *73-74, 75-76 u*	5	8
____ 9070	Rock Island SP-type Caboose, *73-74*	13	17
____ 9071	Santa Fe Bobber Caboose, *74 u, 77-78*	7	9
____ 9073	Coca-Cola SP-type Caboose, *74 u, 75*	30	35
____ 9075	Rock Island SP-type Caboose, *75-76 u*	13	17
____ 9076	"We The People" SP-type Caboose, *75 u*	19	28
____ 9077	D&RGW SP-type Caboose, *76-83, 84-91 u*	7	8
____ 9078	Rock Island Bobber Caboose, *76-77*	5	7
____ 9079	GTW Hopper (027), *77*	28	32
____ 9080	Wabash SP-type Caboose, *77*	9	10
____ 9085	Santa Fe Work Caboose, *79-82*	4	5
____ 9090	General Mills Mini-Max Car, *71*	27	32
____ 9106	Miller Vat Car, *84-85*	33	52
____ 9107	Dr Pepper Vat Car, *86-87*	30	36
____ 9110	B&O Quad Hopper, *71*	25	30
____ 9111	N&W Quad Hopper, *72-75*	15	20
____ 9112	D&RGW Covered Quad Hopper, *73-75*	20	23
____ 9113	Norfolk & Western Quad Hopper (SSS), *73*	27	32
____ 9114	Morton Salt Covered Quad Hopper, *74-76*	18	27
____ 9115	Planter's Covered Quad Hopper, *74-76*	21	33
____ 9116	Domino Sugar Covered Quad Hopper, *74-76*	22	29
____ 9117	Alaska Covered Quad Hopper (SSS), *74-76*	29	33

	MODERN 1970-2021	Esc	Mint	
9119	Detroit & Mackinac Covered Hopper, *75 u*		20	
9120	Northern Pacific Flatcar with trailers, *70-71*	33	38	
9121	L&N Flatcar with bulldozer and scraper, *71-79*	47	54	
9122	Northern Pacific Flatcar with trailers, *72-75*	19	32	
9123	C&O Auto Carrier, 3-tier, *72 u, 73-74*	18	27	
9124	P&LE Flatcar with logs, *73-74*	18	25	
9125	Norfolk & Western Auto Carrier, 2-tier, *73-77*	23	28	
9126	C&O Auto Carrier, 3-tier, *73-75*	23	34	
9128	Heinz Vat Car, *74-76*	28	37	
9129	N&W Auto Carrier, 3-tier, *75-76*	17	19	
9130	B&O Quad Hopper, *70*	23	24	
9131	D&RGW Gondola with canisters, *73-77*	5	8	
9132	Libby's Vat Car (SSS), *75-77*	16	23	
9133	BN Flatcar with trailers, *76-77, 80*	20	28	
9134	Virginian Covered Quad Hopper, *76-77*		32	
9135	N&W Covered Quad Hopper, *70 u, 71, 75*	17	26	
9136	Republic Steel Gondola with canisters, *72-76, 79*	9	11	
9138	Sunoco 3-D Tank Car (SSS), *78*	33	37	
9139	PC Auto Carrier, 3-tier, *76-77*	21	29	
9140	Burlington Gondola with canisters, *70, 73-82, 87-89*	7	9	
9141	BN Gondola with canisters, *70-72*	8	10	
9143	CN Gondola with canisters, *71-73 u*	30	34	
9144	D&RGW Gondola with canisters (SSS), *74-76*	9	13	
9145	ICG Auto Carrier, 3-tier, *77-80*	21	29	
9146	Mogen David Vat Car, *77-81*	21	26	
9147	Texaco 1-D Tank Car, *77-78*	46	63	
9148	Du Pont 3-D Tank Car, *77-81*	25	28	
9149	CP Rail Flatcar with trailers, *77-78*	22	35	
9150	Gulf 1-D Tank Car, *70 u, 71*	22	28	
9151	Shell 1-D Tank Car, *72*	27	31	
9152	Shell 1-D Tank Car, *73-76*	25	34	
9153	Chevron 1-D Tank Car, *74-76*	28	35	
9154	Borden 1-D Tank Car, *75-76*	33	47	
9156	Mobilgas 1-D Tank Car, *76-77*	30	40	
9157	C&O Crane Car, *76-78, 81-82*	35	44	
9158	PC Flatcar with shovel, *76-77, 80*	40	55	
9159	Sunoco 1-D Tank Car, *76*	35	50	
9160	Illinois Central N5c Caboose, *70-72*	17	23	
9161	CN N5c Caboose, *72-74*	14	25	
9162	PRR N5c Caboose, *72-76*	25	30	
9163	Santa Fe N5c Caboose, *73-76*	17	24	
9165	Canadian Pacific N5c Caboose (SSS), *73*	21	30	
9166	D&RGW SP-type Caboose (SSS), *74-75*	20	25	
9167	Chessie System N5c Caboose, *74-76*	24	31	
9168	Union Pacific N5c Caboose, *75-77*	17	19	
9169	Milwaukee Road SP-type Caboose (SSS), *75*	16	19	
9170	N&W N5c Caboose "1776," *75*	27	30	
9171	MP SP-type Caboose, *75 u, 76-77*	19	20	
9172	Penn Central SP-type Caboose, *75 u, 76-77*	23	31	
9173	Jersey Central SP-type Caboose, *75 u, 76-77*	22	33	
9174	NYC (P&E) Bay Window Caboose, *76*	65	70	
9175	Virginian N5c Caboose, *76-77*	24	26	
9176	BAR N5c Caboose, *76 u*	16	30	
9177	Northern Pacific Bay Window Caboose (SSS), *76*	25	35	

			Esc	Mint
____	9178	ICG SP-type Caboose, *76-77*	19	24
____	9179	Chessie System Bobber Caboose, *76*	7	11
____	9180	Rock Island N5c Caboose, *77-78*	12	23
____	9181	B&M N5c Caboose, *76 u, 77*	28	49
____	9182	N&W N5c Caboose, *76 u, 77-80*	20	26
____	9183	Mickey Mouse N5c Caboose, *77-78*	32	50
____	9184	Erie Bay Window Caboose, *77-78*	24	30
____	9185	GTW N5c Caboose, *77*	21	28
____	9186	Conrail N5c Caboose, *76 u, 77-78*	27	29
____	9187	Gulf, Mobile & Ohio SP-type Caboose, *77*	10	16
____	9188	GN Bay Window Caboose, *77*	22	27
____	9189	Gulf 1-D Tank Car, *77*	40	60
____	9193	Budweiser Vat Car, *83-84*	92	121
____	9200	Illinois Central Boxcar, *70-71*	19	25
____	9201	Penn Central Boxcar, *70*	17	25
____	9202	Santa Fe Boxcar, *70*	20	24
____	9203	Union Pacific Boxcar, *70*		21
____	9204	Northern Pacific Boxcar, *70*		21
____	9205	Norfolk & Western Boxcar, *70*	22	25
____	9206	Great Northern Boxcar, *70-71*		20
____	9207	Soo Line Boxcar, *71*	11	18
____	9208	CP Rail Boxcar, *71*	21	23
____	9209	Burlington Northern Boxcar, *71-72*	16	21
____	9210	B&O DD Boxcar, *71*	16	20
____	9211	Penn Central Boxcar, *71*	17	28
____	9213	M&StL Covered Quad Hopper (SSS), *78*	20	29
____	9214	Northern Pacific Boxcar, *71-72*	16	21
____	9215	Norfolk & Western Boxcar, *71*	19	24
____	9216	Great Northern Auto Carrier, 3-tier, *78*	25	39
____	9217	Soo Line Operating Boxcar, *82-84*	29	36
____	9218	Monon Operating Boxcar, *81*	25	30
____	9219	Missouri Pacific Operating Boxcar, *83*	27	33
____	9220	Borden Operating Milk Car, *83-86*	95	113
____	9221	Poultry Dispatch Operating Chicken Car, *83-85*	45	50
____	9222	L&N Flatcar with trailers, *83-84*	38	60
____	9223	Reading Operating Boxcar, *84*	33	40
____	9224	Churchill Downs Operating Horse Car, *84-86*	85	110
____	9225	Conrail Operating Barrel Car, *84*	42	55
____	9226	Delaware & Hudson Flatcar with trailers, *84-85*	31	34
____	9228	Canadian Pacific Operating Boxcar, *86*	24	37
____	9229	Express Mail Operating Boxcar, *85-86*	21	27
____	9230	Monon Boxcar (SSS), *71, 72 u*	17	24
____	9231	Reading Bay Window Caboose, *79*	24	32
____	9232	Allis-Chalmers Condenser Car, *80-81, 83 u*	42	50
____	9233	Depressed Center Flatcar with transformer, *80*	55	65
____	9234	Radioactive Waste Car, *80*	53	78
____	9235	Union Pacific Derrick Car, *83-84*	16	22
____	9236	C&NW Derrick Car, *83-85*	22	30
____	9238	Northern Pacific Log Dump Car, *84*	16	24
____	9239	Lionel Lines N5c Caboose, *83 u*	50	60
____	9240	NYC Operating Hopper, *86*	32	39
____	9240	NYC Hopper (O27), *87 u*	20	29
____	9241	PRR Log Dump Car, *85-86*	21	27
____	9250	WaterPoxy 3-D Tank Car, *70-71*	23	34

		Esc	Mint	
9260	Reynolds Aluminum Covered Quad Hopper, *75-77*	19	22	___
9261	Sun-Maid Raisins Covered Quad Hopper, *75 u, 76*	22	29	___
9262	Ralston Purina Covered Quad Hopper, *75 u, 76*	36	58	___
9263	PRR Covered Quad Hopper, *75 u, 76-77*	23	30	___
9264	Illinois Central Covered Quad Hopper, *75 u, 76-77*	28	39	___
9265	Chessie System Covered Quad Hopper, *75 u, 76-77*	21	27	___
9266	Southern "Big John" Covered Quad Hopper, *76*	46	65	___
9267	Alcoa Covered Quad Hopper (SSS), *76*	20	25	___
9268	Northern Pacific Bay Window Caboose, *77 u*	33	40	___
9269	Milwaukee Road Bay Window Caboose, *78*	34	47	___
9270	Northern Pacific N5c Caboose, *78*	14	27	___
9271	M&StL Bay Window Caboose (SSS), *78-79*	18	30	___
9272	New Haven Bay Window Caboose, *78-80*	20	34	___
9273	Southern Bay Window Caboose, *78 u*	36	45	___
9274	Santa Fe Bay Window Caboose, *78 u*	40	47	___
9276	Peabody Quad Hopper, *78*	19	28	___
9277	Cities Service 1-D Tank Car, *78*	41	45	___
9278	Life Savers 1-D Tank Car, *78-79*	117	157	___
9279	Magnolia 3-D Tank Car, *78, 79 u*	13	19	___
9280	Santa Fe Operating Stock Car (O27), *77-81*	17	24	___
9281	Santa Fe Auto Carrier, 3-tier, *78-80*	21	27	___
9282	GN Flatcar with trailers, *78-79, 81-82*	22	28	___
9283	Union Pacific Gondola with canisters, *77*	15	21	___
9284	Santa Fe Gondola with canisters, *77*	16	27	___
9285	ICG Flatcar with trailers, *77*	47	48	___
9286	B&LE Covered Quad Hopper, *77*	14	26	___
9287	Southern N5c Caboose, *77 u, 78*	18	30	___
9288	Lehigh Valley N5c Caboose, *77 u, 78, 80*	25	31	___
9289	C&NW N5c Caboose, *77 u, 78, 80*	25	36	___
9290	Union Pacific Operating Barrel Car, *83*	65	75	___
9300	PC Log Dump Car, *70-75, 77*	18	24	___
9301	U.S. Mail Operating Boxcar, *73-84*	32	42	___
9302	L&N Searchlight Car, *72 u, 73-78*	21	24	___
9303	Union Pacific Log Dump Car, *74-78, 80*	17	22	___
9304	C&O Coal Dump Car, *74-78*	11	23	___
9305	Santa Fe Operating Cowboy Car (O27), *80-82*	16	23	___
9306	Santa Fe Flatcar with horses, *80-82*	18	26	___
9307	Erie Animated Gondola, *80-84*	55	70	___
9308	Aquarium Car, *81-84*	125	129	___
9309	TP&W Bay Window Caboose, *80-81, 83 u*	19	25	___
9310	Santa Fe Log Dump Car, *78 u, 79-83*	13	24	___
9311	Union Pacific Coal Dump Car, *78 u, 79-82*	13	24	___
9312	Conrail Searchlight Car, *78 u, 79-83*	18	27	___
9313	Gulf 3-D Tank Car, *79 u*	43	50	___
9315	Southern Pacific Gondola with canisters, *79 u*	16	23	___
9316	Southern Pacific Bay Window Caboose, *79 u*	47	50	___
9317	Santa Fe Bay Window Caboose, *79*	21	36	___
9320	Fort Knox Mint Car, *79 u*	110	135	___
9321	Santa Fe 1-D Tank Car (FARR 1), *79*	25	31	___
9322	Santa Fe Covered Quad Hopper (FARR 1), *79*	30	38	___
9323	Santa Fe Bay Window Caboose (FARR 1), *79*	39	49	___
9324	Tootsie Roll 1-D Tank Car, *79-81*	67	96	___
9325	Norfolk & Western Flatcar with fences, *79-81 u*	6	10	___
9326	Burlington Northern Bay Window Caboose, *79-80*	34	44	___

	No.	Description	Esc	Mint
____	9327	Bakelite 3-D Tank Car, *80*	19	29
____	9328	Chessie System Bay Window Caboose, *80*	33	42
____	9329	Chessie System Crane Car, *80*	40	47
____	9330	Kickapoo Dump Car, *72, 79*	3	7
____	9331	Union 76 1-D Tank Car, *79*	39	44
____	9332	Reading Crane Car, *79*	37	50
____	9333	Southern Pacific Flatcar with trailers, *79-80*	33	47
____	9334	Humble 1-D Tank Car, *79*	21	26
____	9335	B&O Log Dump Car, *86*	16	22
____	9336	CP Rail Gondola with canisters, *79*	20	29
____	9338	Pennsylvania Power & Light Quad Hopper, *79*	60	75
____	9339	GN Boxcar (O27), *79-83, 85 u, 86*	8	10
____	9340	Illinois Central Gondola with canisters (O27), *79-81, 82 u, 83*	5	9
____	9341	ACL SP-type Caboose, *79-82, 86 u 87-90*	6	8
____	9344	Citgo 3-D Tank Car, *80*	23	38
____	9345	Reading Searchlight Car, *84-85*	20	25
____	9346	Wabash SP-type Caboose, *79*	6	10
____	9348	Santa Fe Crane Car (FARR 1), *79 u*	60	70
____	9349	San Francisco Mint Car, *80*	55	70
____	9351	PRR Auto Carrier, 3-tier, *80*	23	40
____	9352	Trailer Train Flatcar with C&NW trailers, *80*	29	55
____	9353	Crystal Line 3-D Tank Car, *80*	18	26
____	9354	Pennzoil 1-D Tank Car, *80, 81 u*	60	85
____	9355	Delaware & Hudson Bay Window Caboose, *80*	37	45
____	9357	Smokey Mountain Bobber Caboose, *79*	8	10
____	9359	National Basketball Association Boxcar (O27), *79-80 u*	19	24
____	9360	National Hockey League Boxcar (O27), *79-80 u*	21	26
____	9361	C&NW Bay Window Caboose, *80*	47	50
____	9362	Major League Baseball Boxcar (O27), *79-80 u*	17	21
____	9363	N&W Log Dump Car "9325" (O27), *79*	4	7
____	9364	N&W Crane Car "9325" (O27), *79*	7	9
____	9365	Toys "R" Us Boxcar (O27), *79 u*	30	37
____	9366	UP Covered Quad Hopper (FARR 2), *80*	19	23
____	9367	Union Pacific 1-D Tank Car (FARR 2), *80*	21	30
____	9368	Union Pacific Bay Window Caboose (FARR 2), *80*	30	36
____	9369	Sinclair 1-D Tank Car, *80*	60	85
____	9370	Seaboard Gondola with canisters, *80*	19	21
____	9371	Atlantic Sugar Covered Quad Hopper, *80*	19	22
____	9372	Seaboard Bay Window Caboose, *80*	32	38
____	9373	Getty 1-D Tank Car, *80-81, 83 u*	31	42
____	9374	Reading Covered Quad Hopper, *80-81, 83 u*	39	40
____	9376	Soo Line Boxcar (O27), *81 u*	40	50
____	9378	Derrick Car, *80-82*	18	22
____	9379	Santa Fe Gondola with canisters, *80-81, 83 u*	22	30
____	9380	NYNH&H SP-type Caboose, *80-81*	7	10
____	9381	Chessie System SP-type Caboose, *80*	7	9
____	9382	Florida East Coast Bay Window Caboose, *80*	34	48
____	9383	UP Flatcar with trailers (FARR 2), *80 u*	27	34
____	9384	Great Northern Operating Hopper, *81*	50	55
____	9385	Alaska Gondola with canisters, *81*	27	34
____	9386	Pure Oil 1-D Tank Car, *81*	38	50
____	9387	Burlington Bay Window Caboose, *81*	46	52
____	9388	Toys "R" Us Boxcar (O27), *81 u*	38	45
____	9389	Radioactive Waste Car, *81-82*	65	80

| --- | --- | --- |
9398 PRR Coal Dump Car, *83-84*	28	38 ___
9399 C&NW Coal Dump Car, *83-85*	17	22 ___
9400 Conrail Boxcar, *78*	14	20 ___
9401 Great Northern Boxcar, *78*	18	23 ___
9402 Susquehanna Boxcar, *78*	30	33 ___
9403 Seaboard Coast Line Boxcar, *78*	12	17 ___
9404 NKP Boxcar, *78*	19	21 ___
9405 Chattahoochee Boxcar, *78*	14	19 ___
9406 D&RGW Boxcar, *78-79*	17	21 ___
9407 Union Pacific Stock Car, *78*	18	25 ___
9408 Lionel Lines Circus Stock Car (SSS), *78*	31	40 ___
9411 Lackawanna Phoebe Snow Boxcar, *78*	35	43 ___
9412 RF&P Boxcar, *79*	21	27 ___
9413 Napierville Junction Boxcar, *79*	18	24 ___
9414 Cotton Belt Boxcar, *79*	19	23 ___
9415 Providence & Worcester Boxcar, *79*	17	25 ___
9416 MD&W Boxcar, *79, 81*	13	19 ___
9417 CP Rail Boxcar, *79*	45	50 ___
9418 FARR Boxcar, *79 u*	50	60 ___
9419 Union Pacific Boxcar (FARR 2), *80*	10	17 ___
9420 B&O Sentinel Boxcar, *80*	21	26 ___
9421 Maine Central Boxcar, *80*	10	17 ___
9422 EJ&E Boxcar, *80*	12	20 ___
9423 NYNH&H Boxcar, *80*	14	22 ___
9424 TP&W Boxcar, *80*	17	21 ___
9425 British Columbia DD Boxcar, *80*	27	35 ___
9426 Chesapeake & Ohio Boxcar, *80*	19	30 ___
9427 Bay Line Boxcar, *80-81*	12	17 ___
9428 TP&W Boxcar, *80-81, 83 u*		23 ___
9429 "The Early Years" Boxcar, *80*	14	27 ___
9430 "The Standard Gauge Years" Boxcar, *80*	15	25 ___
9431 "The Prewar Years" Boxcar, *80*	14	25 ___
9432 "The Postwar Years" Boxcar, *80*	24	55 ___
9433 "The Golden Years" Boxcar, *80*	33	43 ___
9434 Joshua Lionel Cowen "The Man" Boxcar, *80 u*	29	37 ___
9436 Burlington Boxcar, *81*	25	30 ___
9437 Northern Pacific Stock Car, *81*	22	36 ___
9438 Ontario Northland Boxcar, *81*	25	31 ___
9439 Ashley Drew & Northern Boxcar, *81*	11	19 ___
9440 Reading Boxcar, *81*	50	65 ___
9441 Pennsylvania Boxcar, *81*	32	42 ___
9442 Canadian Pacific Boxcar, *81*	13	21 ___
9443 Florida East Coast Boxcar, *81*	19	24 ___
9444 Louisiana Midland Boxcar, *81*	14	18 ___
9445 Vermont Northern Boxcar, *81*	14	17 ___
9446 Sabine River & Northern Boxcar, *81*	15	21 ___
9447 Pullman Standard Boxcar, *81*	16	21 ___
9448 Santa Fe Stock Car, *81-82*	34	40 ___
9449 Great Northern Boxcar (FARR 3), *81*	27	31 ___
9450 Great Northern Stock Car (FARR 3), *81 u*	50	60 ___
9451 Southern Boxcar (FARR 4), *83*	26	32 ___
9452 Western Pacific Boxcar, *82-83*	12	16 ___
9453 MPA Boxcar, *82-83*	14	19 ___
9454 New Hope & Ivyland Boxcar, *82-83*	21	27 ___

			Esc	Mint
____	9455	Milwaukee Road Boxcar, *82-83*	15	19
____	9456	PRR DD Boxcar (FARR 5), *84-85*	24	30
____	9461	Norfolk & Southern Boxcar, *82*	25	43
____	9462	Southern Pacific Boxcar, *83-84*	18	23
____	9463	Texas & Pacific Boxcar, *83-84*	15	19
____	9464	NC&StL Boxcar, *83-84*	16	22
____	9465	Santa Fe Boxcar, *83-84*	12	19
____	9466	Wanamaker Boxcar, *82 u*	60	70
____	9467	Tennessee World's Fair Boxcar, *82 u*	26	31
____	9468	Union Pacific DD Boxcar, *83*	31	34
____	9469	NYC Pacemaker Boxcar (std O), *84-85*	37	53
____	9470	Chicago Beltline Boxcar, *84*	15	20
____	9471	Atlantic Coast Line Boxcar, *84*	13	20
____	9472	Detroit & Mackinac Boxcar, *84*	22	26
____	9473	Lehigh Valley Boxcar, *84*	15	28
____	9474	Erie-Lackawanna Boxcar, *84*	31	35
____	9475	D&H "I Love NY" Boxcar, *84 u*	28	37
____	9476	PRR Boxcar (FARR 5), *84-85*	27	36
____	9480	MN&S Boxcar, *85-86*	15	18
____	9481	Seaboard System Boxcar, *85-86*	15	18
____	9482	Norfolk & Southern Boxcar, *85-86*	13	17
____	9483	Manufacturers Railway Boxcar, *85-86*	14	19
____	9484	Lionel 85th Anniversary Boxcar, *85*	22	26
____	9486	GTW "I Love Michigan" Boxcar, *86*	23	34
____	9490	Christmas Boxcar for Lionel Employees, *85 u*		1800
____	9491	Christmas Boxcar, *86 u*	26	37
____	9492	Lionel Lines Boxcar, *86*	23	29
____	9500	Milwaukee Road Passenger Coach, *73*	28	75
____	9501	Milwaukee Road Passenger Coach, *73 u, 74-76*	33	37
____	9502	Milwaukee Road Observation Car, *73*	30	48
____	9503	Milwaukee Road Passenger Coach, *73*	33	48
____	9504	Milwaukee Road Passenger Coach, *73 u, 74-76*	33	37
____	9505	Milwaukee Road Passenger Coach, *73 u, 74-76*	35	38
____	9506	Milwaukee Road Combination Car, *74 u, 75-76*	32	37
____	9507	PRR Passenger Coach, *74-75*	34	55
____	9508	PRR Passenger Coach, *74-75*	32	50
____	9509	PRR Observation Car, *74-75*	41	60
____	9510	PRR Combination Car, *74 u, 75-76*	30	47
____	9511	Milwaukee Road Passenger Coach, *74 u*	33	48
____	9513	PRR Passenger Coach, *75-76*	25	44
____	9514	PRR Passenger Coach, *75-76*	23	36
____	9515	PRR Passenger Coach, *75-76*	22	34
____	9516	B&O Passenger Coach, *76*	27	42
____	9517	B&O Passenger Coach, *75*	45	65
____	9518	B&O Observation Car, *75*	45	65
____	9519	B&O Combination Car, *75*	55	85
____	9521	PRR Baggage Car, *75 u, 76*	65	95
____	9522	Milwaukee Road Baggage Car, *75 u, 76*	65	80
____	9523	B&O Baggage Car, *75 u, 76*	60	70
____	9524	B&O Passenger Coach, *76*	27	37
____	9525	B&O Passenger Coach, *76*	30	43
____	9527	Milwaukee Road Campaign Observation Car, *76 u*	38	60
____	9528	PRR Campaign Observation Car, *76 u*	48	75
____	9529	B&O Campaign Observation Car, *76 u*	35	59

No.	Description		
9530	Southern Baggage Car, *77-78*	45	
9531	Southern Combination Car, *77-78*	29	
9532	Southern Passenger Coach, *77-78*	33	47
9533	Southern Passenger Coach, *77-78*	27	38
9534	Southern Observation Car, *77-78*	31	47
9536	Blue Comet Baggage Car, *78-80*	39	55
9537	Blue Comet Combination Car, *78-80*	35	50
9538	Blue Comet Passenger Coach, *78-80*	35	47
9539	Blue Comet Passenger Coach, *78-80*	35	48
9540	Blue Comet Observation Car, *78-80*	21	40
9541	Santa Fe Baggage Car, *80-82*	21	30
9545	Union Pacific Baggage Car, *84*	135	200
9546	Union Pacific Combination Car, *84*	85	105
9547	Union Pacific Observation Car, *84*	85	105
9548	UP Placid Bay Passenger Coach, *84*	90	110
9549	UP Ocean Sunset Passenger Coach, *84*	85	105
9551	W&ARR Baggage Car, *77 u, 78-80*	36	48
9552	W&ARR Passenger Coach, *77 u, 78-80*	46	60
9553	W&ARR Flatcar with horses, *77 u, 78-80*	32	50
9554	Chicago & Alton Baggage Car, *81*	55	85
9555	Chicago & Alton Combination Car, *81*	50	75
9556	Chicago & Alton Wilson Passenger Coach, *81*	50	75
9557	Chicago & Alton Webster Groves Passenger Coach, *81*	45	65
9558	Chicago & Alton Observation Car, *81*	50	75
9559	Rock Island Baggage Car, *81-82*	42	65
9560	Rock Island Passenger Coach, *81-82*	43	65
9561	Rock Island Passenger Coach, *81-82*	42	65
9562	N&W Baggage Car "577," *81*	80	110
9563	N&W Combination Car "578," *81*	80	105
9564	N&W Passenger Coach "579," *81*	90	100
9565	N&W Passenger Coach "580," *81*	85	100
9566	N&W Observation Car "581," *81*	90	95
9567	N&W Vista Dome Car "582," *81 u*	160	255
9569	PRR Combination Car, *81 u*	115	160
9570	PRR Baggage Car, *79*	85	115
9571	PRR Passenger Coach, *79*	125	145
9572	PRR Passenger Coach, *79*	110	125
9573	PRR Vista Dome Car, *79*	95	120
9574	PRR Observation Car, *79*	75	100
9575	PRR Passenger Coach, *79-80 u*	100	135
9576	Burlington Baggage Car, *80*	145	175
9577	Burlington Passenger Coach, *80*	95	105
9578	Burlington Passenger Coach, *80*	105	110
9579	Burlington Vista Dome Car, *80*	95	110
9580	Burlington Observation Car, *80*	95	110
9581	Chessie System Baggage Car, *80*	55	62
9582	Chessie System Combination Car, *80*	47	55
9583	Chessie System Passenger Coach, *80*	40	47
9584	Chessie System Passenger Coach, *80*	31	37
9585	Chessie System Observation Car, *80*	55	65
9586	Chessie System Diner, *86 u*	85	90
9588	Burlington Vista Dome Car, *80 u*	110	120
9589	Southern Pacific Baggage Car, *82-83*	110	135
9590	Southern Pacific Combination Car, *82-83*	90	105

		Esc	Mint
	thern Pacific Pullman Passenger Coach, 82-83	85	105
	thern Pacific Pullman Passenger Coach, 82-83	85	105
	uthern Pacific Observation Car, 82-83	100	130
	C Baggage Car, 83-84	105	130
	/C Combination Car, 83-84	75	85
	YC Wayne County Passenger Coach, 83-84	80	95
9597	NYC Hudson River Passenger Coach, 83-84	70	85
9598	NYC Observation Car, 83-84	75	85
9599	Chicago & Alton Diner, 86 u	80	90
9600	Chessie System Hi-Cube Boxcar, 75 u, 76-77	19	25
9601	ICG Hi-Cube Boxcar, 75 u, 76-77	20	21
9602	Santa Fe Hi-Cube Boxcar, 75 u, 76-77	17	20
9603	Penn Central Hi-Cube Boxcar, 76-77	12	18
9604	Norfolk & Western Hi-Cube Boxcar, 76-77	23	26
9605	NH Hi-Cube Boxcar, 76-77	17	21
9606	Union Pacific Hi-Cube Boxcar, 76 u, 77	10	17
9607	Southern Pacific Hi-Cube Boxcar, 76 u, 77	12	15
9608	Burlington Northern Hi-Cube Boxcar, 76 u, 77	21	23
9610	Frisco Hi-Cube Boxcar, 77	25	34
9620	NHL Wales Boxcar, 80	27	35
9621	NHL Campbell Boxcar, 80	27	34
9622	NBA Western Boxcar, 80	24	30
9623	NBA Eastern Boxcar, 80	26	34
9624	National League Baseball Boxcar, 80	27	34
9625	American League Baseball Boxcar, 80	27	35
9626	Santa Fe Hi-Cube Boxcar, 82-84	10	14
9627	Union Pacific Hi-Cube Boxcar, 82-83	15	21
9628	Burlington Northern Hi-Cube Boxcar, 82-84	14	19
9629	Chessie System Hi-Cube Boxcar, 83-84	24	36
9660	Mickey Mouse Hi-Cube Boxcar, 77-78	34	46
9661	Goofy Hi-Cube Boxcar, 77-78	53	61
9662	Donald Duck Hi-Cube Boxcar, 77-78	38	49
9663	Dumbo Hi-Cube Boxcar, 77 u, 78	43	58
9664	Cinderella Hi-Cube Boxcar, 77 u, 78	56	86
9665	Peter Pan Hi-Cube Boxcar, 77 u, 78	49	77
9666	Pinocchio Hi-Cube Boxcar, 78	119	168
9667	Snow White Hi-Cube Boxcar, 78	365	471
9668	Pluto Hi-Cube Boxcar, 78	149	193
9669	Bambi Hi-Cube Boxcar, 78 u	67	105
9670	Alice In Wonderland Hi-Cube Boxcar, 78 u	61	91
9671	Fantasia Hi-Cube Boxcar, 78 u	56	91
9672	Mickey Mouse 50th Anniversary Hi-Cube Boxcar, 78 u	372	472
9700	Southern Boxcar, 72-73	22	30
9701	B&O DD Boxcar, 72	14	19
9702	Soo Line Boxcar, 72-73	15	21
9703	CP Rail Boxcar, 72	34	44
9704	Norfolk & Western Boxcar, 72	10	17
9705	D&RGW Boxcar, 72	13	20
9706	C&O Boxcar, 72	12	19
9707	MKT Stock Car, 72-75	14	22
9708	U.S. Mail Toy Fair Boxcar, 73 u	85	95
9708	U.S. Mail Boxcar, 72-75	18	23
9709	BAR State of Maine Boxcar (SSS), 72-74	29	32
9710	Rutland Boxcar (SSS), 72-74	24	28

		Esc	Mint	
9711	Southern Boxcar, *74-75*	19	25	___
9712	B&O DD Boxcar, *73-74*	31	34	___
9713	CP Rail "Season's Greetings" Boxcar, *74 u*	95	120	___
9713	CP Rail Boxcar, *73-74*	24	30	___
9714	D&RGW Boxcar, *73-74*	16	20	___
9715	C&O Boxcar, *73-74*	17	22	___
9716	Penn Central Boxcar, *73-74*	15	20	___
9717	Union Pacific Boxcar, *73-74*	21	25	___
9718	Canadian National Boxcar, *73-74*	23	31	___
9719	New Haven DD Boxcar, *73 u*	23	32	___
9723	Western Pacific Toy Fair Boxcar, *74 u*	20	60	___
9723	Western Pacific Boxcar (SSS), *73-74*	27	29	___
9724	Missouri Pacific Boxcar (SSS), *73-74*	21	24	___
9725	MKT Stock Car (SSS), *73-75*	15	18	___
9726	Erie-Lackawanna Boxcar (SSS), *78*	25	30	___
9729	CP Rail Boxcar, *78*		34	___
9730	CP Rail Boxcar, *74-75*	23	27	___
9731	Milwaukee Road Boxcar, *74-75*	16	21	___
9732	Southern Pacific Boxcar, *79 u*	24	31	___
9734	Bangor & Aroostook Boxcar, *79*	30	38	___
9735	Grand Trunk Western Boxcar, *74-75*	15	21	___
9737	Vermont Central Boxcar, *74-76*	27	34	___
9738	Illinois Terminal Boxcar, *82*	33	45	___
9739	D&RGW Boxcar (SSS), *74-76*	17	25	___
9740	Chessie System Boxcar, *74-75*	15	19	___
9742	M&StL Boxcar, *73 u*	12	19	___
9742	M&StL "Season's Greetings" Boxcar, *73 u*	85	105	___
9743	Sprite Boxcar, *74 u, 75*	19	27	___
9744	Tab Boxcar, *74 u, 75*	17	24	___
9745	Fanta Boxcar, *74 u, 75*	19	29	___
9747	Chessie System DD Boxcar, *75-76*	24	28	___
9748	CP Rail Boxcar, *75-76*	16	20	___
9749	Penn Central Boxcar, *75-76*	16	21	___
9750	DT&I Boxcar, *75-76*	13	20	___
9751	Frisco Boxcar, *75-76*	21	23	___
9752	L&N Boxcar, *75-76*	20	23	___
9753	Maine Central Boxcar, *75-76*	16	22	___
9754	NYC Pacemaker Boxcar (SSS), *75-77*	20	30	___
9755	Union Pacific Boxcar, *75-76*	20	24	___
9757	Central of Georgia Boxcar, *74 u*	16	17	___
9758	Alaska Boxcar (SSS), *75-77*	24	31	___
9759	Paul Revere Boxcar, *75 u*	36	43	___
9760	Liberty Bell Boxcar, *75 u*	30	40	___
9761	George Washington Boxcar, *75 u*	36	43	___
9762	Toy Fair Boxcar, *75 u*	125	170	___
9763	D&RGW Stock Car, *76-77*	15	20	___
9764	GTW DD Boxcar, *76-77*	40	63	___
9767	Railbox Boxcar, *76-77*	15	20	___
9768	B&M Boxcar, *76-77*	18	27	___
9769	B&LE Boxcar, *76-77*	13	21	___
9770	Northern Pacific Boxcar, *76-77*	14	18	___
9771	Norfolk & Western Boxcar, *76-77*	16	24	___
9772	Great Northern Boxcar, *76*	60	85	___
9773	NYC Stock Car, *76*	32	39	___

			Esc	Mint
____	9775	M&StL Boxcar (SSS), *76*	19	23
____	9776	SP Overnight Boxcar (SSS), *76*	32	34
____	9777	Virginian Boxcar, *76-77*	22	25
____	9778	"Season's Greetings" Boxcar, *75 u*	165	185
____	9780	Johnny Cash Boxcar, *76 u*	50	61
____	9781	Delaware & Hudson Boxcar, *77-78*	19	23
____	9782	Rock Island Boxcar, *77-78*	14	17
____	9783	B&O Time-Saver Boxcar, *77-78*	18	27
____	9784	Santa Fe Boxcar, *77-78*	13	17
____	9785	Conrail Boxcar, *77-78*	20	23
____	9786	C&NW Boxcar, *77-79*	18	27
____	9787	Jersey Central Boxcar, *77-79*	12	19
____	9788	Lehigh Valley Boxcar, *77-79*	17	21
____	9789	Pickens Boxcar, *77*	25	33
____	9801	B&O Sentinel Boxcar (std O), *73-75*	18	26
____	9802	Miller High Life Reefer (std O), *73-75*	32	36
____	9803	Johnson Wax Boxcar (std O), *73-75*	27	33
____	9805	Grand Trunk Western Reefer (std O), *73-75*	20	31
____	9806	Rock Island Boxcar (std O), *74-75*	38	46
____	9807	Stroh's Beer Reefer (std O), *74-76*	70	82
____	9808	Union Pacific Boxcar (std O), *75-76*	36	50
____	9809	Clark Reefer (std O), *75-76*	33	41
____	9811	Pacific Fruit Express Reefer (FARR 2), *80*	26	33
____	9812	Arm & Hammer Reefer, *80*	24	30
____	9813	Ruffles Reefer, *80*	20	28
____	9814	Perrier Reefer, *80*	21	30
____	9815	NYC "Early Bird" Reefer (std O), *84-85*	34	40
____	9816	Brach's Candy Reefer, *80*	21	26
____	9817	Bazooka Bubble Gum Reefer, *80*	24	31
____	9818	Western Maryland Reefer, *80*	18	23
____	9819	Western Fruit Express Reefer (FARR 3), *81*	22	29
____	9820	Wabash Gondola with coal (std O), *73-74*	24	38
____	9821	SP Gondola with coal (std O), *73-75*	28	32
____	9822	GTW Gondola with coal (std O), *74-75*	24	29
____	9823	Santa Fe Flatcar with crates (std O), *75-76*	34	44
____	9824	NYC Gondola with coal (std O), *75-76*	41	56
____	9825	Schaefer Reefer (std O), *76-77*	45	60
____	9826	P&LE Boxcar (std O), *76-77*	34	39
____	9827	Cutty Sark Reefer, *84*	38	48
____	9828	J&B Reefer, *84*	37	49
____	9829	Dewar's White Label Reefer, *84*	43	48
____	9830	Johnnie Walker Red Label Reefer, *84*	38	54
____	9831	Pepsi Cola Reefer, *82*	87	98
____	9832	Cheerios Reefer, *82*	169	194
____	9833	Vlasic Pickles Reefer, *82*	23	29
____	9834	Southern Comfort Reefer, *83-84*	34	47
____	9835	Jim Beam Reefer, *83-84*	48	64
____	9836	Old Grand-Dad Reefer, *83-84*	44	54
____	9837	Wild Turkey Reefer, *83-84*	71	105
____	9840	Fleischmann's Gin Reefer, *85*	39	44
____	9841	Calvert Gin Reefer, *85*	44	49
____	9842	Seagram's Gin Reefer, *85*	44	49
____	9843	Tanqueray Gin Reefer, *85*	45	51
____	9844	Sambuca Reefer, *86*	37	49

MODERN 1970-2021		Esc	Mint	
9845	Baileys Irish Cream Reefer, *86*	72	97	___
9846	Seagram's Vodka Reefer, *86*	41	49	___
9847	Wolfschmidt Vodka Reefer, *86*	38	43	___
9849	Lionel Lines Reefer, *83 u*	20	32	___
9850	Budweiser Reefer, *72 u, 73-75*	62	73	___
9851	Schlitz Reefer, *72 u, 73-75*	30	36	___
9852	Miller Reefer, *72 u, 73-77*	32	38	___
	(A) Caramel-colored body	29	34	___
	(B) White body, black logo border	23	28	___
9853	Cracker Jack Reefer, *72 u, 73-75*			___
9854	Baby Ruth Reefer, *72 u, 73-76*	22	26	___
9855	Swift Reefer, *72 u, 73-77*	23	28	___
9856	Old Milwaukee Reefer, *75-76*	33	40	___
9858	Butterfinger Reefer, *73 u, 74-76*	22	28	___
9859	Pabst Reefer, *73 u, 74-75*	43	50	___
9860	Gold Medal Reefer, *73 u, 74-76*	12	21	___
9861	Tropicana Reefer, *75-77*	23	35	___
9862	Hamm's Reefer, *75-76*	35	42	___
9863	REA Reefer (SSS), *74-76*	24	28	___
9866	Coors Reefer, *76-77*	42	58	___
9867	Hershey's Reefer, *76-77*	79	92	___
9869	Santa Fe Reefer (SSS), *76*	32	37	___
9870	Old Dutch Cleanser Reefer, *77-78, 80*	15	21	___
9871	Carling Black Label Reefer, *77-78, 80*	33	45	___
9872	Pacific Fruit Express Reefer, *77-79*	24	28	___
9873	Ralston Purina Reefer, *78*	25	38	___
9874	Miller Lite Beer Reefer, *78-79*	58	63	___
9875	A&P Reefer, *78-79*	23	31	___
9876	Vermont Central Reefer, *78*	26	31	___
9877	Gerber Reefer, *79-80*	68	78	___
9878	Good and Plenty Reefer, *79*	24	31	___
9879	Hills Bros. Reefer, *79-80*	24	29	___
9880	Santa Fe Reefer (FARR 1), *79*	27	31	___
9881	Rath Packing Reefer, *79 u*	23	31	___
9882	NYC "Early Bird" Reefer, *79*	25	29	___
9883	Nabisco Oreo Reefer, *79*	92	99	___
9884	Fritos Reefer, *81-82*	26	34	___
9885	Lipton Tea Reefer, *81-82*	30	38	___
9886	Mounds Reefer, *81-82*	24	30	___
9887	Fruit Growers Express Reefer (FARR 4), *83*	29	38	___
9888	Green Bay & Western Reefer, *83*	42	49	___
11000	Holiday Express Freight Set, *08*		280	___
11004	NASCAR Diesel Freight Set, *06-07*		300	___
11005	Dale Earnhardt Jr. Diesel Freight Set, *06-07*		240	___
11006	Lionel Lion Set, *03 u*		230	___
11006	Kasey Kahne Expansion Pack, *06-07*		130	___
11007	Dale Earnhardt Sr. Expansion Pack, *06-07*		130	___
11008	Dale Earnhardt Jr. Expansion Pack, *06-07*		130	___
11009	Tony Stewart Expansion Pack, *06-07*		130	___
11010	Jimmie Johnson Expansion Pack, *06-07*		130	___
11011	Jeff Gordon Expansion Pack, *06-07*		130	___
11020	Harry Potter Hogwarts Express Steam Passenger Set, *08-13*		330	___
11025	Jimmie Johnson 2006 Champion Boxcar, *07*		45	___
11038	Snow-covered Straight Track 4-pack, *08*		14	___

| --- | --- | --- | --- |
_____	**11041** Holiday Calliope Car, _08_		45
_____	**11067** Lionel Bear, _08_		25
_____	**11077** Harry Potter Figures, _08_		27
_____	**11096** Engineer Hat, _08_		18
_____	**11097** Pennsylvania Flyer Steam Freight Set		
_____	**11098** Holiday Toy Soldier Car, _08_		50
_____	**11099** Pennsylvania Flyer Steam Freight Set		
_____	**11100** PRR 2-8-2 Mikado Locomotive "9631," _CC, 07_		370
_____	**11101** LL 2-8-4 Berkshire Locomotive "737," _CC, 06_		350
_____	**11103** Southern PS-4 4-6-2 Pacific Locomotive "1403," _CC, 06_		1000
_____	**11104** UP Big Boy Locomotive "4014," _CC, 06_		1800
_____	**11105** NYC L-2A 4-8-2 Mohawk Locomotive "2770," _CC, 06_		1100
_____	**11107** LionMaster SP Cab Forward Locomotive "4276," RailSounds, _06-07_		850
_____	**11108** C&O F-19 4-6-2 Pacific Locomotive "494," _CC, 06-07_		1160
_____	**11109** C&O 0-8-0 Locomotive "79," TrainSounds, _06_		420
_____	**11110** NYC 0-8-0 Locomotive "7805," TrainSounds, _06_		420
_____	**11116** UP 4-8-4 FEF-3 Locomotive "844," gray, _CC, 08-09_		1160
_____	**11117** Santa Fe E6 4-4-2 Atlantic Locomotive "1484," _CC, 07-09_		600
_____	**11119** Southern 0-8-0 Locomotive "6535," _TrainSounds, 07_		420
_____	**11122** UP Big Boy Locomotive "4024," _CC, 06_		1700
_____	**11123** UP Big Boy Locomotive "4023," _CC, 06_		1700
_____	**11126** UP Big Boy Locomotive "4012," _CC, 06_		1700
_____	**11127** SP GS-4 4-8-4 Northern Locomotive "4436," _CC, 07-09_		1200
_____	**11128** C&O F-19 4-6-2 Pacific Locomotive "490," _CC, 07_		1160
_____	**11131** UP 4-8-4 FEF-3 Locomotive "844," _black, CC, 08-09_		1160
_____	**11132** Reading 2-8-0 Consolidation Locomotive "1914," RailSounds, _08_		450
_____	**11133** NYC 2-8-0 Consolidation Locomotive "1149," RailSounds, _08_		450
_____	**11134** WM 2-8-0 Consolidation Locomotive "729," RailSounds, _08_		450
_____	**11135** B&O 2-8-0 Consolidation Locomotive "2784," RailSounds, _08_		450
_____	**11136** WP 2-8-2 Mikado Locomotive "322," _CC, 08_		800
_____	**11137** UP 2-8-2 Mikado Locomotive "1925," _CC, 08_		800
_____	**11138** ATSF 2-8-2 Mikado Locomotive "3156," _CC, 08_		800
_____	**11139** MILW 2-8-2 Mikado Locomotive "462," _CC, 08_		800
_____	**11140** Cass Scenic Shay Locomotive "7," _CC, 07_		800
_____	**11141** Birch Valley Lumber Shay Locomotive "5," _CC, 07_		800
_____	**11142** Hogwarts Express Add-on 2-pack, _09-10_		120
_____	**11143** SP AC-4 Cab Forward Locomotive "4100," _CC, 08_		1670
_____	**11146** Pere Marquette 2-8-4 Berkshire Locomotive "1225," _CC, 08_		1290
_____	**11147** PRR 4-8-2 Mib Locomotive "6750," _CC, 08_		1290
_____	**11148** NYC Dreyfuss J-3a 4-6-4 Hudson Locomotive "5448," _CC, 08_		1130
_____	**11149** LionMaster UP Big Boy 4-8-8-4 Locomotive "4006," _CC, 08_		860
_____	**11150** NYC F-12e 4-6-0 10-wheel Locomotive "827," _CC, 08_		700
_____	**11151** Polar Express Tender, RailSounds, _08-10_		440
_____	**11152** D&RGW LionMaster 4-6-6-4 Challenger Locomotive "3805," _CC, 09_		900
_____	**11153** Stourbridge Lion Steam Locomotive, _09-10_		430
_____	**11154** PRR CC2s 0-8-8-0 Mallet Locomotive "8183," _CC, 09-10_		2000
_____	**11155** ATSF 2-10-10-2 Mallet Locomotive "3000," _CC, 09-10_		2500
_____	**11156** C&O 4-6-0 Ten-Wheeler Locomotive, _CC, 10_		740
_____	**11157** WM Shay Locomotive "6," _CC, 10_		800
_____	**11162** Lone Ranger Add-on 3-pack, _10_		165
_____	**11164** Dewitt Clinton Passenger Set, _10_		630
_____	**11165** Dewitt Clinton Add-on Coach, _10_		70
_____	**11166** CSX Merger Freight 2-pack #1, _10-11_		130

		Esc	Mint
11167	CSX Merger Freight 2-pack #2, *10-11*		105 ___
11168	CSX Merger Freight 2-pack #3, *10-11*		130 ___
11169	Strasburg Freight Add-on 2-pack, *10*		100 ___
11170	Three Rivers Fast Freight Set, *10-12*		400 ___
11172	Santa Fe 4-4-2 Steam Freight Set, *13*		200 ___
11173	Texan Freight Add-on 2-pack, *10-11*		130 ___
11174	Maple Leaf Freight Add-on 2-pack, *10-11*		110 ___
11175	Operation Eagle Justice Add-on 2-pack, *10-11*		125 ___
11180	Motor City Express Diesel Freight Train Set, *CC, 12-13*		1175 ___
11181	CN GP9 Diesel Piggyback Train Set, *CC, 12*		850 ___
11182	Dixie Special FT Diesel Freight Set, *11*		700 ___
11183	Lincoln Funeral Train, *13*		1140 ___
11194	Texas Special Diesel Passenger Set, *CC, 13-14*		1110 ___
11195	PRR Diesel Passenger Set, *CC, 13-14*		1110 ___
11199	UP NW2 Diesel Switcher Work Train Set, *CC, 12*		600 ___
11200	UP LionMaster Challenger Locomotive "3985," *CC, 10*		900 ___
11201	WM LionMaster Challenger Locomotive "1204," *CC, 10*		900 ___
11202	CP 4-6-0 Ten-Wheeler Locomotive "914," *CC, 10*		740 ___
11203	Pere Marquette Berkshire Locomotive "1225," *CC, 09*		980 ___
11204	Pere Marquette Tender, RailSounds, *09*		440 ___
11207	PRR LionMaster T1 Duplex Locomotive "5511," *CC, 10*		800 ___
11208	UP LionMaster Big Boy Locomotive "4011," *CC, 10*		900 ___
11209	Vision NYC Hudson Locomotive "5344," *CC, 10*		1600 ___
11210	UP Challenger Locomotive "3967," *CC, 10*		1825 ___
11211	UP 4-6-6-4 Challenger Locomotive "3976," *CC, 10*		1825 ___
11212	NKP Berkshire Locomotive "765," *CC, 10*		1400 ___
11215	LV 4-6-0 Camelback Locomotive "1598," *CC, 10*		550 ___
11216	Jersey Central 4-6-0 Camelback Locomotive, *CC, 10*		550 ___
11217	PRR 4-6-0 Camelback Locomotive "822," *CC, 10*		550 ___
11218	Vision NYC Hudson Locomotive "5331," *CC, 10*		1600 ___
11219	Clinchfield Challenger Locomotive "672," *CC, 10*		1825 ___
11220	UP Challenger Locomotive "3989," *CC, 10*		1825 ___
11221	UP Challenger Locomotive "3983," *CC, 10*		1825 ___
11224	PRR Atlantic Locomotive "460," *CC, 10-11*		700 ___
11225	B&O Atlantic Locomotive "1440," *CC*		700 ___
11226	UP Water Tender, *black, CC, 11*		300 ___
11227	UP Water Tender, *gray, CC, 11*		300 ___
11228	Clinchfield Water Tender, *CC, 11*		300 ___
11229	MILW 4-8-4 Northern Locomotive "261," *CC, 11*		995 ___
11230	MILW 4-8-4 Northern Locomotive "267," *CC, 11*		995 ___
11232	Reading Atlantic Locomotive "351," *CC, 11*		700 ___
11233	Pennsylvania Power & Light 2-Truck Shay Locomotive, *CC, 11*		900 ___
11234	Pennsylvania Power & Light 2-Truck Shay Locomotive, *11*		750 ___
11235	West Side Lumber 2-Truck Shay Steam Locomotive, *CC, 11*		900 ___
11236	West Side Lumber 2-Truck Shay Steam Locomotive, *11*		750 ___
11237	Sugar Pine Lumber Shay Locomotive "4," *CC, 11*		900 ___
11238	Sugar Pine Lumber Shay Locomotive "5," *11*		750 ___
11239	Merrill & Ring Lumber 2-Truck Shay Steam Locomotive, *CC, 11*		900 ___
11240	Merrill & Ring Lumber 2-Truck Shay Steam Locomotive, *11*		750 ___
11247	Erie USRA 0-8-0 Steam Switcher "121," *CC, 11-12*		700 ___
11248	Erie USRA 0-8-0 Steam Switcher "127," *11-12*		550 ___
11249	L&N USRA 0-8-0 Steam Switcher "2119," *CC, 11-12*		700 ___
11250	L&N USRA 0-8-0 Steam Switcher "2121," *11-12*		550 ___

____	**11251**	Pere Marquette USRA 0-8-0 Steam Switcher "1300," *CC, 11-12*	700
____	**11252**	Pere Marquette USRA 0-8-0 Steam Switcher "1307," *11-12*	550
____	**11253**	NH 0-8-0 Steam Switcher "3603," *CC, 11-13*	700
____	**11254**	NH 0-8-0 Steam Switcher "3606," *11-13*	550
____	**11255**	C&O 2-8-2 Mikado Steam Locomotive "1062," *CC, 12*	900
____	**11256**	NH 2-8-2 Mikado Steam Locomotive "3021," *CC, 12*	900
____	**11257**	PRR 2-8-2 Mikado Steam Locomotive "8631," *CC, 12*	900
____	**11258**	Southern 2-8-2 Mikado Steam Locomotive "4501," *CC, 12*	900
____	**11259**	UP 2-8-2 Mikado Steam Locomotive "2840," *CC, 12*	900
____	**11260**	Rio Grande 2-8-2 Mikado Steam Locomotive "1207," *CC, 12*	900
____	**11261**	DM&I 2-8-2 Mikado Steam Locomotive "1305," *CC, 12*	900
____	**11262**	Erie 2-8-2 Mikado Steam Locomotive "3007," *CC, 12*	900
____	**11264**	PRR K4 4-6-2 Pacific Steam Locomotive "1361," *CC, 11*	900
____	**11265**	PRR K4 4-6-2 Pacific Steam Locomotive "1330," *CC, 11*	900
____	**11266**	PRR K4 4-6-2 Pacific Steam Locomotive "1361," *11*	750
____	**11268**	Strasburg 2-6-0 Mogul Steam Locomotive "89," *11*	550
____	**11269**	RI 2-6-0 Mogul Steam Locomotive "750," *11-13*	550
____	**11270**	GN 2-6-0 Mogul Steam Locomotive "453," *11*	550
____	**11271**	C&O 2-6-0 Mogul Steam Locomotive "49," *11-12*	550
____	**11272**	ATSF 2-6-0 Mogul Steam Locomotive "573," *11*	550
____	**11273**	Central Pacific 2-6-0 Mogul Steam Locomotive "1470," *11-13*	550
____	**11274**	MKT USRA 0-8-0 Steam Switcher "46," *CC, 11-12*	700
____	**11275**	MKT 0-8-0 Steam Switcher "51," *CC, 11*	550
____	**11276**	Lionelville & Western 0-8-0 Steam Switcher "1," *CC, 11-13*	700
____	**11277**	Lionelville & Western 0-8-0 Steam Switcher "2," *11-13*	550
____	**11278**	WP 2-8-2 Mikado Steam Locomotive "322," *CC, 11*	900
____	**11279**	WP 2-8-2 Mikado Steam Locomotive "327," *11*	750
____	**11280**	B&O 2-8-2 Mikado Steam Locomotive "4507," *CC, 11*	900
____	**11281**	B&O 2-8-2 Mikado Steam Locomotive "451," *11*	750
____	**11282**	GN 2-8-2 Mikado Steam Locomotive "3125," *CC, 11*	900
____	**11284**	MP 2-8-2 Mikado Steam Locomotive "1310," *CC, 11*	900
____	**11286**	RI 2-8-2 Mikado Steam Locomotive "2302," *CC, 11*	900
____	**11287**	RI 2-8-2 Mikado Steam Locomotive "2305," *11*	750
____	**11288**	T&P 2-8-2 Mikado Steam Locomotive "552," *CC, 11*	900
____	**11289**	T&P 2-8-2 Mikado Steam Locomotive "557," *11*	750
____	**11290**	Bethlehem Steel 2-6-0 Mogul Steam Locomotive "28," *11*	550
____	**11291**	Weyerhaeuser 2-6-0 Mogul Locomotive "288," *11-13*	550
____	**11295**	Elk River Lumber 2-Truck Shay Locomotive "1," *CC, 11*	900
____	**11296**	Elk River Lumber 2-Truck Shay Locomotive "2," *11*	750
____	**11297**	P. Bunyan Lumber 2-Truck Shay Locomotive "18," *CC, 11*	900
____	**11298**	P. Bunyan Lumber 2-Truck Shay Locomotive "23," *11*	750
____	**11299**	C&O 2-6-6-2 Mallet Steam Locomotive "875," *CC, 12*	1300
____	**11300**	PRR 2-10-4 Texas Steam Locomotive "6479," *CC, 11*	1300
____	**11301**	PRR 2-10-4 Texas Steam Locomotive "6498," *CC, 11*	1300
____	**11303**	C&O 2-10-4 Texas Steam Locomotive "3011," *CC, 11*	1300
____	**11304**	C&O 2-10-4 Texas Steam Locomotive "3025," *CC, 11*	1300
____	**11306**	NKP 2-10-4 Texas Steam Locomotive "801," *CC, 11*	1300
____	**11308**	Erie 2-10-4 Texas Steam Locomotive "3405," *CC, 11*	1300
____	**11310**	Pere Marquette 2-10-4 Texas Locomotive "1241," *CC, 11*	1300
____	**11312**	MILW S3 4-8-4 Northern Steam Locomotive "265," *CC, 11*	995
____	**11315**	Pennsylvania-Reading Seashore Atlantic Locomotive, *11*	550
____	**11316**	PRR 4-4-2 Atlantic Steam Locomotive "272," *11*	550
____	**11317**	Southern 4-4-2 Atlantic Steam Locomotive "1910," *11*	550

		Esc	Mint
11318	CN 4-4-2 Atlantic Steam Locomotive "1630," *11*		550 ___
11319	PRR K4 4-6-2 Pacific Locomotive "5409," *13*		900 ___
11320	PRR K4 4-6-2 Pacific Locomotive, *"5436," 13*		750 ___
11321	C&O 2-6-6-2 Mallet Steam Locomotive "1525," *CC, 12*		1300 ___
11322	NKP 2-6-6-2 Mallet Steam Locomotive "943," *CC, 12*		1300 ___
11323	W&LE 2-6-6-2 Mallet Steam Locomotive "8002," *CC, 12*		1300 ___
11327	PRR Prewar K4 4-6-2 Pacific Locomotive "3667," *CC, 11*		900 ___
11328	PRR Prewar K4 4-6-2 Pacific Locomotive "3672," *CC, 11*		900 ___
11329	PRR Prewar K4 4-6-2 Pacific Locomotive "3678," *11*		750 ___
11330	Polar K4 4-6-2 Pacific Locomotive, *CC, 11-14*		900 ___
11331	Polar K4 4-6-2 Pacific Locomotive, *11*		750 ___
11332	ATSF 4-8-4 Northern Steam Locomotive "3751," *CC, 12*		1300 ___
11333	ATSF 4-8-4 Northern Steam Locomotive "3759," *CC, 12*		1300 ___
11334	Southern Crescent Limited 4-6-2 Pacific Locomotive, *CC, 12*		1100 ___
11335	Blue Comet 4-6-2 Pacific Steam Locomotive "832," *CC, 12*		1100 ___
11337	B&O 2-8-8-4 Steam Locomotive "7621," *CC, 12*		1300 ___
11338	Alton Limited 4-6-2 Pacific Steam Locomotive "657," *CC, 12*		1100 ___
11339	N&W 2-6-6-2 Mallet Steam Locomotive "1409," *CC, 12*		1300 ___
11340	B&O 2-8-8-4 Steam Locomotive "659," *CC, 12*		1300 ___
11341	Pilot 4-12-2 Locomotive, *CC, 13*		1300 ___
11342	UP 4-12-2 Steam Locomotive "9004," *CC, 12-13*		1300 ___
11343	UP 4-12-2 Steam Locomotive, black, "9000," *CC, 12-13*		1300 ___
11344	UP 4-12-2 Steam Locomotive, greyhound, "9000," *CC, 12*		1300 ___
11363	Cass Scenic RR 2-Truck Shay Steam Locomotive "3," *CC, 12*		900 ___
11364	Meadow River 2-Truck Shay Steam Locomotive "1," *CC, 12-13*		900 ___
11365	Weyerhaeuser 2-Truck Shay Steam Locomotive "3," *CC, 12-13*		900 ___
11366	Pickering Lumber 2-Truck Shay Locomotive "3," *CC, 12-13*		900 ___
11367	CP 2-Truck Shay Steam Locomotive "111," *CC, 12-13*		900 ___
11368	WM 2-Truck Shay Steam Locomotive "2," *CC, 12*		900 ___
11369	Bethlehem Steel 2-Truck Shay Steam Locomotive "5," *CC, 12-13*		900 ___
11374	DM&I 2-8-8-4 Steam Locomotive "223," *CC, 12*		1300 ___
11375	WP 2-8-8-4 Steam Locomotive "258," *CC, 12*		1300 ___
11376	NP 2-8-8-4 Steam Locomotive "5000," *CC, 12*		1300 ___
11377	GN 2-8-8-4 Steam Locomotive "2060," *CC, 12*		1300 ___
11379	PRR 0-4-0 Shifter Steam Locomotive "112" , *12*		450 ___
11380	PRR 0-4-0 Shifter Steam Locomotive "94," *12*		450 ___
11381	North Pole Central 0-4-0 Switcher (std O), *12*		450 ___
11382	Transylvania 0-4-0 Shifter Steam Locomotive "13," *12*		450 ___
11383	Bethlehem Steel 0-4-0 Shifter Steam Locomotive "134," *12*		450 ___
11384	ATSF 0-4-0 Shifter Steam Locomotive "2301," *13*		450 ___
11385	UP 0-4-0 Shifter Steam Locomotive "206," *13*		450 ___
11386	B&M 2-8-4 Berkshire Steam Locomotive "4018," *CC, 12-13*		1250 ___
11387	ATSF 2-8-4 Berkshire Steam Locomotive "4199," *CC, 12-13*		1250 ___
11388	SP 2-8-4 Berkshire Steam Locomotive "3505," *CC, 12-13*		1250 ___
11389	B&A 2-8-4 Berkshire Steam Locomotive "1404," *CC, 12-13*		1250 ___
11390	Lima Demonstrator 2-8-4 Berkshire Locomotive "1," *CC, 12-13*		1250 ___
11391	IC 2-8-4 Berkshire Steam Locomotive "7020," *CC, 12-13*		1250 ___
11392	Michigan Central 2-8-4 Berkshire Locomotive "1420," *CC, 12-13*		1250 ___
11399	UP H7 Class 2-8-8-2 Steam Locomotive "3595," *CC, 13-14*		1350 ___
11400	C&O H7 Class 2-8-8-2 Steam Locomotive "1578," *CC, 13-14*		1350 ___
11401	Pilot H7 Class 2-8-8-2 Locomotive, *CC, 14-15*		1350 ___
11402	Virginian USRA Y3 2-8-8-2 Locomotive, *CC, 13-14*		1350 ___
11403	Pilot USRA 2-8-8-2 Locomotive, *CC, 13-15*		1350 ___
11404	ATSF USRA Y3 2-8-8-2 Locomotive, *CC, 13-14*		1350 ___

			Esc	Mint
____	**11405**	N&W USRA Y3 2-8-8-2 Locomotive, *CC, 13-14*		1350
____	**11410**	Pilot 4-8-2 Mohawk Locomotive, *CC, 13-15*		1300
____	**11411**	NYC 4-8-2 Mohawk Locomotive "2854," *CC, 12-13*		1300
____	**11412**	NYC 4-8-2 Mohawk Locomotive "2867," *CC, 12-13*		1300
____	**11413**	Pilot 4-8-4 J-Class Locomotive, *CC, 13-15*		1300
____	**11414**	N&W 4-8-4 Steam Locomotive "612," *CC, 12-13*		1300
____	**11415**	Pilot S2 6-8-6 Turbine Locomotive, *CC, 14-15*		1300
____	**11416**	PRR S2 6-8-6 Steam Turbine Locomotive "6200," *CC, 12-14*		1300
____	**11417**	PRR S2 6-8-6 Steam Turbine Locomotive "6200," *CC, 12-13*		1300
____	**11418**	Pilot GS-6 Locomotive, *CC, 13-14*		1300
____	**11419**	SP 4-8-4 GS-2 Locomotive, black, *CC, 12-13*		1300
____	**11420**	SP 4-8-4 GS-2 Locomotive, Daylight, *CC, 12*		1300
____	**11421**	SP 4-8-4 GS-6 Locomotive, black, *CC, 12*		1300
____	**11422**	WP 4-8-4 GS-64 Locomotive "482," *CC, 12*		1300
____	**11423**	CNJ Blue Comet Locomotive "833," *CC, 12-13*		1100
____	**11425**	Alaska 0-4-0 Locomotive, RailSounds, *12-13*		1100
____	**11426**	Rio Grande 0-4-0 Locomotive, RailSounds, *12-13*		450
____	**11427**	SP 0-4-0 Locomotive "14," RailSounds, *12-13*		450
____	**11428**	MILW 0-4-0 Locomotive, RailSounds, *12-13*		450
____	**11429**	Southern 0-4-0 Locomotive, RailSounds, *12-13*		450
____	**11430**	GN 0-4-0 Locomotive "1066," RailSounds, *12-13*		450
____	**11431**	N&W 4-8-4 Locomotive "611," *CC, 12*		1300
____	**11432**	LL S2 6-8-6 Steam Turbine Locomotive, *CC, 13-14*		1300
____	**11433**	PRR S2 6-8-6 Steam Turbine Locomotive CC, *13-14*		1300
____	**11434**	UP Big Boy Locomotive "4006," *CC, 14*		2700
____	**11435**	UP Big Boy Locomotive "4018," *CC, 14*		2700
____	**11436**	UP Big Boy Locomotive "4005," *CC, 14*		2700
____	**11437**	UP Big Boy Locomotive "4014," *CC, 14*		2700
____	**11438**	UP Big Boy Locomotive "4017," *CC, 14*		2700
____	**11446**	UP USRA Y3 2-8-8-2 Locomotive "3671," *CC, 13-14*		1350
____	**11447**	PRR USRA Y3 2-8-8-2 Locomotive "376," *CC, 13-14*		1350
____	**11448**	UP Big Boy Locomotive "4012," *CC, 14*		2700
____	**11449**	UP Big Boy Locomotive "4004," *CC, 14*		2700
____	**11450**	Polar Express Berkshire Scale Locomotive, gold, *CC, 14*		1500
____	**11451**	Polar Express Berkshire Scale Locomotive, black, *CC, 14*		1500
____	**11452**	C&O 2-8-4 Berkshire Locomotive "2687," *CC, 14*		1500
____	**11453**	Erie 2-8-4 Berkshire Locomotive "3321," *CC, 14*		1500
____	**11454**	NKP 2-8-4 Berkshire Locomotive "765," *CC, 14*		1500
____	**11455**	Pere Marquette 2-8-4 Berkshire Locomotive "1225," *CC, 14*		1500
____	**11456**	Pere Marquette 2-8-4 Berkshire Locomotive "1227," *CC, 14*		1500
____	**11462**	SP AC-12 Cab-Forward Locomotive "4291," *CC, 14*		1700
____	**11463**	SP AC-12 Cab-Forward Locomotive "4286," *CC, 14*		1700
____	**11464**	SP AC-12 Cab-Forward Locomotive "4294," *CC, 14*		1700
____	**11465**	SP AC-12 Cab-Forward Locomotive "4275," *CC, 14*		1700
____	**11469**	Pilot AC-12 Cab-Forward Locomotive, *CC, 14-15*		1700
____	**11528**	Frosty the Snowman Figure Pack, *14, 16*		30
____	**11650**	Alderney Dairy General American Milk Car 2-pack (std O), *07*		130
____	**11651**	Freeport General American Milk Car 2-pack (std O), *07*		130
____	**11652**	BNSF Mechanical Reefer 2-pack (std O), *07-09*		140
____	**11653**	SPFE Mechanical Reefer 2-pack (std O), *07*		140
____	**11654**	UPFE Mechanical Reefer 2-pack (std O), *07*		140
____	**11655**	GN WFE Mechanical Reefer 2-pack (std O), *07*		140
____	**11657**	PFE Wood-sided Reefer 3-pack (std O), *06*		190

		Esc	Mint	
11658	John Bull Add-on Coach, *08*		80	___
11700	Conrail Limited Set, *87*	320	370	___
11701	Rail Blazer Set, *87-88*		60	___
11702	Black Diamond Set, *87*	195	265	___
11703	Iron Horse Freight Set, *88-91*	100	105	___
11704	Southern Freight Runner Set (SSS), *87*	210	285	___
11705	Chessie System Unit Train, *88*	360	450	___
11706	Dry Gulch Line Set (SSS), *88*	190	260	___
11707	Silver Spike Set, *88-89*	175	245	___
11708	Midnight Shift Set, *88 u, 89*	60	75	___
11710	CP Rail Freight Set, *89*	375	447	___
11711	Santa Fe F3 Diesel ABA Set, *91*	480	590	___
11712	Great Lakes Express Set (SSS), *90*	260	280	___
11713	Santa Fe Dash 8-40B Set, *90*	395	480	___
11714	Badlands Express Set, *90-91*	49	60	___
11715	Lionel 90th Anniversary Set, *90*	332	382	___
11716	Lionelville Circus Special Set, *90-91*	155	190	___
11717	CSX Freight Set, *90*	230	240	___
11718	Norfolk Southern Dash 8-40C Unit Train, *92*	445	481	___
11719	Coastal Freight Set (SSS), *91*	165	215	___
11720	Santa Fe Special Set, *91*	49	60	___
11721	Mickey's World Tour Train Set, *91, 92 u*	119	154	___
11722	Girls Train Set, *91*	565	828	___
11723	Amtrak Maintenance Train, *91, 92 u*	210	245	___
11724	GN F3 Diesel ABA Set, *92*	730	840	___
11726	Erie-Lackawanna Freight Set, *91 u*	225	275	___
11727	Coastal Limited Set, *92*	90	110	___
11728	High Plains Runner Set, *92*	120	130	___
11733	Feather River Set (SSS), *92*	285	330	___
11734	Erie Alco Diesel ABA Set (FF 7), *93*	250	305	___
11735	NYC Flyer Freight Set "1735WS," *93-99*	125	160	___
11736	Union Pacific Express Set, *93-95*	110	130	___
11738	Soo Line Set (SSS), *93*	250	280	___
11739	Super Chief Set, *93-94*	135	155	___
11740	Conrail Consolidated Set, *93*	200	240	___
11741	Northwest Express Set, *93*	130	155	___
11742	Coastal Limited Set, *93 u*	90	115	___
11743	Chesapeake & Ohio Freight Set, *94*	240	280	___
11744	NYC Passenger/Freight Set (SSS), *94*	295	335	___
11745	U.S. Navy Set, *94-95*	264	308	___
11746	Seaboard Freight Set, *94, 95 u*	90	115	___
11747	Lionel Lines Steam Set, *95*	310	340	___
11748	Amtrak Alco Diesel Passenger Set, *95-96*	130	185	___
11749	Western Maryland Set (SSS), *95*	275	300	___
11750	McDonald's Nickel Plate Special Set, *87 u*	143	153	___
11751	Sears PRR Passenger Set, *87 u*	120	155	___
11752	JCPenney Timber Master Set, *87 u*	75	115	___
11753	Kay Bee Toys Rail Blazer Set, *87 u*	80	100	___
11754	Key America Set, *87 u*	150	165	___
11755	Timber Master Set, *87 u*	150	165	___
11756	Hawthorne Freight Flyer Set, *87-88 u*	65	85	___
11757	Chrysler Mopar Express Set, *88 u*	335	393	___
11758	Desert King Set (SSS), *89*	195	250	___
11759	JCPenney Silver Spike Set, *88 u*	175	250	___

|---|---|---|---|
____ 11761	JCPenney Iron Horse Freight Set, *88 u*	120	125
____ 11762	True Value Cannonball Express Set, *89 u*	95	145
____ 11763	United Model Freight Hauler Set, *88 u*	135	145
____ 11764	Sears Iron Horse Freight Set, *88 u*	155	190
____ 11765	Spiegel Silver Spike Set, *88 u*	175	250
____ 11767	Shoprite Freight Flyer Set, *88 u*	80	125
____ 11769	JCPenney Midnight Shift Set, *89 u*	100	175
____ 11770	Sears Circus Set, *89 u*	185	220
____ 11771	K-Mart Microracers Set, *89 u*	80	110
____ 11772	Macy's Freight Flyer Set, *89 u*	170	220
____ 11773	Sears NYC Passenger Set, *89 u*	175	200
____ 11774	Ace Hardware Cannonball Express Set, *89 u*	145	175
____ 11775	Anheuser-Busch Set, *89-92 u*	265	355
____ 11776	Pace Iron Horse Freight Set, *89 u*	115	135
____ 11777	Sears Lionelville Circus Set, *90 u*	175	190
____ 11778	Sears Badlands Express Set, *90 u*	49	60
____ 11779	Sears CSX Freight Set, *90 u*	190	230
____ 11780	Sears NP Passenger Set, *90 u*	155	190
____ 11781	True Value Cannonball Express Set, *90 u*	75	115
____ 11783	Toys "R" Us Heavy Iron Set, *90-91 u*	138	165
____ 11784	Pace Iron Horse Freight Set, *90 u*	115	135
____ 11785	Costco Union Pacific Express Set, *90 u*	200	230
____ 11789	Sears Illinois Central Passenger Set, *91 u*	170	200
____ 11793	Santa Fe Set, *91 u*	49	60
____ 11794	Mickey's World Tour Set, *91 u*	80	100
____ 11796	Union Pacific Express Set, *91 u*	150	160
____ 11797	Sears Coastal Limited Set, *92 u*	80	100
____ 11800	Toys "R" Us Heavy Iron Thunder Limited Set, *92-93 u*	238	298
____ 11803	Nickel Plate Special Set, *92 u*	135	145
____ 11804	K-Mart Coastal Limited Set, *92 u*	80	100
____ 11809	Village Trolley Set, *95-97*	55	85
____ 11810	Budweiser Modern Era Set, *93-94 u*	222	234
____ 11811	United Auto Workers Set, *93 u*	189	447
____ 11812	Coastal Limited Special Set, *93 u*	95	115
____ 11813	Crayola Activity Train Set, *94 u, 95*	122	148
____ 11814	Ford Limited Edition Set, *94 u*	222	266
____ 11818	Chrysler Mopar Set, *94 u*	230	267
____ 11819	Georgia Power Set, *95 u*	550	575
____ 11820	Red Wing Shoes NYC Flyer Set, *95 u*	264	329
____ 11821	Sears Zenith Set, *95 u*	363	790
____ 11822	Chevrolet Set, *96 u*	287	337
____ 11825	Bloomingdale's Set, *96 u*	0	333
____ 11826	Sears Freight Set, *95-96 u*	0	776
____ 11827	Zenith Employees Set, *96 u*	0	850
____ 11828	NJ Transit Passenger Set, *96 u*		180
____ 11833	NJ Transit GP38 Diesel Passenger Set, *97*	275	300
____ 11837	Union Pacific GP9 Diesel Set, *97*		520
____ 11838	ATSF Warhorse Hudson Freight Set, *97*		810
____ 11839	SP&S 4-6-2 Steam Freight Set, *97*		280
____ 11841	Bloomingdale's Set, *97 u*	150	325
____ 11843	Boston & Maine GP9 Diesel ABA Set, *98*		510
____ 11844	Union Pacific Die-cast Ore Cars 4-pack, *98*		225
____ 11846	Kal Kan Pet Care Train Set, *97 u*	266	873

MODERN 1970-2021		Esc	Mint
11849	Lionel Centennial Series Reefer 4-pack, *98*	0	125 ___
11850	Rice A Roni Trolley Set, *02 u*		268
11851	PFE Reefer 6-pack (std O), *02*	225	255 ___
11852	Clinchfield PS-2 2-bay Hopper, *04*		70
11853	B&M PS-2 2-bay Hopper 2-pack, *05*		128 ___
11854	N&W PS-2 Covered Hopper 2-pack, *04*		70
11855	GN Offset Hopper with coal, 2-pack, *05*		120 ___
11856	Green Bay & Western Offset Hopper 2-pack, *05*		120
11857	Baltimore & Ohio Offset Hopper 2-pack, *05*		120 ___
11858	PRR PS-4 Flatcar with trailers, 2-pack (std O), *05*		160 ___
11859	GN PS-4 Flatcar with trailers (std O), *05*		160 ___
11860	SP PS-4 Flatcar with trailers (std O), *05*		160 ___
11861	C&O PS-4 Flatcar with trailers (std O), *05*		160 ___
11863	Southern Pacific GP9 Diesel "2383," *98*		225 ___
11864	New York Central GP9 Diesel "2383," *98*		275 ___
11865	Alaska GP7 Diesel "1802," *98-99*		90
11866	Govt. of Canada Cylindrical Hopper 2-pack (std O), *05*		120 ___
11867	CN Cylindrical Hopper 2-pack (std O), *05*		120
11868	BN Husky Stack Car 2-pack (std O), *05*		160 ___
11869	SP Husky Stack Car 2-pack (std O), *05*		160
11870	CSX Husky Stack Car 2-pack (std O), *05*		220 ___
11871	TTX Trailer Train Stack Car 2-pack (std O), *05*		160 ___
11872	PFE Orange Steel-sided Reefer 3-pack (std O), *05*		130 ___
11873	C&O Offset Hopper 3-pack (std O), *05*		130
11874	PFE Orange Steel-sided Reefer 3-pack (std O), *05*		130 ___
11875	NP Steel-sided Reefer 3-pack (std O), *05*		130
11876	PFE Silver Steel-sided Reefer 3-pack (std O), *05*		130 ___
11877	C&NW Steel-sided Reefer 3-pack (std O), *05*		130 ___
11878	Santa Fe PS-2 2-bay Covered Hopper 3-pack (std O), *06*		125 ___
11879	MKT PS-2 2-bay Covered Hopper 3-pack (std O), *06*		125 ___
11880	Boraxo PS-2 2-bay Covered Hopper 3-pack (std O), *06*		125 ___
11881	PRR PS-2 2-bay Covered Hopper 3-pack (std O), *06*		125 ___
11882	RI Offset Hopper with gravel, *3-pack (std O), 06*		125 ___
11883	CNJ Offset Hopper 3-pack (std O), *06*		145 ___
11884	Maine Central Offset Hopper 3-pack (std O), *06*		145 ___
11891	Pennsylvania 3-bay Hopper 3-pack (std O), *06*		155 ___
11892	Conrail ACF 3-bay Hopper 3-pack (std O), *06*		155 ___
11893	N&W 3-bay Hopper 3-pack (std O), *06*		155 ___
11894	UP 3-bay Hopper 3-pack (std O), *06*		155 ___
11895	GN Steel-sided Reefer 3-pack (std O), *06*		145 ___
11896	Santa Fe Steel-sided Reefer 3-pack (std O), *06*		145 ___
11897	Pepper Packing Steel-sided Reefer 3-pack (std O), *06*		145 ___
11900	SF Steam Freight Set, *96-01*		130 ___
11903	ACL F3 Diesel ABA Set, *96*		716 ___
11905	U.S. Coast Guard Set, *96*	165	185 ___
11906	Factory Selection Special Set, *95 u*		85
11909	N&W J 4-8-4 Warhorse Set, *96*	560	720 ___
11910	Lionel Lines Set (027), *96*	140	160 ___
11912	"57" Switcher Service Exclusive, *96*		310 ___
11913	SP GP9 Diesel Freight Set, *97*		440 ___
11914	NYC GP9 Diesel Freight Set, *97*		370 ___
11918	Conrail SD20 Service Exclusive "X1144" (SSS), *97*		255 ___
11919	Docksider Set, *97*		70 ___
11920	Port of Lionel City Dive Team Set, *97*		185 ___

| --- | --- | --- | --- |
____ 11921	Lionel Lines Freight Set, *97*		130
____ 11929	ATSF Warbonnet Passenger Set, *97-99*		132
____ 11930	ATSF Warbonnet Passenger Car 2-pack, *97-99*		80
____ 11931	Chessie Flyer Freight Set "1931S," *97-99*		165
____ 11933	Dodge Motorsports Freight Set, *96 u*	100	331
____ 11934	Virginian Electric Locomotive Freight Set, *97-99*		260
____ 11935	NYC Flyer Freight Set, *97*		155
____ 11936	Little League Baseball Steam Set, *97*	244	316
____ 11939	SP&S 4-6-2 Steam Freight Set, *97*		220
____ 11940	Southern Pacific SD40 Warhorse Coal Set, *98*		600
____ 11944	Lionel Lines 4-4-2 Steam Freight Set, *98*		175
____ 11956	UP GP9 Diesel Set, *97*	330	380
____ 11957	Mobil Oil Steam Special Set, *97*	0	443
____ 11971	D&H 4-4-2 Steam Freight Set, *98*	125	155
____ 11972	Alaska GP7 Diesel Set, *98-99*	180	215
____ 11974	Station Accessory Set, *98*		22
____ 11975	Freight Accessory Pack, *98*		23
____ 11977	NP Freight Cars 4-pack, *98*		170
____ 11979	N&W 4-4-2 Steam Freight Set, *98*		75
____ 11981	1998 Holiday Trolley Set, *98*		75
____ 11982	New Jersey Transit Ore Car Set, *98*		250
____ 11983	Farmrail Agricultural Set, *99*	0	492
____ 11984	Corvette GP7 Diesel Set, *99*		455
____ 11988	NYC Firecar "18444" and Instruction Car "19853," *99*		210
____ 12000	NY Yankees Berkshire Passenger Set, *13*		380
____ 12004	Philadelphia Phillies Berkshire Passenger Set, *13*		380
____ 12008	Boston Red Sox Berkshire Passenger Set, *13*		380
____ 12012	Chicago Cubs Berkshire Passenger Set, *13*		380
____ 12013	NY Mets and Yankees Subway Series Set, *13*		400
____ 12014	10" Straight Track (FasTrack), *03-20*		6
____ 12015	O36 Curved Track (FasTrack), *03-20*		6
____ 12016	10" Terminal Track (FasTrack), *03-14, 16, 18-20*		6
____ 12017	O36 Manual Switch, left hand (FasTrack), *03-20*		50
____ 12018	O36 Manual Switch, right hand (FasTrack), *03-20*		50
____ 12019	90-degree Crossover (FasTrack), *03-20*		26
____ 12020	5" Uncoupling Track (FasTrack), *03-20*		42
____ 12022	O36 Half Curved Track (FasTrack), *03-14, 16, 18-20*		5
____ 12023	O36 Quarter Curved Track (FasTrack), *03-14, 16, 18-20*		5
____ 12024	5" Straight Track (FasTrack), *03-17, 18-20*		5
____ 12025	4½" Straight Track (FasTrack), *03-14, 16, 18-20*		5
____ 12026	1¾" Straight Track (FasTrack), *03-14, 16, 18-20*		5
____ 12027	10" Insulated Track (FasTrack), *03-14, 16, 18-20*		5
____ 12028	Inner Passing Loop Track Pack (FasTrack), *03-16, 18-20*		115
____ 12029	Accessory Activator Pack (FasTrack), *03-20*		21
____ 12030	Figure 8 Track Pack (FasTrack), *03-16, 18-20*		75
____ 12031	Outer Passing Loop Track Pack (FasTrack), *03-16, 18-20*		145
____ 12032	10" Straight Track 4-pack (FasTrack), *03-20*		22
____ 12033	O36 Curved Track, card of 4 (FasTrack), *03-20*		22
____ 12035	FasTrack Lighted Bumper 2-pack, *05-20*		33
____ 12036	Grade Crossing 2-pack (FasTrack), *05-16, 18-20*		19
____ 12037	Graduated Trestle Set (FasTrack), *05-16, 18-20*		85
____ 12038	Elevated Trestle Set (FasTrack), *05-16, 18-20*		45
____ 12039	Railer (FasTrack), *04-16, 18-20*		10

	MODERN 1970-2021	Esc	Mint	
12040	O Gauge Transition Piece (FasTrack), *04-14, 16, 18-20*		10	___
12041	072 Curved Track (FasTrack), *04-14, 16, 18-20*		8	___
12042	30" Straight Track (FasTrack), *04-14, 16, 18-20*		15	___
12043	048 Curved Track (FasTrack), *04-14, 16, 18-20*		6	___
12044	Siding Track Add-on Track Pack (FasTrack), *04-16, 18-20*		120	___
12045	036 Remote Switch, left hand (FasTrack), *04-17*		95	___
12046	036 Remote Switch, right hand (FasTrack), *04-17*		95	___
12047	072 Wye Remote Switch (FasTrack), *04-14*		97	___
12048	072 Remote Switch, left hand (FasTrack), *04-14*		104	___
12049	072 Remote Switch, right hand (FasTrack), *04-14*		104	___
12050	22½-degree Crossover (FasTrack), *04-14, 16, 18-20*		48	___
12051	45-degree Crossover (FasTrack), *04-14, 16, 18-20*		27	___
12052	Grade Crossing with flashers (FasTrack), *05-16, 18-20*		100	___
12053	Accessory Power Wire (FasTrack), *04-20*		5	___
12054	Operating Track with half straight (FasTrack), *05-20*		45	___
12055	072 Half Curved Track (FasTrack), *04-14, 16, 18-20*		7	___
12056	060 Curved Track (FasTrack), *05-14, 16, 18-20*		8	___
12057	060 Remote Switch, left hand, *05-14*		104	___
12058	060 Remote Switch, right hand (FasTrack), *05-14*		104	___
12059	Earthen Bumper (FasTrack), *04-16, 18-20*		12	___
12060	Block Section (FasTrack), *05-14, 16, 18-20*		11	___
12061	084 Curved Track (FasTrack), *05-14, 16, 18-20*		8	___
12062	Grade Crossing with gates and flashers (FasTrack), *06-14, 18, 20*		168	___
12065	048 Remote Switch, left hand (FasTrack), *07-14*		104	___
12066	048 Remote Switch, right hand (FasTrack), *07-14*		104	___
12073	1 3/8" Track Section (FasTrack), *07-14, 16, 18-20*		5	___
12074	1 3/8" Track Section, no roadbed (FasTrack), *07-14, 16, 18-20*		5	___
12080	42" Path Remote Switch, right hand, *07-12*		80	___
12081	42" Path Remote Switch, left hand, *07-12*		80	___
12700	Erie Magnetic Gantry Crane, *87*	125	150	___
12701	Operating Fueling Station, *87*	60	74	___
12702	Control Tower, *87*	60	75	___
12703	Icing Station, *88-89*	60	65	___
12704	Dwarf Signal, *88-93*	9	11	___
12705	Lumber Shed Kit, *88-99*		9	___
12706	Barrel Loader Building Kit, *87-99*		10	___
12707	Billboards, *set of 3, 87-99*		5	___
12708	Street Lamps, set of 3, *88-93*	6	9	___
12709	Banjo Signal, *87-91, 95-00*		29	___
12710	Engine House Kit, *87-91*	21	25	___
12711	Water Tower Kit, *87-99*		13	___
12712	Automatic Ore Loader, *87-88*	17	21	___
12713	Automatic Gateman, *87-88, 94-00*	30	40	___
12714	Crossing Gate, *87-91, 93-19*		50	___
12715	Illuminated Bumpers, set of 2, *87-15*		13	___
12716	Searchlight Tower, *87-89, 91-92*	15	22	___
12717	Nonilluminated Bumpers, set of 3, *87-17*		7	___
12718	Barrel Shed Kit, *87-99*		10	___
12719	Animated Refreshment Stand, *88-89*	65	70	___
12720	Rotary Beacon, *88-89*	40	45	___
12721	Illuminated Extension Bridge, rock piers, *89*	26	38	___
12722	Roadside Diner, smoke, *88-89*	27	38	___
12723	Microwave Tower, *88-91, 94-95*	14	19	___

		Esc	Mint
____ 12724	Double Signal Bridge, *88-90*	39	50
____ 12725	Lionel Tractor and Trailer, *88-89*	10	18
____ 12726	Grain Elevator Kit, *88-91, 94-99*		36
____ 12727	Operating Semaphore, *89-99*		26
____ 12728	Illuminated Freight Station, *89*	29	38
____ 12729	Mail Pickup Set, *88-91, 95*	12	16
____ 12730	Lionel Girder Bridge, *88-03, 08-20*		21
____ 12731	Station Platform, *88-00*		8
____ 12732	Coal Bag, *88-20*		7
____ 12733	Watchman Shanty Kit, *88-99*		5
____ 12734	Passenger/Freight Station, *89-99*		18
____ 12735	Diesel Horn Shed, *88-91*	19	24
____ 12736	Coaling Station Kit, *88-91*	21	31
____ 12737	Whistling Freight Shed, *88-99*		28
____ 12739	Lionel Gas Company Tractor and Tanker, *89*	20	25
____ 12740	Genuine Wood Logs, set of 3, *88-92, 94-95, 97-99*		5
____ 12741	Union Pacific Intermodal Crane, *89*	165	185
____ 12742	Gooseneck Lamps, set of 2, *89-00*		21
____ 12743	Track Clips, dozen (O), *89-16*		12
____ 12744	Rock Piers, set of 2, *89-92, 94-05, 08, 11-15, 18-20*		15
____ 12745	Barrel Pack, set of 6, *89-20*		8
____ 12746	Operating/Uncoupling Track (O27), *89-16*		10
____ 12748	Illuminated Passenger Platform, *89-99*		18
____ 12749	Rotary Radar Antenna, *89-92, 95*	28	38
____ 12750	Crane Kit, *89-91*	8	10
____ 12751	Shovel Kit, *89-91*	8	10
____ 12752	History of Lionel Trains Video, *89-92, 94*	19	21
____ 12753	Ore Load, set of 2, *89-91, 95*	1	2
____ 12754	Graduated Trestle Set, 22 pieces, *89-15*		27
____ 12755	Elevated Trestle Set, 10 pieces, *89-15*		27
____ 12756	The Making of the Scale Hudson Video, *91-94*	20	22
____ 12759	Floodlight Tower, *90-00*		25
____ 12760	Automatic Highway Flasher, *90-91*	23	27
____ 12761	Animated Billboard, *90-91, 93, 95*	12	23
____ 12763	Single Signal Bridge, *90-91, 93*	31	35
____ 12767	Steam Clean and Wheel Grind Shop, *92-93, 95*	240	290
____ 12768	Burning Switch Tower, *90, 93*	85	90
____ 12770	Arch-Under Bridge, *90-03, 08-20*		30
____ 12771	Mom's Roadside Diner, smoke, *90-91*	34	50
____ 12772	Truss Bridge, flasher and piers, *90-16, 18, 20*		70
____ 12773	Freight Platform Kit, *90-98*		32
____ 12774	Lumber Loader Kit, *90-99*		19
____ 12777	Chevron Tractor and Tanker, *90-91*	9	15
____ 12778	Conrail Tractor and Trailer, *90*	9	16
____ 12779	Lionelville Grain Company Tractor and Trailer, *90*	11	19
____ 12780	RS-1 50-watt Transformer, *90-93*	95	130
____ 12781	N&W Intermodal Crane, *90-91*	145	160
____ 12782	Lift Bridge, *91-92*	428	518
____ 12783	Monon Tractor and Trailer, *91*	11	19
____ 12784	Intermodal Containers, set of 3, *91*	12	17
____ 12785	Lionel Gravel Company Tractor and Trailer, *91*	9	15
____ 12786	Lionel Steel Company Tractor and Trailer, *91*	10	16
____ 12791	Animated Passenger Station, *91*	45	60

	MODERN 1970-2021	Esc	Mint	
12794	Lionel Tractor, *91*	7	13	___
12795	Cable Reels, pair, *91-98*	3	5	___
12798	Forklift Loader Station, *92-95*	33	44	___
12800	Scale Hudson Replacement Pilot Truck, *91 u*	13	17	___
12802	Chat & Chew Roadside Diner, smoke and lights, *92-95*	41	50	___
12804	Highway Lights, set of 4, *92-99, 02-04, 13-18, 20*	9	27	___
12805	Intermodal Containers, set of 3, *92*	10	14	___
12806	Lionel Lumber Company Tractor and Trailer, *92*	10	15	___
12807	Little Caesars Tractor and Trailer, *92*	9	14	___
12808	Mobil Tractor and Tanker, *92*	8	13	___
12809	Animated Billboard, *92-93*	12	22	___
12810	American Flyer Tractor and Trailer, *94*	12	18	___
12811	Alka Seltzer Tractor and Trailer, *92*	11	19	___
12812	Illuminated Freight Station, *93-00*		27	___
12818	Animated Freight Station, *92, 94-95*	50	60	___
12819	Inland Steel Tractor and Trailer, *92*	9	16	___
12821	Lionel Catalog Video, *92*	13	17	___
12826	Intermodal Containers, set of 3, *93*	10	16	___
12831	Rotary Beacon, *93-95*	22	32	___
12832	Block Target Signal, *93-98*		25	___
12833	RoadRailer Tractor and Trailer, *93*	9	15	___
12834	Pennsylvania Magnetic Gantry Crane, *93*	130	170	___
12835	Operating Fueling Station, *93*	55	60	___
12836	Santa Fe Quantum Tractor and Trailer, *93*	8	14	___
12837	Humble Oil Tractor and Tanker, *93*	9	16	___
12838	Crate Load, set of 2, *93-97*		3	___
12839	Grade Crossings, set of 2, *93-16*		7	___
12840	Insulated Straight Track (O), *93-16*		8	___
12841	Insulated Straight Track (O27), *93-16*		5	___
12842	Dunkin' Donuts Tractor and Trailer, *92 u*	13	25	___
12843	Die-cast Sprung Trucks, pair, *93-99*		10	___
12844	Coil Covers, pair (O), *93-98*		3	___
12847	Animated Ice Depot, *94-99*		65	___
12848	Lionel Oil Company Derrick, *94*	55	75	___
12849	Lionel Controller with wall pack, *94, 95 u*		NRS	___
12852	Die-cast Intermodal Trailer Frame, *94-01*		6	___
12853	Coil Covers, pair (std O), *94-98*		7	___
12854	U.S. Navy Tractor and Tanker, *94-95*		33	___
12855	Intermodal Containers, set of 3, *94-95*	9	13	___
12860	Lionel Visitor's Center Tractor and Trailer, *94 u*	10	14	___
12861	Lionel Leasing Company Tractor, *94*	8	13	___
12862	Oil Drum Loader, *94-95*	75	85	___
12864	Little Caesars Tractor and Trailer, *94*	8	14	___
12865	Wisk Tractor and Trailer, *94*	12	55	___
12866	TMCC 135-watt PowerHouse Power Supply, *94 u, 95-03*		46	___
12867	TMCC 135 PowerMaster Power Distribution Center, *94 u, 95-04*		49	___
12868	TMCC CAB-1 Remote Controller, *94 u, 95-09*		115	___
12869	Marathon Oil Tractor and Tanker, *94*	15	22	___
12873	Operating Sawmill, *95-97*		70	___
12874	Classic Street Lamps, set of 3, *94-00*		13	___
12877	Operating Fueling Station, *95*	75	85	___
12878	Control Tower, *95*	49	60	___
12881	Chrysler Mopar Tractor and Trailer, *94 u*	46	57	___

			Esc	Mint
____	**12882**	Lighted Billboard, *95*	9	14
____	**12883**	Dwarf Signal, *95-20*		27
____	**12884**	Truck Loading Dock Kit, *95-98*		16
____	**12885**	40-watt Control System, *94 u, 95-05*		35
____	**12886**	Floodlight Tower, *95-98*		31
____	**12888**	Railroad Crossing Flasher, *95-20*		56
____	**12889**	Operating Windmill, *95-98*		34
____	**12890**	Big Red Control Button, *94 u, 95-00*		43
____	**12891**	Lionel Refrigerator Lines Tractor and Trailer, *95*	12	16
____	**12892**	Automatic Flagman, *92-98*		25
____	**12893**	TMCC PowerMaster Power Adapter Cable, *94 u, 95-13, 17-20*		20
____	**12894**	Signal Bridge, *95-01*		22
____	**12895**	Double-track Signal Bridge, *95-00*		44
____	**12896**	Tunnel Portals, pair, *95-19*		20
____	**12897**	Engine House Kit, *96-98*		29
____	**12898**	Flagpole, *95-97*		9
____	**12899**	Searchlight Tower, *95-98*	10	25
____	**12900**	Crane Kit, *95-98*		8
____	**12901**	Shovel Kit, *95-98*		7
____	**12902**	Marathon Oil Derrick, *94 u, 95*	109	161
____	**12903**	Diesel Horn Shed, *95-98*		29
____	**12904**	Coaling Station Kit, *95-98*		19
____	**12905**	Factory Kit, *95-98*		20
____	**12906**	Maintenance Shed Kit, *95-98*		20
____	**12907**	Intermodal Containers, set of 3, *95*	9	14
____	**12911**	TMCC Command Base, *95-09*		80
____	**12912**	Oil Pumping Station, *95-98*	38	65
____	**12914**	SC-1 Switch and Accessory Controller, *95-98*		35
____	**12915**	Log Loader, *96*		115
____	**12916**	Water Tower, *96-97*		56
____	**12917**	Animated Switch Tower, *96-98*		29
____	**12922**	NYC Operating Gantry Crane, coil covers, *96*	75	90
____	**12923**	Red Wing Shoes Tractor and Trailer, *95 u*	34	38
____	**12925**	42" Diameter Curved Track Section (O), *96-16*		4
____	**12926**	Globe Street Lamps, set of 3, *96-03, 08-09, 16-20*		25
____	**12927**	Yard Light, set of 3, *96-19*		27
____	**12929**	Rail-truck Loading Dock, *96*		44
____	**12930**	Lionelville Oil Company Derrick, *95 u, 96*	55	75
____	**12931**	Electrical Substation, *96*		22
____	**12932**	Laimbeer Packaging Tractor and Trailer Set, *96*		14
____	**12933**	GM Parts Tractor and Trailer, *95*		NRS
____	**12935**	Zenith Tractor and Trailer, *96*		25
____	**12936**	SP Intermodal Crane, *97*		195
____	**12937**	NS Intermodal Crane, *97*		200
____	**12938**	PowerStation Controller and PowerHouse 135-watt Power Supply, *97-00*		150
____	**12943**	Illuminated Station Platform, *97-00*		24
____	**12944**	Sunoco Oil Derrick, *97*		85
____	**12945**	Sunoco Pumping Oil Station, *97*		80
____	**12948**	Bascule Bridge, *97*	75	315
____	**12949**	Billboards, set of 3, *97-00*		7
____	**12951**	Airplane Hangar Kit, *97-98*		29
____	**12952**	Big L Diner Kit, *97*		24

		Esc	Mint	
12953	Linex Gas Tall Oil Tank, *97*		9	___
12954	Linex Gas Wide Oil Tank, *97*		10	___
12955	Road Runner and Wile E. Coyote Ambush Shack, *97*		100	___
12958	Industrial Water Tower, *97-98*		50	___
12960	Rotary Radar Antenna, *97*		26	___
12961	Newsstand with diesel horn, *97*		30	___
12962	LL Passenger Service Train Whistle, *97-99*		30	___
12964	Donald Duck Radar Antenna, *97*		72	___
12965	Goofy Rotary Beacon, *97*		58	___
12966	Rotary Aircraft Beacon, *97-00*		35	___
12968	Girder Bridge Building Kit, *97*		22	___
12969	TMCC Command Set, *97-09*		148	___
12974	Blinking Light Billboard, *97-00*		15	___
12975	Steiner Victorian Building Kit, *97-98*		33	___
12976	Dobson Victorian Building Kit, *97-98*		24	___
12977	Kindler Victorian Building Kit, *97-98*		35	___
12982	Culvert Loader, conventional, *98-00*		190	___
12983	Culvert Unloader, conventional, *99*		185	___
12987	Intermodal Containers, set of 3, *98*		15	___
12989	Lionel Tractor and Trailer, *98*		16	___
12991	Linex Gas Tractor-Tanker, *98*		16	___
14000	Operating Forklift Platform, *00*		160	___
14001	Operating Belt Lumber Loader, *00*		95	___
14002	ZW Amp/Volt Meter, *00-04*		80	___
14003	80-watt Transformer/Controller, *00-03*		70	___
14004	Operating Coal Loader, *00*		135	___
14005	Operating Coal Ramp, *00*		130	___
14018	ElectroCoupler Kit for Command Upgradeable GP9s, *00*		20	___
14062	31" Path Remote Switch, left hand, *01-14*		55	___
14063	31" Path Remote Switch, right hand, *01-14*		75	___
14065	Nuclear Reactor, *00*		233	___
14071	Yard Light 3-pack, *00-18*		35	___
14072	Haunted House, *01*		181	___
14073	History of Lionel, *The First 90 Years Video, 00*		15	___
14075	A Century of Lionel, *1900-1969 Video, 00*		15	___
14076	A Century of Lionel, *1970-2000 Video, 00*		15	___
14077	ZW Amp/Volt Meter, *00-03*		70	___
14078	Die-cast Sprung Trucks, *00-05, 07-20*		24	___
14079	Operating North Pole Pylon, *01*		70	___
14080	Hobo Hotel, *01*	30	65	___
14081	Shell Oil Derrick, *01*		100	___
14082	Pedestrian Walkover, speed sensor, *01-03*		50	___
14083	Pedestrian Walkover, *01-03, 08, 12-16*		55	___
14084	Lionel Heliport, *01*		85	___
14085	Newsstand, *01*		75	___
14086	Water Tower, *00*		105	___
14087	Lighthouse, *01*		95	___
14090	Banjo Signal, *01-20*		60	___
14091	Automatic Gateman, *01-03, 07-09*		38	___
14092	Floodlight Tower, *01-05, 08-16*		48	___
14093	Single Signal Bridge, *01-04, 08*		22	___
14094	Double Signal Bridge, *01-04, 08*		30	___
14095	Illuminated Station Platform, *01-04*		20	___
14096	Station Platform, *01-04*		10	___

		Esc	Mint
____	**14097** Rotary Aircraft Beacon, *01-04, 07-10*		40
____	**14098** Auto Crossing Gate 2-pack, *01-19*		100
____	**14099** Block Target Signal, *01-04, 07-08*		22
____	**14100** Blinking Light Billboard, *01-03*		23
____	**14101** Red Baron Pylon, *01*		85
____	**14102** Rocket Launcher, *01*		250
____	**14104** Burning Switch Tower, *00*		70
____	**14105** Aquarium, *01*		175
____	**14106** Operating Freight Station, *00*		70
____	**14107** Coaling Station, *01-03*		95
____	**14109** Carousel, *01*		230
____	**14110** Operating Ferris Wheel, *01-02, 04*		170
____	**14111** 1531R Controller, *00-17*		46
____	**14112** Lighted Lockon, *01-10, 13-16*		6
____	**14113** Engine Transfer Table, *01*		210
____	**14114** Engine Transfer Table Extension, *01*		75
____	**14116** PRR Die-cast Girder Bridge, *01*		20
____	**14117** NYC Die-cast Girder Bridge, *01*		20
____	**14119** Gooseneck Lamps, set of 2, *01-04, 07*		22
____	**14121** Classic Billboards, set of 3, *01-03*		10
____	**14124** ZW Controller with 2 transformers, *01*		300
____	**14125** Christmas Tree with 400E Train, *00*		65
____	**14126** Exploding Ammo Dump		55
____	**14133** Madison Hobby Shop, *01*		290
____	**14134** Triple Action Magnetic Crane, *01*		230
____	**14135** NS Black Die-cast Girder Bridge, *02*		15
____	**14137** Die-cast Girder Bridge, *01-07*		25
____	**14138** Snap-On Tool Animated Billboard, *01 u*		NRS
____	**14142** Industrial Smokestack, *02-04*		50
____	**14143** Industrial Tank, *02-04*		40
____	**14145** Operating Lumberjacks, *02-03*		65
____	**14147** Die-cast Old Style Clock Tower, *02-04, 08-19*		47
____	**14148** Operating Billboard Signmen, *02-03*		60
____	**14149** Scale-sized Banjo Signal, *02-05*		40
____	**14151** Mainline Dwarf Signal, *02-08*		43
____	**14152** Passenger Station, *02-04*		37
____	**14153** Lion Oil Derrick, *02-03*		50
____	**14154** Water Tower, *01-02*		65
____	**14155** Floodlight Tower, *02-03*		55
____	**14156** Lion Oil Diesel Fueling Station, *02-03*		70
____	**14157** Coal Loader, *01-03*		120
____	**14158** Icing Station, *01-02*		75
____	**14159** Animated Billboard, *02-04*		20
____	**14160** Frank's Hotdog Stand, *03-04*		55
____	**14161** Smoking Hobo Shack, *02*		60
____	**14162** Missile Launching Platform, *02-03*		48
____	**14163** Industrial Power Station, *02-03*		550
____	**14164** Lionelville Bandstand, *02*		140
____	**14166** Train Orders Building, *04-05*		49
____	**14167** Operating Lift Bridge, *02*		380
____	**14168** Operating Harry's Barber Shop, *02-04*		100
____	**14170** Amusement Park Swing Ride, *03-04*		150
____	**14171** Pirate Ship Ride, *02-04*		130

		Esc	Mint	
14172	NYC Railroad Tugboat, *02*		180	___
14173	Drawbridge, *02-04*		70	___
14175	Santa Fe Die-cast Girder Bridge, *01-03*		17	___
14176	Norfolk Southern Die-cast Girder Bridge, *02-03*		18	___
14178	TMCC Direct Lockon, *02-03*		25	___
14179	TMCC Track Power Controller, *02-13*		230	___
14180	B&O Railroad Tugboat, *02-03*		155	___
14181	TMCC Action Recorder Controller, *02-13*		115	___
14182	TMCC Accessory Switch Controller, *02-13*		115	___
14183	TMCC Accessory Motor Controller, *02-13*		115	___
14184	TMCC Block Power Controller, *02-12*		90	___
14185	TMCC Operating Track Controller, *02-13*		100	___
14186	TMCC Accessory Voltage Controller, *02-13*		160	___
14187	TMCC How-to Video, *02-04*		11	___
14189	TMCC Track Power Controller, *02-13*		175	___
14190	The Lionel Train Book, *04-14*		30	___
14191	TMCC Command Base Cable, 6 feet, *02-13*		14	___
14192	TMCC 3-wire Command Base Cable, *02-13*		15	___
14193	TMCC Controller to Controller Cable, 1 foot, *02-13*		6	___
14194	TMCC TPC Cable Set, *02-13*		16	___
14195	TMCC Command Base Cable, 20 feet, *02-07*		12	___
14196	TMCC Controller to Controller Cable, 6 feet, *02-13*		9	___
14197	TMCC Controller to Controller Cable, 20 feet, *02-07*		9	___
14198	CW-80 80-watt Transformer, *03-18*	65	150	___
14199	Playground Swings, *03-04, 08-09*		50	___
14201	Burning Switch Tower, *05*		70	___
14202	Water Tower, *05*		140	___
14203	Amusement Park Swing Ride, *06-07*		230	___
14209	U.S. Steel Gantry Crane, *05*		180	___
14210	Pony Ride, *06-07*		70	___
14211	Road Crew, *07-08*		90	___
14214	Lionelville Mini Golf, *06*		80	___
14215	Tug-of-War, *06-08*		60	___
14217	Helicopter Pylon, *06-09*		140	___
14218	Downtown People Pack, *06-19*		27	___
14219	Ice Rink, *06-08*		80	___
14220	Lionelville Water Tower, *06-08*		21	___
14221	Witches Cauldron, *06-08*		70	___
14222	Die-cast Girder Bridge, *06-09*		30	___
14225	Sunoco Industrial Tank, *06-09*		70	___
14227	Yard Tower, *06-08*		45	___
14229	Crossing Shanty, *06-09*		20	___
14230	Milk Bottle Toss Midway Game, *06*		20	___
14231	Cotton Candy Midway Booth, *06*		20	___
14236	Operating Freight Station, *06-07*		105	___
14237	Rocket Launcher, *06-07*		320	___
14240	Ice Block Pack, *06-20*		6	___
14241	Work Crew People Pack, *06-19*		27	___
14242	Hard Rock Cafe, *06*		50	___
14243	U.S. Army Water Tower, *06-08*		95	___
14244	Ammo Loader, *06-07*		105	___
14251	Die-cast Sprung Trucks, rotating bearing caps, *07-20*		25	___
14255	Sand Tower, *06-18*		35	___
14257	Passenger Station, *06-13*		60	___

	No.	Description	Esc	Mint
___	14258	North Pole Passenger Station, *06-10*		53
___	14259	Christmas People Pack, *06-12*		23
___	14260	Christmas Tractor and Trailer, *06-08*		25
___	14261	Christmas Tree Lot, *06*		70
___	14262	Elevated Tank, *07*		70
___	14265	Sawmill with sound, *08*		130
___	14267	Sir Topham Hatt Gateman, *07-12*		80
___	14273	Polar Express Add-on Figures, *06-07, 12-14, 16-19*		30
___	14289	Operating Santa Gateman, *08*		80
___	14290	UPS Store, *06*		30
___	14291	Operating Milk Loading Depot, K-Line, *08*		100
___	14294	993 Legacy Expansion Set, *07-16, 18-20*		335
___	14295	990 Legacy Command Set, *07-16, 18-20*		400
___	14297	Halloween Witch Pylon, *07-08*	0	150
___	14500	KCS F3 Diesel AA Set, Railsounds, *CC, 01*	380	660
___	14512	F3 Diesel ABA Demonstrator "291," *CC, 01*	360	425
___	14517	Santa Fe F3 Diesel B Unit "2343C," *powered, 01*		280
___	14518	CP F3 Diesel B Unit "2373C," RailSounds, *CC, 01*		345
___	14520	Texas Special F3 Diesel B Unit, RailSounds, *01*		360
___	14521	Rock Island E6 Diesel AA Set, *01*		530
___	14524	Atlantic Coast Line E6 Diesel AA Set, *01*		630
___	14536	Santa Fe F3 Diesel AA Set, RailSounds, *CC, 03-04*		800
___	14539	Santa Fe F3 Diesel B Unit, *03*		300
___	14540	D&RGW F3 Diesel B Unit, RailSounds, *CC, 01*		315
___	14541	C&O F3 Diesel B Unit, RailSounds, *CC, 01*		300
___	14542	KCS F3 Diesel B Unit "2388C," RailSounds, *CC, 01*		375
___	14543	SP F3 Diesel B Unit, RailSounds, *CC, 01*		282
___	14544	Southern E6 AA Diesel Set, *CC, 02*		560
___	14547	Burlington E5 AA Diesel Set, *CC, 02*		570
___	14552	NYC F3 Diesel AA Set, RailSounds, *CC, 03-04*		740
___	14555	NYC F3 Diesel B Unit, *03*		200
___	14557	WP F3 Diesel B Unit, nonpowered, *03-04*		190
___	14558	B&O F3 Diesel B Unit, nonpowered, *03-04*		155
___	14559	D&RGW F3 Diesel AA Set, *01*		620
___	14560	NP F3 Diesel A Unit "2390B," *freight, 02*		175
___	14561	NP F3 Diesel A Unit "2390B," *passenger, 02*		190
___	14562	Milwaukee Road F3 Diesel A Unit "75C," *02*		190
___	14563	Erie-Lackawanna F3 Diesel A Unit "7094," *02*		175
___	14564	CP F3 Diesel B Unit "237C," *CC, 02*		350
___	14565	B&O F3 Diesel AA Set, *03-04*		650
___	14568	WP F3 Diesel AA Set, *03-04*		780
___	14571	Santa Fe PA Diesel AA Set, *CC, 03*		660
___	14574	D&H PA Diesel AA Set, *CC, 03*		580
___	14584	Wabash F3 Diesel A Unit, nonpowered, *03*		180
___	14586	D&H PB Unit, *03*		125
___	14587	Santa Fe PB Unit, *03*		125
___	14588	Santa Fe F3 Diesel ABA Set, *CC, 04-05*		980
___	14592	PRR F3 Diesel ABA Set, *CC, 04-05*		750
___	14596	NH Alco PA Diesel AA Set, *04-05*		700
___	14599	NH Alco PB Diesel B Unit "0767-B," *04-05*		150
___	15000	D&RGW Waffle-sided Boxcar, *95*	12	18
___	15001	Seaboard Waffle-sided Boxcar, *95*	14	19
___	15002	Chesapeake & Ohio Waffle-sided Boxcar, *96*	16	20

		Esc	Mint	
15003	Green Bay & Western Waffle-sided Boxcar, *96*	16	20	___
15004	Bloomingdale's Boxcar, *97 u*		40	___
15005	"I Love NY" Boxcar, *97 u*		65	___
15008	CP Rail Boxcar		30	___
15013	L&N Waffle-sided Boxcar "102402," *00*		29	___
15014	Seaboard Waffle-sided Boxcar "125925," *00*		25	___
15015	C&NW Waffle-sided Boxcar "161013," *03*		18	___
15016	IC Waffle-sided Boxcar "12981," *04*		20	___
15017	CSX Waffle-sided Boxcar, *05*		27	___
15018	D&H Waffle-sided Boxcar "24052," *06*		30	___
15020	NH Waffle-sided Boxcar, *07*		30	___
15021	MKT Waffle-sided Boxcar, *08*		35	___
15024	UP Waffle Boxcar "960860," *09-11*		40	___
15028	Southern Waffle-sided Boxcar "539889," *10*		40	___
15029	Western & Atlantic Wood-sided Reefer, *10*		53	___
15033	MTK Stock Car, *10*		65	___
15038	CSX Hi-Cube Boxcar, *11-12*		40	___
15039	NS Waffle-sided Boxcar, *11-12*		40	___
15041	BNSF Hi-Cube Boxcar, *10*		50	___
15042	CSX Waffle-sided Boxcar, *11*		40	___
15051	Lionel Lines Boxcar, *11-12*		40	___
15052	Amtrak Hi-Cube Boxcar, *11-12*		40	___
15053	REA Waffle-sided Boxcar, *11-12*		40	___
15054	C&NW Wood-sided Reefer, *11-12*		40	___
15060	K-Line Boxcar, *06*		40	___
15063	U.S.A.F. Minuteman Boxcar, *11*		55	___
15069	Coke Wood-sided Reefer #1, *09-16*		65	___
15071	Coca-Cola Christmas Boxcar, *12*		70	___
15072	Halloween Boxcar, *09-11*		55	___
15074	Mr. Goodbar Wood-sided Reefer, *09-11*		55	___
15075	Boy Scouts of America Eagle Scout Boxcar, *11-14*		60	___
15077	ATSF Stock Car , *11*		55	___
15078	Pabst Wood-sided Reefer, *11*		65	___
15079	Schlitz Wood-sided Reefer, *11*		58	___
15080	C&O 40' Boxcar, *11*		55	___
15083	CP Rail Waffle-sided Boxcar, *13*		43	___
15084	GN Hi-Cube Boxcar, *13-14*		43	___
15086	Alaska Wood-Sided Reefer, *12*		40	___
15091	Angela Trotta Thomas "High Hopes" Hi-Cube Boxcar, *12*		55	___
15094	Sleepy Hollow Halloween Reefer, *14-15*		60	___
15095	1953 Lionel Catalog Art Reefer, *13*		55	___
15096	Hershey's Kisses Christmas Boxcar, *12*		70	___
15097	Peanuts Christmas Boxcar, *12-13*		70	___
15098	Lone Ranger Boxcar, *12-14*		60	___
15100	Amtrak Passenger Coach, *95-97*		35	___
15101	Reading Baggage Car (O27), *96*		34	___
15102	Reading Combination Car (O27), *96*		23	___
15103	Reading Passenger Coach (O27), *96*		23	___
15104	Reading Vista Dome Car (O27), *96*		26	___
15105	Reading Full Vista Dome Car (O27), *96*		26	___
15106	Reading Observation Car (O27), *96*		23	___
15107	Amtrak Vista Dome Car, *96*		38	___
15108	Northern Pacific Vista Dome Car, *96*		34	___
15109	ATSF Combine Car "2407," *97*		35	___

		Esc	Mint
___ **15110**	ATSF Vista Dome Car 2404," *97*		35
___ **15111**	ATSF Observation Car "2406," *97*		35
___ **15112**	ATSF Albuquerque Coach "2405," *97*		34
___ **15113**	ATSF Culebra Vista Dome Car "2404," *97*		34
___ **15114**	NJ Transit Coach "5610," *96 u*		45
___ **15115**	NJ Transit Coach "5611," *96 u*		45
___ **15116**	NJ Transit Coach "5612," *96 u*		45
___ **15117**	Annie Passenger Coach, *97*		26
___ **15118**	Clarabel Passenger Coach, *97*		26
___ **15122**	NJ Transit Passenger Coach "5613," *97 u*		45
___ **15123**	NJ Transit Passenger Coach "5614," *97 u*		45
___ **15124**	NJ Transit Passenger Coach "5615," *97 u*		45
___ **15125**	Amtrak Observation Car, *97 u*		50
___ **15126**	Stars & Stripes Abraham Lincoln General Coach, *99*		60
___ **15127**	Stars & Stripes Ulysses S. Grant General Coach, *99*		60
___ **15128**	Pride of Richmond Robert E. Lee General Coach, *99*		60
___ **15129**	Pride of Richmond Jefferson Davis General Coach, *99*		60
___ **15136**	Custom Series Short Observation Car, blue, *99*		40
___ **15137**	Custom Series Short Observation Car, red, *99*		34
___ **15138**	Pratt's Hollow Baggage Car, *98*		100
___ **15139**	Pratt's Hollow Vista Dome Car, *98*		100
___ **15140**	Pratt's Hollow Coach, *98*		100
___ **15141**	Pratt's Hollow Observation, *98*		100
___ **15142**	U.S. Army Baby Heavyweight Coach, *00*		50
___ **15143**	U.S. Army Baby Heavyweight Coach, *00*		50
___ **15153**	Pullman Baby Madison Set 4-pack, *01*		190
___ **15163**	T&P Baby Heavyweight Coach, *01*		30
___ **15166**	Union Pacific Whistling Baggage Car, *04*		41
___ **15169**	C&O Streamliner Car 4-pack, *03*		140
___ **15170**	L&N Streamliner Car 4-pack, *03*		140
___ **15180**	NYC Streamliner Car 4-pack, *04*		340
___ **15185**	UP Streamliner Car 4-pack, *04*		340
___ **15300**	NYC Superliner Aluminum Passenger Car 4-pack, *02*		360
___ **15301**	NYC Manhattan Superliner Passenger Coach, *02*		90
___ **15302**	NYC Queens Superliner Passenger Coach, *02*		90
___ **15304**	NYC Staten Island Superliner Passenger Coach, *02*		90
___ **15305**	NYC Brooklyn Superliner Passenger Coach, *02*		90
___ **15311**	CB&Q California Zephyr Aluminum Passenger Car 4-pack, *03*		350
___ **15312**	Santa Fe Super Chief Aluminum Passenger Car 4-pack, *03*		275
___ **15313**	D&H Aluminum Passenger Car 4-pack, *03*		415
___ **15314**	Amtrak Superliner 2-pack, *03*		220
___ **15315**	Santa Fe Superliner 2-pack, *03*		200
___ **15316**	NYC Superliner 2-pack, *03*		195
___ **15317**	Southern Aluminum Passenger Car 4-pack, *03*		350
___ **15318**	Lionel Lines Aluminum Passenger Car 2-pack, *03*		125
___ **15319**	Santa Fe Superliner Aluminum Passenger Car 2-pack, *03*		145
___ **15326**	NYC 20th Century Limited Aluminum Passenger Car 6-pack, *02*		485
___ **15333**	N&W Powhatan Arrow Aluminum Passenger Car 6-pack, *02*		435
___ **15340**	PRR South Wind Aluminum Passenger Car 6-pack, *02*		435
___ **15379**	Lionel Lines Silver Valley Aluminum Combination Car, *03*		100
___ **15380**	Lionel Lines Silver Spoon Aluminum Diner, *03*		100
___ **15381**	Santa Fe Aluminum Baggage Car "2571," *03*		100
___ **15382**	Santa Fe Regal Dome Aluminum Vista Dome Car, *03*		100

No.	Description	Esc	Mint	
15383	NYC 20th Century Limited Diner, StationSounds, *03*		195	___
15384	N&W Powhatan Arrow Diner, StationSounds, *03*		190	___
15385	Pennsylvania South Wind Diner, StationSounds, *03*		190	___
15394	Amtrak Streamliner Car 4-pack, *03-04*		450	___
15395	Alaska Streamliner Car 4-pack, *03-04*		355	___
15396	Amtrak Superliner Diner, StationSounds, *03*		220	___
15397	Santa Fe Superliner Diner, StationSounds, *03*		200	___
15398	NYC Superliner Diner, StationSounds, *03*		200	___
15405	50th Anniversary Hillside Heavyweight Diner, StationSounds, *02*		195	___
15406	Blue Comet Giacobini Heavyweight Diner, StationSounds, *02*		300	___
15504	Alton Limited Diner, StationSounds, *03*		230	___
15507	Phantom III Passenger Car 4-pack (15508 Baggage, 15509 Vista Dome, 15510 Coach, 15511 Observation), *02*		245	___
15512	Phantom II Passenger Car 4-pack, *02*		250	___
15517	Southern Crescent Limited Heavyweight Passenger Car 2-pack, *03-04*		205	___
15520	Southern Crescent Limited Heavyweight Diner, StationSounds, *03-04*		220	___
15521	NYC 20th Century Limited Heavyweight Passenger Car 4-pack, *04*		345	___
15526	Santa Fe Chief Heavyweight Passenger Car 4-pack, *04*		370	___
15538	NYC 20th Century Limited Heavyweight Passenger Car 2-pack, *04*		200	___
15541	NYC 20th Century Limited Heavyweight Diner, StationSounds,*04*		200	___
15542	Santa Fe Chief Heavyweight Passenger Car 2-pack, *04*		195	___
15545	Santa Fe Chief Heavyweight Diner, StationSounds, *04*		200	___
15546	Napa Valley Wine Train Heavyweight 2-pack, *05*		250	___
15549	Napa Valley Wine Train Diner, StationSounds, *05*		280	___
15554	Pennsylvania Heavyweight Car 3-pack (std O), *05*		375	___
15558	Pennsylvania Heavyweight Add-on Coach (std O), *05*		140	___
15559	PRR Reading Seashore Heavyweight Car 3-pack (std O), *05*		370	___
15563	PRR Reading Seashore Heavyweight Add-on Coach, *05*		130	___
15564	LIRR Heavyweight Car 3-pack (std O), *05*		370	___
15568	LIRR Heavyweight Add-on Coach (std O), *05*		130	___
15570	LIRR Heavyweight Car 3-pack (std O), *06*		230	___
15574	LIRR Heavyweight Car Add-on (std O), *06*		140	___
15575	C&O Heavyweight Diner, StationSounds (std O), *06-07*		295	___
15576	C&O Heavyweight Passenger Car 2-pack (std O), *06-07*		265	___
15577	NYC Heavyweight 3-pack (std O), *05-06*		370	___
15581	NYC Heavyweight Add-on Coach (std O), *05-06*		130	___
15584	Amtrak Acela Passenger Car 3-pack (std O), *06*		580	___
15588	Southern Heavyweight Passenger Car 4-pack, *06*		495	___
15593	Southern Heavyweight Passenger Car 2-pack, *06*		265	___
15596	Southern Heavyweight Diner, StationSounds, *06*		295	___
15597	C&O Heavyweight Passenger Car 4-pack (std O), *06-07*		495	___
15906	RailSounds Trigger Button, *90-95*		12	___
16000	PRR Vista Dome Car (O27), *87-88*	37	55	___
16001	PRR Passenger Coach (O27), *87-88*	33	41	___
16002	PRR Passenger Coach (O27), *87-88*	24	29	___
16003	PRR Observation Car (O27), *87-88*	24	29	___
16009	PRR Combination Car (O27), *88*	36	38	___
16010	Virginia & Truckee Passenger Coach (SSS), *88*	36	47	___
16010	Railbox Modern Boxcar 6-pack, LionScale, *16*		360	___
16011	Virginia & Truckee Passenger Coach (SSS), *88*	36	47	___
16012	Virginia & Truckee Baggage Car (SSS), *88*	36	47	___
16013	Amtrak Combination Car (O27), *88-89*	21	34	___

| --- | --- | --- | --- |
___ 16014	Amtrak Vista Dome Car (027), *88-89*	21	34
___ 16015	Amtrak Observation Car (027), *88-89*	21	34
___ 16016	NYC Baggage Car (027), *89*	36	55
___ 16017	NYC Combination Car (027), *89*	21	29
___ 16018	NYC Passenger Coach (027), *89*	21	29
___ 16019	NYC Vista Dome Car (027), *89*	21	29
___ 16020	NYC Passenger Coach (027), *89*	23	33
___ 16020	BNSF Modern Boxcar 6-pack, LionScale, *16*		360
___ 16021	NYC Observation Car (027), *89*	20	28
___ 16022	Pennsylvania Baggage Car (027), *89*	27	38
___ 16023	Amtrak Passenger Coach (027), *89*	21	30
___ 16024	Northern Pacific Diner (027), *92*	39	44
___ 16027	LL Combination Car (027, SSS), *90*	39	48
___ 16028	LL Passenger Coach (SSS, 027), *90*	35	42
___ 16029	LL Passenger Coach (SSS, 027), *90*	35	42
___ 16030	LL Observation Car (SSS, 027), *90*	35	42
___ 16030	CSX Modern Boxcar 6-pack, LionScale, *16*		360
___ 16031	Pennsylvania Diner (027), *90*	35	39
___ 16033	Amtrak Baggage Car (027), *90*	28	38
___ 16034	NP Baggage Car (027), *90-91*	30	45
___ 16035	NP Combination Car (027), *90-91*	18	26
___ 16036	NP Passenger Coach (027), *90-91*	21	30
___ 16037	NP Vista Dome Car (027), *90-91*	18	26
___ 16038	NP Passenger Coach (027), *90-91*	17	25
___ 16039	NP Observation Car (027), *90-91*	21	30
___ 16040	Southern Pacific Baggage Car, *90-91*	22	30
___ 16040	NS Modern Boxcar 6-pack, LionScale, *16*		360
___ 16041	NYC Diner (027), *91*	37	47
___ 16042	Illinois Central Baggage Car (027), *91*	24	34
___ 16043	Illinois Central Combination Car (027), *91*	22	30
___ 16044	Illinois Central Passenger Coach (027), *91*	24	34
___ 16045	Illinois Central Vista Dome Car (027), *91*	22	30
___ 16046	Illinois Central Passenger Coach (027), *91*	24	34
___ 16047	Illinois Central Observation Car (027), *91*	24	34
___ 16048	Amtrak Diner (027), *91-92*	33	40
___ 16049	Illinois Central Diner (027), *92*	27	38
___ 16050	C&NW Baggage Car "6620," *93*	44	55
___ 16050	AT&SF 3-bay Offset Hopper 6-pack, LionScale, *16*		330
___ 16051	C&NW Combination Car "6630," *93*	40	50
___ 16052	C&NW Passenger Coach "6616," *93*	34	42
___ 16053	C&NW Passenger Coach "6602," *93*	37	46
___ 16054	C&NW Observation Car "6603," *93*	38	47
___ 16055	Santa Fe Passenger Coach (027), *93-94*	29	38
___ 16056	Santa Fe Vista Dome Car (027), *93-94*	25	32
___ 16057	Santa Fe Passenger Coach (027), *93-94*	30	40
___ 16058	Santa Fe Combination Car (027), *93-94*	27	35
___ 16059	Santa Fe Vista Dome Car (027), *93-94*	26	34
___ 16060	Santa Fe Observation Car (027), *93-94*	25	31
___ 16060	B&O 3-bay Offset Hopper 6-pack, LionScale, *16*		330
___ 16061	N&W Baggage Car "6061," *94*	60	85
___ 16062	N&W Combination Car "6062," *94*	38	50
___ 16063	N&W Passenger Coach "6063," *94*	43	55
___ 16064	N&W Passenger Coach "6064," *94*	43	55
___ 16065	N&W Observation Car "6065," *94*	36	48

		Esc	Mint	
16066	NYC Combination Car "6066" (SSS), *94*	55	70	___
16067	NYC Passenger Coach "6067" (SSS), *94*	38	47	___
16068	UP Baggage Car "6068" (O27), *94*	50	65	___
16069	UP Combination Car "6069" (O27), *94*	36	43	___
16070	UP Passenger Coach "6070" (O27), *94*	36	43	___
16070	B&M 3-bay Offset Hopper 6-pack, LionScale, *16*		330	___
16071	UP Diner "6071" (O27), *94*	36	46	___
16072	UP Vista Dome Car "6072" (O27), *94*	36	43	___
16073	UP Passenger Coach "6073" (O27), *94*	36	42	___
16074	UP Observation Car "6074" (O27), *94*	36	43	___
16075	Missouri Pacific Baggage Car "6620," *95*	44	55	___
16076	Missouri Pacific Combination Car "6630," *95*	34	41	___
16077	Missouri Pacific Passenger Coach "6616," *95*	34	41	___
16078	Missouri Pacific Passenger Coach "7805," *95*	34	39	___
16079	Missouri Pacific Observation Car "6609," *95*	34	41	___
16080	New Haven Baggage Car "6080" (O27), *95*	35	44	___
16080	C&O 3-bay Offset Hopper 6-pack #1, LionScale, *16*		330	___
16081	New Haven Combination Car "6081" (O27), *95*	28	37	___
16082	New Haven Passenger Coach "6082" (O27), *95*	28	37	___
16083	New Haven Vista Dome Car "6083" (O27), *95*	30	39	___
16084	New Haven Full Vista Dome Car "6084" (O27), *95*	33	39	___
16086	New Haven Observation Car "6086" (O27), *95*	31	40	___
16087	NYC Baggage Car "6087" (SSS), *95*	48	65	___
16088	NYC Passenger Coach "6088" (SSS), *95*	36	43	___
16089	NYC Diner "6089" (SSS), *95*	36	43	___
16090	NYC Observation Car "6090" (SSS), *95*	38	46	___
16090	C&O 3-bay Offset Hopper 6-pack #2, LionScale, *16*		330	___
16091	NYC Passenger Cars, *set of 4 (SSS)*, *95*	140	165	___
16092	Santa Fe Full Vista Dome Car (O27), *95*	30	38	___
16093	Illinois Central Full Vista Dome Car (O27), *95*	29	38	___
16094	Pennsylvania Full Vista Dome Car (O27), *95*	30	39	___
16095	Amtrak Combination Car (O27), *95*	19	23	___
16096	Amtrak Vista Dome Car (O27), *95*	19	23	___
16097	Amtrak Observation Car (O27), *95*	19	23	___
16098	Amtrak Passenger Coach, *95-97*	20	33	___
16099	Amtrak Vista Dome Car, *95-97*	20	33	___
16100	Alaska RR 3-bay 9-panel Hopper 6-pack, LionScale, *16*		330	___
16102	Southern 3-D Tank Car (SSS), *87*	23	30	___
16103	Lehigh Valley 2-D Tank Car (O27), *88*	19	25	___
16104	Santa Fe 2-D Tank Car (O27), *89*	19	23	___
16105	D&RGW 3-D Tank Car (SSS), *89*	48	65	___
16106	Mopar Express 3-D Tank Car, *88 u*	105	156	___
16107	Sunoco 2-D Tank Car (O27), *90*	16	20	___
16108	Racing Fuel 1-D Tank Car "6108" (O27), *89 u, 92 u*	9	13	___
16109	B&O 1-D Tank Car (SSS), *91*	29	34	___
16110	Circus Animals Operating Stock Car "1989" (O27), *89 u*	24	34	___
16110	Chessie 3-bay 9-panel Hopper 6-pack, LionScale, *16*		330	___
16111	Alaska 1-D Tank Car, *90-91*	22	27	___
16112	Dow Chemical 3-D Tank Car, *90*	20	26	___
16113	Diamond Shamrock 2-D Tank Car (O27), *91*	20	25	___
16114	Hooker Chemicals 1-D Tank Car (O27), *91*	13	17	___
16115	MKT 3-D Tank Car, *92*	13	16	___
16116	U.S. Army 1-D Tank Car, *91 u*	36	42	___
16119	MKT 2-D Tank Car (O27), *92, 93 u*	14	19	___

16120	Southern 3-bay 9-panel Hopper 6-pack, LionScale, *16*		330
16121	C&NW Stock Car (SSS), *92*	33	43
16123	Union Pacific 3-D Tank Car, *93-95*	16	22
16124	Penn Salt 3-D Tank Car, *93*	21	26
16125	Virginian Stock Car, *93*	19	24
16126	Jefferson Lake 3-D Tank Car, *93*	22	26
16127	Mobil 1-D Tank Car, *93*	28	33
16128	Alaska 1-D Tank Car, *94*	24	29
16129	Alaska 1-D Tank Car (027), *93 u, 94*	21	28
16130	SP Stock Car (027), *93 u, 94*	10	13
16130	WM 3-bay 9-panel Hopper 6-pack, LionScale, *16*		330
16131	T&P Reefer, *94*	19	24
16132	Deep Rock 3-D Tank Car, *94*	25	30
16133	Santa Fe Reefer, *94*	22	28
16134	Reading Reefer, *94*	17	21
16135	C&O Stock Car, *94*	23	27
16136	B&O 1-D Tank Car, *94*	28	32
16137	Ford 1-D Tank Car "12," *94 u*	34	39
16138	Goodyear 1-D Tank Car, *95*	28	34
16140	Domino Sugar 1-D Tank Car, *95*	24	29
16140	Klemme Coop PS-2CD Covered Hopper 6-pack, LionScale, *16*		360
16141	Erie Stock Car, *95*	22	30
16142	Santa Fe 1-D Tank Car, *95*	26	30
16143	Reading Reefer, *95*	18	23
16144	San Angelo 3-D Tank Car, *95*	22	25
16146	Dairy Despatch Reefer, *95*	15	20
16147	Clearly Canadian 1-D Tank Car (027), *94 u*	25	40
16149	Zep Chemical 1-D Tank Car (027), *95 u*	71	87
16150	Sunoco 1-D Tank Car "6315," *97*	35	38
16150	D&RGW PS-2CD Covered Hopper 6-pack, LionScale, *16*		360
16152	Sunoco 3-D Tank Car "6415," *97*		26
16153	AEC Reactor Fluid 1-D Tank Car "6515-1," *97*		94
16154	AEC Reactor Fluid 1-D Tank Car "6515-2," *97*	0	108
16155	AEC Reactor Fluid 1-D Tank Car "6515-3," *97*	0	109
16157	Gatorade Little League Baseball 1-D Tank Car "6315," *97 u*	0	64
16160	AEC Tank Car "6515" with reactor fluid, *98*		85
16160	MILW PS-2CD Covered Hopper 6-pack, LionScale, *16*		360
16162	Hooker 1-D Tank Car "6315-1," *97*		50
16163	Hooker 1-D Tank Car "6315-2," *97*		50
16164	Hooker 1-D Tank Car "6315-3," *97*		50
16165	Mobilfuel 3-D Tank Car "6415," *97 u*		50
16170	RFMX PS-2CD Covered Hopper 6-pack, LionScale, *16*		360
16170	RFMX PS-2CD Covered Hopper 6-pack, LionScale, *16*		360
16171	Alaska 1-D Tank Car "6171," *98-99*		33
16173	Harold the Helicopter Flatcar, *98*	45	60
16175	NJ Transit Port Morris Ore Car "9125," *98*		45
16176	NJ Transit Raritan Yard Ore Car "9126," *98 u*		45
16177	NJ Transit Gladstone Yard Ore Car "9127," *98 u*		45
16178	NJ Transit Bay Head Yard Ore Car "9128," *98 u*		45
16179	NJ Transit Dover Yard Ore Car "9129," *98 u*		45
16180	Tabasco 1-D Tank Car, *98*	69	86
16181	Biohazard Tank Car with Lights, *98*	0	90
16182	Gatorade 1-D Tank Car "6315," *98 u*		64
16187	Linex 3-D Tank Car "6425," *99*		30

		Esc	Mint	
16188	Kodak 1-D Tank Car "6515," *99*	74	91	___
16199	UP 1-D Tank Car "6035," *99-00*		25	___
16200	Rock Island Boxcar (027), *87-88*	5	10	___
16201	Wabash Boxcar (027), *88-91*	7	10	___
16203	Key America Boxcar (027), *87 u*	45	65	___
16204	Hawthorne Boxcar (027), *87 u*	50	85	___
16205	Mopar Express Boxcar "1987" (027), *87-88 u*	55	65	___
16206	D&RGW Boxcar (SSS), *89*	37	42	___
16207	True Value Boxcar (027), *88 u*	32	115	___
16208	PRR Auto Carrier, 3-tier, *89*	24	37	___
16209	Disney Magic Boxcar (027), *88 u*	90	110	___
16211	Hawthorne Boxcar (027), *88 u*	45	65	___
16213	Shoprite Boxcar (027), *88 u*	55	80	___
16214	D&RGW Auto Carrier, *90*	24	32	___
16215	Conrail Auto Carrier, *90*	27	38	___
16217	Burlington Northern Auto Carrier, *92*	24	36	___
16219	True Value Boxcar (027), *89 u*	55	75	___
16220	Ace Hardware Boxcar (027), *89 u*	58	81	___
16221	Macy's Boxcar (027), *89 u*	55	80	___
16222	Great Northern Boxcar (027), *90-91*	8	15	___
16223	Budweiser Reefer, *89-92 u*	68	90	___
16224	True Value "Lawn Chief" Boxcar (027), *90 u*	45	60	___
16225	Budweiser Vat Car, *90-91 u*	130	169	___
16226	Union Pacific Boxcar "6226" (027), *90-91 u*	15	19	___
16227	Santa Fe Boxcar (027), *91*	13	17	___
16228	Union Pacific Auto Carrier, *92*	26	33	___
16229	Erie-Lackawanna Auto Carrier, *91 u*	45	55	___
16232	Chessie System Boxcar, *92, 93 u, 94, 95 u*	25	30	___
16233	MKT DD Boxcar, *92*	20	29	___
16234	ACY Boxcar (SSS), *92*	34	41	___
16235	Railway Express Agency Reefer, *92*	19	23	___
16236	NYC Pacemaker Boxcar, *92 u*	18	24	___
16237	Railway Express Agency Boxcar, *92 u*	21	23	___
16238	NYNH&H Boxcar, *93-95*		3	___
16239	Union Pacific Boxcar, *93-95*	15	20	___
16241	Toys "R" Us Boxcar, *92-93 u*	35	45	___
16242	Grand Trunk Western Auto Carrier, *93*	35	40	___
16243	Conrail Boxcar, *93*	26	34	___
16244	Duluth, South Shore & Atlantic Boxcar, *93*	20	24	___
16245	Contadina Boxcar, *93*	16	20	___
16247	ACL Boxcar, *94*	15	19	___
16248	Budweiser Boxcar, *93-94 u*	52	70	___
16249	United Auto Workers Boxcar, *93 u*		55	___
16250	Santa Fe Boxcar (027), *93 u, 94*	8	10	___
16251	Columbus & Greenville Boxcar, *94*	8	15	___
16252	U.S. Navy Boxcar "6106888," *94-95*		30	___
16253	Santa Fe Auto Carrier, *94*	32	38	___
16255	Wabash DD Boxcar, *95*	20	26	___
16256	Ford DD Boxcar, *94 u*	30	34	___
16257	Crayola Boxcar, *94 u, 95*	17	23	___
16258	Lehigh Valley Boxcar, *95*	17	22	___
16259	Chrysler Mopar Boxcar, *97 u*	33	43	___
16260	Chrysler Mopar Auto Carrier, *96 u*	59	69	___
16261	Union Pacific DD Boxcar, *95*	26	29	___

			Esc	Mint
____	**16263**	ATSF Boxcar, *96-99*		25
____	**16264**	Red Wing Shoes Boxcar, *95*	26	32
____	**16265**	Georgia Power "Atlanta, '96" Boxcar, *95 u*	200	236
____	**16266**	Crayola Boxcar, *95*	17	23
____	**16267**	Sears Zenith Boxcar, *95-96 u*		55
____	**16268**	GM/AC Delco Boxcar, *95 u*		51
____	**16269**	Lionel Lines Boxcar, *96*		10
____	**16272**	Christmas Boxcar, *97*		36
____	**16273**	Lionel Employee Christmas Boxcar, *97*		55
____	**16274**	Marvin the Martian Boxcar, *97*		60
____	**16279**	Dodge Motorsports Boxcar, *96 u*	147	189
____	**16284**	Galveston Wharves Boxcar, *98*		28
____	**16285**	Savannah State Docks Boxcar, *98*		26
____	**16291**	Christmas Boxcar, *98*		34
____	**16292**	Lionel Employee Christmas Boxcar, *98*	309	369
____	**16293**	JCPenney Boxcar, *97*		100
____	**16294**	Pedigree Boxcar, *97*	148	168
____	**16295**	Kal Kan Boxcar, *97*	151	171
____	**16296**	Whiskas Boxcar, *97*	142	168
____	**16297**	Sheba Boxcar, *97*	136	160
____	**16298**	Mobil Boxcar, *97*		50
____	**16300**	Rock Island Flatcar with fences (027), *87-88*	8	10
____	**16301**	Lionel Barrel Ramp Car, *87*	14	19
____	**16303**	PRR Flatcar with trailers, *87*	26	33
____	**16304**	RI Gondola with cable reels (027), *87-88*	5	9
____	**16305**	Lehigh Valley Ore Car, *87*	80	130
____	**16306**	Santa Fe Barrel Ramp Car, *88*	12	16
____	**16307**	NKP Flatcar with trailers, *88*	30	40
____	**16308**	Burlington Northern Flatcar with trailer, *88-89*	20	25
____	**16309**	Wabash Gondola with canisters, *88-91*	9	13
____	**16310**	Mopar Express Gondola with canisters, *87-88 u*	35	39
____	**16311**	Mopar Express Flatcar with trailers, *87-88 u*	116	160
____	**16313**	PRR Gondola with cable reels (027), *88 u, 89*	5	10
____	**16314**	Wabash Flatcar with trailers, *89*	26	30
____	**16315**	PRR Flatcar with fences (027), *88 u, 89*	7	9
____	**16317**	PRR Barrel Ramp Car, *89*	18	22
____	**16318**	LL Depressed Center Flatcar with cable reels, *89*	22	26
____	**16320**	Great Northern Barrel Ramp Car, *90*	13	19
____	**16323**	Lionel Lines Flatcar with trailers, *90*	21	25
____	**16324**	PRR Depressed Center Flatcar with cable reels, *90*	16	20
____	**16325**	Microracers Exhibition Ramp Car, *89 u*	21	28
____	**16326**	Santa Fe Depressed Center Flatcar with cable reels, *91*	16	21
____	**16327**	"The Big Top" Circus Gondola with canisters, *89 u*	19	24
____	**16328**	NKP Gondola with cable reels, *90-91*	17	23
____	**16329**	SP Flatcar with horses (027), *90-91*	19	24
____	**16330**	MKT Flatcar with trailers, *91*	25	30
____	**16332**	LL Depressed Center Flatcar with transformer, *91*	28	33
____	**16333**	Frisco Bulkhead Flatcar with lumber, *91*	17	22
____	**16334**	C&NW Flatcar Set ("16337, 16338") with trailers, *91*	55	60
____	**16335**	NYC Pacemaker Flatcar with trailer (SSS), *91*	46	65
____	**16336**	UP Gondola "6336" with canisters, *90-91 u*	17	21
____	**16339**	Mickey's World Tour Gondola with canisters (027), *91, 92 u*	17	21
____	**16341**	NYC Depressed Center Flatcar with transformer, *92*	29	32
____	**16342**	CSX Gondola with coil covers, *92*	18	23

16343	Burlington Gondola with coil covers, *92*	20	23	___
16347	Ontario Northland Bulkhead Flatcar with pulp load, *92*	22	26	___
16348	Erie Liquefied Petroleum Car, *92*	23	25	___
16349	Allis Chalmers Condenser Car, *92*	28	35	___
16350	CP Rail Bulkhead Flatcar with lumber, *91 u*	20	29	___
16351	Flatcar with U.S. Navy submarine, *92*	27	33	___
16352	U.S. Military Flatcar with cruise missile, *92*	33	43	___
16353	B&M Gondola with coil covers, *91 u*	33	39	___
16355	Burlington Gondola, *92, 93 u, 94-95*	11	17	___
16356	MKT Depressed Center Flatcar with cable reels, *92*	17	21	___
16357	L&N Flatcar with trailer, *92*	24	31	___
16358	L&N Gondola with coil covers, *92*	17	21	___
16359	Pacific Coast Gondola with coil covers (SSS), *92*	33	38	___
16360	N&W Maxi-Stack Flatcar Set ("16361, 16362") with containers, *93*	44	55	___
16363	Southern TTUX Flatcar Set ("16364, 16365") with trailers, *93*	38	49	___
16367	Clinchfield Gondola with coil covers, *93*	18	21	___
16368	MKT Liquid Oxygen Car, *93*	21	22	___
16369	Amtrak Flatcar with wheel load, *92 u*	19	28	___
16370	Amtrak Flatcar with rail load, *92 u*	19	28	___
16371	BN I-Beam Flatcar with load, *92 u*	24	29	___
16372	Southern I-Beam Flatcar with load, *92 u*	24	34	___
16373	Erie-Lackawanna Flatcar with stakes, *93*	19	23	___
16374	D&RGW Flatcar with trailer, *93*	25	28	___
16375	NYC Bulkhead Flatcar, *93-95*	21	25	___
16376	UP Flatcar with trailer, *93-95*	31	37	___
16378	Toys "R" Us Flatcar with trailer, *92-93 u*	60	95	___
16379	NP Bulkhead Flatcar with pulp load, *93*	16	23	___
16380	UP I-Beam Flatcar with load, *93*	20	26	___
16381	CSX I-Beam Flatcar with load, *93*	20	25	___
16382	Kansas City Southern Bulkhead Flatcar, *93*	14	18	___
16383	Conrail Flatcar with trailer, *93*	50	58	___
16384	Soo Line Gondola with cable reels, *93*	14	19	___
16385	Soo Line Ore Car, *93*	65	75	___
16386	SP Flatcar with lumber, *94*	15	19	___
16387	KCS Gondola with coil covers, *94*	13	16	___
16388	LV Gondola with canisters, *94*	16	20	___
16389	PRR Flatcar with wheel load, *94*	27	32	___
16390	Flatcar with water tank, *94*	24	27	___
16391	Lionel Lines Gondola, *93 u*		15	___
16392	Wabash Gondola with canisters (O27), *93 u, 94*	7	9	___
16393	Wisconsin Central Bulkhead Flatcar, *94*	13	19	___
16394	Vermont Central Bulkhead Flatcar, *94*	20	30	___
16395	CP Flatcar with rail load, *94*	18	23	___
16396	Alaska Bulkhead Flatcar, *94*	17	22	___
16397	Milwaukee Road I-Beam Flatcar with load, *94*	30	34	___
16398	C&O Flatcar with trailer, *94*	80	85	___
16399	Western Pacific I-Beam Flatcar with load, *94*	31	35	___
16400	PRR Hopper (O27), *88 u, 89*	15	18	___
16402	Southern Quad Hopper with coal (SSS), *87*	30	42	___
16406	CSX Quad Hopper with coal, *90*	29	34	___
16407	B&M Covered Quad Hopper (SSS), *91*	28	37	___
16408	UP Hopper "6408" (O27), *90-91 u*	17	21	___
16410	MKT Hopper (O27), *92, 93 u*	19	24	___
16411	L&N Quad Hopper with coal, *92*	28	32	___

			Esc	Mint
___	**16412**	C&NW Covered Quad Hopper, *94*	16	21
___	**16413**	Clinchfield Quad Hopper with coal, *94*	16	22
___	**16414**	CCC&StL Hopper (O27), *94*	18	25
___	**16416**	D&RGW Covered Quad Hopper, *95*	16	20
___	**16417**	Wabash Quad Hopper with coal, *95*	19	21
___	**16418**	C&NW Hopper with coal (O27), *95*	15	21
___	**16419**	Tennessee Central Hopper, *96*		17
___	**16420**	WM Quad Hopper with coal (SSS), *95*	30	34
___	**16421**	WM Quad Hopper with coal (SSS), *95*	30	33
___	**16422**	WM Quad Hopper with coal (SSS), *95*		33
___	**16423**	WM Quad Hopper with coal (SSS), *95*		30
___	**16424**	WM Covered Quad Hopper (SSS), *95*	34	39
___	**16425**	WM Covered Quad Hopper (SSS), *95*	25	29
___	**16426**	WM Covered Quad Hopper (SSS), *95*	24	27
___	**16427**	WM Covered Quad Hopper (SSS), *95*	27	30
___	**16429**	WM Quad Hopper with coal, set of *2*		70
___	**16430**	Georgia Power Quad Hopper "82947" with coal, *95 u*		109
___	**16431**	Lionel Corporation 2-bay Hopper "6456-1," *96*		30
___	**16432**	Lionel Corporation 2-bay Hopper "6456-2," *96*		64
___	**16433**	Lionel Corporation 2-bay Hopper "6456-3," *96*		18
___	**16434**	LV 2-bay Hopper "6456," "TLDX," *97*		25
___	**16435**	Virginian 2-bay Hopper "6456-1," *97*		30
___	**16436**	N&W 2-bay Hopper "6456-2," *97*		33
___	**16437**	C&O 2-bay Hopper "6456-3," *97*		33
___	**16438**	Frisco 4-bay Covered Hopper "87538," *98*		34
___	**16439**	Southern 4-bay Covered Hopper "77836," *98*		34
___	**16440**	Alaska 2-bay Hopper "7100," *98-99*		35
___	**16441**	New York Central 4-bay Hopper, *99*		26
___	**16442**	Bethlehem Gondola "6462" (SSS), *99*		40
___	**16443**	GN 2-bay Hopper "172364," *99-00*		20
___	**16444**	CNJ 2-bay Hopper "643," *00*		20
___	**16445**	Frisco 2-bay Hopper "93108," *00*		20
___	**16446**	Burlington 2-bay Hopper, *00*		20
___	**16447**	PRR Tuscan 2-bay Hopper, *00 u*		30
___	**16448**	PRR Gray 2-bay Hopper, *00 u*		30
___	**16449**	PRR Black 2-bay Hopper, *00 u*		30
___	**16450**	PRR Green 2-bay Hopper, *00 u*		30
___	**16451**	Lionel Mines 2-bay Hopper, *00 u*		50
___	**16453**	SP 2-bay Hopper "460604," *01*		15
___	**16454**	Bethlehem Steel Hopper "41025," *01*		37
___	**16455**	Pioneer Seed 2-bay Hopper, *00 u*		50
___	**16456**	B&O 2-bay Hopper, *01*		20
___	**16459**	LV 2-bay Hopper "51102," *01*		23
___	**16460**	Reading 2-bay Hopper "79636," *02*		25
___	**16463**	Rio Grande Icebreaker Tunnel Car "18936," *02*		32
___	**16464**	NYC Icebreaker Tunnel Car "X3200," *02*		32
___	**16465**	WP 2-bay Hopper "100340," *03*		19
___	**16466**	Pennsylvania Icebreaker Tunnel Car, *03*		33
___	**16467**	"Naughty and Nice" Hopper 2-pack, *02*		60
___	**16469**	B&O Hopper "435351," *02*		22
___	**16470**	"Naughty and Nice" Ore Car 2-pack, *03*		43
___	**16473**	Rock Island Ore Car "99122," *03*		18
___	**16474**	Alaska Ore Car "16474," *04*		21
___	**16475**	Santa Fe Hopper "16475," *04*		18

		Esc	Mint
16480	Lionelville Snow Transport Quad Hopper, *04*		45 ___
16482	Norfolk Southern Hopper, traditional, *05*		27 ___
16487	Alaska 2-bay Hopper, *05*		35 ___
16489	BNSF Ore Car, traditional, *05*		15 ___
16490	Sodor Mining Hopper, *05, 13*		35 ___
16491	CNJ Hopper "60714," *06*		30 ___
16492	C&NW Ore Car "114023," *06*		30 ___
16493	Christmas Ice Breaker Car, *06*		55 ___
16500	Rock Island Bobber Caboose, *87-88*	9	13 ___
16501	Lehigh Valley SP-type Caboose, *87*	19	24 ___
16503	NYC Transfer Caboose, *87*	16	22 ___
16504	Southern N5c Caboose (SSS), *87*	17	30 ___
16505	Wabash SP-type Caboose, *88-91*	10	15 ___
16506	Santa Fe Bay Window Caboose, *88*	18	28 ___
16507	Mopar Express SP-type Caboose, *87-88 u*	42	54 ___
16508	Lionel Lines SP-type Caboose "6508," *89 u*	13	17 ___
16509	D&RGW SP-type Caboose (SSS), *89*	19	24 ___
16510	New Haven Bay Window Caboose, *89*	25	30 ___
16511	PRR Bobber Caboose, *88 u, 89*	9	13 ___
16513	Union Pacific SP-type Caboose, *89*	14	21 ___
16515	Lionel Lines SP-type Caboose, RailScope, *89*	20	23 ___
16516	Lehigh Valley SP-type Caboose, *90*	15	26 ___
16517	Atlantic Coast Line Bay Window Caboose, *90*	21	26 ___
16518	Chessie System Bay Window Caboose, *90*	41	50 ___
16519	Rock Island Transfer Caboose, *90*	13	17 ___
16520	"Welcome to the Show" Circus SP-type Caboose, *89 u*	13	21 ___
16521	PRR SP-type Caboose, *90-91*	8	11 ___
16522	"Chills & Thrills" Circus N5c Caboose, *90-91*	10	15 ___
16523	Alaska SP-type Caboose, *91*	24	31 ___
16524	Anheuser-Busch SP-type Caboose, *89-92 u*	36	47 ___
16525	D&H Bay Window Caboose (SSS), *91*	30	39 ___
16526	Kansas City Southern SP-type Caboose, *91*	17	21 ___
16528	UP SP-type Caboose "6528," *90-91 u*	17	21 ___
16529	Santa Fe SP-type Caboose "16829," *91*	9	13 ___
16530	Mickey's World Tour SP-type Caboose "16830," *91, 92 u*	13	17 ___
16531	Texas & Pacific SP-type Caboose, *92*	18	23 ___
16533	C&NW Bay Window Caboose, *92*	22	30 ___
16534	Delaware & Hudson SP-type Caboose, *92*	14	19 ___
16535	Erie-Lackawanna Bay Window Caboose, *91 u*	42	50 ___
16536	Chessie System SP-type Caboose, *92, 93 u, 94, 95 u*		23 ___
16537	MKT SP-type Caboose, *92, 93 u*	17	21 ___
16538	L&N Bay Window Caboose "1041," *92 u*	29	33 ___
16539	WP Steelside Caboose "539," smoke, SSS (std O), *92*	50	55 ___
16541	Montana Rail Link Extended Vision Caboose "10131" with smoke, *93*	55	65 ___
16543	NYC SP-type Caboose, *93-95*		20 ___
16544	Union Pacific SP-type Caboose, *93-95*	22	26 ___
16546	Clinchfield SP-type Caboose, *93*	22	26 ___
16547	"Happy Holidays" SP-type Caboose, *93-95*	46	55 ___
16548	Conrail SP-type Caboose, *93*	15	20 ___
16549	Soo Line Work Caboose, *93*	18	26 ___
16550	U.S. Navy Searchlight Caboose, *94-95*	16	21 ___
16551	Budweiser SP-type Caboose, *93-94 u*	30	33 ___
16552	Frisco Searchlight Caboose, *94*	23	26 ___

			Esc	Mint
___	16553	United Auto Workers SP-type Caboose, *93 u*		40
___	16554	GT Extended Vision Caboose "79052," smoke, *94*	40	47
___	16555	C&O SP-type Caboose, *94*	22	26
___	16557	Ford SP-type Caboose, *94 u*	19	24
___	16558	Crayola SP-type Caboose, *94 u, 95*	17	21
___	16559	Seaboard Center Cupola Caboose "5658," *95*	23	24
___	16560	Chrysler Mopar Caboose, *94 u*	24	26
___	16561	UP Center Cupola Caboose "25766," *95*	27	31
___	16562	Reading Center Cupola Caboose, *95*	25	29
___	16563	Lionel Lines SP-type Caboose, *95*	22	26
___	16564	Western Maryland Center Cupola Caboose (SSS), *95*	30	34
___	16565	Milwaukee Road Bay Window Caboose, *95*	50	60
___	16566	U.S. Army SP-type Caboose "907," *95*		28
___	16568	ATSF SP-type Caboose, *96-99*		23
___	16571	Georgia Power SP-type Caboose "52789," *95 u*		68
___	16575	Sears Zenith SP-type Caboose, *95*		38
___	16577	U.S. Coast Guard Work Caboose, *96*		26
___	16578	Lionel Lines SP-type Caboose, *95 u*		20
___	16579	GM/AC Delco, SP-type Caboose, *95*		35
___	16580	SP-type Caboose, *96-99*		11
___	16581	UP Illuminated Caboose, *96*		30
___	16586	SP Illuminated Caboose "6357," *97*		42
___	16590	Dodge Motorsports SP-type Caboose "6950," *96*		58
___	16591	Little League Baseball SP-type Caboose "6397," *97*		45
___	16593	Lionel Belt Line Caboose "6257," *98*		32
___	16594	Caboose "6357," *98*		29
___	16600	Illinois Central Coal Dump Car, *88*	14	23
___	16601	Canadian National Searchlight Car, *88*	19	24
___	16602	Erie-Lackawanna Coal Dump Car, *87*	16	26
___	16603	Detroit Zoo Giraffe Car (O27), *87*	40	49
___	16604	NYC Log Dump Car, *87*	15	27
___	16605	Bronx Zoo Giraffe Car (O27), *88*	39	44
___	16606	Southern Searchlight Car, *87*	13	21
___	16607	Southern Coal Dump Car "16707" (SSS), *87*	18	26
___	16608	Lehigh Valley Searchlight Car, *87*	16	30
___	16609	Lehigh Valley Derrick Car, *87*	22	30
___	16610	Track Maintenance Car, *87-88*	15	25
___	16611	Santa Fe Log Dump Car, *88*	15	23
___	16612	Soo Line Log Dump Car, *89*	14	24
___	16613	MKT Coal Dump Car, *89*	17	26
___	16614	Reading Cop and Hobo Car (O27), *89*	24	25
___	16615	Lionel Lines Extension Searchlight Car, *89*	20	28
___	16616	D&RGW Searchlight Car (SSS), *89*	22	30
___	16617	C&NW Boxcar with ETD, *89*	23	34
___	16618	Santa Fe Track Maintenance Car, *89*	11	19
___	16619	Wabash Coal Dump Car, *90*	14	25
___	16620	C&O Track Maintenance Car, *90-91*	16	19
___	16621	Alaska Log Dump Car, *90*	24	31
___	16622	CSX Boxcar with ETD, *90-91*	20	28
___	16623	MKT DD Boxcar with ETD, *91*	16	23
___	16624	NH Cop and Hobo Car (O27), *90-91*	23	31
___	16625	NYC Extension Searchlight Car, *90*	22	30
___	16626	CSX Searchlight Car, *90*	18	26
___	16627	CSX Log Dump Car, *90*	19	23

		Esc	Mint	
16628	Cop and Hobo Circus Gondola, *90-91*	36	43	___
16629	Operating Circus Elephant Car (O27), *90-91*	38	50	___
16630	SP Operating Cowboy Car (O27), *90-91*	22	26	___
16631	RI Boxcar, steam RailSounds, *90*	110	130	___
16632	BN Boxcar, diesel RailSounds, *90*	90	100	___
16634	WM Coal Dump Car, *91*	26	32	___
16636	D&RGW Log Dump Car, *91*	19	25	___
16637	WP Extension Searchlight Car, *91*	27	30	___
16638	Operating Circus Animal Car (O27), *91*	50	55	___
16639	B&O Boxcar, steam RailSounds, *91*	100	120	___
16640	Rutland Boxcar, diesel RailSounds, *91*	100	120	___
16641	Toys "R" Us Giraffe Car (O27), *90-91 u*	48	68	___
16642	Mickey's World Tour Goofy Car (O27), *91, 92 u*	33	41	___
16644	Amtrak Crane Car, *91, 92 u*	36	42	___
16645	Amtrak Searchlight Caboose, *91*	27	30	___
16649	Railway Express Agency Boxcar, steam RailSounds, *92*	110	140	___
16650	NYC Pacemaker Boxcar, diesel RailSounds, *92*	100	135	___
16651	Operating Circus Clown Car (O27), *92*	24	30	___
16652	Radar Car, *92*	25	29	___
16653	Western Pacific Crane Car (SSS), *92*	44	60	___
16655	Steam Tender "1993," RailSounds, *93*	115	140	___
16656	Burlington Log Dump Car, *92 u*	18	25	___
16657	Lehigh Valley Coal Dump Car, *92 u*	22	29	___
16658	Erie-Lackawanna Crane Car, *93*	47	65	___
16659	Union Pacific Searchlight Car, *93-95*	15	18	___
16660	Fire Car with ladders, *93-94*	28	33	___
16661	Flatcar with boat, *93*	20	22	___
16662	Bugs Bunny and Yosemite Sam Outlaw Car (O27), *93-94*	28	30	___
16663	Missouri Pacific Searchlight Car, *93*	16	19	___
16664	L&N Coal Dump Car, *93*	22	25	___
16665	Maine Central Log Dump Car, *93*	23	27	___
16666	Toxic Waste Car, *93-94*	25	32	___
16667	Conrail Searchlight Car, *93*	27	30	___
16668	Ontario Northland Log Dump Car, *93*	20	24	___
16669	Soo Line Searchlight Car, *93*	17	21	___
16670	TV Car, *93-94*	12	22	___
16673	Lionel Lines Tender, whistle, *94-97*	33	42	___
16674	Pinkerton Animated Gondola, *94*	28	32	___
16675	Great Northern Log Dump Car, *94*	21	25	___
16676	Burlington Coal Dump Car, *94*	23	28	___
16677	NATO Flatcar with Royal Navy submarine, *94*	34	44	___
16678	Rock Island Searchlight Car, *94*	12	23	___
16679	U.S. Mail Operating Boxcar, *94*	45	50	___
16680	Cherry Picker Car, *94*	25	28	___
16681	Aquarium Car, *95*	35	44	___
16682	Lionelville Farms Operating Stock Car (O27), *94*	23	27	___
16683	Los Angeles Zoo Elephant Car (O27), *94*	22	26	___
16684	U.S. Navy Crane Car, *94-95*	35	40	___
16685	Erie Extension Searchlight Car, *95*	30	34	___
16686	Mickey Mouse Animated Boxcar, *95*	32	38	___
16687	U.S. Mail Operating Boxcar, *94*	29	37	___
16688	Fire Car with ladders, *94*	35	43	___
16689	Toxic Waste Car, *94*	29	32	___
16690	Bugs Bunny and Yosemite Sam Outlaw Car (O27), *94*	30	34	___

			Esc	Mint
MODERN 1970-2021				
___	**16701**	Southern Tool Car (SSS), *87*	43	55
___	**16702**	Amtrak Bunk Car, *91, 92 u*	25	27
___	**16703**	NYC Tool Car, *92*	24	31
___	**16704**	TV Car, *94*	27	29
___	**16705**	Chesapeake & Ohio Cop and Hobo Car, *95*	28	34
___	**16706**	Animal Transport Service Giraffe Car, *95*	27	30
___	**16708**	C&NW Track Maintenance Car, *95*	24	31
___	**16709**	New York Central Derrick Car, *95*	22	28
___	**16710**	U.S. Army Operating Missile Car, *95*	40	42
___	**16711**	Pennsylvania Searchlight Car, *95*	27	31
___	**16712**	Pinkerton Animated Gondola, *95*	34	39
___	**16715**	ATSF Log Dump Car, *96-99*		24
___	**16717**	Jersey Central Crane Car, *96*		41
___	**16718**	USMC Missile Launching Flatcar, *96*	26	31
___	**16719**	Exploding Boxcar, *96*		38
___	**16720**	Lionel Lines Searchlight Car "3650," *96-97*		50
___	**16724**	Mickey and Friends Submarine Car, *96*		39
___	**16725**	Rhino Transport Car, *97*		31
___	**16726**	U.S. Army Fire Ladder Car, *96*		43
___	**16734**	U.S. Coast Guard Searchlight Car, *96*		30
___	**16735**	U.S. Coast Guard Flatcar with radar, *96*	28	35
___	**16736**	U.S. Coast Guard Derrick Car, *96*		34
___	**16737**	Road Runner and Wile E. Coyote Gondola "3444," *96*		72
___	**16738**	Pepe LePew Boxcar "3370," *96*		40
___	**16739**	Foghorn Leghorn Poultry Car "6434," *96*		44
___	**16740**	Lionel Corporation Mail Car "3428," *96*		37
___	**16741**	Union Pacific Illuminated Bunk Car, *97*		25
___	**16742**	Trout Ranch Aquarium Car "3435," *96*		32
___	**16744**	Port of Lionel City Searchlight Car, *97*		30
___	**16745**	Port of Lionel City Flatcar with radar, *97*		30
___	**16746**	Port of Lionel City Derrick Car, *97*		30
___	**16747**	Breyer Animated Horse Car "6473," *97*		34
___	**16748**	U.S. Forest Service Log-Dump Car "3361," *97*		30
___	**16749**	Midget Mines Ore-Dump Car "3479," *97*		36
___	**16750**	Lionel City Aquarium Car "3436," *97*		32
___	**16751**	AIREX Sports Channel TV Car "3545," *97*		25
___	**16752**	Marvin the Martian Missile Launching Flatcar "6655," *97*	142	167
___	**16754**	Porky Pig and Instant Martians Flatcar "6805," *97*	137	185
___	**16755**	Daffy Duck Animated Balloon Car "3470," *97*	141	178
___	**16760**	Pluto and Cats Animated Gondola "3444," *97*		55
___	**16765**	Bureau of Land Management Log Car "3351," *98*		30
___	**16766**	Bureau of Land Management Ore Car "3479," *98*		31
___	**16767**	New York Central Ice Docks Ice Car "6352," *98*		47
___	**16776**	Holiday Boxcar, RailSounds, *98*		68
___	**16777**	Animated Cola Car and Platform, *98*		100
___	**16782**	Bethlehem Ore Dump Car "3479," *99*		95
___	**16783**	Westside Lumber Log Dump Car "3351," *99*		32
___	**16784**	Pratt's Hollow Seed Dump Car "3479," *99*		36
___	**16785**	"Happy Holidays" Music Reefer "5700," *99*		100
___	**16789**	Easter Operating Boxcar, *99*		39
___	**16790**	UP Stock Car "3356," Crowsounds, *99*		90
___	**16791**	New York City Lights Boxcar, *99*		44
___	**16792**	Constellation Boxcar "9600," *99*		37
___	**16793**	Animated Glow-in-the-Dark Alien Boxcar, *99*		44

		Esc	Mint
MODERN 1970-2021			
16794	Wicked Witch Halloween Boxcar, *99*		46 ___
16795	Elf Chasing Rudolph Gondola "6462," *99*		55 ___
16796	Snowman Loading Ice Car "6352," *99*		55 ___
16805	Budweiser Malt Nutrine Reefer "3285," *91-92 u*	82	109 ___
16806	Toys "R" Us Boxcar, *92 u*	21	26 ___
16807	H.J. Heinz Reefer "301," *93*	23	27 ___
16808	Toys "R" Us Boxcar, *93 u*	28	30 ___
16817	Ambassador 1-D Tank Car, *00 u*		178 ___
16818	Engineer Award Tank Car, *00 u*		715 ___
16819	JLC Award Tank Car, *00 u*		760 ___
16820	Ambassador Boxcar, *00 u*	322	533 ___
16822	CSX Water Tower, *08*		23 ___
16824	O36 Command Control Switch, left hand (FasTrack), *09-14*		110 ___
16825	O36 Command Control Switch, right hand (FasTrack), *09-14*		110 ___
16826	O72 Command Control Switch, left hand (FasTrack), *09-14*		120 ___
16827	O72 Command Control Switch, right hand (FasTrack), *09-14*		120 ___
16828	O60 Command Control Switch, left hand (FasTrack), *09-14*		120 ___
16829	O60 Command Control Switch, right hand (FasTrack), *09-14*		120 ___
16830	O48 Command Control Switch, left hand (FasTrack), *09-14*		120 ___
16831	O48 Command Control Switch, right hand (FasTrack), *09-14*		120 ___
16832	O72 Command Control Wye Switch (FasTrack), *09-14*		115 ___
16834	O48 Half-Curved Track (FasTrack), *09-14, 16, 18-20*		6 ___
16835	O48 Quarter-Curved Track (FasTrack), *09-14, 16, 18-20*		5 ___
16836	Christmas Girder Bridge, *09*		21 ___
16837	Christmas Operating Billboard, *09*		45 ___
16841	Halloween Gateman, *09*		80 ___
16842	Big Moe Crane, *10*		70 ___
16843	City and Western Diorama, *10-11*		15 ___
16845	Bookstore, *09-10*		60 ___
16846	Burning Hobo Depot, *09*		90 ___
16847	Legacy Hotel, *10-11*		70 ___
16848	Creature Comforts Pet Store, sound, *09-10*		80 ___
16849	Rotary Dumper with coal conveyor, *CC, 10*		600 ___
16850	Operating Wind Turbine, 3-pack, *09-11*		225 ___
16851	Sunoco Cylindrical Oil Tank, gray, *10-11*		100 ___
16852	Sunoco Cylindrical Oil Tank, yellow, *10-11*		90 ___
16853	Polar Express Diorama, *09-11, 13*		18 ___
16854	MTA LIRR Blinking Billboard, *09*		30 ___
16855	MTA LIRR Illuminated Station Platform, *09*		37 ___
16856	MTA LIRR Passenger Station, *09*		60 ___
16857	Thomas & Friends Diorama, *10-16, 20*		18 ___
16859	Grand Central Terminal, *09*		1500 ___
16861	50,000-gallon Water Tank, *09-11*		150 ___
16863	Santa's Christmas Wish Station, *09-11*		125 ___
16868	Straight O Gauge Tunnel, *09-17*		55 ___
16871	Winter Wonderland Diorama, *09-11*		15 ___
16872	Illuminated Christmas Station Platform, *09*		35 ___
16873	Bathtub Gondola Coal Load 3-pack, *10-19*		20 ___
16874	Coaling Station, *10-11*		80 ___
16880	Freight Platform, *10-12*		30 ___
16881	Barrel Shed, *10-11*		30 ___
16882	12" Covered Bridge, *10-18*		60 ___
16883	Neil's Guitar Shop, *10-11*		60 ___
16889	Coal Tipple Pack, *11-20*		15 ___

		Esc	Mint
___ **16891**	Tank Car Accident, *10-11*		130
___ **16896**	Flagpole with lights, *10-16*		28
___ **16897**	75th Anniversary Gateman, *10*		80
___ **16903**	CP Bulkhead Flatcar with pulp load (SSS), *94*	22	25
___ **16904**	NYC Pacemaker Flatcar Set with trailers, *94*	55	60
___ **16907**	Flatcar with farm tractors, *94*	27	33
___ **16908**	U.S. Navy Flatcar "04039" with submarine, *94-95*	39	46
___ **16909**	U.S. Navy Gondola "16556" with canisters, *94-95*	16	22
___ **16910**	Missouri Pacific Flatcar with trailer, *94*	22	27
___ **16911**	B&M Flatcar with trailer, *94*	28	34
___ **16912**	CN Maxi-Stack Flatcar Set with containers, *94*	70	75
___ **16915**	Lionel Lines Gondola (O27), *93-94 u*	7	10
___ **16916**	Ford Flatcar with trailer, *94 u*	38	45
___ **16917**	Crayola Gondola with crayons, *94 u, 95*	8	9
___ **16919**	Chrysler Mopar Gondola with coil covers, *94-96*	33	36
___ **16922**	Chesapeake & Ohio Flatcar with trailer, *95*	25	31
___ **16923**	Intermodal Service Flatcar with wheel chocks, *95*	15	22
___ **16924**	Lionel Corporation Flatcar "6424" with trailer, *96*		24
___ **16925**	New York Central Flatcar with trailer, *95*	65	85
___ **16926**	Frisco Flatcar with trailers, *95*	24	31
___ **16927**	New York Central Flatcar with gondola, *95*	17	22
___ **16928**	Soo Line Flatcar with dump bin (O27), *95*	12	15
___ **16929**	BC Rail Gondola with cable reels, *95*	21	25
___ **16930**	Santa Fe Flatcar with wheel load, *95*	20	25
___ **16932**	Erie Flatcar with rail load, *95*	17	22
___ **16933**	Lionel Lines Flatcar with autos, *95*	23	25
___ **16934**	Pennsylvania Flatcar with Ertl road grader, *95*	28	39
___ **16935**	UP Depressed Center Flatcar with Ertl bulldozer, *95*	22	35
___ **16936**	Sealand Maxi-Stack Flatcar Set with containers, *95*	70	85
___ **16939**	U.S. Navy Flatcar "04040" with boat, *95*	25	30
___ **16940**	ATSF Flatcar with trailer, *96-99*		40
___ **16941**	ATSF Flatcar with autos, *96-99*		25
___ **16943**	Jersey Central Gondola, *96*		18
___ **16944**	Georgia Power Depressed Center Flatcar "31438" with transformer, *95 u*		50
___ **16945**	Georgia Power Depressed Center Flatcar "31950" with cable reels, *95 u*		53
___ **16946**	C&O F9 Well Car "3840," *96*		31
___ **16951**	Southern I-Beam Flatcar "9823" with load, *97*		25
___ **16952**	U.S. Navy Flatcar with Ertl helicopter, *96*		25
___ **16953**	NYC Flatcar with Red Wing Shoes trailer, *95 u*	39	45
___ **16954**	NYC Flatcar "6424" with Ertl scraper, *96*		30
___ **16955**	ATSF Flatcar with Ertl Challenger, *96*		30
___ **16956**	Zenith Flatcar with trailer, *95 u*	50	141
___ **16957**	Depressed Center Flatcar "6461" with Ertl Case tractor, *96*		29
___ **16958**	Flatcar with Ertl New Holland loader, *96*		26
___ **16960**	U.S. Coast Guard Flatcar with boat, *96*		40
___ **16961**	GM/AC Delco Flatcar with trailer, *95*		73
___ **16963**	Lionel Corporation Flatcar "6411," *96-97*		34
___ **16964**	Lionel Corporation Gondola "6462," *97*		22
___ **16965**	Scout Flatcar "6424" with stakes, *96-97*		20
___ **16967**	Depressed Center Flatcar "6461" with transformer, *96*		21
___ **16968**	Depressed Center Flatcar "6461" with Ertl Helicopter, *96*		35
___ **16969**	Flatcar "6411" with Beechcraft Bonanza, *96*		33

MODERN 1970-2021		Esc	Mint	
16970	LA County Flatcar "6424" with motorized powerboat, *96*		20	___
16971	Port of Lionel City Flatcar with boat, *97*		35	___
16972	P&LE Gondola "6462," *97*		22	___
16975	Well Car Doublestack Set, *97*		75	___
16978	MILW Flatcar "6424" with P&H shovel, *97*		43	___
16980	Speedy Gonzales Missile Flatcar "6823," *97*	0	56	___
16982	BC Rail Bulkhead Flatcar "9823" with lumber, *97*		28	___
16983	PRR F9 Well Car "6983" with cable reels, *97*		39	___
16986	Sears Zenith Bulkhead Flatcar, *96 u*		45	___
16987	Musco Lighting Bulkhead Flatcar, *97 u*		35	___
16997	Lionel Lines Recovery Crane Car, *99*		50	___
17002	Conrail 2-bay ACF Hopper (std O), *87*	42	47	___
17003	Du Pont 2-bay ACF Hopper (std O), *90*	39	45	___
17004	MKT 2-bay ACF Hopper (std O), *91*	23	27	___
17005	Cargill 2-bay ACF Hopper (std O), *92*	29	37	___
17006	Soo Line 2-bay ACF Hopper (std O, SSS), *93*	31	36	___
17007	GN 2-bay ACF Hopper "173872" (std O), *94*	26	31	___
17008	D&RGW 2-bay ACF Hopper "10009" (std O), *95*		31	___
17009	New York Central 2-bay ACF Hopper, *96*		35	___
17010	Govt. of Canada ACF 2-bay Covered Hopper "7000," *98*		32	___
17010	NP PS-1 Boxcar 6-pack, LionScale, *17*		360	___
17011	NP ACF 2-bay Covered Hopper "75052," *98*		44	___
17012	Govt. of Canada ACF 2-bay Covered Hopper "7001," *98*		30	___
17013	NYC Graffiti 2-bay Covered Hopper "7000," *99*		55	___
17014	Graffiti 2-bay Covered Hopper "7000" (std O), *99*		45	___
17015	Corning 2-bay Hopper "90409" (std O), *01*		40	___
17016	C&NW 2-bay Hopper "96644" (std O), *01*		46	___
17017	Chessie System 2-bay Hopper "605527" (std O), *02*		32	___
17018	Nickel Plate Road Offset Hopper "33074," *02*		43	___
17019	Santa Fe Offset Hopper "78299," *02*		43	___
17020	Frisco Offset Hopper "92092," *02*		43	___
17020	UP PS-1 Boxcar 6-pack, LionScale, *17*		360	___
17021	NYC Offset Hopper "867999," *02*		43	___
17022	Burlington 2-bay ACF Hopper "183925" (std O), *03*		30	___
17023	BNSF 2-bay Hopper "409038" (std O), *04*		30	___
17024	Reading Offset Hopper "81089" (std O), *03-04*		43	___
17025	C&O Offset Hopper "300027" (std O), *03-04*		43	___
17026	D&H Offset Hopper "7215" (std O), *03-04*		41	___
17027	IC Offset Hopper "92142" (std O), *03-04*		49	___
17028	GE PS-2 2-bay Covered Hopper "326" (std O), *03-04*		35	___
17029	CNJ PS-2 2-bay Covered Hopper "803" (std O), *03-04*		35	___
17030	MILW PS-2 2-bay Covered Hopper "99708" (std O), *03-04*		35	___
17030	Reading PS-1 Boxcar 6-pack, LionScale, *17*		360	___
17031	SP PS-2 2-bay Covered Hopper "401306" (std O), *03-04*		38	___
17038	Clinchfield PS-2 Covered Hopper, *05*		70	___
17039	Boston & Maine PS-2 2-bay Covered Hopper, *05*		55	___
17040	Norfolk & Western PS-2 2-bay Covered Hopper, *05*		55	___
17040	NYC PS-1 Boxcar 6-pack, LionScale, *17*		360	___
17041	Great Northern Offset Hopper, *05*		60	___
17042	Green Bay & Western Offset Hopper, *05*		60	___
17043	Baltimore & Ohio Offset Hopper, *05*		60	___
17050	NYC 14-panel Hopper 6-pack, LionScale, *17*		330	___
17060	D&RGW 14-panel Hopper 6-pack, LionScale, *17*		330	___
17063	Santa Fe PS-2 2-bay Covered Hopper "82297" (std O), *06*		55	___

			Esc	Mint
____	**17064**	MKT PS-2 2-bay Covered Hopper "1311" (std-O), *06*		55
____	**17065**	Boraxo PS-2 2-bay Covered Hopper "31062" (std O), *06*		55
____	**17066**	PRR PS-2 2-bay Covered Hopper "256177" (std O), *06*		55
____	**17067**	Rock Island Offset Hopper "89500" with gravel (std O), *06*		65
____	**17068**	CNJ Offset Hopper "61261" (std O), *06*		65
____	**17069**	Maine Central Offset Hopper "3785" (std O), *06*		65
____	**17070**	P&LE Offset Hopper "4990" (std O), *06*		65
____	**17070**	Conrail 14-panel Hopper 6-pack, LionScale, *17*		330
____	**17080**	EL 14-panel Hopper 6-pack, LionScale, *17*		330
____	**17083**	C&O Offset Hopper "47386" (std O), *05*		40
____	**17090**	Trailer Train 50' Flatcar 6-pack, *17*		330
____	**17100**	Chessie System 3-bay ACF Hopper	49	85
____	**17100**	BN 50' Flatcar 6-pack, *17*		330
____	**17101**	Chessie System 3-bay ACF Hopper (std O), *88*	37	45
____	**17102**	Chessie System 3-bay ACF Hopper (std O), *88*	35	41
____	**17103**	Chessie System 3-bay ACF Hopper (std O), *88*	31	34
____	**17104**	Chessie System 3-bay ACF Hopper (std O), *88*	38	46
____	**17105**	Chessie System 3-bay ACF Hopper (std O), *88*	39	46
____	**17107**	Sinclair 3-bay ACF Hopper (std O), *89*	40	48
____	**17108**	Santa Fe 3-bay ACF Hopper (std O), *90*	42	48
____	**17109**	N&W 3-bay ACF Hopper (std O), *91*	24	31
____	**17110**	UP Hopper with coal (std O), *91*	24	30
____	**17110**	AT&SF 50' Flatcar 6-pack, *17*		330
____	**17111**	Reading Hopper with coal (std O), *91*	23	28
____	**17112**	Erie-Lack. 3-bay ACF Hopper (std O), *92*	24	34
____	**17113**	LV Hopper with coal (std O), *92-93*	25	32
____	**17114**	Peabody Hopper with coal (std O), *92-93*	26	30
____	**17118**	Archer Daniels Midland 3-bay ACF Hopper "60029" (std O), *93*	28	35
____	**17120**	CSX Hopper "295110" with coal (std O), *94*	28	30
____	**17120**	PRR 50' Flatcar 6-pack, *17*		330
____	**17121**	ICG Hopper "72867" with coal (std O), *94*	26	33
____	**17122**	RI 3-bay ACF Hopper "800200" (std O), *94*	32	39
____	**17123**	Cargill Covered Grain Hopper "844304" (std O), *95*	25	34
____	**17124**	Archer Daniels Midland 3-bay ACF Hopper "50224" (std O), *95*	24	30
____	**17127**	Delaware & Hudson 3-bay Hopper, *96*		34
____	**17128**	Chesapeake & Ohio 3-bay Hopper, *96*		30
____	**17129**	WM 3-bay Hopper "9300" with coal (std O), *97*		34
____	**17130**	ACFX ACF 4-bay Covered Hopper 6-pack, LionScale, *17*		360
____	**17132**	PRR 3-bay ACF Hopper "260815," *98*		40
____	**17133**	BNSF ACF 3-bay Covered Hopper "403698," *98*		38
____	**17134**	BNSF 3-bay Covered Hopper "403698" (std O), *01*		38
____	**17135**	BNSF ACF 3-bay Covered Hopper with ETD, *98*		39
____	**17137**	Cargill 3-bay Covered Hopper "1219" (std O), *99*		45
____	**17138**	Farmers Elevator 3-bay Covered Hopper (std O), *99*		45
____	**17139**	"Grain Train" 3-bay Hopper "BLMR 1025," *99-00*		39
____	**17140**	Virginian 3-bay Hopper 6-pack, "5260-5265," *99*		230
____	**17140**	GN ACF 4-bay Covered Hopper 6-pack, LionScale, *17*		360
____	**17147**	C&O 3-bay Hopper 6-pack, "156330-156335," *99*		230
____	**17150**	AT&SF ACF 4-bay Covered Hopper 6-pack, LionScale, *17*		360
____	**17154**	Alberta Cylindrical Hopper "628373" (std O), *01*		40
____	**17155**	Shell Cylindrical Hopper "3527" (std O), *01*		40
____	**17156**	ACF Pressureaide 3-bay Hopper "59267" (std O), *01*		27
____	**17157**	Wonder Bread "56670" 3-bay Hopper (std O), *01*		45
____	**17158**	Conrail Coal Hopper "487739" (std O), *01*		42

MODERN 1970-2021		Esc	Mint
17159	N&W Coal Hopper "1776" (std O), *01*		45 ___
17160	C&NW (UP) B145ACF 4-bay Covered Hopper 6-pack, LionScale, *17*		360 ___
17163	C&O 3-bay Hopper (std O), *01*		30 ___
17170	General Mills 3-bay Covered Hopper (std O), *00 u*		60 ___
17170	PFE 57' Mechanical Reefer, *17*		390 ___
17171	Lionel Lion Cylindrical Hopper (std O), *01*		45 ___
17172	CP Rail Cylindrical Hopper "385206" (std O), *02*		37 ___
17173	Govt. of Canada Cylindrical Hopper "111031" (std O), *02*		33 ___
17174	GN 3-bay Hopper "171250" (std O), *02*		29 ___
17175	IC PS-2CD 4427 Covered Hopper "57031" (std O), *02*		40 ___
17176	Cargill PS-2CD 4427 Covered Hopper "2514" (std O), *02*		46 ___
17177	PS-2CD 4427 Covered Hopper "2500" (std O), *02*		40 ___
17178	Santa Fe PS-2CD 4427 Covered Hopper "304774" (std O), *02*		40 ___
17179	Indianapolis Power & Light Coal Hopper "10074" (std O), *02*		40 ___
17180	Rock Island Coal Hopper "700665" (std O), *02*		40 ___
17180	SPFE 57' Mechanical Reefer 6-pack, LionScale, *17*		390 ___
17181	NYC 4-bay ACF Centerflow Hopper "892138" (std O), *03*		45 ___
17182	Sigco Hybrids 4-bay ACF Centerflow Hopper "1100" (std O), *03*		46 ___
17183	C&O Hopper "156341" (std O), *01*		30 ___
17184	Virginian Hopper "5271" (std O), *01*		30 ___
17185	LLCX Bathtub Gondola "877900" (std O), *01*		36 ___
17186	Cannonaide 4-bay ACF Centerflow Hopper "96169" (std O), *03*		40 ___
17187	Rio Grande 4-bay ACF Centerflow Hopper "15521" (std O), *03*		40 ___
17188	Govt. of Canada 3-bay Cylindrical Hopper (std O), *03*		48 ___
17189	Saskatchewan Grain 3-bay Cylindrical Hopper (std O), *03*		48 ___
17190	Soo/CP 3-bay ACF Hopper "119303" (std O), *03*		37 ___
17190	UPFE 57' Mechanical Reefer 6-pack, LionScale, *17*		390 ___
17191	BN PS-2CD 4427 Hopper "450669" (std O), *03-04*		45 ___
17192	Lehigh Valley PS-2CD 4427 Hopper "51118" (std O), *03-04*		40 ___
17193	Chessie System/WM PS-2CD 4427 Hopper "4673" (std O), *03-04*		30 ___
17194	MKT PS-2CD 4427 Hopper "1122" (std O), *03-04*		40 ___
17195	L&N 3-bay Hopper "240850" (std O), *04*		40 ___
17196	Firestone 4-bay Hopper "53240" (std O), *04*		40 ___
17197	Diamond Chemicals 4-bay Hopper "53286" (std O), *04*		40 ___
17198	Hercules 4-bay Hopper "50503" (std O), *04*		40 ___
17199	Conrail 4-bay Hopper "888367" (std O), *04*		46 ___
17200	Canadian Pacific Boxcar (std O), *89*	26	32 ___
17200	BNFE 57' Mechanical Reefer 6-pack, LionScale, *17*		390 ___
17201	Conrail Boxcar (std O), *87*	33	38 ___
17202	Santa Fe Boxcar (std O), diesel RailSounds, *90*	80	85 ___
17203	Cotton Belt DD Boxcar (std O), *91*	33	38 ___
17204	Missouri Pacific DD Boxcar (std O), *91*	27	30 ___
17207	C&IM DD Boxcar (std O), *92*	36	42 ___
17208	Union Pacific DD Boxcar (std O), *92*	35	40 ___
17209	B&O DD Boxcar "296000" (std O), *93*	37	43 ___
17210	Chicago & Illinois Midland Boxcar "16021" (std O), *92 u*	30	39 ___
17210	BN 100-Ton, 4-Bay Hopper 6-pack, *17*		330 ___
17211	Chicago & Illinois Midland Boxcar "16022" (std O), *92 u*	30	39 ___
17212	Chicago & Illinois Midland Boxcar "16023" (std O), *92 u*	24	31 ___
17213	Susquehanna Boxcar "501" (std O), *93*	28	31 ___
17214	Railbox Boxcar (std O), diesel RailSounds, *93*	75	85 ___
17216	PRR DD Boxcar "60155" (std O), *94*	34	38 ___
17217	New Haven State of Maine Boxcar "45003" (std O), *95*	28	35 ___
17218	BAR State of Maine Boxcar "2184" (std O), *95*	23	36 ___

| --- | --- | --- | --- |
____	**17219** Tazmanian Devil 40th Birthday Boxcar (std O), *95*	40	50
____	**17220** Pennsylvania Boxcar (std O), *96*		23
____	**17220** CSX 100-Ton, 4-Bay Hopper 6-pack, *17*		330
____	**17221** NYC Boxcar (std O), *96*		34
____	**17222** Western Pacific Boxcar (std O), *96*	28	34
____	**17223** Milwaukee Road DD Boxcar (std O), *96*		34
____	**17224** Central of Georgia Boxcar "9464-197" (std O), *97*	15	29
____	**17225** Penn Central Boxcar "9464-297" (std O), *97*	13	26
____	**17226** Milwaukee Road Boxcar "9464-397" (std O), *97*		23
____	**17227** UP DD Boxcar "9200" (std O), *97*		35
____	**17230** NS 100-Ton, 4-Bay Hopper 6-pack, *17*		330
____	**17231** Wisconsin Central DD Boxcar "9200" with auto frames, *98*		40
____	**17232** SP/UP Merger DD Boxcar "9200," *98*		33
____	**17233** Western Pacific Boxcar "9464-198," *98*		27
____	**17234** Port Huron & Detroit Boxcar "9464-298," *98*		33
____	**17235** Boston & Maine Boxcar "9464-398," *98*		41
____	**17239** ATSF "Texas Chief" Boxcar "9464-1," *97*		50
____	**17240** ATSF "Super Chief" Boxcar "9464-2," *97*		50
____	**17240** UP 100-Ton, 4-Bay Hopper 6-pack, *17*		330
____	**17241** ATSF" El Capitan" Boxcar "9464-3," *97*		50
____	**17242** ATSF "Grand Canyon" Boxcar "9464-4," *97*		60
____	**17243** NP Boxcar "8722," *98*		48
____	**17244** Santa Fe "Chief" Boxcar, *98*		37
____	**17245** C&O Boxcar with Chessie kitten, *98*		44
____	**17246** NYC Pacemaker Rolling Stock 4-pack, *98*		200
____	**17247** NYC 9464 Boxcar "174940," *98*		135
____	**17248** NYC 9464 Boxcar "174945," *98*		115
____	**17249** NYC 9464 Boxcar "174949," *98*		60
____	**17250** UP Boxcar "507406" (std O), *99*		45
____	**17250** AT&SF Stockcar 6-pack, *17*		360
____	**17251** BNSF Boxcar "103277," *99*		41
____	**17252** NS Boxcar "564824" (std O), *99*		41
____	**17253** CSX Boxcar "141756" (std O), *99*		35
____	**17254** UP Boxcar "551967" (std O), *99*		42
____	**17255** Chevy DD Boxcar "9200" (std O), *99*		38
____	**17257** Atlantic Coast Line Boxcar "28809" (std O), *99*		36
____	**17258** D&H 9464 Boxcar "29055" std O, *99*		41
____	**17259** MKT 9464 Boxcar "1422" (std O), *99*		34
____	**17260** CP Rail 9464 Boxcar "286138" (std O), silver, *00*		45
____	**17260** PRR Stockcar 6-pack, *17*		360
____	**17261** CP Rail 9464 Boxcar "85154," green, *00*		44
____	**17262** CP Rail 9464 Boxcar "56776," red (std O), *00*		48
____	**17263** NYC Boxcar "45725" (std O), *00*		46
____	**17264** C&O Boxcar "6054" (std O), *00*		44
____	**17265** U.S. Army Boxcar (std O), *00*		35
____	**17266** Monon Boxcar "911" (std O), *00*		45
____	**17268** C&O 9464 Boxcar "12700" (std O), *01*		44
____	**17269** Western Maryland 9464 Boxcar "29140" (std O), *01*		44
____	**17270** B&O Time-Saver 9464 Boxcar "467439" (std O), *01*		42
____	**17270** Nickel Plate Road Stockcar 6-pack, *17*		360
____	**17271** "The Rock" Boxcar "300324" (std O), *01*		37
____	**17272** Railbox Boxcar "15150" (std O), *01*		27
____	**17273** DT&I DD Boxcar "26852" (std O), *01*		44
____	**17274** Soo Line DD Boxcar "177587" (std O), *01*		42

		Esc	Mint
17275	NYC PS-1 Boxcar "175008" (std O), *02*		43 ___
17276	Cotton Belt PS-1 Boxcar "75000" (std O), *02*		44 ___
17277	Rio Grande PS-1 Boxcar "69676" (std O), *02*		40 ___
17278	WP PS-1 Boxcar "1953" (std O), *02*		44 ___
17279	Ontario Northland Boxcar "7428" (std O), *02*		40 ___
17280	Santa Fe Boxcar "600194" with auto frames (std O), *02*		45 ___
17280	UP Stockcar 6-pack, *17*		360 ___
17281	PRR DD Boxcar "83158" (std O), *04*		42 ___
17282	UP DD Boxcar "160300" (std O), *04*		42 ___
17283	GM&O DD Boxcar "9077" (std O), *04*		41 ___
17284	Erie DD Boxcar "66000" (std O), *04*		41 ___
17285	CSX Big Blue Boxcar "151296" (std O), *03*		36 ___
17287	BAR Boxcar "5976" (std O), *03*		35 ___
17288	NYC PS-1 Boxcar "175012" (std O), *03-04*		38 ___
17289	GN PS-1 Boxcar "18485" (std O), *03*		40 ___
17290	Seaboard PS-1 Boxcar "24452" (std O), *03-04*		42 ___
17290	Portland Terminal Wood-chip Hopper 6-pack, *17*		360 ___
17291	RI PS-1 Boxcar "21110" (std O), *03-04*		42 ___
17292	B&M PS-1 Boxcar "76182" (std O), *04*		34 ___
17293	IC PS-1 Boxcar "400666" (std O), *04*		40 ___
17294	TP&W PS-1 Boxcar "5036" (std O), *04*		36 ___
17295	Santa Fe PS-1 Boxcar "276749" (std O), *04*		40 ___
17297	UP PS-1 Boxcar, *03*		100 ___
17300	Canadian Pacific Reefer (std O), *89*	28	33 ___
17300	Chessie System Wood-chip Hopper 6-pack, *17*		360 ___
17301	Conrail Reefer (std O), *87*	35	42 ___
17302	Santa Fe Reefer with ETD (std O), *90*	35	41 ___
17303	C&O Reefer "7890" (std O), *93*	23	30 ___
17304	Wabash Reefer "26269" (std O), *94*	29	37 ___
17305	Pacific Fruit Express Reefer "459400" (std O), *94*	27	40 ___
17306	Pacific Fruit Express Reefer "459401" (std O), *94*	19	27 ___
17307	Tropicana Reefer "300" (std O), *95*	44	65 ___
17308	Tropicana Reefer "301" (std O), *95*	22	35 ___
17309	Tropicana Reefer "302" (std O), *95*	21	29 ___
17310	Tropicana Reefer "303" (std O), *95*	20	27 ___
17310	GM&O Wood-chip Hopper 6-pack, *17*		360 ___
17311	REA Reefer (std O), *96*	28	30 ___
17314	PFE Reefer "9800-198," *98*		42 ___
17315	PFE Reefer "9800-298," *98*		39 ___
17316	NP Reefer "98583," *98*		50 ___
17317	PRR Reefer FGE "91904," *98*		36 ___
17318	UP Reefer "170650" (std O), *99*		47 ___
17319	PFE Reefer 6-pack (std O), *01*		300 ___
17320	WM Wood-chip Hopper 6-pack, *17*		360 ___
17331	Hood's General American Milk Car "802" (std O), *02*		100 ___
17332	Pfaudler General American Milk Car "501" (std O), *02*		70 ___
17334	REA General American Milk Car "1741" (std O), *02*		100 ___
17335	New Haven General American Milk Car "102" (std O), *02*		75 ___
17336	PFE Steel-sided Reefer "17760" (std O), *03*		45 ___
17337	CN Steel-sided Reefer "209712" (std O), *03*		38 ___
17338	Merchants Dispatch Transit Steel-sided Reefer "12322" (std O), *03*		39 ___
17339	Burlington Steel-sided Reefer "74825" (std O), *03*		45 ___
17340	White Bros. General American Milk Car "891" (std O), *03*		44 ___
17341	Dairymen's League General American Milk Car "779" (std O), *03*		43 ___

MODERN 1970-2021		Esc	Mint
17342	Miller Beer Steel-sided Reefer (std O), *03 u*	0	63
17343	Miller Beer Steel-sided Reefer (std O), *03 u*		64
17349	NYC General American Milk Car "6581" (std O), *03 u*		42
17350	Hood's General American Milk Car "503" (std O), *03 u*		45
17351	Santa Fe Steel-sided Reefer "3526" (std O), *04*		43
17352	PFE Steel-sided Reefer "20043" (std O), *04*		41
17353	Needham Packing Steel-sided Reefer "60507" (std O), *04*		44
17354	Swift Steel-sided Reefer "15392" (std O), *04*		42
17355	Hood's Steel-sided Reefer "550" (std O), *04*		40
17356	Nestle Nesquik Steel-sided Reefer (std O), *04*		44
17357	Borden's Steel-sided Reefer "522" (std O), *04*		47
17358	Fairfield Farms Steel-sided Reefer (std O), *04*		44
17360	Hood's General American Milk Car "810" (std O), *03*		46
17361	Hood's General American Milk Car "811" (std O), *03*		43
17362	Pfaudler General American Milk Car "502" (std O), *03*		47
17363	Pfaudler General American Milk Car "503" (std O), *03*		40
17364	REA General American Milk Car "1742" (std O), *03*		38
17365	REA General American Milk Car "1743" (std O), *03*		44
17366	NH General American Milk Car "103" (std O), *03*		43
17367	NH General American Milk Car "104" (std O), *03*		47
17368	White Brothers General American Milk Car "892" (std O), *03*		43
17369	White Brothers General American Milk Car "893" (std O), *03*		47
17370	Dairymen's League General American Milk Car "780" (std O), *03*		47
17371	Dairymen's League Milk Car "781" (std O), *03*		47
17372	NYC General American Milk Car "6582" (std O), *03*		47
17373	NYC General American Milk Car "6583" (std O), *03*		40
17374	Hood's General American Milk Car "504" (std O), *03*		43
17375	Hood's General American Milk Car "505" (std O), *03*		47
17377	Railway Express Operating Milk Car "302" (std O), *05*		172
17378	Supplee General American Milk Car (std O), *05*		63
17379	NP Steel-sided Reefer "91353" (std O), *05*		60
17380	PFE Silver Steel-sided Reefer "45698" (std O), *05*		60
17381	North Western Steel-sided Reefer "751" (std O), *05*		40
17397	PFE Steel-sided Reefer "47767" (std O), *05*		45
17398	A&P General American Milk Car "737" (std O), *06*		65
17399	Bowman Dairy General American Milk Car "117" (std O), *06*		65
17400	CP Rail Gondola with coal (std O), *89*	30	34
17401	Conrail Gondola with coal (std O), *87*	24	26
17402	Santa Fe Gondola with coal (std O), *90*	19	25
17403	Chessie System Gondola "371629" with coil covers (std O), *93*	18	25
17404	ICG Gondola "245998" with coil covers (std O), *93*	26	32
17405	Reading Gondola "24876" with coil covers (std O), *94*	27	31
17406	PRR Gondola "385405" with coil covers (std O), *95*	37	42
17407	NKP Gondola with scrap load		24
17408	Cotton Belt Gondola "9820" with scrap load (std O), *97*		32
17410	UP Gondola "903004" with scrap load (std O), *99*		30
17412	Gondola, blue, online store, *98*		20
17413	Service Center Gondola with parts load (SSS), *00*		24
17414	Nickel Plate PS-5 Gondola "44801" (std O), *01-02*		40
17415	Frisco PS-5 Gondola "61878" (std O), *01-02*		35
17416	D&H Gondola "14011" with scrap load (std O), *01*		33
17417	BN Rotary Bathtub Gondola 3-pack, *01*		140
17421	CSX Rotary Bathtub Gondola 3-pack, *01*		135

	MODERN 1970-2021	Esc	Mint	
17425	Western Maryland PS-5 Gondola "354903" (std O), *01-02*		36	___
17426	Maine Central PS-5 Gondola "1116" (std O), *01-02*		40	___
17427	CSX Rotary Bathtub Gondola Add-on Unit (std O), *02*		47	___
17428	BN Rotary Bathtub Gondola Add-on Unit (std O), *02*		42	___
17429	Conrail Rotary Bathtub Gondola 3-pack (std O), *02-03*		115	___
17433	BNSF Rotary Bathtub Gondola 3-pack (std O), *02-03*		145	___
17439	UP PS-5 Gondola "229606" (std O), *03*		35	___
17440	Algoma Central PS-5 Gondola "801" (std O), *03*		32	___
17441	Conrail Rotary Bathtub Gondola "507673" (std O), *03*		39	___
17442	BNSF Rotary Bathtub Gondola "668330" (std O), *03*		46	___
17443	NS Rotary Bathtub Gondola 3-pack (std O), *03*		90	___
17447	UP Rotary Bathtub Gondola 3-pack (std O), *03*		100	___
17457	GN PS-5 Gondola "72839" (std O), *03*		35	___
17458	Reading PS-5 Gondola "33267" (std O), *03*		35	___
17459	CP Rail PS-5 Gondola "338966" (std O), *04*		35	___
17460	NYC PS-5 Gondola "749592" (std O), *04*		40	___
17461	Pennsylvania PS-5 Gondola "374256" (std O), *04*		36	___
17462	Santa Fe PS-5 Gondola "167340" (std O), *04*		35	___
17463	NS Bathtub Gondola "10303" (std O), *04*		40	___
17464	UP Bathtub Gondola "28100" (std O), *04*		35	___
17465	CP Rail Bathtub Gondola 3-pack (std O), *04*		105	___
17470	CP Rail Bathtub Gondola, *05*		50	___
17471	Burlington PS-5 Gondola with covers (std O), *05*		44	___
17472	New Haven PS-5 Gondola with covers (std O), *05*		53	___
17473	NYC PS-5 Gondola "502351" (std O), *06-07*		65	___
17474	D&H PS-5 Gondola "13816" (std O), *06-07*		65	___
17475	Koppers PS-5 Gondola "213" (std O), *06-07*		65	___
17477	L&N PS-5 Gondola "170012" (std O), *06-07*		46	___
17478	N&W PS-5 Gondola "275005" with containers (std O), *08*		70	___
17479	LV PS-5 Gondola "33455" with containers (std O), *08*		70	___
17480	RI PS-5 Gondola with coke containers (std O), *08-09*		70	___
17488	UP Bathtub Gondola 3-pack (std O), *09*		190	___
17500	CP Flatcar with logs (std O), *89*	17	29	___
17501	Conrail Flatcar with stakes (std O), *87*	37	45	___
17502	Santa Fe Flatcar with trailer (std O), *90*	70	75	___
17503	NS Flatcar with trailer (std O), *92*	55	65	___
17504	NS Flatcar with trailer (std O), *92*	55	65	___
17505	NS Flatcar with trailer (std O), *92*	50	55	___
17506	NS Flatcar with trailer (std O), *92*	46	55	___
17507	NS Flatcar with trailer (std O), *92*	50	55	___
17510	NP Flatcar "61200" with logs (std O), *94*	31	36	___
17511	WM Flatcar with logs, set of 3 (std O), *95*		145	___
17512	WM Flatcar with logs (std O), *95*	35	41	___
17513	WM Flatcar with logs (std O), *95*	43	50	___
17514	WM Flatcar with logs (std O), *95*	39	45	___
17515	Norfolk Southern Flatcar with tractors (std O), *95*	24	42	___
17516	T&P Flatcar "9823" with 2 Beechcraft Bonanzas (std O), *97*		50	___
17517	WP Flatcar "9823" with Ertl Caterpillar frontloader (std O), *97*		39	___
17518	PRR Flatcar "9823" with 2 Corgi Mack trucks (std O), *97*	29	50	___
17522	Flatcar with Plymouth Prowler, *98*		41	___
17527	Flatcar with 2 Dodge Vipers, *98*		38	___
17529	ATSF Flatcar "90010" with Ford milk truck, *99*		55	___
17533	MTTX Ford Flatcar with auto frames, *99*		38	___

			Esc	Mint
	MODERN 1970-2021			
___	**17534** Diamond T Flatcar with Mack trucks "9823," *99*			55
___	**17536** Route 66 Flatcar "9823-3" with 2 luxury coupes, *99*			37
___	**17537** Route 66 Flatcar "9823-4" with 2 touring coupes, *99*			32
___	**17538** NYC Flatcar with Ford tow truck, *99*			43
___	**17539** Flatcar "9823" with 2 Corvettes (std O), *99*			70
___	**17540** Flatcar "9823" with 2 Corvettes (std O), *99*			70
___	**17546** LL Recovery Flatcar "6424" with rail load, *99*			50
___	**17547** Lionel Lines Recovery Flatcar "6429" with machinery, *99*			50
___	**17548** Route 66 Flatcar "9823-6" with 2 luxury coupes, *99*			42
___	**17549** Route 66 Flatcar "9823-5" with station wagon and trailer, *99*			42
___	**17550** BN Center Beam Flatcar "6216" with lumber (std O), *99*			39
___	**17551** NYC Flatcar with NYC pickups "499," *99*			49
___	**17553** Trailer Train Flatcar "98102" with combine (std O), *99*			125
___	**17554** GN Flatcar "61042" with logs, *00*			32
___	**17555** Ford Mustang Flatcar with 2 cars (std O), *01*			NRS
___	**17556** Ford Mustang Flatcar with 2 cars (std O), *01*			NRS
___	**17557** Route 66 Flatcar "9823-7" with black sedans, *99-00*			39
___	**17558** Route 66 Flatcar "9823-8" with brown sedans, *99*			39
___	**17559** Route 66 Flatcar "9823-9" with 2 wagons (std O), *01*			40
___	**17560** Route 66 Flatcar "9823-10" with 2 sedans (std O), *01*			40
___	**17563** Santa Fe Flatcar "90011" with pickup trucks (std O), *01*			49
___	**17564** West Side Lumber Shay Log Car 3-pack #2 (std O), *01*			95
___	**17568** PRR Flatcar "470333" with pickup trucks (std O), *02*			50
___	**17571** UP Flatcar "909231" with pickup trucks (std O), *03*			50
___	**17572** Pioneer Seed Flatcar with pedal cars, *02 u*			220
___	**17573** WM PS-4 Flatcar "2631" (std O), *03*			35
___	**17574** Santa Fe PS-4 Flatcar "90081" (std O), *03*			35
___	**17575** NYC PS-4 Flatcar "506098" (std O), *03*			40
___	**17576** Ontario Northland PS-4 Flatcar "2020" (std O), *03*			35
___	**17577** B&O PS-4 Flatcar "8651" (std O), *04*			35
___	**17578** B&M PS-4 Flatcar "34007" (std O), *04*			35
___	**17579** Milwaukee Road PS-4 Flatcar "64073" (std O), *04*			35
___	**17580** UP PS-4 Flatcar "54603" (std O), *04*			35
___	**17581** GN Flatcar "X4168" with pickup trucks (std O), *04*			42
___	**17582** PRR PS-4 Flatcar "469617" with trailers (std O), *05*			110
___	**17583** GN PS-4 Flatcar with trailers, *05*			80
___	**17584** SP PS-4 Flatcar with trailers, *05*			80
___	**17585** C&O PS-4 Flatcar "81000" with trailers (std O), *05*			80
___	**17586** BN Husky Stack Car "63322" (std O), *05*			80
___	**17587** SP Husky Stack Car "513915" (std O), *05*			80
___	**17588** CSX Husky Stack Car "620350" (std O), *05*			80
___	**17589** TTX Trailer Train Husky Stack Car "456249" (std O), *05*			65
___	**17600** NYC Wood-sided Caboose (std O), *87 u*		35	45
___	**17601** Southern Wood-sided Caboose (std O), *88*		35	44
___	**17602** Conrail Wood-sided Caboose (std O), *87*		65	75
___	**17603** RI Wood-sided Caboose (std O), *88*		19	34
___	**17604** Lackawanna Wood-sided Caboose (std O), *88*		42	53
___	**17605** Reading Wood-sided Caboose (std O), *89*		34	37
___	**17606** NYC Steel-sided Caboose, smoke (std O), *90*		49	65
___	**17607** Reading Steel-sided Caboose, smoke (std O), *90*		55	65
___	**17608** C&O Steel-sided Caboose, smoke (std O), *91*		46	55
___	**17610** Wabash Steel-sided Caboose, smoke (std O), *91*		39	55
___	**17611** NYC Wood-sided Caboose "6003" (std O), *90 u*		40	55
___	**17612** NKP Steel-sided Caboose, smoke (FF 6), *92*		60	65

MODERN 1970-2021	Esc	Mint
17613 Southern Steel-sided Caboose "7613," smoke (std O), *92*	60	65 ___
17615 NP Wood-sided Caboose, smoke (std O), *92*	65	70 ___
17617 D&RGW Steel-sided Caboose (std O), *95*	50	55 ___
17618 Frisco Wood-sided Caboose (std O), *95*	65	75 ___
17620 NP Wood-sided Caboose "1746," *98*		70 ___
17623 Farmrail Extended Vision Caboose, *99*		74 ___
17624 Conrail Extended Vision Caboose "6900," *99*		43 ___
17625 Burlington Northern Steel-sided Caboose "7606," *99*		65 ___
17626 Service Center Extended Vision Caboose (SSS), *00*		29 ___
17627 C&O Extended Vision Caboose, *01*		65 ___
17628 BNSF Extended Vision Caboose, *01*		65 ___
17629 Santa Fe Extended Vision Caboose, *01*		80 ___
17630 UP Extended Vision Caboose, *01*		85 ___
17631 Virginian Bay Window Caboose, *01*		85 ___
17632 CSX Bay Window Caboose, *01*		75 ___
17633 NYC Bay Window Caboose, *01*		90 ___
17634 Delaware & Hudson Bay Window Caboose, *01*		75 ___
17635 100th Anniversary Die-cast Gold Caboose, *00*		345 ___
17636 NYC Die-cast Caboose "18096," *00-01*		100 ___
17637 NYC "Quicker via Peoria" Die-cast Caboose, *00*		135 ___
17638 RI Extended Vision Caboose "17011" (std O), *02*		55 ___
17639 Chessie Extended Vision Caboose "3322" (std O), *02*		55 ___
17640 CP Extended Vision Caboose "434604" (std O), *02*		57 ___
17641 Soo Line Extended Vision Caboose "2" (std O), *02*		55 ___
17642 Conrail Bay Window Caboose "21023" (std O), *02*		65 ___
17643 NKP Bay Window Caboose "480" (std O), *02*		60 ___
17644 Erie Bay Window Caboose "C307," *(std O), 02*		55 ___
17645 N&W Bay Window Caboose "C-6," *(std O), 02*		55 ___
17646 UP Bay Window Caboose "24555," *(std O), 02*		65 ___
17647 B&O Caboose "C-2820" (std O), *03-04*		65 ___
17648 Chessie System Caboose "C-2800" (std O), *03-04*		75 ___
17649 Lionel Lines Caboose "7649" (std O), *03-04*		65 ___
17650 Rio Grande Extended Vision Caboose "01500" (std O), *03*		65 ___
17651 BN Extended Vision Caboose "10531" (std O), *03-05*		80 ___
17652 NYC Bay Window Caboose "20200" (std O), *03*		75 ___
17653 SP Bay Window Caboose "1337" (std O), *03*		65 ___
17654 Alaska Extended Vision Caboose "989" (std O), *03*		75 ___
17655 WP Bay Window Caboose "448" (std O), *03-04*		75 ___
17657 Norman Rockwell Holiday Caboose, *03*		30 ___
17658 Burlington Extended Vision Caboose "13611" (std O), *04*		70 ___
17659 CN Extended Vision Caboose "79646" (std O), *04*		70 ___
17660 Seaboard Extended Vision Caboose "5700" (std O), *04*		65 ___
17661 C&NW Bay Window Caboose "10871" (std O), *04*		65 ___
17662 PC Bay Window Caboose "21001" (std O), *04*		65 ___
17663 Southern Bay Window Caboose "X546" (std O), *04*		65 ___
17664 B&O Caboose "C-2824" (std O), *03-04*		65 ___
17665 Chessie System Caboose "C-2802" (std O), *03-04*		75 ___
17669 NYC Bay Window Caboose, smoke, *05*		85 ___
17670 CP Rail Bay Window Caboose, smoke, *05*		85 ___
17671 BN Extended Vision Caboose, *05*		85 ___
17672 GN Extended Vision Caboose "X-106" (std O), *05*		85 ___
17673 Santa Fe Extended Vision Caboose, *05*		85 ___
17674 Reading Extended Vision Caboose "94119" (std O), *05*		75 ___
17675 Rio Grande Extended Vision Caboose "01507" (std O), *06*		90 ___

			Mint
___	**17676**	NYC Bay Window Caboose "20300," *07*	60
___	**17677**	Erie-Lack. Bay Window Caboose "C359" (std O), *06*	90
___	**17678**	B&O I-12 Caboose "C2421" (std O), *06*	90
___	**17679**	Long Island Bay Window Caboose "C-62" (std O), *06*	90
___	**17682**	Reading Northeastern Caboose "92841" (std O), *06-07*	85
___	**17683**	Chessie System Northeastern Caboose "1893" (std O), *07*	85
___	**17684**	Conrail Northeastern Caboose "18873" (std O), *07*	85
___	**17685**	Jersey Central Northeastern Caboose "91533" (std O), *07*	85
___	**17690**	UP CA-4 Caboose "3826" (std O), *06*	90
___	**17691**	UP CA-4 Caboose "25103" (std O), *06*	90
___	**17692**	LL CA-4 B22 Caboose "7629" (std O), *06*	90
___	**17693**	Chessie Extended Vision Caboose "3285" (std O), *06*	90
___	**17694**	NS Extended Vision Caboose "555582" (std O), *06*	90
___	**17695**	Alaska I-12 Caboose "1001" (std O), *06*	90
___	**17696**	CP Bay Window Caboose "437266" (std O), *06*	90
___	**17697**	CN Extended Vision Caboose "78128" (std O), *06*	90
___	**17699**	UP Ca-4 Caboose "25193" (std O), *07*	90
___	**17700**	UP ACF 40-ton Stock Car "47456" (std O), *01-02*	85
___	**17701**	Rio Grande ACF 40-ton Stock Car "39269" (std O), *01-02*	60
___	**17702**	CP ACF 40-ton Stock Car "277083" (std O), *01-02*	75
___	**17703**	NYC ACF 40-ton Stock Car "23334" (std O), *01-02*	85
___	**17703**	Crayola 2-bay Hopper, LionScale, *17-18*	70
___	**17704**	B&O ACF 40-ton Stock Car "110234" (std O), *02*	40
___	**17705**	CB&Q ACF 40-ton Stock Car "52886" (std O), *02*	40
___	**17707**	PRR ARF 40-ton Stock Car "128994" (std O), *03*	35
___	**17708**	CP Rail ACF 40-ton Stock Car "277313" (std O), *03*	38
___	**17709**	UP Stock Car "48154" (std O), *04*	45
___	**17710**	Great Northern Stock Car "56385" (std O), *04*	40
___	**17711**	C&O ACF 40-ton Stock Car "95237" (std O), *06*	60
___	**17712**	N&W ACF 40-ton Stock Car "33000" (std O), *06*	60
___	**17713**	MKT ACF 40-ton Stock Car "47150" (std O), *06*	60
___	**17714**	CN 40-ton Stock Car "172755" (std O), *06*	60
___	**17715**	MP 40-ton Stock Car "52428" (std O), *06*	60
___	**17716**	CGW 40-ton Stock Car "838," *08*	60
___	**17717**	UP 40-ton Stock Car "48217," *08*	60
___	**17718**	NS Heritage 3-bay Hopper 2-pack (std O), *12*	160
___	**17719**	C&BQ ACF Stock Car "52925" (std O), *09*	70
___	**17720**	UP ACF Stock Car (std O), *10*	70
___	**17721**	Postwar Scale Stock Car 2-pack, *10-11*	140
___	**17724**	CN Scale Steel-sided Reefer "210552," (std O), *11*	80
___	**17725**	NP Scale Steel-sided Reefer "98528," (std O), *11*	80
___	**17726**	IC Scale Steel-sided Reefer "16644," (std O), *11*	80
___	**17727**	Mopac/Wabash Scale Steel-sided Reefer "30790," (std O), *11*	80
___	**17729**	C&O Scale PS-1 Boxcar "2992" (std O), *12*	70
___	**17730**	Seaboard Scale Round-roof Boxcar "19293" (std O), *11*	70
___	**17731**	Pere Marquette Scale Boxcar "81805" (std O), *12*	70
___	**17732**	L&N Scale PS-1 Boxcar "4798" (std O) , *12*	70
___	**17733**	PRR Scale Round-roof Boxcar "78948" (std O), *11*	70
___	**17734**	PRR Scale Round-roof Boxcar "76644" (std O), *11*	70
___	**17735**	PRR Round-roof DD Boxcar "77851" (std O), *12*	70
___	**17736**	PRR Round-roof DD Boxcar "60156" (std O), *12*	70
___	**17737**	N&W Scale Round-roof Boxcar "46494" (std O), *11*	70
___	**17738**	NP Round-roof DD Boxcar "39300" (std O), *12*	70

MODERN 1970-2021		Esc	Mint
17739	DT&I Round-roof DD Boxcar "12250" (std O), *12*		70 ___
17740	Alaska Scale Round-roof Boxcar "27781" (std O), *11*		70 ___
17741	Santa Fe Scale Slogan Reefer 5-car Set (std O), *12*		320 ___
17747	Santa Fe Scale Boxcar "39009" (std O), *12*		70 ___
17748	Grave's Mortuary Supply Scale PS-1 Boxcar (std O), *12-13*		70 ___
17749	Erie Scale PS-1 Boxcar "90300" (std O), *12*		70 ___
17750	NYC Round-roof DD Boxcar "77147" (std O), *12*		70 ___
17751	NKP Scale PS-1 Boxcar "6605" (std O), *12*		70 ___
17752	Polar Round-roof Boxcar "1202" (std O), *12-13, 16-17*		70 ___
17753	LV Scale PS-1 Boxcar "65124" (std O), *12*		70 ___
17754	EL DD Boxcar "65000" (std O), *12*		75 ___
17755	D&H DD Boxcar "25025" (std O), *12*		75 ___
17756	CP Rail DD Boxcar "42630" (std O), *12*		75 ___
17757	Milwaukee Road DD Boxcar "13441" (std O), *12*		75 ___
17758	ATSF Map and Slogan Reefer 3-pack, *12*		190 ___
17762	BN 57' Mechanical Reefer "9618" (std O), *12*		85 ___
17763	NYC 57' Mechanical Reefer "6762" (std O), *12*		85 ___
17764	ATSF 57' Mechanical Reefer "56244" (std O), *12*		85 ___
17765	Virginian Round-roof DD Boxcar "3131" (std O), *13-14*		80 ___
17766	NH Round-roof Boxcar "39303" (std O), *13*		70 ___
17767	SP Round-roof DD Boxcar "166052" (std O), *13-14*		80 ___
17768	Grave's Mortuary Supply Round-roof Boxcar (std O), *13*		70 ___
17769	D&RGW PS-1 Boxcar "60046" (std O), *13*		70 ___
17770	MILW PS-1 Boxcar "8777" (std O), *13*		70 ___
17771	CNJ PS-1 Boxcar "23522" (std O), *13-14*		80 ___
17772	Central of Georgia PS-1 Boxcar (std O), *13*		70 ___
17773	D&M Round-roof Boxcar "3148" (std O), *13-14*		80 ___
17774	D&M PS-1 Boxcar "2833" (std O), *13*		70 ___
17775	NS Heritage 3-bay Hopper 3-pack (std O), *13-15*		240 ___
17779	NS Heritage 3-bay Hopper 3-pack (std O), *13-15*		240 ___
17783	NS Heritage 3-bay Hopper 3-pack (std O), *13-15*		240 ___
17787	NS Heritage 3-bay Hopper 3-pack (std O), *13*		240 ___
17791	NS Heritage 3-bay Hopper 3-pack (std O), *13*		240 ___
17795	NS Heritage 3-bay Hopper 3-pack (std O), *13*		240 ___
17800	Ontario Northland Ore Car "6126," *00*		30 ___
17801	CN Ore Car "345165," *00*		37 ___
17802	CP Ore Car "377249," *00*		28 ___
17803	DMIR Ore Car "31456," *00*		30 ___
17804	UP Ore Car "8023," *01*		29 ___
17805	CP Rail Ore Car "377238," *01*		29 ___
17806	UP Ore Car "27250," *03*		30 ___
17807	BN Ore Car "95887," *02*		28 ___
17900	Santa Fe Unibody Tank Car (std O), *90*	37	46 ___
17901	Chevron Unibody Tank Car (std O), *90*	26	32 ___
17902	NJ Zinc Unibody Tank Car (std O), *91*	26	34 ___
17903	Conoco Unibody Tank Car (std O), *91*	24	29 ___
17904	Texaco Unibody Tank Car (std O), *92*	39	48 ___
17905	Archer Daniels Midland Unibody Tank Car (std O), *92*	24	33 ___
17906	SCM Unibody Tank Car "78286" (std O), *93*	47	55 ___
17908	Marathon Oil Unibody Tank Car (std O), *95*	55	60 ___
17909	Hooker Chemicals Unibody Tank Car (std O), *96*		55 ___
17910	Sunoco Unibody Tank Car "7900," *97*		37 ___
17913	J.M. Huber Tank Car, *98*		29 ___

	MODERN 1970-2021	Esc	Mint
___	**17914** Englehard Tank Car, *98*		36
___	**17915** Gulf Unibody Tank Car "8438," *00*		43
___	**17916** Burlington Unibody Tank Car "130000," *00*	24	38
___	**17918** Southern Unibody Tank Car, *01*		32
___	**17919** Koppers Unibody Tank Car, *01*		39
___	**17924** Safety Kleen Unibody Tank Car "77603" (std O), *02*		40
___	**17925** Beefmaster Unibody Tank Car "120021" (std O), *02*		38
___	**17926** Cargill Unibody 1-D Tank Car "5836" (std O), *03*		40
___	**17927** Union Starch Unibody 1-D Tank Car "59137" (std O), *03*		35
___	**17928** Merck 1-D Tank Car "25421" (std O), *03*		35
___	**17929** Wyandotte Chemicals 1-D Tank Car "1325" (std O), *03*		34
___	**17930** CSX Unibody Tank Car "993369" (std O), *04*		35
___	**17931** UP Unibody Tank Car "6" (std O), *04*		35
___	**17932** CIBRO TankTrain Intermediate Car "26263" (std O), *04*		35
___	**17933** GATX TankTrain Intermediate Car 3-pack (std O), *04*		100
___	**17946** Candy Cane Unibody Tank Car, *04*		60
___	**17948** Philadelphia Quartz 1-D Tank Car "806" (std O), *06*		55
___	**17949** Skelly Oil 1-D Tank Car "2293" (std O), *06*		55
___	**17950** ADM Unibody Tank Car "19020" (std O), *06*		60
___	**17951** Cerestar Unibody Tank Car "190177" (std O), *06*		60
___	**17959** Dow 1-D Tank Car "310101" (std O), *07*		55
___	**17960** Amaizo 1-D Tank Car "15440" (std O), *07*		55
___	**17962** Domino Sugar 1-D Tank Car "3008" (std O), *07*		60
___	**17966** Procor 1-D Tank Car "82607" (std O), *07*		60
___	**17972** Union Starch 1-D Tank Car "724" (std O), *08*		60
___	**17973** UP 1-D Tank Car "907838" (std O), *08*		60
___	**17975** Cargill Foods Unibody Tank Car 3-pack (std O), *08-09*		195
___	**17976** Huber Unibody Tank Car 3-pack (std O), *08-09*		195
___	**17983** GATX TankTrain Intermediate Car 3-pack, *08*		195
___	**18000** PRR 0-6-0 Locomotive "8977," *89, 91*	258	405
___	**18001** Rock Island 4-8-4 Locomotive "5100," *87*	305	315
___	**18002** NYC 4-6-4 Locomotive "785," *87 u*	510	576
___	**18003** DL&W 4-8-4 Locomotive "1501," *88*	235	294
___	**18004** Reading 4-6-2 Locomotive "8004," *89*	185	205
___	**18005** NYC 4-6-4 Locomotive "5340," display case, *90*	705	799
___	**18006** Reading 4-8-4 Locomotive "2100," *89 u*	490	528
___	**18007** Southern Pacific 4-8-4 Locomotive "4410," *91*	374	392
___	**18008** Disneyland 35th Anniversary 4-4-0 Locomotive, display case, *90*	268	318
___	**18009** NYC 4-8-2 Locomotive "3000," *90 u, 91*	370	561
___	**18010** PRR 6-8-6 Steam Turbine Locomotive "6200," *91-92*	900	1041
___	**18010** L&NE AC-2 Covered Hopper 6-pack, *18*		360
___	**18011** Chessie System 4-8-4 Locomotive "2101," *91*	440	536
___	**18012** NYC 4-6-4 Locomotive "5340," *90*	710	900
___	**18013** Disneyland 35th Anniversary 4-4-0 Locomotive, *90*	255	300
___	**18014** Lionel Lines 2-6-4 Locomotive "8014," *91*	145	190
___	**18016** Northern Pacific 4-8-4 Locomotive "2626," *92*	385	440
___	**18018** Southern 2-8-2 Locomotive "4501," *92*	640	650
___	**18020** N&W AC-2 Covered Hopper 6-pack, *18*		360
___	**18022** Pere Marquette 2-8-4 Locomotive "1201," *93*	550	650
___	**18023** Western Maryland Shay Locomotive "6," *92*	1050	1350
___	**18024** Sears T&P 4-8-2 Locomotive "907," display case, *92 u*	750	790
___	**18025** T&P 4-8-2 Locomotive "907," *92 u*		640
___	**18026** NYC 4-6-4 Dreyfuss Hudson Locomotive, 2-rail, *92 u*		2350

	MODERN 1970-2021	Esc	Mint
18027	NYC 4-6-4 Dreyfuss Hudson Locomotive, 3-rail, *93 u*		1450 ___
18028	Smithsonian PRR 4-6-2 Locomotive "3768," 2-rail, *93 u*		2150 ___
18029	NYC 4-6-4 Dreyfuss Hudson Locomotive, 3-rail, *93 u*	1900	2150 ___
18030	Frisco 2-8-2 Locomotive "4100," *93 u*	530	625 ___
18030	Pere Marquette AC-2 Covered Hopper 6-pack, *18*		360 ___
18031	2-10-0 Bundesbahn BR-50 Locomotive, 2-rail, *93 u*		NRS ___
18034	Santa Fe 2-8-2 Locomotive "3158," *94*	540	620 ___
18035	2-10-0 Reichsbahn BR-50 Locomotive, 2-rail, *93 u*		NRS ___
18036	2-10-0 French BR-50 Locomotive, 2-rail, *93 u*		NRS ___
18040	N&W 4-8-4 Locomotive "612," *95*	640	710 ___
18040	WM AC-2 Covered Hopper 6-pack, *18*		360 ___
18042	Boston & Albany 4-6-4 Locomotive "618," *95*		250 ___
18043	Chesapeake & Ohio 4-6-4 Locomotive "490," *95*	680	750 ___
18044	Southern 4-6-2 Locomotive "1390," *96*		255 ___
18045	Commodore Vanderbilt Locomotive "777," *96*		678 ___
18046	Wabash 4-6-4 Locomotive "700," *96*	190	375 ___
18049	N&W Warhorse 4-8-4 Locomotive "600," *96*		490 ___
18050	JCPenney 4-6-2 Locomotive "2055," *96*	235	245 ___
18050	Continental Grain ACF 3-Bay Covered Hopper 6-pack, *18*		360 ___
18052	Pennsylvania Torpedo Locomotive "238E," *97*		455 ___
18054	NYC 0-4-0 Switcher "1665," black, *97*		145 ___
18056	NYC J1-e Hudson Locomotive "763E," Vanderbilt tender, *97*		603 ___
18060	PRR ACF 3-Bay Covered Hopper 6-pack, *18*		360 ___
18062	ATSF 4-6-4 Hudson Locomotive "3447," *97*		680 ___
18063	NYC 4-6-4 Commodore Vanderbilt Locomotive, *99*		952 ___
18064	NYC 4-8-2 Mohawk L-3A Locomotive "3005," tender, *98*	275	450 ___
18067	NYC Weathered Commodore Vanderbilt Scale Hudson Locomotive, *97*		840 ___
18070	Tenneco ACF 3-Bay Covered Hopper 6-pack, *18*		360 ___
18071	SP Daylight Locomotive "4449," *98*		680 ___
18072	Lionel Lines Torpedo Locomotive, tender, *98*		360 ___
18079	NYC 2-8-2 Mikado Locomotive "1967," *99*		710 ___
18080	D&RGW 2-8-2 Mikado Locomotive "1210," *99*		720 ___
18080	BN ACF 3-Bay Covered Hopper 6-pack, *18*		360 ___
18082	NYC 4-6-4 Hudson Locomotive "5404," *99*		230 ___
18083	C&O 4-6-4 Hudson Locomotive "305," *99*		205 ___
18084	Santa Fe 4-6-4 Hudson Locomotive "305," *99*		225 ___
18085	NH 4-6-2 Pacific Locomotive "1334," *99*		275 ___
18086	NYC 4-6-2 Pacific Locomotive "4929," *99*		235 ___
18087	Santa Fe 4-6-2 Pacific Locomotive "3448," *99*		265 ___
18088	SP 4-6-2 Pacific Locomotive "1407," *99*		350 ___
18089	CNJ 4-6-0 Camelback Locomotive "771," *99*		405 ___
18090	Vesuvius Crucible PS-1 Boxcar 6-pack, *18*		360 ___
18091	PRR 4-6-0 Camelback Locomotive "821," *99*		405 ___
18092	SP 4-6-0 Camelback Locomotive "2283," *99*		395 ___
18093	C&NW 4-6-0 Camelback Locomotive "3006," *99*		285 ___
18094	B&O 4-4-2 E6 Atlantic Locomotive, *CC, 99-00*		345 ___
18095	PRR 4-4-2 E6 Atlantic Locomotive, *CC, 99-00*	275	455 ___
18096	ATSF 4-4-2 E6 Atlantic Locomotive, *CC, 99-00*		370 ___
18097	CNJ 4-6-0 Camelback Locomotive "770," *99*		330 ___
18098	PRR 4-6-0 Camelback Locomotive "820," *99*		355 ___
18099	SP 4-6-0 Camelback Locomotive "2282," *99*		360 ___
18100	Santa Fe F3 Diesel A Unit "8100" (see 11711)		NRS ___

		Esc	Mint
____	**18100** EJ&E PS-1 Boxcar 6-pack, *18*		360
____	**18100** Monon PS-1 Boxcar 6-pack, *18*		360
____	**18101** Santa Fe F3 Diesel B Unit "8101" (see 11711)		NRS
____	**18102** Santa Fe F3 Diesel A Unit "8102," dummy (see 11711)		NRS
____	**18103** Santa Fe F3 Diesel B Unit "8103," dummy, *91 u*	180	190
____	**18104** GN F3 Diesel A Unit "366A," dummy (see 11724)		500
____	**18105** GN F3 Diesel B Unit "370B," dummy (see 11724)		NRS
____	**18106** GN F3 Diesel A Unit "351C," dummy (see 11724)		NRS
____	**18107** D&RGW Alco PA1 Diesel ABA Set, *92*	640	740
____	**18108** Great Northern F3 Diesel B Unit "371B," *93*	85	105
____	**18109** Erie Alco Diesel A Unit "725A" (see 11734)		NRS
____	**18110** Erie Alco Diesel B Unit "725B" (see 11734)		160
____	**18111** Erie Alco Diesel A Unit "736A," dummy (see 11734)		NRS
____	**18115** Santa Fe F3 Diesel B Unit, *93*	90	115
____	**18116** Erie-Lackawanna Alco PA1 Diesel AA Set, *93*	450	490
____	**18120** Rutland PS-1 Boxcar 6-pack, *18*		360
____	**18121** Santa Fe F3 Diesel B Unit "200A," *94*	75	95
____	**18122** Santa Fe F3 Diesel B Unit "200B," *95*	140	150
____	**18123** ACL F3 Diesel A Unit "342" (see 11903)		NRS
____	**18124** ACL F3 Diesel B Unit "342B" (see 11903)		NRS
____	**18125** ACL F3 Diesel A Unit "343," dummy (see 11903)		NRS
____	**18128** Santa Fe F3 Diesel A Unit "2343," *96*		435
____	**18129** Santa Fe F3 Diesel B Unit "2343C," *96*		245
____	**18130** Santa Fe F3 Diesel AB Set, *96*		580
____	**18130** NYC AAR 3-Bay Hopper 6-pack, *18*		360
____	**18131** NP F3 Diesel AB Set, "2390A, 2390C," *97*	295	360
____	**18132** NP F3 Diesel A Unit, powered		300
____	**18133** NP F3 Diesel B Unit, dummy		150
____	**18134** Santa Fe F3 Diesel A Unit "2343," dummy, *97*		195
____	**18136** Santa Fe F3 Diesel B Unit "2343C," *97*	135	240
____	**18138** Milwaukee Road F3 Diesel A Unit "75A," *98*		400
____	**18139** Milwaukee Road F3 Diesel B Unit "2378B," *98*		250
____	**18140** Milwaukee Road F3 Diesel AB Set, *98*	390	600
____	**18140** Nickel Plate Road AAR 3-Bay Hopper 6-pack, *18*		360
____	**18145** NP F3 Diesel A Unit "2390A," *97*	300	360
____	**18146** NP F3 Diesel B Unit "2390C," *97*		170
____	**18147** NP F3 Diesel AB Set, *97*	450	580
____	**18149** UP Veranda Gas Turbine Locomotive "61," *98*	860	900
____	**18150** LG Everist AAR 3-Bay Hopper 6-pack, *18*		360
____	**18154** Deluxe Santa Fe FT Diesel AA Set, *98-00*		375
____	**18155** Deluxe Santa Fe FT Diesel A Unit, powered (see 18154)		NRS
____	**18156** Deluxe Santa Fe FT Diesel A Unit, dummy (see 18154)		NRS
____	**18157** Santa Fe FT Diesel AA Set, *98-00*		240
____	**18158** Santa Fe FT Diesel A Unit, powered (see 18157)		NRS
____	**18159** Santa Fe FT Diesel A Unit, dummy (see 18157)		NRS
____	**18160** NYC Deluxe FT Diesel AA Set, "1602, 1603," *98-00*		500
____	**18160** UP AAR 3-Bay Hopper 6-pack, *18*		360
____	**18163** NYC FT Diesel AA Set, "1600, 2400," *98-00*		300
____	**18166** B&O FT Diesel AA Set, *CC, 99-00*		340
____	**18169** B&O FT Diesel AA Set, traditional, *99-00*		240
____	**18189** Army of Potomac Operating Stock Car, *99*		45
____	**18190** McNeil's Rangers Operating Stock Car "2," *99*		45
____	**18191** WP F3 Diesel AA Set, *98*	153	570

		Esc	Mint	
MODERN 1970-2021				
18192	WP F3 Diesel A Unit, powered, *98*		485	___
18193	WP F3 Diesel A Unit, dummy, *98*		495	___
18197	WP F3 Diesel B Unit "2355C," *99*	88	255	___
18198	WP F3 Diesel B Unit "2345C" CC, *99*		360	___
18200	Conrail SD40 Diesel "8200," *87*	180	200	___
18201	Chessie System SD40 Diesel "8201," *88*	245	340	___
18202	Erie-Lack. SD40 Diesel Unit "8459," dummy, *89 u*	90	140	___
18203	CP Rail SD40 Diesel "8203," *89*	195	250	___
18204	Chessie SD40 Diesel Unit "8204," dummy, *90 u*	135	190	___
18205	Union Pacific Dash 8-40C Diesel "9100," *89*	275	335	___
18206	Santa Fe Dash 8-40B Diesel "8206," *90*	195	235	___
18207	Norfolk Southern Dash 8-40C Diesel "8689," *92*	230	270	___
18208	BN SD40 Diesel Dummy Unit "8586," *91 u*	115	165	___
18209	CP Rail SD40 Diesel Dummy Unit "8209," *92 u*	135	165	___
18210	Illinois Central SD40 "6006," *93*	220	250	___
18210	Northwestern Refrigerated Wood-sided Refrigerator Car 6-pack, *18*		360	___
18211	Susquehanna Dash 8-40B Diesel "4002," *93*	145	165	___
18212	Santa Fe Dash 8-40B Diesel Dummy Unit "8212," *93*	155	180	___
18213	Norfolk Southern Dash 8-40C Diesel "8688," *94*	225	240	___
18214	CSX Dash 8-40C Diesel "7500," *94*	235	255	___
18215	CSX Dash 8-40C Diesel "7643," *94*	240	260	___
18216	Conrail SD-60M Diesel "5500," *94*	355	380	___
18217	Illinois Central SD40 Diesel "6007," *94*	170	175	___
18218	Susquehanna Dash 8-40B Diesel "4004," *94*	205	225	___
18219	C&NW Dash 8-40C Diesel "8501," *95*	325	330	___
18220	C&NW Dash 8-40C Diesel "8502," *95*	215	315	___
18220	PFE Wood-sided Refrigerator Car 6-pac, *18*		360	___
18221	D&RGW SD50 Diesel "5512," *95*	455	520	___
18222	D&RGW SD50 Diesel "5517," *95*	280	325	___
18223	Milwaukee Road SD40 Diesel "154," *95*	375	380	___
18224	Milwaukee Road SD40 Diesel "155," *95*	240	265	___
18226	GE Dash 9 Diesel, *97*		295	___
18228	SP Dash 9 Diesel "8228," gray with red nose, *97*		340	___
18229	SP SD40 Diesel "7333," *98*	300	425	___
18230	Swift Wood-sided Refrigerator Car 6-pac, *18*		360	___
18231	BNSF Dash 9 Diesel "739," *98*		435	___
18232	Soo Line SD60 Diesel "5500," *97*		350	___
18233	BNSF Dash 9 Diesel "745," *98*		330	___
18234	BNSF Dash 9 Diesel "740," *CC, 98-99*		405	___
18235	BNSF Dash 9 Diesel 2-pack, "739, 740," *98*		710	___
18238	Conrail SD70 Diesel "4145," *99-00*		300	___
18240	Conrail Dash 8-40B Diesel "5065" CC, *98*		260	___
18240	Rath Wood-sided Refrigerator Car 6-pac, *18*		360	___
18241	BN SD70 Diesel "9413," *99-00*		345	___
18245	PRR Alco PA1 Diesel AA Set, *99*		495	___
18248	PRR Alco PB-1 Diesel "5750B," *99*		215	___
18249	Erie Alco PB-1 Diesel "850B," *00*		250	___
18250	BNSF SD70 Diesel "9870," *99-00*		365	___
18251	CSX SD60 Diesel "8701," *99-00*		300	___
18252	Amtrak Dash 9 Diesel, *CC, 99*		285	___
18253	BNSF Dash 9 Diesel, *CC, 99*		305	___
18254	ATSF Dash 9 Diesel, *CC, 99*		340	___
18255	NS Dash 9 Diesel, *CC, 99*		315	___

		Esc	Mint
____ 18256	Amtrak Dash 9 Diesel, traditional, *99*		200
____ 18257	BNSF Dash 9 Diesel, traditional, *99*		190
____ 18258	ATSF Dash 9 Diesel, traditional, *99*		205
____ 18259	NS Dash 9 Diesel, traditional, *99*		215
____ 18260	Conrail SD70 Diesel "4144," *99-00*		280
____ 18261	BN SD60 Diesel "9412," *99-00*		255
____ 18262	BNSF SD70 Diesel "9869," *99-00*		250
____ 18263	CSX SD60 Diesel "8700," *99-00*		255
____ 18264	Southern Pacific SD70M Diesel "8238," *99-00*		245
____ 18265	Southern Pacific SD70M Diesel "9803," *99-00*		340
____ 18266	Norfolk Southern SD60 Diesel "6552," *CC, 01-02*		400
____ 18268	Lionel Centennial SD90MAC Diesel, *CC, 00*		420
____ 18269	UP SD90MAC Diesel "8006," *CC, 00*		405
____ 18271	CP SD90MAC Diesel "9129," *CC, 00*		440
____ 18273	UP SD40 Diesel "8071," *99-00*		330
____ 18274	Burlington U30C Diesel "891," *CC, 01*		370
____ 18276	Seaboard U30C Diesel "7274," *CC, 01*		325
____ 18278	UP U30C Diesel "2938," *CC, 01*		330
____ 18280	Maersk SD70 Diesel, *CC, 00*		345
____ 18281	BNSF Dash 9-44CW Diesel "788," *CC, 00*		340
____ 18282	BNSF Dash 9-44CW Diesel "789," traditional, *00*		225
____ 18283	CSX Dash 9-44CW Diesel "9019," *CC, 00*		340
____ 18284	CSX Dash 9-44CW Diesel "9020," traditional, *00*		300
____ 18285	UP Dash 9-44C Diesel "9659," *CC, 01*		325
____ 18286	UP Dash 9-44CW Diesel "9717," *CC, 01*		355
____ 18287	CN Dash 9-44C Diesel "2529," *CC, 01*		460
____ 18288	Odyssey System SD70 Diesel, *CC, 00 u*		400
____ 18290	Amtrak Dash 8-32BWH Diesel "509," *CC, 01*		325
____ 18291	BNSF Dash 8-32BWH Diesel "580," *CC, 02*		340
____ 18292	Chessie GE U30C Diesel "3312," *CC, 02*		340
____ 18293	Santa Fe U30C Diesel, *CC, 03*		395
____ 18294	Alaska SD70MAC Diesel "4005," *CC, 01-02*		435
____ 18295	Conrail SD80MAC Diesel "7200," *CC, 02-03*		365
____ 18296	CSX SD80MAC Diesel "801," *CC, 02-03*		405
____ 18297	NYC SD80MAC Diesel "9914," *CC, 02-03*		405
____ 18298	UP "Desert Victory" SD40-2 Diesel "3593," *CC, 02-03*		380
____ 18299	CP Rail SD40-2 Diesel "5420," *CC, 02-03*		375
____ 18300	PRR GG1 Electric Locomotive "8300," *87*	285	335
____ 18301	Southern FM Train Master Diesel "8301," *88*	150	204
____ 18302	GN EP-5 Electric Locomotive "8302" (FF 3), *88*	190	250
____ 18303	Amtrak GG1 Electric Locomotive "8303," *89*	275	338
____ 18304	Lackawanna MU Commuter Car Set, *91*	380	435
____ 18305	Lackawanna MU Commuter Car Dummy Set, *92*	230	255
____ 18306	PRR MU Commuter Car Set, *92*	260	330
____ 18307	PRR FM Train Master Diesel "8699," *94*	170	202
____ 18308	PRR GG1 Electric Locomotive "4866," *92*	193	278
____ 18309	Reading FM Train Master Diesel "863," *93*	173	212
____ 18310	PRR MU Commuter Car Dummy Set, *93*	265	345
____ 18311	Disney EP-5 Electric Locomotive "8311," *94*	303	412
____ 18313	Pennsylvania GG1 Electric Locomotive "4907," *96*	75	297
____ 18314	PRR GG1 Electric Locomotive "2332," 5 gold stripes, *97*	300	507
____ 18315	Virginian E33 Electric Locomotive "2329," *97*		240
____ 18319	New Haven EP-5 Electric Locomotive, *99*	200	365

	MODERN 1970-2021	Esc	Mint
18321	CNJ Train Master Diesel "2341," 99		405 ___
18322	Lackawanna Train Master Diesel "2321," 99		465 ___
18326	PRR Congressional GG1 Electric Locomotive, 00		600 ___
18327	Virginian FM Train Master Diesel "2331," 99-00		410 ___
18328	NH MU Commuter Car Set, CC, 00		385 ___
18331	Reading MU Commuter Car Set, CC, 00		460 ___
18334	NH MU Commuter Car Dummy Set, CC, 01		180 ___
18337	Reading MU Commuter Car Dummy Set, CC, 01		200 ___
18343	PRR GG1 Electric Locomotive "2332," CC, 01		610 ___
18344	LIRR MU Commuter Car Set, powered, CC, 01		470 ___
18347	IC MU Commuter Car Set, powered, CC, 01		470 ___
18351	NYC S1 Electric Locomotive, 03		400 ___
18352	JCPenney SP MU Commuter Car, display case, 02		140 ___
18353	Pennsylvania E33 Electric Locomotive "4403," CC, 02		280 ___
18354	PRR GG1 Electric Locomotive "4918," tuscan, CC, 04		790 ___
18355	PRR GG1 Electric Locomotive "4876," green, CC, 04		900 ___
18356	Penn Central GG1 Electric Locomotive "4901," CC, 04		1050 ___
18364	PRR BB1 Electric Locomotive "3900," CC, 05-07		530 ___
18367	LIRR BB3 Electric Locomotive "328 A," CC, 05		530 ___
18371	PRR GG1 Electric Locomotive "4912," tuscan, 5 stripes, CC, 05-07		780 ___
18372	PRR GG1 Electric Locomotive "4925," green, 1 stripe, CC, 05-07		780 ___
18373	NYC S2 Electric Locomotive "125," CC, 05-07		410 ___
18374	PRR GG1 Electric Locomotive "4866," silver, CC, 06-08		900 ___
18375	Lackawanna FM Train Master Diesel "850," CC, 06		400 ___
18376	Lackawanna FM Train Master Diesel "851," nonpowered (std O), 06		130 ___
18378	New York City R27 Subway Car 2-pack, 07		360 ___
18384	MILW EP-2 Electric Locomotive, CC, 07-08		950 ___
18385	NYC H-16-44 Diesel "7001," 07-09		202 ___
18386	NYC H-16-44 Diesel "7002," nonpowered (std O), 07-09		123 ___
18389	MILW EP-2 Electric Locomotive "E-1," CC, 07-08		950 ___
18399	NH EF-4 Rectifier Locomotive "306," CC, 09		360 ___
18400	Santa Fe Vulcan Rotary Snowplow "8400," 87	135	170 ___
18401	Workmen Handcar, 87-88	30	37 ___
18402	Lionel Lines Burro Crane, 88	65	80 ___
18403	Santa Claus Handcar, 88	26	29 ___
18404	San Francisco Trolley "8404," 88	55	85 ___
18405	Santa Fe Burro Crane, 89	70	83 ___
18406	Track Maintenance Car, 89, 91	34	49 ___
18407	Snoopy and Woodstock Handcar, 90-91	91	108 ___
18408	Santa Claus Handcar, 89	26	35 ___
18410	PRR Burro Crane, 90	100	115 ___
18411	Canadian Pacific Fire Car, 90	70	98 ___
18413	Charlie Brown and Lucy Handcar, 91	40	68 ___
18416	Bugs Bunny and Daffy Duck Handcar, 92-93	124	175 ___
18417	Section Gang Car, 93	65	80 ___
18419	Lionelville Electric Trolley "8419," 94	75	90 ___
18421	Sylvester and Tweety Handcar, 94	44	50 ___
18422	Santa and Snowman Handcar, 94	32	37 ___
18423	On-track Step Van, 95	23	28 ___
18424	On-track Pickup Truck, 95	20	25 ___
18425	Goofy and Pluto Handcar, 95	45	58 ___
18426	Santa and Snowman Handcar, 95	25	30 ___
18427	Tie-Jector Car "55," 97		60 ___
18429	Workmen Handcar, 96	28	34 ___

		Esc	Mint
___ **18430**	Crew Car, *96*		28
___ **18431**	Trolley Car, *96-97*		46
___ **18433**	Mickey and Minnie Handcar, *96-97*	48	87
___ **18434**	Porky and Petunia Handcar, *96*		35
___ **18436**	Dodge Ram Track Inspection Vehicle, *97*		39
___ **18438**	PRR High-rail Inspection Vehicle, *98*		50
___ **18439**	Union Pacific High-rail Inspection Vehicle, *98*		42
___ **18440**	NJ Transit High-rail Inspection Vehicle, *98*		50
___ **18444**	Lionelville Fire Car (SSS), *98*		150
___ **18445**	NYC Fire Car, *98*		90
___ **18446**	Postwar "58" GN Rotary Snowplow, *99*		181
___ **18447**	Executive Inspection Vehicle, *99*		125
___ **18452**	Boston Trolley "3321," *99-00*		65
___ **18454**	Executive Inspection Vehicle, blue, *00*		105
___ **18455**	NYC Tie-Jector Car "X-2," *00-01*		74
___ **18456**	Postwar "59" Minuteman Motorized Unit, *01-02*		290
___ **18457**	Postwar "65" Handcar, *00-01*		45
___ **18458**	Postwar "53" D&RGW Snowplow, *00*		160
___ **18459**	Christmas Handcar, *01*		35
___ **18461**	Track Cleaning Car, *02-03*		90
___ **18463**	Hot Rod Inspection Vehicle, *01-02*		100
___ **18464**	Postwar "54" Track Ballast Tamper, *02-03*		170
___ **18465**	Postwar "50" Gang Car, *03*		78
___ **18466**	UP Rotary Snow Plow, *01-02*		150
___ **18467**	Train Robbery Handcar, *02*		45
___ **18468**	CN Railroad Speeder, *03-04*		49
___ **18469**	Chessie System Railroad Speeder, *03-04*		49
___ **18470**	Postwar "52" Fire Car, *02*		105
___ **18471**	UP GP20 Diesel "1977," *03*		105
___ **18473**	Lehigh Valley GP38 Diesel "310," *03*		160
___ **18474**	Postwar "41" U.S. Army Switcher, *03-04*		145
___ **18475**	Toy Story Handcar, *03*		55
___ **18476**	Mickey and Minnie Mouse Handcar, *03-04*	0	60
___ **18480**	Hobo Motorized Handcar, *03-04*		35
___ **18481**	Christmas Yuletide Trolley, *03*		50
___ **18482**	New Haven Rail Bonder "16," *04*		35
___ **18483**	C&O Ballast Tamper "48," *04*		55
___ **18484**	NS Dodge Inspection Vehicle, *04-05*		55
___ **18485**	NYC Gang Car, *04-05*		100
___ **18486**	Donald and Daisy Duck Handcar, *04-05*		63
___ **18487**	Postwar "56" M&StL Mine Transport Car, *04-05*		230
___ **18489**	Great Northern Rail Bonder "HR-73," *04*		35
___ **18490**	UP Ballast Tamper, *04-05*		150
___ **18491**	MOW Ballast Tamper "325," *04*		44
___ **18492**	MOW Rail Bonder "58," *04*		35
___ **18493**	Santa's Speeder, *05*		60
___ **18497**	N&W Speeder "541005," traditional, *05*		65
___ **18498**	New York Central Rotary Snowplow, *05*		210
___ **18500**	Milwaukee Road GP9 Diesel "8500" (FF 2), *87*	175	230
___ **18501**	WM NW2 Switcher "8501" (FF 4), *89*	185	215
___ **18502**	LL 90th Anniversary GP9 Diesel "1900," *90*	148	173
___ **18503**	Southern Pacific NW2 Switcher "8503," *90*	250	280
___ **18504**	Frisco GP7 Diesel "504" (FF 5), *91*	155	240

MODERN 1970-2021		Esc	Mint
18505	NKP GP7 Diesel Set "400, 401" *(FF 6)*	295	365 ___
18506	CN Budd RDC Set, "D202, D203"	210	261 ___
18507	CN Budd RDC Baggage Car "D202," powered, *92*	50	75 ___
18508	CN Budd RDC Passenger Dummy Unit "D203," *92*	125	150 ___
18510	CN Budd RDC Passenger Dummy Unit "D200"	50	75 ___
18511	CN Budd RDC Passenger Dummy Unit "D250"	50	75 ___
18512	CN Budd RDC Dummy Set, "D200, D250," *93*	125	195 ___
18513	NYC GP7 Diesel "7420," *94*	90	125 ___
18514	Missouri Pacific GP7 Diesel "4124," *95*	245	310 ___
18515	Lionel Steel Vulcan Diesel "57" (SSS), *96*		190 ___
18516	Phantom III Locomotive, *CC, 02*		345 ___
18550	JCPenney MILW GP9 Diesel "8500," display case, *87 u*	180	245 ___
18551	JCPenney Susquehanna RS3 Diesel "8809," display case, *89 u*	180	195 ___
18552	JCPenney DM&IR SD18 Diesel "8813," display case, *90 u*	170	195 ___
18553	Sears UP GP9 Diesel "150," display case, *91 u*	100	150 ___
18554	JCPenney GM&O RS3 "721," display case, *92-93 u*	160	180 ___
18555	Sears C&IM SD9 Diesel "52," *92 u*	165	190 ___
18556	Sears Chicago & Illinois Midland Freight Car Set, *92 u*	110	120 ___
18557	Chessie System 4-8-4 Locomotive "2101," display case, export, *92 u*		NRS
18558	JCPenney MKT GP9 Diesel "91," display case, *94 u*	160	180 ___
18562	SP GP9 Diesel "2380," *96*		195 ___
18563	NYC GP9 Diesel "2380," *96*		230 ___
18564	CP GP9 Diesel "2380," *97*		265 ___
18565	Milwaukee Road GP9 Diesel "2338," *97*		220 ___
18566	CR SD20 Diesel "8495" (SSS), *97*		150 ___
18567	PRR GP9 Diesel "2028," *97*		225 ___
18569	CB&Q GP9 Diesel "2380," *98*		190 ___
18573	Santa Fe GP9 Diesel "2380," *98*		155 ___
18574	Milwaukee Road GP20 Diesel "975," *98*		250 ___
18575	Custom Series I GP9 Diesel "2398," *98*		350 ___
18576	SP GP9 Diesel B Unit "2385," nonpowered, *98*		135 ___
18577	NYC GP9 Diesel B Unit "2385," nonpowered, *98*		145 ___
18579	MILW GP9 Diesel "2384," nonpowered, *99*		135 ___
18580	Pennsylvania GP9 Diesel B Unit "2027," *98*		165 ___
18582	Seaboard NW2 Switcher, *98*	250	455 ___
18583	AEC Switcher "57," *98*		211 ___
18585	Centennial SD40 Diesel, *99*		450 ___
18587	NKP Alco C420 Switcher "577," *CC, 99-01*	215	255 ___
18588	D&H Alco C420 Switcher "412," *CC, 99-01*	250	275 ___
18589	LV Alco C420 Switcher "409," *CC, 99-01*	255	300 ___
18590	NKP Alco C420 Switcher "578," traditional, *99-01*		170 ___
18591	D&H Alco C420 Switcher "411," traditional, *99-01*		215 ___
18592	LV Alco C420 Switcher "410," traditional, *99-01*		175 ___
18596	D&H Alco RS-11 Switcher "5001," *CC, 99-01*		370 ___
18598	NYC Alco RS-11 Switcher "8010," *CC, 99-01*		380 ___
18599	C&O GP38 Diesel "3855," *99-00*		145 ___
18600	ACL 4-4-2 Locomotive "8600," *87 u*	65	75 ___
18601	Great Northern 4-4-2 Locomotive "8601," *88*	80	95 ___
18602	PRR 4-4-2 Locomotive "8602," *87*	75	85 ___
18604	Wabash 4-4-2 Locomotive "8604," *88-91*	65	75 ___
18605	Mopar Express 4-4-2 Locomotive "1987," *87-88 u*	75	120 ___
18606	NYC 2-6-4 Locomotive "8606," *89*	170	190 ___
18607	Union Pacific 2-6-4 Locomotive "8607," *89*	130	155 ___

			Esc	Mint
____	**18608**	D&RGW 2-6-4 Locomotive "8608" (SSS), *89*	90	105
____	**18609**	Northern Pacific 2-6-4 Locomotive "8609," *90*	170	195
____	**18610**	Rock Island 0-4-0 Locomotive "8610," *90*	105	115
____	**18611**	Lionel Lines 2-6-4 Locomotive (SSS), *90*	125	140
____	**18612**	C&NW 4-4-2 Locomotive "8612," *89*	75	100
____	**18613**	NYC 4-4-2 Locomotive "8613," *89 u*	75	95
____	**18614**	Circus Train 4-4-2 Locomotive "1989," *89 u*	95	125
____	**18615**	GTW 4-4-2 Locomotive "8615," *90*	70	85
____	**18616**	Northern Pacific 4-4-2 Locomotive "8616," *90 u*	85	110
____	**18617**	Adolphus III 4-4-2 Locomotive, *89-92 u*	100	125
____	**18620**	Illinois Central 2-6-2 Locomotive "8620," *91*	165	190
____	**18622**	Union Pacific 4-4-2 Locomotive "8622," *90-91 u*	65	80
____	**18623**	Texas & Pacific 4-4-2 Locomotive "8623," *92*	80	110
____	**18625**	Illinois Central 4-4-2 Locomotive "8625," *91 u*	70	95
____	**18626**	Delaware & Hudson 2-6-2 Locomotive "8626," *92*	105	115
____	**18627**	C&O 4-4-2 Locomotive "8627" or "8633," *92, 93 u, 94, 95 u*	75	95
____	**18628**	MKT 4-4-2 Locomotive "8628," *92, 93 u*	70	85
____	**18630**	C&NW 4-6-2 Locomotive "2903," *93*	325	370
____	**18632**	NYC 4-4-2 Locomotive "8632," *93-95*	75	95
____	**18632**	C&O Columbia 4-4-2 Locomotive "8632," *97-99*	75	95
____	**18633**	C&O 4-4-2 Locomotive "8633," *94-95*	65	85
____	**18633**	UP 4-4-2 Locomotive "8633," *93-95*	65	85
____	**18635**	Santa Fe 2-6-4 Locomotive "8625," *93*	135	155
____	**18636**	B&O 4-6-2 Locomotive "5300," *94*	295	315
____	**18637**	United Auto Workers 4-4-2 Locomotive "8633," *93 u*		90
____	**18638**	Norfolk & Western 2-6-4 Locomotive "638," *94*	170	220
____	**18639**	Reading 4-6-2 Locomotive "639," *95*	145	170
____	**18640**	Union Pacific 4-6-2 Locomotive "8640," *95*	110	130
____	**18641**	Ford 4-4-2 Locomotive "8641," *94 u*	65	85
____	**18642**	Lionel Lines 4-6-2 Locomotive, *95*	110	130
____	**18644**	ATSF 4-4-2 Columbia Locomotive "8644," *96-99*	75	90
____	**18648**	Sears Zenith 4-4-2 Locomotive "8632," *96 u*		140
____	**18649**	Chevrolet 4-4-2 Locomotive "USA-1," *96 u*		150
____	**18650**	LL 4-4-2 Columbia Locomotive "X-1110," *96-99*	95	120
____	**18653**	B&A 4-6-2 Pacific Locomotive "2044," *97*		140
____	**18654**	SP 4-6-2 Pacific Locomotive "2044," *97*		140
____	**18656**	Bloomingdale's 4-4-2 Columbia Locomotive "8632," *96*		112
____	**18657**	Sears Zenith 4-4-2 Columbia Locomotive "8632," *96*		120
____	**18658**	LL Little League 4-4-2 Columbia Locomotive "X-1110," *97*		90
____	**18660**	CN 4-6-2 Locomotive "2044," tender, *98*		175
____	**18661**	N&W 4-6-2 Locomotive "2044," tender, *98*		160
____	**18662**	Pennsylvania 0-4-0 Switcher, *98*	165	230
____	**18666**	SP&S 4-6-2 Pacific Locomotive "2044," *97*		200
____	**18668**	Bloomingdale's 4-4-2 Columbia Locomotive "8632," *97*		130
____	**18669**	JCPenney IC 4-6-2 Pacific Locomotive "2099," *98*		205
____	**18670**	D&H Columbia 4-4-2 Locomotive "1400," *98*		80
____	**18671**	N&W Columbia 4-4-2 Locomotive "1201," *98*		70
____	**18678**	Quaker Oats Columbia 4-4-2 Locomotive "8632," *98*		162
____	**18679**	JCPenney T&P 4-6-2 Locomotive "2000," traditional, *99, 00 u*		250
____	**18681**	PRR 4-4-2 Locomotive "460," *99*		75
____	**18682**	Santa Fe 4-4-2 Columbia Locomotive "524," traditional, *00-01*		70
____	**18696**	ACL 4-6-4 Locomotive "1800," *01*		120
____	**18697**	Santa Fe 4-6-4 Locomotive "3465," *01*		100
____	**18699**	Alaska 4-4-2 Locomotive "64," *01*		105

MODERN 1970-2021		Esc	Mint	
18700	Rock Island 0-4-0T Locomotive "8700," *87-88*	36	43	___
18701	Polar Express LionScale 3-Bay Covered Hopper, *18*		65	___
18702	V&TRR 4-4-0 Locomotive "8702" (SSS), *88*	160	195	___
18703	Merry Christmas LionScale 3-Bay Covered Hopper, *18*		60	___
18704	Lionel Lines 2-4-0 Locomotive, *89 u*	36	43	___
18704	Halloween ELX 3-Bay Hopper, LionScale, *18*		65	___
18705	Neptune 0-4-0T Locomotive "8705," *90-91*	35	42	___
18706	Santa Fe 2-4-0 Locomotive "8706," *91*	36	43	___
18707	Mickey's World Tour 2-4-0 Locomotive "8707," *91, 92 u*	58	68	___
18709	Lionel Employee Learning Center 0-4-0T Locomotive, *92 u*		140	___
18710	SP 2-4-0 Locomotive "2000," *93*	30	38	___
18711	Southern 2-4-0 Locomotive "2000," *93*	30	38	___
18712	Jersey Central 2-4-0 Locomotive "2000," *93*	30	38	___
18713	Chessie System 2-4-0 Locomotive "1993," *94-95*	30	38	___
18716	Lionelville Circus 4-4-0 Locomotive, *90-91*	90	110	___
18718	LL 0-4-0 Dockside Switcher "8200," *97-98*		40	___
18719	Thomas the Tank Engine "1," *97*		158	___
18720	Union 4-4-0 General Locomotive "1865," *99*		175	___
18721	Confederate 4-4-0 General Locomotive "1861," *99*		175	___
18722	Percy the Tank Engine "6," *99*		170	___
18723	Union Pacific 4-4-0 General Locomotive, *05*		100	___
18730	Transylvania RR 4-4-0 Locomotive "13," traditional, *05*		105	___
18732	North Pole Central 4-4-0 Locomotive "25," *06*		110	___
18733	Percy the Tank Engine "6," *05-12*		120	___
18734	James the Tank Engine "5," *06-12*		120	___
18741	Thomas the Tank Engine, *08-13*		120	___
18745	Hallow's Eve 4-6-0 Steam Locomotive, *11-12*		190	___
18753	Route of the Reindeer RS3 Diesel, *11*		190	___
18754	Polar Express 2-8-4 Berkshire Steam Locomotive, *11, 13*		300	___
18755	C&O Berkshire Steam Locomotive "2751," TrainSounds, *11*		290	___
18771	Percy, remote system, *13-16*		140	___
18774	James, remote system, *13-16*		140	___
18775	Diesel, remote system, *13-16*		140	___
18799	Bethlehem Steel Switcher "44," *99*		100	___
18800	Lehigh Valley GP9 Diesel "8800," *87*	80	95	___
18801	Santa Fe U36B Diesel "8801," *87*	100	120	___
18802	Southern GP9 Diesel "8802" (SSS), *87*	100	115	___
18803	Santa Fe RS3 Diesel "8803," *88*	90	105	___
18804	Soo Line RS3 Diesel "8804," *88*	95	115	___
18805	Union Pacific RS3 Diesel "8805," *89*	100	125	___
18806	New Haven SD18 Diesel "8806," *89*	100	115	___
18807	Lehigh Valley RS3 Diesel "8807," *90*	90	120	___
18808	ACL SD18 Diesel "8808," *90*	85	105	___
18809	Susquehanna RS3 Diesel "8809," *89 u*		130	___
18810	CSX SD18 Diesel "8810," *90*	95	130	___
18811	Alaska SD9 Diesel "8811," *91*	95	135	___
18812	Kansas City Southern GP38 Diesel "4000," *91*	120	140	___
18813	DM&IR SD18 Diesel "8813," *90 u*	90	145	___
18814	D&H RS3 Diesel "8814" (SSS), *91*	90	120	___
18815	Amtrak RS3 Diesel "1815," *91, 92 u*	100	130	___
18816	C&NW GP38-2 Diesel "4600," *92*	105	130	___
18817	UP GP9 Diesel "150" (see 18553), *91 u*		135	___
18819	L&N GP38-2 Diesel "4136," *92*	115	145	___
18820	WP GP9 Diesel "8820" (SSS), *92*	120	140	___

|---|---|---|---|---|
___	18821	Clinchfield GP38-2 Diesel "6005," *93*	125	150
___	18822	Gulf, Mobile & Ohio RS3 Diesel "721," *92-93 u*		NRS
___	18823	Chicago & Illinois Midland SD9 Diesel "52," *92 u*		235
___	18824	Montana Rail Link SD9 Diesel "600," *93*	185	230
___	18825	Soo Line GP38-2 Diesel "4000" (SSS), *93*	120	145
___	18826	Conrail GP7 Diesel "5808," *93*	100	120
___	18827	"Happy Holidays" RS3 Diesel "8827," *93*	165	220
___	18830	Budweiser GP9 Diesel "1947," *93-94 u*	125	165
___	18831	SP GP20 Diesel "4060," *94*	105	120
___	18832	PRR RSD-4 Diesel "8446," *95*	110	135
___	18833	Milwaukee Road RS3 Diesel "2487," *94*	100	110
___	18834	C&O SD28 Diesel "8834," *94*	110	140
___	18835	NYC RS3 Diesel "8223" (SSS), *94*	135	195
___	18836	CN (Grand Trunk) GP38-2 Diesel "5800," *94*	135	160
___	18837	"Happy Holidays" RS3 Diesel "8837," *94-95*	150	190
___	18838	Seaboard RSC-3 Diesel "1538," *95*	110	140
___	18840	U.S. Army GP7 Diesel "1821," *95*	85	124
___	18841	Western Maryland GP20 Diesel "27" (SSS), *95*	120	150
___	18842	JCPenney B&LE SD38 Diesel "868," *95 u*		265
___	18843	Great Northern RS3 Diesel "197," *96*		145
___	18845	D&RGW RS3 Diesel "5204," *97*		100
___	18846	Lionel Centennial Series GP9 Diesel, *98*	0	427
___	18847	Santa Fe H-12-44 Switcher "602," *99*		385
___	18848	PRR H-12-44 Switcher "9087," *99*		420
___	18853	JCPenney Santa Fe GP9 Diesel "2370," *97 u*		150
___	18854	UP GP9 Diesel Dummy Set, "2380, 2387," *97*		450
___	18856	NJ Transit GP38-2 Diesel "4303," *99*		315
___	18857	Union Pacific GP9 Diesel "2397," *97*		240
___	18858	Lionel Centennial GP20 Diesel, *98*		450
___	18859	Phantom II, *99*		360
___	18860	Pratt's Hollow Collection I: Phantom, *98*		400
___	18864	Southern Pacific GP9 Diesel B Unit, *98*		140
___	18865	New York Central GP9 Diesel B Unit, *98*		170
___	18866	Milwaukee Road GP7 Diesel "2383," *98*		205
___	18868	NJ Transit GP38-2 Diesel "4300," *98 u*		140
___	18870	Pennsylvania GP9 Diesel "2029," *98*		180
___	18872	Wabash GP7 Diesel Set, "453, 454, 455," *99*		560
___	18876	C&NW H-12-44 Switcher "1053," *99*	125	319
___	18877	Union Pacific GP9 Diesel "2399," nonpowered, *99*		175
___	18878	Alaska GP7 Diesel "1803," *99*		115
___	18879	B&O GP9 Diesel "5616," *99*		260
___	18881	Custom GP9 Diesel "5616," *99*		350
___	18892	Burlington GP9 Diesel "2328," *99*		205
___	18897	Christmas GP7 Diesel "1999," *99*		200
___	18900	PRR Switcher "8900," *88 u, 89*	26	34
___	18903	Amtrak "Mopar Express," *99*		500
___	18905	PRR 44-ton Switcher "9312," *92*	80	116
___	18906	Erie-Lackawanna RS3 Diesel "8906," *91 u*	70	90
___	18907	Rock Island 44-ton Switcher "371," *93*	95	110
___	18910	CSX Switcher "8910," *93*	40	46
___	18911	UP Switcher "8911," *93*	33	37
___	18912	Amtrak Switcher "8912," *93*	37	43
___	18913	Santa Fe Alco Diesel A Unit "8913," *93-94*	55	65
___	18915	WM Alco Diesel A Unit "8915," *93*	65	80

		Esc	Mint	
18916	WM Alco Diesel A Unit "8916," dummy, *93*	38	42	___
18917	Soo Line NW2 Switcher, *93*	65	75	___
18918	B&M NW2 Switcher "8918," *93*	75	90	___
18919	Santa Fe Alco Diesel A Unit "8919," dummy, *93-94*	36	55	___
18920	Frisco NW2 Switcher "254," *94*	70	75	___
18921	C&NW NW2 Switcher "1017," *94*	60	80	___
18922	New Haven Alco Diesel A Unit "8922," *94*	75	105	___
18923	New Haven Alco Diesel A Unit "8923," dummy, *94*	50	55	___
18924	IC Switcher "8924," *94-95*	37	44	___
18925	D&RGW Switcher "8925," *94-95*	32	37	___
18926	Reading Switcher "8926," *94-95*	31	39	___
18927	U.S. Navy NW2 Switcher "65-00637," *94-95*	65	85	___
18928	C&NW NW2 Switcher Calf Unit, *95*	50	55	___
18929	B&M NW2 Switcher Calf Unit, *95*	44	49	___
18930	Crayola Switcher, *94 u, 95*	27	30	___
18931	Chrysler Mopar NW2 Switcher "1818," *94 u*	76	88	___
18932	Jersey Central NW2 Switcher "8932," *96*		65	___
18933	Jersey Central NW2 Switcher Calf Unit "8933," *96*		55	___
18934	Reading Alco Diesel A-A Set, *1995*			___
18936	Amtrak Alco Diesel A Unit "8936," *95*		65	___
18937	Amtrak FA2 Alco Diesel, nonpowered, *95-97*		50	___
18938	U.S. Navy NW2 Switcher Calf Unit, *95*	55	65	___
18939	Union Pacific NW2 Switcher Set, *96*		145	___
18943	Georgia Power NW2 Switcher "1960," *95 u*		170	___
18946	U.S. Coast Guard NW2 Switcher "8946," *96*		80	___
18947	Port of Lionel City Alco FA2 Diesel "2030," *97*		70	___
18948	Port of Lionel City Alco FB2 Diesel "2030B," *97*		45	___
18952	ATSF Alco PA1 Diesel "2000," *97*		345	___
18953	NYC Alco PA1 Diesel "2000," *97*		260	___
18954	ATSF Alco FA2 Diesel "212," *powered, 97-99*		80	___
18955	NJ Transit NW2 Switcher "500," *96 u*		110	___
18956	Dodge Motorsports NW2 Switcher "8956," *96 u*		172	___
18959	New York Central NW2 Switcher "622," *97*		475	___
18961	Erie Alco PA1 Diesel "850," *98*		315	___
18965	Santa Fe Alco PB1 Diesel, *98*		255	___
18966	New York Central Alco BP1 Diesel "2008," *98*		250	___
18971	Alco Diesel A Unit, nonpowered, *98*		60	___
18973	RI Alco FA2 Diesel "2031," powered, *98-99*		NRS	___
18974	RI Alco FA2 Diesel Dummy Unit, *98-99*		NRS	___
18975	Southern 44-ton Switcher "1955," *99*		190	___
18978	C&O NW2 Switcher "624," *99-00*		410	___
18981	Pennsylvania Railroad Speeder "16," *04*		45	___
18982	Santa Fe Railroad Speeder "122," *04-05*		65	___
18988	MP15 Diesel, K-Line, *06*		140	___
18989	Bethlehem Steel Plymouth Switcher, traditional, K-Line, *06*		100	___
18992	SP S2 Diesel Switcher "1440," *CC, 08*		410	___
18993	C&NW S2 Diesel Switcher "1031," *CC, 08*		410	___
18994	Lionel Lines FA Diesel, traditional, *08-09*		90	___
19000	Blue Comet Diner, *87 u*	60	75	___
19001	Southern Diner, *87 u*	55	65	___
19002	Pennsylvania Diner, *88 u*	29	41	___
19003	Milwaukee Road Diner, *88 u*	29	44	___
19010	B&O Diner, *89 u*	36	55	___
19011	Lionel Lines Baggage Car, *93*	184	299	___

		Esc	Mint
____ 19015	Lionel Lines Passenger Coach, *91*	125	180
____ 19016	Lionel Lines Passenger Coach, *91*	100	135
____ 19017	Lionel Lines Passenger Coach, *91*	85	110
____ 19018	Lionel Lines Observation Car, *91*	95	120
____ 19019	SP Baggage Car "9019," *93*	120	153
____ 19023	SP Passenger Coach "9023," *92*	125	160
____ 19024	SP Passenger Coach "9024," *92*	85	100
____ 19025	SP Passenger Coach "9025," *92*	100	115
____ 19026	SP Observation Car "9026," *92*	85	100
____ 19038	Adolphus Busch Observation Car, *92-93 u*		85
19039	Pere Marquette Baggage Car, *93*		75
19040	Pere Marquette Passenger Coach "1115," *93*		75
19041	Pere Marquette Passenger Coach "1116," *93*		75
19042	Pere Marquette Observation Car "36," *93*		75
19047	Baltimore & Ohio Combination Car "9047," *96*		55
19048	Baltimore & Ohio Passenger Coach "9048," *96*		50
19049	Baltimore & Ohio Diner "9049," *96*		42
19050	Baltimore & Ohio Observation Car "9050," *96*		42
19056	NYC Heavyweight Baggage Car, *96*		105
19057	NYC Willow Run Heavyweight Coach, *96*		95
19058	NYC Willow Trail Heavyweight Coach, *96*		90
19059	NYC Seneca Valley Heavyweight Observation Car, *96*		100
19060	Pullman Heavyweight Set, *96*		473
19061	Wabash Passenger Set, *97*		235
19062	Wabash City of Columbia Coach "2361," *97*		90
19063	Wabash City of Danville Coach "2362," *97*		75
19064	Wabash REA Baggage Car "2360," *97*		47
19065	Wabash Windy City Observation Car "2363," *97*		90
19066	Commodore Vanderbilt Pullman Heavyweight 2-pack, *97*		190
19067	Commodore Vanderbilt Willow River Pullman "2543," *97*		115
19068	Commodore Vanderbilt Willow Valley Pullman "2544," *97*		100
19069	Pullman Baby Madison Set "9500-02," *97*		155
19070	Baby Madison Combination Car "9501," *97*		40
19071	Laurel Gap Baby Madison Coach "9500," *97*		34
19072	Laurel Summit Baby Madison Coach "9500," *97*		40
19073	Catskill Valley Baby Madison Observation Car "9502," *97*		34
19074	Legends of Lionel Madison Set, *97*		385
19075	Mazzone Lionel Legends Coach "2621," *97*		105
19076	Caruso Lionel Legends Coach "2624," *97*		90
19077	Raphael Lionel Legends Coach "2652," *97*		90
19078	Cowen Lionel Legends Observation Car "2600," *97*		95
19079	NYC Heavyweight Passenger Car Set, *97*		275
19080	NYC Heavyweight REA Baggage Car "2564," *97*		100
19081	NYC Park Place Heavyweight Coach "2565," *97*		100
19082	NYC Star Beam Heavyweight Coach "2566," *97*		100
19083	NYC Hudson Valley Heavyweight Observation Car "2567," *97*		100
19087	C&O Heavyweight Passenger Car 4-pack, *"2571-74," 97*		290
19088	C&O Heavyweight Baggage Car "2571," *97*		100
19089	C&O Heavyweight Sleeper Car "2572," *97*		100
19090	C&O Heavyweight Diner "2573," *97*		110
19091	C&O Heavyweight Observation Car "2574," *97*		100
19093	Commodore Vanderbilt Heavyweight Sleeper Car 2-pack, *98*		170
19094	Commodore Vanderbilt Niagara Falls Sleeper, *98*		75
19095	Commodore Vanderbilt Highland Falls Sleeper, *98*		75

		Esc	Mint	
19096	Legends of Lionel Madison Car 2-pack, 98		130	___
19097	Bonnano Lionel Legends Coach "2653," 98		80	___
19098	Pagano Lionel Legends Coach "2654," 98		105	___
19099	PRR Liberty Gap Baggage Car "2623," 99		80	___
19100	Amtrak Baggage Car "9100," 89	125	165	___
19101	Amtrak Combination Car "9101," 89	75	85	___
19102	Amtrak Passenger Coach "9102," 89	75	85	___
19103	Amtrak Vista Dome Car "9103," 89	70	90	___
19104	Amtrak Diner "9104," 89	65	80	___
19105	Amtrak Full Vista Dome Car "9105," 89 u	70	80	___
19106	Amtrak Observation Car "9106," 89	75	90	___
19107	SP Full Vista Dome Car, 90 u	70	88	___
19108	N&W Full Vista Dome Car "576," 91 u	75	85	___
19109	Santa Fe Baggage Car "3400," 91	225	300	___
19110	Santa Fe Combination Car "3500," 91	80	110	___
19111	Santa Fe Diner "601," 91	100	135	___
19112	Santa Fe Passenger Coach, 91	125	175	___
19113	Santa Fe Vista Dome Car, 91	100	135	___
19116	Great Northern Baggage Car "1200," 92	135	165	___
19117	Great Northern Combination Car "1240," 92	65	80	___
19118	Great Northern Passenger Coach "1212," 92	75	95	___
19119	Great Northern Vista Dome Car "1322," 92	75	95	___
19120	Great Northern Observation Car "1192," 92	75	95	___
19121	Union Pacific Vista Dome Car "9121," 92 u	90	100	___
19122	D&RGW California Zephyr Baggage Car, 93	170	210	___
19123	D&RGW California Zephyr Silver Bronco Vista Dome Car, 93	95	115	___
19124	D&RGW California Zephyr Silver Colt Vista Dome Car, 93	95	115	___
19125	D&RGW California Zephyr Silver Mustang Vista Dome Car, 93	100	125	___
19126	D&RGW California Zephyr Silver Pony Vista Dome Car, 93	95	115	___
19127	D&RGW California Zephyr Vista Dome Car, 93	85	100	___
19128	Santa Fe Full Vista Dome Car "507," 92 u	175	185	___
19129	IC Full Vista Dome Car "9129," 93	75	85	___
19130	Lackawanna Passenger Cars, set of 4, 94	280	350	___
19131	Lackawanna Baggage Car "2000" (see 19130)		150	___
19132	Lackawanna Diner "469" (see 19130)		100	___
19133	Lackawanna Passenger Coach "260" (see 19130)		100	___
19134	Lackawanna Observation Car "789" (see 19130)		85	___
19135	Lackawanna Combination Car "425," 94	85	100	___
19136	Lackawanna Passenger Coach "211," 94	65	75	___
19137	New York Central Roomette Car, 95	90	105	___
19138	Santa Fe Roomette Car, 95	75	95	___
19139	N&W Baggage Car "577," 95	150	200	___
19140	N&W Combination Car "494," 95	60	80	___
19141	N&W Diner "495," 95	105	135	___
19142	N&W Passenger Coach "538," 95	75	95	___
19143	N&W Passenger Coach "537," 95	75	95	___
19144	N&W Observation Car "582," 95	80	95	___
19145	C&O Combination Car "1403," 96		65	___
19146	C&O Passenger Coach "1623," 96		60	___
19147	C&O Passenger Coach "1803," 96		55	___
19148	C&O Chessie Club Coach "1903," 96		55	___
19149	C&O Coach/Diner "1950," 96		50	___
19150	C&O Observation Car "2504," 96		55	___
19151	Norfolk & Western Duplex Roomette car, 96		108	___

			Esc	Mint
___	19152	Union Pacific Duplex Roomette Car, 96		75
___	19153	C&O Passenger Cars, set of 4, 96		340
___	19154	Atlantic Coast Line Passenger Car Set, 96		340
___	19155	ACL Combination Car "101," 96		90
___	19156	ACL Talladega Diner, 96		90
___	19157	ACL Moultrie Coach, 96		95
___	19158	ACL Observation Car "256," 96		90
___	19159	N&W Passenger Cars, set of 4, 95 u	300	385
___	19160	LL REA Baggage Car, 96		90
___	19161	LL Silver Mesa Coach, 96		80
___	19162	LL Silver Sky Vista Dome Car, 96		75
___	19163	LL Silver Rail Observation Car, 96		75
___	19164	Chesapeake & Ohio Passenger Cars, 96		160
___	19165	ATSF Super Chief Set, 96		305
___	19166	NP Vista Dome Car Set, 97		305
___	19167	NP Pullman Coach "2571," 97		105
___	19168	NP Pullman Coach "2571," 97		105
___	19169	NP Pullman Coach "2570," 97		95
___	19170	NP Pullman Coach "2571," 97		100
___	19171	NYC Streamliner Car 4-pack, 97		285
___	19172	NYC Aluminum Passenger/Baggage Car "2570," 97		95
___	19173	NYC Manhattan Island Aluminum Passenger Diner, 97		100
___	19174	NYC Queensboro Bridge Aluminum Passenger Coach, 97		100
___	19175	NYC Windgate Brook Aluminum Observation Car, 97		90
___	19176	ATSF Indian Arrow Diner "2572," 97		90
___	19177	ATSF Grass Valley Coach "2573," 97		90
___	19178	ATSF Citrus Valley Coach "2574," 97		90
___	19179	ATSF Vista Heights Coach "2575," 97		90
___	19180	ATSF Surfliner Passenger Car 4-pack, 97		250
___	19181	GN Empire Builder Prairie View Full Vista Dome Car, 98		75
___	19182	GN Empire Builder River View Full Vista Dome Car, 98		75
___	19183	GN Empire Builder Vista Dome Car 2-pack, 98		125
___	19184	Milwaukee Road Passenger Car 4-pack, 99		390
___	19185	MILW Red River Valley Aluminum Passenger Coach "194," 99		125
___	19186	MILW Aluminum Coach/Diner "170," 99		110
___	19187	MILW Cedar Rapids Aluminum Observation Car "186 ," 99		120
___	19188	MILW Aluminum REA Passenger/Baggage Car "1336," 99		95
___	19194	KCS Aluminum Passenger Car 4-pack, 00		380
___	19200	Tidewater Southern Boxcar, 87	14	21
___	19201	Lancaster & Chester Boxcar, 87	23	37
___	19202	PRR Boxcar, 87	22	30
___	19203	D&TS Boxcar, 87	11	18
___	19204	Milwaukee Road Boxcar (FF 2), 87	29	41
___	19205	Great Northern DD Boxcar (FF 3), 88	20	24
___	19206	Seaboard System Boxcar, 88	18	23
___	19207	CP Rail DD Boxcar, 88	17	22
___	19208	Southern DD Boxcar, 88	11	13
___	19209	Florida East Coast Boxcar, 88	15	19
___	19210	Soo Line Boxcar, 89	19	23
___	19211	Vermont Railway Boxcar, 89	18	21
___	19212	PRR Boxcar, 89	21	25
___	19213	SP&S DD Boxcar, 89	16	19
___	19214	Western Maryland Boxcar (FF 4), 89	23	27
___	19215	Union Pacific DD Boxcar, 90	17	21

		Esc	Mint	
19216	Santa Fe Boxcar, *90*	17	22	___
19217	Burlington Boxcar, *90*	16	21	___
19218	New Haven Boxcar, *90*	16	20	___
19219	Lionel Lines 1900-1906 Boxcar, diesel RailSounds, *90*	120	145	___
19220	Lionel Lines 1926-1934 Boxcar, *90*	27	30	___
19221	Lionel Lines 1935-1937 Boxcar, *90*	27	30	___
19222	Lionel Lines 1948-1950 Boxcar, *90*	27	30	___
19223	Lionel Lines 1979-1989 Boxcar, *90*	18	25	___
19228	Cotton Belt Boxcar, *91*	16	22	___
19229	Frisco Boxcar, diesel RailSounds (FF 5), *91*	75	90	___
19230	Frisco DD Boxcar (FF 5), *91*	21	26	___
19231	TA&G DD Boxcar, *91*	13	16	___
19232	Rock Island DD Boxcar, *91*	17	20	___
19233	Southern Pacific Boxcar, *91*	15	19	___
19234	NYC Boxcar, *91*	60	65	___
19235	MKT Boxcar, *91*	55	65	___
19236	NKP DD Boxcar (FF 6), *92*	22	30	___
19237	C&IM Boxcar, *92*	17	24	___
19238	Kansas City Southern Boxcar, *92*	18	23	___
19239	Toronto, Hamilton & Buffalo DD Boxcar, *92*	15	20	___
19240	Great Northern DD Boxcar, *92*	15	20	___
19241	Mickey Mouse 60th Anniversary Hi-Cube Boxcar, *91 u*	135	180	___
19242	Donald Duck 50th Anniversary Hi-Cube Boxcar, *91 u*	143	152	___
19243	Clinchfield Boxcar "9790," *91 u*	35	41	___
19244	L&N Boxcar "9791," *92*	35	38	___
19245	Mickey's World Tour Hi-Cube Boxcar, *92 u*	35	40	___
19246	Disney World 20th Anniversary Hi-Cube Boxcar, *92 u*	33	40	___
19247	Postwar "6464" Series Boxcar Set I, 3 cars, *93*	445	610	___
19248	Western Pacific Boxcar "6464," *93*	75	95	___
19249	Great Northern Boxcar "6464," *93*	75	95	___
19250	M&StL Boxcar "6464," *93*	80	105	___
19251	Montana Rail Link DD Boxcar "10001," *93*	21	27	___
19254	Erie Boxcar (FF 7), *93*	21	25	___
19255	Erie DD Boxcar (FF 7), *93*	22	26	___
19256	Goofy Hi-Cube Boxcar, *93*	23	26	___
19257	Postwar "6464" Series Boxcar Set II, 3 cars, *94*	80	97	___
19258	Rock Island Boxcar "6464," *94*	25	34	___
19259	Western Pacific Boxcar "6464100," *94*	33	46	___
19260	Western Pacific Boxcar "6464100," *94*	35	49	___
19261	Perils of Mickey Hi-Cube Boxcar #1, *93*	20	30	___
19262	Perils of Mickey Hi-Cube Boxcar #2, *93*	20	28	___
19263	NYC DD Boxcar (SSS), *94*	36	42	___
19264	Perils of Mickey Hi-Cube Boxcar #3, *94*	28	31	___
19265	Mickey Mouse 65th Anniversary Hi-Cube Boxcar, *94*	22	44	___
19266	Postwar "6464" Series Boxcar Set III, 3 cars, *95*	75	90	___
19267	NYC Pacemaker Boxcar "6464125," *95*	37	42	___
19268	Missouri Pacific Boxcar "6464150," *95*	25	29	___
19269	Rock Island Boxcar "6464," *95*	25	26	___
19270	Donald Duck 60th Anniversary Hi-Cube Boxcar, *95*	30	34	___
19271	Minnie Mouse Hi-Cube Boxcar, *95*	21	43	___
19272	Postwar "6464" Series Boxcar Set IV, 3 cars, *96*	70	85	___
19273	BAR State of Maine Boxcar "6464275," *96*		35	___
19274	SP Overnight Boxcar "6464225," *96*		28	___
19275	Pennsylvania Boxcar "6464," *96*		44	___

|---|---|---|---|---|
___	**19276**	Postwar "6464" Series Boxcar Set V, 3 cars, *96*	65	85
___	**19277**	Rutland Boxcar "6464-300," *96*		26
___	**19278**	B&O Boxcar "6464-325," *96*		30
___	**19279**	Central of Georgia Boxcar "6464-375," *96*		29
___	**19280**	Mickey's Wheat Hi-Cube Boxcar, *96*		32
___	**19281**	Mickey's Carrots Hi-Cube Boxcar, *96*		40
___	**19282**	Santa Fe "Super Chief" Boxcar "6464-196," *96*		24
___	**19283**	Erie Boxcar "6464-296," *96*		22
___	**19284**	Northern Pacific Boxcar "6464-396," *96*		29
___	**19285**	B&A State of Maine Boxcar "6464-275," *96*		27
___	**19286**	Tweety and Sylvester Boxcar, *96*		46
___	**19287**	NYC/PC Merger Boxcar "6464-125X" (SSS), *97*	50	75
___	**19288**	PRR/CR Merger Boxcar "6464-200X" (SSS), *97*	43	56
___	**19289**	Monon "Hoosier Line" Boxcar "6464," *97*		27
___	**19290**	Seaboard "Silver Meteor" Boxcar "6464," *97*		24
___	**19291**	GN Boxcar "6464-397," *97*		26
___	**19292**	Postwar "6464" Series Boxcar Set VI, 3 cars, *97*		90
___	**19293**	MKT Boxcar "6464-350," *97*	28	32
___	**19294**	B&O Boxcar "6464-400," *97*	27	34
___	**19295**	NH Boxcar "6464-425," *97*	25	34
___	**19300**	PRR Ore Car, *87*	15	23
___	**19301**	Milwaukee Road Ore Car, *87*	20	25
___	**19302**	Milwaukee Road Quad Hopper with coal (FF 2), *87*	24	35
___	**19303**	Lionel Lines Quad Hopper with coal, *87 u*	20	31
___	**19304**	GN Covered Quad Hopper (FF 3), *88*	18	25
___	**19305**	Chessie System Ore Car, *88*	18	23
___	**19307**	B&LE Ore Car with load, *89*	19	25
___	**19308**	GN Ore Car with load, *89*	18	23
___	**19309**	Seaboard Covered Quad Hopper, *89*	16	19
___	**19310**	L&C Quad Hopper with coal, *89*	16	30
___	**19311**	SP Covered Quad Hopper, *90*	13	17
___	**19312**	Reading Quad Hopper with coal, *90*	21	36
___	**19313**	B&O Ore Car with load, *90-91*	20	25
___	**19315**	Amtrak Ore Car with load, *91*	22	30
___	**19316**	Wabash Covered Quad Hopper, *91*	18	23
___	**19317**	Lehigh Valley Quad Hopper with coal, *91*	47	55
___	**19318**	NKP Quad Hopper with coal (FF 6), *92*	30	34
___	**19319**	Union Pacific Covered Quad Hopper, *92*	19	23
___	**19320**	PRR Ore Car with load, *92*	21	30
___	**19321**	B&LE Ore Car with load, *92*	21	30
___	**19322**	C&NW Ore Car with load, *93*	27	34
___	**19323**	Detroit & Mackinac Ore Car with load, *93*	20	29
___	**19324**	Erie Quad Hopper with coal (FF 7), *93*	25	33
___	**19325**	N&W 4-bay Hopper "6446-1" with coal, *97*		65
___	**19326**	N&W 4-bay Hopper "6446-2" with coal, *96*		60
___	**19327**	N&W 4-bay Hopper "6446-3" with coal, *96*		60
___	**19328**	N&W 4-bay Hopper "6446-4" with coal, *96*		60
___	**19329**	N&W 4-bay Hopper "6436" with coal, *97*		55
___	**19330**	Cotton Belt 4-bay Hopper "64661" with coal, *98*		45
___	**19331**	Cotton Belt 4-bay Hopper "64662" with coal, *98*		45
___	**19332**	Cotton Belt 4-bay Hopper "64663" with coal, *98*		45
___	**19333**	Cotton Belt 4-bay Hopper "64664" with coal, *98*		45
___	**19338**	Cotton Belt 4-bay Hopper 2-pack, *99*		120
___	**19339**	Cotton Belt 4-bay Hopper "64469," *99*		NRS

| --- | --- | --- | --- |
19340	Cotton Belt 4-bay Hopper "64470," *99*		NRS ___
19341	LV 2-bay Hopper "6456," *99*		30 ___
19344	D&RGW 3-bay Cylindrical Hopper "15990," *99-00*		42 ___
19345	CN 3-bay Cylindrical Hopper "370708," *99-00*		95 ___
19346	PRR 4-bay Hopper with coal "744433," *01*		40 ___
19347	LV 2-bay Hopper "643657," *01*		40 ___
19348	Duluth, Missabe & Iron Range Ore Car "28000," *03*		25 ___
19349	U.S. Steel Ore Car "19349," *03*		29 ___
19350	Postwar "6636" Alaska Quad Hopper, *03*		34 ___
19357	N&W Hopper "6446-25," Archive Collection, *07*		50 ___
19361	Twizzlers Quad Hopper, *10*		55 ___
19362	Coursers Christmas Hopper with gifts, *10*		60 ___
19364	Milk Duds Covered Hopper, *11*		55 ___
19365	Coca-Cola Quad Hopper, *10*		60 ___
19366	Santa's Little Hopper, *10-11*		55 ___
19367	ATSF Quad Hopper, *11*		60 ___
19368	Southern Offset Hopper "106723," (std O), *11*		70 ___
19369	Alaska Quad Hopper "20756," *12*		60 ___
19371	Burlington Northern I-Beam Car, *04*		60 ___
19374	NS Bathtub Gondola 2-pack (std O), *15*		140 ___
19377	DETX Bathtub Gondola 2-pack (std O), *15*		140 ___
19380	CSX Bathtub Gondola 2-pack (std O), *15*		140 ___
19383	UP PS-4 Flatcar "57125" (std O), *13*		70 ___
19384	ATSF PS-4 Flatcar "90088" (std O), *13*		70 ___
19385	CNJ PS-4 Flatcar "339" (std O), *13*		70 ___
19386	BN PS-4 Flatcar "613200" (std O), *13*		70 ___
19388	BN 89' Auto Carrier (std O), *13-14*		110 ___
19389	SP 89' Auto Carrier (std O), *13-14*		110 ___
19390	CP 89' Auto Carrier (std O), *13-14, 16*		110 ___
19391	Soo Line 89' Auto Carrier (std O), *13-14, 16*		110 ___
19393	BNSF Auto Carrier 2-pack (std O), *12*		220 ___
19394	UP Auto Carrier 2-pack (std O), *12*		220 ___
19395	Grand Trunk Auto Carrier 2-pack (std O), *12*		220 ___
19396	CSX Auto Carrier 2-pack (std O), *12*		220 ___
19397	CN Auto Carrier 2-pack (std O), *12*		220 ___
19398	Conrail Auto Carrier 2-pack (std O), *12*		220 ___
19400	Milwaukee Road Gondola with cable reels (FF 2), *87*	23	31 ___
19401	GN Gondola with coal (FF 3), *88*	14	16 ___
19402	GN Crane Car (FF 3), *88*	47	65 ___
19403	WM Gondola with coal (FF 4), *89*	20	25 ___
19404	Trailer Train Flatcar with WM trailers (FF 4), *89*	29	33 ___
19405	Southern Crane Car, *91*	42	65 ___
19406	West Point Mint Car, *91 u*	38	50 ___
19408	Frisco Gondola with coil covers (FF 5), *91*	26	31 ___
19409	Southern Flatcar with stakes, *91*	18	22 ___
19410	NYC Gondola with canisters, *91*	47	55 ___
19411	NKP Flatcar with Sears trailer (FF 6), *92*	50	59 ___
19412	Frisco Crane Car, *92*	49	65 ___
19413	Frisco Flatcar with stakes, *92*	16	21 ___
19414	Union Pacific Flatcar with stakes (SSS), *92*	19	26 ___
19415	Erie Flatcar with trailer "7200" (FF 7), *93*	28	39 ___
19416	ICG TTUX Flatcar Set with trailers (SSS), *93*	70	75 ___
19419	Charlotte Mint Car, *93*	25	32 ___
19420	Lionel Lines Vat Car, *94*	18	22 ___

			Esc	Mint
____	19421	Hirsch Brothers Vat Car, *95*	16	21
____	19423	Circle L Racing Flatcar "6424" with stock cars, *96*		27
____	19424	Edison Electric Depressed Center Flatcar "6461" with transformer, *97*		31
____	19427	Evans Auto Loader "6414," *99*		55
____	19428	Evans Boat Loader "6414," *99*		70
____	19429	Culvert Gondola "6342," *98-99*		48
____	19430	ATSF Flatcar "6411" with Beechcraft Bonanza, *98*		47
____	19438	Christmas Gondola (std O), *98*		42
____	19439	Flatcar with safes, *98*		35
____	19440	Flatcar with FedEx trailer, *98*		34
____	19441	Lobster Vat Car, *98*		35
____	19442	Water Supply Flatcar with tank (SSS), *98*		31
____	19444	Flatcar with VW Bug, *98*		38
____	19445	Borden Milk Tank Car "520," *99*		38
____	19446	Pittsburgh Paint Vat Car, *99*		43
____	19447	Mama's Baked Beans Vat Car, *99*		35
____	19448	Easter Gondola "6462" with candy, *99*		27
____	19449	Liquified Gas Tank Car "6469," *99*		31
____	19450	Barrel Ramp Car "6343," *99*		31
____	19451	Wheel Car "6262," *99*		32
____	19454	PRR Flatcar "6424" with gondola, *99*		25
____	19455	Lionel Lines Flatcar "6430" with Cooper-Jarrett trailers, *99*		60
____	19457	Lionel Lines Extension Searchlight Car, *99*		40
____	19459	Valentine Gondola "6462" with candy, *99*		50
____	19471	Mobil Flatcar with 2 trailers, *00 u*		96
____	19472	Mobil Bulkhead Flatcar with tank, *00 u*		68
____	19474	L&N Flatcar "6424" with trailer frames, *99*		26
____	19476	Zoo Gondola "6462" with animals, *99-00*		43
____	19477	Monday Night Football Flatcar with trailer, *01*		30
____	19478	Culvert Gondola "6342," *99*		45
____	19479	Borden Milk Car "521," *00*		38
____	19480	Valentine's Vat Car "6475," *99-00*		30
____	19481	Easter Vat Car, *99-00*		38
____	19482	NYC Flat with trailer "6424," *00*		50
____	19483	VW Beetle Flatcar, *00*		48
____	19484	Flatcar "6264" with timber, *00*		34
____	19485	PRR Culvert Gondola "347004," *01*		41
____	19486	NYC Lumber Flatcar, *01*		34
____	19487	Flatcar "6800" with airplane, *00*		41
____	19489	Evans Auto Loader "500085," *00*		50
____	19490	Postwar "6475" Libby's Vat Car, *01-02*		36
____	19491	Christmas Vat Car, *01*		30
____	19492	WM Skeleton Log Car 3-pack, *01*		95
____	19496	Westside Lumber Skeleton Log Car 3-pack, *01*		112
____	19500	Milwaukee Road Reefer (FF 2), *87*	30	39
____	19502	C&NW Reefer, *87*	30	33
____	19503	Bangor & Aroostook Reefer, *87*	22	25
____	19504	Northern Pacific Reefer, *87*	16	22
____	19505	Great Northern Reefer (FF 3), *88*	29	35
____	19506	Thomas Newcomen Reefer, *88*	18	23
____	19507	Thomas Edison Reefer, *88*	21	27
____	19508	Leonardo da Vinci Reefer, *89*	19	27
____	19509	Alexander Graham Bell Reefer, *89*	17	20

MODERN 1970-2021		Esc	Mint
19510	PRR Stock Car (FARR 5), *89 u*	18	26 ___
19511	WM Reefer (FF 4), *89*	22	28 ___
19512	Wright Brothers Reefer, *90*	17	21 ___
19513	Ben Franklin Reefer, *90*	17	20 ___
19515	Milwaukee Road Stock Car (FF 2), *90 u*	33	41 ___
19516	George Washington Reefer, *89 u, 91*	14	19 ___
19517	Civil War Reefer, *89 u, 91*	14	19 ___
19518	Man on the Moon Reefer, *89 u, 91*	13	17 ___
19519	Frisco Stock Car (FF 5), *91*	26	31 ___
19520	CSX Reefer, *91*	18	23 ___
19522	Guglielmo Marconi Reefer, *91*	19	23 ___
19523	Dr. Robert Goddard Reefer, *91*	19	23 ___
19524	Delaware & Hudson Reefer (SSS), *91*	29	32 ___
19525	Speedy Alka Seltzer Reefer, *91 u*	31	32 ___
19526	Jolly Green Giant Reefer, *91 u*	21	33 ___
19527	Nickel Plate Road Reefer (FF 6), *92*	20	29 ___
19528	Joshua L. Cowen Reefer, *92*	23	28 ___
19529	A.C. Gilbert Reefer, *92*	18	23 ___
19530	Rock Island Stock Car, *92 u*	34	38 ___
19531	Rice Krispies Reefer, *92 u*	23	33 ___
19532	Hormel Reefer "901," *92 u*	18	24 ___
19535	Erie Reefer (FF 7), *93*	23	26 ___
19536	Soo Line REA Reefer (SSS), *93*	25	30 ___
19538	Hormel Reefer "102," *94*	22	25 ___
19539	Heinz Reefer, *94*	38	47 ___
19540	Broken Arrow Ranch Stock Car "3356," *97*		28 ___
19552	Rutland Reefer "395" (std O), *00*		32 ___
19553	ATSF Stock Car "23003," *00*		37 ___
19554	Postwar Celebration Milk Car "36621," *00*		125 ___
19555	Swift Reefer "5839," red, *01*		33 ___
19556	Swift Reefer "1020," silver, *01*		31 ___
19557	Circus Stock Car "6376," *00*		32 ___
19558	Postwar "6556" MKT Stock Car, *02*		27 ___
19559	MKT Stock Car, girls set add-on, *02*		95 ___
19560	NP 2-door Stock Car "6356," Archive Collection, *02*		33 ___
19561	Norman Rockwell Holiday Reefer, *03*		25 ___
19562	Norman Rockwell Holiday Reefer, *03*		25 ___
19563	Norman Rockwell Holiday Reefer, *03*		25 ___
19564	Postwar "6672" Santa Fe Reefer, *03*		35 ___
19565	Burlington Reefer "6672," Archive Collection, *03*		35 ___
19567	Postwar "6572" Railway Express Agency Reefer, *05*		45 ___
19568	GN Reefer, Archive Collection, *05*		45 ___
19569	Pillsbury Reefer, traditional, *05*		53 ___
19570	Nestle Nesquik Reefer, traditional, *05*		53 ___
19572	NYC Reefer "6672," Archive Collection, *06*		45 ___
19573	Postwar "6356" NYC Stock Car, *06-07*		50 ___
19574	GN Stock Car, *08*		50 ___
19575	REA Reefer "6721," *08-09*		50 ___
19576	Alaska Reefer, *08*		50 ___
19577	Krey's Reefer, *10-11*		60 ___
19578	Granny Smith Apples Wood-sided Reefer, *10-11*		53 ___
19585	NS Transparent Instruction Car, *10-11*		75 ___
19586	Alaska Husky Transport Car, *10-11*		75 ___
19587	Hershey's Chocolate Wood-sided Reefer, *10*		75 ___

		Esc	Mint
19588	Santa's Wish Transparent Gift Car, *10*		75
19589	Blood Transfusion Bunk Car, *10-11*		60
19590	Wood-sided Reefer 2-pack, *10*		110
19593	Hershey's Kisses Wood-sided Reefer, *11-15*		60
19594	York Peppermint Patty Wood-sided Reefer, *10-11*		55
19599	Old Glory Reefers, set of 3, *89 u, 91*	37	43
19600	Milwaukee Road 1-D Tank Car (FF 2), *87*	33	40
19601	North American 1-D Tank Car (FF 4), *89*	17	29
19602	Johnson 1-D Tank Car (FF 5), *91*	24	30
19603	GATX 1-D Tank Car (FF 6), *92*	32	41
19604	Goodyear 1-D Tank Car (SSS), *93*	33	36
19605	Hudson's Bay 1-D Tank Car (SSS), *94*	25	29
19607	Sunoco 1-D Tank Car "6315," *96*		23
19608	Sunoco Aviation Services 1-D Tank Car "6315" (SSS), *97*		38
19611	Gulf Oil 1-D Tank Car "6315," *98*		33
19612	Gulf Oil 3-D Tank Car "6425," *98*		30
19614	BASF 1-D Tank Car "UTLX 78252," *99-00*		25
19615	Vulcan Chemicals 1-D Tank Car, *99-00*		25
19621	Centennial 1-D Tank Car "6015-1," *99*		55
19622	Centennial 1-D Tank Car "6015-2," *99*		62
19623	Centennial 1-D Tank Car "6015-3," *99*		62
19624	Centennial 1-D Tank Car "6015-4," *99*		58
19625	Ethyl Tank Car " 6236," *01*		31
19626	Diamond Chemical Tank Car "19419," *01*		29
19627	Shell 1-D Tank Car "1227," *01*		37
19628	Lion Oil 1-D Tank Car "2256," *01*		35
19634	General American 1-D Tank Car, *01*		30
19635	U.S. Army 1-D Tank Car "10936," *01*		31
19636	Hooker Chemicals 1-D Tank Car "6180," *01*		36
19637	GATX TankTrain Intermediate Car "44589" (std O), *02*		55
19638	CN TankTrain Intermediate Car "75571" (std O), *02*		65
19639	GATX TankTrain Intermediate Car 3-pack (std O), *02*		140
19644	Union Texas 1-D Tank Car "9922," *02*		33
19645	Penn Salt 1-D Tank Car "4730," *02*		33
19646	CN TankTrain Intermediate Car "75571" (std O), *03*		45
19647	GATX TankTrain Intermediate Car "44589" (std O), *03*		45
19649	Scrooge McDuck Mint Car, *05*	0	199
19651	Santa Fe Tool Car, *87*	30	35
19652	Jersey Central Bunk Car, *88*	25	33
19653	Jersey Central Tool Car, *88*	26	28
19654	Amtrak Bunk Car, *89*	22	25
19655	Amtrak Tool Car, *90-91*	23	30
19656	Milwaukee Road Bunk Car, smoke, *90*	40	50
19657	Wabash Bunk Car, smoke, *91-92*	36	42
19658	Norfolk & Western Tool Car, *91*	24	29
19660	Mint Car, *98*		40
19663	Pratt's Hollow Bunk Car "5717," *99*		40
19664	Ambassador Award Bunk Car, bronze, *99 u*	0	445
19665	Ambassador Engineer Bunk Car, silver, *99 u*		610
19666	Ambassador Cowen Bunk Car, gold, *99 u*		440
19667	Wellspring Gold Bullion Car, *99*		58
19669	King Tut Museum Car "9660," *99*		70
19670	NY Federal Reserve Bullion Car "6445," *00*		44
19671	Lionel Model Shop Display Car "6445-01," *99-00*		50

MODERN 1970-2021		Esc	Mint
19672	Lionel Mines Mint Car, *00 u*		250 ___
19673	Wellspring Capital Management Mint Car, *99 u*		220 ___
19674	Lionel Lines Platinum Car, *00*		43 ___
19675	Lionel Model Shop Display "6445-2," *01*		42 ___
19676	Philadelphia Mint Car, *01*		40 ___
19677	Fort Knox Mint Car "6445," *00*		50 ___
19678	U.S. Army Bunk Car, *02*		45 ___
19679	St. Louis Federal Reserve Mint Car, *02*		38 ___
19681	Area 51 Alien Suspension Car, *02*		47 ___
19682	Alaska Klondike Mining Mint Car, *02*		40 ___
19683	Pony Express Mint Car, *02*		50 ___
19686	Chicago Federal Reserve Mint Car "6445," *03-04*		45 ___
19687	UP Bunk Car "3887," smoke, *03*		40 ___
19688	Postwar "6445" Fort Knox Mint Car, *02-03*		39 ___
19689	CIBRO TankTrain Intermediate Car 3-pack (std O), *03*		100 ___
19694	Pony Express Mint Car, *03*		50 ___
19696	U.S. Savings Bond Mint Car, *00*		150 ___
19697	U.S. Bureau of Engraving and Printing Mint Car "19697," *04*		40 ___
19698	San Francisco Federal Reserve Mint Car, *04*		40 ___
19700	Chessie System Extended Vision Caboose, *88*	43	50 ___
19701	Milwaukee Road N5c Caboose (FF 2), *88*	50	65 ___
19702	PRR N5c Caboose, *87*	44	55 ___
19703	GN Extended Vision Caboose (FF 3), *88*	42	49 ___
19704	WM Extended Vision Caboose, smoke (FF 4), *89*	42	49 ___
19705	CP Rail Extended Vision Caboose, smoke, *89*	43	47 ___
19706	UP Extended Vision Caboose "9706," smoke, *89*	40	56 ___
19707	SP Work Caboose with searchlight, smoke, *90*	55	60 ___
19708	Lionel Lines Bay Window Caboose, *90*	43	46 ___
19709	PRR Work Caboose, smoke, *89, 91*	49	70 ___
19710	Frisco Extended Vision Caboose, smoke (FF 5), *91*	43	47 ___
19711	NS Extended Vision Caboose, smoke, *92*	47	65 ___
19712	PRR N5c Caboose, *91*	44	47 ___
19714	NYC Work Caboose with searchlight, smoke, *92*	100	130 ___
19715	DM&IR Extended Vision Caboose "C-217," *92 u*	50	60 ___
19716	IC Extended Vision Caboose "9405," smoke, *93*	105	135 ___
19717	Susquehanna Bay Window Caboose "0121," *93*	44	55 ___
19718	C&IM Extended Vision Caboose "74," *92 u*	38	45 ___
19719	Erie Bay Window Caboose "C-300" (FF 7), *93*	47	55 ___
19720	Soo Line Extended Vision Caboose (SSS), *93*	32	41 ___
19721	GM&O Extended Vision Caboose "2956," *93 u*	47	50 ___
19723	Disney Extended Vision Caboose, *94*	36	45 ___
19724	JCPenney MKT Extended Vision Caboose "125," *94 u*	38	43 ___
19726	NYC Bay Window Caboose (SSS), *95*	50	60 ___
19727	Pennsylvania N5c Caboose "477938," *96*		30 ___
19728	N&W Bay Window Caboose, *96*		70 ___
19732	ATSF Bay Window Caboose "6517," *96*		43 ___
19733	New York Central Caboose "6357," *96*		30 ___
19734	Southern Pacific Caboose "6357," *96*		26 ___
19736	PRR N5c Caboose "6417," *97*		27 ___
19737	Lackawanna Searchlight Caboose "2420," *97*		75 ___
19738	Conrail N5c Caboose "6417" (SSS), *97*		55 ___
19739	NYC Wood-sided Caboose "6907," *97*		60 ___
19740	Virginian N5c Caboose "6427," *97 u*		65 ___
19741	Pennsylvania N5c Caboose "6417," 98		50 ___

	MODERN 1970-2021	Esc	Mint
___ 19742	Erie Bay Window Caboose "C301," Caboose Talk, 98		95
___ 19748	SP&S Bay Window Caboose "6517," 97 u		50
___ 19749	SP Bay Window Caboose "6517," 98		100
___ 19750	Holiday Music Bay Window Caboose, 98		160
___ 19751	PRR N5c Caboose "492418," 98		30
___ 19752	NP Bay Window Caboose "407," 98		50
___ 19753	UP Extended Vision Caboose "25641," 98		55
___ 19754	NYC Caboose "20112," 98		55
___ 19755	Centennial Porthole Caboose, 99		68
___ 19756	Lionel Lines Bay Window Caboose, 99		50
___ 19758	DL&W Work Caboose "6419," 99		55
___ 19759	Corvette N5c Caboose, 99		60
___ 19772	Lionel Visitor's Center Vat Car, 99 u		40
___ 19773	Lionel Kids Club Barrel Ramp Car "6343," 96 u		48
___ 19778	Case Cutlery Wood-sided Caboose "1889" (std O), 99 u		NRS
___ 19779	SP Bay Window Caboose "1908," 99		65
___ 19780	LV Porthole Caboose "641751," 99-00		43
___ 19781	Vapor Records Holiday Porthole Caboose "6417," 99-00		62
___ 19782	NYC Bay Window Caboose "21719," 00		65
___ 19783	Ford Mustang Extended Vision Caboose, 01		50
___ 19785	SP Bay Window Caboose "6517," 00		55
___ 19786	PRR Extended Vision Caboose, 00 u		40
___ 19787	PRR Extended Vision Caboose "477927," 01		40
___ 19790	Postwar "6417" Lehigh Valley Caboose, 02		41
___ 19792	Postwar "C301" Erie Bay Window Caboose, 03		45
___ 19796	C&O Bay Window Caboose, 03		50
___ 19800	Circle L Ranch Operating Cattle Car, 88	75	95
___ 19801	Poultry Dispatch Chicken Car, 87	20	27
___ 19802	Carnation Milk Car, 87	87	102
___ 19803	Reading Ice Car, 87	38	44
___ 19804	Wabash Operating Hopper, 87	25	34
___ 19805	Santa Fe Operating Boxcar, 87	28	36
___ 19806	PRR Operating Hopper, 88	28	32
___ 19807	PRR Extended Vision Caboose, smoke, 88	39	47
___ 19808	NYC Ice Car, 88	38	49
___ 19809	Erie-Lackawanna Operating Boxcar, 88	27	35
___ 19810	Bosco Milk Car, 88	80	89
___ 19811	Monon Brakeman Car, 90	50	55
___ 19813	Northern Pacific Ice Car, 89 u	41	46
___ 19815	Delaware & Hudson Brakeman Car, 92	49	60
___ 19816	Madison Hardware Operating Boxcar "190991," 91 u	90	105
___ 19817	Virginian Ice Car, 94	31	35
___ 19818	Dairymen's League Milk Car "788," 94	65	80
___ 19819	Poultry Dispatch Car (SSS), 94	36	43
___ 19820	Die-cast Tender, RailSounds II, 95-96		175
___ 19821	UP Operating Boxcar, 95	31	36
___ 19822	Pork Dispatch Car, 95	29	39
___ 19823	Burlington Ice Car, 94 u, 95	39	49
___ 19824	U.S. Army Target Launcher, 96		32
___ 19825	Generator Car, 96		48
___ 19827	NYC Operating Boxcar, 97		37
___ 19828	C&NW Animated Stock Car "3356" and Stockyard, 96-97		100
___ 19830	U.S. Mail Operating Boxcar "3428," 97		39
___ 19831	GM Generator Car "3530," power pole and wire, 97		44

		Esc	Mint	
19832	Cola Ice Car "6352," 97		47	___
19833	Tender "2426RS," RailSounds II, 97		240	___
19834	LL 6-wheel Crane Car "2460," 97		60	___
19835	FedEx Animated Boxcar "3464X," 97		38	___
19837	Bucyrus 6-wheel Crane Car "2460," 99		49	___
19845	Aquarium Car "3435," CC, 98		151	___
19846	Animated Giraffe Car "3376C," 98		105	___
19850	Stock Car "33760," RailSounds, 00		130	___
19853	Firefighting Instruction Generator Car (SSS), 98		60	___
19854	Lionelville Fire Car (SSS), 98		55	___
19855	Christmas Aquarium Car, 98		60	___
19856	Mermaid Transport, 98		65	___
19857	NYC Firefighting Instruction Car "19853," 98-99		175	___
19858	Lionelville Operating Searchlight Car "19854," 99		65	___
19859	REA Boxcar "6267," steam RailSounds, 99		170	___
19860	Conrail Boxcar "169671," diesel RailSounds, 99		140	___
19864	Animated Ostrich Boxcar, 99		37	___
19867	Operating Poultry Dispatch Car "3434," 99		48	___
19868	Shark Aquarium Car "3435," 99		190	___
19869	Alien Aquarium Car "3435," 99		49	___
19877	ATSF Operating Barrel Car, 99		55	___
19878	Operating Helium Tank Flatcar "3362," 99		40	___
19880	Lionel Lines Extension Searchlight Car, 00		50	___
19882	Sanderson Farms Poultry Car "3434," 99		41	___
19883	LL Bucyrus Erie Crane Car "64608," 99		45	___
19884	Atlantis Travel Aquarium Car, 00 u		95	___
19885	N&W Operating Hopper Car, 00		31	___
19886	Seaboard Boxcar "16126," steam RailSounds, 00		140	___
19887	SP Boxcar "651663," diesel RailSounds, 00		140	___
19888	Christmas Music Boxcar, 01		65	___
19889	PRR Bay Window Caboose "477719," Crewtalk, 00		140	___
19890	Santa Fe Bay Window Caboose "999211," Crewtalk, 00		100	___
19894	Hood's Operating Milk Car with platform, 03-04		95	___
19895	3356 Santa Fe Horse Car with corral, 04		120	___
19896	USMC Missile Launch Sound Car "45," 03-04		165	___
19897	NYC Crane Car, TMCC, 04		255	___
19898	Nestle Nesquik Operating Milk Car with platform, 04		95	___
19899	Pennsylvania Crane Car "19899" CC, 03-05		260	___
19900	Toy Fair Boxcar, 87 u	65	80	___
19901	"I Love Virginia" Boxcar, 87	25	35	___
19902	Toy Fair Boxcar, 88 u	55	80	___
19903	Christmas Boxcar, 87 u	22	34	___
19904	Christmas Boxcar, 88 u	32	43	___
19905	"I Love California" Boxcar, 88	20	24	___
19906	"I Love Pennsylvania" Boxcar, 89	26	32	___
19907	Toy Fair Boxcar, 89 u	38	55	___
19908	Christmas Boxcar, 89 u	30	39	___
19909	"I Love New Jersey" Boxcar, 90	19	25	___
19910	Christmas Boxcar, 90 u	35	38	___
19911	Toy Fair Boxcar, 90 u	75	95	___
19912	"I Love Ohio" Boxcar, 91	21	28	___
19913	Christmas Boxcar, 91	34	52	___
19913	Lionel Employee Christmas Boxcar, 91 u	150	200	___
19914	Toy Fair Boxcar, 91 u	38	50	___

			Esc	Mint
	MODERN 1970-2021			
___	**19915**	"I Love Texas" Boxcar, *92*	35	60
___	**19916**	Lionel Employee Christmas Boxcar, *92 u*	190	220
___	**19917**	Toy Fair Boxcar, *92 u*	45	53
___	**19918**	Christmas Boxcar, *92 u*	49	70
___	**19919**	"I Love Minnesota" Boxcar, *93*	40	60
___	**19920**	Lionel Visitor's Center Boxcar, *92 u*	16	28
___	**19921**	Lionel Employee Christmas Boxcar, *93 u*	140	185
___	**19922**	Christmas Boxcar, *93*	33	41
___	**19923**	Toy Fair Boxcar, *93 u*	65	95
___	**19925**	Lionel Employee Learning Center Boxcar, *93 u*	55	63
___	**19926**	"I Love Nevada" Boxcar, *94*	21	26
___	**19927**	Lionel Visitor's Center Boxcar, *93 u*	26	33
___	**19928**	Lionel Employee Christmas Boxcar, *94 u*	205	230
___	**19929**	Christmas Boxcar, *94*	30	40
___	**19931**	Toy Fair Boxcar, *94 u*	49	65
___	**19932**	Lionel Visitor's Center Boxcar, *94 u*	26	33
___	**19933**	"I Love Illinois" Boxcar, *95*	21	27
___	**19934**	Lionel Visitor's Center Boxcar, *95 u*	18	22
___	**19937**	Toy Fair Boxcar, *95 u*	55	75
___	**19938**	Christmas Boxcar, *95*	26	34
___	**19939**	Lionel Employee Christmas Boxcar, *95 u*	100	128
___	**19941**	"I Love Colorado" Boxcar, *95*	23	30
___	**19942**	"I Love Florida" Boxcar, *96*	19	27
___	**19943**	"I Love Arizona" Boxcar, *96*	20	25
___	**19944**	Lionel Visitor's Center Tank Car, *96 u*		35
___	**19945**	Holiday Boxcar, *96*		29
___	**19946**	Lionel Employee Christmas Boxcar, *96 u*		195
___	**19947**	Lionel Toy Fair Boxcar, *96 u*		200
___	**19948**	Visitor's Center Flatcar with trailer, *96 u*		34
___	**19949**	"I Love NY" Boxcar, *97*		50
___	**19950**	"I Love Montana" Boxcar, *97*		30
___	**19951**	"I Love Massachusetts" Boxcar, *98*		26
___	**19952**	"I Love Indiana" Boxcar, *98*		31
___	**19955**	Lionel Visitor's Center Gondola with coil covers, *98 u*		20
___	**19956**	Toy Fair Boxcar "777," *98 u*		65
___	**19957**	Ambassador Caboose, *97 u*		488
___	**19958**	Ambassador Caboose, silver (std O), *98 u*		558
___	**19959**	Ambassador Caboose, gold (std O), *98 u*	0	756
___	**19964**	U.S. JCI Senate Boxcar, *92 u*	55	63
___	**19968**	"I Love Maine" Boxcar, *99*		40
___	**19969**	"I Love Vermont" Boxcar, *99*		40
___	**19970**	"I Love New Hampshire" Boxcar, *99*		34
___	**19971**	"I Love Rhode Island" Boxcar, *99*		34
___	**19976**	Lionel Employee Holiday Boxcar, *99 u*		150
___	**19977**	Toy Fair Boxcar, *99 u*		50
___	**19981**	Lionel Centennial Boxcar, *99*		36
___	**19982**	Lionel Centennial Boxcar, *99*		36
___	**19983**	Lionel Centennial Boxcar, *99*		36
___	**19984**	Lionel Centennial Boxcar, *99*		36
___	**19985**	"I Love Georgia" Boxcar, *99-00*		45
___	**19986**	"I Love North Carolina" Boxcar, *99-00*		40
___	**19987**	"I Love South Carolina" Boxcar, *99-00*		40
___	**19988**	"I Love Tennessee" Boxcar, *99-00*		55
___	**19989**	Toy Fair Boxcar, *00 u*		55

19996	Toy Fair Boxcar, *01 u*		50 ___
19997	Lionel Employee Boxcar, *01 u*		125 ___
19998	Christmas Boxcar, *01*		33 ___
19999	Lionel Visitor's Center 4-bay Hopper, *02 u*		153 ___
20000	PRR Senator Coach 4-pack (std O), *13, 15*		640 ___
20005	SP Sunset Limited Coach 4-pack (std O), *13, 15*		640 ___
20010	UP City of Los Angeles Coach 4-pack (std O), *13, 15*		640 ___
20015	B&O Capitol Limited Coach 4-pack (std O), *13*		640 ___
20020	FEC City of Miami Coach 4-pack (std O), *13*		640 ___
20025	KCS Southern Belle Coach 4-pack (std O), *13*		640 ___
20030	MILW Olympian Coach 4-pack (std O), *13, 15*		640 ___
21029	World of Little Choo Choo Set, *94u, 95*	36	43 ___
21141	North Dakota State Quarter Gondola Bank, *07*		60 ___
21142	South Dakota State Quarter Hopper Bank, *07*		60 ___
21163	SuperStreets FasTrack Grade Crossing, *08-10*		20 ___
21164	SuperStreets 10" Transition to FasTrack, *08-10*		9 ___
21165	SuperStreets Transition to FasTrack, 2 pieces, *08-10*		17 ___
21168	City Traction Trolley Add-on, *08*		75 ___
21169	City Traction Speeder Add-on, *08*		75 ___
21170	NYC 15" Heavyweight Passenger Car 4-pack, *07*		250 ___
21175	NYC 15" Heavyweight Passenger Car 2-pack, *07*		125 ___
21198	ATSF Alco Diesel AA Set, *horn, 08*		200 ___
21199	ATSF Midnight Chief Streamliner Car 4-pack, *08*		200 ___
21204	ATSF Midnight Chief Streamliner Car 2-pack, *08*		100 ___
21207	SP Diesel Work Train, *07*		175 ___
21212	NH Diesel Freight Set, *07*		250 ___
21217	Southern Diesel Executive Inspection Train, *07*		175 ___
21229	Ringling Bros. S2 Diesel Switcher, *horn, 07*		80 ___
21230	Ringling Bros. Porter Locomotive, *07*		105 ___
21231	Ringling Bros. Streamliner Car 4-pack, *07*		210 ___
21234	Ringling Bros. Streamliner Car 2-pack, *07*		105 ___
21237	Ringling Bros. Flatcar with 3 wagons, *07*		50 ___
21238	Ringling Bros. Flatcar with 3 wagons, *07*		50 ___
21239	Ringling Bros. Flatcar with crates, *07*		45 ___
21240	Ringling Bros. Flatcar with front end loader and poles, *07*		45 ___
21252	Boy Flying Kite, *08*		60 ___
21253	Operating Bunk Car Yard Office, *07*		80 ___
21261	SuperStreets 2.5" Straight-to-Curve Connector, 4 pieces, *08-10*		9 ___
21265	Operating Voltmeter Car, *07*		75 ___
21266	SuperStreets Intersection, 4 pieces, *08-10*		40 ___
21267	PRR Boxcab Electric Locomotive, *horn, 07*		77 ___
21271	WP Operating Coal Dump Car with vehicle, *07*		33 ___
21276	Congressional Diner, *smoke, 07*		110 ___
21277	Operating Flagman's Shanty, *08*		70 ___
21279	Roach Wranglers Pest Control Van, *08*		30 ___
21281	SuperStreets D21 Curve, *08-10*		3 ___
21282	SuperStreets 2.5" Curve-to-Curve Connector, 4 pieces, *08-10*		9 ___
21283	SuperStreets Tubular Track Grade Crossing, *08-10*		18 ___
21284	SuperStreets 10" Tubular Transition, *08-10*		8 ___
21285	SuperStreets 10" Tubular Transition, *2 pieces, 08-10*		14 ___
21286	SuperStreets Intersection, *08-10*		10 ___
21287	SuperStreets Y Roadway, *08-10*		12 ___
21288	SuperStreets O Gauge Conversion Pins, *08-10*		2 ___
21289	SuperStreets Connector Pins, *08-10*		2 ___

___	21290	SuperStreets Hookup Wires, 2 pieces, *08-10*	3
___	21291	Dogbone Expander pack, *08-10*	25
___	21296	City Traction Classic Truck, *07*	30
___	21298	NYC 4-6-4 Hudson Locomotive "5279," CC, *07*	500
___	21316	PE RS3 Diesel "2815," CC, *07*	350
___	21324	Acrobats and Clowns Figures, 10 pieces, *08-10*	12
___	21325	Ringmaster Circus Figures, 5, with accessories, *08-10*	12
___	21326	PRR 15" Interurban Car 2-pack, *07*	200
___	21354	Fresh Never Frozen Fish Transport Car, *07*	80
___	21355	Dump Bin, *08-10*	20
___	21358	Special Addition Boxcar, Girl, *08-10*	25
___	21359	Special Addition Boxcar, Boy, *08-10*	25
___	21368	Passenger Coach Figures, 9 pieces, *08-10*	11
___	21369	Walking Figures, 8 pieces, *08-10*	11
___	21370	Sitting Figures, 6, with benches, *08-10*	11
___	21371	Standing Figures, 8 pieces, *08-10*	11
___	21372	Railroad Station Figures, 6, with accessories, *08-10*	11
___	21373	School Figures, 7, with accessories, *08-10*	11
___	21374	Service Station Figures, 5, with accessories, *08-10*	11
___	21375	Police Figures, 10, with dog, *08*	20
___	21376	Seated Passenger Figures, 40 pieces, *08*	27
___	21377	Mounted Police, 3, with horses, *08-10*	11
___	21378	Factory, *08-10*	18
___	21379	Police Station, *08-10*	16
___	21380	Colonial House, *08-10*	16
___	21381	Suburban Station, *08-10*	16
___	21382	School, *08-10*	17
___	21383	Suburban Ranch House, *08-10*	15
___	21384	Service Station with gas pumps, *08-10*	17
___	21385	Barn and Chicken Coop, *08-10*	20
___	21386	Firehouse, *08-10*	17
___	21387	Church, *08-10*	15
___	21388	Country L-shaped Ranch House, *08-10*	16
___	21389	Supermarket, *08-10*	12
___	21390	Diner, *08-10*	15
___	21394	Rotating Beacon, *08-09*	31
___	21396	Single Tunnel Portals, *pair, 08-10*	15
___	21397	SuperSnap 31" Remote Switch, left hand, *08-09*	55
___	21398	SuperSnap 31" Remote Switch, right hand, *08-09*	55
___	21399	SuperSnap 72" Remote Switch, left hand, *08-09*	70
___	21400	SuperSnap 72" Remote Switch, right hand, *08-09*	70
___	21412	NYC Plymouth Switcher Freight Set, *07*	155
___	21430	SuperStreets D16 Curve, *08-10*	2
___	21431	SuperStreets 10" Straight Track, *08-10*	2
___	21432	SuperStreets D16 Curved Track, 8 pieces, *08-10*	18
___	21433	SuperStreets 5" Straight Track, 4 pieces, *08-10*	14
___	21434	SuperStreets 10" Straight Track, *8 pieces, 08-10*	19
___	21435	World War II Seated Soldiers, 9, with benches, *08-09*	20
___	21436	Rings and Things Circus Accessories, *08-09*	10
___	21438	Remote Controller, *07-10*	35
___	21442	City Figures, 7, with scooter, *08-10*	11
___	21443	Factory Figures, 6, with accessories, *08-10*	11
___	21444	Church Figures, 5, with accessories, *08-10*	11
___	21445	Firefighting Figures, 11, with accessories, *08-10*	20

21449	Operating Loading Platform with flatcar, *07-08*	80	___
21450	Unloading Station with dump bins, *07*	100	___
21451	Girder Bridge with stone piers, *07*	40	___
21452	Graduated Trestle Set, 26 pieces, *07*	50	___
21453	Elevated Trestle Set, 10 pieces, *07*	40	___
21454	Double Tunnel Portals, 2 pieces, *08-10*	20	___
21456	UPS Step Van, *07*	30	___
21469	Ringling Bros. Flatcar, white, with container, *07*	45	___
21470	Ringling Bros. Flatcar, blue, with container, *07*	45	___
21471	Ringling Bros. Flatcar with 2 trailers, *08-10*	60	___
21472	Ringling Bros. Flatcar with 2 trailers, *08-10*	60	___
21476	Strasburg Plymouth Diesel Switcher, *07*	100	___
21494	WM RS3 Diesel "189," *CC, 07*	350	___
21529	Montana State Quarter Boxcar Bank, *08*	45	___
21542	Washington State Quarter Tank Car Bank, *08*	45	___
21543	Boyd Bros. Ford Classic Truck, *08*	33	___
21549	Ringling Bros. Crew Bus, *08*	33	___
21552	S.W.A.T. Team Step Van, *08*	30	___
21560	Reading Flatcar with rail load, *07*	25	___
21567	School Bus SuperStreets Set, *08*	110	___
21568	Dirty Dogz Van SuperStreets Set, *08*	100	___
21569	Angelo's Pizza Delivery Van, *08*	30	___
21570	Flying Colors Painting Van, *08*	30	___
21571	SuperStreets 10" Insulated Roadway, 2 pieces, *08-10*	8	___
21572	SuperStreets 5" Straight School, 2 pieces, *08-10*	8	___
21573	SuperStreets 5" Straight Stop Ahead, 2 pieces, *08-10*	8	___
21574	SuperStreets 5" Straight Crosswalk, 2 pieces, *08-10*	8	___
21575	SuperStreets 10" Crossing, 2 pieces, *08-10*	10	___
21576	SuperStreets Skid Mark Roadway Pack, *08-10*	13	___
21577	Snack-On Step Van, *08*	30	___
21582	Keystone Coal Porter Locomotive, *08*	100	___
21583	Keystone Coal Freight Car 4-pack, *08*	100	___
21590	ATSF "Midnight Chief" 2-bay Hopper "162277," *08*	25	___
21591	ATSF "Midnight Chief" Flatcar "94468" with trailer, *08*	43	___
21592	ATSF "Midnight Chief" Caboose, *08*	25	___
21593	ATSF "Midnight Chief" Boxcar "621593," *08*	35	___
21594	NYC Empire State Express 15" Aluminum Car 4-pack, *08-09*	420	___
21599	SP flatcar with wheel load, *07*	35	___
21600	B&M RS3 Diesel "1538," *CC, 08-09*	350	___
21607	Jack Frost Hopper "327" with sugar load, *08*	25	___
21609	Elephants and Giraffes, 2 pair, *08-10*	13	___
21610	Lions and Tigers, 2 pair, *08-10*	13	___
21611	Horses, 4 pieces, *08*	13	___
21621	ATSF Operating Boxcar "22658," *08-09*	90	___
21623	Rutland Operating Milk Car with platform, *08-10*	150	___
21626	Rath Wood-sided Reefer "622," *09*	45	___
21627	Greenlee Packing Wood-sided Reefer "3862," *10*	45	___
21628	CNJ Reefer "1438," *08-09*	35	___
21629	C&O Reefer "7783," *08-09*	35	___
21630	UP Stock Car "42005," *09*	45	___
21631	Reading Boxcar "107984," *08-09*	35	___
21632	GN Boxcar "34285," *08-09*	35	___
21633	RI "Route of the Rockets" Boxcar "21110," *09-10*	40	___
21634	Tidewater Flying A 1-D Tank Car "1367," *09*	40	___

			Esc	Mint
___	21635	Southern Depressed Center Flatcar, 2 transformers, *09*		43
___	21636	NS Flatcar with bulkheads and stakes, *08-09*		35
___	21637	Ontario Northland Ribbed Hopper with coal, *09*		40
___	21639	Pan Am Boxcar "32126," *08-09*		55
___	21640	UP Modern Steel-sided Reefer "499030," *08-09*		55
___	21641	Ringling Bros. Merchandise Flatcar, *08*		50
___	21643	PRR Die-cast Gondola with covers, *09*		73
___	21644	PRR 16-wheel Flatcar with transformer, *08-09*		80
___	21646	DT&I Work Crane and Boom Car, *09*		85
___	21649	City Traction Trolley with Ringling Bros. banner, *08-09*		80
___	21651	Moo-Town Creamery Step Van, *08-09*		38
___	21656	Quikrete Step Van, *08-09*		42
___	21658	Ringling Bros. Vintage Truck, *08-09*		42
___	21659	DT&I Flatcar "90059" with Ford trailer, *08-09*		60
___	21662	Moo-Town Creamery Vending Machine, *08-09*		13
___	21663	Moo-Town Creamery Bunk Car Ice Cream Shop, *08-09*		115
___	21664	RI Operating Coal Dump Car with vehicle, *09*		40
___	21665	Alaska Operating Log Dump Car with vehicle, *09*		40
___	21667	Red River Lumber Boxcab Diesel with horn, *08-09*		100
___	21668	CP Operating Hopper "9628," *08-09*		45
___	21675	Mountain View Creamery Loading Depot, *08-10*		130
___	21676	Beaver Creek Logging Die-cast Porter Locomotive, *08-09*		120
___	21677	Ford Factory, *09*		22
___	21679	Assured Comfort HVAC Van, *08-09*		38
___	21680	Division of Prisons Bus SuperStreets Set, *08-09*		150
___	21688	Ringling Bros. Heavyweight Coach 2-pack, *08-11*		240
___	21691	Ringling Bros. Flatcar with 2 trailers, *08-10*		60
___	21692	C&NW MP15 Diesel with Ringling Bros. banner, *08-09*		140
___	21693	Southern MP15 Diesel Pair, powered and dummy, *10*		200
___	21696	Ford Flatcar with 2 trucks, *08-09*		53
___	21698	Lionel Van SuperStreets Set, *08-10*		130
___	21701	Star Spangled GG1 Electric Locomotive "4837," *08-10*		260
___	21702	Milwaukee Road Girder Bridge, *08-09*		15
___	21703	ATSF Black Mesa Aluminum Business Car, *09-10*		160
___	21704	C&O Double Searchlight Car with vehicle, *08-09*		50
___	21706	Chatham Police Van, *08-09*		38
___	21707	NYC Aluminum Business Car, *09*		160
___	21708	CN Operating Log Dump Car, *10*		120
___	21709	PRR Girder Bridge, *08-09*		15
___	21715	Ringling Bros. Stock Car, *08-09*		60
___	21717	Pullman-Standard 1-D Tank Car, *08-09*		35
___	21719	NYC Bay Window Caboose, *99*		70
___	21720	Ringling Bros. Billboard Set #2, *08-09*		10
___	21721	Warning Sign Pack, 12 pieces, *08-10*		25
___	21730	Regulatory Sign Pack, 12 pieces, *08-10*		25
___	21738	Railroad Crossing Sign Pack, 6 pieces, *08-10*		21
___	21750	NKP Rolling Stock 4-pack, *98*		160
___	21751	PRR Rolling Stock 4-pack, *98*		145
___	21752	Conrail Unit Trailer Train, *98*		285
___	21753	Service Station Fire Rescue Train, *98*	500	585
___	21754	BNSF 3-bay Covered Hopper 2-pack (std O), *98*		65
___	21755	4-bay Covered Hoppers 2-pack, *98*		65
___	21756	6464-style Overstamped Boxcars 2-pack, *98*		65
___	21757	UP Freight Car Set, *98*		188

No.	Description	Esc	Mint	
21758	Bethlehem Steel "44" (SSS), 99		375	___
21759	Canadian Pacific F3 Diesel Passenger Set, 99		930	___
21761	B&M Boxcar Set, 4-pack, 99		180	___
21763	New Haven Freight Set, 99		265	___
21766	ACL Passenger Car 2-pack, 99		385	___
21769	Centennial 1-D Tank Car Set, 4-pack, 99	0	240	___
21770	NYC Reefer Set, 4-pack, 99		225	___
21771	D&RGW Stock Car Set, 4-pack, 99		230	___
21774	Custom Series Consist I, 3-pack, 99		150	___
21775	Train Wreck Recovery Set, 99		190	___
21778	ATSF Train Master Diesel Freight Set, 99		NRS	___
21779	Seaboard Freight Car Set, 99		280	___
21780	NYC Aluminum Passenger Car 2-pack, 99		160	___
21781	Case Cutlery Freight Set, 99 u	0	1034	___
21782	PRR Congressional Set, 00		930	___
21783	Monday Night Football 2-pack, 01-02		50	___
21784	QVC PRR Coal Freight Steam Set, 00 u		360	___
21785	QVC Gold Mine Freight Steam Set, 00 u		300	___
21786	Santa Fe F3 Diesel ABBA Passenger Set, 00		1500	___
21787	Blue Comet Steam Passenger Set, 01-02		1050	___
21788	Postwar Missile Launch Freight Set, 02-03		350	___
21789	Norfolk Southern Piggyback Set, CC (SSS), 01		370	___
21790	CN TankTrain Dash 9 Diesel Freight Set, 02		630	___
21791	Freedom Train Diesel Passenger Set, RailSounds, 03		540	___
21792	C&O Coal Hopper 6-pack #2 (std O), 01		145	___
21793	Virginian Coal Hopper 6-pack #2 (std O), 01		160	___
21794	Pioneer Seed GP7 Diesel Freight Set, 01 u	0	925	___
21795	Case Farmall Freight Set, 01 u	0	995	___
21796	NJ Medical Steam Freight Set, 01 u		483	___
21797	SP Daylight Passenger Set, 01		670	___
21852	MILW PS-2CD Hopper 3-pack (std O), 06		155	___
21853	BNSF PS-2CD Hopper 3-pack (std O), 06		155	___
21854	N&W PS-2CD Hopper 3-pack (std O), 06		155	___
21855	A&P Milk Car 3-pack, 06		150	___
21856	Bowman Dairy Milk Car 3-pack (std O), 06		150	___
21857	Western Dairy Milk Car 3-pack (std O), 06		150	___
21858	NP PS-4 Flatcar with trailers, 2-pack (std O), 06		170	___
21859	C&NW PS-4 Flatcar with trailers, 2-pack (std O), 06		170	___
21860	UP PS-4 Flatcar with trailers, 2-pack (std O), 06		170	___
21861	PRR PS-4 Flatcar with trailers (std O), 06		170	___
21863	ADM Unibody Tank Car 3-pack (std O), 06		135	___
21864	Cerestar Unibody Tank Car 3-pack (std O), 06		135	___
21865	Coe Rail Husky Stack Car 2-pack (std O), 06		170	___
21866	Santa Fe Husky Stack Car 2-pack (std O), 06		170	___
21872	C&O Offset Hopper 3-pack (std O), 05		130	___
21873	P&LE Offset Hopper 3-pack (std O), 06		145	___
21874	TTX Trailer Train 2-pack (std O), 06		170	___
21875	CSX Husky Stack Car 2-pack (std O), 06		170	___
21876	Disney Villain Hi-Cube Boxcar 3-pack, 05-06		135	___
21877	Domino Sugar 1-D Tank Car 3-pack (std O), 07		135	___
21878	Procor 1-D Tank Car 3-pack (std O), 07		135	___
21879	C&EI Offset Hopper 3-pack (std O), 07		145	___
21880	Erie Offset Hopper 3-pack (std O), 07		145	___
21881	Frisco Offset Hopper 3-pack (std O), 07-08		200	___

		Esc	Mint
___ 21882	Chessie System Offset Hopper 3-pack (std O), *07*		145
___ 21883	C&O 3-bay Hopper 2-pack (std O), *07-08*		140
___ 21884	Pennsylvania Power & Light 3-bay Hopper 2-pack (std O), *07*		140
___ 21885	Santa Fe 3-bay Hopper 2-pack (std O), *07*		140
___ 21886	C&NW 3-bay Hopper 2-pack (std O), *07-08*		140
___ 21888	IMC Canada Cylindrical Hopper 2-pack, *06*		130
___ 21893	Greenbrier Husky Stack Car 2-pack (std O), *07*		170
___ 21894	CSX Husky Stack Car 2-pack (std O), *07*		170
___ 21895	BN Husky Stack Car 2-pack (std O), *07*		170
___ 21896	Arizona & California Husky Stack Car 2-pack (std O), *07*		170
___ 21897	REA PS-4 Flatcar with trailers, 2-pack (std O), *07-08*		170
___ 21898	NYC PS-4 Flatcar with trailers, 2-pack (std O), *07-08*		170
___ 21899	Lackawanna PS-4 Flatcar with trailers, 2-pack (std O), *07*		170
___ 21900	Civil War Union Train Set, *99*		375
___ 21901	Civil War Confederate Train Set, *99*		375
___ 21902	MILW PS-4 Flatcar with trailers, 2-pack (std O), *07-08*		170
___ 21902	Construction Zone Set, *99 u*		87
___ 21904	UP PS-2 Covered Hopper 2-pack (std O), *07*		120
___ 21904	Safari Adventure Set, *99 u*		90
___ 21905	NYC Flyer Set, *99 u*		100
___ 21909	AGFA Film Steam Freight Set, *98 u*		1413
___ 21914	Lionel Lines Freight Set, *99*		120
___ 21916	Lionel Village Trolley, *99*		75
___ 21917	N&W Freight Set, *99*		70
___ 21918	PC PS-2 Covered Hopper 2-pack (std O), *07*		120
___ 21918	Thomas Circus Play Set, *00*		100
___ 21921	Imco PS-2 Covered Hopper 2-pack (std O), *07-08*		120
___ 21924	Holiday Trolley Set, *99*		65
___ 21925	Thomas the Tank Engine Island of Sodor Train Set, *99-00*		150
___ 21930	NYC PS-2 Covered Hopper 2-pack (std O), *07*		120
___ 21932	JCPenney NYC Freight Flyer Steam Set, *00 u*		170
___ 21934	Custom Series Consist II, 3-pack, *99*		140
___ 21936	Looney Tunes Train Set, *00 u*		400
___ 21937	NYC Steel-sided Reefer 2-pack (std O), *07*		130
___ 21939	Dubuque Steel-sided Reefer 2-pack (std O), *07-08*		130
___ 21940	ADM Steel-sided Reefer 2-pack (std O), *07*		130
___ 21941	National Car Steel-sided Reefer 2-pack (std O), *07*		130
___ 21944	"Celebrate a Lionel Christmas" Steam Set, *00-01*		165
___ 21945	Christmas Trolley Set, *00*		100
___ 21948	NYC Freight Flyer Set, *air whistle, 00*		240
___ 21950	Maersk SD70 Diesel Maxi-Stack Set, *00*	560	700
___ 21951	World War II Troop Train, *00*		410
___ 21952	Lionel Lines Service Station Special Set, *00*		294
___ 21953	Ford Mustang GP7 Diesel Set, *CC, 01*		345
___ 21955	D&RGW F3 Diesel AA Passenger Set, *CC, 01*		740
___ 21956	New York Central Freight Set, *99-00*		355
___ 21969	Lionel Village Trolley Set, *00*		85
___ 21970	SP RS3 Diesel Freight Set, *horn, 00-01*		110
___ 21971	Pennsylvania Flyer Steam Set, *00*		150
___ 21972	Frisco GP7 Diesel Freight Set, *horn, 00*		150
___ 21973	ATSF Passenger Set, RailSounds, *00-01*		375
___ 21974	ATSF Passenger Set, SignalSounds, *00-01*		240
___ 21975	Burlington Steam Freight Set, SignalSounds, *00*		275
___ 21976	Centennial Steam Freight Starter Set, *00*	0	663

21977	NYC Train Master Steam Freight Set, *99-00*		620 ___
21978	ATSF Train Master Diesel Freight Set, *99-00*		500 ___
21981	JCPenney NYC Flyer Set, *00 u*		150 ___
21988	NYC Freight Set, RailSounds, *00*		325 ___
21989	Burlington Steam Freight Set, RailSounds, *00*		338 ___
21990	NYC Flyer Freight Set, RailSounds, *00*		175 ___
21999	Whirlpool Steam Freight Set, *00 u*	0	740 ___
22103	PRR A5 Scale Switcher "411," CC, *08-09*		330 ___
22104	PRR Freight Car 3-pack, *08*		135 ___
22105	NYC Empire State Express 4-6-4 Hudson Locomotive "5429," CC, *08-09*		420 ___
22113	NYC Empire State Express 15" Aluminum Car 2-pack, *08-10*		210 ___
22116	Ringling Bros. Diesel Freight Set, *08-10*		245 ___
22121	Ringling Bros. Freight Set, *08-10*		390 ___
22126	Ringling Bros. Expansion Pack, *08-10*		135 ___
22131	NH Streamliner Car 3-pack, *07*		150 ___
22135	CB&Q S2 Diesel Switcher "9305," horn, *07*		80 ___
22136	Erie S2 Diesel Switcher "522," horn, *07*		80 ___
22137	Alaska MP15 Diesel "1552," horn, *07*		100 ___
22138	Astoria Heat & Power Porter Locomotive "4," *07*		100 ___
22139	LIRR Speeder, *08*		50 ___
22140	CNJ Boxcab Diesel "1000," horn, *08*		90 ___
22141	Lackawanna 15" Interurban Car 2-pack, *07*		200 ___
22142	FEC Operating Dump Car, *07*		70 ___
22143	B&A Operating Log Dump Car, *08-09*		70 ___
22144	Alaska Operating Coal Dump Car with vehicle, *08*		33 ___
22145	WM Operating Log Dump Car with vehicle, *08*		33 ___
22146	PFE Operating Boxcar, *08*		80 ___
22147	B&O Operating Hopper with coal, *08*		35 ___
22148	GN Operating Hopper with coal, *08*		35 ___
22149	Dairymen's League Operating Milk Car, green, with platform, *08*		140 ___
22150	D&RGW Bunk Car, smoke, *08*		65 ___
22151	Alaska Searchlight Car with vehicle, *08*		45 ___
22152	NKP 2-bay Outside-braced Hopper "31299," *08*		50 ___
22153	L&N 2-bay Offset Hopper "78660," *08*		50 ___
22154	D&H 2-bay Rib Side Hopper "5737," *07*		50 ___
22155	Erie-Lack. 2-bay Aluminum Hopper "21353," *08*		60 ___
22156	ACF Demonstrator 2-bay Aluminum Hopper "44586," *07*		60 ___
22157	GN Aluminum Tank Car "74787," *08*		60 ___
22158	MILW Bulkhead Flatcar "967116" with wood, *08-09*		43 ___
22159	BNSF Flatcar "585011" with trailer, *08*		43 ___
22160	UP Flatcar "58059" with container, *08*		43 ___
22161	Conrail Flatcar "705910" with NS container, *08*		43 ___
22162	Foppiano Wine 3-D Tank Car "1112," *08*		45 ___
22163	PRR Weed Control Car "6321226," *07*		45 ___
22166	PRR Reefer "19492," *08*		25 ___
22167	Seaboard Reefer "16622," *08*		25 ___
22168	N&W Boxcar "645772," *08*		25 ___
22169	ATSF Reefer "11744," *07*		25 ___
22170	P&LE Reefer "22300," *07*		25 ___
22171	B&O DD Boxcar "495289," *08*		25 ___
22172	CB&Q Stock Car "52731," *08*		25 ___
22174	Erie-Lack. Transfer Caboose, *07*		25 ___
22176	PRR Caboose "478884," *07*		25 ___

			Esc	Mint
___	**22177**	L&N Caboose "100," *07*		25
___	**22179**	NYC Depressed Center Flatcar "66256" with 2 girders, *08*		25
___	**22180**	IC Depressed Center Flatcar with 2 transformers, *07*		25
___	**22182**	RI Gondola "180043" with coils, *08*		25
___	**22184**	B&O Covered Hopper "604321," *08*		25
___	**22185**	UP Covered Hopper "53186," *08*		25
___	**22186**	P&LE (NYC) Gondola "17243," *08-09*		35
___	**22187**	PRR 2-D Tank Car "6351815," *07*		25
___	**22188**	Deep Rock 3-D Tank Car "2152," *08*		25
___	**22189**	NP Java Diner, smoke, *08*		110
___	**22190**	C&O Operating Billboard, *08*		65
___	**22191**	Operating Passenger Station, *08-09*		105
___	**22192**	Hot Box Operating BBQ Shack, *07*		80
___	**22193**	Cold Drinks Vending Machine, *08*		12
___	**22194**	Water Tower with light, *08-09*		20
___	**22199**	City Traction Trolley Barn, *08-09*		65
___	**22202**	Loading Ramp, *08-10*		20
___	**22203**	Dairymen's League Operating Milk Car, white, with platform, *07*		140
___	**22204**	Snacks Vending Machine, *08*		12
___	**22205**	Soup and Sandwich Vending Machine, *08*		12
___	**22206**	PRR Crew Bus, *08*		30
___	**22222**	Ringling Bros. Speeder Chase Set, *08-10*		92
___	**22225**	Ringling Bros. Jomar Heavyweight Private Car, *08-11*		120
___	**22226**	Ringling Bros. 18" Caledonia Heavyweight Private Car, *08*		100
___	**22227**	Ringling Bros. 18" Advertising Car, *08*		100
___	**22228**	Ringling Bros. Flatcar with 3 wagons, *08*		50
___	**22231**	Ringling Bros. Flatcar with 3 wagons, *08*		50
___	**22235**	Ringling Bros. Flatcar with pole wagon and truck, *08*		75
___	**22238**	Ringling Bros. Work Caboose with calliope wagon, *08*		40
___	**22240**	Ringling Bros. Flatcar/Stock Car with wagon, *08*		50
___	**22243**	Ringling Bros. Human Cannonball Car, *08*		45
___	**22244**	Ringling Bros. Operating Searchlight Car with 3 spotlights, *08*		60
___	**22247**	Ringling Bros. Stock Car "54," *08*		50
___	**22248**	Ringling Bros. Stock Car "47," *08*		50
___	**22249**	Ringling Bros. Dining Dept. Billboard Reefer, *08*		80
___	**22250**	Ringling Bros. Dining Dept. Wood-sided Reefer, *08-09*		90
___	**22251**	Ringling Bros. Dormitory Bunk Car "22," *08*		75
___	**22252**	Ringling Bros. Operating Billboard, *08-09*		75
___	**22253**	Ringling Bros. Vintage Billboard Set #1, *08*		9
___	**22255**	Ringling Bros. Aluminum Coach "40010," *08-10*		165
___	**22257**	Ringling Bros. Aluminum Shop Car "63002," *08-10*		165
___	**22258**	Ringling Bros. 18" Aluminum Large Animal Car, *08-10*		165
___	**22259**	Ringling Bros. Flatcar with trailer, *08*		53
___	**22260**	Ringling Bros. Tractor Trailer, *08*		30
___	**22261**	Idaho State Quarter Hopper Bank, *08*		65
___	**22262**	Wyoming State Quarter Tank Car Bank, *08*		50
___	**22263**	Utah State Quarter Boxcar Bank, *08*		45
___	**22264**	SuperStreets Figure-8 Expander Pack, *08-10*		35
___	**22267**	Mulligan Spring Water Step Van, *08*		30
___	**22270**	Quikrete Classic Truck with 2 pallets, *08*		33
___	**22271**	MILW EP-5 Electric Locomotive "E20," *CC, 08-09*		460
___	**22272**	MILW Olympian Hiawatha 18" Aluminum Car 4-pack, *08*		480
___	**22277**	MILW Olympian Hiawatha 18" Aluminum Car 2-pack, *08*		250
___	**22280**	Erie-Lack. RS3 Diesel "933," *CC, 08-09*		350

Number	Description	Esc	Mint
22281	Southern Train Master Diesel "6300," *CC, 08-09*		420 ___
22282	Southern Bay Window Caboose "X270," *08-09*		70 ___
22283	UP S2 Diesel Switcher "1103" and Caboose "25384," *08*		130 ___
22286	GN Boxcab Electric Locomotive "5008-A," horn, *08*		90 ___
22287	North Shore Line 15" Interurban Car 2-pack, *08*		230 ___
22288	Commuter Train Station, 6 road name stickers, *09*		25 ___
22289	Ringling Bros. 18" Aluminum Passenger Car 2-pack, *08*		270 ___
22290	Erie Boxcar "86448" with graffiti, *08*		46 ___
22291	C&NW Stock Car "14303," *08*		46 ___
22292	Land o' Lakes Butter Billboard Reefer, *08*		75 ___
22293	PRR 4-bay Hopper "253776," *08*		65 ___
22294	Montana Rail Link 3-bay Aluminum Hopper "50049," *08*		70 ___
22295	Canada Wheat 4-bay Aluminum Hopper "606418," *08*		73 ___
22296	Eaglebrook Aluminum Tank Car "19039," *08*		70 ___
22297	Petri Wine 3-D Tank Car "904," *08-09*		45 ___
22298	Cotton Belt Offset Cupola Wood-sided Caboose "2230," *08*		80 ___
22299	MILW Bay Window Caboose "980502," *08-09*		70 ___
22300	Detroit, Toledo & Ironton Coil Car "1352," *08*		60 ___
22301	NYC Flatcar "506090" with freight kit, *08*		35 ___
22302	C&O Flatcar "80951" with freight kit, *08*		35 ___
22303	Extruded Aluminum I-Beam, 3 pieces, *08-09*		6 ___
22304	Rails, 12 pieces, *08-09*		6 ___
22305	Small Transformer Load, pair, *08-09*		15 ___
22306	Large Transformer Load, *08*		19 ___
22307	Forklifts, 3, with pallets, *08-09*		27 ___
22308	Loaders with crates, pair, *08-09*		13 ___
22309	Loaders with logs, pair, *08-09*		13 ___
22310	KBL Logistics Container 2-pack, *08*		40 ___
22312	Commemorative Quarter Extended Vision Caboose, *09*		80 ___
22313	ATSF Boxcar "137460," *08*		25 ___
22314	Coastal King Seafood Wood-sided Reefer, *08*		25 ___
22315	Wisconsin & Southern "God Bless America" Boxcar, *09*		43 ___
22316	NP Depressed Center Flatcar "66130" with water tank, *08*		25 ___
22317	U.S. Air Force Hopper "55175" with ballast load, *08*		25 ___
22318	DM&IR Ore Car "29991," *08*		25 ___
22319	Celanese Chemicals 1-D Tank Car "12730," *08*		25 ___
22320	Baldwin Locomotives Works 1-D Tank Car "6809," *08*		25 ___
22321	B&O Operating Boxcar, *08*		45 ___
22322	PRR Operating Ballast Dump Car, *08*		75 ___
22323	FEMA Voltmeter Car, *08*		75 ___
22324	C&NW Cop and Robber Chase Gondola, *08-09*		55 ___
22325	White Milk Cans, *10 pieces, 08-10*		8 ___
22326	Twin Searchlight Tower, *08-10*		33 ___
22327	Tommy's Bunk Car Grill, *08-09*		100 ___
22328	Santa Fe Operating Freight Transfer Platform, *08-09*		130 ___
22329	Dual Track Signal Bridge, *08-10*		45 ___
22330	Stella's Heavyweight Diner, *smoke, 08-09*		140 ___
22331	Coffee Vending Machine, *08*		12 ___
22332	Spring Water Vending Machine, *08*		12 ___
22333	Candy Vending Machine, *08*		12 ___
22334	Ford Plymouth Diesel Switcher and Ore Car 6-pack, *08*		200 ___
22335	NS Operating Paint Shop with boxcar, *08-09*		140 ___
22344	KBL Logistics ISO Tank, *08*		19 ___
22346	Tableau Circus Wagons, *08*		13 ___

		Esc	Mint
___	**22349** Forklift with 6 pallets, *08-09*		23
___	**22350** Twin Lamp Posts, 3 pieces, *08-09*		22
___	**22352** Lamp Posts, 4 pieces, *08-09*		20
___	**22354** Portable Spotlights, 3 pieces, *08-09*		15
___	**22356** High Tension Poles, 4 pieces, *08-09*		8
___	**22358** Rail Yard Signs, 12 pieces, *08-09*		10
___	**22360** Telephone Poles, 6 pieces, *08-09*		7
___	**22362** Girder Bridge, *08-09*		8
___	**22363** Stone Bridge Piers, pair, *08-10*		27
___	**22365** Heavyweight Passenger Coach 6-wheel Scale Trucks, pair, *08-09*		25
___	**22366** Aluminum Passenger Coach 4-wheel Scale Trucks, pair, *08-09*		25
___	**22367** Timkin Scale Sprung Trucks, pair, *08-09*		19
___	**22368** Bettendorf Scale Sprung Trucks, pair, *08-09*		19
___	**22369** Scale Couplers, pair, *08-09*		6
___	**22379** SuperStreets Barricade, 2 pieces, *08-10*		11
___	**22387** Kiosk with 3 vending machines, *08-09*		40
___	**22391** Ford MP15 Diesel "10021," horn, *08*		115
___	**22392** Ford Farming Boxcar "1681," *08*		30
___	**22393** Ford Stampings DD Boxcar "101," *08*		35
___	**22394** Ford 2-bay Covered Hopper "1667," *08*		30
___	**22395** Ford Speeder "14," *08*		65
___	**22396** Ford Water Tower, *08*		25
___	**22397** Ford Rotating Sign Tower, *08*		55
___	**22398** Boyd Bros. and Ford Barn and Chicken Coop, *08*		25
___	**22399** Ford ISO Tank, *08-09*		21
___	**22402** PRR Streamlined K4 4-6-2 Pacific Locomotive, tender, *09-10*		500
___	**22408** Ringling Bros. Tractor Trailer #1, *08-09*		35
___	**22411** Tableau Wagon Set #2, *08-10*		18
___	**22412** PRR Operating Flagman's Shanty, *08-09*		90
___	**22414** Linde Union Carbide Boxcar with aluminum tank, *08-09*		70
___	**22415** Ringling Bros. Flatcar with circus wagon, *08*		50
___	**22417** Ringling Bros. Flatcar with container, *09*		55
___	**22420** PRR Broadway Limited Aluminum Passenger Car 2-pack, *09-10*		300
___	**22423** GN Aluminum Passenger Car 2-pack, *09-10*		360
___	**22426** Ford Gondola "13447" with coils, *08-09*		43
___	**22427** Ford Operating Billboard, *08-09*		75
___	**22428** Ford Tin Sign Replica 4-pack, *08-09*		17
___	**22433** PRR Broadway Limited Aluminum Passenger Car 4-pack, *09-10*		600
___	**22438** Mail Crane, *08-10*		30
___	**22439** Milwaukee Road Aluminum Passenger Car 2-pack, *09-11*		360
___	**22447** Wabash Die-cast 2-bay Ribbed Hopper "37751," *08-09*		60
___	**22449** UP Crew Bus, *08-09*		38
___	**22450** Seaboard Die-cast Hopper with gravel, *10*		80
___	**22454** Oklahoma State Quarter Die-cast Hopper Bank, *08-09*		75
___	**22455** New Mexico State Quarter Die-cast Gondola Bank, *08-09*		74
___	**22456** Arizona State Quarter Tank Car Bank, *08-09*		55
___	**22457** Alaska State Quarter Boxcar Bank, *09*		55
___	**22458** Hawaii State Quarter Die-cast Hopper Bank, *09*		75
___	**22459** Southern Aluminum Passenger Car 2-pack #1, *09*		300
___	**22460** Southern Aluminum Passenger Car 2-pack #2, *09*		300
___	**22461** Scale Skeleton Log Car 4-pack, *08-09*		160
___	**22467** Railroad Water Tower, *08-09*		23
___	**22468** Fast Eddie's Used Car Lot with 2 die-cast vehicles, *08-09*		50
___	**22469** Cola Illuminated Vending Machine, *08-09*		13

		Mint
22470	SuperStreets Guard Rails, *08-10*	20 ___
22472	Ringling Bros. Tin Sign Replica 4-pack, *08-09*	17 ___
22477	Lionel Tin Sign Replica 4-pack, *08-09*	15 ___
22482	Vintage Tin Sign Replica 4-pack, *08-09*	15 ___
22487	Scooter Gang with scooters, *09-10*	13 ___
22492	Airport Revolving Searchlight, *10*	40 ___
22493	Ringling Bros. Lighted Clown Wood-sided Reefer, *09*	75 ___
22494	Ford Flatcar with 2 Thunderbird convertibles, *09*	53 ___
22496	Vita O Flavored Water Vending Machine, *09*	13 ___
22497	Top Pop Soda Illuminated Vending Machine, *09*	13 ___
22498	Ringling Bros. Flatcar with 3 circus wagons, *09-10*	55 ___
22500	Defense Dept. Flatcar with 2 jeeps and soldier, *09*	50 ___
22501	C&NW Railroad Van, *CC, 09-10*	100 ___
22502	Ringling Bros. Flatcar with 3 circus wagons, *09-10*	55 ___
22504	Ford Water Tower with vintage Ford logo, *09-10*	25 ___
22505	Sparkling Springs Beverage Truck, *09*	45 ___
22506	SuperStreets Fishtail Roadway, *09*	25 ___
22507	Ringling Bros. Flatcar with boxcar and ticket wagon, *09*	60 ___
22509	Pallet Pack with banded loads, *09*	20 ___
22510	Lionel Step Van, *CC, 09-10*	100 ___
22511	BNSF Flatcar with helicopter, *09*	50 ___
22513	Ringling Bros. Heavyweight Advertising Car, *09*	120 ___
22514	NYC Girder Bridge, *09-10*	15 ___
22515	Milwaukee Road/REA Scale Boxcar "6436," *09*	55 ___
22516	BNSF MP15 Diesel "3704" with horn, *09*	120 ___
22517	Quick Lane Ford Motorcraft Auto Parts Van, *09-10*	42 ___
22518	Lionel Tank Container Leasing ISO Tank, *09-10*	23 ___
22519	Roma Wine Wood-sided Billboard Reefer, *09-10*	70 ___
22520	WWII Soldiers in Action, 10 pieces, *09-10*	20 ___
22521	1959 Ford Billboard Set, *09*	10 ___
22523	American Flyer Vintage Truck, *09*	38 ___
22524	Ford Coil Car "749772," *09*	73 ___
22525	Vermont Railway Operating Boxcar "177," *09*	50 ___
22526	Crabby Matt's Smoking Heavyweight Diner, *09*	150 ___
22527	Toledo, *Peoria & Western Boxcar "5067," 09-10*	55 ___
22528	GN Stock Car "55973," *09-10*	55 ___
22529	U.S. Army 1-D Tank Car "11278," *09*	35 ___
22530	Milwaukee Road Aluminum Coach "627," *09-11*	180 ___
22531	Southern Girder Bridge, *09*	15 ___
22532	Montana Rail Link 1-D Tank Car "100017," *09*	35 ___
22533	GN Aluminum Coach "1377," *09-10*	180 ___
22534	SuperStreets D16 Curve Guard Rails, *09-10*	20 ___
22536	SuperStreets D21 Curve Guard Rails, *09-10*	22 ___
22538	Ford Modern Aluminum Tank Car "30166," *09*	90 ___
22539	BNSF Flatcar "922267" with Ford trailer, *09-10*	60 ___
22542	PRR Flatcar "480227" with freight kit, *09*	40 ___
22543	Biodiesel 2-D Tank Car "1544," *09*	40 ___
22544	Ringling Bros. Wood-sided Gondola with equipment, *09*	63 ___
22548	Kiosk #2 with 3 illuminated vending machines, *09*	40 ___
22553	Convenience Mart, *09-10*	25 ___
22554	Auto Parts Store, *09-10*	20 ___
22555	Ringling Bros. Tractor with Gold Tour container, *09-10*	55 ___
22558	PRR Flatcar "469301" with milk containers, *09*	50 ___
22559	UP Gondola "229794" with freight kit, *09-10*	80 ___

		Mint
22560	CB&Q Wood-sided Gondola "85150" with spools, *09-10*	60
22561	Gondola Scrap Load, *09*	9
22562	Operation Lifesaver Boxcar with flashing LEDs, *09*	65
22563	Ringling Bros. Handcar and Trailer Set, *10-11*	70
22566	SuperStreets 2.5" Straight Roadway, 4 pieces, *10*	12
22568	Generators, 2 pieces, *09*	9
22570	Large transformer, *09*	22
22571	Cage Wagon Set, *09-10*	18
22573	Display Base, *09*	20
22574	Ringling Bros. Flatcar "39" with trailer, *09*	60
22577	Biodiesel Storage Tank with 2 figures, *09-10*	40
22578	Ringling Bros. Heavyweight Coach "70," *09*	120
22579	Circus Horses, 4 pieces, *09-10*	15
22580	Bollards and Chains, *09-10*	20
22582	Pipe Stack Load, *09*	30
22583	KBL Operating Wind Turbine, *09-10*	75
22584	KBL Die-cast 16-wheel Flatcar "34807," *09*	85
22587	Old Reading Flatcar Foot Bridge with stone piers, *09-10*	50
22590	Roadside Fender Bender, *09-10*	75
22592	SuperStreets D16 Turn Roadways, left and right, *10*	35
22595	SuperStreets D21 Turn Roadways, left and right, *10*	39
22598	SuperStreets Adjustable Straight Kit, *09-10*	20
22600	Wire Spool Load, 6 pieces, *09*	20
22610	Napa Valley Wine Train Alco FA Diesel AA Set, *10*	230
22613	Napa Valley Wine Train 15" Passenger Car 4-pack, *10*	450
22618	Signal Oil Co. 1-D Tank Car, *10*	40
22619	PRR Paoli MU Commuter Train 2-pack, *10*	290
22622	RR Paoli Motorized Combine, *10*	200
22623	PRR Commuter Train Station, *10*	35
22624	NH Die-cast Plymouth Switcher with snowplow, *10*	160
22625	Ringling Bros. 18" Aluminum Generator Car, *10-11*	180
22627	Ringling Bros. Lighted Clown Wood-sided Reefer, *10-11*	90
22628	Ringling Bros. 18" Aluminum Advertising Car, *10-11*	180
22629	Ringling Bros. Stock Car, *10-11*	60
22630	Ringling Bros. Tractor and Trailer, *10-11*	35
22633	Ringling Bros. 18" Aluminum Coach, *10-11*	180
22634	Ringling Bros. 18" Heavyweight Advertising Car, *10-11*	146
22635	Ringling Bros. Operating Dual Searchlight Car, *10-11*	60
22637	Quikrete Step Van, *10*	48
22638	PRR Crew Bus, *10*	45
22639	B&O Boxcab Diesel "195," *10*	100
22640	Central of Georgia Boxcar "5823," *10*	45
22641	New Haven Boxcar "36438," *10*	45
22642	Ringling Bros. Operating Large Animal Feed Car, *10-11*	150
22643	Ford MP15 Diesel "10022," *10-11*	135
22644	Ford Motorcraft 48' Aluminum Tank Car, *10-11*	95
22645	Ringling Bros. Operating Tent Pole Dump Car, *10-11*	130
22646	Ford Speeder, *10-11*	75
22647	Rock Island Gondola "180044," *10*	35
22648	PRR Gondola "353381," *10*	35
22651	Central Vermont Operating Milk Car with platform, *10*	175
22653	Starlite Diner with parking lot, *10*	200
22654	Ringling Bros. Flatcar with 3 circus wagons, *10-11*	60

		Esc	Mint	
22656	Ringling Bros. Flatcar with 3 circus wagons, *10-11*		60	___
22658	Operating Flagman's Shanty, *10*		100	___
22659	Union 76 1-D Tank Car "6322," *10*		40	___
22660	Moose Pond Creamery Operating Loading Depot, *10*		140	___
22661	WM 2-Bay Covered Hopper "5051," *10*		35	___
22662	PRR Reefer "19494," *10*		45	___
22663	New Haven Illuminated Caboose, *10*		40	___
22667	Acme Scrap Platform Crane, *10*		60	___
22670	ATSF Operating Boxcar, *10*		140	___
22671	Smoking Southern Bay Window Caboose, *10*		90	___
22672	Ringling Bros. 18" Sarasota Observation Car, *10-11*		146	___
22673	Ford Water Tower with light, *10*		27	___
22674	MILW 21" Aluminum Passenger Car 2-pack, *10-11*		400	___
22679	Ringling Bros. Operating Billboard, *10-11*		100	___
22902	Quonset Hut, *98-99*		22	___
22907	Die-cast Girder Bridge, *98-01*		10	___
22910	Gilbert Tractor Trailer, *98*		20	___
22914	PowerHouse Lockon, *98-01*		24	___
22915	Municipal Building, *98-99*		28	___
22916	190-watt Power Accessory System, *98*		425	___
22918	Locomotive Backshop, *98*	300	460	___
22919	ElectroCouplers Kit for GP9 Diesel, *98-00*		20	___
22922	Intermodal Crane, *98*		195	___
22931	Die-cast Cantilever Signal Bridge, *98-06*		35	___
22934	Walkout Cantilever Signal, *98-03*		42	___
22936	Coaling Tower, 3 pieces, *98*		85	___
22940	Mast Signal, *98-00*		37	___
22942	Accessories Box, *98-01*		20	___
22944	Automatic Operating Semaphore, *98-03, 08*		35	___
22945	Block Target Signal, *98-00*		39	___
22946	Automatic Crossing Gate and Signal, *98-99*		45	___
22947	Auto Crossing Gate, *98-00*		36	___
22948	Gooseneck Street Lamps, set of 2, *98-00*		30	___
22949	Highway Lights, set of 4, *98-99*		20	___
22950	Classic Street Lamps, set of 3, *98-02*		20	___
22951	Dwarf Signal, *98-00*		24	___
22952	Classic Billboards, set of 3, *98-00*		15	___
22953	Linex Gasoline Tall Oil Tank, *98-99*		6	___
22954	Linex Gasoline Wide Oil Tank, *98-99*		6	___
22955	ElectroCouplers Kit for J Class and B&A tenders, *98-00*		20	___
22956	ElectroCouplers Kit for NW2 Switcher, *98*		20	___
22957	ElectroCouplers Kit for F3 Diesel, *98-01*		20	___
22958	ElectroCouplers Kit for Dash 9 Diesel, *98-01*		20	___
22959	ElectroCoupler Conversion Kit for Atlantic Locomotive, *98-01*		13	___
22960	Trainmaster Command Basic Upgrade Kit, *98-01*		34	___
22961	Standard GP9 Diesel B Unit Upgrade Kit, *98-01*		30	___
22962	Deluxe GP9 Diesel B Unit Upgrade Kit, black trucks, *98-01*		44	___
22963	RailSounds Upgrade Kit, steam RailSounds, *98-01*		55	___
22964	RailSounds Upgrade Kit, diesel RailSounds, *98-01*		55	___
22965	Culvert Loader, *CC*, *98-01*		255	___
22966	Figure-8 Add-on Track Pack (O27), *98-16*		17	___
22967	Double Loop Add-on Track Pack (O27), *98-16*		62	___

			Esc	Mint
___	**22968**	Double Loop Track Pack (O27), *98-03*		65
___	**22969**	Deluxe Complete Track Pack (O), *98-16*		120
___	**22972**	Bascule Bridge, *98-99*		337
___	**22973**	Lionel Corporation Tractor and Trailer, *98*		15
___	**22975**	Culvert Unloader, *CC, 99-00*		225
___	**22979**	GP9 Diesel B-Unit Deluxe Upgrade Kit, silver trucks, *98-01*		34
___	**22980**	TMCC SC-2 Switch Controller, *99-16*		130
___	**22982**	Postwar ZW Controller and Transformer Set, *98*		265
___	**22983**	180-watt PowerHouse Power Supply, *99-16. 18*		125
___	**22990**	Flatcar with Route 66 autos, 4-pack, *99*		37
___	**22991**	Christmas Tree and Blue Comet Train, *99-00*		60
___	**22993**	Route 66 Sinclair Dino Cafe, *99-00*		210
___	**22997**	Oil Drum Loader, *99-00*		100
___	**22998**	Triple Action Magnetic Crane, *99*		220
___	**22999**	Sound Dispatching Station, *99-00*		90
___	**23000**	NYC Dreyfuss Hudson Operating Base, 2-rail, *92 u*		190
___	**23001**	NYC Dreyfuss Hudson Operating Base, 3-rail, *93 u*		190
___	**23002**	NYC Hudson Operating Base, *92 u, 93-94*		190
___	**23003**	PRR B-6 Switcher Operating Base, *92 u, 93-94*		190
___	**23004**	NP 4-8-4 Operating Base, *92 u, 93-94*		190
___	**23005**	Reading T-1 Operating Base, *92 u, 93-94*		190
___	**23006**	Chessie System T-1 Operating Base, *92 u, 93-94*		190
___	**23007**	SP Daylight Operating Base, *92 u, 93-94*		190
___	**23008**	NYC L-3 Mohawk Operating Base, *92 u, 93-94*		190
___	**23009**	PRR S2 Turbine Locomotive Operating Base, *92 u, 93-94*		190
___	**23010**	31" Remote Switch, left hand (O), *95-99*	30	37
___	**23011**	31" Remote Switch, right hand (O), *95-99*	20	30
___	**23012**	F3 Diesel ABA Operating Base, *92 u, 93-94*		190
___	**24018**	PRR Boxcar, *05*		25
___	**24101**	Mainline Color Position Signal, *04-08*		25
___	**24102**	Industrial Water Tower, *03*		55
___	**24103**	Double Floodlight Tower, *03, 05-09*		42
___	**24104**	Hobo Tower, *03-05*		70
___	**24105**	Track Gang, *03-06*		70
___	**24106**	Exploding Ammunition Dump, *02*		25
___	**24107**	Missile Firing Range Set, *02*		60
___	**24108**	World War II Pylon, *03*		80
___	**24109**	Santa Fe Railroad Tugboat, *03*		125
___	**24110**	Pennsylvania Railroad Tugboat, *03*		118
___	**24111**	Swing Bridge, *03*		215
___	**24112**	Oil Field with bubble tubes, *03*		44
___	**24113**	Lionelville Ford Auto Dealership, *03*		225
___	**24114**	AMC/ARC Gantry Crane, *CC, 03*		195
___	**24115**	AMC/ARC Log Loader, *CC, 03, 06-07*		140
___	**24117**	Illuminated Covered Bridge, *02-16, 18-20*		75
___	**24119**	Big Bay Lighthouse, *04-05*		170
___	**24122**	Lionelville People Pack, *03, 08-09, 15-17*		27
___	**24123**	Passenger Station People Pack, *03, 08-09, 15-20*		27
___	**24124**	Carnival People Pack, *03, 08-11, 13-16, 18-20*	5	27
___	**24130**	TMCC 135/180 PowerMaster, *04-12*		79
___	**24131**	Dumbo Pylon, *03*		70
___	**24134**	Bethlehem Steel Gantry Crane, *02*		200
___	**24135**	Lionel Lighthouse, *02-03*		100

	MODERN 1970-2021	Esc	Mint	
24137	Mr. Spiff and Puddles, *03, 08*		34	___
24138	Playtime Playground, *03, 08*		50	___
24139	Duck Shooting Gallery, *03*		110	___
24140	Charles Bowdish Homestead, *03*		60	___
24147	Lionel Sawmill, *03*		90	___
24148	Coal Tipple Coal Pack, *602, 08-10, 13-20*		15	___
24149	NYC Hobo Hotel, *02*		42	___
24151	Hobo Campfire, *03*		25	___
24152	Conveyor Lumber Loader, *03*		65	___
24153	Railroad Control Tower, *03, 08-10*		40	___
24154	Maiden Rescue, *03*		35	___
24155	Blinking Light Billboard, *04-10*		21	___
24156	Lionelville Street Lamps, set of 4, *04-05, 07-19*		30	___
24159	Illuminated Station Platform, *04-08*		32	___
24160	Rub-a-Dub-Dub, *04*		42	___
24161	Test O' Strength, *04-06*		70	___
24164	Summer Vacation, *04-05*		80	___
24168	Tire Swing, *04-05*		70	___
24170	Rover's Revenge, *04-05*		70	___
24171	Campbell's Soup Water Tower, *04*		45	___
24172	Balancing Man, *04-05*		70	___
24173	Derrick Platform, *03-05*		60	___
24174	Icing Station, *04-06*		100	___
24176	Irene's Diner, *06-07*		65	___
24177	Hot Air Balloon Ride, *04, 06*		95	___
24179	Scrambler Amusement Ride, *04-07*		165	___
24180	Choo Choo Barn Lionelville Zoo, *04-05*		105	___
24182	Lionelville Firehouse, *04*		100	___
24183	Lionelville Gas Station, *04, 06-09*		115	___
24187	Classic Billboard Set: 3 stands and 5 inserts, *04-08*		10	___
24190	Station Platform, *05-09*		17	___
24191	Park People Pack, *04-18*		27	___
24192	Park Benches People Pack, *04-09*		23	___
24193	Railroad Yard People Pack, *04-08, 14-18*		27	___
24194	Civil Servants People Pack, *04-18*		27	___
24196	Farm People Pack, *04-09*		23	___
24197	City Accessory Pack, *04-17*		27	___
24200	Lionel FasTrack Book, *07-10, 13-15*		35	___
24201	UPS Centennial Operating Billboard Signmen, *07*		100	___
24203	Polar Express Original Figures, 4 pieces, *08-14, 16, 20*		30	___
24204	Christmas Tractor Trailer with trees, *08*		25	___
24205	Classic Billboard Set, *08-10*		20	___
24206	MOW Gantry Crane, *08*		280	___
24212	Lionel Art Blinking Billboard, *08-09*		23	___
24213	Universal Lockon, *12-16*		4	___
24214	Postwar "395" Floodlight Tower, *08*		75	___
24215	MTA Metro-North Passenger Station, *07*		53	___
24218	Sunoco Elevated Tank, *08-09*		75	___
24219	PRR Plastic Girder Bridge, *08*		18	___
24220	ATSF Girder Bridge, *08-09*		18	___
24221	UP Die-cast Girder Bridge, *08*		30	___
24222	UPS Die-cast Girder Bridge, *08*		30	___
24223	Santa's Sleigh Pylon, *08*		150	___
24224	Postwar "38" Water Tower, *08-09*		150	___

		Esc	Mint
___ **24226**	Christmas Toy Store, *08*		52
___ **24227**	Halloween Animated Billboard, *08-09*		54
___ **24228**	Christmas Operating Billboard, *08*		38
___ **24229**	Pennsylvania Water Tower, *08-09*		23
___ **24230**	Maiden Rescue, *08*		60
___ **24232**	Burning Switch Tower, *08*		80
___ **24233**	Exploding Ammunition Dump, *08*		36
___ **24234**	Missile Firing Range, *08*		43
___ **24235**	UPS Water Tower, *08*		80
___ **24236**	Wimpy's All-Star Burger Stand, *08*		97
___ **24238**	Sunoco Oil Derrick, *08*		90
___ **24240**	MTA Metro-North Blinking Billboard, *07*		21
___ **24242**	Postwar "352" Icing Station, *08*		100
___ **24243**	Rosie's Roadside Diner, *08*		85
___ **24244**	Commuter People, *08, 13-18*		27
___ **24245**	MTA Metro-North Illuminated Station Platform, *07*		32
___ **24248**	Manual Crossing Gate, *08-19*		20
___ **24250**	Mainline Gooseneck Lamps, pair, *08-09*		32
___ **24251**	Polar Express Caribou, *08-14, 16-20*		27
___ **24252**	Polar Express Wolves and Rabbits, *08-14, 16-20*		27
___ **24264**	Halloween People, *08-12*		23
___ **24265**	Trick or Treat People, *08-13*		23
___ **24270**	Operating Forklift Platform, *08-09*		280
___ **24272**	Train Orders Building, *08*		80
___ **24273**	Christmas Water Tower, *08-10*		23
___ **24274**	Christmas Girder Bridge, *08*		18
___ **24279**	PowerMaster Bridge, *08-13*		55
___ **24283**	NYC Girder Bridge, *09-10*		21
___ **24284**	Halloween Girder Bridge, *09-11*		21
___ **24285**	CP Rail Girder Bridge, *08-09*		30
___ **24286**	Polar Express Girder Bridge, *09-14*		21
___ **24287**	ATSF Blinking Light Water Tower, *09*		30
___ **24288**	NYC Blinking Light Water Tower, *09*		30
___ **24293**	Legacy Module Garage, *08-09*		50
___ **24294**	AEC Nuclear Reactor, *09-10*		325
___ **24295**	Cowen's Corner Hobby Shop, *09*		420
___ **24296**	Engine House, *09-12, 14*		70
___ **24299**	Main Street Ice Cream Parlor, *08*		37
___ **24500**	D&RGW Alco PA Diesel AA Set, *04*		530
___ **24503**	D&RGW Alco PB Diesel, *04*		150
___ **24504**	Santa Fe E6 Diesel AA Set, *CC, 03*		530
___ **24507**	Milwaukee Road E6 Diesel AA Set, *CC, 03*		530
___ **24511**	Burlington FT Diesel AA Set, RailSounds, *03*		225
___ **24516**	Santa Fe F3 Diesel B Unit, *03*		235
___ **24517**	NYC F3 Diesel B Unit "2404," powered, *CC, 03*		250
___ **24518**	WP F3 Diesel B Unit, *03*		275
___ **24519**	B&O F3 Diesel B Unit, *03*		270
___ **24520**	Alaska F3 Diesel AA Set, *03*		650
___ **24521**	Alaska F3 Diesel B Unit, nonpowered, *03*		200
___ **24522**	Alaska F3 Diesel B Unit "1519," powered, *CC, 03*		300
___ **24528**	Postwar "2379T" Rio Grande F3 Diesel A Unit, nonpowered, *04*		175
___ **24529**	Santa Fe F3 Diesel AA Set, *CC, 04*		690
___ **24532**	Santa Fe F3 Diesel B Unit "18A," nonpowered, *04*		150

		Esc	Mint	
24533	Santa Fe F3 Diesel B Unit "18B," *04*		200	___
24534	Erie-Lack. F3 Diesel ABA Set, *CC, 05*		900	___
24538	Erie-Lack. F3 Diesel B Unit "8042," powered, *CC, 05*		225	___
24544	NYC FA2 Diesel AA Set, *CC, 05*		600	___
24547	NYC FB2 Diesel B Unit "3330" (std O), *05*		150	___
24548	CN FPA-4 Diesel AA Set, *CC, 05*		600	___
24551	CN FPB-4 Diesel B Unit "6865" (std O), *05*		150	___
24552	UP F3 Diesel ABA Set, *CC, 05*		680	___
24556	UP F3 Diesel B Unit "900C," powered, *CC, 05*		285	___
24562	Santa Fe F3 Diesel B Unit, powered, *04-05*		300	___
24563	PRR F3 Diesel B Unit, powered, *04-05*		195	___
24570	Santa Fe FT Diesel B Unit, nonpowered, *05*		85	___
24573	Postwar "2383C" Santa Fe F3 Diesel B Unit, nonpowered, *05*		180	___
24574	UP E7 Diesel AA Set, *CC, 06*		700	___
24577	UP E7 Diesel B Unit "990," nonpowered (std O), *06*		150	___
24578	UP E7 Diesel B Unit "988," powered, *06*		300	___
24579	NYC E7 Diesel AA Set, *CC, 06*		700	___
24582	NYC E7 Diesel B Unit "4105," nonpowered (std O), *06*		150	___
24583	NYC E7 Diesel B Unit "4104," powered, *06*		300	___
24584	Pennsylvania F7 Diesel ABA Set, *CC, 06*		900	___
24588	Pennsylvania F7 Diesel B Unit "9643B," powered, *06-07*		300	___
24589	Santa Fe F7 Diesel ABA Set, *CC, 06-07*		900	___
24593	Santa Fe F7 Diesel B Unit "332B," powered, *06-07*		300	___
24594	PRR F7 Diesel Breakdown B Unit, RailSounds, *06-07*		160	___
24595	Santa Fe F7 Diesel Breakdown B Unit, RailSounds, *06-07*		270	___
24596	UP E7 Diesel Breakdown B Unit, RailSounds, *06*		270	___
24597	NYC E7 Diesel Breakdown B Unit, RailSounds, *06*		270	___
24928	Franklin Mutual Bank, *08*		60	___
25003	WP Boxcar, orange with silver feather, *05*		30	___
25008	Holiday Boxcar, *06*		50	___
25009	Santa Fe Hi-Cube Boxcar "14064," *06*		30	___
25010	NP Boxcar "48189," *06*		30	___
25011	Angela Trotta Thomas "Santa's Break" Boxcar, *06*		50	___
25014	PRR Boxcar, silver, *10*		30	___
25016	ATSF Boxcar, *10*		35	___
25022	NYC Boxcar, *06*		35	___
25025	Reading Boxcar "106502," *07-08*		35	___
25026	RI Hi-Cube Boxcar, *07-08*		35	___
25030	Billboard Boxcar with catalog art, *06*		20	___
25033	Holiday Boxcar, *07*		50	___
25034	Angela Trotta Thomas "Santa's Workshop" Boxcar, *07*		50	___
25035	Disney Holiday Boxcar, *06*		50	___
25041	UPS Centennial Boxcar #1, *06*		60	___
25042	UPS Centennial Boxcar #2, *07*		60	___
25043	Macy's Parade Boxcar, *06*		40	___
25047	"It's a Wonderful Life" Bedford Falls Boxcar			___
25048	It's a Wonderful Life Happy Holidays Boxcar			___
25050	British Columbia Hi-Cube Boxcar "8008," *08*		35	___
25051	Seaboard Boxcar, *08*		35	___
25052	Disney Holiday Boxcar, *07*		75	___
25053	NYC DD Boxcar "75500," *08*		55	___
25054	Angela Trotta Thomas "Christmas Memories" Boxcar, *08*		55	___
25057	PRR Boxcar "19751," *08*		20	___

			Esc	Mint
____	25058	Santa Fe Boxcar, *10*		30
____	25059	Democrat 2008 Election Boxcar, *08*		50
____	25060	Republican 2008 Election Boxcar, *08*		50
____	25061	Holiday Boxcar, *08*		55
____	25063	Conrail Boxcar "25063," *09*		40
____	25064	CP Rail Hi-Cube Boxcar, *09-10*		40
____	25065	Disney Holiday Boxcar, *08*		40
____	25066	Holiday Boxcar, *09*		65
____	25067	Angela Trotta Thomas "General Delivery" Boxcar, *09*		65
____	25068	D&H Boxcar, *08 u*		60
____	25077	Milwaukee Road Boxcar "8484," *09-10*		40
____	25087	Wabash Boxcar "6439," *10-11*		40
____	25093	Seaboard Boxcar, *10*		30
____	25095	Texas Special Boxcar, *10*		100
____	25096	CN Boxcar, *10*		45
____	25103	Chessie "Steam Special" Madison Car 2-pack, *05*		100
____	25106	Pennsylvania Madison Car 4-pack, *05*		210
____	25111	Pennsylvania Madison Car 2-pack, *05*		120
____	25114	Lionel Lines Passenger Car 3-pack, *05*		120
____	25118	Lionel Lines Passenger Car 2-pack, *05*		80
____	25121	Southern Streamliner Car 4-pack, *05*		210
____	25126	Southern Streamliner Car 2-pack, *05-06*		120
____	25134	Polar Express Add-on Diner, *05-14, 16-17*		70
____	25135	Polar Express Add-on Baggage Car, *05-14,16-17*		70
____	25142	NYC Combination Car, "5018"		
____	25143	NYC Coach, "3807"		
____	25148	B&O Madison Car 4-pack, *06-07*		220
____	25153	B&O Madison Car 2-pack, *06-07*		125
____	25156	California Zephyr Streamliner Car 4-pack (std O), *06-07*		220
____	25161	California Zephyr Streamliner Car 2-pack, *06-07*		125
____	25164	UP Madison Car 4-pack, *06-07*		220
____	25169	UP Madison Car 2-pack, *06-07*		125
____	25176	B&O Baggage Car, TrainSounds, *06-07*		160
____	25177	UP Baggage Car, TrainSounds, *06-07*		160
____	25178	California Zephyr Streamliner Baggage Car, TrainSounds, *06-07*		160
____	25186	Polar Express Hot Chocolate Car Add-on, *06-14, 16-17*		70
____	25187	GN Streamliner Car 4-pack, *07*		220
____	25188	GN Streamliner Car 2-pack, *07*		125
____	25189	GN Streamliner Baggage Car, TrainSounds, *07*		160
____	25196	North Pole Central Vista Dome Car, *07-08*		45
____	25197	North Pole Central Baggage Car, *07-10*		45
____	25198	PRR Vista Dome Car "4058," *07-08*		45
____	25199	PRR Baggage Car "9359," *07-09*		45
____	25404	FEC Champion Aluminum Passenger Car 2-pack, *04-05*		290
____	25407	FEC Champion Aluminum Diner, StationSounds, *04-05*		290
____	25408	Santa Fe El Capitan Aluminum Passenger Car 2-pack, *05*		290
____	25411	Santa Fe El Capitan Aluminum Diner, StationSounds, *05*		290
____	25412	B&O Columbian Aluminum Passenger Car 2-pack, *05*		275
____	25415	B&O Columbian Aluminum Diner, StationSounds, *05*		290
____	25416	SP Daylight Aluminum Passenger Car 2-pack, *04-05*		290
____	25419	SP Daylight Aluminum Diner, StationSounds, *04-05*		290
____	25420	PRR Trail Blazer Aluminum Passenger Car 2-pack, *04-05*		290
____	25423	PRR Trail Blazer Aluminum Diner, StationSounds, *04-05*		290

MODERN 1970-2021

		Esc	Mint
25433	UP City of Denver Aluminum Passenger Car 4-pack (std O), 05	1000	___
25438	Union Pacific Aluminum Passenger Car 2-pack, 05	250	___
25441	UP City of Denver 18" Aluminum Diner, StationSounds, 05	290	___
25446	Santa Fe Super Chief Streamliner Car 2-pack, 05	150	___
25450	PRR Congressional Aluminum Passenger Car 4-pack (std O), 06-07	580	___
25455	PRR Congressional Aluminum Passenger Car 2-pack (std O), 06-07	300	___
25458	PRR Congressional Diner, StationSounds (std O), 06-07	300	___
25473	NYC Commodore Vanderbilt Aluminum Passenger Car 2-pack (std O), 06	300	___
25476	NYC Commodore Vanderbilt Diner, StationSounds (std O), 06	300	___
25496	Texas Special 21" Streamliner Diner, StationSounds (std O), 07	300	___
25503	Santa Fe Heavyweight Passenger Car 4-pack (std O), 07-09	495	___
25504	Santa Fe Heavyweight Passenger Car 2-pack (std O), 07-09	265	___
25505	Santa Fe Heavyweight Diner, StationSounds (std O), 07-09	295	___
25506	SP Heavyweight Passenger Car 4-pack (std O), 07	495	___
25507	SP Heavyweight Passenger Car 2-pack (std O), 07-08	265	___
25508	SP Heavyweight Diner, StationSounds (std O), 07-08	295	___
25512	Texas Special Streamliner Car 2-pack (std O), 07	300	___
25514	Best Friend of Charleston Coach, 08	125	___
25515	MILW Heavyweight Passenger Car 4-pack (std O), 07	495	___
25516	MILW Heavyweight Passenger Car 2-pack (std O), 07	265	___
25517	MILW Heavyweight Diner, StationSounds (std O), 07-08	295	___
25518	PRR Heavyweight Passenger Car 4-pack (std O), 07	495	___
25519	PRR Heavyweight Passenger Car 2-pack (std O), 07	265	___
25520	PRR Heavyweight Diner, StationSounds (std O), 07-08	295	___
25521	B&O Heavyweight Passenger Car 4-pack (std O), 07	495	___
25522	B&O Heavyweight Passenger Car 2-pack (std O), 07	265	___
25523	B&O Heavyweight Diner, StationSounds (std O), 07-08	295	___
25559	Phantom IV Passenger Car 4-pack, 08	380	___
25574	UP Streamlined Diner, StationSounds (std O), 08	325	___
25575	Polar Express Heavyweight Car 2-pack, 09	400	___
25576	Polar Express Scale Observation Car, 14, 16	210	___
25578	Polar Express Heavyweight Add-on Coach, 09	200	___
25582	New York City Transit R30 Subway 2-pack, 10	400	___
25586	Polar Express Heavyweight Baggage Car, 10, 12-14	210	___
25587	Polar Express Abandoned Toy Car, 10, 13	200	___
25595	New York City Transit R16 Subway 2-pack, 10	400	___
25598	Polar Express Heavyweight Combination Car, 12-14	210	___
25600	Postwar Scale CP 18" Aluminum Passenger Car 4-pack , 11	640	___
25605	Postwar Scale CP 18" Aluminum Passenger Car 2-pack , 11	320	___
25608	ATSF Super Chief 18" Aluminum Passenger Cars 4-pack, 11	640	___
25613	ATSF Super Chief 18" Aluminum Passenger Cars 2-pack, 11	320	___
25616	UP 18" Passenger Car 2-pack (std O), 11	320	___
25619	PRR "Lindbergh Special" Passenger Car 2-pack, 11	280	___
25622	Milwaukee Road 18" Passenger Car 4-pack, 11	640	___
25623	Milwaukee Road 18" Passenger Car 2-pack, 11	320	___
25630	Polar Express Scale Heavyweight Diner, 12-14, 16	210	___
25631	Lionel Funeral Set Add-on 2-pack (std O), 13	300	___
25635	PRR Red Arrow Heavyweight Coach 3-pack (std O), 13	430	___
25639	PRR Red Arrow Heavyweight Diner (std O), 13	150	___
25646	ATSF Scout Heavyweight Coach 4-pack (std O), 12-14	550	___
25651	ATSF Scout Heavyweight Coach 2-pack (std O), 12-14	280	___
25654	Southern Crescent Limited Heavyweight Passenger Car 2-pack, 12	550	___
25655	Blue Comet Heavyweight Passenger Car 2-pack, 12-13	550	___
25656	Alton Limited Heavyweight Passenger Car 2-pack, 12-14	550	___

			Esc	Mint
____	**25665**	Amtrak Acela Passenger Car 2-pack, *12*		500
____	**25713**	NYC 20th Century Limited Heavyweight Passenger Car 4-pack (std O), *12-14*		550
____	**25714**	NYC 20th Century Limited Van Twiller Combo Car (std O), *12*		140
____	**25715**	NYC 20th Century Limited Schuyler Mansion Sleeper Car (std O), *12*		140
____	**25716**	NYC 20th Century Limited Macomb House Sleeper Car (std O), *12*		140
____	**25717**	NYC 20th Century Limited Catskill Valley Observation Car (std O), *12*		140
____	**25718**	NYC 20th Century Limited Heavyweight Passenger Car 2-pack, *12-14*		280
____	**25719**	NYC 20th Century Limited Baggage Car "4857" (std O), *12*		140
____	**25720**	NYC 20th Century Limited Poplar Highlands Sleeper Car (std O), *12*		140
____	**25721**	NYC 20th Century Limited Heavyweight Diner "655" (std O), *12*		280
____	**25722**	D&RGW California Zephyr 18" Aluminum Passenger Car 4-pack, *12*		640
____	**25727**	WP California Zephyr 18" Aluminum Passenger Car 2-pack, *12*		320
____	**25731**	CB&Q California Zephyr 18" Aluminum Passenger Car 2-pack, *12*		320
____	**25757**	Texas Special Passenger Car 2-pack, *13-14*		400
____	**25760**	PRR Passenger Car 2-pack, *13-14*		400
____	**25773**	SAL Round-roof Boxcar "19297" (std O), *14*		80
____	**25790**	NYC 20th Century Limited Heavyweight Diner (std O), *12*		140
____	**25795**	Polar Express 10th Anniversary Scale Coach, *14*		215
____	**25795**	Polar Express Gold Coach, *17*		200
____	**25796**	Polar Express 10th Anniversary Scale Observation Car, *14, 16*		215
____	**25930**	John Adams Boxcar, *13, 15-16*		70
____	**25931**	Andrew Johnson Boxcar, *13, 15-16*		70
____	**25932**	Calvin Coolidge Boxcar, *13, 15-16*		70
____	**25933**	Harry S. Truman Boxcar, *13, 15-16*		70
____	**25934**	Santa Fe Reefer 3-pack, *14-17*		145
____	**25938**	PRR Freight Expansion 3-pack, *13*		155
____	**25942**	Western Freight Expansion 3-pack, *13-16*		155
____	**25946**	SP Hi-Cube Boxcar "128132," *13, 15*		50
____	**25947**	North Pole Express Jack Frost Reefer, *13*		43
____	**25958**	Gingerbread Dough Vat Car, *13-14*		60
____	**25959**	Gingerbread 3-D Tank Car, *13*		55
____	**25960**	Christmas Tree Transparent Boxcar, *13-14*		75
____	**25961**	Thanksgiving on Parade Boxcar, *13*		60
____	**25962**	Thanksgiving Poultry Car, *13*		70
____	**25963**	A Christmas Story 30th Anniversary Boxcar, *13-14*		65
____	**25964**	Silver Bell Casting Co. Ore Car, *13*		55
____	**25965**	Polar Express 10th Anniversary Boxcar, *13*		65
____	**25972**	MILW Scale Round-roof Boxcar (std O), *15*		50
____	**25973**	Seaboard Round-roof Boxcar "19297" (std O), *14*		80
____	**25977**	A Christmas Story Leg Lamp Mint Car, *13*		80
____	**26000**	C&O Flatcar with pipes, *01*		20
____	**26001**	BP Flatcar "6424" with trailers, *01 u*		150
____	**26002**	Monopoly Flatcar with airplane, *00 u*		NRS
____	**26003**	Lackawanna Flatcar with NH trailer, *01*		60
____	**26004**	Conrail Flatcar "71693" with trailer, *01*		50
____	**26005**	Nickel Plate Flatcar with trailer, *01*		55
____	**26006**	Southern Flatcar "50126" with trailer, *01*		50
____	**26007**	NW Flatcar "203029" with trailer, *01*		50
____	**26008**	Farmall Flatcar, *01 u*		NRS
____	**26011**	B&M Bulkhead Flatcar, *01 u*		NRS
____	**26013**	CN Flatcar with Zamboni ice resurfacing machine, *01*		48
____	**26014**	JCPenney Flatcar, *01 u*		145
____	**26016**	Soo Line Flatcar with trucks, *01 u*		NRS

		Esc	Mint
26017	Soo Line Flatcar with trailer, *01 u*	NRS	___
26018	Soo Line Flatcar with trailer, *01 u*	NRS	___
26019	Alaska Gondola "13801," *02*		30 ___
26020	Postwar "3830" Flatcar with submarine, *02*		46 ___
26021	CN Flatcar with trailer, *02*		44 ___
26022	PFE Flatcar with trailer, *02*		32 ___
26023	Postwar "6816" Flatcar with bulldozer, *02*		65 ___
26024	Postwar "6817" Flatcar with scraper, *02*		65 ___
26025	Postwar "6407" Flatcar with rocket, *02*		42 ___
26026	Postwar "6413" Flatcar with Mercury capsules, *02*		95 ___
26027	Flatcar "6425" with U.S. Army boat, *02*		30 ___
26028	Conrail Well Car "768121," *02*		40 ___
26030	NYC Flatcar "601172" with stakes and bulkheads, *02*		22 ___
26033	NYC Gondola "6462," *01*		30 ___
26035	LL Flatcar with traffic helicopter, *01*		50 ___
26039	Lions Flatcar with 2 Zamboni ice resurfacing machines, *02*		39 ___
26042	B&O Gondola "601272" with canisters, *03*		19 ___
26043	Seaboard Flatcar "48109" with trailer, *03*		30 ___
26044	NYC Flatcar "506089" with trailers, *03*		35 ___
26045	Postwar "2411" Flatcar with pipes, *03*		40 ___
26046	Postwar "6561" Flatcar with cable reels, *03*		30 ___
26047	Postwar "2461" Flatcar with transformer, *03*		25 ___
26048	Postwar "6801" Flatcar with boat, *02*		29 ___
26049	Speedboat Willie Flatcar with boat, *03*		29 ___
26053	PRR Gondola with canisters, *04, 05*		20 ___
26056	Southern Bulkhead Flatcar "50125," *02*		19 ___
26057	SP Flatcar "599365" with tractors, *02*		37 ___
26058	SP Flatcar "599366" with trailer frames, *02*		35 ___
26061	Lionelville Tree Transport Gondola, *03*		40 ___
26062	NYC Gondola "26062" with cable reels, *03*		19 ___
26063	Pennsylvania Bulkhead Flatcar "26063," *03*		19 ___
26064	Rock Island Flatcar "90088" with trailer, *04*		34 ___
26065	REA Flatcar with trailers "TLCX2," *04*		35 ___
26066	Great Northern Bulkhead Flatcar "26066," *04*		20 ___
26067	Southern Gondola "60141" with cable reels, *04*		20 ___
26070	Nestle Nesquik Flatcar "26070" with trailer, *03*		70 ___
26077	LL Flatcar "6424" with autos, girls set add-on, *03*		44 ___
26078	LL Flatcar "6801" with boat, boys set add-on, *03*		40 ___
26080	NJ Medical School Flatcar with handcar, *03*		80 ___
26082	Frisco Auto Carrier, 2-tier, *04*		20 ___
26085	New York Auto Carrier, 2-tier, *05*		27 ___
26086	Alaska Flatcar with bulkheads, *05*		25 ___
26087	Rock Island Gondola with canisters, traditional, *05*		27 ___
26091	Elvis Flatcar with tractor and trailer, traditional, *05*		60 ___
26096	BNSF Screened Auto Carrier, *04*		55 ___
26099	PRR Auto Carrier "500423," 3-tier, *07*		30 ___
26100	PRR 1-D Tank Car, *00*		27 ___
26101	Lenoil 1-D Tank Car "6015," *00*		34 ___
26102	AEC Glow-in-Dark 1-D Tank Car, *00*		58 ___
26103	GATX Tank Train 1-D Tank Car "44588," *00*		34 ___
26107	BP Petroleum 3-D Tank Car, *00 u*		99 ___
26108	Lionel Visitor's Center Reefer "206482," *00 u*		38 ___
26109	NYC (P&LE) 1-D Tank Car, *00*		42 ___
26110	SP 3-D Tank Car "6415," *00-01*		15 ___

		Esc	Mint
___ 26111	Frisco Tank Car, *00*		29
___ 26112	Gulf Oil Tank Car, *00*		40
___ 26113	U.S. Army 1-D Tank Car, *00*		35
___ 26114	Service Station 1-D Tank Car (SSS), *00*		32
___ 26115	Lionel Centennial Tank Car, *00 u*		90
___ 26116	Pepe LePew 1-D Tank Car, *00 u*		85
___ 26118	NYC Tank Car "101900," *01*		23
___ 26119	Protex 3-D Tank Car "1054," *00*		29
___ 26120	KCS Tank Car "1229," *00*		32
___ 26122	Pioneer Seed Tank Car, *00*		NRS
___ 26123	Santa Fe Stock Car "23002," *01*		35
___ 26124	C&O 1-D Tank Car "X1019," *01*		30
___ 26125	Winter Wonderland Clear Tank Car with confetti, *00*		50
___ 26126	Cheerios Boxcar, *98*		70
___ 26127	Wellspring Capital Management Tank Car with confetti, *00 u*	0	233
___ 26131	Santa Fe 1-D Tank Car "335268," *02*		22
___ 26132	UP 1-D Tank Car "69015, *02*		40
___ 26133	Tootsie Roll 1-D Tank Car "26133," *02*		40
___ 26135	Whirlpool Tank Car, *01*		NRS
___ 26136	Southern 1-D Tank Car "8790011," *03*		20
___ 26137	Jack Frost 1-D Tank Car "106," *03*		32
___ 26138	Nestle Nesquik 1-D Tank Car "26138," *03*		40
___ 26139	Lionel Lines Stock Car "26139" with horses, *03*		39
___ 26141	Whirlpool 1-D Tank Car, *03 u*		97
___ 26144	Chessie System 1-D Tank Car "2233," *02*		22
___ 26145	Do It Best 1-D Tank Car, *03 u*		82
___ 26146	Do It Best 1-D Tank Car, *03 u*		95
___ 26147	Diamond Chemicals 1-D Tank Car "6315," Archive Collection, *02*		33
___ 26149	Egg Nog 1-D Tank Car, *03*		43
___ 26150	Alaska 3-D Tank Car "26150," *03*		23
___ 26151	NP Wood-sided Reefer "26151," *03*		19
___ 26152	Morton Salt 1-D Tank Car "26152," *04*		40
___ 26153	Pillsbury 1-D Tank Car "26153," *04*		40
___ 26154	NYC 3-D Tank Car "26154," *04*		25
___ 26155	Pennsylvania 1-D Tank Car "26155," *04*		20
___ 26156	North Western Wood-sided Reefer "15356," *04*		20
___ 26157	Ballyhoo Brothers Circus Stock Car "26157," *04*		35
___ 26158	Campbell's Soup 1-D Tank Car, *04*		35
___ 26164	LL 1-D Tank Car "6315," girls set add-on, *03*		43
___ 26167	New Haven 1-D Tank Car, traditional, *05*		27
___ 26168	Conrail 3-D Tank Car, traditional, *05*		27
___ 26169	Santa Fe Wood-sided Reefer, traditional, *05*		27
___ 26171	Alaska 1-D Tank Car, *05*		30
___ 26176	Tidmouth Milk 1-D Tank Car, *05*		35
___ 26179	GN 3-D Tank Car, *06*		30
___ 26180	DM&IR 1-D Tank Car "S15," *06*		30
___ 26181	NYC Wood-sided Reefer, *06*		30
___ 26193	UP 1-D Tank Car, *07*		15
___ 26196	Candy Cane 1-D Tank Car, *06*		60
___ 26197	D&H 1-D Tank Car "55," *07-08*		35
___ 26198	D&RGW 3-D Tank Car, *07*		30
___ 26199	WP PFE Wood-sided Reefer "55327," *07*		30
___ 26200	NKP Boxcar "18211," *98*		35
___ 26201	Operation Lifesaver Boxcar, *98*		29

		Esc	Mint
26203	D&H Boxcar "1829," 98		25 ___
26204	Alaska Boxcar "10806," 98-99		35 ___
26205	Rocky & Bullwinkle Boxcar, 99		36 ___
26206	Curious George Boxcar, 99		40 ___
26208	Vapor Records Boxcar #2, 98		60 ___
26214	Celebrate the Century Stamp Boxcar, 98 u		97 ___
26215	AEC Glow-in-the-Dark Boxcar, 98		105 ___
26216	Cheerios Boxcar, 98 u		80 ___
26218	Quaker Oats Boxcar, 98 u		460 ___
26219	Ace Hardware Boxcar, 98 u		NRS ___
26220	Smuckers Boxcar, 98 u		92 ___
26222	Penn Central Boxcar "125962," 99		31 ___
26223	FEC Boxcar "5027," 99		31 ___
26224	D&H Boxcar, 99		24 ___
26228	Vapor Records Holiday Boxcar, 99 u		130 ___
26230	AEC Glow-in-the-Dark Boxcar #2, 99		59 ___
26232	Martin Guitar Lumber Boxcar "9823," 99		50 ___
26234	NYC Boxcar, 99		29 ___
26235	Valentine Boxcar, 99		40 ___
26236	Aircraft Boxcar, 99		28 ___
26237	Boy Scout Boxcar, 99		85 ___
26238	Detroit Historical Museum Boxcar, 99		29 ___
26239	M.A.D.D. Boxcar, 99		19 ___
26240	RailBox Boxcar, 99-00		24 ___
26241	Norfolk & Western Boxcar, 99-00		17 ___
26242	D.A.R.E. Boxcar, 99		30 ___
26243	Christmas Boxcar, 99		35 ___
26244	Woody Woodpecker Boxcar, 99		43 ___
26247	Lionel Lines Boxcar, 99		38 ___
26253	Acme Explosives Boxcar, 99 u		NRS ___
26254	Keebler Boxcar, 99 u		NRS ___
26255	NYC Boxcar "200495," 99 u		30 ___
26256	Salvation Army Charity Boxcar, 99		29 ___
26257	Wheaties Boxcar, 99		86 ___
26264	Lionel Station Boxcar, 99		44 ___
26265	NYC Pacemaker Boxcar, 00		30 ___
26271	AEC Glow-in-the-Dark Boxcar, 99		62 ___
26272	Christmas Boxcar, 00		42 ___
26275	Boy Scout Boxcar, 00		55 ___
26276	C&O Boxcar "23296," 99-00		23 ___
26277	UP Boxcar "491050," 00		20 ___
26278	Cap'n Crunch Christmas Boxcar, 99		680 ___
26280	Tinsel Town Express Boxcar, music, 00		50 ___
26284	Toy Fair Preview Boxcar, 99 u		725 ___
26285	NYC Pacemaker Boxcar, 00		40 ___
26288	AEC Glow-in-Dark Boxcar, 99		55 ___
26290	SP Boxcar, 00		20 ___
26291	Pennsylvania Boxcar "47158," 00		20 ___
26292	Frisco Boxcar "22015," 00		20 ___
26293	Burlington Boxcar, 00		30 ___
26294	Centennial Express Boxcar, 00		NRS ___
26295	Trainmaster Boxcar, 99 u		55 ___
26296	Service Station Boxcar Set (SSS), 00		105 ___
26298	Taz Bobbing Boxcar, 00		70 ___

		Esc	Mint
_____ 26300	UPS Flatcar with trailers, *04*		50
_____ 26301	UPS Flatcar with airplane, traditional, *05*		53
_____ 26302	Troublesome Truck #1, *05*		35
_____ 26303	Troublesome Truck #2, *05*		35
_____ 26305	SP Auto Carrier, 2-tier, *06*		30
_____ 26306	D&RGW Gondola "56135" with canisters, *06*		30
_____ 26307	Chessie System Bulkhead Flatcar, *06*		30
_____ 26308	Hard Rock Cafe Flatcar with billboards, *06*		55
_____ 26309	Alaska Depressed Center Flatcar with cable reels, *06*		50
_____ 26310	CGW Flatcar "3707" with trailer, *06*		55
_____ 26311	Santa Fe Flatcar with pickups, *06*		60
_____ 26317	AEC Gondola with toxic waste containers		30
_____ 26318	AEC Gondola with toxic waste containers		30
_____ 26330	Gondola with trees and presents, *06*		60
_____ 26331	Lionel Lines Bulkhead Flatcar, *07*		30
_____ 26332	CP Rail Gondola "337061" with canisters, *07*		30
_____ 26335	Domino Sugar Flatcar with trailer, *07-08*		60
_____ 26355	Kasey Kahne Auto Loader		
_____ 26357	CSX Flatcar "600514" with pipes, *07-08*		50
_____ 26366	REA Flatcar with trailers, *07*		60
_____ 26367	Santa's Egg Nog Flatcar with container, *07*		60
_____ 26368	Gondola with trees and presents, *07*		60
_____ 26378	Conrail Auto Carrier "786414," 2-tier, *08*		35
_____ 26379	PRR Gondola with cable reels, *08-09*		35
_____ 26380	NYC Bulkhead Flatcar, *08*		35
_____ 26389	ATSF Flatcar "108477" with 2 pickups, *08*		60
_____ 26390	ATSF Flatcar with bulkheads, *09-10*		40
_____ 26391	NYC Gondola "263910" with containers, *09*		40
_____ 26392	BNSF Auto Carrier, *09*		40
_____ 26400	C&NW Hopper, *07-08*		35
_____ 26401	NP Ore Car "78540," *08*		35
_____ 26410	Chessie System Hopper "47806," *08*		35
_____ 26411	Lionel Lines Ore Car "2026," *08-09*		35
_____ 26412	Chessie System 4-bay Hopper "60573," *08*		35
_____ 26418	B&M Hopper, *09*		40
_____ 26421	PRR Ore Car, *11*		40
_____ 26422	White Pass Ice Breaker Car, *09*		50
_____ 26423	Soo Line Ore Car, *10*		40
_____ 26424	LV Hopper, *11*		30
_____ 26425	UP Hopper, *11*		40
_____ 26429	PRR Hopper, *11*		40
_____ 26435	B&M Ice Breaker Hopper , *11*		50
_____ 26437	CSX Hopper, *11*		40
_____ 26439	Central of Georgia Hopper, *11-12*		40
_____ 26443	M&StL Ore Car "6700," *11*		40
_____ 26445	Polar Hopper with presents, *11-14*		60
_____ 26446	Thomas & Friends Troublesome Trucks Christmas 2-pack, *11-15*		70
_____ 26448	U.S. Army Gondola with reels, *11*		40
_____ 26449	CN Hi-Cube Boxcar "799346," *13*		55
_____ 26451	DM&IR Ore Car "28003," *13*		43
_____ 26452	PRR Hopper "153935," *13*		43
_____ 26457	PRR Ore Car, *12*		40
_____ 26473	Lackawanna NS Heritage 2-bay Hopper, *13*		55
_____ 26474	NYC NS Heritage Quad Hopper, *13*		55

		Esc	Mint
26477	Monopoly Electric Company Hopper, *13*		65 ___
26481	Boy Scouts of America Christmas Gondola, *13*		65 ___
26488	Hershey's Ice Breakers Hopper, *13*		66 ___
26489	Hershey's Chistmas Bells Boxcar, *13*		65 ___
26491	Pennsylvania Power & Light Gondola with canisters, *13*		43 ___
26492	Area 51 3-D Tank Car, *13*		43 ___
26493	Monopoly Water Works 3-D Tank Car, *13*		65 ___
26494	PRR Truss Rod Gondola with vats, *13*		60 ___
26495	C&NW Poultry Car, *13*		60 ___
26496	Lionelville Aquarium Co. Fish Food Vat Car, *13-16*		65 ___
26497	Bethlehem Steel Depressed Flatcar with reels, *13*		43 ___
26499	CN Hi-Cube Boxcar "799346," *14*		55 ___
26502	UP Bay Window Caboose "6517," *97*		47 ___
26503	ATSF High-Cupola Caboose "7606R," *97*		85 ___
26504	Mobil Oil Square Window Caboose "6257," *97 u*		37 ___
26505	Rescue Unit Caboose, *98*		50 ___
26506	N&W Square Window Caboose "562748," *98*		15 ___
26507	D&H Square Window Caboose "35707," *98*		20 ___
26508	Alaska Square Window Caboose "1081," *98*		28 ___
26511	Quaker Oats Square Window Caboose, *98 u*		52 ___
26513	NYC Emergency Caboose "26505," *99*		47 ___
26515	Lionel Lines Bobber Caboose, *99*		10 ___
26516	Safari Bobber Caboose, *99 u*		10 ___
26519	Christmas Work Caboose "6496," *99*		41 ___
26520	Bethlehem Steel Work Caboose "6130" (SSS), *99*		55 ___
26523	Keebler Cheezit Square Window Caboose, *99 u*		NRS ___
26524	NYC Square Window Caboose "295," *99 u*		20 ___
26526	Santa Fe Square Window Caboose "999471," *01*		30 ___
26527	Christmas Work Caboose with presents, *02*		27 ___
26528	PRR Square Window Caboose "6257," *99*		21 ___
26530	LL Square Window Caboose "6257," *99*		22 ___
26532	NYC Square Window Caboose "296," *00*		20 ___
26533	SP Square Window Caboose, *00*		20 ___
26534	PRR Square Window Caboose "6257," *00*		20 ___
26535	Frisco Square Window Caboose "1700," *00*		20 ___
26536	Centennial Express Square Window Caboose, *00*		NRS ___
26537	Lionel Mines Square Window Caboose, *00 u*		45 ___
26539	Whirlpool Square Window Caboose, *00 u*		NRS ___
26542	ACL Square Window Caboose "069," *01*		31 ___
26543	GN Square Window Caboose "X66," *00-01*		28 ___
26544	Alaska Square Window Caboose "1084," *01*		25 ___
26545	Snap-On Square Window Caboose, *00 u*		NRS ___
26548	Pioneer Seed Square Window Caboose, *00 u*		NRS ___
26549	PRR Square Window Caboose "4977947," *01*		20 ___
26550	NYC Square Window Caboose "19293," *01*		20 ___
26551	Chessie System Center Cupola Caboose, *01*		25 ___
26552	Santa Fe Square Window Caboose "999472," *01*		25 ___
26553	C&O Center Cupola Caboose "A918," *01*		30 ___
26554	Monopoly Short Line Square Window Caboose, *00 u*		NRS ___
26556	NH Center Cupola Caboose, *01*		35 ___
26557	Farmall Square Window Caboose, *01 u*		NRS ___
26559	N&W Center Cupola Caboose "518408," *01*		20 ___
26560	B&M Square Window Caboose, *01 u*		20 ___
26564	Soo Line Center Cupola Caboose, *01 u*		20 ___

Esc Mint

		Esc	Mint
____ 26565	Lionel Employee Square Window Caboose, *01 u*		165
____ 26566	WP Square Window Caboose "731," *02*		25
____ 26568	NKP Square Window Caboose "1155," *02*		25
____ 26569	Southern Square Window Caboose "252," *02*		25
____ 26570	B&O Square Window Caboose "295," *02*		25
____ 26572	Lionel 20th Century Square Window Caboose, *00 u*		25
____ 26580	Wabash Square Window Caboose "2805," *03*		22
____ 26581	C&O Square Window Caboose "C-1831," *03*		20
____ 26582	L&N Square Window Caboose "318," *03*		20
____ 26583	PRR Square Window Caboose "477814," *03*		25
____ 26594	Ontario Northland Work Caboose "26594," *03*		25
____ 26595	UP Caboose "26595," *03*		18
____ 26596	NYC Caboose "17716," *04*		25
____ 26597	Great Northern Caboose "X295," *04*		25
____ 26598	UP Caboose "26598," *04*		25
____ 26599	DM&IR Work Caboose "26599," *04*		25
____ 26600	American Fire and Rescue Water Tank Car, *09-11*		55
____ 26603	LV Depressed Flatcar with reels, *09*		40
____ 26604	Halloween Spooky Grave Gondola, *09*		58
____ 26609	NYC Gondola with Pacemaker canisters		40
____ 26612	Christmas Gifts Gondola, *09*		60
____ 26614	Tupelo Dairy Farms Milk Car, *10-11*		60
____ 26616	UP Bulkhead Flatcar with pipes, *10*		40
____ 26617	B&O Depressed Center Flatcar with generator, *10*		40
____ 26629	PRR Flatcar with generators		35
____ 26638	Pennsylvania Power & Light Flatcar with reels, *11*		40
____ 26639	Cities Service 3-Tier Auto Carrier, *11-12*		40
____ 26640	CN Maple Syrup Barrel Ramp Car, *11-12*		40
____ 26641	Coca-Cola Flatcar with trailer, *11*		78
____ 26642	CN Jet Snowblower, *11-12*		65
____ 26643	D&RGW Jet Snowblower, *11-13*		65
____ 26644	BNSF Flatcar with generator, *11*		40
____ 26645	BNSF Flatcar with trailer, *11*		40
____ 26646	Pennsylvania Power & Light Flatcar with transformer, *11-12*		40
____ 26647	IC Bulkhead Flatcar with pipes, *11*		40
____ 26649	Erie-Lack. Gondola with canisters, *11*		40
____ 26650	M&StL Flatcar with pipes, *11*		40
____ 26651	ATSF Scout Heavyweight Passenger Car 2-pack (std O), *12*		280
____ 26652	NYC Gondola with canisters, *11*		40
____ 26653	PC Flatcar with generator, *11*		35
____ 26654	Boy Scouts Flatcar with Pinewood Derby Kit, *11-13*		75
____ 26660	Coca-Cola Vat Car, *11-16*		75
____ 26661	Reindeer Feed Barrel Ramp Car, *09*		60
____ 26665	Hershey's Special Dark Flatcar with trailer, *11*		60
____ 26666	Boy Scouts Flatcar with trailer, *11*		70
____ 26667	Flatcar with Santa's sleigh, *12*		70
____ 26668	Strasburg Flatcar with wheels, *11*		55
____ 26669	U.S. Navy Flatcar with Shark submarine, *12-13*		60
____ 26673	B&M Flatcar with Milk Tank, *12*		60
____ 26675	Monopoly Auto Loader, *12*		80
____ 26676	Heinz Baked Beans Vat Car, *12*		60
____ 26677	LIRR Gondola with canisters, *12*		40
____ 26679	ATSF Gondola with reels, *12-13*		55

No.	Description	Esc	Mint	
26683	Christmas Track Maintenance Car, *12-13*		67	___
26685	Flatcar with Santa's plane, *12*		55	___
26686	Hershey's Cocoa Vat Car, *12-13*		63	___
26687	Lone Ranger Gondola with gunpowder vats, *12-14*		65	___
26691	UP Flatlcar w/Trailers, *2012*			___
26692	UP Gondola w/Coil Covers, *2012*			___
26693	Hershey's Krackel Piggyback Flatcar with trailer, *12-13*		78	___
26694	Carnegie Science Center Flatcar with submarine, *13*		70	___
26696	NJ Transit Gondola with wood ties, *12*		75	___
26699	PRR Flatcar with wheel load, *12-14*		55	___
26706	Lighted Christmas Boxcar, *00*		47	___
26707	Lionel Steel Operating Welding Flatcar "1108," *00*		90	___
26709	Flatcar "6511" with psychedelic submarine, *99*		32	___
26710	Southern Stock Car, Carsounds, *99*		95	___
26712	Churchill Downs Horse Car "6473," *99-00*		38	___
26713	Shay Log Car 3-pack, *99*		105	___
26714	Westside Lumber Flatcar with logs (std O), *99*		45	___
26715	Westside Lumber Flatcar with logs (std O), *99*		45	___
26716	Westside Lumber Flatcar with logs (std O), *99*		45	___
26717	Orion Star Boxcar 9600, *00*		30	___
26718	Christmas Boxcar, RailSounds, *00*		160	___
26719	Bobbing Ghost Halloween Boxcar, *00*		46	___
26721	Lionel Lines Coal Dump Car "3379," *00*		31	___
26722	Lionel Lines Log Dump Car "3351," *00*		31	___
26723	Lion Chasing Trainer Gondola "3444," *00*		49	___
26724	Veterans Day Boxcar, *00*		70	___
26725	NYC Jumping Hobo Boxcar "88160," *00*		38	___
26726	T. Rex Bobbing Boxcar, *00*		41	___
26727	San Francisco City Lights Boxcar, *00*		50	___
26736	Lionel Birthday Boxcar, *02 u*		40	___
26737	Operating Santa Gondola "6462," *00 u*		65	___
26738	Lionel Mines Gondola, *00 u*		NRS	
26739	Santa and Snowman Boxcar, *00*		46	___
26740	Reindeer Car, *00*		43	___
26741	Operating Santa Boxcar, *00*		50	___
26743	Christmas Reindeer Car, *01*		55	___
26745	Traveling Aquarium Car "506," *01*		70	___
26746	Bobbing Vampire Boxcar, *01*		46	___
26747	Halloween Bats Aquarium Car, *01*		75	___
26748	T&P Operating Hopper Car "9699," *01*		38	___
26749	Alaska Log Dump Car, *01*		29	___
26751	Chessie Coal Dump Car, *01*		27	___
26752	Christmas Aquarium Car, *01*		55	___
26753	Christmas Operating Dump Car, *01*		43	___
26757	Operating Barrel Car "35621," *00*		55	___
26758	AEC Nuclear Gondola "719766," *01*		95	___
26759	Postwar "3459" Coal Dump Car, *02*		60	___
26760	Postwar "3461" Log Dump Car, *02*		60	___
26761	AEC Security Caboose 3535, *01*		64	___
26762	Postwar "3665" Minuteman Car, *01*		55	___
26763	Postwar "6448" Exploding Boxcar, *01*		40	___
26764	Bethlehem Steel Operating Welding Car, *01*		75	___
26765	Postwar "3370" Sheriff and Outlaw Car, *01-02*	40	49	___

		Esc	Mint
26766	Priority Mail Operating Boxcar, *01-02*		32
26768	Postwar "6520" Searchlight Car, *02*		49
26769	Santa Fe Crane Car "199793," *CC, 03*		255
26770	Wabash Brakeman Car "3424," *01*		70
26773	Chessie Searchlight Car, *01*		20
26774	Santa Fe Log Dump Car, *01*		25
26775	U.S. Army Searchlight Car, *00*		50
26776	U.S. Army Operating Boxcar "26413," *00*		55
26777	U.S. Flag Boxcar, *01 u*		250
26779	Burlington Operating Hopper "189312," *02*		40
26780	Postwar "3376" Bronx Zoo Giraffe Car, *02*	35	36
26781	Postwar "3540" Operating Radar Car, *02*		35
26782	Lenny the Lion Bobbing Head Car, *02*		38
26784	Stingray Express Aquarium Car, *02*		35
26785	Flatcar with powerboat, *02*		31
26786	Lionelville Operating Parade Car, *02*		40
26787	Erie Jumping Hobo Boxcar, *01-02*		43
26788	Christmas Music Boxcar, *02*		46
26789	Kiss Kringle Chase Gondola, *02*		35
26790	Lighted Christmas Boxcar, *02*		34
26791	UP Animated Gondola, *02*	40	50
26792	REA Operating Boxcar "6299," *03*		39
26793	Alaska Extension Searchlight Car, *01*		44
26794	Postwar "6352" PFE Ice Car, *01-02*		85
26795	NYC Stock Car "3121," Cattle Sounds, *02*		50
26796	Lionel Farms Poultry Dispatch Car, *01*		55
26797	GN Log Dump Car "60011," *02*		48
26798	Bethlehem Steel Coal Dump Car "26798," *02*		70
26801	Jumping Bart Simpson Boxcar, *04*		44
26802	Simpsons Animated Gondola, *04*		46
26803	Santa Fe Derrick Car "26803," *04*		25
26804	NYC Coal Dump Car "26804," *04*		22
26805	Pennsylvania Log Dump Car "26805," *04*		24
26806	Pillsbury Operating Boxcar "3428," Archive Collection, *04*		40
26807	Blue Chip Line Motorized Animated Gondola, *04*		40
26808	Egg Nog Barrel Car, *04*		55
26809	Santa's Extension Searchlight Car, *04*		42
26810	NYC Operating Searchlight Car, *05*		33
26811	Pennsylvania Coal Dump Car, *05*		33
26812	Santa Fe Log Dump Car, *05*		33
26813	Lionel Lines Derrick Car, *05*		33
26814	NYC Walking Brakeman Car "174226," *05*		40
26815	PRR "Workin' on the Railroad" Boxcar "24255," *05*		42
26816	REA Boxcar, *steam TrainSounds, 05*		105
26817	Alaska Boxcar, *diesel TrainSounds, 05*		145
26818	Christmas Music Boxcar, *05*		63
26819	Holiday Animated Gondola, *05*		55
26820	Penguin Transport Aquarium Car, *05*		60
26821	NP Moe & Joe Lumber Flatcar, *05*		75
26826	Alaska Searchlight Car, *05*		40
26827	UPS Operating Boxcar "9237," Archive Collection, *05*		62
26828	Tornado Chaser Radar Tracking Car, *05*		63
26829	UPS Holiday Operating Boxcar, *05*		59
26832	Lionel Lines Tender, TrainSounds, *07-08*		105

		Esc	Mint
26833	Wellspring Radar Car, *04*		70 ___
26834	PFE Ice Car "20042" (std O), *05-06*		63 ___
26835	MOW Track Cleaning Car, *05*		140 ___
26836	Halloween Boxcar, SpookySounds, *05*		105 ___
26841	PRR Log Dump Car, *05*		27 ___
26842	NYC Coal Dump Car, *05*		27 ___
26845	Southern Derrick Car, *06*		35 ___
26846	GN Coal Dump Car, *06*		38 ___
26847	C&O Coal Dump Car, *06-07*		80 ___
26848	Lionel Lines Moe & Joe Flatcar, *06*		80 ___
26849	SP Log Dump Car, *06-07*		80 ___
26850	D&RGW Searchlight Car, *06*		75 ___
26851	WM Log Dump Car, *06*		35 ___
26852	Postwar "3562-25" Santa Fe Barrel Car, *06*		75 ___
26853	SeaWorld Aquarium Car, *06*		75 ___
26854	UP Walking Brakeman Car, *06-07*		75 ___
26855	Halloween Animated Gondola, *06*		65 ___
26856	Christmas Chase Gondola, *06*		65 ___
26857	Alien Radar Tracking Car, *06*		65 ___
26858	Christmas Music Boxcar, *06*		65 ___
26859	Christmas Parade Boxcar, *06*		75 ___
26860	B&O Boxcar "466035," steam TrainSounds (std O), *06-07*		75 ___
26861	Santa Fe Boxcar, diesel TrainSounds (std O), *06-07*		110 ___
26862	Hard Rock Cafe Boxcar, *06*		35 ___
26863	Railway Express Operating Milk Car with platform, *06*		140 ___
26864	Domino Sugar Operating Boxcar, *06-07*		40 ___
26865	CP Animated Caboose, *06-07*		80 ___
26867	Boxcar, AlienSounds, *06-07*		110 ___
26868	U.S. Steel Operating Welding Car, *06*		75 ___
26869	REA Jumping Hobo Boxcar, *06-07*		70 ___
26870	Christmas Dump Car with presents, *06*		80 ___
26871	PRR Tender, steam TrainSounds (std O), *06*		105 ___
26872	U.S. Army Security Car, *06*		75 ___
26876	Missile Firing Trail Car, *06*		75 ___
26877	U.S. Army Missile Launch Car, *06-07*		190 ___
26888	Weyerhaeuser Timber Co. Log Car		40 ___
26889	Weyerhaeuser Timber Co. Log Car		40 ___
26891	PRR Coal Dump Car, *05*		30 ___
26897	Great Western Flatcar with handcar, *07*		65 ___
26898	NYC Log Dump Car, *05*		25 ___
26905	Bethlehem Steel Gondola "6462" with canisters, *98*		29 ___
26906	SP Flatcar "9823" with Corgi '57 Chevy, *98*		40 ___
26908	TTUX Flatcar "6300" with Apple trailers, *98*		70 ___
26913	East St. Louis Gondola "9820," *98*		29 ___
26920	Union Pacific Die-cast Ore Car "64861," *97*		70 ___
26921	Union Pacific Die-cast Ore Car "64862," *97*		55 ___
26922	Union Pacific Die-cast Ore Car "64863," *97*		65 ___
26923	Union Pacific Die-cast Ore Car "64864," *97*		55 ___
26924	Union Pacific Die-cast Ore Car "64865," *97*		55 ___
26925	Union Pacific Die-cast Ore Car "64866," *97*		60 ___
26926	Union Pacific Die-cast Ore Car, *98*		55 ___
26927	Union Pacific Die-cast Ore Car, *98*		55 ___
26928	Union Pacific Die-cast Ore Car, *98*		55 ___
26929	Union Pacific Die-cast Ore Car, *98*		40 ___

	MODERN 1970-2021	Esc	Mint
____	**26936** Die-cast Tank Car 4-pack, *98*		335
____	**26937** Die-cast Hopper 4-pack, *98*		325
____	**26938** NYC Reefer, *99*		80
____	**26940** Rio Grande Stock Car "37710," *99*		80
____	**26946** D&H Semi-Scale Hopper "9642"		85
____	**26947** Gulf Die-cast Tank Car, *98*		120
____	**26948** P&LE Die-cast Hopper, *98*		65
____	**26949** NP Flatcar with trailer "6424-2017," *98*		47
____	**26950** NP Flatcar with trailer "6424-2016," *98*		47
____	**26951** TTX Flatcar "475185" with PRR trailer, *98*		55
____	**26952** J.B. Hunt Flatcar with trailer, *98*		40
____	**26953** J.B. Hunt Flatcar with trailer, *98*		40
____	**26954** J.B. Hunt Flatcar with trailer, *98*		40
____	**26955** J.B. Hunt Flatcar with trailer, *98*		40
____	**26956** C&O Gondola (O27), *98-99*		15
____	**26957** Delaware & Hudson Flatcar with stakes, *98*		20
____	**26971** Lionel Steel 16-wheel Depressed Center Flatcar, *98*		135
____	**26972** Pony Express Animated Gondola, *98*		36
____	**26973** Getty Die-cast Tank Car 3-pack, *98*		270
____	**26974** Getty Die-cast 1-D Tank Car "4003," *98*		80
____	**26975** Getty Die-cast 1-D Tank Car "4004," *98*		90
____	**26976** Getty Die-cast 1-D Tank Car "4005," *98*		80
____	**26977** Sinclair Die-cast Tank Car 3-pack, *98*		275
____	**26978** Sinclair Tank Car UTLX "64026," *98*		105
____	**26979** Sinclair Tank Car UTLX "64027," *98*		85
____	**26980** Sinclair Tank UTLX "64028," *98*		90
____	**26981** Gulf Die-cast Tank Car 2-pack, *99*		165
____	**26985** B&O Die-cast Hopper 2-pack, *99*		160
____	**26987** Chessie System (B&O) Die-cast 4-bay Hopper "235154," *99*		90
____	**26991** Lionelville Ladder Fire Car, *99*		47
____	**26992** NYC Reefer, *99*		75
____	**26993** NYC Reefer, *99*		85
____	**26994** NYC Reefer, *99*		135
____	**26995** Rio Grande Stock Car "37714," *99*		80
____	**26996** Rio Grande Stock Car "37715," *99*		80
____	**26997** Rio Grande Stock Car "37716," *99*		80
____	**27000** C&EI Offset Hopper "97393" (std O), *07*		65
____	**27001** Erie Offset Hopper "28001" (std O), *07*		65
____	**27002** Frisco Offset Hopper "92399" (std O), *07*		65
____	**27003** Chessie System Offset Hopper "234355" (std O), *07*		65
____	**27016** UP PS-2 Covered Hopper "1312" (std O), *07-08*		60
____	**27019** Imco PS-2 Covered Hopper "41001" (std O), *07-08*		60
____	**27022** PC PS-2 Covered Hopper "74217" (std O), *07*		60
____	**27025** NYC PS-2 Covered Hopper "883180" (std O), *07*		60
____	**27029** ATSF Offset Hopper 3-pack (std O), *08-09*		200
____	**27030** Monon Offset Hopper 3-pack (std O), *08-09*		200
____	**27031** MoPac Offset Hopper 3-pack (std O), *08-09*		200
____	**27032** NYC Offset Hopper 3-pack (std O), *08-09*		200
____	**27033** Chessie System PS-2 Hopper 3-pack (std O), *08-09*		180
____	**27034** Nickel Plate Road PS-2 Hopper 3-pack (std O), *08-09*		180
____	**27053** CB&Q ACF 2-bay Covered Hopper "183925" (std O), *08-09*		55
____	**27059** Bakelite Plastics PS-2 Hopper "61445" (std O), *10-11*		70
____	**27061** Clinchfield Freight Car 2-pack (std O), *10*		150

27064	PRR Flatcar with PRR piggyback trailers (std O), *12*	98 ___
27065	SP Flatcar with SP piggyback trailers (std O), *12*	98 ___
27066	IC Flatcar with IC piggyback trailers (std O), *12*	98 ___
27067	C&O Flatcar with REA piggyback trailers (std O), *12*	98 ___
27068	ATSF Flatcar with Santa Fe piggyback trailers (std O), *12*	98 ___
27069	Conrail PS-2 Hopper "878330" (std O), *12-13*	70 ___
27070	N&W Scale Offset Hopper "279850" (std O), *12*	70 ___
27071	CSX 4-Bay Covered Hopper "256300" (std O), *12*	90 ___
27072	C&NW Scale PS-1 Boxcar "7" (std O), *12-13*	70 ___
27073	PRR Scale Offset Hopper 3-pack (std O), *12*	200 ___
27077	L&N Scale Offset Hopper "88494" (std O), *12-13*	70 ___
27078	Frisco Scale 3-Bay Open Hopper "88299" (std O), *12-14*	75 ___
27079	NYC Boxcar, *09*	30 ___
27080	Lionel Vision Boxcar, *14-15*	60 ___
27081	BN PS-2 Hopper "424796" (std O), *12-13*	70 ___
27082	Grand Trunk 4-Bay Covered Hopper "38111" (std O), *12*	90 ___
27083	RI PS-2 Hopper "500751" (std O), *12-13*	70 ___
27084	Seaboard 8000-gallon 1-D Tank Car "27084" (std O), *12*	70 ___
27085	Wabash PS-2 Hopper "30425" (std O), *12-13*	70 ___
27086	Grand Trunk 60' Boxcar "383575" (std O), *12, 14*	85 ___
27087	CN 60' Boxcar "799424" (std O), *12, 14*	85 ___
27088	MKT PS-5 Gondola "12447" (std O), *12-13*	65 ___
27089	LIRR PS-5 Gondola "6053" (std O), *12*	65 ___
27090	NP 8000-gallon 1-D Tank Car "27090" (std O), *12*	70 ___
27091	WM Scale 3-Bay Open Hopper "85125" (std O), *12*	80 ___
27092	CSX Heritage 60' Boxcar "176740" (std O), *12*	85 ___
27093	Boy Scouts PS-2 Hopper "2013" (std O), *13*	70 ___
27094	BNSF PS-2 Hopper 2-pack (std O), *13-14*	130 ___
27095	KCS PS-2 Hopper 2-pack (std O), *13*	130 ___
27096	C&NW PS-2 Hopper 2-pack (std O), *13*	130 ___
27099	North Pole Central PS-1 Boxcar "125025" (std O), *13*	70 ___
27100	C&NW PS-2CD 4427 Hopper "450669" (std O), *04*	40 ___
27101	Morton Salt PS-2CD 4427 Hopper "504" (std O), *04*	43 ___
27102	Pillsbury PS-2CD 4427 Hopper "3980" (std O), *04*	42 ___
27103	Soo Line PS-2CD 4427 Hopper "70207" (std O), *04*	49 ___
27104	Wabash Cylindrical Hopper "33007" (std O), *03*	43 ___
27105	PC Cylindrical Hopper "884312" (std O), *03*	42 ___
27113	Govt. of Canada Cylindrical Hopper, *04-05*	60 ___
27114	Canadian National Cylindrical Hopper, *04-05*	60 ___
27115	D&H 3-bay ACF Hopper "3454" (std O), *05-06*	65 ___
27116	NYC 3-bay ACF Hopper "886270" (std O), *05-06*	65 ___
27117	DM&IR 3-bay ACF Hopper "5017" (std O), *05*	65 ___
27118	WP 3-bay ACF Hopper "11774" (std O), *05-06*	65 ___
27129	N&W 3-bay ACF Hopper "10717" (std O), *06*	70 ___
27130	PRR 3-bay ACF Hopper "180658" (std O), *06*	70 ___
27131	Conrail 3-bay ACF Hopper "473877" (std O), *06*	70 ___
27132	UP 3-bay ACF Hopper "18137" (std O), *06*	70 ___
27133	MILW PS-2CD Hopper "98606" (std O), *06*	70 ___
27134	BNSF PS-2CD Hopper "414367" (std O), *06*	70 ___
27135	N&W PS-2CD Hopper "71573" (std O), *06*	70 ___
27142	CP Rail 3-bay Hopper, *06*	48 ___
27146	CP Soo 3-bay Hopper, *06*	48 ___
27165	C&O 3-bay Hopper "86912" (std O), *07*	70 ___
27166	Pennsylvania Power & Light 3-bay Hopper "347" (std O), *07*	70 ___

		Esc	Mint
___	27167	Santa Fe 3-bay Hopper "178558" (std O), *07-08*	70
___	27168	C&NW 3-bay Hopper "135000" (std O), *07*	70
___	27169	CN Cylindrical Hopper "370708" (std O), *06*	65
___	27172	IMC Canada Cylindrical Hopper "45726" (std O), *06*	65
___	27177	Union Starch Cylindrical Hopper 3-pack (std O), *08*	210
___	27186	PRR Cylindrical Hopper 3-pack (std O), *08*	210
___	27187	TH&B Cylindrical Hopper 3-pack (std O), *08*	210
___	27188	KCS 3-bay Covered Hopper 3-pack, *08*	225
___	27189	BNSF 3-bay Aluminum Covered Hopper 3-pack, *08*	225
___	27190	C&NW PS-2CD Covered Hopper 3-pack (std O), *08*	225
___	27191	RI PS-2CD Covered Hopper 3-pack, *08*	225
___	27192	NP PS-2CD Covered Hopper 3-pack (std O), *08*	225
___	27203	NYC DD Boxcar "75509" (std O), *05*	63
___	27204	Grand Trunk Western DD Boxcar "596377" (std O), *05*	63
___	27205	D&RGW DD Boxcar "63798" (std O), *05*	40
___	27206	UP PS 60' Boxcar "960342" (std O), *08*	75
___	27207	IC PS 60' Boxcar "44295" (std O), *08*	75
___	27208	ATSF PS 60' Boxcar "37287" (std O), *08*	75
___	27209	D&RGW PS 60' Boxcar "63835" (std O), *08*	75
___	27210	PRR PS-1 Boxcar "47009" (std O), *05*	60
___	27211	MKT PS-1 Boxcar "948" (std O), *05*	60
___	27212	Rutland PS-1 Boxcar "358" (std O), *05*	60
___	27213	N&W DD Boxcar, *05*	35
___	27214	Chessie System PS-1 Boxcar "23770" (std O), *06*	60
___	27215	Rock Island PS-1 Boxcar "57607" (std O), *06*	60
___	27216	Erie-Lack. PS-1 Boxcar "84433" (std O), *06*	60
___	27217	Frisco PS-1 Boxcar "17826" (std O), *06*	19
___	27218	Santa Fe DD Boxcar "9870" (std O), *06-07*	70
___	27219	GN DD Boxcar "35449" (std O), *06-07*	70
___	27220	L&N DD Boxcar "41237" (std O), *06-07*	70
___	27221	CB&Q DD Boxcar "48500" (std O), *06-07*	70
___	27224	CGW PS-1 Boxcar "5180" (std O), *06*	60
___	27225	WP PS-1 Boxcar "19528" (std O), *06*	60
___	27226	NH PS-1 Boxcar "32196" (std O), *06*	60
___	27227	UP PS-1 Boxcar "100306" (std O), *06*	60
___	27228	UP DD Boxcar "454400" (std O), *07*	70
___	27229	Nickel Plate Road DD Boxcar "87100" (std O), *08*	70
___	27230	LV DD Boxcar "8505" (std O), *08*	70
___	27231	GN USRA Double-sheathed Boxcar (std O), *07*	65
___	27232	UP USRA Double-sheathed Boxcar (std O), *07*	65
___	27233	Cotton Belt USRA Double-sheathed Boxcar (std O), *07*	65
___	27234	C&NW USRA Double-sheathed Boxcar (std O), *07*	65
___	27235	Railbox Boxcar "10011" (std O), *07*	55
___	27239	SP DD Boxcar "232852" with auto rack (std O), *08*	75
___	27240	Pere Marquette DD Boxcar with auto rack (std O), *08*	75
___	27241	C&O PS-1 Boxcar "18719," *08*	60
___	27242	LV PS-1 Boxcar "62080," *08*	60
___	27243	SP PS-1 Boxcar "128131," *08*	60
___	27244	GN PS-1 Boxcar "39404," *08*	60
___	27246	SP Double-sheathed Boxcar "133" (std O), *08*	70
___	27247	MP Double-sheathed Boxcar "45111" (std O), *08*	70
___	27249	GN Express Boxcar "2500" (std O), *08*	65
___	27250	CN Express Boxcar "11061" (std O), *08-09*	65

27251	WP Express Boxcar "220116," *08-09*	65 ___
27254	Western Pacific UP Heritage Boxcar (std O), *09-11, 13*	85 ___
27259	PRR ACF Stock Car "128988" (std O), *10*	70 ___
27260	ATSF Tool Car "190021" (std O), *09-10*	80 ___
27261	D&RGW Double-sheathed Boxcar "3282," *09*	80 ___
27263	Polar Railroad PS-1 Boxcar, *09*	70 ___
27264	C&O Double-sheathed Boxcar "3502," *10*	80 ___
27265	Virginian PS-1 Boxcar "63300" (std O), *10*	70 ___
27266	PRR Express Boxcar "504141" (std O), *10*	70 ___
27267	SP UP Heritage 60' Boxcar "6991" (std O), *10*	85 ___
27270	B&O PS-1 Boxcar 2-pack (std O), *10-11*	140 ___
27273	Ann Arbor PS-1 Boxcar "1314" (std O), *11*	70 ___
27274	Polar Railroad Double-sheathed Boxcar "1201," *10*	70 ___
27275	SP Overnight PS-1 Boxcar "97938" (std O), *10*	70 ___
27276	NKP Double-sheathed Boxcar "10580" (std O), *10-11*	70 ___
27277	WP Scale PS-1 Boxcar "1925" (std O), *11*	70 ___
27278	Cryo-Trans Trans-Mechanical Reefer (std O), *10*	95 ___
27282	UP DD Boxcar "163100" (std O), *10*	70 ___
27283	Postwar Scale Boxcar 2-pack, *10*	140 ___
27286	Postwar Scale 6464 Boxcar 2-pack #2, *11-13*	140 ___
27287	LV Boxcar and Caboose Set (std O), *10-11*	160 ___
27289	Jersey Central Boxcar and Caboose Set (std O), *10-11*	160 ___
27291	PRR Double-sheathed Boxcar "539335" (std O), *10-11*	70 ___
27294	ATSF 57' Mechanical Reefer "3006" (std O), *10*	85 ___
27296	Cryo-Trans 57' Mechanical Reefer (std O), *11*	85 ___
27299	WM Steel-sided Reefer (std O), *11*	80 ___
27300	Western Dairy General American Milk Car (std O), *06*	65 ___
27305	GN Steel-sided Reefer "70290" (std O), *06*	65 ___
27306	Santa Fe Steel-sided Reefer "3494" (std O), *06*	42 ___
27307	Pepper Packing Steel-sided Reefer "2330" (std O), *06*	65 ___
27327	BNSF Mechanical Reefer "798870" (std O), *07*	70 ___
27328	SP Fruit Express Reefer "456465" (std O), *07-09*	70 ___
27329	UP Fruit Express Reefer "55962" (std O), *07*	70 ___
27330	Great Northern WFE Reefer "8873" (std O), *07-08*	70 ___
27331	Alderney Dairy General American Milk Car (std O), *07*	65 ___
27332	Freeport General American Milk Car (std O), *07*	65 ___
27345	Milwaukee Road 40' Steel-sided Reefer "5317" (std O), *12*	80 ___
27349	ADM Steel-sided Reefer "7019" (std O), *07*	65 ___
27350	National Car Steel-sided Reefer "2430" (std O), *07*	48 ___
27355	NYC Steel-sided Reefer "2570" (std O), *07-08*	65 ___
27358	Dubuque Steel-sided Reefer "63648" (std O), *07*	65 ___
27361	PFE Wood-sided Reefer "97680" (std O), *06*	65 ___
27364	Erie URTX Steel-sided Reefer (std O), *11*	80 ___
27365	Sheffield Farms Milk Car 2-pack (std O), *08*	140 ___
27368	CNJ 40' Steel-sided Reefer "1443" (std O), *12*	80 ___
27369	Borden's Milk Car 2-pack (std O), *08*	140 ___
27372	PFE Steel-sided Reefer 3-pack (std O), *08*	210 ___
27373	MILW Reefer 3-pack (std O), *08-09*	225 ___
27374	Alaska Reefer 3-pack (std O), *08-09*	225 ___
27375	NP Reefer 3-pack (std O), *08-09*	225 ___
27394	Detroit, Toledo & Ironton Steel-sided Reefer (std O), *09-10*	80 ___
27395	Amtrak ExpressTrak Baggage Car, *10*	75 ___
27396	C&NW UP Heritage Mechanical Reefer (std O), *10*	85 ___

		Esc	Mint
____	**27409** ATSF Water Tank Car "100844" (std O), *09-10*		70
____	**27410** 30,000-gallon Ethanol Tank Car 3-pack, sound, *09*		270
____	**27411** 30,000-gallon Ethanol Tank Car 3-pack, *09*		210
____	**27412** GATX TankTrain Car "53782" (std O), *10*		70
____	**27418** PRR NS Heritage Unibody Tank Car (std O), *10*		70
____	**27419** Pennsylvania Power & Light 3-bay Open Hopper, *08*		80
____	**27421** MoPac UP Heritage Cylindrical Hopper (std O), *09-11*		80
____	**27422** N&W 3-bay Open Hopper "1776" (std O), *09*		80
____	**27424** Penn Central PS-2 Hopper "440774" (std O), *10-11*		80
____	**27425** Saskatchewan Cylindrical Hopper "397015" (std O), *09*		80
____	**27426** Stourbridge Lion Anthracite Coal Car 2-pack, *09-10*		130
____	**27429** MKT UP Heritage PS2-CD Hopper (std O), *09*		80
____	**27431** CSX B&O Quad Hopper, *11*		50
____	**27432** UP 3-bay Open Hopper "78123" (std O), *10*		80
____	**27433** Conrail NS Heritage Cylindrical Hopper (std O), *10-11*		80
____	**27434** D&RGW UP Heritage PS2-CD Hopper (std O), *10*		80
____	**27435** Polar Railroad Tank Car, *09*		70
____	**27436** Alberta Cylindrical Hopper "396363" (std O), *10*		80
____	**27438** Virginian NS Heritage 3-bay Open Hopper (std O), *10*		80
____	**27439** NS Heritage Unibody Tank Car "14098" (std O), *10*		70
____	**27440** BN Cylindrical Hopper "458456" (std O), *10*		80
____	**27441** D&M PS-2 Hopper "6133" (std O), *11*		70
____	**27445** N&W NS Heritage PS-2CD Hopper (std O), *10*		80
____	**27446** Southern NS Heritage Cylindrical Hopper (std O), *10*		80
____	**27448** PRR NS Heritage 3-Bay Open Hopper (std O), *11*		80
____	**27449** UP Boy Scouts 100th Anniversary Cylindrical Hopper (std O), *11*		80
____	**27450** NW NS Heritage 3-Bay Open Hopper (std O), *11*		80
____	**27451** Conrail NS Heritage Unibody 1-D Tank Car (std O), *11*		70
____	**27452** PRR NS Heritage PS-1 Boxcar "45540" (std O), *11*		70
____	**27453** NS Heritage PS-1 Boxcar "67850" (std O), *11*		70
____	**27454** CP Cylindrical Hopper (std O), *11*		80
____	**27455** Amtrak 57' Mechanical Reefer (std O), *11*		85
____	**27456** Soo Line PS2 Covered Hopper "70702" (std O), *11*		70
____	**27457** NS 3-Bay Open Hopper "148028" (std O), *11*		80
____	**27458** UP Mechanical Reefer "457244" (std O), *11*		85
____	**27459** WP DD Boxcar "19404" (std O), *11*		70
____	**27460** M&StL Double-sheathed Boxcar "26002" (std O), *11*		70
____	**27461** UP ACF 4-Bay Covered Hopper "91341" (std O), *11*		85
____	**27462** Chessie ACF 4-Bay Covered Hopper "601878" (std O), *11*		85
____	**27463** PRR ACF 3-Bay Covered Hopper "259900" (std O), *11-12*		80
____	**27464** BNSF ACF 3-Bay Covered Hopper "453403" (std O), *11*		80
____	**27465** CSX 89' Auto Rack Car "604540" (std O), *12-13*		150
____	**27466** UP 89' Auto Rack Car (std O), *12-13*		150
____	**27467** ATSF 89' Auto Rack Car (std O), *12-13*		150
____	**27468** Grand Truck 89' Auto Rack Car (std O), *12-13*		150
____	**27469** Frisco Cylindrical Hopper "81021" (std O), *11*		80
____	**27470** MKT Scale 1-D Tank Car (std O), *11*		70
____	**27471** DT&I 3-Bay Hopper "2070" (std O), *11*		80
____	**27472** CP Scale 1-D Tank Car "9943" (std O), *11*		70
____	**27473** Conrail 89' Auto Rack Car "456249" (std O), *12*		150
____	**27474** SP Cylindrical Hopper "491020" (std O), *11*		80
____	**27475** Lionelville & Western Scale 1-D Tank Car "2747" (std O), *11*		80
____	**27476** U.S. Army Scale 1-D Tank Car (std O), *11*		70

		Esc	Mint	
27477	D&RGW 3-Bay Hopper "14901" (std O), *11*		80	___
27478	NYC 3-Bay Hopper "922158" (std O), *11*		80	___
27479	BN Scale 3-Bay Open Hopper "516400" (std O), *12*		80	___
27480	NKP Scale Offset Hopper "33060" (std O), *12*		70	___
27481	W&LE Scale Offset Hopper "62240" (std O), *12*		70	___
27482	CP Scale Offset Hopper "354000" (std O), *12*		70	___
27483	SP Unibody 1-D Tank Car "67200" (std O), *12*		70	___
27484	D&H Unibody 1-D Tank Car "59" (std O), *12*		70	___
27485	KCS Unibody 1-D Tank Car "996" (std O), *12*		70	___
27488	Clinchfield CSX Heritage 3-Bay Open Hopper (std O), *12*		80	___
27489	Chessie System CSX Heritage 3-Bay Open Hopper (std O), *12*		80	___
27490	ATSF 3-Bay Covered Hopper "314000" (std O), *12-13*		85	___
27491	GN 3-Bay Covered Hopper "171400" (std O), *12*		85	___
27492	CN 89' Auto Rack Car "710833" (std O), *12*		150	___
27493	CN PS-4 Flatcar with piggyback trailers (std O), *12*		98	___
27494	CN PS-4 Flatcar with piggyback trailers (std O), *12*		98	___
27495	CN PS-4 Flatcar with piggyback trailers (std O), *12*		98	___
27496	Polar PS-2 Covered Hopper "1245" (std O), *12, 14*		70	___
27497	UP Offset Hopper "74556" (std O), *12*		80	___
27498	DM&I 8000-gallon 1-D Tank Car "S19" (std O), *12*		70	___
27499	Monon Scale PS-1 Boxcar "916" (std O), *12*		70	___
27510	WP PS-4 Flatcar "2001" (std O), *05-06*		53	___
27511	P&LE PS-4 Flatcar "1154" (std O), *05-06*		35	___
27512	Reading PS-4 Flatcar "9314" (std O), *05*		53	___
27513	UP 40' Flatcar "51219" (std O), *06*		55	___
27514	CP 40' Flatcar "307401" (std O), *06*		55	___
27515	Pennsylvania 40' Flatcar "473567" (std O), *06*		55	___
27516	N&W 40' Flatcar "32900" (std O), *06*		55	___
27517	NP PS-4 Flatcar "62829" with trailers (std O), *06*		85	___
27518	C&NW PS-4 Flatcar "44503" with trailers (std O), *06*		85	___
27519	UP PS-4 Flatcar "53007" with trailers (std O), *06*		85	___
27520	Coe Rail Husky Stack Car "5540" (std O), *06*		85	___
27521	Santa Fe Husky Stack Car "254220" (std O), *06*		85	___
27535	UP PS-4 Flatcar "53008" with trailers (std O), *07*		65	___
27536	UP PS-4 Flatcar "53009" with trailers (std O), *08*		65	___
27537	UP Flatcar with wood load, *06*		39	___
27541	NYC 40' Flatcar "496299" with load (std O), *07*		63	___
27542	NH 40' Flatcar "17808" with load (std O), *07-08*		70	___
27543	ATSF 40' Flatcar "191549" with load (std O), *07-08*		70	___
27544	GT 40' Flatcar "64301" with load (std O), *07-08*		70	___
27545	REA PS-4 Flatcar "81003" with trailers (std O), *07-08*		85	___
27546	Greenbrier Husky Stack Car "1993" (std O), *07*		85	___
27552	Arizona & California Husky Stack Car (std O), *07*		85	___
27562	NYC PS-4 Flatcar "506075" with trailers (std O), *07-08*		85	___
27563	Lackawanna PS-4 Flatcar "16540" with trailers (std O), *07*		85	___
27564	Milwaukee Road PS-4 Flatcar with trailers "64074" (std O), *07-08*		85	___
27583	UP 40' Flatcar "59292" with load (std O), *08*		70	___
27584	Reading Flatcar with covered load (std O), *08-09*		70	___
27585	B&M 40' Flatcar "33773" with stakes (std O), *08-09*		65	___
27586	Cass Scenic Skeleton Log Car 3-pack, *07*		170	___
27587	Birch Valley Lumber Skeleton Log Car 3-pack, *07*		170	___
27594	Wabash PS-4 Flatcar with stakes (std O), *08-09*		65	___
27600	RI Bay Window Caboose "17070" (std O), *07*		90	___

___	**27601** MILW Extended Vision Caboose "992300" (std O), *07*		90
___	**27603** MP UP Heritage Ca-4 Caboose "2891" (std O), *08*		95
___	**27604** UP Caboose "3881" (std O), *08*		90
___	**27605** Pere Marquette Northeastern Caboose "A986" (std O), *08*		90
___	**27606** LL Northeastern Caboose "4679" (std O), *08*		90
___	**27607** Monongahela NS Heritage Caboose (std O), *12*		95
___	**27608** WM Caboose "1863" (std O), *08*		85
___	**27609** B&O Caboose "C-2445" (std O), *07*		90
___	**27612** WP Bay Window Caboose "446" (std O), *08*		90
___	**27615** NYC Bay Window Caboose "20383" (std O), *07*		90
___	**27617** D&H Bay Window Caboose "35725" (std O), *08*		90
___	**27618** MKT UP Heritage Ca-4 Caboose "8891" (std O), *08*		95
___	**27619** WP UP Heritage Ca-4 Caboose "3891" (std O), *08*		95
___	**27623** N&W Northeastern Caboose "500837" (std O), *09*		90
___	**27624** D&RGW UP Heritage CA-4 Caboose (std O), *09*		95
___	**27625** C&NW UP Heritage CA-4 Caboose (std O), *09*		95
___	**27626** SP UP Heritage CA-4 Caboose (std O), *09*		95
___	**27628** Wabash Northeastern Caboose "02222" (std O), *09-10*		90
___	**27629** C&O Northeastern Caboose (std O), *10*		90
___	**27630** Virginian NS Heritage CA-4 Caboose (std O), *10*		95
___	**27631** NS Heritage CA-4 Caboose (std O), *10*		95
___	**27633** UP CA-3 Caboose (std O), *10*		95
___	**27634** ATSF Extended Vision Caboose (std O), *10*		85
___	**27635** B&O I-12 Caboose (std O), *10*		85
___	**27636** NKP Northeastern Caboose (std O), *10-11*		85
___	**27638** Southern NS Heritage CA-4 Caboose (std O), *10-11*		95
___	**27639** N&W NS Heritage CA-4 Caboose (std O), *10*		95
___	**27640** Clinchfield Northeastern CA-3 Caboose, *10-11*		90
___	**27642** Virginian Scale Caboose with smoke, *10-13*		90
___	**27645** UP Boy Scouts 100th Anniversary Ca-3 Caboose (std O), *11*		95
___	**27648** PRR NS Heritage Ca-3 Caboose (std O), *11*		95
___	**27649** Baldwin Locomotive Works I-12 Caboose "6000" (std O), *12-13*		85
___	**27650** CSX Heritage Scale Bay Window Caboose "2510" (std O), *12*		90
___	**27651** B&O CSX Heritage I-12 Caboose (std O), *11*		90
___	**27652** CSX Heritage Chessie System Scale Caboose (std O), *12*		90
___	**27653** Family Lines CSX Heritage Ca-4 Caboose (std O), *11*		90
___	**27654** CSX/Clinchfield Scale Bay-Window Caboose (std O), *12*		90
___	**27655** WM CSX Heritage Extended Vision Caboose (std O), *11*		90
___	**27658** Pennsylvania Power & Light Work Caboose (std O), *11*		80
___	**27659** Bethlehem Steel Work Caboose (std O), *11*		80
___	**27660** UP George Bush Extended Vision Caboose (std O), *11*		90
___	**27661** KCS Extended Vision Caboose (std O), *11*		90
___	**27662** GTW Northeastern Caboose (std O), *11*		90
___	**27663** IC Extended Vision Caboose (std O), *11*		90
___	**27664** Lionel & Western Northeastern Caboose (std O), *11-12*		90
___	**27665** BN Bicentennial Extended Vision Caboose (std O), *11*		90
___	**27666** NH Scale Northeastern Caboose "C-666" (std O), *12*		90
___	**27667** UP Scale Ca-4 Caboose "3857" (std O), *12-13*		95
___	**27668** UP Scale Ca-3 Caboose "3779" (std O), *12-13*		95
___	**27669** PC Scale Northeastern Caboose "18420" with smoke (std O), *12-13*		90
___	**27670** CP Scale Northeastern Caboose "400501" (std O), *12-13*		90
___	**27671** West Side Lumber Scale Work Caboose "8" (std O), *12*		80
___	**27672** Weyerhaeuser Timber Scale Work Caboose "12" (std O), *12-13*		80

		Esc	Mint
27673	NYC Scale Northeastern Caboose "20090" (std O), *12*	90	___
27674	Elk River Lumber Work Caboose "6" (std O), *12, 14*	80	___
27676	CN Wood-Sided Caboose (std O), *12*	90	___
27677	UP Work Caboose "907306" (std O), *12*	80	___
27678	ATSF Wood-Sided Caboose "1790" (std O), *12*	85	___
27679	NP Wood-Sided Caboose "1282" (std O), *12*	85	___
27680	GN Wood-Sided Caboose "X499" (std O), *12*	85	___
27681	Southern NS Heritage Caboose (std O), *12*	95	___
27682	Conrail NS Heritage Caboose (std O), *12*	95	___
27683	Erie NS Heritage Caboose (std O), *12, 14-15*	95	___
27684	Illinois Terminal NS Heritage Caboose (std O), *12, 14-15*	95	___
27685	Central of Georgia NS Heritage Caboose (std O), *12*	95	___
27686	LV NS Heritage Caboose (std O), *12*	95	___
27687	Reading NS Heritage Caboose (std O), *13-15*	95	___
27688	NYC NS Heritage Caboose (std O), *13*	95	___
27689	Wabash NS Heritage Caboose (std O), *13-15*	95	___
27690	Virginian NS Heritage Caboose (std O), *13*	95	___
27691	PRR NS Heritage Caboose (std O), *12*	95	___
27692	N&W NS Heritage Caboose (std O), *12*	95	___
27693	CNJ NS Heritage Caboose (std O), *13-14*	95	___
27694	NS Heritage Caboose (std O), *12*	95	___
27695	DL&W NS Heritage Caboose (std O), *13-15*	95	___
27696	Savannah & Atlanta NS Heritage Caboose (std O), *13-15*	95	___
27697	Nickel Plate Road NS Heritage Caboose (std O), *12*	95	___
27698	Interstate NS Heritage Caboose (std O), *12*	95	___
27699	PC NS Heritage Caboose (std O), *13*	95	___
27702	Maersk Husky Stack Car 2-pack (std O), *09*	225	___
27705	ATSF Wedge Plow Flatcar "191369" (std O), *09*	90	___
27706	ATSF Idler Flatcar "191852" with load (std O), *09*	75	___
27707	UP Husky Stack Car 2-pack (std O), *09-10*	225	___
27710	No. 6464 Variation Boxcar 2-pack #2, *09*	110	___
27767	Santa Fe Passenger 4-pack, *11-12*	240	___
27771	Postwar "6572" REA Reefer, *11-13*	60	___
27772	Santa Fe Baggage Car and Diner 2-pack, *11-12*	120	___
27775	Postwar "2414" Santa Fe Blue-stripe Coach, *11-13*	60	___
27776	No. 6464 Variation Boxcar 2-pack #3, *11*	105	___
27779	Postwar Archive UP Caboose "8561," *11-12*	48	___
27791	Archive 6464-50 M&StL Boxcar, *12*	55	___
27792	Archive Pastel Freight Car 3-pack, *12*	170	___
27800	B&M Gondola with coke containers, *09-11*	80	___
27816	D&RGW Flatcar "22177" with pipes, *09-10*	80	___
27820	Wabash PS-4 Flatcar with piggyback trailers (std O), *09-10*	98	___
27824	MILW 40' Flatcar with metal pipes (std O), *10*	80	___
27825	West Side Lumber Skeleton Log Car, *11*	70	___
27826	CP Skeleton Log Car 2-pack (std O), *10*	133	___
27827	UP Bathtub Gondola "28081" (std O), *10*	65	___
27828	CN Bathtub Gondola "193140" (std O), *10*	65	___
27829	WM Skeleton Log Car 2-pack, *10*	133	___
27834	Pere Marquette PS-5 Gondola "18400," *11*	70	___
27835	P. Bunyan Lumber Skeleton Log Car, *11-12*	70	___
27836	Elk River Lumber Skeleton Log Car "11203" (std O), *11*	70	___
27837	B&M PS-4 Flatcar with bulkheads (std O), *10-11*	80	___
27838	PRR PS-4 Flatcar with bulkheads (std O), *10*	80	___

____	**27840** Polar Railroad PS-4 Flatcar with trailers, *10*	98
____	**27841** CSX Bathtub Gondola 2-pack (std O), *11*	130
____	**27842** UP Scale Flatcar with bulkheads "15775" (std O), *11*	70
____	**27843** WP Scale PS-5 Gondola "6774" (std O), *11*	70
____	**27844** BNSF Bathtub Gondola 3-pack (std O), *10*	200
____	**27848** Virginian NS Heritage 60' Boxcar (std O), *11*	85
____	**27849** Southern NS Heritage 60' Boxcar (std O), *11*	85
____	**27850** CSX 60' Boxcar "196911" (std O), *11*	85
____	**27851** BNSF Bathtub Gondola 2-pack, *11*	130
____	**27854** B&O Double-sheathed Boxcar "196500" (std O), *11*	70
____	**27855** NYC 60' DD Boxcar "53423" (std O), *11*	85
____	**27856** KCS PS-1 Boxcar "18741" (std O), *11*	70
____	**27857** PRR DD Boxcar "81919" (std O), *11, 14*	75
____	**27858** MP DD Boxcar "90103" (std O), *11*	70
____	**27860** Sugar Creek Lumber Skeleton Log Car "1749" (std O), *11*	70
____	**27863** Merrill & Ring Lumber Skeleton Log Car, *11-12*	70
____	**27868** NS Bathtub Gondola 2-pack (std O), *11*	130
____	**27871** NS 60' Boxcar "499646" (std O), *11*	85
____	**27872** Polar Hot Cocoa Milk Car, *11, 13*	70
____	**27873** Polar Reindeer Stock Car, *11, 13*	70
____	**27874** Grove's Mortuary Double-sheathed Boxcar (std O), *11*	70
____	**27875** NYC DD Boxcar "45395" (std O), *11*	70
____	**27876** State of Maine PS-1 Boxcar "5141" (std O), *11*	70
____	**27877** NH DD Boxcar "40510" (std O), *11*	70
____	**27882** Southern ACF 40-ton Stock Car "45655" (std O), *11*	70
____	**27883** T&P ACF 40-ton Stock Car "24042" (std O), *11*	70
____	**27884** RI ACF 40-ton Stock Car "77601" (std O), *11*	70
____	**27885** ATSF ACF 40-ton Stock Car "60390" (std O), *11*	70
____	**27886** GN PS-1 Boxcar "11310" (std O), *11*	70
____	**27887** D&RGW PS-5 Gondola "56316" with covers (std O), *11*	65
____	**27888** LIRR 40' Flatcar with wheels (std O), *11*	70
____	**27889** Erie 40' Flatcar "6361" with wheels (std O), *11*	70
____	**27890** L&N 40' Flatcar "22269" with wheels (std O), *11*	70
____	**27891** NKP Heritage PS-4 Flatcar with trailers (std O), *11*	98
____	**27892** Conrail PS-5 Gondola "612690" with covers (std O), *11*	65
____	**27893** GTW PS-1 Boxcar "516650" (std O), *11*	70
____	**27894** C&O PS-5 Gondola "362600" with covers (std O), *11*	65
____	**27895** ATSF PS-4 Bulkhead Flatcar "90085" (std O), *11*	80
____	**27896** CP 40' Flatcar with pipe load (std O), *11*	80
____	**27899** UP Scale PS-1 Boxcar "196889" (std O), *12*	70
____	**27903** Sager Place Observation Car, *09*	65
____	**27912** Postwar "2445" Elizabeth Coach, *08*	60
____	**27917** Postwar "2550" Baggage-Mail Rail Diesel Car, nonpowered, *13-14*	70
____	**27928** UP Boy Scouts 100th Anniversary PS-1 Boxcar (std O), *11*	70
____	**27929** Postwar Nos. 2484/2485 UP Passenger Car 2-pack, *12-13*	120
____	**27935** Postwar "6820" Aerial Missile Transport Car, *13*	60
____	**27941** Postwar "3854" Merchandise Car, *12*	75
____	**27946** Postwar "6050-25" Christmas Savings Boxcar, *13-14*	55
____	**27947** Postwar "6473-25" Reindeer Transport Car, *13*	60
____	**27948** Postwar "6464-25" Great Northern Christmas Boxcar, *13*	60
____	**27949** Postwar "3854-25" PRR Christmas Merchandise Car, *13-14*	75
____	**27953** Reading PS-2 Hopper 2-pack (std O), *13-14*	140
____	**27962** L&N PS-2 Hopper 2-pack (std O), *13-14*	140

MODERN 1970-2021	Esc	Mint	
27965	P&WV Offset Hopper 3-pack (std O), *13-15*		210 ___
27969	N&W Offset Hopper 3-pack (std O), *13-15*		210 ___
27973	C&O Offset Hopper 3-pack (std O), *13-15*		210 ___
27977	GN Offset Hopper 3-pack (std O), *13-15*		210 ___
27981	PRR USRA Double-sheathed Boxcar (std O), *13*		70 ___
27982	SP USRA Double-sheathed Boxcar (std O), *13-14*		80 ___
27983	UP USRA Double-sheathed Boxcar (std O), *13-14*		70 ___
27984	Procor 30,000-gallon 1-D Tank Car 3-pack (std O), *13*		240 ___
27988	UTLX 30,000-gallon 1-D Tank Car 3-pack (std O), *13*		240 ___
27992	ADM 30,000-gallon 1-D Tank Car 3-pack (std O), *13*		240 ___
27996	ACFX 30,000-gallon 1-D Tank Car 3-pack (std O), *13*		240 ___
28000	C&NW 4-6-4 Hudson Locomotive "3005," *99*		205 ___
28004	B&O 4-4-2 E6 Atlantic Locomotive, *traditional, 99-00*		410 ___
28005	PRR 4-4-2 E6 Atlantic Locomotive, traditional, *99-00*		345 ___
28006	ATSF 4-4-2 E6 Atlantic Locomotive, traditional, *99-00*		285 ___
28007	NYC 4-6-4 Hudson Locomotive "5406," *99*		380 ___
28008	C&O 4-6-4 Hudson Locomotive "306," *99*		345 ___
28009	Santa Fe 4-6-4 Hudson Locomotive "3463," *99*		330 ___
28011	C&O 2-6-6-6 Allegheny Locomotive "1601," *99*		1800 ___
28012	4-6-4 Commodore Vanderbilt Locomotive, red, *00 u*		1700 ___
28013	NH 4-6-2 Pacific Locomotive "1335," *99*		325 ___
28014	NYC 4-6-2 Pacific Locomotive "4930," *99*		305 ___
28015	Santa Fe Pacific 4-6-2 Pacific Locomotive "3449," *99*		340 ___
28016	Southern 4-6-2 Pacific Locomotive "1407," *99*		345 ___
28017	Case Cutlery 4-6-2 Pacific Locomotive, *99 u*		313 ___
28018	Reading 4-6-0 Camelback Locomotive "571," *CC, 01*		495 ___
28020	Lionel Lines 4-6-2 Pacific Locomotive "3344," *99*		250 ___
28022	West Side Lumber Shay Locomotive "800," *99*		810 ___
28023	PRR K4 4-6-2 Pacific Locomotive "3755," *CC, 99*		375 ___
28024	4-6-4 Commodore Vanderbilt Locomotive, blue, *00 u*		1663 ___
28025	PRR K4 4-6-2 Pacific Locomotive, traditional, *99*		330 ___
28026	LL 4-6-2 Pacific Locomotive, *CC, 99*		325 ___
28027	NYC 4-6-4 Hudson Locomotive "5413," *00*		590 ___
28028	Virginian 2-6-6-6 Allegheny Locomotive "1601," *99*		1318 ___
28029	UP 4-8-8-4 Big Boy Locomotive "4006," *99-00*		1500 ___
28030	NYC 4-6-4 Hudson Locomotive "5450," gray, *CC, 00*		315 ___
28032	B&O 4-6-2 Pacific Locomotive, *CC, 00*		315 ___
28033	B&O 4-6-2 Pacific Locomotive, traditional, *00*		195 ___
28034	UP 4-6-2 Pacific Locomotive, *CC, 00*		310 ___
28035	UP 4-6-2 Pacific Locomotive, traditional, *00*		210 ___
28036	SP 2-8-0 Consolidation Locomotive "2685," *CC, 00-01*		270 ___
28037	SP 2-8-0 Consolidation Locomotive "2686," traditional, *00-01*		295 ___
28038	UP 2-8-0 Consolidation Locomotive "324," *CC, 00-01*		315 ___
28039	UP 2-8-0 Consolidation Locomotive "326," traditional, *00-01*		240 ___
28044	NYC 4-6-4 Hudson Locomotive , *04*		250 ___
28051	B&O 2-8-8-4 EM-1 Articulated Locomotive "7617," *00*		970 ___
28052	N&W 2-6-6-4 Class A Locomotive "1218," *00*		870 ___
28055	GN 4-6-4 Hudson Locomotive "1725," traditional, *00-01*		170 ___
28057	Southern 4-8-2 Mountain Locomotive "1491," *CC, 00*		690 ___
28058	NH 4-8-2 Mountain Locomotive "3310," *CC, 00*		670 ___
28059	WP 4-8-2 Mountain Locomotive "179," *CC, 00*		630 ___
28062	LL Gold-plated 700E J-1E 4-6-4 Hudson Locomotive, display case, *00*		1050 ___
28063	PRR T-1 4-4-4-4 Duplex Locomotive "5511," *CC, 00*		910 ___

| --- | --- | --- | --- |
___	**28064** UP Challenger Coal Tender "3985," CC, 00 u	1350	1800
___	**28065** NYC Hudson 4-6-4 Locomotive "5412," RailSounds, 00		290
___	**28066** B&O President Polk 4-6-2 Locomotive, CC, 01		750
___	**28067** Erie 4-6-2 Locomotive "2934," CC, 01		570
___	**28068** D&RGW 4-6-4 Hudson Locomotive, traditional, 01 u		300
___	**28070** SP Daylight 4-4-2 Atlantic Locomotive "3000," CC, 01		425
___	**28071** NP 4-4-2 Atlantic Locomotive "604," CC, 01		415
___	**28072** NYC 4-6-4 Hudson J3a Locomotive "5444," CC, 01		790
___	**28074** NP 2-8-4 Berkshire Locomotive "759," CC, 01		640
___	**28075** C&O 2-6-6-2 Locomotive "1521," CC, 01		930
___	**28076** NKP 2-6-6-2 Locomotive "921," CC, 01		960
___	**28077** UP 4-6-6-4 Challenger Locomotive "3983," CC, 01		680
___	**28078** PRR 2-10-4 J1a Locomotive "6496," CC, 01		880
___	**28079** C&O 2-10-4 Class T Locomotive "3004," CC, 01		882
___	**28080** NYC 0-8-0 Locomotive "7745," CC, 01-02		540
___	**28081** C&O 0-8-0 Locomotive "75," CC, 01-02		520
___	**28084** NYC Dreyfuss Hudson 4-6-4 Locomotive "5452," CC, 01-02		790
___	**28085** N&W 2-8-8-2 Y6b Class Locomotive "2200," CC, 03		1207
___	**28086** PRR H9 Consolidation Locomotive "1111," CC, 01		480
___	**28087** UP Auxiliary Tender, yellow, CC, 01		210
___	**28088** N&W Auxiliary Water Tender, CC, 01-02		200
___	**28089** PRR 4-4-4-4 T-1 Duplex Locomotive "5511," 2-rail, 00		1150
___	**28090** UP Challenger Oil Tender "3977," 2-rail, 00 u		1800
___	**28098** NYC 4-6-0 10-wheel Locomotive "1916," CC, 01-02		520
___	**28099** UP Challenger Oil Tender "3977," CC, 00 u		1700
___	**28200** D&H U30C Diesel "702," CC (SSS), 02		375
___	**28201** UP SD90MAC Diesel "8049," 03		345
___	**28202** Conrail SD80MAC Diesel "7203," 03		325
___	**28203** CSX SD80MAC Diesel "803," 03		325
___	**28204** NS SD80MAC Diesel "7201," 03		345
___	**28205** Chessie System SD9 Diesel "1833," CC, 03		230
___	**28207** Erie-Lackawanna U33C Diesel "3304," CC, 02		355
___	**28208** BN U33C Diesel "5734," CC, 02		355
___	**28211** CP SD90MAC Diesel "9107," 03		300
___	**28213** Amtrak GE Dash 8 Diesel "516," CC, 02		300
___	**28214** BNSF GE Dash 8 Diesel "582," CC, 02		325
___	**28215** B&O GP30 Diesel "6939," CC, 02		315
___	**28216** Reading GP30 Diesel "5518," CC, 02		315
___	**28217** Rio Grande GP30 Diesel "3013," CC, 02		315
___	**28218** Lehigh Valley Alco C420 Switcher "407," CC, 04		325
___	**28219** Seaboard Alco C420 Switcher "136," CC, 04		300
___	**28222** Santa Fe Dash 9 Diesel "605," CC, 05		250
___	**28223** BNSF SD70MAC Diesel "9433," CC, 05		250
___	**28224** Jersey Central SD40-2 Diesel "3067," CC, 04		350
___	**28225** SPSF SD40T-2 Diesel "8521," CC, 04-05		430
___	**28226** NS SD80MAC Diesel "7204," CC, 04-05		430
___	**28227** UP SD70MAC Diesel "4979," CC, 04		375
___	**28228** C&NW Dash 9-44CW Diesel "8669," CC, 03		350
___	**28229** SP Dash 9-44CW Diesel "8132," CC, 03		350
___	**28230** Amtrak Dash 8 Diesel "505," CC, 04		295
___	**28235** Great Northern U33C Diesel "2543," CC, 05		455
___	**28237** Reading U30C Diesel "6301," CC, 05		455
___	**28239** Union Pacific SD70 Diesel, TMCC, 04		360

		Esc	Mint
28241	C&NW U30C Diesel "935," *CC, 06*		455 ___
28242	SP U33C Diesel "8773," *CC, 06*		475 ___
28243	LIRR Alco C420 Hi-nose Switcher "206," *CC, 06*		420 ___
28244	N&W Alco C420 Hi-nose Switcher "417," *CC, 06-07*		420 ___
28245	Chessie System SD40T-2 Diesel "7617," RailSounds, *06*		265 ___
28246	Chessie System SD40T-2 Diesel "7618," nonpowered (std O), *06*		160 ___
28247	Rio Grande SD40T-2 Diesel "5348," RailSounds, *06*		265 ___
28248	Rio Grande SD40T-2 Diesel "5349," nonpowered (std O), *06*		160 ___
28250	N&W Alco C420 Hi-nose Switcher "416," nonpowered (std O), *06-07*		160 ___
28251	LIRR Alco C420 Hi-nose Switcher "206," nonpowered (std O), *06*		160 ___
28252	SP U33C Diesel "8774," nonpowered (std O), *06*		160 ___
28253	C&NW U30C Diesel "936," nonpowered (std O), *06*		160 ___
28255	UP SD40T-2 Diesel "4551," traditional, *CC, 07-08*		265 ___
28256	UP SD40T-2 Diesel "4596," nonpowered (std O), *07*		170 ___
28257	NS SD40-2 Diesel "3340," *CC, 06*		430 ___
28258	NS SD40-2 Diesel "3341," nonpowered (std O), *06*		170 ___
28259	CN SD40-2 Diesel "5383," *CC, 06*		430 ___
28260	CN SD40-2 Diesel "5384," nonpowered (std O), *06*		170 ___
28261	UP (MP) SD70ACe Diesel "1982," *CC, 07*		450 ___
28262	UP (WP) SD70ACe Diesel "1983," *CC, 07*		450 ___
28263	UP (MKT) SD70ACe Diesel "1988," *CC, 07*		450 ___
28264	UP "Building America" SD70ACe Diesel "8348," *CC, 07*		450 ___
28265	MILW U30C Diesel "5657," *CC, 07*		455 ___
28266	MILW U30C Diesel "5657," nonpowered (std O), *07-08*		170 ___
28267	Conrail U30C Diesel "6837," *CC, 07*		455 ___
28268	Conrail U30C Diesel "6838," nonpowered (std O), *07-08*		170 ___
28269	ATSF Dash 8-40BW Diesel "562," *CC, 08*		500 ___
28270	ATSF Dash 8-40CW Diesel "563," nonpowered, *08*		220
28272	"I Love USA" SD60 Diesel "1776," traditional, *06*		250
28279	UP SD70ACe Diesel "1989," *CC, 07*		450
28280	UP (C&NW) SD70ACe Diesel "1995," *CC, 07*		450
28281	UP (SP) SD70ACe Diesel "1996," *CC, 07*		450
28283	UP "Building America" SD70AC3 Diesel, nonpowered (std O), *07*		170
28284	Ferromex SD70ACe Diesel "4011," *CC, 08*		495
28287	KCS SD70ACe Diesel "4050," *CC, 08*		495
28292	Chessie System U30C Diesel "3312," *CC, 02*		300 ___
28293	Santa Fe U28CG Diesel "354," *CC, 02*		375
28295	Conrail LionMaster SD80MAC Diesel, nonpowered, *08*		200
28296	UP AC6000 Diesel "7526," *CC, 08*		660 ___
28297	SP GP9 Diesel "446," *CC, 10*		390
28298	CSX AC6000 Diesel "608," *CC, 08*		660 ___
28299	CSX AC6000 Diesel "609," nonpowered, *08*		220
28300	NS Dash 9 Diesel "9607," nonpowered, *08*		220
28302	BNSF SD70ACe Diesel "9380," *CC, 08*		495 ___
28305	CSX AC6000 Diesel "610," nonpowered, RailSounds, *08*		430 ___
28306	GE ES44AC Evolution Hybrid Diesel "2010," *CC, 09-10*		1000 ___
28307	Wabash Train Master Diesel "550," *CC, 09-10*		495 ___
28311	UP DD35A Diesel, *CC, 11*		600 ___
28312	BN SD60 Diesel "8301," *CC, 09*		800 ___
28314	UP 3GS21B Genset Switcher "2701," *CC, 10*		675 ___
28316	PRR NS Heritage SD70ACe Diesel "1854," *CC, 10*		500 ___
28318	Conrail NS Heritage SD70ACe Diesel "1209," *CC, 10*		500 ___
28320	CP Evolution Hybrid Diesel, *10*		875 ___

			Mint
___	28323	NS Genset Switcher, *CC, 11*	800
___	28327	UP AC6000 Diesel "7050," *CC, 10*	700
___	28328	UPAC6000 Diesel "7055," nonpowered, *CC, 10*	350
___	28330	UP SD70ACe Diesel "8444," *CC, 10*	500
___	28331	CSX AC6000 Diesel "618," *CC, 10*	700
___	28333	Virginian NS Heritage SD70ACe Diesel, *CC, 10*	500
___	28334	NS Heritage SD70ACe Diesel "1982," *CC, 10*	500
___	28338	PRR NS Heritage SD70ACe Diesel, *CC, 11*	500
___	28339	ATSF AC6000 Diesel "9876," *CC, 10*	550
___	28340	WP GP7 Diesel "705," *CC, 10*	450
___	28343	Amtrak Dash 9 Diesel "519," *CC, 10*	500
___	28344	Southern NS Heritage SD70ACe Diesel, *CC, 10*	500
___	28345	N&W NS Heritage SD70ACe Diesel "247," *CC, 10*	500
___	28347	UP Boy Scouts 100th Anniversary ES44AC Diesel, *CC, 11*	875
___	28350	BNSF ES44AC Diesel, *CC, 11*	850
___	28351	KCS ES44AC Diesel "4655," *CC, 11*	850
___	28353	Erie GP7 Diesel, *CC, 11*	450
___	28354	CSX Genset Switcher "1303," *CC, 11*	800
___	28355	BNSF Genset Switcher "1249," *CC, 11*	800
___	28356	CSX SD60 Diesel, *CC, 11*	500
___	28357	CSX SD60 Diesel, *CC, 11*	500
___	28358	Soo Line SD60 Diesel, *CC, 11*	500
___	28359	Soo Line SD60 Diesel, *CC, 11*	500
___	28360	WP GP7 Diesel "707," *CC, 11*	450
___	28361	WM GP7 Diesel "21," *CC, 11*	450
___	28362	WM GP7 Diesel "23," *CC, 11*	450
___	28363	BN SD60 Diesel "8302," *CC, 11*	500
___	28364	BNSF Dash-9 Diesel "4081," *CC, 11*	500
___	28365	BNSF Dash-9 Diesel "5121," *CC, 11*	500
___	28366	CN Dash-9 Diesel "2643," *CC, 11*	500
___	28367	CN Dash-9 Diesel "2692," *CC, 11*	500
___	28368	Amtrak Dash-9 Diesel, *CC, 11*	500
___	28369	NYC DD35A Diesel "9950," *CC, 11*	600
___	28370	UP DD35 Diesel "84," *CC, 12*	600
___	28371	UP DD35A Diesel "72," *CC, 11*	600
___	28372	NYC DD35A Diesel "9955," *CC, 11*	600
___	28373	C&NW UP Heritage SD70ACe Diesel, *CC, 11*	500
___	28374	SP UP Heritage SD70ACe Diesel, *CC, 11*	500
___	28375	Katy UP Heritage SD70ACe Diesel, *CC, 11*	500
___	28376	MoPac UP Heritage SD70ACe Diesel, *CC, 11*	500
___	28377	Rio Grande UP Heritage SD70ACe Diesel, *CC, 11*	500
___	28378	WP UP Heritage SD70ACe Diesel, *CC, 11*	500
___	28380	NYC DD35A Diesel, nonpowered, *11*	440
___	28381	ATSF GP30 Diesel, *CC, 11*	500
___	28382	U.S. Army Genset Switcher, *CC, 11*	800
___	28383	Conrail Genset Switcher, *CC, 11*	800
___	28384	CN Genset Switcher "7990," *CC, 11-12*	800
___	28385	ATSF GP30 Diesel "1214," *CC, 11*	500
___	28386	ATSF GP30 Diesel "2710," *11*	380
___	28387	ATSF GP30 Diesel "2715," nonpowered, *11*	240
___	28388	ICG GP30 Diesel "2268," *CC, 11*	500
___	28389	ICG GP30 Diesel "2271," *CC, 11*	500
___	28390	UP DD35 Diesel "79," nonpowered, *12*	440
___	28394	ICG GP30 Diesel "2277," *11*	380

		Mint	
28395	ICG GP30 Diesel "2279," nonpowered, *11*	240	___
28396	UP ES44AC Diesel "7454," *CC, 11*	850	___
28397	UP ES44AC Diesel "7459," *CC, 11*	850	___
28398	BNSF ES44AC Diesel "6436," *CC, 11*	850	___
28399	KCS ES44AC Diesel "4682," *CC, 11*	850	___
28400	Amtrak Rail Bonder, *05*	65	___
28403	Pennsylvania Ballast Tamper, traditional, *05-06*	105	___
28404	Maintenance Car, *05*	105	___
28405	Picatinny Arsenal Switcher, *CC, 05*	290	___
28406	CSX Rail Bonder "92794," traditional, *05*	65	___
28407	UP Speeder, *05*	65	___
28408	CNJ Speeder "MW840," traditional, *06*	70	___
28409	Conrail Rail Bonder "X409," traditional, *06*	70	___
28411	U.S. Army Missile Launcher Locomotive, *06-07*	300	___
28412	Santa's Speeder, *06*	70	___
28413	Milwaukee Road Snowplow "X903," traditional, *06*	210	___
28414	Lionel Lines Burro Crane, traditional, *06*	160	___
28415	Third Avenue Trolley "1651," traditional, *06*	70	___
28416	Hobo Handcar, traditional, *06*	70	___
28417	Christmas Rotary Snowplow, *06*	180	___
28418	Christmas Trolley, *06*	70	___
28419	Lionel Lines Speeder, *07-08*	70	___
28420	D&RGW Handcar, *07-08*	70	___
28421	Fort Collins Trolley, *07*	73	___
28422	PRR Burro Crane, *07-08*	160	___
28423	Alaska Rotary Snowplow, *06-07*	220	___
28424	Postwar "51" Navy Switcher, *07*	210	___
28425	Polar Express Elf Handcar, *06-20*	100	___
28427	Christmas Snowplow, *08-10*	210	___
28428	Halloween Handcar, *07*	70	___
28430	Wellspring Capital Management Trolley, *06*	85	___
28432	Bethlehem Steel Switcher, traditional, *07*	210	___
28434	Christmas Trolley, *07*	70	___
28438	Portland Birney Trolley, *08-09*	65	___
28440	PRR Inspection Vehicle, *08-09*	170	___
28441	Transylvania Trolley, *08*	75	___
28442	Postwar "50" Gang Car, *08*	120	___
28444	NH Handcar, *08-09*	75	___
28445	AEC Burro Crane Car	100	___
28446	Silver Bell Trolley, *09*	90	___
28447	4850TM Factory Trackmobile, *CC, 10*	300	___
28448	CSX 4850TM Trackmobile, *CC, 10*	300	___
28449	UP 4850TM Trackmobile, *CC, 10*	300	___
28450	CP Rail Trackmobile, *CC, 11*	300	___
28451	Christmas Track Cleaning Car, *10-13*	150	___
28452	MOW Early Era Inspection Vehicle, *10*	130	___
28453	PRR Early Era Inspection Vehicle, *10*	130	___
28454	CP Early Era Inspection Vehicle, *10*	130	___
28455	NYC Trackmobile, *CC, 11-13*	300	___
28456	Coca-Cola Trolley, *10*	90	___
28457	B&M Rotary Snowplow "8457," *11*	250	___
28466	U.S. Army Trackmobile, *CC, 11*	300	___
28467	PRR Trackmobile, *CC, 11*	300	___
28468	Amtrak Trackmobile, *CC, 11*	300	___

		Mint
28469	BNSF Trackmobile, *CC, 11*	300
28470	NYC Early Era Inspection Vehicle , *11*	130
28471	ATSF Early Era Inspection Vehicle, *CC, 11*	130
28472	Southern Early Era Inspection Vehicle, *11*	130
28473	GN Early Era Inspection Vehicle, *CC, 11*	130
28474	North Pole Central Elf Handcar, *11*	80
28475	UP Early Era Inspection Vehicle, *11*	130
28476	IC Early Era Inspection Vehicle, *11*	130
28478	Frisco Early Era Inspection Vehicle, *CC, 11*	130
28479	Christmas Early Era Inspection Vehicle, *11*	130
28480	Grand Trunk Early Era Inspection Vehicle, *CC, 11*	130
28500	Mopac GP20 Diesel "2274," *99-00*	205
28501	ATSF GP9 Diesel "2924," traditional, *99*	200
28502	ATSF GP9 Diesel "2925," *CC, 99-00*	255
28503	ACL GP7 Diesel, *CC, 00*	245
28504	ACL GP7 Diesel, traditional, *00*	170
28505	Monon Alco C420 Switcher "505," *CC, 00-01*	230
28506	Monon Alco C420 Switcher "506," traditional, *00-01*	170
28507	NH Alco C420 Switcher "2556," *CC, 00-01*	275
28508	NH Alco C420 Switcher "2557," traditional, *00-01*	290
28509	FEC GP7 Diesel Set, *99*	560
28514	B&O GP9 Diesel "6590," *00*	85
28515	Lionel Service Station Alco C420 Switcher, *CC, 00*	205
28516	Lehigh & Hudson River Alco C420 Diesel, *00*	160
28517	C&NW GP7 Diesel "1518," *CC, 00-01*	275
28518	PRR EP-5 Electric Locomotive "2352," *CC, 00*	410
28519	NP GP9 Diesel "2349," *CC, 01*	290
28521	SP Alco RS-11 Switcher "5725," *CC, 01-02*	280
28522	MP Alco RS-11 Switcher "4611," *CC, 01-02*	305
28523	Soo SD40-2 Diesel "6622," *CC, 01*	375
28524	Chessie SD40-2 Diesel "7616," *CC, 01*	355
28527	AEC GP9 Diesel "2001," *CC, 01*	400
28529	Norfolk Southern GP9 Diesel, *CC, 02*	200
28530	NP Alco S4 Diesel "722," *CC, 02*	285
28531	Santa Fe Alco S2 Switcher "2337," *CC, 02*	285
28532	LV Alco S2 Switcher "150," *CC, 02*	280
28533	Seaboard Air Line Alco S4 Diesel "1489," *CC, 02*	290
28536	Rock Island GP7 Diesel "1274," *CC, 02-03*	230
28538	WP Alco S2 Switcher "553," *CC, 03*	340
28539	B&O Alco S2 Switcher "9045," *CC, 03*	320
28540	UP SD40T-2 Diesel "4455," *CC, 03*	390
28541	SP SD40T-2 Diesel "8239," *CC, 03*	400
28542	Rio Grande SD40T-2 Diesel "5350," *CC, 03*	400
28543	Ontario Northland RS3 Diesel "1308," *03*	80
28544	Pennsylvania Alco RS-11 Switcher "8618," *CC, 04*	350
28545	NP Alco RS-11 Switcher "900," *CC, 03*	325
28548	Chessie System S4 Diesel "9009," *CC, 05*	400
28553	PRR Alco RS-11 Switcher "8620," traditional, *07-08*	285
28554	Pennsylvania Alco RS-11 Switcher "8618," nonpowered, *CC, 07*	170
28554	PRR RS-11 Diesel "8621," nonpowered, *08*	170
28555	Alaska GP38-2 Diesel "2001," *CC, 06*	400
28556	Alaska GP38-2 Diesel "2002," nonpowered (std O), *06*	160
28557	CP GP30 Diesel "5000," *CC, 06-07*	400

		Esc	Mint
28558	CP GP30 Diesel "5001," nonpowered (std O), *06-07*		150 ___
28559	Chessie System GP30 Diesel "3044," *CC, 06-07*		400 ___
28560	Chessie System GP30 Diesel "3045," nonpowered (std O), *06-07*		150 ___
28561	NYC GP7 Diesel "5628," *CC, 07-08*		340 ___
28562	NYC GP7 Diesel "5629," nonpowered (std O), *07*		170 ___
28563	GN GP7 Diesel "626," *CC, 07*		400 ___
28564	GN GP7 Diesel "627," nonpowered (std O), *07*		170 ___
28565	RI GP7 Diesel "1265," *CC, 07*		400 ___
28566	RI GP7 Diesel "1266," nonpowered (std O), *07*		170 ___
28567	UP GP7 Diesel "105," *CC, 07*		400 ___
28568	UP GP7 Diesel "106," nonpowered (std O), *07*		170 ___
28570	D&RGW GP7 Diesel "5101," *CC, 08*		440 ___
28573	PRR GP7 Diesel "8512," *CC, 08*		440 ___
28578	D&H GP38-2 Diesel "7307," *CC, 08*		440 ___
28587	PRR GP7 Diesel "8510," *CC, 10*		450 ___
28592	N&W GP7 Diesel "2446," *CC, 09*		500 ___
28594	White Pass & Yukon NW2 Diesel Switcher, traditional, *09-10*		300 ___
28595	ATSF SD40 Diesel "5004," *CC, 09*		380 ___
28596	Erie GP7 Diesel "1210," *CC, 11*		450 ___
28598	ATSF GP7 Diesel "2791," *CC, 10*		450 ___
28599	Erie GP9 Diesel "1261," *CC, 10*		390 ___
28612	WP 4-4-2 Atlantic Locomotive, traditional, *02*		80 ___
28613	Reading 0-6-0 Dockside Switcher "1251," traditional, *04*		100 ___
28615	B&O 4-6-4 Hudson Locomotive, traditional, *02*		225 ___
28616	Nickel Plate 2-8-4 Berkshire Locomotive, traditional, *02*		190 ___
28617	Southern 2-8-4 Berkshire Locomotive, traditional, *02*		235 ___
28624	Santa Fe 0-6-0 Dockside Switcher "2174," traditional, *04*		175 ___
28625	Wabash 4-4-2 Atlantic Locomotive "8625," traditional, *03*		85 ___
28626	PRR 4-6-4 Hudson Locomotive "626," traditional, *03*		175 ___
28627	C&O 2-8-4 Berkshire Locomotive "2755," traditional, *03*		200 ___
28628	L&N 2-8-4 Berkshire Locomotive "1970," traditional, *03*	150	200 ___
28633	JCPenney B&O 2-8-4 Berkshire Locomotive, *07*		135 ___
28636	D&RGW 4-4-2 Atlantic Locomotive "8636," traditional, *04*		95 ___
28637	UP 4-6-4 Hudson Locomotive "673," traditional, *04*		160 ___
28638	GN 2-8-4 Berkshire Locomotive "3414," traditional, *04*		200 ___
28639	NYC 2-8-4 Berkshire Locomotive "9401," traditional, *04*		200 ___
28646	North Pole Central 2-8-4 Berkshire "1900," traditional, *04*		230 ___
28649	Polar Express 2-8-4 Berkshire Locomotive, *03, 10*		120 ___
28650	NYC 0-6-0 Dockside Switcher "X-8688," traditional, *05*		80 ___
28651	Bethlehem Steel 0-6-0 Dockside Switcher "72," traditional, *05*		80 ___
28652	LL 4-4-2 Locomotive "8652," traditional, *05*		105 ___
28655	Erie 2-8-4 Berkshire Locomotive "3338," traditional, *05*		240 ___
28656	PRR 2-8-4 Berkshire Locomotive "56," traditional, *05*		240 ___
28660	North Pole Central 0-6-0 Dockside Switcher "25," traditional, *05*		105 ___
28661	Santa Fe 0-4-0 Locomotive "2300" traditional, *05*		160 ___
28662	C&O 0-4-0 Locomotive "39," traditional, *05*		160 ___
28674	C&O 0-6-0 Dockside Switcher "67," traditional, *06-07*		110 ___
28675	SP 0-6-0 Dockside Switcher "675," traditional, *06-07*		110 ___
28676	U.S. Steel 0-6-0 Dockside Switcher "76," traditional, *06-07*		110 ___
28677	WM 4-4-2 Atlantic Locomotive "103," traditional, *06*		110 ___
28678	Rio Grande 0-4-0 Locomotive "55," traditional, *06-07*		170 ___
28679	U.S. Army Transportation Corps 0-4-0 Locomotive "40," traditional, *06*		170 ___
28680	Reading 0-4-0 Locomotive "1152," traditional, *06*		170 ___

		Esc	Mint
28681	Virginian 2-8-4 Berkshire Locomotive "509," traditional, 06		260
28683	B&O 2-8-2 Mikado Locomotive "1520," TrainSounds, 06-07		260
28684	UP 2-8-2 Mikado Locomotive "2498," TrainSounds, 06-07		260
28693	B&O 4-4-2 Locomotive "28," traditional, 05		105
28694	NYC 4-4-2 Atlantic Locomotive "8637," traditional, 06		100
28695	Halloween 0-6-0 Dockside Switcher "X-131," traditional, 06-07		85
28699	Holiday 2-8-2 Mikado Locomotive "25," red, RailSounds, 08		260
28700	CB&Q 0-8-0 Locomotive "543," RailSounds, 05		650
28701	NP 0-8-0 Locomotive "1178," RailSounds, 05		650
28702	Boston & Albany 0-8-0 Locomotive "53," RailSounds, 05		650
28704	PRR 4-4-2 Atlantic Locomotive "68," CC, 05		550
28706	PRR Reading Seashore 4-4-2 Atlantic Locomotive "6064," CC, 05		550
28742	B&O 4-6-0 Camelback Locomotive "1630," CC, 03		335
28743	B&O 4-6-0 Camelback Locomotive "1632," traditional, 03		300
28744	D&H 4-6-0 Camelback Locomotive "548," CC, 03		325
28745	D&H 4-6-0 Camelback Locomotive "555," traditional, 03		300
28746	Erie 4-6-0 Camelback Locomotive "860," CC, 03		375
28747	Erie 4-6-0 Camelback Locomotive "878," traditional, 03		300
28748	Jersey Central 4-6-0 Camelback Locomotive "772," CC, 03		300
28749	Jersey Central 4-6-0 Camelback Locomotive "773," traditional, 03		300
28750	Lackawanna 4-6-0 Camelback Locomotive "690," CC, 03		375
28751	Lackawanna 4-6-0 Camelback Locomotive "1031," traditional, 03		300
28752	LIRR 4-6-0 Camelback Locomotive "126," CC, 03		300
28753	LIRR 4-6-0 Camelback Locomotive "127," traditional, 03		300
28754	NYO&W 4-6-0 Camelback Locomotive "249," CC, 03		300
28755	NYO&W 4-6-0 Camelback "253" Locomotive, traditional, 03		300
28756	PRR Reading Seashore 4-6-0 Camelback Locomotive "6000," CC, 03		325
28757	PRR Reading Seashore 4-6-0 Camelback Locomotive "6001," traditional, 03		300
28758	Susquehanna 4-6-0 Camelback Locomotive "30," CC, 03		305
28759	Susquehanna 4-6-0 Camelback Locomotive "36," traditional, 03		300
28800	N&W GP7 Diesel "507," 99-00		80
28801	Lionel Lines 44-ton Switcher, 99		135
28806	Jersey Central FM H16-44 Diesel "1516," CC, 01		335
28811	Santa Fe FM H16-44 Diesel "3003," CC, 01		290
28813	Milwaukee Road FM H16-44 Diesel "406," CC, 01		280
28815	B&O GP30 Diesel "6935," CC, 02		295
28817	Reading GP30 Diesel "5513," CC, 02		310
28819	Rio Grande GP30 Diesel "3013," CC, 02		310
28821	GT GP7 Diesel "4438," 01		100
28822	Southern RS3 Diesel "2127," 01		70
28823	Virginian Electric Locomotive "234," 01		122
28826	Pioneer Seed GP7 Diesel "2001," traditional, 00 u		NRS
28827	Chessie GP38 Diesel, traditional, 01		100
28830	Soo Line GP9 Diesel, traditional, 01 u		NRS
28831	Conrail U36B Diesel "2971," traditional, 02		100
28832	Santa Fe RS3 Diesel "2099," traditional, 02		70
28836	NYC FM H-16-44 Diesel "7000," CC, 02		330
28837	NH FM H-16-44 Diesel "591," CC, 02		325
28838	UP FM H-16-44 Diesel "1340," CC, 02		325
28839	Alaska GP 30 Diesel "2000," CC, 04		315
28840	Burlington GP30 Diesel "945," CC, 03		325
28841	Seaboard GP30 Diesel "1315," CC, 03		220
28842	C&O GP9 Diesel, horn, 04		160

		Esc	Mint	
28843	Southern GP38 Diesel, horn, *04*		140	__
28845	Amtrak RS3 Diesel "106," *03*		70	__
28846	Western Pacific U36B Diesel "3067," traditional, *04*		100	__
28847	DM & IR GP38 Diesel "203," traditional, *04*		170	__
28848	JCPenney Santa Fe GP38 Diesel, *04*		125	__
28849	Western Maryland GP7 Diesel, horn, *04*		185	__
28850	NYC GP30 Diesel "6115," *CC, 04*		360	__
28851	Pennsylvania RS3 Diesel, *04*		75	__
28852	CSX U36B Diesel "1976," traditional, *05*		140	__
28853	Santa Fe GP38 Diesel "2371," traditional, *05*		210	__
28857	Alaska GP9 Diesel, *05*		125	__
28859	Pennsylvania GP30 Diesel "2206," nonpowered, *06*		160	__
28860	UP GP30 Diesel "844," *CC, 06*		360	__
28861	UP GP30 Diesel "845," nonpowered (std O), *06*		150	__
28862	CSX GP30 Diesel "4249," *CC, 06*		400	__
28863	CSX GP30 Diesel "4250," nonpowered (std O), *06*		150	__
28864	UP RS3 Diesel "1195," traditional, *06*		85	__
28865	GN GP9 Diesel "688," traditional, *06*		160	__
28866	NYC GP20 Diesel "6110," traditional, *06*		140	__
28868	ATSF GP38 Diesel		140	__
28873	NYC RS3 Diesel "8226," traditional, *06*		85	__
28874	UP GP9 Diesel "178," traditional, *06-07*		210	__
28875	Santa Fe GP20 "1107," traditional, *06*		140	__
28876	GN FT Diesel "418," traditional, *07-08*		245	__
28879	UPS Centennial GP38 Diesel, traditional, *06*		210	__
28881	Conrail GP20 Diesel "2107," traditional, *07*		140	__
28882	Alaska RS3 Diesel "1079," traditional, *07*		85	__
28883	Diesel, *07-13*		120	__
28884	PRR GP38 Diesel "2389," traditional, *08-09*		210	__
28886	RI RS3 Diesel "492," traditional, *08*		95	__
28887	Southern RS3 Diesel "2028," traditional, *08*		95	__
28890	CN GP9 Diesel "4573," traditional, *08*		210	__
28897	Seaboard U36B Diesel "1762," traditional, *08*		140	__
28900	Iron 'Arry and Iron Bert 2-pack, *08-09*		240	__
28905	ATSF FT Diesel "160," nonpowered, *09-10*		120	__
29000	PRR Caleb Strong Madison Coach "2622," *99*		80	__
29001	PRR Villa Royal Madison Coach "2621," *99*		80	__
29002	PRR Philadelphia Madison Coach "2624," *99*	30	80	__
29003	PRR Madison Car 4-pack, *98*		220	__
29004	NYC Heavyweight Passenger Car 2-pack, *99*		170	__
29007	NYC Pullman Passenger Car 2-pack, *98 u*		95	__
29008	NYC Heavyweight Diner "383," *98*		95	__
29009	NYC Van Twiller Heavyweight Combination Car, *98*		95	__
29010	C&O Heavyweight Passenger Car 2-pack, *99*		150	__
29039	Lionel Lines Recovery Combination Car "9501," *99*		NRS	__
29041	Alaska Streamliner Car 4-pack, *99-00*		230	__
29042	Alaska Streamliner Baggage Car "6310," *99-00*		50	__
29043	Alaska Streamliner Coach "5408," *99-00*		65	__
29044	Alaska Streamliner Vista Dome Car "7014," *99-00*		65	__
29046	B&O Streamliner Car 4-pack, *99-00*		165	__
29047	B&O Streamliner Baggage Car, *99-00*		35	__
29048	B&O Streamliner Coach, *99-00*		50	__
29049	B&O Streamliner Vista Dome Car, *99-00*		50	__
29050	B&O Streamliner Observation Car, *99-00*		40	__

____	**29051** ATSF Streamliner Car 4-pack, *99-00*		200
____	**29052** ATSF Streamliner Baggage Car, *99-00*		40
____	**29053** ATSF Streamliner Coach, *99-00*		60
____	**29054** ATSF Streamliner Vista Dome Car, *99-00*		60
____	**29055** ATSF Streamliner Observation Car, *99-00*		40
____	**29056** NYC Streamliner Car 4-pack, *99-00*		180
____	**29057** NYC Streamliner Baggage Car, *99-00*		40
____	**29058** NYC Streamliner Coach, *99-00*		50
____	**29059** NYC Streamliner Vista Dome Car, *99-00*		50
____	**29060** NYC Streamliner Observation Car, *99-00*		45
____	**29061** PRR Madison Passenger Car 4-pack, *99-00*		190
____	**29062** PRR Indian Point Madison Baggage Car, *99-00*		50
____	**29063** PRR Christopher Columbus Madison Coach, *99-00*		50
____	**29064** PRR Andrew Jackson Madison Coach, *99-00*		50
____	**29065** PRR Broussard Madison Observation Car, *99-00*		50
____	**29066** CNJ Madison Passenger Car 4-pack, *99-00*		210
____	**29067** CNJ Madison Baggage Car "420," *99-00*		50
____	**29068** CNJ Beachcomber Madison Coach, *99-00*		50
____	**29069** CNJ Echo Lake Madison Coach, *99-00*		50
____	**29070** CNJ Madison Observation Car "1178," *99-00*		50
____	**29071** NYC Baby Madison Car 4-pack, *00*		155
____	**29072** NYC Baby Madison Baggage Car "1001," *00*		50
____	**29073** NYC Baby Madison Coach "1005," *00*		50
____	**29074** NYC Baby Madison Coach "1006," *00*		50
____	**29075** NYC Detroit Baby Madison Observation Car "1019," *00*		40
____	**29076** Southern Baby Madison Car 4-pack, *00*		155
____	**29077** Southern Delaware Madison Baggage Car "702," *00*		30
____	**29078** Southern North Carolina Madison Coach "800," *00*		50
____	**29079** Southern Maryland Madison Coach "801," *00*		50
____	**29080** Southern Madison Observation Car "1100," *00*		40
____	**29081** ATSF Baby Madison Car 4-pack, *00*		160
____	**29082** ATSF Baby Madison Baggage Car "1765," *00*		30
____	**29083** ATSF Baby Madison Coach "3040," *00*		50
____	**29084** ATSF Baby Madison Coach "1535," *00*		50
____	**29085** ATSF Baby Madison Observation Car "10," *00*		45
____	**29086** Madison Car 3-pack, *99*		280
____	**29090** Lionel Liontech Madison Car "2656," *99*		75
____	**29091** Lawrence Cowen Lionel Legends Madison Coach "2657," *99-00*		75
____	**29105** PRR Trail Blazer Aluminum Passenger Car 4-pack, *04-05*		550
____	**29108** Searchlight Car, *00*		30
____	**29110** B&O Columbian Aluminum Passenger Car 4-pack, *04*		425
____	**29115** SP Daylight Aluminum Passenger Car 4-pack, *04-05*		550
____	**29122** Erie-Lack. F3 Diesel AB Passenger Set, *99*		840
____	**29123** Erie-Lack. Aluminum Coach/Baggage Car "203," *99*		100
____	**29124** Erie-Lack. Aluminum Coach/Diner "770," *99*		100
____	**29125** Erie-Lack. Eleanor Lord Aluminum Coach, *99*		100
____	**29126** Erie-Lack. Tavern Lounge Aluminum Observation Car "789," *99*		125
____	**29127** ACL Aluminum Baggage Car "152," *99*		NRS
____	**29128** ACL North Hampton Aluminum Coach, *99*		NRS
____	**29129** Texas Special Passenger Car 4-pack, *99*	650	700
____	**29130** Texas Special Edward Burleson Aluminum Coach "1200," *99*		115
____	**29131** Texas Special David G. Burnett Aluminum Coach "1201," *99*		115
____	**29132** Texas Special J. Pinckney Henderson Aluminum Coach "1202," *99*		115

|---|---|---|---|
29133	Texas Special Stephen F. Austin Aluminum Observation Car "1203," *99*		100
29135	California Zephyr Silver Poplar Aluminum Vista Dome Car, *99*		150
29136	California Zephyr Silver Palm Aluminum Vista Dome Car, *99*		150
29137	California Zephyr Silver Tavern Aluminum Vista Dome Car, *99*		150
29138	California Zephyr Silver Planet Aluminum Vista Dome Car, *99*		150
29139	Kughn Lionel Legends Madison Car "2655," *99*		113
29140	NYC Castleton Bridge Aluminum Sleeper Car, *99*		120
29141	NYC Martin Van Buren Aluminum Combination Car, *99*		120
29142	CP Skyline Aluminum Vista Dome Car "596," *99*		125
29143	CP Banff Park Aluminum Observation Car, *99*		125
29144	Santa Fe El Capitan Aluminum Passenger Car 4-pack, *04*		400
29149	CB&Q California Zephyr Aluminum Passenger Car 2-pack, *03*		300
29152	Santa Fe Super Chief Aluminum Passenger Car 2-pack, *03*		190
29155	D&H Aluminum Passenger Car 2-pack, *03*		190
29158	Southern Aluminum Passenger Car 2-pack, *03*		205
29165	Amtrak Superliner Passenger Car 2-pack, Phase IV, *04*		195
29168	Amtrak Superliner Diner, StationSounds, Phase IV, *04*		200
29169	Alaska Superliner Passenger Car 2-pack, *04*		200
29172	Alaska Superliner Diner, StationSounds, *04*		200
29182	N&W Powhatan Arrow Aluminum Passenger Car 4-pack (std O), *05*		550
29187	N&W Powhatan Arrow Aluminum Passenger Car 2-pack (std O), *05*		290
29190	N&W Powhatan Arrow Aluminum Diner, StationSounds, *05*		290
29191	MILW Hiawatha Passenger Car 4-pack, *06*		370
29196	MILW Hiawatha Passenger Car 2-pack, *06*		190
29199	MILW Hiawatha Diner, StationSounds, *06*		190
29202	Santa Fe Map Boxcar "6464," *97 u*		53
29203	Maine Central Boxcar "6464-597," *97 u*		35
29205	Mickey Mouse Hi-Cube Boxcar "9555," *97*		70
29206	Vapor Records Boxcar #1, *97*		90
29209	Postwar "6464" Boxcar Series VII, 3 cars, *98*		95
29210	GN Boxcar "6464-450," *98*		33
29211	B&M Boxcar "6464-475," *98*		27
29212	Timken Boxcar "6464-500," *98*		28
29213	ATSF Grand Canyon Route 6464 Boxcar "6464-198," *98*		26
29214	Southern 6464 Boxcar "6464-298," *98*		27
29215	Canadian Pacific 6464 Boxcar "6464-398," *98*		26
29217	1997 Toy Fair Airex Boxcar, *97*		78
29218	Vapor Records Boxcar "6464-496," *97 u*		85
29220	Lionel Centennial Series Hi-Cube Boxcar Set, 4 cars, *97*		235
29221	Centennial Series Hi-Cube Boxcar "9697-1," *97*		65
29222	Centennial Series Hi-Cube Boxcar "9697-2," *97*		72
29223	Centennial Series Hi-Cube Boxcar "9697-3," *97*		65
29224	Centennial Series Hi-Cube Boxcar "9697-4," *97*		62
29225	H.O.R.D.E. Music Festival Boxcar, *97*	48	70
29229	Vapor Records Holiday Car, *98*		160
29231	Halloween Animated Boxcar, *98*		42
29233	Conrail PC Overstamped Boxcar "6464-598," *98*		38
29234	Conrail Erie Overstamped Boxcar "6464-698," *98*		32
29235	NYC Boxcar "6464-510," *99*		47
29236	MKT Boxcar "6464-515," *99*		40
29237	M&StL Boxcar "6464-525," *99*		25
29247	Mainline Classic Street Lamps, 3 pieces, *08-16, 18-20*		40

___	**29250**	Phoebe Snow Boxcar "6464-199," 99	41
___	**29251**	BN Boxcar "6464-299," 99	31
___	**29252**	CP Boxcar "6464-399," 99	33
___	**29253**	B&M Boxcar "76032," 99	50
___	**29254**	B&M Boxcar "76033," 99	50
___	**29255**	B&M Boxcar "76034," 99	50
___	**29256**	B&M Boxcar "76035," 99	50
___	**29257**	Southern Boxcar "9464-199," 99	38
___	**29258**	Reading Boxcar "9464-299," 99	36
___	**29259**	NP Bicentennial Boxcar "9464-399," 99	34
___	**29265**	Maine Central Boxcar "8661," 99	36
___	**29266**	Frisco Boxcar "8722," 99	36
___	**29267**	No. 6464 Boxcar 3-pack, Series VIII, 99	85
___	**29268**	Rio Grande Boxcar "63067," 99	40
___	**29271**	Lionel Cola Tractor and Trailer, 98	12
___	**29279**	Conrail Jersey Central Overstamped Boxcar "6464-28X," 99	40
___	**29280**	Conrail LV Overstamped Boxcar "6464-31X," 99	41
___	**29281**	Conrail Overstamped Boxcar 2-pack, 99	70
___	**29282**	Postwar "6464" Boxcar 3-pack, 99	130
___	**29283**	NYC Boxcar, 99	55
___	**29284**	GN Boxcar, 99	40
___	**29285**	Seaboard Boxcar, 99	36
___	**29286**	Overstamped Boxcar 2-pack, 99	65
___	**29287**	NH PC Overstamped Boxcar "6464-29X," 99	18 34
___	**29288**	Conrail Reading Overstamped Boxcar "6464-32X," 99	38
___	**29289**	Postwar "6464" Series IX, 3 cars, 99-00	70
___	**29290**	D&RGW Boxcar "6464-650," 00	41
___	**29291**	ATSF Boxcar "6464-700," 00	38
___	**29292**	NH Boxcar "6464-725," 00	39
___	**29293**	NH Boxcar "6464-425," 99	95
___	**29294**	Hellgate Bridge Boxcar "1900-2000," 99 u	38
___	**29295**	PRR "Don't Stand Me Still" Boxcar "24018," 99-00	65
___	**29296**	PRR "Merchandise" Boxcar "29296," 99-00	65
___	**29297**	PRR "No Damage" Boxcar "47158," 99-00	65
___	**29298**	Lionel Boxcar "6464-2000," 00	46
___	**29300**	50th Anniversary Clear Shell Aquarium Car, 10	85
___	**29301**	Postwar "3662" Transparent Milk Car with platform, 11, 13	155
___	**29302**	Christmas Music Reefer, 10	75
___	**29303**	North Pole Central Crane Car, 10-11	65
___	**29305**	UP Chisholm Trail Stock Car, Cattle Sounds, 11, 13	200
___	**29306**	PRR Hi-Cube Lighted Garland Boxcar, 10-11	70
___	**29309**	GN Pullman-Standard Diesel Freight Set, CC, 13	830
___	**29310**	Marine Science Deep Sea Exhibition Aquarium Car, 11	75
___	**29311**	Strasburg Derrick Car, 11	45
___	**29312**	Santa's Operating Boxcar, 11-12	75
___	**29314**	SP DD Boxcar "214051" (std O), 13-14	75
___	**29317**	CN DD Boxcar "214051" (std O), 13-14	75
___	**29320**	CNJ DD Boxcar "214051" (std O), 13-14	75
___	**29320**	UP Walking Brakeman Car, 2012	
___	**29320**	CNJ Walking Brakeman Car, 14	40
___	**29321**	Ice Skating Aquarium Car, 12	80
___	**29322**	Koi Aquarium Car, 13-14	80
___	**29323**	UP DD Boxcar "500019" (std O), 13-14	75
___	**29324**	Walking Zombie Brakeman Car, 12	80

	MODERN 1970-2021	Mint	
29326	NP "Pig Palace" Operating Stock Car "84144," 12	200	___
29327	Bethlehem Steel Operating Hopper "2025," 12	60	___
29328	Beatles "Nothing is Real" Aquarium Car, 12-13	85	___
29329	Peanuts Halloween Aquarium Car, 12-13	85	___
29333	ATSF 89' Auto Carrier 2-pack (std O), 13-14, 16	220	___
29338	BN 89' Auto Carrier 2-pack (std O), 13-14	220	___
29344	C&NW DD Boxcar "57766" (std O), 13	75	___
29345	ATSF 89' Auto Carrier (std O), 13-14	110	___
29346	Soo Line 89' Auto Carrier 2-pack (std O), 13-16	220	___
29349	SP 89' Auto Carrier 2-pack (std O), 13-16	220	___
29364	NYC Water Level Steam Freight Set, CC, 12-13	1600	___
29365	N&W Pocahontas Steam Passenger Set, CC, 12	1950	___
29366	SP TankSet Diesel Set, CC, 12	850	___
29372	BNSF 89' Auto Carrier "300267" (std O), 13	110	___
29373	CN 89' Auto Carrier "710771" (std O), 13, 16	110	___
29376	Conrail 89' Auto Carrier "964444" (std O), 13	110	___
29377	CP 89' Auto Carrier 2-pack (std O), 13-14, 16	220	___
29380	CSX 89' Auto Carrier "604544" (std O), 13	110	___
29381	GTW 89' Auto Carrier "50450" (std O), 14-15	110	___
29382	UP 89' Auto Carrier "604545" (std O), 13	110	___
29384	DL&W USRA Double-sheathed Boxcar "44153" (std O), 13	70	___
29385	ATSF USRA Double-sheathed Boxcar "39012" (std O), 13	70	___
29386	PRR PS-4 Flatcar with stakes "469614" (std O), 13	70	___
29387	GN PS-4 Flatcar with stakes "629387" (std O), 13	70	___
29400	Bethlehem Steel Slag Car 3-pack (std O), 03	185	___
29404	Bethlehem Steel Hot Metal Car 3-pack (std O), 03	210	___
29408	PRR Coil Car, 01	40	___
29411	Sherwin-Williams Vat Car, 02	35	___
29412	Tabasco Brand Vat Car, 02	36	___
29413	Airex Boat Loader Car "29413," 02	42	___
29414	PRR Evans Auto Loader "480123," 01	56	___
29415	WM Skeleton Log Car 3-pack #2 (std O), 02	90	___
29419	West Side Lumber Skeleton Log Car 3-pack #2 (std O), 02	90	___
29423	Wellspring Capital Management Happy Holidays Vat Car, 03 u	255	___
29424	Meadow River Lumber Skeleton Log Car 3-pack (std O), 03	90	___
29429	Campbell's Soup Vat Car "29429," 03	38	___
29430	Meadow River Lumber Skeleton Log Car 3-pack #2 (std O), 03	90	___
29434	Weyerhauser Skeleton Log Car 3-pack, 05	100	___
29438	Trailer Train Flatcar with 2 UP trailers, 03	60	___
29439	Postwar "6414" Evans Auto Loader, 02	43	___
29441	UP Flatcar "53471" with grader, 02	43	___
29442	CSX Flatcar "600513" with backhoe, 02	43	___
29453	Elk River Lumber Skeleton Log Car 3-pack #2 (std O), 03	90	___
29457	NS Flatcar "157590" with Caterpillar loader, 03	42	___
29458	BNSF Flatcar "922268" with Caterpillar truck, 03	44	___
29459	Water Barrel Car "1878," Archive Collection, 03	40	___
29460	LL Flatcar "3460" with trailers, Archive Collection, 03	39	___
29461	Postwar "6500" Flatcar with red-and-white airplane, 03	32	___
29462	Postwar "6500" Flatcar with white-and-red airplane, 03	31	___
29463	Postwar "6414" Evans Auto Loader, 03	30	___
29464	U.S. Army Vat Car "29464," 04	35	___
29465	U.S. Steel Slag Car 3-pack (std O), 04-05	160	___
29469	U.S. Steel Hot Metal Car 3-pack (std O), 04-05	190	___
29473	Youngstown Sheet & Tube Slag Car 3-pack (std O), 03	150	___

____	29477	Youngstown Sheet & Tube Hot Metal Car 3-pack (std O), *03*	170
____	29481	Cass Scenic Railroad Skeleton Log Car 3-pack (std O), *03*	80
____	29487	Boat-loader with 4 boats, *04*	65
____	29488	Cass Scenic Railroad Skeleton Log Car 3-pack #2 (std O), *04*	90
____	29492	Pickering Lumber Skeleton Log Car 3-pack #1 (std O), *04*	100
____	29496	Pickering Lumber Skeleton Log Car 3-pack #2 (std O), *04*	90
____	29602	Celanese Chemicals 1-D Tank Car, *05*	45
____	29603	Comet 1-D Tank Car, *traditional, 05*	53
____	29604	Meadow Brook Molasses 1-D Tank Car, traditional, *05*	53
____	29606	Elvis Presley Gold Record Transport Car, *04*	120
____	29607	Las Vegas Mint Car, traditional, *05*	58
____	29609	Alien Suspension Car, *06*	60
____	29610	Dixie Honey 1-D Tank Car, *06*	60
____	29611	Sunoco 1-D Tank Car, *06*	60
____	29612	Las Vegas Poker Chip Car, *06*	40
____	29613	Postwar "6463" Rocket Fuel 2-D Tank Car, *06*	75
____	29617	Cities Service Tank Car, *06-07*	48
____	29618	Hooker Chemicals 3-D Tank Car, *07*	60
____	29619	Grave's Formaldehyde 1-D Tank Car, *07*	60
____	29622	Fort Knox Mint Car, lilac, Archive Collection, *07*	60
____	29624	Monopoly Mint Car with money, *08*	65
____	29626	"Case Closed" Mint Car with shredded documents, *08*	109
____	29628	Poinsettia Mint Car, *09*	70
____	29629	AEC Glow-in-the-Dark Tank Car, *09-10*	65
____	29633	Christmas Ornament Lighted Mint Car, *10*	70
____	29634	Federal Reserve Bailout Mint Car, *10*	70
____	29635	Monopoly "Go To Jail" Mint Car, *10*	70
____	29636	Vampire Transport Mint Car, *10-11*	70
____	29637	Candy Cane 2-D Tank Car, *10-11*	55
____	29640	Coca-Cola Tank Car, *10*	65
____	29642	Jolly Rancher 1-D Tank Car, *11*	55
____	29643	Hershey's Syrup 1-D Tank Car, *11*	58
____	29644	ATSF 1-D Tank Car, *11*	55
____	29645	Atlantic City Casino Mint Car, *11*	70
____	29646	Alaska Oil 2-D Tank Car, *11*	50
____	29647	Gingerbread Man Mint Car, *11*	70
____	29649	Lionel SP Smoke Pellets Mint Car, *12-13*	70
____	29650	Cleveland Federal Reserve Mint Car, *11*	70
____	29651	Richmond Federal Reserve Mint Car, *12*	70
____	29654	Boston Federal Reserve Mint Car, *13*	70
____	29655	PRR 16-wheel Flatcar with girders "469846," *12*	75
____	29656	ATSF 16-wheel Flatcar with transformer "90096," *12*	75
____	29671	Smoke Pellet Mint Car #2, *13-15*	70
____	29694	Hershey's Mint Car, *14*	0	95
____	29695	Trailer Set Maxi-Stack Pair "48," *13*	120
____	29697	Santa's Flatcar with submarine, *13*	70
____	29698	Tree Topper Star Transport Car, *13-14*	80
____	29699	Silver and Gold Christmas Mint Car, *13-14*	70
____	29703	PRR Porthole Caboose, *01*	45
____	29708	C&O Bay Window Caboose "8315," *04*	45
____	29709	Pennsylvania N5c Caboose "477938," *04*	40
____	29711	Santa Fe Bay Window Caboose, *05*	60
____	29712	Postwar "2420" Searchlight Caboose, *04*	50
____	29718	N&W Work Caboose, *06*	48

29719	Santa Fe Caboose "6427," Archive Collection, *06*		48 ___
29726	Virginian Caboose "6427," Archive Collection, *06-07*		50 ___
29727	"I Love U.S.A." Bay Window Caboose "1985," *06*		60 ___
29729	Bethlehem Steel Searchlight Caboose, *06*		90 ___
29732	PRR Caboose "477871," *08*		45 ___
29733	White Pass & Yukon Extended Vision Caboose, *09-10*		90 ___
29734	PRR NS Heritage CA-4 Caboose (std O), *10*		95 ___
29735	Conrail NS Heritage CA-4 Caboose (std O), *10*		95 ___
29737	ATSF Bay Window Caboose, traditional, *10-11*		70 ___
29739	B&M Transfer Caboose, *11*		50 ___
29765	TankSet Add-on 3-pack (std O), *12*		240 ___
29771	CN TankSet 2-pack (std O), *12*		160 ___
29774	GATX TankSet 2-pack (std O), *12*		160 ___
29777	Cibro TankSet 2-pack (std O), *12*		160 ___
29786	Bethlehem Steel PS-2 3-bay Hopper (std O), *13*		80 ___
29787	PRR PS-2 3-bay Hopper (std O), *13*		80 ___
29791	Wizard of Oz Anniversary Boxcar, *13-15*		70 ___
29792	Angela Trotta Thomas "Toyland Express" Boxcar, *13*		65 ___
29793	Where the Wild Things Are Boxcar, *13-15*		70 ___
29800	MOW Crane Car, TMCC, *04*		250 ___
29804	UP Crane Car "JPX 250," *CC, 05*		320 ___
29805	Conrail Crane Car "50202," *CC, 05*		320 ___
29806	Weyerhaeuser Log Dump Car, *05*		75 ___
29807	DM&IR Coal Dump Car, *05*		75 ___
29808	Candy Cane Dump Car, *05*		55 ___
29809	Dump Car with presents, *05*		60 ___
29810	Operating Egg Nog Car with platform, *05*		140 ___
29811	Merchant's Despatch Transit Hot Box Reefer "12425," *05*		85 ___
29811	LCCA Merchandise Dispatch Refrigerator Car w/Hot box, *2008u*		110 ___
29812	Santa Fe Hot Box Reefer "20699," *05*		90 ___
29813	Santa Fe Boom Car "19144," Crane Sounds, *05*		210 ___
29814	Pennsylvania Boom Car "491063," Crane Sounds, *05*		210 ___
29815	NYC Boom Car "X923," Crane Sounds, *05*		210 ___
29816	MOW Boom Car "X-816," Crane Sounds, *05*		210 ___
29817	UP Boom Car "909438," Crane Sounds, *05*		210 ___
29818	Conrail Boom Car, Crane Sounds, *05*		210 ___
29821	Postwar "2460" Lionel Lines Crane Car, gray cab, *05*		43 ___
29822	Postwar "773W" NYC Tender, whistle, *05*		48 ___
29823	Postwar "3484" Pennsylvania Operating Boxcar, *05*		38 ___
29827	Postwar "3419" Helicopter Launching Car, *06*		49 ___
29828	Postwar "3666" Minuteman Car with cannon, *06*		85 ___
29829	Postwar "6905" Radioactive Waste Car, *06*		85 ___
29830	PFE Hot Box Reefer "5890" (std O), *06*		105 ___
29831	Swift Hot Box Reefer "15342" (std O), *06*		150 ___
29832	Chessie System Crane Car "940504," *CC, 06*		320 ___
29833	Chessie System Boom Car "940561," *CC, 06*		210 ___
29834	LL Bay Window Caboose "834," TrainSounds (std O), *06-07*		110 ___
29835	SP Bay Window Caboose "4667," TrainSounds (std O), *06-07*		160 ___
29839	Cherry Picker Car, *06*		63 ___
29849	Lionel Lines Crane Car, silver cab, *06*		60 ___
29850	N&W J Class Tender, air whistle, *06-07*		70 ___
29853	Postwar "6651" Big John Cannon Car, *08*		75 ___
29854	Satellite Launching Car, *07*		70 ___
29855	Lionel Lines Operating Milk Car with platform, *07*		140 ___

			Mint
___	29856	Monon Operating Boxcar, 06-07	65
___	29857	Lionel Lines Boom Car, 06-07	55
___	29858	CP Rail Crane Car "414475," CC, 07	320
___	29859	CP Rail Boom Car "412567," CC, 07	210
___	29865	Southern Operating Barrel Car, 07-08	75
___	29866	Pirates Aquarium Car, 07	75
___	29867	NYC Jet Snow Blower "X27207," 07	120
___	29868	Alaska Jet Snow Blower, 07	120
___	29869	Bethlehem Steel Crane Car, 06	60
___	29870	MOW Jet Snow Blower "MWX-16," 07	120
___	29874	Peanuts Halloween Aquarium Car, 12	85
___	29877	Southern Crane Car "D76," CC, 08	350
___	29882	Witches Operating Brew Car, 08	150
___	29884	CNJ Twin Dump Car, 08	85
___	29885	BN Crane Car "S-104," CC, 10	340
___	29886	BN Boom Car "S-1040," CC, 10	220
___	29888	Postwar "3494-625" Soo Lines Operating Boxcar, 08	70
___	29893	PRR Operating Stock Car "129893," RailSounds, 09	150
___	29894	Christmas Chase Gondola, 09	65
___	29895	Christmas Operating Snow Globe Car, 10	75
___	29897	CSX Chessie System Research Car "3440," 11	65
___	29900	"I Love Wisconsin" Boxcar, 01	35
___	29901	"I Love Kentucky" Boxcar, 01	30
___	29902	"I Love Iowa" Boxcar, 01	31
___	29903	"I Love Missouri" Boxcar, 01	31
___	29904	2002 Toy Fair Boxcar, 02	22
___	29906	"I Love Connecticut" Boxcar, 02	33
___	29907	"I Love West Virginia" Boxcar, 02	33
___	29908	"I Love Delaware" Boxcar, 02	33
___	29909	"I Love Maryland" Boxcar, 02	65
___	29910	Toy Fair Centennial Boxcar, 03	40
___	29912	"I Love Alabama" Boxcar, 03	30
___	29913	"I Love Mississippi" Boxcar, 03	35
___	29914	"I Love Louisiana" Boxcar, 03	35
___	29915	"I Love Arkansas" Boxcar, 03	30
___	29918	2003 Toy Fair Boxcar, 03	48
___	29919	2004 Toy Fair Boxcar, 04	37
___	29920	"I Love North Dakota" Boxcar, 03	35
___	29921	"I Love South Dakota" Boxcar, 03	40
___	29922	"I Love Nebraska" Boxcar, 03	30
___	29923	"I Love Kansas" Boxcar, 03	30
___	29924	2004 Lionel Employee Christmas Boxcar, 2004u	110
___	29925	Toy Fair Polar Express Boxcar, 05	250
___	29927	"I Love Washington" Boxcar, 05	45
___	29928	"I Love Oregon" Boxcar, 05	40
___	29929	"I Love Idaho" Boxcar, 05	45
___	29930	"I Love Utah" Boxcar, 05	45
___	29932	"I Love Oklahoma" Boxcar, 06	45
___	29933	"I Love New Mexico" Boxcar, 06	45
___	29934	"I Love Hawaii" Boxcar, 06	45
___	29935	"I Love Alaska" Boxcar, 06	45
___	29936	"I Love Wyoming" Boxcar, 06	45
___	29937	2006 Toy Fair Boxcar, 06	38
___	29942	Santa Fe Railroad Art Boxcar, 06	50

29943	Texas Special Railroad Art Boxcar, *06*		50 ___
29944	1957 Lionel Art Boxcar, *06*		50 ___
29945	1947 Lionel Art Boxcar, *06*		50 ___
29949	Weyerhaeuser Timber Skeleton Log Car 3-pack #2 (std O), *03*		90 ___
29949	2007 Lionel Employee Christmas Boxcar, *2007u*		60 ___
29950	1948 Lionel Art Boxcar, *08*		50 ___
29951	1954 Lionel Art Boxcar, *08*		50 ___
29952	GN Art Boxcar, *08*		50 ___
29953	SP Art Boxcar, *08*		50 ___
29954	Dealer Christmas Boxcar, *07*		75 ___
29954	2007 Lionel Dealer Appreciation Boxcar, *2007u*		30 ___
29955	Dealer Boxcar, *08*		75 ___
29955	2008 Lionel Dealer Appreciation Boxcar, *2008u*		70 ___
29956	2008 Lionel Employee Christmas Boxcar, *2008u*		60 ___
29958	Dealer Boxcar, *09*		50 ___
29958	2009 Lionel Dealer Appreciation Boxcar, *2009u*		40 ___
29959	1952 Lionel Art Boxcar, *09*		58 ___
29960	Rock Island Art Boxcar, *09-10*		58 ___
29961	Meet the Beatles Boxcar 2-pack, *10-14*		130 ___
29965	Lionel Art Boxcar 2-pack, *10-11*		116 ___
29968	Beatles "A Hard Day's Night" Boxcar, *11-14*		65 ___
29969	Beatles "Something New" Boxcar, *11-14*		65 ___
29973	NYC Pacemaker Boxcar "175005," *11*		60 ___
29974	SP Boxcar "128133," *11*		60 ___
29975	Holiday Boxcar, *11*		60 ___
29976	Holiday Boxcar, *12-13*		65 ___
29978	Railroad Museum of Pennsylvania Boxcar, *12*		65 ___
29979	Angela Trotta Thomas "Christmas Morning" Boxcar, *12-13*		60 ___
29980	Elvis Presley 35th Anniversary Boxcar, *12*		70 ___
29982	CV Milk Car "575" (std O), *16*		80 ___
29985	B&M Milk Car "1903" (std O), *16*		80 ___
29989	PFE Steel-sided Refrigerator Car 3-pack (std O), *14-15*		240 ___
29994	U.S. Army Boxcar, *13-15*		70 ___
29995	U.S. Navy Boxcar, *13-15*		70 ___
29996	U.S. Marines Boxcar, *13-15*		70 ___
29997	U.S. Air Force Boxcar, *13-15*		70 ___
29998	U.S. National Guard Boxcar, *13-16*		70 ___
29999	U.S. Coast Guard Boxcar, *13-16*		70 ___
30000	PRR Keystone Super Freight Steam Train, TMCC, *05*		450 ___
30001	Santa Fe El Capitan Passenger Set, TrainSounds, *05-10*		370 ___
30002	Neil Young's Greendale Diesel Freight Set, *04*		420 ___
30003	Pennsylvania Flyer Operating Freight Expansion Pack, *05*		99 ___
30004	Pennsylvania Flyer Passenger Expansion Pack, *05-08*		120 ___
30005	Disney Passenger Train, *05*		190 ___
30007	NYC Flyer Operating Freight Expansion Pack, *05*		99 ___
30008	NYC Flyer Passenger Expansion Pack, *05-08*		120 ___
30011	Holiday Expansion Pack, *05*		100 ___
30012	Thomas the Tank Engine Expansion Pack, *05-13, 16*		150 ___
30016	NYC Flyer Steam Freight Set, *06-08*		290 ___
30018	Pennsylvania Flyer Steam Freight Set, *06-07*		200 ___
30020	North Pole Central Christmas Steam Train, *06-07*		220 ___
30021	Cascade Range Steam Logging Train, *06-08*		190 ___
30022	Southwest Diesel Freight Set, TrainSounds, *06*		295 ___
30024	UP Fast Freight Steam Set, TrainSounds, *06-07*		340 ___

Esc Mint

			Esc	Mint
___	30025	Chesapeake Super Freight Steam Set, TMCC, *06-07*		475
___	30026	CP Diesel Freight Set, TMCC, *06*		540
___	30034	Great Western Train Set with Lincoln Logs, *07-09*		230
___	30035	Sodor Freight Expansion Pack, *06-09*		120
___	30036	Great Western Expansion Pack, *07-08*		120
___	30037	Pennsylvania Flyer Operating Freight Expansion Pack, *06-08*		120
___	30038	NYC Flyer Operating Freight Expansion Pack, *06-08*		120
___	30039	North Pole Central Passenger Expansion Pack, *06-11*		110
___	30040	North Pole Central Freight Expansion Pack, *06-11*		110
___	30041	Southwest Diesel Freight Expansion Pack, *06*		110
___	30042	Cascade Range Expansion Pack, *06*		110
___	30044	NYC Empire Builder Steam Freight Set, TMCC, *06*		2800
___	30045	Alaska Steam Work Train, *07-09*		270
___	30046	Alaska Work Train Expansion Pack, *07-08*		110
___	30047	Northwest Special Diesel Freight Set, TrainSounds, *07-08*		295
___	30048	Northwest Special Freight Expansion Pack, *07-08*		110
___	30049	D&RGW Fast Freight Set, TrainSounds, *08-09*		320
___	30050	Pennsylvania Super Freight Set, *CC, 08*		450
___	30051	UP Diesel Freight Set, TMCC, *07*		500
___	30056	Halloween Steam Freight Set, *07-10*		225
___	30061	UPS Centennial Stream Freight Set, *07-08*		230
___	30063	It's a Wonderful Life Christmas Steam Freight Set		225
___	30064	Pennsylvania Speeder Set, traditional, K-Line, *06*		75
___	30065	Best Friend of Charleston Locomotive, *07*		425
___	30068	North Pole Central Christmas Freight Set, *08*		220
___	30069	Thomas & Friends Passenger Train, *08-12*		170
___	30070	Lionel Lines 4-4-2 Steam Freight Set, *07*		300
___	30076	Disney Christmas Train, *07*		400
___	30081	UP Merger Special GP38 Freight Set, *08*		300
___	30082	UP Heritage Freight Car 3-pack, *08*		100
___	30084	British Great Western Shakespeare Express Passenger Train, *08*		300
___	30085	MTA Metro-North M-7 Commuter Car Set, *07-08*		280
___	30087	Alien Spaceship Recovery Freight Set, *08-09*		230
___	30088	John Bull Passenger Train, *08*		430
___	30089	Pennsylvania Flyer Freight Set, *08-10*		200
___	30091	ATSF Steam Freight Set, *08-09*		270
___	30094	Chicago & North Western Passenger Set, *08*		150
___	30096	Pennsylvania Keystone Special Steam Freight Set, *09*		260
___	30103	NYC 0-8-0 Steam Freight Set, *09-10*		300
___	30108	American Fire and Rescue GP20 Freight Set, *09-10*		400
___	30109	Nutcracker Route Christmas Train Set, *10-11*		270
___	30111	Pullman Passenger Expansion Pack, *09-16*		155
___	30112	Eastern Freight Expansion Pack, *09-17*		155
___	30114	MTA LIRR M-7 Commuter Set, *09*		320
___	30116	Lone Ranger Wild West Freight Set, *09-13*		400
___	30118	A Christmas Story Steam Freight Set, *09-12*		330
___	30120	Menards C&NW Steam Passenger Set, *09*		250
___	30121	ATSF Baby Madison Car 3-pack, *10-11*		190
___	30122	Wizard of Oz Steam Freight Set, *10-12*		310
___	30123	Boy Scouts of America Steam Freight Set, *10*		310
___	30124	Thunder Valley Quarry Steam Freight Set, *10-11*		300
___	30125	Rio Grande Ski Train, TrainSounds, *10-11*		340
___	30126	Pennsylvania Flyer Steam Freight Set, *10*		230
___	30127	Scout Steam Freight Set, *10-12*		200

		Esc	Mint
MODERN 1970-2021			
30128	Western Freight Expansion Pack, *10-12*		138 ___
30131	Chessie System Merger Diesel Freight Set, *10*		300 ___
30133	Strasburg Steam Passenger Set, *10-13*		330 ___
30135	Scout Freight Expansion Pack, *11-15*		115 ___
30136	Thunder Valley Quarry Freight Car Add-on 2-pack, *10-11*		110 ___
30138	Chessie System Merger Freight Car Add-on 2-pack, *10-11*		120 ___
30139	Santa Fe Flyer Steam Freight Set, *10*		270 ___
30141	Sodor Tank and Wagon Expansion Pack, *10-16*		150 ___
30142	Texas Special Freight Set, TrainSounds, *10-11*		700 ___
30144	Operation Eagle Justice Diesel Freight Set, *10-11*		500 ___
30145	Maple Leaf Diesel Freight Set, *10-11*		550 ___
30146	Menards Soo Line Freight Set, *10*	175	275 ___
30147	MTA Long Island M-7 Commuter Set, *11*		320 ___
30153	CSX Diesel Freight Set, *11*		330 ___
30154	BNSF Diesel Freight Set, *11*		340 ___
30155	M&StL Diesel Freight Set, *11-12*		230 ___
30156	NYC Flyer Freight Set, TrainSounds, *11*		300 ___
30157	M&StL Flatcar and Erie-Lack. Gondola 2-pack, *11-15*		110 ___
30158	Norfolk Southern GP38 Diesel Freight Train Set, *11*		320 ___
30159	Wabash Blue Bird Passenger Set, *11-12*		360 ___
30161	Boy Scouts Steam Freight Set, *11-13*		320 ___
30162	Thomas & Friends Christmas Set , *13-15*		200 ___
30164	Santa's Flyer Steam Freight Set, *11-13*		250 ___
30165	Candy Cane Transit Commuter 2-pack, *11-13*		180 ___
30166	Coca-Cola 125th Anniversary Steam Set, *11-12*		350 ___
30167	SP Merger Steam Freight Train Set , *12*		400 ___
30168	Rio Grande General Set, TrainSounds, *11-12*		300 ___
30169	NJ Transit Train Set, *11*		350 ___
30170	Sodor Freight 3-pack, *11-13*		100 ___
30171	GG1 Electric Freight Train Set, *11-13*		550 ___
30173	Santa Fe Flyer Freight Set, *11-12*		270 ___
30174	Pennsylvania Flyer Freight Set, *11-13*		290 ___
30178	ATSF Super Chief Diesel Passenger Train Set, *12-13*		400 ___
30179	RI Rocket Diesel Freight Train Set, *12-13*		400 ___
30180	Horseshoe Curve Steam Freight Train Set, *12-13*		440 ___
30181	CP Diesel Passenger Set, RailSounds, *13, 15*		450 ___
30183	Scout Remote Steam Freight Set , *13, 15*		220 ___
30184	Polar Express Steam Freight Set , *13*		420 ___
30185	NJ Transit Diesel MOW Train Set, *12-13*		350 ___
30186	KCS Southern Belle Diesel Freight Train Set, *12-13*		350 ___
30187	Titanic Centennial Diesel Freight Train Set, *12-13*		450 ___
30188	UP Flyer Steam Freight Train Set, *12-13*		330 ___
30189	LIRR Diesel Passenger Train Set, *12-13*		330 ___
30190	Thomas & Friends Set, LionChief, *12-16*		200 ___
30191	Sodor Work Set 3-pack, *12-15*		100 ___
30193	Peanuts Christmas Steam Freight Set, *12-15*		370 ___
30194	North Pole Express Steam Freight Set, *12-13*		290 ___
30195	Grand Central Express Diesel Passenger Train Set, *12-14*		440 ___
30196	Hershey's Steam Freight Train Set, *12-13*		312 ___
30200	NYC Flyer Steam Freight Train Set, *12-13*		350 ___
30205	Silver Bells Christmas Steam Freight Set, *513-14*		240 ___
30206	Area 51 RS3 Diesel Freight Set, *13*		250 ___
30207	Santa Fe RS3 Diesel Freight Set, *13*		200 ___
30210	CP Rail Grain SetDiesel Freight Set, *13*		390 ___

		Mint
30211	BNSF Maxi Stack Diesel Freight Set, *13*	440
30213	Northeast NS Heritage Diesel Freight Set, *13*	410
30214	Peanuts Halloween Steam Freight Set, *13, 15-16*	320
30217	SP Black Widow Diesel Freight Set, *13, 15*	460
30218	Polar Express Steam Passenger Set, *13-16*	400
30218	Polar Express Steam Passenger Set w/Personalized Tender, LionChief, *18*	440
30219	Gingerbread Junction Steam Freight Set, *13-14*	290
30220	Polar Express 10th Anniversary Passenger Set, *13-14, 16*	500
30221	Diesel Remote Control Set, *13-16*	200
30222	Percy Remote Control Set, *13-15*	200
30223	James Remote Control Set, *13-15*	200
30224	Pennsylvania Limited Steam Passenger Set, *13*	340
30225	Medal of Honor Train, *13*	430
30226	NS Diesel Freight Set, RailSounds, *13*	410
30228	Chattanooga Express Steam Passenger Set, *13*	250
30233	Pennsylvania Flyer Remote Steam Freight Set, *13-17*	280
31569	Western & Atlantic Passenger Car 2-pack, *08*	100
31700	Postwar Girls Freight Set, *01*	570
31701	Postwar Boys Freight Set, *02*	345
31704	Alton Limited Steam Passenger Set, *02*	870
31705	50th Anniversary Hudson Passenger Set, *02*	910
31706	UP Burro Crane Set, *02*	210
31707	C&O Diesel Freight Set, *03*	280
31708	Postwar "1805" Marines Missile Launch Train, *03*	400
31710	BN Diesel Coal Train, RailSounds, *03*	690
31711	Postwar "1563W" Wabash Diesel Freight Set, RailSounds, *03*	570
31712	UP Alco PA Diesel Passenger Set, RailSounds, *03*	1495
31713	Southern Crescent Limited Steam Passenger Set, RailSounds, *03*	1195
31714	Amtrak Acela Diesel Passenger Set, RailSounds, *04-05*	2000
31715	Fire Rescue Steam Freight Set, *02*	300
31716	Fire Rescue Steam Freight Set, *03*	280
31717	CP Rail Snow Removal Train, *03*	255
31718	SP "Oil Can" Tank Train Freight Set, *03*	1600
31719	Western Maryland Fireball Diesel Freight Set, *04*	290
31720	FEC Champion Diesel Passenger Set, RailSounds, *04*	900
31721	Postwar "13138" Majestic Electric Freight Set, RailSounds, *04*	580
31724	Nabisco 3-car Passenger Set, *03*	110
31727	Postwar "2291W" Rio Grande Diesel Freight Set, RailSounds, *04*	640
31728	Elvis "He Dared to Rock" Steam Freight Set, *04*	325
31730	Norman Rockwell Boxcar 4-pack, *05*	95
31733	Jones & Laughlin Steel Slag Train, *05*	250
31734	Chessie Steam Special Passenger Set, TMCC, *05*	405
31735	Chessie Diesel Freight Set, TMCC, *05-06*	670
31736	CP Diesel Grain Train, TMCC, *05*	700
31737	Napa Valley Wine Train, TMCC, *05*	900
31739	Postwar "13150" Hudson Steam Freight Set, Super O, *05*	940
31740	Postwar "2519W" Virginian Diesel Freight Set, TMCC, *05-07*	620
31742	Postwar "2544W" Santa Fe Super Chief Diesel Passenger Set, *05*	700
31746	GN Mountain Mover Steam Freight Set, *12-13*	430
31747	Pennsylvania Electric Ballast Train, TMCC, *06*	550
31748	Santa Fe U28CG Diesel Freight Set (std O), TMCC, *06-07*	770
31749	Pennsylvania Diesel Coal Train, TMCC, *06*	770
31750	NYC Hotbox Reefer Steam Freight Set, TMCC, *06-07*	530

		Esc	Mint
31751	New York City Transit Authority R27 Subway Train, *CC, 07*		700 ___
31752	B&O Diesel Freight Set, TMCC, *06-07*		740 ___
31753	GN Diesel Freight Set, TMCC, *06-08*		740 ___
31754	Postwar "2545WS" N&W Space Freight Set, TMCC, *06-07*		960 ___
31755	Texas Special Diesel Passenger Set, *CC, 07-08*		1280 ___
31757	Postwar "2289WS" Berkshire Freight Set, *CC, 07*		750 ___
31758	Postwar "2270W" Jersey Central Diesel Passenger Car Set, *CC, 08*		750 ___
31760	CSX SD40-2 Diesel Husky Stack Car Set, *CC, 07-08*		770 ___
31765	Postwar "11268" C&O Diesel Freight Set, *08*		580 ___
31767	Bethlehem Steel Rolling Stock Set, K-Line, *06*		100 ___
31768	B&O Rolling Stock Set, K-Line, *06*		100 ___
31772	Conrail LionMaster Diesel Freight Set, *CC, 08-09*		535 ___
31773	NS Dash 9 Diesel TankTrain Set, *CC, 08*		785 ___
31774	AEC Burro Crane Set, traditional, *09-11*		260 ___
31775	"1562" Burlington GP Passenger Set, *08*		470 ___
31776	"2219W" Lackawanna Train Master Freight Set, *08*		415 ___
31777	"2124W" GG1 Passenger Set, *08*		470 ___
31778	"1484WS" Steam Passenger Set, *08*		610 ___
31779	Amtrak HHP-8 Amfleet Passenger Set, *CC, 09*		500 ___
31782	ATSF Crane Car and Boom Car (std O), *CC, 09-10*		560 ___
31783	BNSF Ice Cold Express Diesel Freight Set, *CC, 10*		1000 ___
31784	No. 1593 UP Work Train Set, *09*		470 ___
31787	CN SD70M-2 Diesel Coal Train, *CC, 09*		800 ___
31790	PRR GG1 Passenger Set, *10*		500 ___
31791	NYC LionMaster Diesel Freight Set, *CC, 10*		700 ___
31793	White Pass & Yukon Freight Car Add-on 3-pack, *10-11, 13*		195 ___
31795	Pere Marquette Freight Car 3-pack (std O), *10-11*		210 ___
31796	Feather Route Freight Car 3-pack (std O), *10-11*		210 ___
31797	New York City Transit R16 Subway Set, *CC, 10*		800 ___
31799	GN Empire Steam Freight Express Set, *10*		430 ___
31901	Christmas Steam Freight Set, *02*		145 ___
31902	PRR K4 Freight Set, *01-02*		580 ___
31904	C&O Steam Freight Set, RailSounds, *01*		400 ___
31905	NH Diesel Freight Set, *CC, 01*		660 ___
31907	PRR Atlantic Freight Set, *01 u*		400 ___
31908	Reading Hobo Express Freight Set, *01 u*		365 ___
31909	Santa Fe Shell Tank Car Freight Set, *01 u*		320 ___
31910	Soo Line Diesel Freight Set, *01 u*		365 ___
31911	Snap-On Anniversary Steam Freight Set, *00 u*		615 ___
31913	PRR Flyer Steam Freight Set, *01*		145 ___
31914	NYC Flyer Steam Freight Set, RailSounds, *01-02*		170 ___
31915	Chessie GP38 Diesel Freight Set, *01-02*		155 ___
31916	Santa Fe Steam Freight Set, *01*		300 ___
31918	C&O Steam Freight Set, SignalSounds, *01*		315 ___
31919	T&P Steam Passenger Set, RailSounds, *01*		210 ___
31920	L.L. Bean Freight Set, *01 u*		270 ___
31922	Snap-On Tool Diesel Freight Set, *01 u*		360 ___
31923	PRR Flyer Freight Set, *01 u*		130 ___
31924	Union Pacific RS3 Diesel Freight Set, *02*		95 ___
31926	Area 51 FA Diesel Freight Set, *02*		160 ___
31928	Great Train Robbery Set, *02*		180 ___
31931	Ballyhoo Brothers Circus Train, *02*		190 ___
31932	NYC Limited Passenger Set, RailSounds, *02*		285 ___

		Esc	Mint
____ **31933**	Santa Fe Steam Freight Set, RailSounds, *02*		320
____ **31934**	Lionel 20th Century Express Steam Freight Set, *00 u*		285
____ **31936**	Pennsylvania Flyer Steam Freight Set, *03-05*		190
____ **31938**	Southern Diesel Freight Set, *03-04*		160
____ **31939**	Great Train Robbery Steam Freight Set, *03*		185
____ **31940**	NYC Flyer Steam Freight Set, RailSounds, *03*		225
____ **31941**	Winter Wonderland Railroad Christmas Train, *03*		150
____ **31942**	Norman Rockwell Christmas Train, *03*		330
____ **31944**	NYC Limited Diesel Passenger Set, RailSounds, *03*		250
____ **31945**	Santa Fe Steam Super Freight Set, RailSounds, *03*		350
____ **31946**	Disney Christmas Steam Train, *04-05*		310
____ **31947**	World of Disney Steam Freight Set, *03*		215
____ **31950**	Kraft Holiday UP RS3 Diesel Freight Set, *02 u*		149
____ **31952**	Great Northern Glacier Route Diesel Freight Set, *03-04*		110
____ **31953**	"Riding the Rails" Hobo Train Set, *03-04*		225
____ **31956**	Thomas the Tank Engine Set, *04-07*		195
____ **31958**	Santa Fe Flyer Steam Freight Set, RailSounds, *04*		205
____ **31960**	Polar Express Steam Passenger Set, *04-13*		420
____ **31961**	Bloomingdale's Pennsylvania Flyer Steam Freight Set, *02 u*		160
____ **31962**	Nickel Plate Road Super Freight Set, RailSounds, *04*		350
____ **31963**	Southern Pacific Overnight Steam Freight Set, *04*		340
____ **31966**	Holiday Tradition Steam Freight Set, *04-05*		210
____ **31969**	NYC Flyer Steam Freight Set, RailSounds, *04*		205
____ **31976**	Yukon Special Diesel Freight Set, *05*		225
____ **31977**	New York Central Flyer Steam Freight Set, *05*		250
____ **31985**	Santa Fe Steam Fast Freight Set, TrainSounds, *05*		320
____ **31987**	Mickey's Holiday Express Train, *04*		280
____ **31989**	UP Overland Freight Express Set, *04*		880
____ **31990**	Copper Range Steam Freight Mine Set, *05*		175
____ **31993**	NS Black Diamond Diesel Freight Set, TMCC, *05*		500
____ **32900**	DC Billboard, *99*		24
____ **32902**	Construction Zone Signs, set of 6, *99-19*		10
____ **32904**	Hellgate Bridge, *99*	235	415
____ **32905**	Irvington Factory, *99-00*		295
____ **32910**	Rotary Coal Tipple with bathtub gondola, *02*		442
____ **32919**	Animated Maiden Rescue, *99*		65
____ **32920**	Animated Pylon with airplane, *99*		130
____ **32921**	Electric Coaling Station, *99-01*		125
____ **32922**	Highway Barrels, set of 6, *99-18, 20*		10
____ **32923**	Accessory Transformer, *99-03, 06-16*		46
____ **32929**	Icing Station with Santa, *99*		90
____ **32930**	Power Supply Set with ZW controller and 2 power supplies, *99-02, 06-09*	240	425
____ **32933**	Christmas Stocking Hanger Set, 4-piece, *99-00*		50
____ **32934**	Stocking Hanger, gondola, *99-00*		15
____ **32935**	Stocking Hanger, boxcar, *99-00*		15
____ **32960**	Hindenburger Cafe, *99*		195
____ **32961**	Route 66 UFO Cafe, *99*		200
____ **32987**	Hobo Campfire, *99-00*	25	45
____ **32988**	Postwar "192" Railroad Control Tower, *99-00*		75
____ **32989**	Postwar "464" Sawmill, *99-00*		75
____ **32990**	Linex Oil Derrick, *99-00*		55
____ **32991**	WLLC Radio Station, *99*		75
____ **32996**	Postwar "362" Barrel Loader, *00*		125

	MODERN 1970-2021	Esc	Mint
32997	Aluminum Rico Station, *00*		300 ___
32998	Hobby Shop, *99-00*		300 ___
32999	Hellgate Bridge, *99-00*		400 ___
33000	GP9 Diesel "3000," RailScope video camera system, *88-90*	125	170 ___
33002	RailScope Television Monitor, *88-90*	45	70 ___
34102	Amtrak Shelter, *04-08*		25 ___
34108	Lionelville Suburban House, *03*		20 ___
34109	Lionelville Large Suburban House, *03*		15 ___
34110	Lionelville Estate House, *03*		30 ___
34111	Lionelville Deluxe Fieldstone House, *03*		17 ___
34112	Lionelville Fieldstone House, *03*		17 ___
34113	Lionelville Large Suburban House, *03*		17 ___
34114	Late Illuminated Station and Terrace, red trim, *03*		475 ___
34117	Early Illuminated Station and Terrace, green trim, *03*		475 ___
34120	TMCC Direct Lockon, *04-16, 18-19*		56 ___
34121	Lionelville Bungalow, *04*		20 ___
34122	Lionelville Bungalow with garage, *04*		20 ___
34123	Lionelville Bungalow with addition, *04*		20 ___
34124	Lionelville Anastasia's Bakery, *04*		20 ___
34125	Lionelville Cotton's Candy, *04*		20 ___
34126	Lionelville Market, *04*		20 ___
34127	Lionelville O'Grady's Tavern, *04*		22 ___
34128	Lionelville Pharmacy, *04*		15 ___
34129	Lionelville Kiddie City Toy Store, *04*		20 ___
34130	Lionelville Jim's 5&10, *04*		25 ___
34131	Lionelville Al's Hardware, *04*		30 ___
34144	Santa Fe Scrap Yard, *05-06*		80 ___
34145	New Haven Scrap Yard, *06*		100 ___
34149	Sly Fox and the Hunter, *05-07*		80 ___
34150	Reading Room, *05-06*		70 ___
34158	Ring Toss Midway Game, *05-06*		20 ___
34159	Camel Race Midway Game, *05-06*		20 ___
34162	Operating Oil Pump, *04-09*		53 ___
34163	Speeder Shed, *04-06*		30 ___
34164	Nutcracker Operating Gateman, *05-08*		80 ___
34190	Carousel, *04-06*		165 ___
34191	Hobo Depot, *04-05*		70 ___
34192	Operating Lumberjacks, *04-06*		60 ___
34193	UPS Animated Billboard, *04*		30 ___
34194	UPS Package Station, *05*		120 ___
34195	UPS People Pack, *06-09, 11*		27 ___
34210	TMCC Direct Lockon, *09*		52 ___
34359	2011 Lionel Dealer Appreciation Boxcar, *2011u*		40 ___
34360	2012 Lionel Dealer Appreciation Boxcar, *2012u*		40 ___
34500	Rio Grande FT Diesel "5484," traditional, *06*		245 ___
34501	Southern FT Diesel "4102," traditional, *06*		400 ___
34504	B&O F3 Diesel A Unit "2368," nonpowered, *06-07*		200 ___
34505	B&O E7 Diesel AA Set, *CC, 07*		700 ___
34508	PRR E7 Diesel AA Set, *CC, 07*		700 ___
34509	PRR E7 Diesel B Unit, nonpowered (std O), *07*		170 ___
34510	PRR E7 Diesel B Unit, powered, *CC, 07*		300 ___
34511	NYC F7 Diesel ABA Set, *CC, 07-08*		900 ___
34512	NYC F7 Diesel B Unit "2439," powered, *CC, 07-08*		300 ___
34513	WP F7 Diesel ABA Set, *CC, 07-08*		900 ___

		Esc	Mint
____ 34514	WP F7 Diesel B Unit "918C," powered, *CC, 07-08*		300
____ 34515	NYC F7 Diesel Breakdown B Unit "2440," RailSounds, *07*		270
____ 34518	PRR E7 Diesel Breakdown B Unit, RailSounds, *07*		270
____ 34519	NYC Sharknose RF-16 Diesel AA Set, *CC, 07-08*		630
____ 34520	NYC Sharknose Diesel B Unit "3818," nonpowered (std O), *07-08*		160
____ 34521	Santa Fe F3 Diesel A Unit "17," traditional, *07*		265
____ 34522	Santa Fe F3 Diesel B Unit "17," nonpowered (std O), *07*		150
____ 34544	ATSF F3 Diesel B Unit, *CC, 08*		270
____ 34545	D&RGW F3 Diesel B Unit, *CC, 08*		270
____ 34546	Southern F3 Diesel B Unit, *CC, 08*		270
____ 34547	Texas Special F3 Diesel B Unit, *CC, 08*		270
____ 34559	Archive New Haven F3 Diesel AA Set, *10*		500
____ 34564	SP Alco PA Diesel AA Set, *CC, 10-11*		750
____ 34567	SP Alco PB B Unit, *CC, 10-11*		400
____ 34568	ATSF Alco PA AA Diesel Set, *CC, 11*		750
____ 34569	ATSF Alco PB Diesel, *CC, 11*		400
____ 34570	B&O FA Diesel AA Set, *CC, 10*		650
____ 34573	Postwar Scale ATSF F3 AA Diesel Set, *CC, 11*		700
____ 34576	Postwar Scale NYC F3 AA Diesel Set, *CC, 11*		700
____ 34579	Postwar Scale ATSF F3 B Unit, *CC, 11*		380
____ 34580	Postwar Scale NYC F3 B Unit, *CC, 11*		380
____ 34581	Postwar "2331" Virginian Train Master Diesel, *CC, 10*		495
____ 34582	Postwar "2373" CP F3 Diesel AA Set, *CC, 10*		700
____ 34585	Postwar "2375" CP F3 B Unit, *CC, 10*		380
____ 34586	Postwar "2378" MILW F3 Diesel AB Set, *CC, 10*		700
____ 34589	Postwar "2377" MILW F3 A, powered, *CC, 10*		425
____ 34594	UP Alco PA AA Diesel Set, *CC, 11*		750
____ 34597	UP Alco PB Diesel, *CC, 11*		400
____ 34600	SP GP30 Diesel "5010," *CC, 11*		500
____ 34601	SP GP30 Diesel "5012," *CC, 11*		500
____ 34602	SP GP30 Diesel "5014," *11*		380
____ 34603	SP GP30 Diesel "5017," nonpowered, *11*		240
____ 34604	Conrail GP30 Diesel "2178," *CC, 11*		500
____ 34605	Conrail GP30 Diesel "2180," *CC, 11*		500
____ 34606	Conrail GP30 Diesel "2182," *11*		380
____ 34607	Conrail GP30 Diesel "2185," nonpowered, *11*		240
____ 34608	Lionelville & Western GP30 Diesel "1100," *CC, 11*		450
____ 34609	Lionelville & Western GP30 Diesel "1103," *CC, 11*		450
____ 34610	Lionelville & Western GP30 Diesel "1107," *11*		330
____ 34611	Lionelville & Western GP30 Diesel "1112," nonpowered, *11*		190
____ 34612	NS SD70M-2 Diesel "2658," *CC, 11*		550
____ 34613	NS SD70M-2 Diesel "2663," *CC, 11*		550
____ 34614	CN SD70M-2 Diesel "8020," *CC, 11*		550
____ 34615	CN SD70M-2 Diesel "8024," *CC, 11*		550
____ 34616	FEC SD70M-2 Diesel "101," *CC, 11*		550
____ 34617	FEC SD70M-2 Diesel "103," *CC, 11*		550
____ 34618	George Bush SD70ACe Diesel "4141," *CC, 11*		550
____ 34619	NH SD70ACe Diesel "8696," *CC, 11*		550
____ 34620	NH SD70ACe Diesel "8699," *CC, 11*		550
____ 34623	Texas Special SD70ACe Diesel "6340," *CC, 11*		550
____ 34624	Texas Special SD70ACe Diesel "6344," *CC, 11*		550
____ 34625	NP F3 AA Diesel Set, *CC, 11*		700
____ 34628	NP F3 Diesel B Unit "6005C," *CC, 11*		380
____ 34629	NP F3 Diesel B Unit "6006C," nonpowered, *11*		240

		Esc	Mint
34630	Frisco F3 AA Diesel Set, *CC, 11*		700 ___
34633	Frisco F3 Diesel B Unit, *CC, 11*		380 ___
34634	Frisco F3 Diesel B Unit, nonpowered, *11*		260 ___
34635	ATSF F3 AA Diesel Set, *CC, 11*		700 ___
34638	ATSF F3 Diesel B Unit, *CC, 11*		380 ___
34639	ATSF F3 Diesel B Unit, nonpowered, *11*		240 ___
34640	GTW F3 AA Diesel Set, *CC, 11*		700 ___
34643	GTW F3 Diesel B Unit, *CC, 11*		380 ___
34644	GTW F3 Diesel B Unit, nonpowered, *11*		260 ___
34645	CN F3 AA Diesel Set, *CC, 11*		700 ___
34648	CN F3 Diesel B Unit, *CC, 11*		380 ___
34649	CN F3 Diesel B Unit, nonpowered, *11*		260 ___
34650	MILW DD35A Diesel "1535," *CC, 11*		600 ___
34651	MILW DD35A Diesel "1537," nonpowered, *11*		440 ___
34662	RI GP9 Diesel "1331," *CC, 12-13*		480 ___
34663	RI GP9 Diesel "1327," *CC, 12-13*		480 ___
34664	GN GP9 Diesel "688," *CC, 12-13*		480 ___
34665	GN GP9 Diesel "695," *CC, 12-13*		480 ___
34666	L&N GP9 Diesel "504," *CC, 12-13*		480 ___
34667	L&N GP9 Diesel "525," *CC, 12-13*		480 ___
34668	CN GP90 Diesel "4463," *CC, 12*		480 ___
34669	CN GP90 Diesel "4455," *CC, 12*		480 ___
34670	C&O GP9 Diesel "6240," *CC, 12-13*		480 ___
34671	C&O GP9 Diesel "6243," *CC, 12*		480 ___
34672	PRR Baldwin Centipede Diesel AA, *CC, 12-13*		2200 ___
34673	UP Baldwin Centipede Diesel AA, *CC, 12*		2200 ___
34676	PRR Baldwin Centipede Diesel "5821," *CC, 12-14*		1100 ___
34677	Seaboard Baldwin Centipede Diesel "4503," *CC, 12-14*		1100 ___
34680	NdeM Baldwin Centipede Diesel "6402," *CC, 12-14*		1100 ___
34681	UP GP9 Diesel "256," *CC, 12*		480 ___
34682	UP GP9 Diesel "261," *CC, 12*		480 ___
34683	PRR Baldwin Centipede Diesel AA, *CC, 12-13*		2200 ___
34686	Baldwin Demonstrator Centipede AA, *CC, 12*		2200 ___
34689	WM F7 AA Diesel Set, *CC, 12-13*		730 ___
34692	WM F7 B Unit "410," *CC, 12-13*		400 ___
34693	WM F7 B Unit, *12-13*		250 ___
34694	L&N F7 AA Diesel Set, *CC, 12*		730 ___
34697	L&N F7 B Unit "900," *CC, 12-13*		400 ___
34698	L&N F7 B Unit, *12-13*		250 ___
34701	PRR Baldwin RF-16 Diesel AA Set, *CC, 12-14*		730 ___
34704	PRR Baldwin RF-16 Diesel B Unit, *CC, 12-14*		400 ___
34705	PRR Baldwin RF-16 Diesel B Unit, nonpowered, *12-14*		250 ___
34731	NH Alco RS-11 Diesel "1413," nonpowered, *12*		240 ___
34732	LV Alco RS-11 Diesel "7640," *CC, 12*		480 ___
34733	LV Alco RS-11 Diesel "7642," *CC, 12*		480 ___
34734	LV Alco RS-11 Diesel "7643," nonpowered, *12*		240 ___
34735	ATSF GP9 Diesel "726," *CC, 12*		480 ___
34736	ATSF GP9 Diesel "741," *CC, 12*		480 ___
34737	NP GP9 Diesel "202," *CC, 12*		480 ___
34738	NP GP9 Diesel "317," *CC, 12-13*		480 ___
34739	RI GP9 Diesel "1325," nonpowered, *12*		240 ___
34740	GN GP9 Diesel "668," nonpowered, *12*		240 ___
34741	L&N GP9 Diesel "531," nonpowered, *12*		240 ___
34742	CN GP90 Diesel "4527," nonpowered, *12*		240 ___

| --- | --- | --- | --- |
___	**34743** C&O GP9 Diesel "6249," nonpowered, *12*		240
___	**34744** UP GP9 Diesel "268," nonpowered, *12*		240
___	**34745** Monon Alco C-420 Diesel "509," *CC, 12-13*		530
___	**34746** Monon Alco C-420 Diesel "512," *CC, 12-13*		530
___	**34747** Monon Alco C-420 Diesel "514," nonpowered, *12-13*		260
___	**34748** LV Alco C-420 Diesel "404," *CC, 12*		530
___	**34749** LV Alco C-420 Diesel "412," *CC, 12*		530
___	**34750** LV Alco C-420 Diesel "414," nonpowered, *12*		260
___	**34754** Alaska Alco C-420 Diesel "1210," *CC, 12*		530
___	**34755** Alaska Alco C-420 Diesel "1214," *CC, 12*		530
___	**34756** Alaska Alco C-420 Diesel "1217," nonpowered, *12*		260
___	**34757** Seaboard Alco C-420 Diesel "127," *CC, 12-13*		530
___	**34758** Seaboard Alco C-420 Diesel "129," *CC, 12-13*		530
___	**34759** Seaboard Alco C-420 Diesel "134," nonpowered, *12-13*		260
___	**34760** NKP Alco C-420 Diesel "578," *CC, 12-13*		530
___	**34761** NKP Alco C-420 Diesel "575," *CC, 12-13*		530
___	**34762** NKP Alco C-420 Diesel "572," nonpowered, *12-13*		260
___	**34763** CNJ Scale NW2 Diesel Switcher "1060," *CC, 12*		470
___	**34764** CNJ Scale NW2 Diesel Switcher "1061," *CC, 12*		470
___	**34765** KCS Scale NW2 Diesel Switcher "1221," *CC, 12*		470
___	**34766** KCS Scale NW2 Diesel Switcher "1224," *CC, 12*		470
___	**34767** L&N Scale NW2 Diesel Switcher "2203," *CC, 12*		470
___	**34768** L&N Scale NW2 Diesel Switcher "2206," *CC, 12*		470
___	**34769** MKT Scale NW2 Diesel Switcher "8," *CC, 12*		470
___	**34770** MKT Scale NW2 Diesel Switcher "12," *CC, 12*		470
___	**34771** Reading Scale NW2 Diesel Switcher "102," *CC, 12*		470
___	**34772** Reading Scale NW2 Diesel Switcher "104," *CC, 12*		470
___	**34773** PRR Scale NW2 Diesel Switcher "9163," *CC, 12*		470
___	**34774** PRR Scale NW2 Diesel Switcher "9171," *CC, 12*		470
___	**34775** N&W SD40-2 Diesel "6106," nonpowered, *12-13*		240
___	**34776** N&W SD40-2 Diesel "6121," *CC, 12-13*		530
___	**34777** N&W SD40-2 Diesel "6109," *CC, 12-14*		530
___	**34778** CSX SD40-2 Diesel "8023," nonpowered, *12-13*		240
___	**34779** CSX SD40-2 Diesel "8028," *CC, 12-13*		530
___	**34780** CSX SD40-2 Diesel "8033," *CC, 12-13*		530
___	**34781** BN SD40-2 Diesel "7140," nonpowered, *12-13*		240
___	**34782** BN SD40-2 Diesel "7153," *CC, 12-13*		530
___	**34783** BN SD40-2 Diesel "7162," *CC, 12-13*		530
___	**34784** Frisco SD40-2 Diesel "957," *CC, 12-13*		530
___	**34785** Frisco SD40-2 Diesel "950," nonpowered, *12-13*		240
___	**34786** Frisco SD40-2 Diesel "952," *CC, 12-13*		530
___	**34787** C&NW SD40-2 Diesel "6816," nonpowered, *12-13*		240
___	**34788** C&NW SD40-2 Diesel "6820," *CC, 12-13*		530
___	**34789** C&NW SD40-2 Diesel "6832," *CC, 12-13*		530
___	**34790** MKT SD40-2 Diesel "602," nonpowered, *12-13*		240
___	**34791** MKT SD40-2 Diesel "609," *CC, 12-13*		530
___	**34792** MKT SD40-2 Diesel "620," *CC, 12-13*		530
___	**35100** NYC Vista Dome Car "7012," *07-09*		45
___	**35101** NYC Baggage Car "5028," *07*		40
___	**35102** Santa Fe El Capitan Streamliner Diner, *07*		65
___	**35124** Alton Limited Madison Passenger Car 4-pack, *08-10*		240
___	**35128** ATSF El Capitan Baggage Car "2103," *08*		70
___	**35129** ATSF El Capitan Vista Dome Car "3153," *08*		70
___	**35130** Polar Express Disappearing Hobo Car, *08-14, 16-17*		75

		Esc	Mint
35133	MTA Metro-North M-7 Commuter Add-on 2-pack, *07-08*		85 ___
35134	North Pole Central Vista Dome Car, *08*		45 ___
35135	North Pole Central Diner, *08-10*		45 ___
35167	PRR Diner "2044," *10*		52 ___
35168	PRR Coach "4046," *09*		52 ___
35173	North Pole Central Blitzen Coach, *09*		45 ___
35174	MTA LIRR M-7 Add-on 2-pack, *09*		98 ___
35184	Western & Atlantic Baggage Car, *09*		60 ___
35185	Great Western Passenger Car 2-pack, *09*		100 ___
35193	PRR Streamliner 4-pack, *10-11*		250 ___
35200	Strasburg Observation Car, *10*		60 ___
35205	D&RGW Pikes Peak Add-on Coach, *10-11*		70 ___
35211	Strasburg Passenger Car Add-on 2-pack, *10*		100 ___
35214	Rio Grande Winter Park Diner, *11*		70 ___
35219	Hallow's Eve Express Passenger Car 2-pack, *11*		120 ___
35229	Hogwarts Express Dementors Coach, *11-15*		60 ___
35239	NJ Transit 2-pack Passenger Car Add-on, *11-14*		100 ___
35247	Grand Central Express Passenger Car 2-pack, *12-13*		140 ___
35250	North Pole Coach 2-pack, *12-13*		120 ___
35256	Hallow's Eve Express Passenger Car 2-pack #2, *12*		120 ___
35257	ATSF Vista Dome, *12*		70 ___
35258	ATSF Baggage Car, *12-13*		70 ___
35259	LIRR Passenger Car 2-pack, *12-15*		110 ___
35281	ATSF Super Chief Diner "1495," *13*		70 ___
35282	LIRR Jamaica Coach, *13-15*		60 ___
35283	CP Baggage Car and Diner 2-pack, *13*		130 ___
35286	Peanuts Coach 3-pack, *13*		165 ___
35290	Polar Express Passenger Car Add-on 2-pack, *13-14, 16*		150 ___
35293	Angela Trotta Thomas "Toyland Express" Boxcar, *13*		45 ___
35294	Polar Express Snow Tower, *13-14*		28 ___
35295	Christmas Billboard Set, *13-14, 16*		13 ___
35403	NYC 20th Century Limited 18" Aluminum Passenger Car 4-pack (std O), *08*		625 ___
35408	NYC 20th Century Limited 18" Aluminum Passenger Car 2-pack (std O), *08*		325 ___
35411	NYC 20th Century Limited Diner, StationSounds (std O), *08*		325 ___
35412	Lenny Dean Passenger Coach, *08*		100 ___
35413	LL Streamliner Car 2-pack, *08*		270 ___
35415	UP 18" Streamliner Car 4-pack (std O), *08*		625 ___
35423	UP 18" Streamliner Car 2-pack (std O), *08*		325 ___
35430	Amtrak Coach		45 ___
35431	Amtrak Coach		45 ___
35432	Amtrak Coach		45 ___
35433	Amfleet Phase IVB Coach 2-pack (std O), *10*		140 ___
35445	SP Shasta Daylight 18" Passenger Car 4-pack (std O), *11*		640 ___
35446	SP Shasta Daylight 18" Passenger Car 2-pack (std O), *11*		320 ___
35454	Amfleet Cab Control End Car (std O), *10*		250 ___
35473	Amfleet Capstone Coach 3-pack (std O), *10*		180 ___
35481	NYC Add-on Passenger Car "M-498," *11*		120 ___
35490	Alaska Budd RDC Combination Car "702," nonpowered, *11*		130 ___
35497	RI Budd RDC Combination Car "751," nonpowered, *11*		130 ___
35498	RI Budd RDC Coach "750," nonpowered, *11*		130 ___
35499	Alaska Budd RDC Coach "712," nonpowered, *11*		130 ___
36000	Route 66 Flatcar with 2 red sedans, *98*		44 ___

		Esc	Mint
___ 36001	Route 66 Flatcar with 2 wagons, *98*		42
___ 36002	Pratt's Hollow Passenger Car 4-pack, *98*		445
___ 36006	Uranium Flatcar "6508," *99*		60
___ 36016	Flatcar with propellers, *98*		45
___ 36020	Flatcar "TT-6424" with auto frames, *99*		32
___ 36021	Alaska Flatcar "6424" with airplane, *99*		44
___ 36024	J.B. Hunt Flatcar "64245" with trailer, *99*		44
___ 36025	J.B. Hunt Flatcar "64246" with trailer, *99*		50
___ 36026	Flatcar with J.B. Hunt trailers 2-pack, *99*		85
___ 36027	Tredegar Iron Works Flatcar with cannon, *99*		45
___ 36028	Heavy Artillery Flatcar with cannon, *99*		45
___ 36029	SP Auto Carrier "516712," *99*		44
___ 36030	Troublesome Truck #1, *99*		35
___ 36031	Troublesome Truck #2, *99*		35
___ 36032	Christmas Gondola "6462" with presents, *99*		35
___ 36036	C&O Gondola, *99*		20
___ 36038	Construction Zone Gondola, *99 u*		NRS
___ 36040	Bethlehem Flatcar with block (SSS), *99*		75
___ 36041	Bethlehem Ore Car (SSS), *99*		40
___ 36043	Custom Consist Flatcar with pickup truck, *99*		40
___ 36044	Custom Consist Flatcar with dragster, *99*		40
___ 36045	Flatcar with dragster, *04*		30
___ 36046	Flatcar with custom truck, *04*		30
___ 36047	Construction Zone Gondola, *99 u*		NRS
___ 36048	Construction Zone Gondola, *99 u*		NRS
___ 36054	Archaeological Expedition Gondola with eggs, *00 u*		55
___ 36055	Flatcar with dragster, *01 u*		30
___ 36056	Flatcar with roadster, *01 u*		30
___ 36059	"Season's Greetings" Gondola, *99 u*		50
___ 36062	NYC 6462 Gondola, *99-00*		22
___ 36063	Conrail Gondola "604768," *99-00*		20
___ 36064	Billboard Flatcar "6424," *00*		41
___ 36065	Wabash Flatcar "25536" with trailer, *00*		35
___ 36066	Christmas Gondola with presents, *00*		32
___ 36067	King Auto Sales Flatcar "6424" with pink Cadillac, *00*		40
___ 36068	Pine Peak Tree Transport Gondola, *00*		NRS
___ 36079	Service Station Ltd. Flatcar with trailer, *00*		34
___ 36082	Whirlpool Flatcar with trailer, *00 u*		NRS
___ 36083	Santa Fe Gondola "168998," *01*		17
___ 36084	Grand Trunk Western Coil Car, *00*		32
___ 36085	FEC Coil Car, *00*		29
___ 36086	SP Flatcar with trailer, *01*	34	35
___ 36087	Flatcar "6424" with wooden whistle, *01*		25
___ 36088	Allis Chalmers Condenser Car "6519," *00*		43
___ 36089	Frisco Flatcar with airplane, *00*		35
___ 36090	TT Flatcar "6424" with Pepsi truck, *01*		44
___ 36091	Maersk Flatcar "250129" with die-cast tractors, *00*		55
___ 36092	Maersk Flatcar "250130" with die-cast frames, *00*		55
___ 36093	Soo TT Auto Carrier "906760," *00*		49
___ 36094	PC F9 Well Car "768122," *01*		41
___ 36095	Christmas Chase Gondola, *01*		37
___ 36098	PRR Gondola "385186," *01*		20
___ 36099	NYC Flatcar with stakes and bulkheads, *01*		25
___ 36104	Area 51 3-D Tank Car, *07*		60

		Esc	Mint
36108	Candy Cane 1-D Tank Car, *07*		60 ___
36112	NP 3-D Tank Car, *08*		35 ___
36113	IC 1-D Tank Car, *08*		35 ___
36114	ART Wood-sided Reefer, *08*		35 ___
36117	Lionel Lines 2-D Tank Car, *08*		50 ___
36118	NYC Pastel Stock Car "63561," *08-09*		55 ___
36128	Texas & Pacific 3-D Tank Car, *09*		40 ___
36129	British Columbia 1-D Tank Car, *09*		40 ___
36131	Lackawanna Wood-sided Reefer "7000," *09-10*		40 ___
36145	Philadelphia Quartz 3-D Tank Car "606," *10*		40 ___
36146	Cities Service 1-D Tank Car "11800," *10*		40 ___
36149	Strasburg Wood-sided Reefer "105," *10*		55 ___
36151	Grave's Blood Bank Tank Car, *10*		50 ___
36156	Pennsylvania Power & Light 1-D Tank Car, *10*		40 ___
36162	Diamond Chemicals 3-D Tank Car, *11*		40 ___
36163	Celanese 2-D Tank Car, *11-12*		40 ___
36166	Polar Express Reefer, *11-12*		55 ___
36169	Coca-Cola 3-D Tank Car, *11*		55 ___
36170	Partridge in a Pear Tree Reefer, *11-13*		55 ___
36172	Bubble Yum 1-D Tank Car, *11*		55 ___
36173	Santa's Flyer Hot Cocoa 3-D Tank Car, *11*		40 ___
36176	C&O 1-D Tank Car, *13*		43 ___
36177	WP 3-D Tank Car, *12*		40 ___
36178	Frisco 2-D Tank Car, *12-13*		40 ___
36182	Eggnog Unibody 1-D Tank Car, *12*		70 ___
36191	GN Waffle-sided Boxcar, *13*		43 ___
36195	PRR Flatcar with patrol helicopter, *13*		60 ___
36200	Quaker Life Cereal Boxcar, *00*		500 ___
36203	Whirlpool Boxcar, *00 u*		150 ___
36205	eBay Boxcar, *00*		275 ___
36206	REA Boxcar, *01*		25 ___
36207	Vapor Records Christmas Boxcar, *01*		80 ___
36208	Father's Day Boxcar, *00*		35 ___
36210	Burlington Hi-Cube Boxcar "19825," *01*		40 ___
36211	NP Hi-Cube Boxcar "659999," *01*		33 ___
36212	Lionel Employee Christmas Boxcar, *00 u*		410 ___
36213	Vapor Records Christmas Boxcar, *00*		50 ___
36215	Train Station 25th Anniversary Boxcar, *00 u*		48 ___
36218	Snap-On Boxcar, *00 u*		150 ___
36219	UP Boxcar "183518," *02*		78 ___
36220	Pioneer Seed Boxcar, *00 u*		NRS ___
36221	PRR Boxcar "569356," *01*		20 ___
36222	NYC Boxcar "162440," *01*		20 ___
36223	Chessie System Boxcar, *01*		20 ___
36224	Santa Fe Boxcar "16263," *01*		20 ___
36225	C&O Boxcar "250549," *01*		20 ___
36226	E-Hobbies Boxcar, *01 u*		200 ___
36227	Monopoly Community Chest Boxcar, *00 u*		50 ___
36228	Lionel Visitor Center Boxcar, *01 u*		34 ___
36229	Island Trains 20th Anniversary Boxcar, *01 u*		29 ___
36232	Farmall Boxcar, *01 u*		NRS ___
36236	TM Books "I Love Lionel" Boxcar "7474-1," *01 u*		43 ___
36238	Snap-On Tool Team ASE Racing Boxcar, *01 u*		NRS ___
36239	L.L. Bean Boxcar, *01 u*		150 ___

			Esc	Mint
	MODERN 1970-2021			
___	36240	Do It Best Boxcar, *01 u*		100
___	36242	Erie-Lackawanna Boxcar "73113," *02*		24
___	36243	Christmas Boxcar "2002," *02*		31
___	36244	Teddy Bear Centennial Boxcar, *02*		36
___	36245	Lionel 20th Century Boxcar "1900-1925," *00 u*		30
___	36246	Lionel 20th Century Boxcar "1926-1950," *00 u*		30
___	36247	Lionel 20th Century Boxcar "1951-1975," *00 u*		30
___	36248	Lionel 20th Century Boxcar "1976-2000," *00 u*		30
___	36250	NYC Early Bird Boxcar, *04*		20
___	36253	Christmas Boxcar (O), *03*		32
___	36254	Goofy Hi-Cube Boxcar, *03*		37
___	36255	Donald Duck Hi-Cube Boxcar, *03*		40
___	36256	GN Boxcar "6341," *03*		23
___	36261	PRR Boxcar, *03-05*		15
___	36262	Southern Central of Georgia Boxcar, *03, 04*		20
___	36264	Santa Fe Boxcar "600196, *02*		18
___	36265	Angela Trotta Thomas "Window Wishing" Boxcar, *02*		38
___	36267	Mickey Mouse Hi-Cube Boxcar, *03*		50
___	36270	Angela Trotta Thomas "Home for the Holidays" Boxcar, *02-03*		30
___	36272	New Haven Boxcar "6501," *04*		20
___	36273	Railbox Hi-Cube Boxcar "15000," *04*		21
___	36275	Christmas Boxcar, *04*		35
___	36276	Angela Trotta Thomas "Tis the Season" Boxcar, *04*		34
___	36277	Pluto Hi-Cube Boxcar, *04-05*		50
___	36278	Winnie the Pooh Hi-Cube Boxcar, *04-05*		50
___	36281	B&O Boxcar, *04*		35
___	36291	Simpsons Boxcar, *04-05*		44
___	36294	UP Hi-Cube Boxcar, *traditional, 05*		27
___	36295	CN Boxcar, *traditional, 05*		27
___	36296	2005 Holiday Boxcar, *05*		48
___	36297	Angela Trotta Thomas "Christmas Eve" Boxcar, *05*		48
___	36299	Hammacher Schlemmer Music Boxcar, *04*		65
___	36305	eBay Boxcar, *00 u*		120
___	36500	Western Pacific Caboose "36500," *04*		23
___	36501	D&RGW Caboose "36501," *04*		22
___	36502	Reading Caboose "36502," *04*		25
___	36515	North Pole Central Lines Caboose "36515," *04*		36
___	36519	Lionel Lines Caboose, *04*		22
___	36520	Santa Fe Caboose "36520," *04*		22
___	36525	CSX Work Caboose, lighted, *05*		35
___	36526	Pennsylvania Work Caboose, traditional, *05*		27
___	36527	Santa Fe Work Caboose, traditional, *05*		28
___	36528	Chesapeake & Ohio Work Caboose, traditional, *05*		40
___	36529	North Pole Central Work Caboose with presents, traditional, *05*		38
___	36530	Pennsylvania Caboose, traditional, *05*		33
___	36531	Erie Caboose "C150," traditional, *05*		33
___	36532	SP Caboose "1097," traditional, *05*		48
___	36533	Reading Caboose "92803," traditional, *05*		33
___	36534	NYC Center Cupola Caboose, traditional, *05*		40
___	36535	LL Center Cupola Caboose, traditional, *05*		28
___	36536	Southern Center Cupola Caboose, traditional, *05*		40
___	36544	Alaska Caboose, *05*		35
___	36547	Bethlehem Steel Transfer Caboose, traditional, *05*		40
___	36548	Transylvania RR Work Caboose, traditional, *05*		45

	MODERN 1970-2021	Esc	Mint	
36550	Halloween Transfer Caboose, traditional, *06-07*		45	___
36551	Christmas Caboose, *06*		45	___
36552	U.S. Steel Work Caboose, traditional, *06-07*		45	___
36553	NYC Caboose, *08*		20	___
36554	SP Work Caboose, traditional, *06*		45	___
36555	Pennsylvania Transfer Caboose, *06*		45	___
36556	Lionel Lines Work Caboose, *06-07*		30	___
36557	Rio Grande Work Caboose, traditional, *06*		29	___
36558	Virginian Center Cupola Caboose "316," traditional, *06*		45	___
36559	WM Center Cupola Caboose "1863," traditional, *06*		45	___
36560	C&O Center Cupola Caboose "90876," traditional, *06*		45	___
36562	Army Transportation Work Caboose, traditional, *06*		45	___
36563	Reading Work Caboose, traditional, *06*		45	___
36565	UP SP-type Caboose, traditional, *06*		48	___
36566	NYC SP-type Caboose, traditional, *06*		48	___
36567	GN SP-type Caboose, traditional, *06*		48	___
36571	PRR Caboose, *08*		20	___
36580	B&O Center Cupola Caboose "C2047," traditional, *05*		40	___
36582	C&O Caboose, *05*		22	___
36583	Holiday Caboose, *07*		50	___
36587	SP Caboose "1121," *07-09*		40	___
36589	PRR Work Caboose, *07*		40	___
36590	UP Work Caboose, *07*		45	___
36591	Southern Caboose "X99," *08*		45	___
36592	Santa Fe Caboose "999471," *06*		48	___
36593	NYC Caboose, *06*		48	___
36601	UP Caboose, *06*		48	___
36602	UPS Centennial Caboose, *06*		45	___
36604	Pennsylvania Caboose, *06*		25	___
36607	K-Line Caboose, *06*		40	___
36611	Conrail Caboose "19674," *07*		40	___
36612	Alaska Caboose "1080," *07*		40	___
36613	NYC Caboose, *07*		30	___
36618	It's a Wonderful Life Caboose			___
36622	C&O Caboose "C-1838," *08-09*		40	___
36623	ATSF Caboose, *07-09*		40	___
36624	Lionel Lines Caboose, *08-09*		40	___
36625	B&M Caboose, *08*		50	___
36626	Erie Caboose "C101," *08-09*		45	___
36634	Holiday Porthole Caboose, green, *08*		50	___
36646	Monopoly Caboose, *10*		48	___
36647	Strasburg Caboose, *10*		48	___
36649	Pennsylvania Power & Light Work Caboose, *10*		45	___
36657	Western & Atlantic Caboose, *10-11*		48	___
36659	PRR Illuminated Porthole Caboose, *11*		35	___
36668	CSX Illuminated Square Window Caboose, *10*		35	___
36672	NS Caboose, *11*		25	___
36674	Polar Caboose, *11-12*		53	___
36690	UP Caboose, *2012*			___
36701	Baldwin Locomotive Works Operating Welding Car "36701," *02*		60	___
36702	Bosco Operating Milk Car with platform, *02*		115	___
36703	Circus Horse Car with corral, *06*		150	___
36704	Animated Reindeer Stock Car and Corral, *02*		145	___
36718	AEC Security Caboose, *02*		45	___

	No.	Description	Esc	Mint
___	36719	Lionel Lion Bobbing Head Car, 02		20
___	36720	Aladdin Aquarium Car, 03		40
___	36721	101 Dalmatians Animated Gondola, 03		45
___	36722	Peter Pan Bobbing Head Boxcar, 03		45
___	36726	Santa Fe Searchlight Car "36726," 03		50
___	36727	Weyerhaeuser Moe & Joe Flatcar, 03		65
___	36728	SP Walking Brakeman Boxcar 163143," 03		42
___	36729	Lionel Lines Animated Caboose, 04-05	6	68
___	36730	U.S. Army Missile Launch Sound Car "44," 03		175
___	36731	Motorized Aquarium Car "3435," 03		83
___	36732	C&NW Jumping Hobo Car, 03		41
___	36733	Christmas Music Boxcar, 03		45
___	36734	Santa Fe Operating Searchlight Car "20611," 02		25
___	36735	WP Ice Car "7045," 02		55
___	36736	D&RGW Stock Car "39268," RailSounds, 04		45
___	36738	T&P Poultry Dispatch Car "36738," 02		50
___	36739	Postwar "3461" Lionel Lines Log Dump Car, 03		50
___	36740	Postwar "3469" Lionel Lines Coal Dump Car, 03		49
___	36743	Santa Claus Bobbing Head Boxcar, 03		40
___	36744	Little Mermaid Aquarium Car, 03		55
___	36745	Toy Story Animated Gondola, 03		70
___	36753	LFD Firecar with ladder, 02		60
___	36757	Southern Searchlight Car, 03-04		NRS
___	36758	Patriotic Lighted Boxcar, 02		60
___	36760	B&O Sentinel Operating Brakeman Boxcar "3424," Archive Collection, 02		65
___	36761	Wellspring Capital Management Lighted Boxcar, 02 u		220
___	36764	West Side Lumber Log Dump Car "36764," 03		55
___	36765	Alaska Coal Dump Car "401," 03		50
___	36766	Erie Chase Gondola, 03		50
___	36767	Santa's Radar Tracking Car, 03		40
___	36769	Fourth of July Lighted Boxcar, 03		70
___	36770	American Refrigerator Transit Ice Car "23701," 04		42
___	36771	CN Barrel Car "74208," 04		48
___	36772	Spokane, Portland & Seattle Log Dump Car "36772," 04		46
___	36773	Jersey Central Coal Dump Car "92926," 04		45
___	36774	PRR Moe & Joe Lumber Flatcar, 04		50
___	36775	Santa Fe Animated Caboose "999010," 05		75
___	36776	Santa Fe Walking Brakeman Car "19938," 04		43
___	36778	C&O Searchlight Car "216614," 04		30
___	36780	Sea-Monkeys Motorized Aquarium Car, 04		45
___	36781	Finding Nemo Aquarium Car, 04		50
___	36782	Goofy and Pete Jumping Boxcar, 05		70
___	36783	Disney Operating Boxcar, 04-05		65
___	36784	Monsters Inc. Bobbing Head Boxcar, 04		40
___	36786	Postwar "3494-150" MP Operating Boxcar, 03		40
___	36787	MOW Remote Control Searchlight Car, 04		45
___	36788	Lionel Lines Tender, TrainSounds, 04		75
___	36789	Railbox Boxcar, TrainSounds, 04-05		105
___	36790	Christmas Music Boxcar, 04		70
___	36793	Pennsylvania Derrick Car, 03		22
___	36794	NYC Log Dump Car, 03		25
___	36795	Southern Coal Dump Car, 03		25
___	36796	GN Searchlight Car, 03		24

36797	"Operation Iraqi Freedom" Minuteman Car, *03*	45	___
36803	Santa Animated Caboose, *06*	75	___
36804	Candy Cane Dump Car, *06*	80	___
36805	Reindeer Jumping Boxcar, *06*	70	___
36809	NYC Derrick Car, *07-08*	35	___
36810	PRR Searchlight Car, *07*	35	___
36811	UP Dump Coal Dump Car, *07*	35	___
36812	British Columbia Log Dump Car, *07-08*	35	___
36813	State of Maine Brakeman Car, *08*	80	___
36814	D&RGW Animated Caboose "01415," *07-09*	80	___
36815	Santa Fe Moe & Joe Flatcar, *07-08*	80	___
36816	Virginian Coal Dump Car, *08*	80	___
36818	U.S. Steel Searchlight Car, *07-08*	75	___
36821	"Naughty or Nice" Dump Car, *07*	80	___
36823	Halloween SpookySmoke Boxcar, *07*	115	___
36824	AlienSmoke Boxcar, *07*	110	___
36829	Alien Radioactive Car, *07*	70	___
36830	Trick or Treat Aquarium Car, *07*	75	___
36831	MOW Welding Car, *07-08*	75	___
36833	Christmas Music Boxcar, *07*	65	___
36834	Santa Fe Transparent Instruction Car, *07-08*	65	___
36838	Lionel Power Co. Voltmeter Car, K-Line, *06*	75	___
36839	Operating Milk Car with platform, K-Line, *06*	140	___
36841	Visitor Center 15th Anniversary Lighted Boxcar, *06*	70	___
36847	Polar Express Tender, TrainSounds, *08-14*	130	___
36848	Candy Cane Dump Car, *07*	80	___
36849	Tell-Tale Reindeer Car, *07*	53	___
36850	Santa and Snowman Boxcar, *07*	75	___
36851	Generator Car with Christmas tree, *07*	75	___
36853	U.S. Army Exploding Boxcar, *08*	60	___
36855	GW Horse Car and Corral, *08*	160	___
36856	W&ARR Sheriff and Outlaw Car, *08*	75	___
36857	Bobbing Ghost Boxcar, *08*	65	___
36859	Lionel Lines Aquarium Car, *08*	80	___
36861	PRR Poultry Dispatch Car, *08-09*	80	___
36863	Alien Security Car, *08*	80	___
36864	Bethlehem Steel Searchlight Car, *08*	40	___
36866	WP Coal Dump Car "52369," *08*	40	___
36868	NH Barrel Ramp Car, *08*	40	___
36869	Bobbing Santa Boxcar, *08*	65	___
36870	Postwar "6812" Track Maintenance Car, *08*	65	___
36874	PRR Searchlight Car, *09*	35	___
36875	Polar Express Coach, sound, *08-14, 16*	132	___
36878	NYC Track Cleaning Car, *08*	150	___
36879	REA Ice Car "1221," *08*	65	___
36880	Koi Fish Aquarium Car, *10*	75	___
36881	Christmas Music Boxcar, *08*	70	___
36887	Great Western Animated Gondola, *08-09*	65	___
36888	Casper Aquarium Car, *09-10*	90	___
36889	PRR Barrel Ramp Car, *09-10*	46	___
36893	UP Transparent Instruction Car "195220," *09-10*	75	___
36896	Christmas Music Boxcar, *09*	80	___
36897	Pennsylvania Power & Light Coal Dump Car, *09-10*	46	___
36898	Wisconsin Central Log Dump Car, *09*	46	___

___	**36900**	Depressed Center Flatcar with backshop load, *99*	115
___	**36913**	Allied Chemical 1-D Tank Car 2-pack, *00*	150
___	**36914**	Allied Chemical 1-D Tank Car "68075," die-cast, white, *00*	90
___	**36915**	Allied Chemical 1-D Tank Car "68076," die-cast, white, *00*	90
___	**36916**	Allied Chemical 1-D Tank Car 2-pack, *00*	175
___	**36917**	Allied Chemical 1-D Tank Car "65124," die-cast, black, *00*	95
___	**36918**	Allied Chemical 1-D Tank Car "65125," die-cast, black, *00*	90
___	**36919**	Maersk Maxi-Stack Car, *00*	33
___	**36927**	B&O DC Hopper 6-pack, "435040-45," *01*	520
___	**36935**	Maersk Maxi-Stack Car 2-pack, "250131-32," *00*	135
___	**36937**	SP Maxi-Stack Car "513957," *02*	65
___	**36998**	Gingerbread Man Gateman, *12-13*	80
___	**37001**	No. 3444 Erie Animated Gondola, *09*	70
___	**37002**	Operating Plutonium Car 2-pack, *10-11*	140
___	**37003**	PRR Jet Snow Blower "491252," *09-10*	138
___	**37004**	Area 51 Searchlight Car, *09*	46
___	**37006**	Lionel Flatcar with operating LCD billboard, *09*	180
___	**37009**	Smoking Mount St. Helens Boxcar, *10-11*	125
___	**37010**	Pennsylvania Power & Light Searchlight Car, *10*	46
___	**37011**	B&M Operating Milk Car with platform, *10*	155
___	**37012**	GN Jumping Hobo Boxcar, *10*	75
___	**37015**	Jack-o-Lantern Flatcar, *11-13*	75
___	**37016**	Radioactive Plutonium Flatcar, *11*	70
___	**37017**	Plutonium Boom Car, *11*	70
___	**37022**	ATSF Blinking Billboard, *12*	25
___	**37032**	Postwar "3562" Operating Barrel Car, *11*	75
___	**37033**	Casper Animated Gondola , *11*	70
___	**37035**	Santa's Operating Snow Globe Car, *11*	75
___	**37036**	Halloween Operating Globe Car, *11*	78
___	**37038**	Halloween Searchlight Car, *12-13*	45
___	**37039**	Minuteman Searchlight Car, *11*	45
___	**37040**	UP Derrick Car, *11-12*	46
___	**37041**	Pennsylvania Power & Light Coal Dump Car, *11*	80
___	**37042**	IC Coal Dump Car, *11*	46
___	**37043**	Seaboard Log Dump Car, *11*	46
___	**37044**	CP Rail Log Dump Car, *11, 13*	80
___	**37045**	Beatles Yellow Submarine Aquarium Car, *11*	85
___	**37047**	Santa's Flyer Animated Gondola, *11*	55
___	**37053**	EL Derrick Car, *12*	45
___	**37054**	CSX Coal Dump Car, *12*	46
___	**37055**	SP Log Dump Car, *12*	46
___	**37056**	Zombie Aquarium Car, *12*	80
___	**37057**	Bethlehem Steel Culvert Car, *12*	65
___	**37058**	Ghost Globe Halloween Car, *12-15*	80
___	**37059**	Christmas Snow Globe Car, *12*	85
___	**37060**	LIRR Derrick Car, *13-14*	50
___	**37061**	UP Railroad Speeder, *CC, 12-14*	150
___	**37062**	NS Railroad Speeder, *CC, 12-14*	150
___	**37063**	PRR Railroad Speeder, *CC, 12-14, 16*	150
___	**37064**	CSX Railroad Speeder, *CC, 12-14*	150
___	**37065**	BNSF Railroad Speeder, *CC, 12-14*	150
___	**37066**	MOW Railroad Speeder, *CC, 12-14*	150
___	**37067**	NYC Railroad Speeder, *CC, 12-14*	150

		Esc	Mint
37068	CN Railroad Speeder, *CC, 12-14*		150 ___
37069	Strasburg RR Crane Car, *12*		65 ___
37070	Gingerbread Man and Santa Animated Gondola, *12*		55 ___
37071	MOW Searchlight Car, *12*		46 ___
37073	U.S. Marine Corps Cannon Car, *12*		75 ___
37075	Boy Scouts of America Crane Car, *13*		75 ___
37076	Bethlehem Steel Coal Dump Car, *13*		50 ___
37078	RI Searchlight Car, *13*		50 ___
37079	Santa Fe Derrick Car, *13*		50 ___
37081	Peanuts Pumpkin Jack-O-Lantern Car, *13*		85 ___
37082	Peanuts Animated Trick or Treat Chase Gondola, *14-16*		75 ___
37083	Strasburg Coal Dump Car, *13*		50 ___
37084	PRR Cop and Hobo Animated Gondola, *13*		65 ___
37085	BN Log Dump Car, *13*		50 ___
37086	Lionelville Aquarium Co. Aquarium Car, *13*		80 ___
37087	NH Walking Brakeman Car, *13-14*		75 ___
37089	Santa's List Snow Globe Car, *13*		90 ___
37090	Polar Express Searchlight Car, *13*		60 ___
37094	Wizard of Oz Aquarium Car, *13-15*		85 ___
37095	North Pole Sleigh Repair Welding Car, *13*		85 ___
37097	Where the Wild Things Are Aquarium Car, *13-15*		85 ___
37099	North Pole Central EV Caboose "2510" (std O), *13*		95 ___
37100	Barrel Loader Building, *12-14*		43 ___
37101	Smiley Water Tower, *12-14*		23 ___
37102	Watchman Shanty, *12-14*		30 ___
37103	O31 Curved Track (FasTrack), *13-14, 16, 19-20*		5 ___
37110	FasTrack Terminal, LionChief, *14-16, 18-20*		9 ___
37112	Helicopter 2-pack, *13-20*		35 ___
37115	Pedestrian Walkover, green, *16-18*		55 ___
37120	Railroad Crossing Signs, *13-20*		10 ___
37121	Christmas Station Platform, *13*		25 ___
37122	Santa Fe Blinking Billboard, *13*		25 ___
37123	Weyerhaeuser Timber Operating Sawmill, *12-13*		140 ___
37124	West Side Lumber Operating Sawmill, *12-13*		140 ___
37125	Legacy Writable Utility Mobile, *12-16, 20*		20 ___
37127	Angela Trotta Thomas Gallery, *12*		75 ___
37129	Boy Scouts of America Girder Bridge, *13*		23 ___
37130	Boy Scouts of America Covered Bridge, *13*		60 ___
37139	Tis the Season Accessories, *12-13*		310 ___
37140	All Aboard Accessories, *12-13*		65 ___
37141	Rail Yard Accessories, *12-13*		277 ___
37142	Welcome Home Accessories, *12-13*		154 ___
37146	Legacy PowerMaster, *12-16, 18-20*		100 ___
37147	CAB-1L/Base-1L Command Set, *12-16, 18-20*		250 ___
37149	FasTrack Modular Layout Straight Section Kit, *13*		200 ___
37150	FasTrack Modular Layout Template, *13-16*		30 ___
37151	Christmas Classic Street Lamps, *14, 16-20*		40 ___
37152	Operating Coaling Station, *13-14*		180 ___
37153	FasTrack Modular Layout 45-Degree Reversible Corner Kit, *13*		225 ___
37154	FasTrack Modular Layout 45-Degree Corner Kit, *13*		225 ___
37155	CAB-1L Remote Controller, *12-16, 20*		150 ___
37156	Base-1L, *12-16*		125 ___
37158	Hershey's Water Tower, *13*		30 ___
37159	Peanuts Figure Pack, *13-15*		30 ___

		Esc	Mint
___	**37160** Strasburg Girder Bridge, *13*		21
___	**37161** Container 4-pack, *13*		40
___	**37162** Lionelville Water Tower, *13*		25
___	**37163** LIRR Girder Bridge, *13*		21
___	**37164** NS Girder Bridge, *13*		21
___	**37165** CP Water Tower, *13*		25
___	**37166** Crossing Shanty, *13-14, 16*		25
___	**37167** Freight Platform, *13*		30
___	**37169** Peanuts Psychiatric Booth, *13-16*		40
___	**37172** Gooseneck Lamp 2-pack, *13-20*		34
___	**37173** Globe Lamp 3-pack, *13-14, 16-19*		25
___	**37174** Classic Street Lamp 3-pack, black, *13-14, 16-20*		40
___	**37176** Santa Fe Shanty, *13*		25
___	**37183** Polar Express 10th Anniversary Pewter Snowman and Children Figure Pack, *13-14,16-17*		37
___	**37184** Christmas Half Covered Bridge, *13*		43
___	**37185** Christmas Railroad Signs, *13-14, 16-18*		10
___	**37187** Kris Kringle's Kloseout Shop, *13*		50
___	**37191** 36-watt Power Supply, LionChief, *14*		36
___	**37195** Grand Central Terminal 100th Anniversary, *13-15*		280
___	**37196** Christmas Extension Bridge, *13, 16-18*		15
___	**37197** North Pole Central Girder Bridge, *13-14, 16-17*		30
___	**37530** Santa Animated Caboose, *11*		80
___	**37807** Station Platform, *10-15*		23
___	**37808** Sunoco Spherical Oil Tank, *10-11*		100
___	**37810** Curved O Gauge Tunnel, *11-17*		65
___	**37813** Christmas Tractor and Trailer with trees, *10*		27
___	**37814** Christmas Crossing Shanty, *10-14*		30
___	**37816** Rockville Bridge, *11-12*		700
___	**37820** Lionel Auto Loader Cars 4-pack, *12-13, 16-17*		25
___	**37821** Smoke Fluid Loader, *11*		250
___	**37826** Classic Travel Billboard Set, *11-14*		13
___	**37827** Coca-Cola Covered Bridge, *11*		45
___	**37828** Vintage Boy Scouts Figure Pack, *11-14*		30
___	**37829** Polar Express Station Platform, *11-18*		40
___	**37831** NJ Transit Blinking Light Water Tower, *11-12*		30
___	**37834** Lionel Boat 4-pack, *11-20*		25
___	**37836** Monopoly Auto 4-pack, *12*		25
___	**37837** Polar Express Straight Tunnel, *12-14*		80
___	**37840** Santa Fe Diorama, *12-17*		15
___	**37841** Premium Smoke Fluid, *12-16*		7
___	**37842** CN Tractor with piggyback trailer, *12, 15*		90
___	**37846** PRR Tractor Trailer, *12*		90
___	**37847** SP Tractor Trailer, *12*		90
___	**37848** IC Tractor Trailer, *12*		90
___	**37849** ATSF Tractor Trailer, *12*		90
___	**37850** REA Tractor Trailer, *12*		90
___	**37851** Scale Telephone Poles, *12-20*		37
___	**37852** Christmas People Pack, *12-14, 16-18*		20
___	**37853** Alien Billboard , *13, 15*		13
___	**37854** Classic Christmas Billboard , *12*		11
___	**37855** Lionel Airplane 2-pack, *12-20*		37
___	**37900** Silver Truss Bridge, *11*		70

37901	Lehigh Valley Tugboat, *10*	270
37902	Illuminated Barge, *10*	180
37903	Cell Tower, *10-16, 18-20*	70
37904	Boy Scouts Billboard Set, *10*	13
37907	Christmas Street Lamps with wreaths, *10-14*	30
37909	North Pole Central Jet Snowblower, *11-14*	138
37910	Operating Lighthouse, *10*	180
37911	D&RGW Blinking Light Water Tower, *10-11*	30
37912	Lighted Coaling Tower, *10-15*	180
37913	Hopper Shed, *10-15*	35
37914	Illuminated Work House, *10-18*	40
37916	Beige Brick Suburban House, *10*	80
37917	Red Brick Suburban House, *10*	80
37919	Operating Sawmill, *10*	130
37920	Bascule Bridge, *10*	350
37921	ZW-L Transformer, *11-16, 18-20*	900
37923	Coca-Cola Blinking Light Water Tower, *11*	28
37928	Passenger Station, sounds, *11*	90
37929	Coca-Cola Diner, *11, 13*	75
37930	Rotary Aircraft Beacon, *11-12*	81
37933	MG Switch Tower, *11-13*	300
37935	Operating Track Gang, *11*	100
37939	Scale Telephone Poles, *11-20*	43
37940	PRR Hobo Hotel, *12*	150
37941	House Under Construction, *11*	90
37942	Christmas Hobo Hotel, *12-13*	150
37944	Weathered 50,000-gallon Water Tank, *11-12*	170
37946	House Under Construction #2, *12-13*	90
37947	GW-180 180-watt Transformer, *12-20*	280
37948	Boy Scouts Flagpole with lights, *11*	30
37951	Postwar "342" Culvert Loader, *11*	165
37952	Postwar "345" Culvert Unloader, *11*	190
37953	Jacobs Pharmacy, *11*	50
37954	Halloween Station Platform, *11-13*	35
37955	Sodor Station Platform, *11-15*	35
37957	Deluxe Holiday House, *11*	85
37958	SP Scrap Yard, *11-14*	110
37959	Midway Basketball Shot Game, *11-13*	21
37960	Burning Switch Tower, *11-13*	100
37961	NYC Scrap Yard, *11-13*	110
37962	NJ Transit Station Platform, *11*	37
37964	Archive Operating Freight Terminal, *11-14*	150
37965	Christmas Operating Freight Terminal, *11-14, 16-17*	150
37966	Lionel Cylindrical Oil Tank, *11-17*	100
37967	Boy Scouts Troop Cabin, *12-13*	80
37971	Bethlehem Steel Culvert Loader, *11*	165
37972	Bethlehem Steel Culvert Unloader, *11*	190
37973	Coca-Cola Station Platform, *12*	37
37975	PFE Operating Freight Terminal, *11-16*	150
37977	Hooker Tank Car Accident, *11-17*	130
37978	Deluxe Suburban House, *11-13*	80
37979	Rotary Coal Tipple, *12*	540
37980	Operating Coal Conveyor, *12*	90
37984	Santa's Repair Work House, *12-14*	40

			Esc	Mint
___	37985	Operating Wind Turbine, *12-15*		75
___	37986	NJ Transit Blinking Billboard, *12-13*		28
___	37989	Sodor Train Shed, *12-16*		60
___	37992	Coca-Cola Blinking Light Billboard, *10-11*		28
___	37993	Snoopy and the Red Baron Animated Pylon, *12*		160
___	37994	Deluxe Holiday House #2, *12-14*		120
___	37995	Illuminated Scale Telephone Poles, *12-20*		50
___	37996	Postwar 192 Control Tower, *12*		70
___	37997	Christmas Lawn Figure Pack, *12-14, 16-18*		20
___	37998	Halloween Haunted Passenger Station, *12-13, 15*		75
___	38004	Virginian 4-6-0 10-wheel Locomotive "203," *CC, 01-02*		570
___	38005	Long Island 4-6-0 10-wheel Locomotive "138," *CC, 01-02*		510
___	38007	UP Auxiliary tender, black, *CC, 01*		200
___	38008	UP Auxiliary tender, gray, *CC, 01*		205
___	38009	D&RGW 4-6-6-4 Challenger Locomotive "3803," *CC, 01*		1550
___	38010	Clinchfield 4-6-6-4 Challenger Locomotive "673," *CC, 01*		1400
___	38012	Wheeling & Lake Erie 2-6-6-2 Locomotive "8005," *CC, 01*		610
___	38013	D&H 4-6-6-4 Challenger Locomotive "1527," *CC, 01*		720
___	38014	D&RGW 4-6-6-4 Challenger Locomotive "3800," *CC, 01*		710
___	38015	NYC 4-6-4 Hudson Locomotive "773," *CC, 01*		900
___	38016	Southern 0-8-0 Yard Goat Locomotive "6536," *CC, 01-02, 05*		530
___	38017	CN 2-6-0 Mogul Locomotive "86," *CC, 03, 05*		600
___	38018	Wabash 2-6-0 Mogul Locomotive "826," *CC, 03*		485
___	38019	B&M 2-6-0 Mogul Locomotive "1455," *CC, 03, 05*		600
___	38020	PRR 4-4-4-4 T1 Duplex Locomotive "5514," *02-03*		630
___	38021	WP 4-6-6-4 Challenger Locomotive "402," *CC, 02*		650
___	38022	WM 4-6-6-4 Challenger Locomotive "1206," *CC, 02*		690
___	38023	UP 4-6-6-4 Challenger Locomotive "3976," *CC, 02*		620
___	38024	PRR 6-4-4-6 S-1 Duplex Locomotive "6100," *TMCC, 03*		1000
___	38025	PRR 4-6-2 K4 Pacific Locomotive "1361," *CC, 02*		950
___	38026	N&W 4-8-4 J Class Northern Locomotive "606," *CC, 02*		1450
___	38027	Meadow River Lumber Heisler Geared Locomotive "6," *CC, 03*		880
___	38028	PRR 6-8-6 S2 Steam Turbine Locomotive, *01*		650
___	38029	UP 4-12-2 Locomotive "9000," *CC, 03*		570
___	38030	Santa Fe 2-8-8-2 Locomotive "1795," *CC, 03*		920
___	38031	SP 2-8-8-4 AC-9 Locomotive "3809," *CC, 04*		1100
___	38032	Virginian 2-8-8-2 Locomotive "741," *CC, 03*		928
___	38036	Long Island 2-8-0 Consolidation Locomotive, *01*		500
___	38037	PRR Reading Seashore 2-8-0 Consolidation Locomotive "6072," *CC, 01*		495
___	38038	D&RGW Auxiliary Water Tender, *01*		230
___	38039	Clinchfield Auxiliary Water Tender, *01*		220
___	38040	LV 4-6-0 Camelback Locomotive, *01*		405
___	38042	C&NW 4-6-0 10-wheel Locomotive "361," *CC, 02*		450
___	38043	Frisco 4-6-0 10-wheel Locomotive "719," *CC, 02*		525
___	38044	PRR 4-6-2 K4 Pacific Locomotive "5385," *CC, 02*		920
___	38045	NYC Hudson J-3a 4-6-4 Locomotive "5418," *CC, 03*		495
___	38046	GN 0-8-0 Locomotive "815," *CC, 02*		530
___	38047	N&W 0-8-0 Locomotive "266," *CC, 02*		550
___	38048	NPR 0-8-0 Locomotive "303," *CC, 02*		530
___	38049	N&W 2-6-6-4 Locomotive "1234," *CC, 02*		690
___	38050	Nickel Plate 2-8-4 Berkshire Locomotive "779," *CC, 03*		925
___	38051	Erie 2-8-4 Berkshire Locomotive "3315," *CC, 03*		810
___	38052	Pere Marquette 2-8-4 Berkshire Locomotive "1225," *CC, 03*		1000

		Esc	Mint	
38053	NYC 4-8-2 Mohawk L-2a Locomotive "2793," CC, 03		915	
38055	Santa Fe 4-8-4 Northern Locomotive "3751," CC, 04		1100	
38056	PRR 4-8-2 Mountain M1a Locomotive "6759," CC, 03		850	
38057	Weyerhaeuser Shay Locomotive, CC, 03		1000	
38058	C&O 2-8-8-2 H7 Locomotive "1580," CC, 04		1200	
38060	UP 2-8-8-2 H7 Locomotive "3590," CC, 04		1200	
38061	Cass Scenic Heisler Geared Locomotive "6," CC, 03		940	
38062	Lionel Lines 4-6-2 Pacific Locomotive "8062," CC, 02-03		275	
38065	UP 2-8-8-2 Mallet Locomotive "3672," CC, 02		1002	
38066	Elk River Shay Locomotive, CC, 03		1000	
38067	MILW 4-6-2 Pacific Locomotive "6316," CC, 03		300	
38068	WM 4-6-2 Pacific Locomotive "204," CC, 03		300	
38069	Erie Hudson Locomotive, whistle, 05		150	
38070	C&O 4-6-2 Pacific Locomotive "489," CC, 04		300	
38071	SP Cab Forward AC-12 Locomotive "4294," CC, 05		1550	
38075	UP 4-8-8-4 Big Boy Locomotive "4024," LionMaster, 03		800	
38076	C&O 2-8-4 Berkshire Locomotive "2699," CC, 04		860	
38077	Virginian 2-8-4 Berkshire Locomotive "508," CC, 04		1000	
38079	SP 4-8-4 Northern GS-2 Locomotive "4410," CC, 04		980	
38080	WP 4-8-4 Northern GS-64 Locomotive "485," CC, 04		1000	
38081	C&O 2-6-6-6 Allegheny Locomotive "1650," CC, 05-07		1700	
38082	Pennsylvania 2-8-8-2 Y3 Locomotive "374," CC, 04		1000	
38083	N&W 2-8-8-2 Y3 Locomotive "2009," CC, 04		910	
38085	NYC 4-6-4 Hudson J-3a Locomotive 5422," CC, 03		495	
38086	B&A 4-6-4 Hudson Locomotive "607," CC, 03		495	
38087	Nickel Plate 2-8-4 Berkshire Locomotive, RailSounds, 05		190	
38088	NYC 2-6-0 Mogul Locomotive "1924," CC, 03, 05		600	
38089	Pennsylvania 4-6-2 Pacific Locomotive "3678," CC, 04		300	
38090	Clinchfield 4-6-6-4 Challenger Locomotive "672" CC, 04		640	
38091	NP 4-6-6-4 Challenger Locomotive "5121," CC, 04		660	
38092	Pickering Lumber Heisler Locomotive "5," CC, 04		1000	
38093	UP 4-6-6-4 Challenger Locomotive "3980," CC, 04		700	
38094	MILW Hiawatha 4-4-2 Atlantic Locomotive, CC, 06		950	
38095	N&W 4-8-4 J Class Locomotive "611," CC, 05-06		1250	
38100	Texas Special F3 Diesel AB Set, 99	860	930	
38103	Texas Special F3 Diesel "2245," 99	435	510	
38114	ATSF FT Diesel B Unit, 99-00		170	
38115	NYC FT Diesel B Unit "2403," nonpowered, 99-00		130	
38116	B&O FT Diesel B Unit, 99-00		130	
38144	C&O F3 Diesel AA Set "7019, 7021," 00		700	
38147	GN Alco FA2 AA Diesel Set, CC, 02		405	
38150	Platinum Ghost "2333," 99		495	
38153	"Spirit of the Century" F3 Diesel AA Set, 99		800	
38160	Pennsylvania Alco FB2 Diesel, 02		125	
38161	MKT Alco FB2 Diesel, 02		125	
38162	Burlington FT Diesel B Unit, 01		NRS	
38167	Burlington FT Diesel AA Set, 01		225	
38176	Pennsylvania Alco FA2 AA Diesel Set, CC, 02		405	
38182	MKT Alco FA2 AA Diesel Set, CC, 02		360	
38188	Southern F3 Diesel ABA Set, 00		557	
38194	GN Alco FB2 Diesel, 02		125	
38195	Santa Fe FT Diesel A Unit "170," 00		125	
38196	Santa Fe FT Diesel A Unit "171," 00		175	

	No.	Description	Esc	Mint
___	38197	SP F3 Diesel ABA Set, *00*		640
___	38202	Wild West Handcar, *10*		75
___	38203	Holly Jolly Trolley 2-car Set, *10*		160
___	38204	ATSF FT B Unit, nonpowered, *10*		120
___	38210	PRR Alco Diesel AA Set, *CC, 10*		400
___	38214	Rio Grande Ski Train FT B Unit, nonpowered, *11*		120
___	38215	ATSF FT Diesel "165," RailSounds, *10-11*		280
___	38216	Rio Grande Ski Train FT A Unit, nonpowered, *11*		120
___	38219	Texan FT B Unit Diesel, nonpowered, *11, 13-14*		120
___	38221	CNJ Alco AA Diesel Set, *11*		300
___	38224	Alaska Alco AA Diesel Set, *11*		300
___	38234	Classic PRR GG1 Electric Locomotive "4866," *12*		330
___	38235	Classic PC GG1 Electric Locomotive "4840," *12*		330
___	38240	Elf Gang Car, *12*		120
___	38241	MOW Gang Car, *12-13*		120
___	38252	CP GE U36B Diesel, *"4245," 13*		
___	38300	Postwar "2331" Virginian Train Master Diesel, *08*	190	210
___	38303	Postwar "2340" GG1 Electric Locomotive, *08*		280
___	38305	Postwar "2338" Milwaukee Road GP7 Diesel, *08*		220
___	38308	Postwar 2146WS Berkshire Passenger Set, *12*		460
___	38310	"2185W" NYC F3 Diesel Freight Set, *09*		600
___	38311	"2276W" B&O RDC Commuter Set, *09*		470
___	38312	"2343" Santa Fe F3 Diesel AA Set, *09*		500
___	38313	B&O Budd RDC 2-pack, *09*		350
___	38323	Postwar "2348" M&StL GP9 Diesel, *CC, 10*		390
___	38324	Postwar 2507W NH F3 Diesel Freight Set, *10*		600
___	38328	Postwar 1623W NP GP9 Diesel Freight Set, *10*		750
___	38329	Postwar 2261W Freight Hauler Set, *10*		610
___	38334	Postwar 11288 Orbitor Diesel Freight Set, *10*		500
___	38338	Postwar 2129WS Berkshire Freight Set, *12*		550
___	38339	Postwar 2505W Virginian Rectifier Freight Set, *10*		470
___	38340	Postwar 1587S Girl's Steam Freight Set, *10*		580
___	38342	Postwar 1619W Santa Fe Freight Set, *10-11*		470
___	38348	Postwar "2339" Transparent Wabash GP7 Diesel, *11*		290
___	38349	Postwar 12885-500 C&O GP7 Freight Set, *11-12*		600
___	38351	Postwar Archive UP GP7 Diesel, *11*		290
___	38353	Postwar X-628 Promotional U.S. Navy Diesel Freight Set, *12-14*		600
___	38354	Postwar 1464W UP Anniversary Alco Diesel Passenger Set, *12-14*		460
___	38357	Postwar 221 U.S. Marine Corps Alco Diesel A Unit, *12-14*		300
___	38358	Postwar 2239 IC F3 Freight Set, *12-14*		600
___	38365	Archive ATSF Black Bonnet F3 AA Diesel Set, *12-14*		500
___	38368	Archive NYC Red Lightning F3 AA Diesel Set, *12-14*		500
___	38371	Postwar 2031 RI Alco Diesel AA Set, *12-13*		400
___	38374	Postwar 221 U.S. Marine Corps Alco Diesel B Unit, *12-14*		120
___	38377	Postwar 2363T F3 A Unit, nonpowered, *12-14*		170
___	38379	Archive ATSF Black Bonnet F3 B Unit, *12-14*		170
___	38380	Archive NYC Red Lightning F3 B Unit, *12-14*		170
___	38386	Postwar "2367" Wabash F3 Diesel AB Units, *12-14*		500
___	38388	Postwar "2367" Wabash F3 Diesel A Unit, nonpowered, *12-14*		170
___	38389	Postwar "2362" UP F3 Diesel AA Set, *14*		460
___	38392	Postwar "2362" F3 Diesel B Unit, nonpowered, *14*		170
___	38393	PRR Round-roof Boxcar "76648" (std O), *14*		80
___	38401	NYC M-497 Jet-Powered Rail Car, *10*		300

		Esc	Mint
38402	Amtrak HHP-8 Electric Locomotive, RailSounds, *10*		400 ___
38403	B&O CSX Heritage AC6000 Diesel "6607," *CC, 11*		550 ___
38404	B&O CSX Heritage AC6000 Diesel "7812," *CC, 11*		550 ___
38405	Chessie System CSX Heritage AC6000 Diesel, *CC, 11-14*		550 ___
38406	Chessie System CSX Heritage AC6000 Diesel, *CC, 11-14*		550 ___
38407	WM CSX Heritage AC6000 Diesel "2652," *CC, 11*		550 ___
38408	WM CSX Heritage AC6000 Diesel "2659," *CC, 11*		550 ___
38409	Clinchfield CSX Heritage AC6000 Diesel, *CC, 11-13*		550 ___
38410	Clinchfield CSX Heritage AC6000 Diesel, *CC, 11-14*		550 ___
38411	Family Lines CSX Heritage AC6000 Diesel "4825," *CC, 11*		550 ___
38412	Family Lines CSX Heritage AC6000 Diesel "4837," *CC, 11*		550 ___
38413	CSX Heritage AC6000 Diesel "607," *CC, 11-13*		550 ___
38414	CSX Heritage AC6000 Diesel "654," *CC, 11-13*		550 ___
38415	PRR U28C Diesel "6531," *CC, 11-12*		530 ___
38416	PRR U28C Diesel "6534," *CC, 11-12*		530 ___
38417	BN Bicentennial U30C Diesel "1776," *CC, 11*		530 ___
38418	BN Bicentennial U30C Diesel "1777," *CC, 11*		530 ___
38419	UP U30C Diesel "2918," *CC, 11-12*		530 ___
38420	UP U30C Diesel "2897," *CC, 11-12*		530 ___
38421	NP U33C Diesel "3305," *CC, 11-12*		530 ___
38422	NP U33C Diesel "3307," *CC, 11-12*		530 ___
38423	Southern U30C Diesel "3801," *CC, 11-12*		530 ___
38424	Southern U30C Diesel "3804," *CC, 11-12*		530 ___
38425	RI Budd RDC Jet Car, *11*		330 ___
38428	Alaska Budd RDC Coach, *11*		300 ___
38429	NYC Budd RDC M-497 Jet Car, *11*		330 ___
38432	MKT H16-44 Diesel "1591," *CC, 11*		500 ___
38433	MKT H16-44 Diesel "1731," *CC, 11*		500 ___
38434	MKT H16-44 Diesel "1732," *11*		380 ___
38435	MKT H16-44 Diesel "1733," nonpowered, *11*		240 ___
38436	LIRR H-16-44 Diesel "1501," *CC, 11*		500 ___
38437	LIRR H-16-44 Diesel "1504," *CC, 11*		500 ___
38438	LIRR H-16-44 Diesel "1507," *11*		380 ___
38439	LIRR H-16-44 Diesel "1509," nonpowered, *11*		240 ___
38440	UP H-16-44 Diesel "1341," *CC, 11*		500 ___
38441	UP H-16-44 Diesel "1342," *CC, 11*		500 ___
38442	UP H-16-44 Diesel "1343," *11*		380 ___
38443	UP H-16-44 Diesel "1344," nonpowered, *11*		240 ___
38444	PRR H16-44 Diesel "8807," *CC, 11*		500 ___
38445	PRR H16-44 Diesel "8810," *CC, 11*		500 ___
38446	PRR H16-44 Diesel "8812," *11*		380 ___
38447	PRR H16-44 Diesel "8815," nonpowered, *11*		240 ___
38452	PC Alco RS-11 Diesel "7605," *CC, 12*		480 ___
38453	PC Alco RS-11 Diesel "7608," *CC, 12*		480 ___
38454	PRR Alco RS-11 Diesel "9622," *CC, 12*		480 ___
38455	PC Alco RS-11 Diesel "7625," nonpowered, *12*		240 ___
38456	N&W Alco RS-11 Diesel "308," *CC, 12-13*		480 ___
38457	N&W Alco RS-11 Diesel "318," *CC, 12*		480 ___
38458	PRR Alco RS-11 Diesel "8631," *CC, 12*		480 ___
38459	N&W Alco RS-11 Diesel "330," nonpowered, *12*		240 ___
38460	NKP Alco RS-11 Diesel "855," *CC, 12*		480 ___
38461	NKP Alco RS-11 Diesel "859," *CC, 12*		480 ___
38462	PRR Alco RS-11 Diesel "8639," nonpowered, *12*		240 ___

___	**38463**	NKP Alco RS-11 Diesel "863," nonpowered, *12*	240
___	**38464**	Alaska Alco RS-11 Diesel "3602," *CC, 12*	480
___	**38465**	Alaska Alco RS-11 Diesel "3604," *CC, 12*	480
___	**38466**	NH Alco RS-11 Diesel "1403," *CC, 12*	480
___	**38467**	Alaska Alco RS-11 Diesel "3607," nonpowered, *12*	240
___	**38468**	Seaboard Alco RS-11 Diesel "101," *CC, 12-13*	480
___	**38469**	Seaboard Alco RS-11 Diesel "102," *CC, 12*	480
___	**38470**	NH Alco RS-11 Diesel "1405," *CC, 12*	480
___	**38471**	Seaboard Alco RS-11 Diesel "104," nonpowered, *12*	240
___	**38472**	C&O Alco S2 Diesel Switcher "5001," *CC, 11*	470
___	**38473**	C&O Alco S2 Diesel Switcher "5505," *CC, 11*	480
___	**38474**	C&O Alco S2 Diesel Switcher "5020," *11*	360
___	**38475**	C&O Alco S2 Diesel Switcher "5027," nonpowered, *11*	220
___	**38476**	CN Alco S2 Diesel Switcher "7946," *CC, 11*	480
___	**38477**	CN Alco S2 Diesel Switcher "7949," *CC, 11*	480
___	**38478**	CN Alco S2 Diesel Switcher "7951," *11*	360
___	**38479**	CN Alco S2 Diesel Switcher "7954," *11*	360
___	**38480**	NYC Alco S2 Diesel Switcher "8504," *CC, 11*	480
___	**38481**	NYC Alco S2 Diesel Switcher "8507," *CC, 11*	480
___	**38482**	NYC Alco S2 Diesel Switcher "8514," *11*	360
___	**38483**	NYC Alco S2 Diesel Switcher "8521," nonpowered, *11*	220
___	**38484**	Southern Alco S2 Diesel Switcher "2209," *CC, 11*	480
___	**38485**	Southern Alco S2 Diesel Switcher "2211," *CC, 11*	480
___	**38486**	Southern Alco S2 Diesel Switcher "2215," *11*	360
___	**38487**	Southern Alco S2 Diesel Switcher "2218," nonpowered, *11*	220
___	**38488**	Mopac Alco S2 Diesel Switcher "9108," *CC, 11*	480
___	**38489**	Mopac Alco S2 Diesel Switcher "9113," *CC, 11*	480
___	**38490**	Mopac Alco S2 Diesel Switcher "9116," *11*	360
___	**38491**	Mopac Alco S2 Diesel Switcher "9131," nonpowered, *11*	220
___	**38493**	ATSF Early Era Inspection Vehicle, *CC, 12*	150
___	**38494**	CP DD35 Diesel "9864," *CC, 12*	600
___	**38495**	CP DD35 Diesel "9868," nonpowered, *12*	440
___	**38496**	SP DD35A Diesel "9903," *CC, 11*	600
___	**38497**	SP DD35A Diesel "9914," nonpowered, *11*	440
___	**38498**	PRR DD35A Diesel "2380," *CC, 11*	600
___	**38499**	PRR DD35A Diesel "2383," nonpowered, *11*	440
___	**38505**	CSX GP-38 Diesel, *11*	140
___	**38521**	PRR GG1 Electric "4839," *11*	330
___	**38522**	Amtrak GG1 Electric "926," *11*	330
___	**38524**	NYC GP35 Diesel "6131," *CC, 12*	500
___	**38525**	NYC GP35 Diesel "6138," *CC, 12*	500
___	**38526**	NYC GP35 Diesel "6147," nonpowered, *12*	260
___	**38527**	UP GP35 Diesel "742," *CC, 12*	500
___	**38528**	UP GP35 Diesel "753," *CC, 12*	500
___	**38529**	UP GP35 Diesel "760," nonpowered, *12*	260
___	**38530**	SP GP35 Diesel "7465," *CC, 12*	500
___	**38531**	SP GP35 Diesel "7474," *CC, 12*	500
___	**38532**	SP GP35 Diesel "7481," nonpowered, *12*	260
___	**38533**	CP GP35 Diesel "5014," *CC, 12*	500
___	**38534**	CP GP35 Diesel "5018," *CC, 12*	500
___	**38535**	CP GP35 Diesel "5023," nonpowered, *12*	260
___	**38536**	PRR GP35 Diesel "2297," *CC, 12*	500
___	**38537**	PRR GP35 Diesel "2302," *CC, 12*	500

		Mint	
38538	PRR GP35 Diesel "2305," *nonpowered, 12*	260	___
38539	N&W Alco RS-11 Diesel "308," *CC, 12*	480	___
38539	Conrail GP35 Diesel "2297," *CC, 12*	500	___
38540	Conrail GP35 Diesel "2302," *CC, 12*	500	___
38541	Conrail GP35 Diesel "2305," *nonpowered, 12*	260	___
38542	Milwaukee Road GP35 Diesel "361," *CC, 12*	500	___
38543	Milwaukee Road GP35 Diesel "363," *CC, 12*	500	___
38544	Milwaukee Road GP35 Diesel "366," *nonpowered, 12*	260	___
38545	Pacific Harbor Line Genset Switcher "31," *CC, 11*	800	___
38546	KCS Genset Switcher "1404," *CC, 11-12*	800	___
38547	Santa Fe Genset Switcher "9910," *CC, 11*	800	___
38548	EL GP35 Diesel "2555," *CC, 12*	500	___
38549	EL GP35 Diesel "2558," *CC, 12*	500	___
38550	EL GP35 Diesel "2561," *nonpowered, 12*	260	___
38558	D&H Baldwin RF-16 Diesel AA Set, *CC, 12*	730	___
38561	D&H Baldwin RF-16 Diesel B Unit, *CC, 12*	400	___
38562	D&H Baldwin RF-16 Diesel B Unit, *nonpowered, 12*	250	___
38563	B&O Baldwin RF-16 Diesel AA Set, *CC, 12-14*	730	___
38566	B&O Baldwin RF-16 Diesel B Unit, *CC, 12-14*	400	___
38567	B&O Baldwin RF-16 Diesel B Unit, *nonpowered, 12-14*	250	___
38568	NYC Baldwin RF-16 Diesel AA Set "3806-3808," *CC, 12-14*	730	___
38571	NYC Baldwin RF-16 Diesel B Unit, *CC, 12-14*	400	___
38572	NYC Baldwin RF-16 Diesel B Unit, *nonpowered, 12-14*	250	___
38573	SP Baldwin RF-16 Diesel AA Set, *CC, 12-14*	730	___
38576	SP Baldwin RF-16 Diesel B Unit, *CC, 12-14*	400	___
38577	SP Baldwin RF-16 Diesel B Unit, *nonpowered, 12-14*	250	___
38579	ATSF GP9 Diesel "744," *nonpowered, 12*	240	___
38580	NP GP9 Diesel "324," *nonpowered, 12*	240	___
38581	CSX SD80MAC Diesel "809," *CC, 12-13*	530	___
38582	CSX SD80MAC Diesel "812," *CC, 12*	530	___
38583	CSX SD80MAC Diesel "804," *nonpowered, 12*	260	___
38584	NS SD80MAC Diesel "7207," *CC, 12*	530	___
38585	NS SD80MAC Diesel "7203," *CC, 12*	530	___
38586	NS SD80MAC Diesel "7209," *nonpowered, 12*	260	___
38587	Conrail SD80MAC Diesel "4126," *CC, 12*	530	___
38588	Conrail SD80MAC Diesel "4129," *CC, 12*	530	___
38589	Conrail SD80MAC Diesel "4103," *nonpowered, 12*	260	___
38593	UP NW2 Diesel Switcher Locomotive "1028," *CC, 12*	470	___
38594	UP NW2 Diesel Switcher Locomotive "1043," *CC, 12*	470	___
38595	CB&Q Scale NW2 Diesel Switcher "9227," *CC, 12*	470	___
38596	CB&Q Scale NW2 Diesel Switcher "9245," *CC, 12*	470	___
38597	CB&Q F3 AA Diesel Set "9962A-9962C," *CC, 12-13*	730	___
38600	UP 0-6-0 Dockside Switcher "87," *traditional, 07-09*	110	___
38601	Lionel Lines 0-6-0 Dockside Switcher, *traditional, 07-09*	110	___
38605	PRR 0-4-0 Locomotive "94," *traditional, 07*	170	___
38606	SP 0-4-0 Locomotive "71," *traditional, 07-08*	170	___
38607	Southern 2-8-4 Berkshire Locomotive "2718," *RailSounds, 07-08*	175	___
38608	LL 2-8-2 Mikado Locomotive "57," *RailSounds, 07*	260	___
38609	NYC 2-8-2 Mikado Locomotive "1843," *CC, 07*	370	___
38610	NKP 2-8-4 Berkshire Locomotive "779," *CC, 07-08*	370	___
38619	Santa Fe 4-6-2 Pacific Locomotive "2037," *traditional, K-Line, 06*	260	___
38620	B&O Porter Locomotive "16," *traditional, K-Line, 06*	100	___
38621	4-6-2 Pacific Locomotive, *traditional, K-Line, 06*	260	___

|---|---|---|---|
___	38626	Holiday 2-8-2 Mikado Locomotive "25," green, RailSounds, *08*	260
___	38627	GN 4-4-2 Atlantic Locomotive "1702," traditional, *08-09*	110
___	38630	U.S. Army 0-6-0 Dockside Switcher "486," traditional, *08-09*	110
___	38634	NYC 4-6-4 Hudson Locomotive "5417," TrainSounds, *07*	200
___	38635	C&O 4-6-4 Hudson Locomotive "309," TrainSounds, *08*	200
___	38636	ATSF 4-6-4 Hudson Locomotive "3459," TrainSounds, *07*	200
___	38637	LL 4-6-4 Hudson Locomotive "5242," TrainSounds, *08*	200
___	38638	UP 4-6-2 Pacific Locomotive "2888," RailSounds, *08*	300
___	38639	Erie 4-6-2 Pacific Locomotive "2939," RailSounds, *08*	300
___	38640	Southern 4-6-2 Pacific Locomotive "1317," RailSounds, *08*	300
___	38641	B&M 4-6-2 Pacific Locomotive "3713," RailSounds, *08*	300
___	38642	PRR 4-6-2 Pacific Locomotive "5385," RailSounds, *08*	300
___	38643	Alaska Mikado 2-8-2 Locomotive "701," *CC, 08-09*	280
___	38644	T&P Mikado 2-8-2 Locomotive "810," *CC, 08-09*	400
___	38649	Christmas 4-6-4 Hudson Locomotive, traditional, *08*	220
___	38651	Lionel Lines 0-8-0 Locomotive "100," traditional, *08-09*	120
___	38654	Bethlehem Steel 0-4-0 Locomotive, traditional, *08-09*	170
___	38657	Alton Limited Pacific 4-6-2 Locomotive "659," traditional, *08*	300
___	38658	W&ARR 4-4-0 General "1892," TrainSounds, *08-09*	165
___	38664	LL 4-4-2 Atlantic Locomotive "1058," traditional, *08-09*	110
___	38671	Santa Flyer 4-6-0 Locomotive, *09*	200
___	38677	Strasburg 0-6-0 Dockside Switcher "1252," *10*	130
___	38678	Monopoly Hudson Locomotive, TrainSounds, *10*	240
___	38679	ATSF 0-4-0 Switcher "1387," *10-11*	190
___	38684	Pennsylvania Power & Light Docksider Switcher, *10*	110
___	38687	Western & Atlantic 0-4-0 Locomotive "1897," *10-11*	190
___	38691	North Pole Central Santa Flyer "2," *10-11*	190
___	38692	Angela Trotta Thomas Signature Express, *10-11*	190
___	38700	CB&Q F3 B Unit "9962B," *CC, 12-13*	400
___	38701	CB&Q F3 B Unit, *12-13*	250
___	38702	D&RGW F3 AA Diesel Set "5531-5533," *CC, 12-14*	730
___	38705	D&RGW F3 B Unit "5532," *CC, 12-14*	400
___	38706	D&RGW F3 B Unit, *12-14*	250
___	38707	WP F3 AB Diesel Set "803A-803B," *CC, 12-14*	730
___	38710	WP F3 A Unit, nonpowered, *12-14*	380
___	38711	WP F3 B Unit "803C," *CC, 12-14*	400
___	38712	Wabash F7 AA Diesel Set "1102A-1102C," *CC, 12-13*	730
___	38715	Wabash F7 B Unit "1102B," *CC, 12-13*	400
___	38716	Wabash F7 B Unit, *12-13*	250
___	38717	Milwaukee Road F7 AA Diesel Set, *CC, 12*	730
___	38720	Milwaukee Road F7 B Unit "109B," *CC, 12*	400
___	38721	Milwaukee Road F7 B Unit, *12*	250
___	38722	Grand Trunk SD80MAC Diesel "9085," *CC, 12*	530
___	38723	Grand Trunk SD80MAC Diesel "9088," *CC, 12*	530
___	38724	Grand Trunk SD80MAC Diesel "9079," nonpowered, *12*	260
___	38725	CB&Q SD80MAC Diesel "9654," *CC, 12*	530
___	38726	CB&Q SD80MAC Diesel "9651," *CC, 12*	530
___	38727	CB&Q SD80MAC Diesel "9660," nonpowered, *12*	260
___	38728	PRR SD80MAC Diesel "9942," *CC, 12*	530
___	38729	PRR SD80MAC Diesel "9945," *CC, 12*	530
___	38730	PRR SD80MAC Diesel "9947," nonpowered, *12-13*	260
___	38731	Polar SD80MAC Diesel, *CC, 12*	530
___	38732	CB&Q BNSF Heritage SD70ACe Diesel "1848," *CC, 12-13*	530

38733	CB&Q BNSF Heritage SD70ACe Diesel "1852," *CC, 12-13*	530 ___
38734	CB&Q BNSF Heritage SD70ACe Diesel "1856," nonpowered, *12-13*	260 ___
38735	ATSF BNSF Heritage SD70ACe Diesel "1996," *CC, 12-13*	530 ___
38736	ATSF BNSF Heritage SD70ACe Diesel "1997," *CC, 12-13*	530 ___
38737	ATSF BNSF Heritage SD70ACe Diesel "1999," nonpowered, *12-13*	260 ___
38738	Frisco BNSF Heritage SD70ACe Diesel "1876," *CC, 12-13*	530 ___
38739	Frisco BNSF Heritage SD70ACe Diesel "1896," *CC, 12-14*	530 ___
38740	Frisco BNSF Heritage SD70ACe Diesel "1916," nonpowered, *12-13*	260 ___
38741	BN BNSF Heritage SD70ACe Diesel "1970," *CC, 12-13*	530 ___
38742	BN BNSF Heritage SD70ACe Diesel "1975," *CC, 12-13*	530 ___
38743	BN BNSF Heritage SD70ACe Diesel "1980," nonpowered, *12-13*	260 ___
38744	GN BNSF Heritage SD70ACe Diesel "1889," *CC, 12-13*	530 ___
38745	GN BNSF Heritage SD70ACe Diesel "1891," *CC, 12-13*	530 ___
38746	GN BNSF Heritage SD70ACe Diesel "1893," nonpowered, *12-13*	260 ___
38747	NP BNSF Heritage SD70ACe Diesel "1870," *CC, 12-13*	530 ___
38748	NP BNSF Heritage SD70ACe Diesel "1872," *CC, 12-13*	530 ___
38749	NP BNSF Heritage SD70ACe Diesel "1875," nonpowered, *12-13*	260 ___
38750	EMD Demonstrator SD70ACe Diesel "2012," *CC, 12-13*	530 ___
38751	CNJ F3 AA Diesel Set, *CC, 13-14*	730 ___
38752	Vision Centipede AA Pilot Diesels, *CC, 13*	2200 ___
38754	C&NW F7 AA Diesel Set, *CC, 13-14*	730 ___
38757	SP F7 AA Diesel Set, *CC, 13-14*	730 ___
38760	CNJ F3 B Unit, *CC, 13-14*	400 ___
38761	CNJ F3 B Unit, *13-14*	250 ___
38762	C&NW F7 B Unit "410," *CC, 13-14*	400 ___
38763	C&NW F7 B Unit, *13-14*	250 ___
38764	SP F7 B Unit "8219," *CC, 13*	400 ___
38765	SP F7 B Unit, *13*	250 ___
38768	N&W GP35 Diesel "1306," *CC, 13-14*	500 ___
38769	N&W GP35 Diesel "1308," nonpowered, *13-14*	260 ___
38770	RI GP35 Diesel "307," *CC, 13-14*	500 ___
38771	RI GP35 Diesel "309," *CC, 13-14*	500 ___
38772	RI GP35 Diesel "323," *nonpowered, 13-14*	260 ___
38773	WP GP35 Diesel "3002," *CC, 13-14*	500 ___
38774	WP GP35 Diesel "3009," *CC, 13-14*	500 ___
38775	WP GP35 Diesel "3014," nonpowered, *13-14*	260 ___
38778	C&NW RS3 Diesel "1621," LionChief, *14-16*	330 ___
38779	NYC RS3 Diesel "8244," LionChief, *14-16*	330 ___
38782	C&BQ GP35 Diesel "990," *CC, 13*	500 ___
38783	C&BQ GP35 Diesel "996," nonpowered, *13*	500 ___
38784	CN GP35 Diesel "4000," *CC, 13*	500 ___
38785	CN GP35 Diesel "4005," *CC, 13*	500 ___
38786	CN GP35 Diesel "4001," nonpowered, *13*	260 ___
38787	D&RGW GP35 Diesel "3031," *CC, 13*	500 ___
38788	D&RGW GP35 Diesel "3034," *CC, 13*	500 ___
38789	D&RGW GP35 Diesel "3038," nonpowered, *13*	260 ___
38790	DT&I GP35 Diesel "351," *CC, 13*	500 ___
38791	DT&I GP35 Diesel "353," *CC, 13*	500 ___
38792	DT&I GP35 Diesel "355," nonpowered, *13*	260 ___
38794	GN GP35 Diesel "3018," *CC, 13-14*	500 ___
38795	GN GP35 Diesel "3036," nonpowered, *13-14*	260 ___
38796	Chessie System GP35 Diesel "1125," *CC, 13*	500 ___
38797	Chessie System GP35 Diesel "1128," *CC, 13*	500 ___

		Esc	Mint
___	**38798** Chessie System GP35 Diesel "1113," nonpowered, *13*		260
___	**38799** N&W GP35 Diesel "1302," *CC, 13-14*		500
___	**38800** B&M Early Era Inspection Vehicle, *CC, 12*		150
___	**38801** KCS Trackmobile, *CC, 12-13*		300
___	**38802** North Pole Central Trackmobile, *CC, 12*		300
___	**38803** MOW Trackmobile, *CC, 12*		300
___	**38804** LIRR Trackmobile, *CC, 12*		300
___	**38805** Conrail Trackmobile, *CC, 12*		300
___	**38806** NS Trackmobile, *CC, 12*		300
___	**38807** NP Trackmobile, *CC, 12-13*		300
___	**38808** Chessie System Trackmobile, *CC, 12*		300
___	**38809** CN Trackmobile, *CC, 12*		300
___	**38810** PRR Early Era Inspection Vehicle, *CC, 12*		150
___	**38811** D&RGW Early Era Inspection Vehicle, *CC, 12*		150
___	**38812** SP Early Era Inspection Vehicle, *CC, 12-13*		150
___	**38813** C&O Early Era Inspection Vehicle, *CC, 12-13*		150
___	**38814** Milwaukee Road Early Era Inspection Vehicle, *CC, 12*		150
___	**38815** Transylvania Early Era Inspection Vehicle, *CC, 12*		150
___	**38816** PRR RS3 Diesel "5620," LionChief, *14-16*		330
___	**38819** D&RGW RS3 Diesel "5202," LionChief, *14-16*		330
___	**38821** AT&SF GP7 Diesel "2656," LionChief, *14-15*		330
___	**38824** NP GP7 Diesel "563," LionChief, *14-15*		330
___	**38825** UP GP7 Diesel "121," LionChief, *14-15*		330
___	**38827** CB&Q GP7 Diesel "1596," LionChief, *14-15*		330
___	**38848** Christmas Pioneer Zephyr Set, *CC, 13-14*		1100
___	**38853** Santa and Mrs. Claus Handcar, *13*		90
___	**38855** GN GP35 Diesel "2519," *CC, 13-14*		500
___	**38856** CB&Q Mark Twain Zephyr, *CC, 13-14*		1100
___	**38860** CB&Q Pioneer Zephyr, *CC, 13-14*		1100
___	**38864** Lionel Lines Zephyr, *CC, 13-14*		1100
___	**38865** L&N GP35 Diesel "1105," *CC, 13*		500
___	**38866** L&N GP35 Diesel "1109," *CC, 13*		500
___	**38867** L&N GP35 Diesel "1114," nonpowered, *13*		260
___	**38868** C&BQ GP35 Diesel "978," *CC, 13*		500
___	**38874** B&O GP9 Diesel "6448," *CC, 13-14*		480
___	**38875** B&O GP9 Diesel "6456," *CC, 13-14*		480
___	**38876** B&O GP9 Diesel "6461," nonpowered, *13-14*		240
___	**38877** B&M GP9 Diesel "1705," *CC, 13*		480
___	**38878** B&M GP9 Diesel "1714," *CC, 13*		480
___	**38879** B&M GP9 Diesel "1722," nonpowered, *13*		240
___	**38883** C&NW GP9 Diesel "701," *CC, 13*		480
___	**38884** C&NW GP9 Diesel "704," *CC, 13*		480
___	**38885** C&NW GP9 Diesel "712," nonpowered, *13*		240
___	**38886** Erie GP9 Diesel "1260," *CC, 13*		480
___	**38887** Erie GP9 Diesel "1263," *CC, 13*		480
___	**38888** Erie GP9 Diesel "1265," nonpowered, *13*		240
___	**38889** Nickel Plate Road GP9 Diesel "514," *CC, 13*		480
___	**38890** Nickel Plate Road GP9 Diesel "452," *CC, 13*		480
___	**38891** Nickel Plate Road GP9 Diesel "457," nonpowered, *13*		240
___	**38892** SP GP9 Diesel "3411," *CC, 13*		480
___	**38893** SP GP9 Diesel "3415," *CC, 13*		480
___	**38894** SP GP9 Diesel "3419," nonpowered, *13*		240
___	**38895** Wabash GP9 Diesel "484," *CC, 13*		480

			Esc	Mint
38896	Wabash GP9 Diesel "488," *CC, 13*			480 ___
38897	Wabash GP9 Diesel "491," nonpowered, *13*			240 ___
38918	Chessie System SD40-2 Diesel "7609," *CC, 13*			530 ___
38919	Chessie System SD40-2 Diesel "7611," *CC, 13*			530 ___
38920	Chessie System SD40-2 Diesel "7614," nonpowered, *13*			240 ___
38921	SP SD40T-2 Diesel Locomotive "8322," *CC, 13*			530 ___
38922	SP SD40T-2 Diesel Locomotive "8326," *CC, 13*			530 ___
38923	SP SD40T-2 Diesel, nonpowered, *13*			260 ___
38924	B&O SD40-2 Diesel "7602," *CC, 13*			530 ___
38925	B&O SD40-2 Diesel "7607," *CC, 13*			530 ___
38926	B&O SD40-2 Diesel "7611," nonpowered, *13*			240 ___
38933	Conrail SD40-2 Diesel "6424," *CC, 13*			530 ___
38934	Conrail SD40-2 Diesel "6437," *CC, 13*			530 ___
38935	Conrail SD40-2 Diesel "6468," nonpowered, *13*			240 ___
38936	UP SD40-2 Diesel "2929," *CC, 13*			530 ___
38937	UP SD40-2 Diesel "2932," *CC, 13*			530 ___
38938	UP SD40-2 Diesel "2947," nonpowered, *13*			240 ___
38939	NS SD40-2 Diesel "3355," *CC, 13*			530 ___
38940	NS SD40-2 Diesel "3365," *CC, 13*			530 ___
38941	NS SD40-2 Diesel "3379," nonpowered, *13*			240 ___
38942	Central of Georgia NS Heritage ES44AC Diesel, *CC, 12*			550 ___
38943	Central of Georgia NS Heritage ES44AC Diesel, *CC, 12*			550 ___
38944	Central of Georgia NS Heritage ES44AC Diesel, nonpowered, *12*			280 ___
38945	Conrail NS Heritage ES44AC Diesel, *CC, 12*			550 ___
38946	Conrail NS Heritage ES44AC Diesel, *CC, 12*			550 ___
38947	Conrail NS Heritage ES44AC Diesel, nonpowered, *12*			280 ___
38948	Interstate NS Heritage ES44AC Diesel Locomotive "8105," *CC, 12*			550 ___
38949	Interstate NS Heritage ES44AC Diesel, *CC, 12*			550 ___
38950	Interstate NS Heritage ES44AC Diesel, nonpowered, *12*			280 ___
38951	LV NS Heritage ES44AC Diesel, *CC, 12*			550 ___
38952	LV NS Heritage ES44AC Diesel, *CC, 12*			550 ___
38953	LV NS Heritage ES44AC Diesel, nonpowered, *12*			280 ___
38954	Nickel Plate Road NS Heritage ES44AC Diesel, *CC, 12*			550 ___
38955	Nickel Plate Road NS Heritage ES44AC Diesel, *CC, 12*			550 ___
38956	Nickel Plate Road NS Heritage ES44AC Diesel, nonpowered, *12*			280 ___
38957	N&W NS Heritage ES44AC Diesel, *CC, 12*			550 ___
38958	N&W NS Heritage ES44AC Diesel, *CC, 12*			550 ___
38959	N&W NS Heritage ES44AC Diesel, nonpowered, *12*			280 ___
38960	PRR NS Heritage ES44AC Diesel, *CC, 12*			550 ___
38961	PRR NS Heritage ES44AC Diesel, *CC, 12*			550 ___
38962	PRR NS Heritage ES44AC Diesel, nonpowered, *12*			280 ___
38963	Southern NS Heritage ES44AC Diesel, *CC, 12*			550 ___
38964	Southern NS Heritage ES44AC Diesel, *CC, 12*			550 ___
38965	Southern NS Heritage ES44AC Diesel, nonpowered, *12*			280 ___
38966	NS Heritage ES44AC Diesel, *CC, 12*			550 ___
38967	NS Heritage ES44AC Diesel, *CC, 12*			550 ___
38968	NS Heritage ES44AC Diesel, nonpowered, *12*			280 ___
38969	North Pole Central GP35 Diesel "2525," *CC, 13*			500 ___
38970	North Pole Central GP35 Diesel "2512," *CC, 13*			500 ___
38971	North Pole Central GP35 Diesel "2513," nonpowered, *13*			260 ___
38972	Reading GP35 Diesel "3625," *CC, 13*			500 ___
38973	Reading GP35 Diesel "3630," *CC, 13*			500 ___
38974	Reading GP35 Diesel "3633," nonpowered, *13*			260 ___

		Esc	Mint
38975	AT&SF GP35 Diesel "3312," *CC, 13*		500
38976	AT&SF GP35 Diesel "3318," *CC, 13*		500
38977	AT&SF GP35 Diesel "3329," nonpowered, *13*		260
38978	Alaska GP35 Diesel "2501," *CC, 13*		500
38979	Alaska GP35 Diesel "2503," *CC, 13*		500
38980	Alaska GP35 Diesel "2502," nonpowered, *13*		260
38981	B&O GP35 Diesel "2506," *CC, 13-14*		500
38982	B&O GP35 Diesel "2511," *CC, 13-14*		500
38983	B&O GP35 Diesel "2517," nonpowered, *13-14*		260
38984	C&O GP35 Diesel "3515," *CC, 13-14*		500
38985	C&O GP35 Diesel "3521," *CC, 13-14*		500
38986	C&O GP35 Diesel "3526," nonpowered, *13-14*		260
38987	MP GP35 Diesel "603," *CC, 13*		500
38988	MP GP35 Diesel "607," *CC, 13*		500
38989	MP GP35 Diesel "611," nonpowered, *13*		260
38990	GM&O GP35 Diesel "603," *CC, 13-14*		500
38991	GM&O GP35 Diesel "607," *CC, 13-14*		500
38992	GM&O GP35 Diesel "611," nonpowered, *13-14*		260
38993	WM GP35 Diesel "3576," *CC, 13*		500
38994	WM GP35 Diesel "3578," *CC, 13*		500
38995	WM GP35 Diesel "3580," nonpowered, *13*		260
38996	CSX GP35 Diesel "4355," *CC, 13*		500
38997	CSX GP35 Diesel "4363," *CC, 13*		500
38998	CSX GP35 Diesel "4390," nonpowered, *13*		260
38999	NS GP35 Diesel "2916," *CC, 13*		500
39008	PRR Heavyweight Passenger Car 4-pack, *00*		225
39009	PRR Indian Rock Heavyweight Combination Car, *00*		50
39010	PRR Andrew Carnegie Heavyweight Passenger Coach, *00*		60
39011	PRR Solomon P. Chase Heavyweight Passenger Coach, *00*		60
39012	PRR Skyline View Heavyweight Observation Car, *00*		50
39013	B&O Heavyweight Passenger Car 4-pack, *00*		400
39014	B&O Harper's Ferry Heavyweight Combination Car, *00*		50
39015	B&O Youngstown Heavyweight Passenger Coach, *00*		50
39016	B&O New Castle Heavyweight Passenger Coach, *00*		50
39017	B&O Chicago Heavyweight Observation Car, *00*		50
39028	LL Heavyweight Passenger Car 3-pack, *00*		195
39029	LL Irvington Heavyweight Coach "2625," *00*		60
39030	LL Madison Heavyweight Coach "2627," *00*		60
39031	LL Manhattan Heavyweight Coach "2628," *00*		60
39032	UP Madison Passenger Car 4-pack, *00*		275
39038	SP Madison Baggage Car "6015," *01*		NRS
39039	SP Madison Coach Car "1978," *01*		NRS
39040	SP Madison Coach "1975," *01*		NRS
39041	SP Madison Observation Car "2951," *01*		NRS
39042	N&W Heavyweight Passenger Car 4-pack, *00*		325
39047	B&O Heavyweight Passenger Car 2-pack, *01*		160
39050	PRR Heavyweight Passenger Car 2-pack, *01*		215
39053	Alaska Streamliner Car 2-pack, *01*		90
39056	NYC Streamliner Car 2-pack, *01*		75
39059	Santa Fe Streamliner Car 2-pack, *01*		100
39062	B&O Streamliner Car 2-pack, *01*		75
39065	PRR Streamliner Car 4-pack, *01*		165
39082	Blue Comet Heavyweight Passenger Car 2-pack, *02*		325

		Esc	Mint
39085	"Freedom Train" Heavyweight Passenger Car 3-pack, *03*		260 ___
39092	PRR Streamliner Car 2-pack, *01*		70 ___
39099	Alton Limited Heavyweight Passenger Car 2-pack, *03*		230 ___
39100	William Penn Congressional Coach, *00*		115 ___
39101	Molly Pitcher Congressional Coach, *00*		100 ___
39102	Betsy Ross Congressional Vista Dome Car, *00*		100 ___
39103	Alexander Hamilton Congressional Observation Car, *00*		100 ___
39104	Phoebe Snow Car, StationSounds, *99*		255 ___
39105	Milwaukee Road Hiawatha Car, StationSounds, *99*		235 ___
39106	CP Aluminum Passenger Car 2-pack, *00*		185 ___
39107	CP Blair Manor Aluminum Passenger Coach "2553," *00*		115 ___
39108	CP Craig Manor Aluminum Passenger Coach "2554," *00*		110 ___
39109	"Spirit of the Century" Aluminum Passenger Car 4-pack, *99*		520 ___
39110	"Spirit of the Century" Full Vista Dome Car, *99-00*		100 ___
39111	"Spirit of the Century" Full Vista Dome Car, *99-00*		100 ___
39112	"Spirit of the Century" Full Vista Dome Car, *99-00*		100 ___
39113	"Spirit of the Century" Skytop Observation Car, *99-00*		100 ___
39118	Texas Special Garland Aluminum Passenger Coach "1203," StationSounds, *99-00*		220 ___
39119	Southern Aluminum Passenger Car 4-pack, *00*		350 ___
39120	Southern Grand Junction Aluminum Passenger/Baggage Car, *00*		280 ___
39121	Southern Charlottesville Aluminum Passenger Coach "812," *00*		90 ___
39122	Southern Roanoke Aluminum Passenger Coach "814," *00*		250 ___
39123	Southern Memphis Aluminum Observation Car "1152," *00*		90 ___
39124	Amtrak Superliner Aluminum Passenger Car 4-pack, *02*		405 ___
39129	Santa Fe Superliner Aluminum Passenger Car 4-pack, *02*		305 ___
39141	RI Aluminum Passenger Car 4-pack, *01*		400 ___
39146	UP Aluminum Passenger Car 4-pack, *01*		285 ___
39151	CP Aluminum Passenger Car 2-pack, *01*		315 ___
39154	PRR Congressional Aluminum Passenger Car 2-pack, *02*		195 ___
39155	PRR Congressional Baggage Car, *02*		105 ___
39156	PRR Robert Morris Congressional Coach, *02*		100 ___
39157	Southern Aluminum Passenger Car 2-pack, *01*		290 ___
39160	KCS Aluminum Passenger Car 2-pack, *01*	200	260 ___
39163	Erie-Lack. Aluminum Passenger Car 2-pack, *01*		230 ___
39166	Texas Special Aluminum Passenger Car 2-pack, *01*	300	430 ___
39169	ACL Aluminum Passenger Car 4-pack, *01*		360 ___
39179	NP Aluminum Passenger Car 2-pack, *02*		305 ___
39182	WP Aluminum Passenger Car 2-pack, *02*		280 ___
39185	Rio Grande Aluminum Passenger Car 2-pack, *02*		290 ___
39194	UP Aluminum Passenger Car 2-pack, *02*		220 ___
39197	CP Aluminum Passenger Coach, StationSounds, *02*		225 ___
39198	PRR Aluminum Passenger Coach, StationSounds, *02*		210 ___
39200	Hellgate Bridge Boxcar #2 "1900-2000," *00 u*		55 ___
39202	Lionel Centennial Boxcar "1900-2000," *00*		46 ___
39203	Postwar "6464" Series X, 3 cars, *01*		115 ___
39204	New Haven Boxcar "6464-725," *01*		44 ___
39205	Alaska Boxcar "6464-825," *01*		55 ___
39206	NYC Boxcar "6464-900," *01*		40 ___
39207	UP Boxcar "508500," red, *00*		50 ___
39208	UP Boxcar "903658," silver, *00*		42 ___
39209	UP Boxcar "500200," yellow, *00*		40 ___
39210	6530 Fire Fighting Car, *00*		37 ___
39211	Postwar "6464" Boxcar 3-pack #2, *00*		85 ___

| --- | --- | --- | --- | --- |
	39212	Postwar "6464" SP&S Boxcar, *00*		NRS
	39213	Postwar "6464" Wabash Boxcar, *00*		NRS
	39214	Postwar "6464" Kansas, Oklahoma & Gulf Boxcar, *00*		NRS
	39216	PRR DD Boxcar "47211," *01*		46
	39220	B&LE Heavyweight Boxcar "82101," *01*		41
	39221	L&N Heavyweight Boxcar "109829," *01*		41
	39222	Conrail Heavyweight Boxcar "269198," *01*		44
	39223	Postwar "6464" Archive Boxcar Set, 3-pack, *02*		125
	39227	Postwar "6468" Automobile Boxcar 3-pack, *01*		95
	39229	B&O DD Boxcar, *01*		40
	39236	WP Boxcar "6464-250," *01*		55
	39238	Elvis Boxcar, *03*		36
	39239	P&LE Boxcar "22300, *02*		35
	39240	Pennsylvania Boxcar "118747," *02*		32
	39241	PC Boxcar "252455," *02*		28
	39242	Postwar "6464" Boxcar 3-pack #1, Archive Collection, *03-04*		80
	39243	Soo Line Boxcar, Archive Collection		35
	39247	NYC DD Boxcar "6468," *02-03*		32
	39248	Lackawanna DD Boxcar with hobo, *03*		45
	39250	Campbell's Kids Centennial Boxcar, *03-04*		40
	39252	Lenny Dean 60th Anniversary Boxcar, *04*		38
	39253	No. 6464 Boxcar 3-pack #2, *Archive Collection, 04*		100
	39257	WP Boxcar "6464-100," *boys set add-on, 03*		50
	39258	Elvis Presley "All Shook Up" Boxcar, *03-04*		40
	39259	Buick Centennial Boxcar, *03*		40
	39260	New Haven Boxcar, *04*		40
	39262	Elvis Presley "Elvis Has Left the Building" Boxcar, *04*		38
	39263	M&StL Boxcar, Postwar Celebration Series, *05*		35
	39267	No. 6464 Boxcar 3-pack #3, Archive Collection, *05*		100
	39271	State of Maine Boxcar, *04*		35
	39273	No. 6464 Boxcar 3-pack #4, Archive Collection, *06*		100
	39281	Florida State University Boxcar, *07*	0	50
	39282	Purdue University Boxcar, *08*		50
	39283	University of Virginia Boxcar, *08*		50
	39284	Penn State University Boxcar, *06-07*		45
	39285	U.S. Military Academy at West Point Boxcar, *08*		50
	39286	University of Illinois Boxcar, *06-07*		45
	39287	University of Alabama Boxcar, *06-07*		45
	39289	University of Oklahoma Boxcar, *06-08*		50
	39290	Postwar "6464" Boxcar 2-pack, rare variations, *08*		100
	39291	University of Michigan Boxcar, *06-07*		45
	39292	Monopoly Boxcar 3-pack, *08*		135
	39296	UPS Centennial Boxcar #3, *08-09*		55
	39297	Macy's Parade Boxcar, *07*		55
	39298	Monopoly Boxcar 3-pack #2, *08*		145
	39299	Lenny Dean Commemorative Boxcar, *08*		50
	39302	University of Maryland Boxcar, *08*		50
	39303	Villanova University Boxcar, *08*		50
	39304	Auburn University Boxcar, *08*		50
	39308	CP Rail "6565" Boxcar "58700," *08-10*		55
	39309	Macy's Parade Boxcar, *08*		50
	39310	Monopoly Boxcar 3-pack #3, *09-10*		170
	39316	New Haven Automobile Boxcar, *09-10*		60
	39317	Wizard of Oz Boxcar #1, *09-10*		60

		Esc	Mint
39318	Wizard of Oz Boxcar #2, *09-10*		60 __
39319	Boy Scouts "Scout Law" Add-on Boxcar, *10*		60 __
39321	Lionel Art Boxcar 2-pack, *10*		116 __
39325	Macy's Parade Boxcar, *09*		45 __
39326	UPS Centennial Boxcar #4, *10-11*		60 __
39328	Monopoly Boxcar 3-pack #4, *10-11*		220 __
39332	Holiday Boxcar, *10*		60 __
39334	Coca-Cola Christmas Boxcar, *10*		70 __
39335	Thomas Kinkade Boxcar, *10, 12*		60 __
39336	Angela Trotta Thomas "My Turn Yet, Dad?" Boxcar, *10*		60 __
39337	George Washington Boxcar, *11-12*		60 __
39338	Abraham Lincoln Boxcar, *11-12*		60 __
39339	Theodore Roosevelt Boxcar, *11-12*		60 __
39340	Thomas Jefferson Boxcar, *11-12*		60 __
39341	2010 Lionel Dealer Appreciation Boxcar, *2010u*		40 __
39342	Strasburg Boxcar, *11*		55 __
39343	New Jersey Central Boxcar, *10*		45 __
39344	Monopoly Boxcar 3-pack #5, *11-12*		165 __
39345	Monopoly Tennessee Avenue Boxcar, *11*		55 __
39346	Monopoly Atlantic Avenue Boxcar, *11*		55 __
39347	Monopoly Illinois Avenue Boxcar, *11*		55 __
39348	Lionel NASCAR Collectables Boxcar, *11-12*		60 __
39350	Thomas Kinkade "All Aboard for Christmas" Boxcar, *12-13*		60 __
39351	Peanuts Thanksgiving Boxcar, *12*		70 __
39354	Monopoly North Carolina Avenue Boxcar, *12*		70 __
39358	Boy Scouts "Prepared For Life" Boxcar, *12*		60 __
39359	Thanksgiving Boxcar, *12*		60 __
39360	Boy Scouts Cub Scout Boxcar, *12-13*		60 __
39361	Coca-Cola Polar Bear Boxcar, *14*		70 __
39362	Thomas Kinkade "Emerald City" Boxcar, *12-15*		75 __
39363	Peanuts Halloween Boxcar, *12*		65 __
39364	Christmas Boxcar, *13*		60 __
39376	Monopoly Boxcar 2-pack, States and Vermont Avenues, *13-15*		140 __
39379	Monopoly Boxcar 2-pack, Mediterranean and St. James Avenues, *13-15*		140 __
39383	Prewar "2719" Boxcar, *13*		65 __
39385	U.S. Navy 1-D Tank Car, *13-15*		70 __
39386	U.S. Marines 1-D Tank Car, *13-15*		70 __
39387	U.S. Air Force 1-D Tank Car, *13-15*		70 __
39388	U.S. National Guard 1-D Tank Car, *13-16*		70 __
39389	U.S. Coast Guard 1-D Tank Car, *13-16*		70 __
39391	U.S. Army Flatcar, *13-16*		70 __
39392	U.S. Navy Flatcar, *13-16*		70 __
39393	U.S. Marines Flatcar, *13-16*		70 __
39394	U.S. Air Force Flatcar, *13-16*		70 __
39395	U.S. National Guard Flatcar, *13-16*		70 __
39396	U.S. Coast Guard Flatcar, *13-16*		70 __
39398	Santa's Flyer Reefer, *13*		43 __
39399	U.S. Army 1-D Tank Car, *13-15*		70 __
39400	Republic Steel Slag Car 3-pack (std O), *04*		100 __
39404	Republic Steel Hot Metal Car 3-pack (std O), *04*		130 __
39411	Jones & Laughline Hot Metal Car 3-pack (std O), *05*		190 __
39423	Postwar "3460" LL Flatcar with trailers, *05*		45 __
39424	U.S. Steel 16-wheel Flatcar with girders, *05*		70 __

		Mint
39425	Hood's Flatcar with milk container, traditional, 05	55
39426	Nestle Nesquik Flatcar with milk container, traditional, 05	55
39428	Bethlehem Steel Slag Car #4 (std O), 05	60
39429	Bethlehem Steel Hot Metal Car #8 (std O), 05	70
39430	Youngstown Sheet & Tube Slag Car #7 (std O), 05	60
39431	Youngstown Sheet & Tube Hot Metal Car #11 (std O), 05	70
39435	Postwar "6477" Flatcar with pipes, 06	50
39436	Postwar "6262" Wheel Car, 06	50
39437	Supplee Flatcar with milk container, 06	60
39439	6827 Flatcar with P&H power shovel, 04	50
39440	6828 Flatcar with P&H truck crane, 04	50
39443	U.S. Steel Slag Car 3-pack #2 (std O), 06	170
39447	Postwar "6561" LL Cable Reel Car, Archive Collection, 06-07	55
39450	Postwar "6414" Evans Auto Loader, Archive Collection, 06	70
39452	White Bros. Flatcar with milk container, 07	60
39457	Postwar "6175" Flatcar with rocket, 08	55
39458	Postwar "6844" Flatcar with missiles, 08	55
39463	Postwar "6430" Flatcar with trailers, 08	55
39468	Allis-Chalmers Car "52369," 08-09	60
39469	Christmas Egg Nog Barrel Car, 08	50
39470	UP Well Car "147128," 08	65
39471	Postwar "6264" Flatcar, 08	60
39472	ATSF Culvert Gondola, 08	60
39473	Play-Doh Vat Car, 08	55
39475	UPS Flatcar with trailer, 08	65
39476	Bethlehem Steel 16-wheel Flatcar, 08	75
39477	Christmas Flatcar with reindeer trailers, 08	60
39478	Postwar "6475" Pickles Vat Car, 08	55
39479	Postwar "6404" Flatcar with brown automobile, 08	50
39480	Western & Atlantic Cannon Flatcar, 09	60
39482	CSX WM Track Maintenance Car "6812," 11	65
39483	CSX P&LE Gondola "69812," 11	65
39484	Cocoa Marsh Vat Car, 10-12	60
39486	Deep Sea Challenger Submarine Car, 11	60
39488	Reese's Vat Car, 10	60
39490	Western & Atlantic Cannonball Flatcar, 10	55
39497	Christmas Reindeer Stock Car, 10-11	60
39498	CNJ Gondola with culvert pipes, 11	55
39499	Alaska Oil Barrel Ramp Car, 11	50
39502	Monongahela NS Heritage ES44AC Diesel, nonpowered, 13	280
39530	PRR 1955 Pickup Truck, CC, 13	180
39531	UP 1955 Pickup Truck, CC, 13	180
39532	ATSF 1955 Pickup Truck, CC, 13-14	180
39533	CP 1955 Pickup Truck, CC, 13-14	180
39534	D&RGW 1955 Pickup Truck, CC, 13	180
39535	GN 1955 Pickup Truck, CC, 13	180
39536	MKT 1955 Pickup Truck, CC, 13-14	180
39537	NYC 1955 Pickup Truck, CC, 13	180
39538	Nickel Plate Road 1955 Pickup Truck, CC, 13	180
39539	NP 1955 Pickup Truck, CC, 13-14	180
39540	Southern 1955 Pickup Truck, CC, 13	180
39541	SP 1955 Pickup Truck, CC, 13-14	180
39542	Weyerhaueser 1955 Pickup Truck, CC, 13-14	180

		Esc	Mint	
39543	Texas Special F3 B Unit, *13-14*		230	___
39544	Texas Special F3 B Unit, *CC, 13-14*		380	___
39547	PRR F3 B Unit, *13-14*		230	___
39548	PRR F3 B Unit, *CC, 13-14*		380	___
39554	NS GP35 Diesel "3918," *CC, 13*		500	___
39555	NS GP35 Diesel "2915," nonpowered, *13*		260	___
39556	CP GP35 Diesel "5004," *CC, 13-14*		500	___
39557	CP GP35 Diesel "5007," *CC, 13-14*		500	___
39558	CP GP35 Diesel "5009," nonpowered, *13-14*		260	___
39562	BN GP35 Diesel "2533," *CC, 13-14*		500	___
39563	BN GP35 Diesel "2509," *CC, 13-14*		500	___
39564	BN GP35 Diesel "2523," nonpowered, *13-14*		260	___
39565	ATSF Dash-9 Diesel "612," *CC, 13*		530	___
39566	ATSF Dash-9 Diesel "623," *CC, 13*		530	___
39567	ATSF Dash-9 Diesel "631," nonpowered, *13*		260	___
39568	BC Rail Dash-9 Diesel "4641," *CC, 13*		530	___
39569	BC Rail Dash-9 Diesel "4647," *CC, 13*		530	___
39570	BC Rail Dash-9 Diesel "4652," nonpowered, *13*		260	___
39571	BNSF Dash-9 Diesel "4023," *CC, 13*		530	___
39572	BNSF Dash-9 Diesel "4037," *CC, 13*		530	___
39573	BNSF Dash-9 Diesel "4046," nonpowered, *13*		260	___
39574	C&NW Dash-9 Diesel "8605," *CC, 13*		530	___
39575	C&NW Dash-9 Diesel "8610," *CC, 13*		530	___
39576	C&NW Dash-9 Diesel "8622," nonpowered, *13*		260	___
39577	SP Dash-9 Diesel "8112," *CC, 13*		530	___
39578	SP Dash-9 Diesel "8123," *CC, 13*		530	___
39579	SP Dash-9 Diesel "8129," nonpowered, *13*		260	___
39580	UP Dash-9 Diesel "9599," *CC, 13*		530	___
39581	UP Dash-9 Diesel "9714," *CC, 13*		530	___
39582	UP Dash-9 Diesel "9717," nonpowered, *13*		260	___
39583	CSX Dash-9 Diesel "9036," *CC, 13*		530	___
39584	CSX Dash-9 Diesel "9048," *CC, 13*		530	___
39585	CSX Dash-9 Diesel "9051," nonpowered, *13*		260	___
39586	NS Dash-9 Diesel "9310," *CC, 13*		530	___
39587	NS Dash-9 Diesel "9322," *CC, 13*		530	___
39588	NS Dash-9 Diesel "9334," nonpowered, *13*		260	___
39589	CN Dash-9 Diesel "2534," *CC, 13*		530	___
39590	CN Dash-9 Diesel "2547," *CC, 13*		530	___
39591	CN Dash-9 Diesel "2570," nonpowered, *13*		260	___
39592	CNJ NS Heritage SD70ACe Diesel "1071," *CC, 13*		530	___
39593	CNJ NS Heritage SD70ACe Diesel "1831," *CC, 13*		530	___
39594	CNJ NS Heritage SD70ACe Diesel "1834," nonpowered, *13*		260	___
39595	DL&W NS Heritage SD70ACe Diesel "1074," *CC, 13*		530	___
39596	DL&W NS Heritage SD70ACe Diesel "1853," *CC, 13*		530	___
39597	DL&W NS Heritage SD70ACe Diesel "1856," nonpowered, *13*		260	___
39598	Monongahela NS Heritage ES44AC Diesel "8025," *CC, 12*		550	___
39599	Monongahela NS Heritage ES44AC Diesel "1901," *CC, 12*		550	___
39600	PRR E8 AA Diesel Set, *CC, 13*		930	___
39603	B&O E9 AA Diesel Set, *CC, 13*		930	___
39606	FEC E9 AA Diesel Set, *CC, 13*		930	___
39609	SP E9 AA Diesel Set, *CC, 13*		930	___
39612	UP E9 AA Diesel Set, *CC, 13*		930	___
39612	SP E9 AA Diesel Set, *CC, 13*		930	___

			MODERN 1970-2021	Mint
____	39615	CB&Q E9 AA Diesel Set, *CC, 13*		930
____	39618	MILW E9 AA Diesel Set, *CC, 13*		930
____	39621	KCS E9 AA Diesel Set, *CC, 13*		930
____	39624	Erie NS Heritage SD70ACe Diesel "1068," *CC, 13*		530
____	39625	Erie NS Heritage SD70ACe Diesel "1832," *CC, 13*		530
____	39626	Erie NS Heritage SD70ACe Diesel "1835," nonpowered, *13*		260
____	39627	Illinois Terminal NS Heritage SD70ACe Diesel "1072," *CC, 13*		530
____	39628	Illinois Terminal NS Heritage SD70ACe Diesel "1896," *CC, 13*		530
____	39629	Illinois Terminal NS Heritage SD70ACe Diesel "1899," nonpowered, *13*		260
____	39630	NYC NS Heritage SD70ACe Diesel "1066," *CC, 13*		530
____	39631	NYC NS Heritage SD70ACe Diesel "1831," *CC, 13*		530
____	39632	NYC NS Heritage SD70ACe Diesel "1834," nonpowered, *13*		260
____	39633	Reading NS Heritage SD70ACe Diesel "1067," *CC, 13*		530
____	39634	Reading NS Heritage SD70ACe Diesel "1833," *CC, 13*		530
____	39635	Reading NS Heritage SD70ACe Diesel "1836," nonpowered, *13*		260
____	39636	Savannah & Atlanta NS Heritage SD70ACe Diesel "1065," *CC, 13*		530
____	39637	Savannah & Atlanta NS Heritage SD70ACe Diesel "1915," *CC, 13*		530
____	39638	Savannah & Atlanta NS Heritage SD70ACe Diesel "1918," nonpowered, *13*		260
____	39639	Virginian NS Heritage SD70ACe Diesel "1069," *CC, 13*		530
____	39640	Virginian NS Heritage SD70ACe Diesel "1907," *CC, 13*		530
____	39641	Virginian NS Heritage SD70ACe Diesel "1910," nonpowered, *13*		260
____	39642	Wabash NS Heritage SD70ACe Diesel "1070," *CC, 13*		530
____	39643	Wabash NS Heritage SD70ACe Diesel "1877," *CC, 13*		530
____	39644	Wabash NS Heritage SD70ACe Diesel "1880," nonpowered, *13*		260
____	39645	PC NS Heritage SD70ACe Diesel "1073," *CC, 13*		530
____	39646	PC NS Heritage SD70ACe Diesel "1968," *CC, 13*		530
____	39647	PC NS Heritage SD70ACe Diesel "1971," nonpowered, *13*		260
____	51008	Burlington Pioneer Zephyr Diesel Passenger Set, RailSounds, *04*		875
____	51009	Prewar "269E" Steam Freight Set, TrainSounds, *06*		630
____	51010	Prewar "246E" Steam Passenger Set, TrainSounds, *07-08*		630
____	51012	Christmas Tinplate Freight Set, *08*		675
____	51014	Prewar "291W" Red Comet Passenger Car Set, *08*		675
____	51220	NYC Imperial Castle Passenger Coach, *93 u*		500
____	51221	NYC Niagara County Passenger Coach, *93 u*		500
____	51222	NYC Cascade Glory Passenger Coach, *93 u*		500
____	51223	NYC City of Detroit Passenger Coach, *93 u*		500
____	51224	NYC Imperial Falls Passenger Coach, *93 u*		500
____	51225	NYC Westchester County Passenger Coach, *93 u*		500
____	51226	NYC Cascade Grotto Passenger Coach, *93 u*		500
____	51227	NYC City of Indianapolis Passenger Coach, *93 u*		500
____	51228	NYC Manhattan Island Observation Car, *93 u*		500
____	51229	NYC Diner "680," *93 u*		500
____	51230	NYC Baggage Car "5017," *93 u*		500
____	51231	NYC Century Club Passenger Coach, *93 u*		500
____	51232	NYC Thousand Islands Observation Car, *93 u*		500
____	51233	NYC Diner "684," *93 u*		500
____	51234	NYC Baggage Car "5020," *93 u*		500
____	51235	NYC Century Tavern Passenger Coach, *93 u*		500
____	51236	NYC City of Toledo Passenger Coach, *93 u*		500
____	51237	NYC Imperial Mansion Passenger Coach, *93 u*		500
____	51238	NYC Imperial Palace Passenger Coach, *93 u*		500
____	51239	NYC Cascade Spirit Passenger Coach, *93 u*		500

		Esc	Mint	
51240	NYC Diner "681," 93 u		500	___
51241	NYC City of Chicago Passenger Coach, 93 u		500	___
51242	NYC Imperial Garden Passenger Coach, 93 u		500	___
51243	NYC Imperial Fountain Passenger Coach, 93 u		500	___
51244	NYC Cascade Valley Passenger Coach, 93 u		500	___
51245	NYC Diner "685," 93 u		500	___
51300	Shell Semi-Scale 1-D Tank Car "8124," 91	50	135	___
51301	Lackawanna Semi-Scale Reefer "7000," 92	119	161	___
51401	PRR Semi-Scale Boxcar "100800," 91	84	128	___
51402	C&O Semi-Scale Stock Car "95250," 92	98	138	___
51501	B&O Semi-Scale Hopper "532000," 91	78	108	___
51502	LL Steel Die-cast Ore Car "6486-3" (SSS), 96		80	___
51503	LL Steel Die-cast Ore Car "6486-1" (SSS), 96		80	___
51504	LL Steel Die-cast Ore Car "6486-2" (SSS), 96		70	___
51600	NYC Depressed Center Flatcar with transformer "6418," 96		105	___
51701	NYC Semi-Scale Caboose "19400," 91	84	123	___
51702	PRR N-8 Caboose "478039," 91-92	300	385	___
52053	TTOS Carail Convention Car, 94			___
52054	Carail Boxcar, 94 u		300	___
52066	Trainmaster Tractor and Trailer, 94 u		120	___
52068	Toy Train Parade Contadina Boxcar "16245," 94	15	28	___
52069	Carail Tractor and Trailer, 94 u		75	___
52070	Knoebel's Boxcar #1, 95 u		92	___
52075	United Auto Workers Boxcar, 95 u		90	___
52082	Steamtown Lackawanna Boxcar, 95 u		90	___
52132	Knoebel's Boxcar #2, 99 u		95	___
52133	Knoebel's Boxcar #3, 98 u		105	___
52134	Knoebel's Boxcar #4, 00 u		100	___
52136A	Christmas Special Tractor and Trailer, 97		NRS	
52136B	Frisco Special Tractor and Trailer, 98		NRS	
52137	Red Wing Shoes Boot Oil Tank Car, 98		65	___
52141	Zep Manufacturing Boxcar, 96		120	___
52158	Monopoly Mint Car "M-0539," 98		340	___
52159	Monopoly Depressed Center Flatcar with transformer, 98		95	___
52160	Monopoly Water Works Tank Car, 98		105	___
52161	Monopoly SP-type Caboose "M-1006," 98		55	___
52168	Carail Flatcar with Trailer "17455," 99 u		120	___
52169	Zep Manufacturing Flatcar with trailer "62734," 99 u		90	___
52181	Monopoly Set #2, 4-pack, 99		295	___
52182	Monopoly Railroads Boxcar "M0636," 99 u		78	___
52183	Monopoly Jail Car "M-1131," 99		75	___
52184	Monopoly Free Parking Flatcar with 2 autos, 99		60	___
52185	Monopoly Chance Gondola "M-0893," 99		50	___
52187	Madison Hardware Flatcar with 2 trailers, 99		98	___
52188	Carail Aquarium with 2 autos, 25th Anniversary, 99		95	___
52189	Monopoly 4-6-4 Hudson Locomotive, 99		550	___
52200	TTOS SW SP Overnight Merchandise Service Boxcar, 2000u		40	___
52207	Lionel Lines SD40 Diesel, traditional, 00		600	___
52208	Lionel Lines Extended Vision Caboose, 00 u		200	___
52218	Monopoly 4-4-2 Steam Freight Set, 00 u		388	___
52219	Monopoly 4-6-4 Hudson Locomotive, bronze, 00 u		530	___
52224A	SP Flatcar with Navajo tractor and trailer, 01		25	___
52224B	SP Flatcar with Trailer Flatcar Service tractor and trailer, 01		25	___
52225	Monopoly 4-6-4 Hudson Locomotive, pewter, 01 u		495	___

___	52231 British Columbia 1-D Tank Car, *00 u*		65
___	52249 Knoebel's Amusement Park 75th Anniversary Boxcar, *01 u*		95
___	52262 Plasticville Boxcar, *01 u*		120
___	52282 Western Pacific Feather Boxcar, red, *03*		365
___	52330 B&O Museum Fundraiser Boxcar, *03 u*		100
___	52334 TTOS Smokey Bear 60th Anniversary 1-D Tank Car, *2004u*		80
___	52335 TTOS Smokey Bear 60th Anniversary Boxcar, *2004u*		70
___	52371 NYC Flatcar with tanker trailer, *05 u*		150
___	52447 LCCA NH Alco Diesel and Passenger Cars, *2009u*		100
___	52495 LCCA UP Water Tower, *2008u*		30
___	58213 LCCA B&M GP7 Diesel, *2015u*		250
___	58253 LCCA Lionel 115th Anniversary Trailer, *2015u*		25
___	58255 LCCA Lionelville Transit Tractor, *2015u*		25
___	58267 LCCA KCS Inspection Truck, *2016u*		125
___	58269 LCCA Tacoma Pickup Truck, *17u*		75
___	58270 LCCA NP Pickup Truck, *17u*		75
___	58504 Lionel Flatcar w/Madison Hardware Trailer, *2015u*		120
___	58513 LCCA Reading Blue Coal 2-bay Hopper w/ETD, *2012u*		75
___	58515 LCCA NS Vulcan Switcher, *2012u*		50
___	58517 NLOE LIRR Alco Diesels, *2013u*		300
___	58527 LCCA Vulcan Switcher, *2013u*		80
___	58528 LCCA Reading Vulcan Switcher, *2014u*		80
___	58539 LCCA Texas Special B-W Caboose, *2013u*		95
___	58545 LCCA Vulcan Switcher, *Gold, 2012u*		75
___	58550 LCCA Texas Special Unibody Tank Car, *2013u*		90
___	58585 LCCA Wabash Auto Loader, *2014u*		125
___	58586 LCCA South Shore Trolley, *2014u*		95
___	58599 LCCA UP Cylindrical Hopper, *2011u*		150
___	59002 LCCA TVRM Boxcar, *2013u*		150
___	59015 LCCA Conway Scenic RR Boxcar, *2015u*		200
___	62162 Postwar "262" Automatic Crossing Gate and Signal, *99-14*		60
___	62180 Railroad Signs, *set of 14, 99-04, 08-20*		10
___	62181 Telephone Pole Set, *99-04, 08-19*		10
___	62283 Die-cast Illuminated Bumpers, *99-17*		27
___	62709 Rico Station Kit, *99-00*		46
___	62716 Short Extension Bridge, *99-03, 07-19*		15
___	62900 Lockon, *99-13*		3
___	62901 Ives Track Clips, *12 pieces (027), 99-10, 13-16*		5
___	62905 Lockon with wires, *99-10, 13-14*		7
___	62909 Smoke Fluid, *99-12*		7
___	62927 Lubrication/Maintenance Set, *99-17, 19-20*		25
___	62985 The Lionel Train Book, *99-03*		12
___	65014 Half Curved Track (027), *99-16*		1
___	65019 Half Straight Track (027), *99-16*		1
___	65020 90-degree Crossover (027), *99-16*		11
___	65021 27" Manual Switch, left hand (027), *99-16*		17
___	65022 27" Manual Switch, right hand (027), *99-16*		18
___	65023 45-degree Crossover (027), *99-16*		11
___	65024 35" Straight Track (027), *99-16*		5
___	65033 27" Diameter Curved Track (027), *99-16*		2
___	65038 9" Straight Track (027), *99-16*		2
___	65041 Insulator Pins, dozen (027), *99-04, 06, 13-14*		3
___	65042 Steel Pins, dozen (027), *99-04, 06-09, 13-14*		3
___	65049 42" Diameter Curved Track (027), *99-16*		3

No.	Description	Mint	
65113	54" Diameter Curved Track (O27), *99-16*	3	___
65121	27" Path Remote Switch, left hand (O27), *99-14*	43	
65122	27" Path Remote Switch, right hand (O27), *99-14*	43	
65149	Uncoupling Track (O27), *99-14*	12	
65165	72" Path Remote Switch, right hand (O), *99-14*	125	
65166	72" Path Remote Switch, left hand (O), *99-14*	125	
65167	42" Remote Switch, right hand (O27), *99-14*	25	
65168	42" Remote Switch, left hand (O27), *99-14*	25	
65500	10" Straight Track (O), *99-16*	2	
65501	31" Diameter Curved Track (O), *99-16*	2	
65504	Half Curved Track (O), *99-16*	2	
65505	Half Straight Track (O), *99-16*	2	
65514	Half Curved Track (O27), *99-03*	3	___
65523	40" Straight Track (O), *99-16*	7	
65530	Remote Control Track (O), *99-16*	38	
65540	90-degree Crossover (O), *99-14*	16	
65543	Insulator Pins, dozen *(O), 99-16*	3	
65545	45-degree Crossover (O), *99-14*	27	
65551	Steel Pins, dozen (O), *99-16*	3	
65554	54" Diameter Curved Track (O), *99-16*	4	
65572	72" Diameter Curved Track (O), *99-16*	5	
65824	NLOE LIRR Hopper w/Coal load, *17u*	95	
71998	LCCA Amtrak Refrigerator Car (Std O), *2010u*	45	
81000	BNSF Waffle-sided Boxcar "496464," *14-15*	50	
81001	SP&S Flatcar with bulkheads, *14-16*	50	
81002	UP 3-D Tank Car , *14-15*	50	
81003	CP Bilevel Auto Carrier, *14-16*	50	
81004	B&O Depressed-Center Flatcar with transformer, *14-15*	50	
81005	Maine Central 2-bay Hopper "1005," *14-16*	50	
81006	PRR Hi-Cube Boxcar "31010," *14-16*	50	
81007	Seaboard Waffle-sided Boxcar "25335," *14-16*	50	
81008	Central of Georgia Boxcar "5818," *14-17*	50	
81009	Southern 2-D Tank Car "951005," *14-16*	50	
81010	FEC Gondola "6121" with reels, *14-16*	50	
81011	PFE Reefer "33280," *14-16*	50	
81012	T&P 1-D Tank Car, *14-16*	50	
81013	Frisco Boxcar "700117," *14-16*	50	
81014	D&RGW Ore Car "31101," *14-15*	50	
81015	B&M Reefer "1878," *14-16*	50	
81016	Coaling Station, *14, 16-20*	110	
81017	Barrel Loading Building, *14-18*	43	
81018	Shell Vat Car, *17*	80	
81019	Short Tunnel, *14-16-17*	45	
81021	B&M Paul Revere GP9 Diesel Freight Set, *14-15*	500	
81023	Jersey Central Yard Boss 0-4-0 Steam Freight Set, *14-15*	500	
81024	Christmas Train Set, *02-04*	150	
81025	Lackawanna Pocono Berkshire Steam Freight Set, *14-15*	480	
81027	Thomas the Tank Engine Set, *01-04*	120	
81028	Marquette GP38 Diesel Freight Set, *14-15*	430	
81029	C&NW Windy City GP38 Diesel Freight Set, *14-15*	400	
81030	UP Gold Coast Flyer Steam Freight Set, *14-15*	455	
81031	Dinosaur Diesel Freight Set, LionChief, *14-16*	175	
81038	MILW Heavy Mikado Locomotive "8693" CC, *15*	1300	
81063	Classic Automatic Gateman, *14-20*	95	___

		Esc	Mint
___	81064 Construction Zone Signs #2, *14-19*		10
___	81066 Milwaukee Road Double-sheathed Boxcar "8775" (std O), *14*		80
___	81067 Monopoly Aquarium Car, *14-15*		85
___	81073 Monopoly Boxcar 2-pack, Ventnor and Indiana Avenues, *14-15*		135
___	81076 Pennsylvania Salt 8,000-gallon 1-D Tank Car "4724" (std O), *14*		73
___	81077 Pere Marquette 8,000-gallon 1-D Tank Car "71710" (std O), *14*		73
___	81078 NYC 8,000-gallon 1-D Tank Car "107898" (std O), *14*		73
___	81079 NKP 8,000-gallon 1-D Tank Car "50277" (std O), *14*		73
___	81080 BN 8,000-gallon 1-D Tank Car "977100" (std O), *14*		73
___	81081 Alaska Steel-sided Reefer "10806" (std O), *14*		80
___	81090 NS Hi-Cube Boxcar 2-pack (std O), *14-15*		190
___	81093 2013 Lionel Dealer Appreciation Boxcar, *2013u*		40
___	81094 Conrail "Big Blue" High-Cube Boxcar Diesel Freight Set, *CC, 14*		970
___	81095 Conrail Hi-Cube Boxcar 2-pack (std O), *14-16*		190
___	81101 Polar Express 10th Anniversary Steam Passenger Set, LionChief, *14-15*		430
___	81113 SP 50' DD Boxcar "214051" (std O), *14-15*		75
___	81122 Christmas Inspection Truck, *15*		180
___	81134 BN SD70MAC Diesel "9424," *CC, 14*		550
___	81135 BN SD70MAC Diesel "9431," *CC, 14*		550
___	81137 BNSF SD70MAC Diesel "9858," *CC, 14*		550
___	81138 BNSF SD70MAC Diesel "9860," *CC, 14*		550
___	81141 Conrail SD70MAC Diesel "4138," *CC, 14*		550
___	81142 PFE Steel-sided Reefers 3-pack (std O), *14*		300
___	81144 CSX SD70MAC Diesel "781," *CC, 14*		550
___	81147 KCS SD7CMAC Diesel "3950," *CC, 14*		550
___	81148 KCS SD7CMAC Diesel "3953," *CC, 14*		550
___	81151 Alaska SD7CMAC Diesel "4002," *CC, 14*		550
___	81152 Alaska SD7CMAC Diesel "4005," *CC, 14*		550
___	81153 CSX SD70MAC Diesel "778," *CC, 14*		550
___	81154 UP ES44AC Diesel "7361," *CC, 14*		550
___	81155 UP ES44AC Diesel "7388," *CC, 14*		550
___	81160 CSX ES44AC Diesel "937," *CC, 14*		550
___	81161 CSX ES44AC Diesel "944," *CC, 14*		550
___	81169 Iowa Interstate ES44AC Diesel "504," *CC, 14*		550
___	81170 Iowa Interstate ES44AC Diesel "507," *CC, 14*		550
___	81171 Ferromex ES44AC Diesel "4617," *CC, 14*		550
___	81172 Ferromex ES44AC Diesel "4626," *CC, 14*		550
___	81176 CN ES44AC Diesel "2812," *CC, 14*		550
___	81177 CN ES44AC Diesel "2818," *CC, 14*		550
___	81179 2-8-2 Heavy Mikado Pilot Locomotive, *CC, 14*		1300
___	81180 2-8-2 Heavy Mikado Locomotive, *CC, 15*		1300
___	81181 Southern 2-8-2 Heavy Mikado Locomotive "4866," *CC, 15*		1300
___	81182 L&N 2-8-2 Heavy Mikado Locomotive "1757," *CC, 14*		1300
___	81183 MP 2-8-2 Heavy Mikado Locomotive "1496," *CC, 14*		1300
___	81184 P&WV 2-8-2 Heavy Mikado Locomotive "1152," *CC, 14*		1300
___	81185 CNJ 2-8-2 Heavy Mikado Locomotive "845," *CC, 14*		1300
___	81186 Frisco 2-8-2 Heavy Mikado Locomotive "4126," *CC, 14*		1300
___	81187 C&IM 2-8-2 Heavy Mikado Locomotive "551," *CC, 14*		1300
___	81188 NYC 2-8-2 Heavy Mikado Locomotive "9506," *CC, 14*		1300
___	81189 CB&Q 2-8-2 Heavy Mikado Locomotive "5509," *CC, 15*		1300
___	81190 WP 2-8-2 Heavy Mikado Locomotive "334," *CC, 15*		1300
___	81191 Erie 2-8-2 Heavy Mikado Locomotive "3207," *CC, 15*		1300
___	81192 GN 2-8-2 Heavy Mikado Locomotive "3148," *CC, 14*		1300

		Esc	Mint	
81193	Wheeling & Lake Erie 2-8-2 Heavy Mikado Locomotive "6012," CC, 15		1300	___
81194	NKP 2-8-2 Heavy Mikado Locomotive "689," CC, 15		1300	___
81195	PRR Boxcar, 14-15		70	___
81196	Timken Boxcar, 14-15		70	___
81197	Santa Fe Boxcar, 14-15		70	___
81198	GN Boxcar, 14-16		70	___
81199	PRR 1-D Tank Car, 14-15		70	___
81200	Timken 1-D Tank Car, 14-16		70	___
81201	GN 1-D Tank Car, 14-16		70	___
81202	Santa Fe 1-D Tank Car, 14-15		70	___
81203	PRR Flatcar, 14-15		70	___
81204	Santa Fe Flatcar, 14-16		70	___
81205	Timken Flatcar, 14-16		70	___
81206	GN Flatcar, 14-16		70	___
81207	CP H-24-66 Train Master Diesel "8900," CC, 14		550	___
81208	CP H-24-66 Train Master Diesel "8903," CC, 14		550	___
81209	CNJ H-24-66 Train Master Diesel "2401," CC, 14		550	___
81210	CNJ H-24-66 Train Master Diesel "2406," CC, 14		550	___
81211	Reading H-24-66 Train Master Diesel "801," CC, 14		550	___
81212	Reading H-24-66 Train Master Diesel "804," CC, 14		550	___
81213	SP H-24-66 Train Master Diesel "4803," CC, 14		550	___
81214	SP H-24-66 Train Master Diesel "4809," CC, 14		550	___
81215	Southern H-24-66 Train Master Diesel "6300," CC, 14		550	___
81216	Southern H-24-66 Train Master Diesel "6303," CC, 14		550	___
81217	N&W H-24-66 Train Master Diesel "151," CC, 14		550	___
81218	N&W H-24-66 Train Master Diesel "164," CC, 14		550	___
81219	Santa Fe E8 Diesel AA Set "84/85," CC, 14		930	___
81222	PC E8 Diesel AA Set "4289/4325," CC, 14		930	___
81225	RI E8 Diesel AA Set "647/648," CC, 14		930	___
81228	C&O E8 Diesel AA Set "4027/4028," CC, 14		930	___
81231	Erie E8 Diesel AA Set "822/823," CC, 14		930	___
81234	MKT E8 Diesel AA Set "131/132," CC, 14		930	___
81237	SAL E8 Diesel AA Set "3051/3055," CC, 14		930	___
81240	Wabash E8 Diesel AA Set "1007/1011," CC, 14		930	___
81243	Pilot M1a 4-8-2 Locomotive, CC, 14		1500	___
81245	PRR M1a 4-8-2 Locomotive "6671," CC, 14		1500	___
81246	PRR M1a 4-8-2 Locomotive "6764," CC, 14		1500	___
81247	PRR M1a Coal Hauler Twin-hopper Steam Freight Set, CC, 14		1800	___
81248	10" Girder Bridge Track, 14-20		25	___
81249	Christmas Girder Bridge Track, 14, 16-18		25	___
81250	FasTrack O-96 Curve, 14, 18-20		7	___
81251	FasTrack O-31 Manual Switch, right-hand, 14-16, 18-20		50	___
81252	FasTrack O-31 Manual Switch, left-hand, 14-16, 18-20		50	___
81253	FasTrack O-31 Remote Switch, right-hand, 14-16, 18-20		110	___
81254	FasTrack O-31 Remote Switch, left-hand, 14-16, 18-20		110	___
81256	Personalized Birthday Message Boxcar, 14-15		85	___
81257	Amtrak Water Tower, 14-18		35	___
81259	PRR Broadway Limited Steam Passenger Set, 14		370	___
81261	NYC Early Bird Special Steam Freight Set, 16-17		380	___
81262	UP Steam Freight Set, LionChief, 15		400	___
81263	CNJ Diesel Passenger Set, LionChief, 14-16		390	___
81264	Western Union Telegraph Steam Freight Set, 14-16		390	___
81266	Amtrak FT Diesel Passenger Set, LionChief, 14-15		460	___

		Mint
81269	PRR Allegheny Hauler Steam Freight Set, *16-17*	420
81270	Bethlehem Steel Steam Work Train, LionChief, *15*	340
81279	Albert Hall European Steam Passenger Set, LionChief, *14-15*	430
81280	Victorian Christmas Steam Passenger Set, *14*	400
81284	Frosty the Snowman Steam Freight Set, LionChief, *14-16*	320
81286	Lionel Junction "Little Steam" Freight Set, *14-15*	175
81287	Lionel Junction UP Steam Freight Set, *14-15*	175
81288	Pet Shop Diesel Freight Set, *14-16*	175
81290	Thomas Kinkade Holiday Covered Bridge, *14*	70
81292	Valley Central 1-D Tank Car "45003," *14-17*	45
81294	LCS Sensor Track, *13-16, 18-20*	95
81295	AT&SF 2-8-2 Locomotive "3158," LionChief, *14-16*	430
81296	GN 2-8-2 Locomotive "3123," LionChief, *14-15*	430
81297	PRR 2-8-2 Locomotive "9633," LionChief, *14-15*	430
81299	Chessie System 2-8-2 Locomotive "2103," LionChief, *14-15*	430
81301	NYC 4-6-4 Locomotive "5421," LionChief, *14-15*	430
81302	C&O 4-6-4 Locomotive "308," LionChief, *14-17*	430
81303	UP 4-6-4 Locomotive "674," LionChief, *14-17*	430
81304	CN 4-6-4 Locomotive "5702," LionChief, *14-17*	430
81307	B&O 4-6-2 Locomotive "5307," LionChief, *14-17*	430
81308	CP 4-6-2 Locomotive "2469," LionChief, *14-17*	430
81309	SP 4-6-2 Locomotive "3106," LionChief, *14-17*	430
81311	Alaska 4-6-2 Locomotive "652," LionChief, *14-17*	430
81313	FasTrack Power Lockon, *15-20*	23
81314	FasTrack Power Block Lockon, *15-20*	40
81315	Coaling Station, *15-17, 19-20*	160
81316	Personalized Christmas Message Boxcar, *15*	80
81317	FasTrack Accessory Activator Track Pack, *15-20*	24
81325	LCS WiFi Module, *13-16, 18-20*	180
81326	LCS Serial Converter #2, *14-16, 18-20*	50
81331	Iron Arry Locomotive with Remote, LionChief, *14-15*	140
81332	Iron Bert Locomotive with Remote, LionChief, *14-15*	140
81373	Candy Cane Flatcar with bulkheads, *15*	60
81395	Thomas Kinkade Christmas Passenger Set, LionChief, *14-15*	380
81419	Alien Ooze 1-D Tank Car, *14-15*	65
81420	PRR Truss-rod Gondola with tarp, *14-16*	65
81422	NS Water Tower, *14*	31
81423	Sodor Coal and Scrap Cars 2-pack, *14-16*	70
81424	Sodor Crane Car and Work Caboose 2-pack, *14*	70
81425	Frosty the Snowman Passenger Station, *14*	65
81426	Frosty the Snowman Animated Gondola, *14*	75
81427	Frosty the Snowman Aquarium Car, *14*	85
81428	Frosty the Snowman Boxcar, *14*	65
81430	Lionelville Shanty, *14*	22
81432	PRR Girder Bridge, *14-15*	21
81433	PRR Crossing Shanty, *14*	22
81434	Pennsylvania Station Platform, *14-15*	23
81435	N&W NS Heritage Quad Hopper with coal, *14-15*	60
81436	Intermodal Container 4-pack, *14*	43
81437	York Peppermint Patty Vat Car, *14-15*	70
81439	Halloween Pumpkinheads Handcar, *14-16*	90
81440	Western Union Handcar, *14-16*	100
81441	North Pole Central Snowplow, *CC , 16-18, 20*	280
81442	PRR Rotary Snowplow "1442," *CC, 16, 18*	280

81443	D&RGW Rotary Snowplow "443," *CC, 16, 18*	280	___
81444	PRR Tie-Jector, *CC, 14-16*	200	___
81445	MOW Tie-Jector, *CC, 14-16*	200	___
81446	Santa Fe Tie-Jector, *CC, 14-16, 18*	200	___
81447	NS Tie-Jector, *CC, 14-16*	200	___
81448	Amtrak Tie-Jector, *CC, 14-16, 18*	200	___
81449	Zombie Motorized Trolley, *14*	100	___
81450	Polar Express Trolley, *14*	110	___
81451	St. Louis Motorized Trolley, *14*	100	___
81452	Neil Young Texas Special F3 AA Diesels, *CC, 13-14*	650	___
81453	Neil Young PRR F3 AA Diesels, *CC, 13-14*	650	___
81462	PRR Broadway Limited Add-on Baggage Car, *14-17*	70	___
81463	CNJ Water Tower, *14-17*	31	___
81464	CNJ Montclair Add-on Passenger Car, *14-16*	60	___
81465	SP Flatcar with piggyback trailers , *14-16*	75	___
81466	BN Maxi-Stack Pair, *14-16*	140	___
81469	GN Bilevel Stock Car "65385," *14-17*	65	___
81470	DC Comics Batman Phantom Train, *16-17*	400	___
81475	DC Comics Batman M7 Subway Set, LionChief, *14-15*	370	___
81479	Batman Add-on M7 Subway Car 2-pack, *14-15*	140	___
81480	John Deere RS-3 Diesel Freight Set, LionChief, *14-16*	320	___
81486	NYC Patrol Flatcar with helicopter, *14-15*	65	___
81487	Ronald Reagan Presidential Boxcar, *14-15*	70	___
81488	Andrew Jackson Presidential Boxcar, *14-16, 18*	70	___
81489	Warren G. Harding Presidential Boxcar, *14-16, 18, 20*	75	___
81490	Dwight D. Eisenhower Presidential Boxcar, *14-16*	70	___
81491	Jersey Central Coal Dump Car, *14-15*	65	___
81492	Strasburg RR Searchlight Car, *14*	50	___
81493	U.S.A.F. Missile Carrying Car, *15-16*	65	___
81494	Santa's Sleigh Rocket Fuel Tank Car, *16*	65	___
81495	40-watt Power Supply, *15-18*	65	___
81496	2014 Lionel Dealer Appreciation Boxcar, *2014u*	40	___
81497	2015 Lionel Dealer Appreciation Boxcar, *2015u*	40	___
81499	LCS Power Supply with DB9 cable, *13-16, 18-20*	37	___
81500	LCS Sensor Track 1' Cable, *13-16, 18-20*	14	___
81501	LCS Sensor Track 3' Cable, *13-16, 18-20*	15	___
81502	LCS Sensor Track 10' Cable, *13-16, 18-20*	19	___
81503	LCS Sensor Track 20' Cable, *13-16, 18-20*	19	___
81504	Ann Arbor FA-2 Diesel AA Set "53/53A," *CC, 14*	750	___
81507	B&O FA-2 Diesel AA Set "817/827," *CC, 14-15*	750	___
81510	Erie FA-2 Diesel AA Set "736A/736D," *CC, 14-15*	750	___
81513	MKT FA-2 Diesel AA Set "331A/331C," *CC, 14*	750	___
81516	NYC FA-2 Diesel AA Set "1075/1078," *CC, 14-15*	750	___
81519	PRR FA-2 Diesel AA Set "9608/9609," *CC, 14-15*	750	___
81522	Ann Arbor FB2 Diesel "53B," *CC, 14*	450	___
81523	B&O FB2 Diesel "817B," *CC, 14-15*	450	___
81524	Erie FB2 Diesel "736B," *CC, 14-15*	450	___
81525	MKT FB2 Diesel "331B," *CC, 14*	450	___
81526	NYC FB2 Diesel "3327," *CC, 14-15*	450	___
81527	PRR FB2 Diesel "9608B," *CC, 14*	450	___
81528	Ann Arbor FB2 Diesel, nonpowered, *14*	350	___
81529	B&O FB2 Diesel, nonpowered, *14-15*	350	___
81530	Erie FB2 Diesel, nonpowered, *14-15*	350	___
81531	MKT FB2 Diesel, nonpowered, *14*	350	___

				Mint
___	81532	NYC FB2 Diesel, nonpowered, *14-15*		350
___	81533	PRR FB2 Diesel, nonpowered, *14-15*		350
___	81534	Christmas Toys Stock Car, *14*		70
___	81545	Operation Eagle Missile Launcher Car, *CC, 15*		350
___	81546	Operation Eagle Sound Car, *CC, 15*		240
___	81568	4th of July Parade Boxcar, *14-16*		80
___	81596	Weathered UP 4-12-2 Locomotive "9000," *CC, 13*		1400
___	81597	Weathered B&O RF-16 Sharknose AA Diesels "855-857," *CC, 13*		830
___	81600	Weathered PRR RF-16 Sharknose AA Diesels "2020A-2021A," *CC, 13*		830
___	81603	72-watt Power Supply, LionChief, *14-20*		55
___	81605	Santa Fe PS-1 Boxcar 5-pack (std O), *14*		380
___	81615	UP 1-D Tank Car, *14*		45
___	81617	Pet Shop 1-D Tank Car, *14-16*		45
___	81619	Reading PS-1 Boxcar "109448" (std O), *14*		80
___	81620	Zombie Figure Pack, *14-15*		23
___	81621	John Deere Billboard Set, *15*		25
___	81622	John Deere Water Tower, *15*		40
___	81625	Amtrak Add-on Baggage Car, *14-16*		85
___	81626	Barrel Shed, *14-16, 18-20*		40
___	81627	Christmas Hopper Shed, *14, 16-17*		45
___	81628	Grain Elevator, *15*		80
___	81629	Lumber Shed Kit, *14-20*		38
___	81635	Water Tower, *14*		35
___	81639	LCS Accessory Switch Controller #2, *14-16, 18-20*		120
___	81640	LCS Block Power Controller #2, *14-16, 18-20*		120
___	81641	Layout Control System Accessory Motor Controller, *17-20*		120
___	81644	Chessie System Baby Madison Passenger Car 3-pack, *14-16*		270
___	81649	SP Baby Madison Passenger Car 3-pack, *14-16*		270
___	81654	Philadelphia Energy Solutions 1-D Tank Car "0765," *15-18*		60
___	81662	FasTrack O-31 Quarter Curved Track, *14, 16, 18-20*		5
___	81668	Philadelphia Energy Solutions 1-D Tank Car "0771," *15-16, 18*		60
___	81680	Dinosaur 1-D Tank Car, *14-16*		45
___	81686	PRR GL-a 2-bay Hopper 3-pack (std O), *14*		220
___	81687	LV GL-a 2-bay Hopper 2-pack (std O), *14-15*		146
___	81688	CB&Q GL-a 2-bay Hopper 3-pack (std O), *14-16*		220
___	81689	C&O GL-a 2-bay Hopper 3-pack (std O), *14-16*		220
___	81693	Aerial Target Launcher, *15-16*		90
___	81699	Polar Express Scale Twin Hopper, *15*		80
___	81703	Santa Fe Hi-Cube Boxcar 2-pack (std O), *14-16*		190
___	81704	Grand Trunk Hi-Cube Boxcar 2-pack (std O), *14-16*		190
___	81705	Milwaukee Road Hi-Cube Boxcar 2-pack (std O), *14-16*		190
___	81706	Frisco Hi-Cube Boxcar 2-pack (std O), *14-16*		190
___	81707	NYC Hi-Cube Boxcar 2-pack (std O), *14-16*		190
___	81708	Santa Fe Hi-Cube Boxcar "36715" (std O), *14-15*		95
___	81710	Milwaukee Road Hi-Cube Boxcar "4980" (std O), *14-15*		95
___	81711	Frisco Hi-Cube Boxcar "9125" (std O), *14-15*		95
___	81712	NYC Hi-Cube Boxcar "67282" (std O), *14-15*		95
___	81723	Postwar "3413" Mercury Capsule Launcher Car, *15*		80
___	81725	UP Operating Merchandise Car, *14-15*		80
___	81726	REA Operating Merchandise Car, *14-15*		80
___	81729	Great Western Passenger Car Add-on 2-pack, *14*		130
___	81733	Christmas Boxcar, *14*		65
___	81734	FasTrack Oval Track and Power Pack, *14-17*		200

		Esc	Mint
81735	FasTrack Figure-8 Track and Power Pack, *14-17*		250 ___
81736	Classic Lionel Catalogs Billboard Pack, *14-15*		13 ___
81737	Passenger Station, *14-15*		60 ___
81738	Lionel Auto Loader Cars 4-pack, *14-15, 17*		25 ___
81739	Santa Fe Baby Madison Passenger Car 3-pack, *14-16*		270 ___
81744	CP Baby Madison Passenger Car 3-pack, *14-16*		270 ___
81749	Pullman Baby Madison Passenger Car 3-pack, *14-16*		270 ___
81754	NYC Baby Madison Passenger Car 3-pack, *14-16*		270 ___
81759	NYC Coach/Diner 2-pack, *14-16*		180 ___
81760	NYC Coach/Baggage Car 2-pack, *14-16*		180 ___
81763	Pullman Baby Madison Passenger Car 3-pack, *14-16*		180 ___
81764	Pullman Coach/Baggage Car 2-pack, *14, 16*		180 ___
81768	Chessie System Coach/Diner 2-pack, *14-16*		180 ___
81769	Chessie System Coach/Baggage Car 2-pack, *14-16*		180 ___
81773	SP Coach/Diner 2-pack, *14-16*		180 ___
81774	SP Coach/Baggage Car 2-pack, *14-16*		180 ___
81778	Santa Fe Coach/Diner 2-pack, *14-16*		180 ___
81779	Santa Fe Coach/Baggage Car 2-pack, *14-16*		180 ___
81783	CP Coach/Diner 2-pack, *14-16*		180 ___
81784	CP Coach/Baggage Car 2-pack, *14-16*		180 ___
81789	NH GL-a 2-bay Hopper 2-pack (std O), *14-16*		146 ___
81793	Berwind GL-a 2-bay Hopper 3-pack (std O), *14-15*		220 ___
81800	Southern 18" Aluminum Observation/Coach Car, *2-pack (std O), 14*		320 ___
81801	Southern 18" Aluminum Combination/Vista Dome Car, *2-pack (std O), 14*		320 ___
81806	PRR N5b Caboose "477814" (std O), *14*		95 ___
81807	Conrail N5b Caboose "22882" (std O), *14-15*		95 ___
81808	PC N5b Caboose "22802" (std O), *14-16*		95 ___
81809	LIRR N5b Caboose "2" (std O), *14-15*		95 ___
81810	Lionel Lines N5b Caboose "1402" (std O), *14-16*		95 ___
81811	Polar Express N5b Caboose, *16*		95 ___
81812	RI 18" Aluminum Observation/Coach Car, 2-pack (std O), *14*		320 ___
81813	RI 18" Aluminum Combination/Vista Dome Car, 2-pack (std O), *14*		320 ___
81818	C&O 18" Aluminum Observation/Coach Car, 2-pack (std O), *14*		320 ___
81819	C&O 18" Aluminum Combination/Vista Dome Car, 2-pack (std O), *14*		320 ___
81824	P&WV GL-a 2-bay Hopper 2-pack (std O), *14-16*		146 ___
81827	PC Round-roof Boxcar "100104" (std O), *14*		80 ___
81828	GN Round-roof Boxcar "5885" (std O), *14*		80 ___
81829	WP Round-roof Boxcar "10211" (std O), *14*		80 ___
81830	MKT 18" Aluminum Observation/Coach Car, *2-pack (std O), 14*		320 ___
81831	MKT 18" Aluminum Baggage/Diner Car, *2-pack (std O), 14*		320 ___
81836	Erie Double-sheathed Boxcar "71107" (std O), *14-15*		80 ___
81837	Frisco Double-sheathed Boxcar "128528" (std O), *14-15*		80 ___
81838	CNJ Double-sheathed Boxcar "14014" (std O), *14-15*		80 ___
81839	Pacific Fright Express Steel-sided Reefer (std O), *14*		80 ___
81840	UP Ca-4 Caboose with smoke "3880" (std O), *14*		90 ___
81841	UP MOW Caboose "903224" (std O), *14*		90 ___
81842	Wabash 18" Aluminum Dome-Observation/Coach Car, 2-pack (std O), *14*		320 ___
81843	Wabash 18" Aluminum Combination/Vista Dome Car, 2-pack (std O), *14*		320 ___
81858	PRR GL-a 2-bay Hopper 3-pack (std O), *14*		220 ___
81862	FasTrack O-31 Curved Track 4-pack, *14, 16, 19-20*		22 ___
81866	RI 18" Aluminum Baggage/Diner Car, 2-pack (std O), *14*		320 ___

| --- | --- | --- | --- |
____ **81869**	C&O 18" Aluminum Baggage/Diner Car, 2-pack (std O), *14*		320
____ **81871**	Loggers Figure Pack, *16-20*		30
____ **81872**	Wabash 18" Aluminum Baggage/Diner Car, 2-pack (std O), *14*		320
____ **81875**	MKT 18" Aluminum Combination/Vista Dome Car, 2-pack (std O), *14*		320
____ **81878**	Southern 18" Aluminum Baggage/Diner Car, 2-pack (std O), *14*		320
____ **81881**	SP Crane Car, *CC, 14-16*		500
____ **81882**	DT&I Crane Car, *CC, 14-16*		500
____ **81883**	CSX Crane Car, *CC, 14-16*		500
____ **81884**	Bethlehem Steel Crane Car, *CC, 14*		500
____ **81885**	MOW Crane Car, *CC, 14-16*		500
____ **81886**	SP Boom Car, RailSounds, *CC, 14-16*		240
____ **81887**	DT&I Boom Car, RailSounds, *CC, 14-16*		240
____ **81888**	CSX Boom Car, RailSounds, *CC, 14-16*		240
____ **81889**	MOW Boom Car, RailSounds, *CC, 14-16*		240
____ **81890**	Bethlehem Steel Boom Car, RailSounds, *CC, 14*		240
____ **81891**	BNSF 52' Gondola "523300" with 3-piece covers (std O), *14*		80
____ **81892**	Bethlehem Steel 52' Gondola "303022" with 3-piece covers (std O), *14*		80
____ **81893**	GTW 52' Gondola "145391" with 3-piece covers (std O), *14*		80
____ **81894**	CSX 52' Gondola "709190" with 3-piece covers (std O), *14*		80
____ **81895**	North Pole Central 52' Gondola "128925" with 3-piece covers (std O), *14*		80
____ **81896**	NYC PS-5 Flatcar "506266" with piggyback trailers (std O), *14*		100
____ **81897**	Milwaukee Road PS-5 Flatcar "64660" with piggyback trailers (std O), *14*		100
____ **81898**	Lionel PS-5 Flatcar with piggyback trailers (std O), *14*		100
____ **81899**	CP PS-5 Flatcar "301000" with piggyback trailers (std O), *14*		100
____ **81900**	UP PS-5 Flatcar "258255" with piggyback trailers (std O), *14*		100
____ **81901**	NYC Tractor and Piggyback Trailer, *14, 17*		90
____ **81902**	Milwaukee Road Tractor and Piggyback Trailer, *14*		90
____ **81903**	Lionel Tractor and Piggyback Trailer, *14*		90
____ **81904**	CP Tractor and Piggyback Trailer, *14-15, 17*		90
____ **81905**	UP Tractor and Piggyback Trailer, *14*		90
____ **81908**	PFE Steel-sided Reefers 3-pack (std O), *14*		240
____ **81912**	New York Yankees Boxcar, *14*		70
____ **81913**	St. Louis Cardinals Boxcar, *14*		70
____ **81914**	Oakland Athletics Boxcar, *14*		70
____ **81915**	San Francisco Giants Boxcar, *14*		70
____ **81916**	Boston Red Sox Boxcar, *14*		70
____ **81917**	Los Angeles Dodgers Boxcar, *14*		70
____ **81918**	Cincinnati Reds Boxcar, *14*		70
____ **81919**	San Diego Padres Boxcar, *14*		70
____ **81920**	Detroit Tigers Boxcar, *14*		70
____ **81921**	Atlanta Braves Boxcar, *14*		70
____ **81922**	Baltimore Orioles Boxcar, *14*		70
____ **81923**	Minnesota Twins Boxcar, *14*		70
____ **81924**	Chicago White Sox Boxcar, *14*		70
____ **81925**	Chicago Cubs Boxcar, *14*		70
____ **81926**	Philadelphia Phillies Boxcar, *14*		70
____ **81927**	Cleveland Indians Boxcar, *14*		70
____ **81928**	New York Mets Boxcar, *14*		70
____ **81929**	Toronto Blue Jays Boxcar, *14*		70
____ **81930**	Miami Marlins Boxcar, *14*		70
____ **81931**	Angels Baseball Boxcar, *14*		70
____ **81932**	Pittsburgh Pirates Boxcar, *14*		70

		Mint
81933	Texas Rangers Boxcar, *14*	70 ___
81934	Milwaukee Brewers Boxcar, *14*	70 ___
81935	Houston Astros Boxcar, *14*	70 ___
81936	Colorado Rockies Boxcar, *14*	70 ___
81937	Tampa Bay Rays Boxcar, *14*	70 ___
81938	Seattle Mariners Boxcar, *14*	70 ___
81939	Washington Nationals Boxcar, *14*	70 ___
81940	Arizona Diamondbacks Boxcar, *14*	70 ___
81941	Kansas City Royals Boxcar, *14*	70 ___
81944	Rotary Beacon, yellow, *14-16, 18-19*	85 ___
81945	Polar Express Scale Coach, *14*	210 ___
81946	FasTrack O-36 Remote Switch, right-hand, *14-16, 18-20*	110 ___
81947	FasTrack O-36 Remote Switch, left-hand, *14-16, 18-20*	110 ___
81948	FasTrack O-48 Remote Switch, right-hand, *14-16, 18-20*	120 ___
81949	FasTrack O-48 Remote Switch, left-hand, *14-16, 19-20*	120 ___
81950	FasTrack O-60 Remote Switch, right-hand, *14-16, 18-20*	120 ___
81951	FasTrack O-60 Remote Switch, left-hand, *14-16, 18-20*	120 ___
81952	FasTrack O-72 Remote Switch, right-hand, *14-16, 18-20*	120 ___
81953	FasTrack O-72 Remote Switch, left-hand, *14-16, 18-20*	120 ___
81954	FasTrack O-72 Remote Switch, wye, *14-16, 18-20*	120 ___
81968	Halloween Pacific Fright Express Caboose (std O), *14*	90 ___
81969	PRR 18" Aluminum Parlor/Coach Car, 2-pack (std O), *14-15*	320 ___
81972	B&O 18" Aluminum Baggage/Sleeper Car, 2-pack (std O), *14*	320 ___
81975	SP 18" Aluminum Sleeper/Coach Car, 2-pack (std O), *14-15*	320 ___
81978	UP 18" Aluminum Sleeper/Coach Car, 2-pack (std O), *14-15*	320 ___
81981	KCS 18" Aluminum Sleeper/Coach Car, 2-pack (std O), *14*	320 ___
81984	Postwar "1887" Christmas Flatcar with reindeer, *14*	70 ___
81985	Postwar "6428" Christmas Mail Car, *14*	60 ___
81986	Christmas Wish 1-D Tank Car, *14*	60 ___
81987	Angela Trotta Thomas "Santa's Letter" Boxcar, *14*	65 ___
81988	Angela Trotta Thomas Christmas Billboard Pack, *14*	15 ___
81990	Christmas Gondola with reindeer feed vats, *14*	65 ___
81992	Santa Claus Bobbing Head Boxcar, *14*	65 ___
81993	North Pole Central Santa Finder Searchlight Car, *14*	55 ___
81999	PRR Gondola with Christmas gifts and trees, *14*	65 ___
82000	PRR Christmas Crane Car, *14*	75 ___
82001	Merry & Bright Hot Cocoa Car, *14*	70 ___
82002	Old St. Nick Operating Billboard, *14, 16*	60 ___
82003	Christmas Blinking Water Tower, *14*	35 ___
82005	Christmas Wreath Clock Tower, *14, 16-17*	43 ___
82008	Bungalow House, *15-17*	80 ___
82009	Suburban House, *15-16*	80 ___
82010	Joe's Bait & Tackle Shop, *15-16*	65 ___
82011	Keystone Cafe, *15-16*	80 ___
82012	Single Floodlight Tower, *15-20*	75 ___
82013	Double Floodlight Tower, *15-19*	90 ___
82014	Postwar "192" Control Tower, *15-16*	100 ___
82015	Wind Turbine, *15-18*	80 ___
82016	Oil Pump, *15-20*	60 ___
82017	Lionel Art Operating Billboard, *15-20*	70 ___
82018	Track Gang, *15-16*	100 ___
82020	Burning Switch Tower, *15-17*	130 ___
82021	Bascule Bridge, *15*	450 ___

		MODERN 1970-2021	Esc	Mint
___	**82022**	Lionel Steel Gantry Crane, *CC, 15-19*		400
___	**82023**	Operating Sawmill, *CC, 15-17*		350
___	**82024**	Postwar "164" Log Loader, *15*		340
___	**82026**	Postwar "497" Coaling Station, *15-17*		300
___	**82028**	Postwar "352" Icing Station, *15-17*		150
___	**82029**	Culvert Loader, *CC, 15-20*		300
___	**82030**	Culvert Unloader, *CC, 15-20*		300
___	**82033**	MOW Trackside Crane, *CC, 16-17, 19*		600
___	**82034**	Loading Station, *16*		350
___	**82035**	Work House, crane sounds, *16-19*		150
___	**82036**	Luxury Diner, *15-17*		80
___	**82038**	8" Female Pigtail Power Cable, *16-17, 19*		10
___	**82039**	36" Male Pigtail Power Cable, *16-18*		11
___	**82043**	Plug-n-play Power Cable Extension, *16-20*		16
___	**82045**	Plug-n-play Control Cable Extension, *16-20*		20
___	**82046**	36" Power Tap Cable, *16-20*		16
___	**82047**	Lionel Lines Log Dump Car, *15-16*		65
___	**82048**	AT&SF Ice Car, *15-17*		75
___	**82049**	Santa's Work Shoppe Log Dump Car, *16*		65
___	**82050**	Santa's Work Shoppe Sawmill, *16-20*		240
___	**82051**	North Pole Central Icing Station, *16-17*		150
___	**82052**	PFE Ice Car, *15-17*		75
___	**82053**	North Pole Central Icing Car, *16-17*		75
___	**82054**	Weyerhaeuser Log Dump Car, *15-17*		65
___	**82055**	Bethlehem Steel Trackside Crane, *CC, 16-19*		600
___	**82056**	Operating Freight Station, *18-19*		110
___	**82064**	Halloween Operating Billboard , *15-19*		80
___	**82066**	PRR Log Dump Car, *15*		65
___	**82067**	Lionel Lines Coal Dump Car, *15-17*		65
___	**82068**	NS Coal Dump Car, *15*		65
___	**82069**	Conrail Coal Dump Car, *15-17*		65
___	**82072**	Philadelphia Quartz Hopper "755," *15-18*		50
___	**82073**	CN Ore Car, *15-17*		50
___	**82074**	SP 1-D Tank Car, *15-17*		50
___	**82075**	NYC Waffle-sided Boxcar, *15-17*		50
___	**82076**	Chessie System Gondola with containers, *16-18*		50
___	**82077**	D&H Hi-Cube Boxcar, *16*		50
___	**82078**	NP 1-D Tank Car, *16*		50
___	**82079**	UP Wood-sided Reefer, *16*		50
___	**82080**	C&NW 3-D Tank Car , *16-18*		50
___	**82081**	CSX Auto Carrier, *16-18*		50
___	**82082**	NS Flatcar with pipes, *16-18*		50
___	**82083**	Central of Georgia Gondola with cable reels, *16*		50
___	**82084**	Virginian Boxcar, *16-18*		50
___	**82085**	AT&SF Waffle-sided Boxcar, *16-17*		50
___	**82086**	MKT Reefer, *16*		50
___	**82087**	WP Depressed Flatcar with generator, *16-18*		50
___	**82088**	Log Pack, *16-20*		10
___	**82091**	PRR Tie Work Car "82091," *14-16*		75
___	**82092**	MOW Tie Work Car "77," *14-16*		75
___	**82093**	AT&SF Tie Work Car "82093," *14-16*		75
___	**82094**	NS Tie Work Car "51," *14-16*		75
___	**82095**	Amtrak Tie Work Car "67," *14-16*		75
___	**82096**	Lionel Steel Culvert Gondola, *15-16*		65

82097	Bucyrus-Erie Gantry Crane, *CC, 15-19*		400 ___
82098	Bucyrus-Erie Culvert Gondola, *15*		65 ___
82099	Zombie Apocalypse Survivors GP38 Diesel Freight Set, LionChief, *15*		440 ___
82100	Polar Express Hero Boy's Home, *16-17*		90 ___
82101	Postwar "6512" Mercury Capsule Astronaut Car, *15-16*		80 ___
82102	Lumberjacks, *15-16*		65 ___
82103	Playground Swing, *15-16*		75 ___
82104	Playground Playtime, *15-16*		100 ___
82105	Tire Swing, *15-16*		100 ___
82106	Pony Ride, *15-17*		75 ___
82107	Tug-of-War, *15-17*		65 ___
82108	Hobo Campfire, *15*		100 ___
82110	Extended Truss Bridge, *15-20*		300 ___
82111	Lionel Industrial Coal 2-bay Hopper "28111," *15-17*		60 ___
82112	B&M Alco S2 Diesel Switcher "1260," *CC, 15*		650 ___
82113	B&M Alco S2 Diesel Switcher "1263," *CC, 15*		650 ___
82114	CB&Q Alco S2 Diesel Switcher "9306," *CC, 15*		650 ___
82115	CB&Q Alco S2 Diesel Switcher "9308," *CC, 15*		650 ___
82116	CP Alco S2 Diesel Switcher "7020," *CC, 15*		650 ___
82117	CP Alco S2 Diesel Switcher "7024," *CC, 15*		650 ___
82118	GM&O Alco S2 Diesel Switcher "1001," *CC, 15*		650 ___
82119	GM&O Alco S2 Diesel Switcher "1007," *CC, 15*		650 ___
82120	GN Alco S2 Diesel Switcher "2," *CC, 15*		650 ___
82121	GN Alco S2 Diesel Switcher "5," *CC, 15*		650 ___
82122	PRR Alco S2 Diesel Switcher "5648," *CC, 15*		650 ___
82123	PRR Alco S2 Diesel Switcher "5652," *CC, 15*		650 ___
82124	South Buffalo Alco S2 Diesel Switcher "102," *CC, 15*		650 ___
82125	South Buffalo Alco S2 Diesel Switcher "104," *CC, 15*		650 ___
82126	UP Alco S2 Diesel Switcher "1111," *CC, 15*		650 ___
82127	UP Alco S2 Diesel Switcher "1138," *CC, 15*		650 ___
82128	C&O GP30 Diesel Locomotive "3011," *CC, 15*		650 ___
82129	C&O GP30 Diesel Locomotive "3018," *CC, 15*		650 ___
82130	EMD Demonstrator GP30 Diesel Locomotive "1962," *CC, 15*		650 ___
82131	TP&W GP30 Diesel Locomotive "700," *CC, 15*		650 ___
82132	PC GP30 Diesel Locomotive "2202," *CC, 15*		650 ___
82133	PC GP30 Diesel Locomotive "2246," *CC, 15*		650 ___
82134	GM&O GP30 Diesel Locomotive "501," *CC, 15*		650 ___
82135	GM&O GP30 Diesel Locomotive "521," *CC, 15*		650 ___
82136	N&W GP30 Diesel Locomotive "522," black, *CC, 15*		650 ___
82137	N&W GP30 Diesel Locomotive "542," blue, *CC, 15*		650 ___
82138	MILW GP30 Diesel Locomotive "344," *CC, 15*		650 ___
82139	MILW GP30 Diesel Locomotive "350," *CC, 15*		650 ___
82140	Southern GP30 Diesel Locomotive "2594," *CC, 15*		650 ___
82141	Southern GP30 Diesel Locomotive "2601," *CC, 15*		650 ___
82142	UP GP30 Diesel Locomotive "803" *CC, 15*		650 ___
82143	UP GP30 Diesel Locomotive "830," *CC, 15*		650 ___
82146	Soo Line PS-1 Boxcar "45025" , *15*		80 ___
82147	N&W PS-1 Boxcar "44292," *15*		80 ___
82148	GB&W PS-1 Boxcar "777," *15*		80 ___
82150	Duluth, South Shore & Atlantic PS-1 Boxcar "15091," *15*		80 ___
82163	B&O NW2 Diesel Locomotive "9555," LionChief, *15-16*		300 ___
82164	BN NW2 Diesel Locomotive "546," LionChief, *15-16*		300 ___
82165	CB&Q NW2 Diesel Locomotive "9412A," LionChief, *15-16*		300 ___
82166	Southern NW2 Diesel Locomotive "2401A," LionChief, *15-16*		300 ___

| --- | --- | --- | --- |
___ 82171	BNSF GP20 Diesel Locomotive "2050," LionChief, 15-17		340
___ 82172	NYC GP20 Diesel Locomotive "2102," LionChief, 15-17		340
___ 82173	NS GP20 Diesel Locomotive "10," LionChief, 15-17		340
___ 82174	NYS&W GP20 Diesel Locomotive "1800," LionChief, 15-17		340
___ 82175	Virginian Rectifier Locomotive "135," LionChief, 15-17		340
___ 82176	N&W Rectifier Locomotive "235," LionChief, 15-17		340
___ 82177	NH Rectifier Locomotive "306," LionChief, 15-17		340
___ 82178	Conrail Rectifier Locomotive "4605," LionChief, 15-17		340
___ 82179	PRR Rectifier Locomotive "4466," LionChief, 15-17		340
___ 82184	PRR B6sb 0-4-0 Locomotive "1670," CC, 15		700
___ 82185	D&RGW Bicentennial Gondola with canisters, 16		50
___ 82186	Patriot Chemicals 1-D Tank Car "2015," 15, 18		60
___ 82187	Bethlehem Steel Water Tower, 15		35
___ 82188	Metro-North M7 Subway Set, LionChief, 15		350
___ 82192	MTA LIRR M7 Set, LionChief, 18-19		400
___ 82196	Metro-North Add-on 2-pack, 15		130
___ 82199	MTA LIRR Add-on Passenger 2-pack, 18		175
___ 82202	UP Big Boy Commemorative CA-4 Caboose, 15		95
___ 82203	Remote Control Box, 15-19		25
___ 82205	BNSF Golden Swoosh ES44AC Diesel Locomotive "7695," CC, 15		650
___ 82206	N&W 2-6-6-4 Locomotive "1218," CC, 16		1000
___ 82207	Iowa Interstate/Rock Island ES44AC Diesel Locomotive "513," CC, 15		650
___ 82208	N&W 2-6-6-4 Locomotive "1212," CC, 16		1000
___ 82209	NS ES44AC Diesel Locomotive "8056," CC, 15		650
___ 82210	NS ES44AC Diesel Locomotive "8065," CC, 15		650
___ 82213	KCS ES44AC Diesel Locomotive "4696," CC, 15		650
___ 82214	KCS ES44AC Diesel Locomotive "4685," CC, 15		650
___ 82215	AT&SF ES44AC Diesel Locomotive "440," CC, 15		650
___ 82216	AT&SF ES44AC Diesel Locomotive "444," CC, 15		650
___ 82218	FEC ES44AC Diesel Locomotive "802," CC, 15		650
___ 82219	FEC ES44AC Diesel Locomotive "804," CC, 15		650
___ 82220	SP Alco PA AA Diesel Locomotive Set "6006, 6015," CC, 15		1000
___ 82223	D&RGW Alco PA AA Diesel Locomotive Set "6001, 6003," CC, 15		1000
___ 82226	LV Alco PA AA Diesel Locomotive Set "601, 602," CC, 15		1000
___ 82229	MP Alco PA AA Diesel Locomotive Set "8018, 8018," CC, 15		1000
___ 82232	NKP Alco PA AA Diesel Locomotive Set "190, 189," CC, 15		1000
___ 82235	PRR Alco PA AA Diesel Locomotive Set "5070A, 5071A," CC, 15		1000
___ 82238	Southern Alco PA AA Diesel Locomotive Set "6900, 6901," CC, 15		1000
___ 82241	Wabash Alco PA AA Diesel Locomotive Set "1020, 1020A," CC, 15		1000
___ 82244	SP Alco PB Diesel Locomotive, CC, 15		530
___ 82245	B&O 2-6-6-4 Locomotive "7620," CC, 16		1000
___ 82246	D&RGW Alco PB Diesel Locomotive, CC, 15		530
___ 82247	AT&SF 2-6-6-4 Locomotive "1798," CC, 16		1000
___ 82248	LV Alco PB Diesel Locomotive, CC, 15		530
___ 82249	Bethlehem Steel Boom Car, 15		55
___ 82250	MP Alco PB Diesel Locomotive, CC, 15		530
___ 82251	Zombie Animated Gondola, 15		75
___ 82252	Nickel Plate Road Alco PB Diesel Locomotive, CC, 15		530
___ 82253	John Deere 1-D Tank Car, 15		65
___ 82254	PRR Alco PB Diesel Locomotive, CC, 15		530
___ 82256	Southern Alco PB Diesel Locomotive, CC, 15		530
___ 82258	Wabash Alco PB Diesel Locomotive, CC, 15		530
___ 82260	PC 50' DD Boxcar "267210" (std O), 16-17		80

		Esc	Mint
82261	Frisco 50' DD Boxcar "7002" (std O), *16-17*		80 __
82263	PRR Scrapyard, *16-17*		130 __
82265	MOW Welding Car, *15-16*		80 __
82266	CN 4-6-0 Steam Locomotive "1158," *CC, 15*		900 __
82267	C&NW 4-6-0 Steam Locomotive "1385," *CC, 15*		900 __
82268	Frisco 4-6-0 Steam Locomotive "633," *CC, 15*		900 __
82269	NP 4-6-0 Steam Locomotive "1382," *CC, 15*		900 __
82270	SP 4-6-0 Steam Locomotive "2353," *CC, 15*		900 __
82271	NYC 4-6-0 Steam Locomotive "1258," *CC, 15*		900 __
82272	NH 4-6-0 Steam Locomotive "816," *CC, 15*		900 __
82273	ACL 4-6-0 Steam Locomotive "1031," *CC, 15*		900 __
82274	Chessie SD40 Diesel Locomotive "7500," *CC, 15*		650 __
82275	Chessie SD40 Diesel Locomotive "7593," *CC, 15*		650 __
82276	BN SD40 Diesel Locomotive "6314," *CC, 15*		650 __
82277	BN SD40 Diesel Locomotive "6320," *CC, 15*		650 __
82278	GT SD40 Diesel Locomotive "5922," *CC, 15*		650 __
82279	GT SD40 Diesel Locomotive "5927," *CC, 15*		650 __
82280	MP SD40 Diesel Locomotive "3007," *CC, 15*		650 __
82281	MP SD40 Diesel Locomotive "3014," *CC, 15*		650 __
82282	Conrail SD40 Diesel Locomotive "6308," *CC, 15*		650 __
82283	Conrail SD40 Diesel Locomotive "6350," *CC, 15*		650 __
82284	Conrail SD40 Diesel Locomotive "6300," *CC, 15*		650 __
82285	SP SD40 Diesel Locomotive "8402," *CC, 15*		650 __
82286	SP SD40 Diesel Locomotive "8451," *CC, 15*		650 __
82287	SP Daylight SD40 Diesel Locomotive "7342," *CC, 15*		650 __
82288	Clinchfield SD40 Diesel Locomotive "3000," *CC, 15*		650 __
82289	Clinchfield SD40 Diesel Locomotive "3006," *CC, 15*		650 __
82290	AT&SF FT AA Diesel Locomotive Set, LionChief, *15-17*		500 __
82293	ACL FT AA Diesel Locomotive Set, LionChief, *15-17*		500 __
82296	Erie FT AA Diesel Locomotive Set, LionChief, *15-17*		500 __
82299	D&RGW FT AA Diesel Locomotive Set, LionChief, *15-17*		500 __
82302	AT&SF FT B Unit, LionChief, *15-17*		280 __
82303	ACL FT B Unit, LionChief, *15-17*		280 __
82304	Erie FT B Unit, LionChief, *15-17*		280 __
82305	D&RGW FT B Unit, LionChief, *15-17*		280 __
82307	PRR B6sb 0-4-0 Locomotive "5244," *CC, 15*		700 __
82308	PRR B6sb 0-4-0 Locomotive "3233," *CC, 15*		700 __
82309	PRR-Reading Seashore Lines B6sb 0-4-0 Locomotive "6096," *CC, 15*		700 __
82310	LIRR B6sb 0-4-0 Locomotive "2015," *CC, 15*		700 __
82311	Polar RR B6sb 0-4-0 Locomotive "2515," *CC, 15*		700 __
82312	UP ACF 40-ton Stock Car "48133," *15*		80 __
82313	GN ACF 40-ton Stock Car "55989," *15*		80 __
82314	MILW ACF 40-ton Stock Car "104954," *15*		80 __
82315	NP ACF 40-ton Stock Car "84161," *15*		80 __
82316	NKP ACF 40-ton Stock Car "42040," *15*		80 __
82324	Chessie Diesel Freight Set, LionChief, *15*		400 __
82330	U.S.A.F. Minuteman Missile Launcher Car, *CC, 15*		350 __
82331	U.S.A.F. Missile Launch Sound Car, *CC, 15*		240 __
82333	Illuminated Hopper Shed, *15-20*		45 __
82334	Ulysses S. Grant Presidential Boxcar, *15*		70 __
82335	Franklin D. Roosevelt Presidential Boxcar, *15*		70 __
82340	N&W Y6b 2-8-8-2 Steam Locomotive "2171," *CC, 15*		2000 __
82341	N&W Y6b 2-8-8-2 Steam Locomotive "2175," *CC, 15*		2000 __

		Mint
___	82342	N&W Y6b 2-8-8-2 Steam Locomotive "2195," *CC, 15*	2000
___	82343	Lionel Steel Welding Car, *15*	80
___	82344	WM Wood Chip Hopper "2945," *15-16*	65
___	82349	Friday the 13th Jason Voorhees Boxcar, *16*	85
___	82394	UP Auxiliary Water Tender "907853," *CC, 15*	380
___	82395	UP Auxiliary Water Tender "907856," *CC, 15*	380
___	82396	UP Commemorative Auxiliary Water Tender "809," *CC, 15*	380
___	82410	Virginian 2-bay Hopper "13168," *16-17*	60
___	82411	N&W 2-bay Hopper "113733," *15-17*	60
___	82412	Reading Birney Trolley, *15, 18*	100
___	82413	Lionel Transit Birney Trolley, *15*	100
___	82414	CNJ 4-6-0 Camelback Locomotive "777," LionChief, *15-16*	440
___	82415	DL&W 4-6-0 Camelback Locomotive "1035," LionChief, *15-17*	440
___	82416	LV 4-6-0 Camelback Locomotive "1602," LionChief, *15-17*	440
___	82417	Philadelphia & Reading 4-6-0 Camelback Locomotive "675," LionChief, *15-17*	440
___	82418	Erie 4-6-0 Camelback Locomotive "861," LionChief, *15-17*	440
___	82419	UP 8-door Hi-Cube Boxcar, *16*	100
___	82420	SP 8-door Hi-Cube Boxcar, *16*	100
___	82421	B&O 8-door Hi-Cube Boxcar, *16*	100
___	82422	PRR 8-door Hi-Cube Boxcar, *16*	100
___	82423	C&NW 8-door Hi-Cube Boxcar, *16*	100
___	82424	Chessie 8-door Hi-Cube Boxcar, *16*	100
___	82425	PC 8-door Hi-Cube Boxcar, *16*	100
___	82426	RI 8-door Hi-Cube Boxcar, *16*	100
___	82427	Patriot U36B Diesel Freight Set, LionChief, *15-17*	360
___	82436	Pennsylvania Keystone GP38 Diesel Freight Set, LionChief, *15*	450
___	82442	Five-Star General Old-Time Steam Set, LionChief, *17-18*	400
___	82447	Sheriff & Outlaw Car, *17*	80
___	82453	Amtrak F40PH Diesel Phase II "200," *CC, 16*	550
___	82454	Amtrak F40PH Diesel Phase II "207," *CC, 16*	550
___	82455	Amtrak F40PH Diesel Phase III "364," *CC, 16*	550
___	82456	Amtrak F40PH Diesel Phase III "388," *CC, 16*	550
___	82460	CSX F40PH Diesel "9998," *CC, 16*	550
___	82461	CSX F40PH Diesel "9999," *CC, 16*	550
___	82473	N&W Early Era Inspection Vehicle, *CC, 15*	200
___	82474	BN Early Era Inspection Vehicle, *CC, 15*	200
___	82475	Bethlehem Steel Early Era Inspection Vehicle, *CC, 15*	200
___	82476	NH Early Era Inspection Vehicle, *CC, 15*	200
___	82477	Virginian Early Era Inspection Vehicle, *CC, 15*	200
___	82478	Reading Early Era Inspection Vehicle, *CC, 15*	200
___	82486	Weathered Virginian USRA Y-3 2-8-8-2 Locomotive "737," *CC, 14*	1450
___	82487	Weathered AT&SF USRA Y-3 2-8-8-2 Locomotive "1797," *CC, 14*	1450
___	82488	Weathered N&W USRA Y-3 2-8-8-2 Locomotive "2029," *CC, 14*	1450
___	82489	MILW 18" Aluminum Coach/Dining Car 2-pack, *14*	320
___	82489	MILW Olympian 18" Aluminum Passenger Car 2-pack, *14-15*	320
___	82494	Turbo Missile Launch Flatcar, *15*	60
___	82495	D&RGW Scrapyard, *16-19*	130
___	82498	Polar Express Mail Car, *16-17*	70
___	82500	Polar Express Covered Bridge, *15*	70
___	82501	Providence & Worcester 89' Auto Carrier "190091," *15-16*	110
___	82502	C&NW 89' Auto Carrier "962255," *15-16*	110
___	82503	Chessie 89' Auto Carrier "255798," *15-16*	110

No.	Description	Esc	Mint
82504	TFM 89' Auto Carrier "987408," 15-16		110
82505	BNSF 89' Auto Carrier "212878," 15-16		110
82506	UP 89' Auto Carrier "992579," 15-16		110
82508	NYC Milk Car "6589" (std O), 16		80
82510	Polar Express Aquarium Car, 16		85
82512	Polar Express Work Caboose with presents, 15		85
82514	Polar Express Reindeer Stock Car, 15		90
82518	Moon Pie Boxcar, 15		85
82528	NYC Empire State Express Steam Passenger Set, CC, 15		1950
82534	NYC J3a 4-6-4 Hudson Locomotive "5429," tender, 15		1500
82535	NYC J3a 4-6-4 Hudson Locomotive "5426," tender, 15		1500
82536	NYC J3a 4-6-4 Hudson Locomotive "5429," tender, 15		1500
82537	NYC J3a 4-6-4 Hudson Locomotive "5426," tender, 15		1500
82543	Postwar "943" Exploding Ammunition Dump, 15-16, 18-20		50
82544	Missile Firing Range, 15-16, 19		65
82545	Santa's Helper Steam Freight Set, 16-17		340
82550	Wabash 21" Streamlined Passenger Car 4-pack, 15		600
82555	Wabash 21" Streamlined Passenger Car 2-pack, 15		300
82558	Southern 21" Streamlined Passenger Car 4-pack, 15		600
82563	Southern 21" Streamlined Passenger Car 4-pack, 15		300
82566	RI 21" Streamlined Passenger Car 4-pack, 15		600
82571	RI 21" Streamlined Passenger Car 4-pack, 15		300
82574	Texas Special 21" Streamlined Passenger Car 4-pack, 15		600
82579	Texas Special 21" Streamlined Passenger Car 4-pack, 15		300
82582	C&O 21" Streamlined Passenger Car 4-pack, 15		600
82587	C&O 21" Streamlined Passenger Car 4-pack, 15		300
82590	Amtrak 21" Passenger Car 4-pack, 16		600
82595	Amtrak 21" Passenger Car 2-pack, 16		300
82598	NYC Empire State Passenger Car Add-on 2-pack, 15		300
82611	PRR GL-a 2-bay Hopper 3-pack, 15		220
82621	Buffalo Creek Flour PS-1 Boxcar "2366," 15		80
82622	U.S. Army PS-1 Boxcar "26875, 15		80
82623	West India Fruit & Steamship Co. PS-1 Boxcar "321," 15		80
82624	Linde Air Products PS-1 Boxcar "3019," 15		80
82625	Air Reduction Products PS-1 Boxcar "100," 15		80
82629	PRR N5b Caboose "478883," 15-16		95
82630	PRR N5b Caboose with trainphone antenna, 15-16		95
82631	B&M N5b Caboose "C-16," 15-16		95
82639	MILW Milk Car "370" (std O), 16, 20		90
82640	UTLX 30,000-Gallon 1-D Tank Car 3-pack, 15		250
82644	Philadelphia Energy Solutions 1-D Tank Car 3-pack , 15		250
82648	Midwest Ethanol Transport 1-D Tank Car 3-pack, 15		250
82652	Global Ethanol Transport 1-D Tank Car 3-pack, 15		250
82656	Conrail 60' Boxcar "216010," 15-17		90
82657	WM 60' Boxcar "38020," 15-17		90
82658	BN 60' Boxcar "355145," 15-17		90
82659	RI 60' Boxcar "33825," 15-17		90
82660	N&W 60' Boxcar "600949," 15-17		90
82661	P&LE PS-5 Gondola and PS-4 Flatcar, 15-16		175
82664	B&LE PS-5 Gondola and PS-4 Flatcar, 15-16		175
82667	DT&I PS-5 Gondola and PS-4 Flatcar, 15-16		175
82670	Conrail PS-5 Gondola and PS-4 Flatcar, 15-16		175
82674	UP Bathtub Gondola 2-pack, 15		140

		Mint
____	**82677** Strasburg 3-D Tank Car, *16*	656
____	**82678** Angela Trotta Thomas Christmas Boxcar, *16*	85
____	**82683** Batman and Flash Justice League Boxcar 2-pack, *15-16*	170
____	**82684** Superman and Green Lantern Justice League Boxcar 2-pack, *15-16*	170
____	**82685** New York Giants Cooperstown Boxcar, *15*	85
____	**82686** Washington Senators Cooperstown Boxcar, *15*	85
____	**82687** Detroit Tigers Cooperstown Boxcar, *15*	85
____	**82688** Pittsburgh Pirates Cooperstown Boxcar, *15*	85
____	**82689** Operation Eagle Missile Carrying Car, *15-17*	65
____	**82690** Coca-Cola Anniversary Bottle Boxcar, *15*	90
____	**82691** Christmas Boxcar, *15*	75
____	**82693** Santa's Helper Crane, *15*	85
____	**82694** UP LionMaster 4-6-6-4 Challenger Locomotive "3985," *CC* , *15*	1000
____	**82695** UP LionMaster 4-6-6-4 Challenger Locomotive "3977," *CC* , *15*	1000
____	**82696** UP LionMaster 4-6-6-4 Challenger Locomotive "3989," *CC* , *15*	1000
____	**82697** D&RGW LionMaster 4-6-6-4 Challenger Locomotive "3803," *CC*, *15*	1000
____	**82698** WM LionMaster 4-6-6-4 Challenger Locomotive "1201," *CC* , *15*	1000
____	**82699** Angela Trotta Thomas Lionelville Christmas Boxcar, *15*	75
____	**82701** Escaping Snowmen Handcar, *15*	90
____	**82702** Ontario Northland PS-4 Flatcar with covered load, *15*	90
____	**82703** BN PS-4 Flatcar with covered load, *15*	90
____	**82704** D&RGW PS-4 Flatcar with covered load, *15*	90
____	**82705** Reading PS-4 Flatcar with covered load, *15*	90
____	**82706** Southern PS-4 Flatcar with covered load, *15*	90
____	**82708** Christmas Gingerbread Shanty, *16-19*	40
____	**82709** PRR Silver & Gold Ore Car 2-pack, *16-17*	130
____	**82710** PRR Ice Breaker Tunnel Car, *16-17*	65
____	**82711** Santa's Favorites Transparent Gift Car, *16*	85
____	**82713** Christmas Music Boxcar, *15*	80
____	**82716** Mickey's Holiday to Remember Freight Set, *16*	400
____	**82717** W. E. Disney Girder Bridge, *16-18*	33
____	**82718** Disney Villains Hi-Cube Boxcar 2-pack, *16-19*	160
____	**82721** Dumbo 75th Anniversary Boxcar, *16-17*	85
____	**82726** Postwar Alco FA Diesel Green Passenger Set, *17-19*	550
____	**82728** Layout Control System Switch Throw Monitor, *17-20*	100
____	**82734** New York Yankees Cooperstown Boxcar, *15*	85
____	**82735** Polar Express Conductor Gateman, *18-20*	120
____	**82736** North Pole Central Water Tower, *15*	40
____	**82737** Coca-Cola Santa Boxcar, *15*	85
____	**82739** North Pole Central Boxcar, *16-18*	80
____	**82740** Winter Wonderland Aquarium Car, *15*	95
____	**82741** Christmas Tinsel Vat Car, *16*	70
____	**82742** Candy Mountain Christmas Quad Hopper, *16-17*	65
____	**82743** Santa's Reindeer Station Platform, *15*	50
____	**82744** Santa Claus Automatic Gateman, *16-17*	100
____	**82745** Christmas Cocoa Barrel Shed, *15*	50
____	**82746** Christmas Floodlight Tower, *16*	75
____	**82747** Christmas Red Arch Under Bridge, *16*	30
____	**82748** Silver Bell Casting Co. Hopper, *15*	70
____	**82749** PRR GG1 Electric "4935," *CC, 16*	1400
____	**82751** PRR GG1 Electric "4913," *CC, 16*	1400
____	**82752** PRR GG1 Electric "4877," *CC, 16*	1400
____	**82754** PC GG1 Electric "4828," *CC, 16*	1400

		Mint	
82755	Amtrak GG1 Electric "926," *CC, 16*	1400	___
82757	CP SD90MAC Diesel "9116," *CC, 16*	650	___
82758	CP SD90MAC Diesel "9130," *CC, 16*	650	___
82759	NS SD90MAC Diesel "7230," *CC, 16*	650	___
82760	NS SD90MAC Diesel "7245," *CC, 16*	650	___
82761	UP SD90MAC Diesel "8130," *CC, 16*	650	___
82762	UP SD90MAC Diesel "8133," *CC, 16*	650	___
82763	UP SD90MAC Diesel "8025," *CC, 16*	650	___
82764	UP SD90MAC Diesel "8055," *CC, 16*	650	___
82765	Indiana SD90MAC Diesel "9003," *CC, 16*	650	___
82766	Indiana SD90MAC Diesel "9006," *CC, 16*	650	___
82767	C&O 2-6-6-6 Locomotive "1601," *CC, 16*	2200	___
82768	C&O 2-6-6-6 Locomotive "1604," *CC, 16*	2200	___
82769	C&O 2-6-6-6 Locomotive "1608," *CC, 16*	2200	___
82770	Virginian 2-6-6-6 Locomotive "906," *CC, 16*	2200	___
82825	CP GP38 Diesel Locomotive "3019," *16-17*	340	___
82826	CSX GP38 Diesel Locomotive "2145," *16-17*	340	___
82827	SP GP38 Diesel Locomotive "4846," *16-18*	340	___
82828	UP GP38 Diesel Locomotive "905," *16-17*	340	___
82840	AT&SF PS-4 Flatcar with trailer (std O), *16*	110	___
82841	E-L PS-4 Flatcar with trailer (std O), *16*	110	___
82842	GN PS-4 Flatcar with trailer (std O), *16*	110	___
82843	WM PS-4 Flatcar with trailer (std O), *16*	110	___
82844	PRR PS-4 Flatcar with trailer (std O), *16*	110	___
82845	B&O Truck with 40' trailer, *16*	90	___
82846	MILW Truck with 40' trailer, *16-17*	90	___
82847	MKT Truck with 40' trailer, *16-17*	90	___
82848	Logging Disconnect with load, *16*	65	___
82849	Logging Disconnect with load 2-pack, *16*	125	___
82850	MILW 40' Flatcar with lumber (std O), *16-17*	90	___
82851	NP 40' Flatcar with lumber (std O), *16-17*	90	___
82852	Meadow River 40' Flatcar with lumber (std O), *16-17*	90	___
82853	Pickering 40' Flatcar with lumber (std O), *16-17*	90	___
82854	PRR 40' Flatcar with lumber (std O), *16*	90	___
82855	ADM Unibody Tank Car "190516" (std O), *16*	75	___
82856	GATX Unibody Tank Car "4415" (std O), *16*	75	___
82857	AFPX Unibody Tank Car "413303" (std O), *16*	75	___
82858	Shell Unibody Tank Car "82858" (std O), *16*	85	___
82859	Engelhard Unibody Tank Car "24586" (std O), *16*	75	___
82860	PC PS-5 Gondola "557065" (std O), *16*	90	___
82861	E-L PS-5 Gondola "14552" (std O), *16*	90	___
82862	Frisco PS-5 Gondola "61442" (std O), *16*	90	___
82863	CB&Q PS-5 Gondola "82050" (std O), *16*	90	___
82864	NYC PS-5 Gondola "712603" (std O), *16*	90	___
82865	PRR N5b Caboose "5017" (std O), *16*	90	___
82866	PRR N5b Caboose "477746" (std O), *16*	90	___
82867	PRR N5b Caboose "477625" (std O), *16*	90	___
82868	NH N5 Caboose "C-507" (std O), *16*	90	___
82869	IR Sensor Track O Gauge Tubular Compatible, *17-20*	95	___
82870	Loading Ramp, *16-20*	25	___
82872	Loader/Unloader Workers Figure Pack, *16-20*	30	___
82873	Loggers Cabin, sound, *16*	140	___
82874	Early Intermodal Work House, sound, *16-19*	130	___

			Mint
___	82877	Thomas Kinkade Polar Express Boxcar, *16*	85
___	82878	Smithsonian Boxcar, *16*	85
___	82879	Coca-Cola Christmas Boxcar, *16-17*	85
___	82883	Legacy 360-watt PowerMaster, *16, 18-20*	220
___	82884	Wabash 21" Streamlined Dining Car, StationSounds, *15*	300
___	82885	Southern 21" Streamlined Dining Car, StationSounds, *15*	300
___	82886	RI 21" Streamlined Dining Car, StationSounds, *15*	300
___	82887	Texas Special 21" Streamlined Dining Car, StationSounds, *15*	300
___	82888	C&O 21" Streamlined Dining Car, StationSounds, *15*	300
___	82889	Amtrak 21" Diner, StationSounds, *16*	300
___	82890	NYC Empire State Express Diner, StationSounds, *15*	300
___	82906	Pluto Walking Brakeman Car, *16-18*	100
___	82908	Mickey's Christmas Shanty, *16-18*	50
___	82913	Winnie the Pooh Boxcar, *16-17*	85
___	82914	Disney Aquarium Car, *16-18*	85
___	82917	Disney Station Platform, *17-19*	55
___	82918	36" Power Cable Extension (3-pin, M/F), *17-20*	12
___	82921	Evil Queen Hi-Cube Boxcar, *17-19*	80
___	82922	Scar Hi-Cube Boxcar, *17-19*	80
___	82925	Scrooge McDuck Mint Car, *17-18*	80
___	82942	James Monroe Presidential Boxcar, *16, 18*	70
___	82943	John F. Kennedy Presidential Boxcar, *16*	70
___	82944	Herbert Hoover Presidential Boxcar, *16*	70
___	82945	James Madison Presidential Boxcar, *16*	70
___	82947	Wonder Woman/Green Arrow Boxcar 2-pack, *16*	170
___	82950	Aquaman/Martian Manhunter Boxcar 2-pack, *16*	170
___	82953	Joker/Lex Luthor Boxcar 2-pack, *16*	170
___	82954	Lionel Christmas Boxcar, *16*	65
___	82958	Christmas Floodlight, *17-18*	75
___	82960	NYC 2-8-2 Steam Locomotive "1548," *16-18*	430
___	82961	UP 2-8-2 Steam Locomotive "2537," *16-18*	430
___	82962	Southern 2-8-2 Steam Locomotive "4501," *16-18*	430
___	82963	Rio Grande 2-8-2 Steam Locomotive "1208," *16-18*	430
___	82964	MILW 4-6-4 Steam Locomotive "125," *16-18*	430
___	82965	AT&SF 4-6-4 Steam Locomotive "3450," *16-18*	430
___	82966	DL&W 4-6-4 Steam Locomotive "1151," *16-18*	430
___	82967	CB&Q 4-6-4 Steam Locomotive "3007," *16-18*	430
___	82968	LL 4-6-2 Steam Locomotive "462," *16-17*	430
___	82969	WM 4-6-2 Steam Locomotive "202," *16-18*	430
___	82970	Reading & Northern 4-6-2 Locomotive "425," *16-17*	450
___	82971	C&NW 4-6-2 Steam Locomotive "600," *16-18*	300
___	82972	Lionel Junction PRR Diesel Freight Set, *16-17*	175
___	82973	PRR A5 0-4-0 Locomotive "3891," *16-18*	450
___	82974	SP A5 0-4-0 Locomotive "1040," *16-18*	450
___	82975	B&O A5 0-4-0 Locomotive "317," *16-18*	450
___	82976	Bethlehem Steel A5 0-4-0 Locomotive "140," LionChief, *16-18*	450
___	82982	Christmas Express Steam Freight Set, LionChief, *17-18*	320
___	82984	NYC RS-3 Diesel Freight Set, *16-17*	260
___	82992	115th Anniversary Boxcar, *16*	90
___	83002	PRR Broadway Limited 21" Diner 2-pack, StationSounds, *16*	450
___	83003	PC 21" StationSounds Diner "4552," *16*	300
___	83006	UP 21" Excursion Diner, StationSounds, *16*	300
___	83007	PRR Broadway Limited 21" Passenger Car 2-pack, *16*	300
___	83010	PC 21" Passenger Car 2-pack, *16*	300

No.	Description	Esc	Mint
83019	UP 21" Excursion Passenger Car 2-pack, *16*		300
83022	PRR Broadway Limited 21" Passenger Car 4-pack, *16*		600
83027	PC 21" Passenger Car 4-pack, *16*		600
83042	UP 21" Excursion Passenger Car 4-pack, *16*		675
83063	AT&SF Super Chief Boxcar "143093," *16-19*		50
83071	Universal Remote, *16-20*		50
83072	PRR "Keystone Special" Steam Freight Set, LionChief, *17-20*		300
83080	Rio Grande 0-4-0 Switcher Freight Set, *16-17*		300
83092	Steel City Switcher Freight Set, *CC, 16*		1300
83102	SP 21" Passenger Car 4-pack, *16*		600
83107	SP 21" Passenger Car 2-pack, *16*		300
83110	SP 21" Diner "290," StationSounds, *16*		300
83111	American Freedom Train 21" Passenger Car 4-pack, *16-17*		675
83116	American Freedom Train 21" Passenger Car 2-pack, *16-17*		300
83119	American Freedom Train 21" Crew Car, *16-17*		300
83120	CSX Office Car Special 21" Passenger Car 4-pack, *16-17*		600
83125	CSX Office Car Special 21" Passenger Car 2-pack, *16-17*		300
83128	CSX Office Car Special 21" Diner, StationSounds, *16-17*		300
83147	Lighted Yard Tower, *16*		60
83148	Christmas Express Boxcar, *16-17*		53
83157	Smithsonian Air & Space Boxcar 2-pack, *16*		170
83162	Nightmare on Elm Street Boxcar, *16*		85
83163	Thomas Kinkade Christmas Boxcar, *16-17*		85
83164	Frosty the Snowman 1-D Tank Car, *16-17*		60
83165	PRR GG1 Electric "4899," *CC, 16*		1400
83166	PRR GG1 Electric "4800," *CC, 16*		1400
83167	Conrail Bicentennial GG1 Electric "4800," *CC, 16*		1400
83168	Iron Workers Figure Pack, *16, 18-20*		30
83169	NYC Flatcar with piggyback trailers, *16-19*		75
83170	Steel Mill Structure, sound, *16-19*		130
83171	MOW Workers Figure Pack, *16-20*		30
83172	MOW Work Structure, *sound, 16-19*		130
83173	Single Signal Bridge, *16-20*		80
83174	Double Signal Bridge, *16-18, 20*		100
83175	Christmas Music Boxcar, *16*		80
83176	Lionel Lines Christmas Caboose, *16-17*		75
83177	Angela Trotta Thomas Caboose, *16-17*		80
83178	Coca-Cola Caboose, *16*		75
83179	Conrail Caboose "23878," *16-19*		75
83180	PRR Caboose "477100," *16-17*		7
83181	AT&SF Caboose "999316," *16-17*		75
83182	ACL Caboose "0634," *16-19*		75
83183	Erie Caboose "C226," *16-19*		75
83184	UP Caboose "25214," *16-18*		75
83185	Polar Express Elves Figure Set, *16-20*		33
83186	NYC Caboose "21777," *16-18*		75
83190	Moon Pie 1-D Tank Car, *16-17*		75
83191	Snow Transport Christmas 1-D Tank Car, *16, 19*		85
83192	Smithsonian Dinosaur Aquarium Car, *16-17*		85
83193	SP GS-4 4-8-4 Locomotive "4449," *CC, 16*		1700
83194	SP GS-4 4-8-4 Locomotive "4449," *CC, 16*		1700
83195	SP GS-4 4-8-4 Locomotive "4443," *CC, 16*		1700
83196	SP GS-4 4-8-4 Locomotive "4444," *CC, 16*		1700
83197	American Freedom Train GS-4 4-8-4 Locomotive, *CC, 16*		1700

____ 83198	Reading T1 4-8-4 Locomotive "2100," *CC, 16*	1700
____ 83199	Reading T1 4-8-4 Locomotive "2119," *CC, 16*	1700
____ 83200	Reading T1 4-8-4 Locomotive "2102," *CC, 16*	1700
____ 83201	Reading T1 4-8-4 Locomotive "2124," *CC, 16*	1700
____ 83202	American Freedom Train T1 4-8-4 Locomotive, *CC, 16*	1700
____ 83203	Chessie T1 4-8-4 Locomotive "2101," *CC, 16*	1700
____ 83204	B&O 0-8-0 Locomotive "1695," *CC, 16*	900
____ 83205	GTW 0-8-0 Locomotive "8380," *CC, 16*	900
____ 83206	Indiana Harbor Belt 0-8-0 Locomotive "312," *CC, 16*	900
____ 83208	Wabash 0-8-0 Locomotive "1526," *CC, 16*	900
____ 83209	Terminal Railroad 0-8-0 Locomotive, *CC, 16*	900
____ 83214	North Pole Central 4-6-2 Locomotive "1225," *16-17*	430
____ 83215	Transformer 2-pack, *16-19*	15
____ 83223	Steel I-Beam 12-pack, *16-20*	15
____ 83230	Amtrak Metal Girder Bridge, *16-20*	43
____ 83231	Polar Express Metal Girder Bridge, *16-17*	43
____ 83232	Bethlehem Steel Metal Girder Bridge, *16-19*	40
____ 83233	CSX Metal Girder Bridge, *16-19*	37
____ 83234	John Deere Plastic Girder Bridge, *16-19*	33
____ 83238	John Deere Flatcar with spreaders, *16-17*	80
____ 83239	Polar Express Bells Mint Car, *16-17*	80
____ 83240	Shell Operating Oil Derrick, *16*	120
____ 83241	Shell Oil Storage Tank with Light, *16*	85
____ 83242	Shell 1-D Tank Car, *16*	75
____ 83243	Shell 3-D Tank Car, *16-17*	75
____ 83244	Shell Elevated Oil Tank, *17*	100
____ 83246	Shell Boxcar, *16*	85
____ 83247	Shell Billboard Pack, *16-17*	25
____ 83248	"It's a Boy" Boxcar, *16*	90
____ 83249	Polar Express Combination Car, *16-17*	70
____ 83250	"It's a Girl" Boxcar, *16*	90
____ 83251	Poultry Dispatch Sweep Car, *16-18*	120
____ 83252	Gold Medal Milk Car with platform, *17-19*	180
____ 83253	D&RGW Searchlight Car, *16-17*	63
____ 83254	Western Union Animated Gondola, *16-18*	70
____ 83256	GN Horse Transport , *16*	80
____ 83257	Bobbing Werewolf Boxcar, *16-17*	75
____ 83258	CP Boom Car, *16*	63
____ 83266	Lionel Junction Santa Fe Steam Freight Set, *16*	175
____ 83275	Sugar Cookie Scented Smoke Fluid, *17-20*	7
____ 83276	Peppermint Scented Smoke Fluid, *17-20*	7
____ 83277	Pine Scented Smoke Fluid, *17-20*	7
____ 83278	Hot Chocolate Scented Smoke Fluid, *17-20*	7
____ 83279	Wood Stove Scented Smoke Fluid, *17-20*	7
____ 83280	Unscented Smoke Fluid, *17-20*	7
____ 83284	Peekaboo Reindeer Operating Boxcar, *16-17*	75
____ 83286	John Deere Steam Freight Set, *16-17*	400
____ 83291	Christmas Half-covered Bridge, *16-19*	70
____ 83292	Christmas Cookies & Candies Store, *16-17*	85
____ 83304	North Pole Elves Work Shanty, *16*	40
____ 83305	Illuminated Winter Covered Bridge, *16-20*	80
____ 83308	North Pole Central Tank Car "122416," *16-17*	75
____ 83311	Santa's Favorites Egg Nog Reefer, *16-18*	65

		Esc	Mint
83312	Santa's Cookies Vat Car, *16-17*		70 ___
83313	Reindeer Express Agency Flatcar with trailer, *16-17*		70 ___
83315	Christmas Toys Stock Car, *16-18*		70 ___
83316	Santa's Sleigh Aquarium Car, *16-18*		80 ___
83317	BNSF 65' Mill Gondola "518357" (std O), *17*		80 ___
83318	C&NW 65' Mill Gondola "342036" (std O), *17*		80 ___
83319	CSX 65' Mill Gondola "491600" (std O), *17*		80 ___
83320	NS 65' Mill Gondola "195015" (std O), *17*		80 ___
83321	SP 65' Mill Gondola "365117" (std O), *17*		80 ___
83322	UP 65' Mill Gondola "96257" (std O), *17*		80 ___
83340	Boxcar Children Boxcar, *16*		85 ___
83347	ACL USRA Double-sheathed Boxcar, *16*		85 ___
83348	B&M USRA Double-sheathed Boxcar, *16*		85 ___
83349	RI USRA Double-sheathed Boxcar, *16*		85 ___
83350	Northwestern Pacific USRA Double-sheathed Boxcar, *16*		85 ___
83351	Wabash USRA Double-sheathed Boxcar, *16*		85 ___
83352	Polar Express USRA Double-sheathed Boxcar, *16*		95 ___
83353	D&RGW Flatcar with snowplow (std O), *16*		95 ___
83354	NYC Flatcar with snowplow (std O), *16*		95 ___
83355	UP Flatcar with snowplow (std O), *16*		95 ___
83356	MOW Flatcar with Snowplow (std O), *16*		95 ___
83357	Reading NE-style Caboose "92882" (std O), *16*		90 ___
83358	Reading NE-style Caboose "92902" (std O), *16*		90 ___
83359	Reading & Northern NE-style Caboose "92884" (std O), *16*		90 ___
83360	C&O NE-style Caboose "90352" (std O), *16*		90 ___
83361	N&W NE-style Caboose "500830" (std O), *16*		90 ___
83362	WM NE-style Caboose "1887" (std O), *16*		90 ___
83368	EL SD45 Diesel Locomotive "3607," *CC, 16*		650 ___
83369	EL SD45 Diesel Locomotive "3618," *CC, 16*		650 ___
83370	EL Bicentennial SD45 Diesel Locomotive "3632," *CC, 16*		650 ___
83371	GN "Hustle Muscle" SD45 Diesel Locomotive "400," *CC, 16*		650 ___
83372	GN SD45 Diesel Locomotive "402," *CC, 16*		650 ___
83373	GN SD45 Diesel Locomotive "407," *CC, 16*		650 ___
83374	PC SD45 Diesel Locomotive "6235," *CC, 16*		650 ___
83375	PC SD45 Diesel Locomotive "6237," *CC, 16*		650 ___
83376	Southern SD45 Diesel Locomotive "3137," *CC, 16*		650 ___
83377	Southern SD45 Diesel Locomotive "3156," *CC, 16*		650 ___
83378	SP SD45 Diesel Locomotive "8801," *CC, 16*		650 ___
83379	SP SD45 Diesel Locomotive "8820," *CC, 16*		650 ___
83380	UP SD45 Diesel Locomotive "1," *CC, 16*		650 ___
83381	UP SD45 Diesel Locomotive "21," *CC, 16*		650 ___
83382	AT&SF NW2 Diesel Locomotive "2405," *CC, 16*		500 ___
83383	B&M NW2 Diesel Locomotive "1200," *CC, 16*		500 ___
83384	B&O NW2 Diesel Locomotive "9527," *CC, 16*		500 ___
83385	CSX NW2 Diesel Locomotive "9565," *CC, 16*		500 ___
83387	NYO&W NW2 Diesel Locomotive "116," *CC, 16*		500 ___
83388	PRR NW2 Diesel Locomotive "9171," *CC, 16*		500 ___
83389	Philadelphia, Bethlehem & New England NW2 Diesel Locomotive "27," *CC, 16*		500 ___
83390	SP NW2 Diesel Locomotive "1423," *CC, 16*		500 ___
83391	SP&S NW2 Diesel Locomotive "41," *CC, 16*		500 ___
83392	Union NW2 Diesel Locomotive "555," *CC, 16*		500 ___
83393	UP NW2 Diesel Locomotive "1011," *CC, 16*		500 ___

|---|---|---|---|
___ 83395	AC&Y H16-44 Diesel "201," *CC, 16*		550
___ 83396	AC&Y H16-44 Diesel "202," *CC, 16*		550
___ 83397	AT&SF H16-44 Diesel "2801," *CC, 16*		550
___ 83398	AT&SF H16-44 Diesel "2807," *CC, 16*		550
___ 83399	B&O H16-44 Diesel "6705," *CC, 16*		550
___ 83400	B&O H16-44 Diesel "6708," *CC, 16*		550
___ 83401	MILW H16-44 Diesel "402," *CC, 16*		550
___ 83402	MILW H16-44 Diesel "404," *CC, 16*		550
___ 83403	DL&W H16-44 Diesel "931," *CC, 16*		550
___ 83404	DL&W H16-44 Diesel "934," *CC, 16*		550
___ 83405	Southern H16-44 Diesel "6547," *CC, 16*		550
___ 83406	Southern H16-44 Diesel "6550," *CC, 16*		550
___ 83426	Johnstown Birney Trolley, *16*		100
___ 83434	Polar Express Passenger Station, *16-17*		90
___ 83435	World War II Pylon, *17*		160
___ 83437	Polar Express Conductor Announcement Car, *16-17, 19*		110
___ 83438	Miller Coors Operating Billboard, *17*		80
___ 83440	Rico Station Kit, *16-18, 20*		60
___ 83442	Large Suburban House, *17-18*		95
___ 83443	Deluxe Bungalow House, *17-18*		95
___ 83444	Illuminated Station Platform, *16-17*		43
___ 83445	Smithsonian Old St. Nick Boxcar, *16-18*		85
___ 83455	Polar Express Operating Billboard, *16-17*		85
___ 83462	Bethlehem Steel Slag Car 3-pack, *16*		240
___ 83466	U.S. Steel Slag Car 3-pack (std O), *16*		240
___ 83470	Slag Car 3-pack (std O), *16*		240
___ 83474	Weathered Slag Car 3-pack (std O), *16*		240
___ 83478	Bethlehem Steel Hot Metal Car 2-pack, *16*		200
___ 83481	U.S. Steel Hot Metal Car 2-pack (std O), *16*		200
___ 83484	Hot Metal Car 2-pack (std O), *16*		200
___ 83487	Weathered Hot Metal Car 2-pack (std O), *16*		200
___ 83490	Lighted Coaling Tower, *16, 18*		180
___ 83491	Boston Red Sox Cooperstown Boxcar, *16*		85
___ 83492	St. Louis Cardinals Cooperstown Boxcar, *16*		85
___ 83493	Philadelphia Phillies Cooperstown Boxcar, *16*		85
___ 83494	Baltimore Orioles Cooperstown Boxcar, *16*		85
___ 83496	Station Platform, *16-18*		40
___ 83497	National Train Day Boxcar, *16-17*		85
___ 83503	Thomas with remote, *16-18*		120
___ 83504	Birthday Thomas with remote, *16-18*		120
___ 83510	Thomas Passenger Set, *LionChief, 16-20*		200
___ 83512	Thomas & Friends Christmas Freight Set, *16-17*		200
___ 83518	PRR Boxcar "83518" (std O), *16*		100
___ 83519	REA SensorCar Steel Reefer "7844" (std O), *16, 19*		130
___ 83520	North Pole Central Flatcar with snowplow, *16*		95
___ 83527	AT&SF PS-1 Boxcar "142501," sound (std O), *16*		130
___ 83528	BAR PS-1 Boxcar "5149," sound (std O), *16*		130
___ 83529	B&O PS-1 Boxcar "467931," sound (std O), *16*		130
___ 83530	BN PS-1 Boxcar "132909," sound (std O), *16*		130
___ 83531	C&NW PS-1 Boxcar "5," sound (std O), *16*		130
___ 83532	NYC PS-1 Boxcar "175001," sound (std O), *16*		130
___ 83533	PRR PS-1 Boxcar "47005," sound (std O), *16*		130
___ 83534	UP PS-1 Boxcar "196883," sound (std O), *16*		130

No.	Description	Esc	Mint
83535	PRR GL-a 2-bay Hopper 3-pack #1 (std O), *16*		220 ___
83539	PRR GL-a 2-bay Hopper 3-pack #2 (std O), *16*		220 ___
83544	PRR N5b Caboose "477797" (std O), *16*		95 ___
83545	PFE Reefer 3-pack (std O), *16*		170 ___
83549	AT&SF Reefer 3-pack (std O), *16*		300 ___
83553	Heisler Log Train Set, *CC, 16*		1450 ___
83555	Red Logging Disconnect Caboose "1" (std O), *16*		40 ___
83556	Brown Logging Disconnect Caboose "6" (std O), *16*		40 ___
83557	Logging Disconnect Boxcar (std O), *16*		40 ___
83558	Logging Disconnect Flatcar (std O), *16*		35 ___
83559	Logging Disconnect Gondola (std O), *16*		40 ___
83560	Logging Disconnect Tank Car (std O), *16*		40 ___
83561	ATSF Express 50' DD Boxcar "1342" (std O), *16-17*		80 ___
83562	CNJ PS-1 Express Boxcar "22487" (std O), *16-17*		80 ___
83563	C&EI PS-1 Express Boxcar "2" (std O), *16-17*		80 ___
83564	GN PS-1 Express Boxcar "2538" (std O), *16-17*		80 ___
83565	KCS PS-1 Express Boxcar "400" (std O), *16-17*		80 ___
83566	SP PS-1 Express Boxcar "5712" (std O), *16-17*		80 ___
83567	T&P PS-1 Express Boxcar "1721" (std O), *16-17*		80 ___
83568	C&S Grain-door PS-1 Boxcar "1650" (std O), *16-17*		80 ___
83569	CP Grain-door PS-1 Boxcar "260293" (std O), *16-17*		80 ___
83570	GN Grain-door PS-1 Boxcar "18119" (std O), *16-17*		80 ___
83571	CGW Grain-door PS-1 Boxcar "5450" (std O), *16-17*		80 ___
83572	IC Grain-door PS-1 Boxcar "19000" (std O), *16-17*		80 ___
83573	MKT Grain-door PS-1 Boxcar "92463" (std O), *16-17*		80 ___
83574	UP CA-4 Caboose "3824" (std O), *16*		90 ___
83575	UP CA-4 Caboose "25121" (std O), *16*		90 ___
83576	B&O Milk Car "847" (std O), *16-17, 20*		90 ___
83577	Supplee Milk Car "7" (std O), *16-17, 20*		90 ___
83578	Hood Milk Car "807" (std O), *16-17, 20*		90 ___
83579	Rutland Milk Car "351" (std O), *16-17, 20*		90 ___
83580	BAR State of Maine 40' Trailer, 2-pack, *16-17*		65 ___
83581	C&NW 40' Trailer, 2-pack, *16-17*		65 ___
83582	PFE 40' Trailer, 2-pack, *16-17*		65 ___
83583	PC 40' Trailer, 2-pack, *16-17*		65 ___
83584	SP 40' Trailer, 2-pack, *16-17*		65 ___
83585	UP 40'Trailer, 2-pack, *16-17*		65 ___
83586	PRR Broadway Limited 21" Passenger Car 2-pack #2 (std O), *16*		300 ___
83589	American Freedom Train Add-On 2-pack #2, *16-17*		300 ___
83592	American Freedom Train Add-On 2-pack #3, *16-17*		300 ___
83595	Conrail Office Car Special Diesel Passenger Set, *CC, 17*		1250 ___
83601	Conrail Office Car Special Add-on 2-pack, *17*		310 ___
83604	Conrail Office Car Special 21" Dome Car "55," StationSounds, *17*		320 ___
83605	Presidents 2-8-2 Mikado Locomotive "1789," *16-17*		430 ___
83606	Halloween 2-8-2 Mikado Locomotive "1031," *16-17*		430 ___
83607	USRA2-8-2 Mikado Locomotive "4500," *16-18*		430 ___
83608	B&O 2-8-2 Mikado Locomotive "4500," *16-17*		430 ___
83609	C&O 2-8-2 Mikado Locomotive "1067," *16-17*		430 ___
83610	MKT 2-8-2 Mikado Locomotive "851," *16-17*		430 ___
83611	NYC Empire State Express 21" Coach 4-pack #2, *17*		620 ___
83616	NYC Empire State Express 21" Combine/Observation Car 2-pack #2, *17*		310 ___
83619	NYC Empire State Express 21" Diner #2, StationSounds, *17*		310 ___
83620	Hogwarts Express Passenger Set, *16-17*		400 ___

			Mint
____	83624	UP Sherman Hill Scout RS-3 Freight Set, *16-17*	500
____	83633	Alaska Gold Mint Car, *17*	70
____	83634	Keystone Smoke Fluid Loader, *16-20*	350
____	83635	North American Smoke Fluid Loader, *16-19*	350
____	83637	Mets-Phillies Mascot Aquarium Car, *16*	85
____	83644	Macy's Dry Goods Boxcar, *2015u*	100
____	83645	Polar Express Boxcar 2-pack, *16-18*	170
____	83648	New York Yankees Subway Set, *16*	390
____	83653	21" Passenger Car Figure Pack, *16-18, 20*	30
____	83655	Hamm's Heritage Beer Wood-sided Reefer, *16-17*	80
____	83656	Coors Heritage Beer Wood-sided Reefer, *16-17*	80
____	83657	Miller Heritage Beer Wood-sided Reefer, *16-17*	80
____	83658	Lionelville School Kit, *16-17*	60
____	83659	PRR Keystone Special Steam Freight Set, *16-17*	280
____	83688	Trackside Railroad Details Pack, *16, 18, 20*	25
____	83689	Angela Trotta Thomas Christmas Covered Bridge, *17-20*	70
____	83690	Company Row House, blue, *16-17*	60
____	83691	Company Row House, yellow, *16-17*	60
____	83692	Company Row House, white, *16-17*	60
____	83693	Company Row House, red, *16-17*	60
____	83694	Toymaker Limited Trolley Set, *18*	200
____	83696	NYC "Pacemaker" Lionel Junction Diesel Freight Set, *17*	175
____	83701	Alaska Gold Mine 0-4-0 Steam Freight Set, LionChief, *17*	320
____	83716	BNSF RS-3 Diesel Scout Freight Set, LionChief, *17*	280
____	83733	Lighted Aquarius Hi-Cube Boxcar, *17*	90
____	83734	Lighted Pegasus Hi-Cube Boxcar, *17*	90
____	83745	Lionelville Hospital Kit, *17-18*	80
____	83751	Yard Tower, *18-19*	65
____	83752	W&A Horse Car and Corral, *17-18*	180
____	83762	Personalized Christmas Boxcar, *16*	90
____	83763	Personalized Holiday Boxcar, *16*	90
____	83764	Happy Birthday Boxcar, *16*	90
____	83765	Anniversary Boxcar, *16-17*	90
____	83766	Personalized Polar Express Baggage Car, *16-18*	95
____	83779	Pearl Harbor 75th Anniversary Boxcar, *16-17*	85
____	83783	Rosie the Riveter Boxcar, *17*	85
____	83784	Heavies and Little Friends Boxcar, *17*	85
____	83785	Doolittle Raid Boxcar, *16-17*	85
____	83786	D-Day Boxcar, *17*	85
____	83788	Uncle Sam "Enlist Now" Boxcar, *16-17*	85
____	83790	Mickey Mouse Happy Holidays Boxcar, *17*	85
____	83791	Donald Duck Happy Holidays Boxcar, *17*	85
____	83792	Goofy Happy Holidays Boxcar, *17*	85
____	83794	75th Anniversary of Bambi Boxcar, *17*	80
____	83795	50th Anniversary of The Jungle Book Boxcar, *17*	80
____	83796	100th Anniversary Moon Pie Boxcar, *17*	85
____	83800	Happy Thanksgiving Boxcar, *17*	80
____	83801	Happy Hanukkah Boxcar, *17*	80
____	83802	Disney Happy Halloween Boxcar, *17*	85
____	83913	Personalized Halloween Boxcar, *17*	95
____	83918	Smithsonian Boxcar, John Bull, *17*	85
____	83923	Angela Trotta Thomas Santa's Cookies Boxcar, *17*	85
____	83924	Caddyshack Boxcar, *17*	80

		Mint
83925	Frosty the Snowman Boxcar, *17*	85 ___
83926	Personalized Polar Express Boxcar, *17-20*	95 ___
83927	Lionel Smoke Fluid 1-D Tank Car, *17*	75 ___
83928	Lionel Paint 1-D Tank Car, *17*	75 ___
83929	Lionel Hydraulic Oil 1-D Tank Car, *17*	75 ___
83938	Harry Potter Hogwarts House Gryffindor Boxcar, *17*	80 ___
83939	Harry Potter Hogwarts House Ravenclaw Boxcar, *17*	80 ___
83940	Harry Potter Hogwarts House Hufflepuff Boxcar, *17*	80 ___
83941	Harry Potter Hogwarts House Slytherin Boxcar, *17*	80 ___
83943	Polar Express Boxcar, *17-18*	85 ___
83944	John Deere Boxcar, *17*	85 ___
83945	Richard Nixon Presidential Boxcar, *17*	70 ___
83946	Jimmy Carter Presidential Boxcar, *17, 19*	70 ___
83947	Woodrow Wilson Presidential Boxcar, *17, 19-20*	75 ___
83948	William Howard Taft Presidential Boxcar, *17, 19-20*	75 ___
83950	Personalized "It's A Boy" Boxcar, *17-20*	90 ___
83951	Personalized "It's A Girl" Boxcar, *17-20*	90 ___
83952	Minnie Mouse Happy Holidays Boxcar, *17*	85 ___
83959	Macy's Parade 90th Anniversary Boxcar, *2016u*	30 ___
83964	Mickey Mouse Christmas Express Steam Freight Set, LionChief, *17-18*	420 ___
83972	Harry Potter Hogwarts Steam Passenger Set, LionChief, *17-19*	420 ___
83974	CSX Diesel Intermodal Set, LionChief, *17-18*	460 ___
83979	Mickey & Friends B337Express Steam Freight Set, LionChief, *17, 19-20*	370 ___
83984	Pennsylvania Flyer 0-8-0 Steam Freight Set, LionChief, *17, 19-20*	300 ___
84000	DETX Rotary Gondola 4-pack (std O), *16-17, 20*	280 ___
84005	CSX Rotary Gondola 4-pack (std O), *16-17, 20*	280 ___
84010	UP Rotary Gondola 4-pack (std O), *16-17, 20*	280 ___
84015	NS Rotary Gondola 4-pack (std O), *16-17, 20*	280 ___
84020	PPLX Rotary Gondola 4-pack (std O), *16-17, 20*	280 ___
84025	PPLX Rotary Gondola 2-pack (std O), *16-17, 20*	140 ___
84028	BNSF Rotary Gondola 4-pack (std O), *16-17, 20*	280 ___
84033	BNSF Rotary Gondola 2-pack (std O), *16-17, 20*	140 ___
84045	BN 21" Passenger Car 4-pack, *17*	620 ___
84050	BN 21" Coach 2-pack, *17*	310 ___
84053	BN 21" Diner, StationSounds , *17*	310 ___
84063	Weathered N&W Y6B 2-8-8-2 Locomotive "2186," *CC, 16*	2200 ___
84064	MILW 4-8-4 Northern Locomotive "261," *CC, 17*	1700 ___
84065	MILW 4-8-4 Northern Locomotive "265," *CC, 17*	1700 ___
84066	MILW 4-8-4 Northern Locomotive "262," *CC, 17*	1700 ___
84067	MILW 4-8-4 Northern Locomotive "260 Hiawatha," *CC, 17*	1700 ___
84068	DL&W 4-8-4 Northern Locomotive "1661," *CC, 17*	1700 ___
84069	B&M 2-6-0 Mogul Locomotive "1397," *CC, 16*	700 ___
84070	CV 2-6-0 Mogul Locomotive "397," *CC, 16*	700 ___
84071	DL&W 2-6-0 Mogul Locomotive "565," *CC, 16*	700 ___
84072	Everett 2-6-0 Mogul Locomotive "11," *CC, 16*	700 ___
84073	GT 2-6-0 Mogul Locomotive "713," *CC, 16*	700 ___
84074	Rutland 2-6-0 Mogul Locomotive "145," *CC, 16*	700 ___
84075	ACL E8 Diesel AA Set "544, 545," *CC, 17*	1000 ___
84078	BN E8 Diesel AA Set "9935, 9940," *CC, 17*	1000 ___
84081	Conrail E8 Diesel AA Set "4020, 4021," *CC , 17*	1000 ___
84084	EMD Demonstrator E8 Diesel A Unit "950," *CC, 17*	650 ___
84085	L&N E8 Diesel AA Set "796, 797," *CC, 17*	1000 ___

| --- | --- | --- | --- |
___	**84088** NYC E8 Diesel AA Set "4036, 4037," *CC, 17*		1000
___	**84091** PRR E8 Diesel AA Set "5763, 5764," *CC, 17*		1000
___	**84094** Arkansas & Missouri SD70ACe Diesel Locomotive "70," *CC, 16*		650
___	**84095** Arkansas & Missouri SD70ACe Diesel Locomotive "71," *CC, 16*		650
___	**84096** BNSF SD70ACe Diesel Locomotive "9372," *CC, 16*		650
___	**84097** BNSF SD70ACe Diesel Locomotive "9385," *CC, 16*		650
___	**84098** CN SD70ACe Diesel Locomotive "8100," *CC, 16*		650
___	**84099** CN SD70ACe Diesel Locomotive "8102," *CC, 16*		650
___	**84100** CSX SD70ACe Diesel Locomotive "4837," *CC, 16*		650
___	**84101** CSX SD70ACe Diesel Locomotive "4843," *CC, 16*		650
___	**84102** EMDX SD70ACe Diesel Locomotive "72," *CC, 16*		650
___	**84103** EMDX SD70ACe Diesel Locomotive "73," *CC, 16*		650
___	**84104** Montana Rail Link SD70ACe Diesel Locomotive "4309" *CC, 16*		650
___	**84105** Montana Rail Link SD70ACe Diesel Locomotive "4312" *CC, 16*		650
___	**84106** UP SD70ACe Diesel Locomotive "8360," *CC, 16*		650
___	**84107** UP SD70ACe Diesel Locomotive "8415," *CC, 16*		650
___	**84108** GN GP7 Diesel "601," *16-18*		330
___	**84109** L&N GP7 Diesel "405," *16-18*		330
___	**84110** Reading GP7 Diesel "619," *16-18*		330
___	**84111** WP GP7 Diesel "707," *16-18*		330
___	**84112** Cotton Belt 50' DD Boxcar "47509" (std O), *16-17*		80
___	**84113** D&RGW 50' DD Boxcar "63689" (std O), *16-17*		80
___	**84114** Seaboard 50' DD Boxcar "10090" (std O), *16-17*		80
___	**84115** PRR K4s 4-6-2 Pacific Locomotive "5385," *CC, 16*		1300
___	**84116** PRR K4s 4-6-2 Pacific Locomotive "5432," *CC, 16*		1300
___	**84117** Burlington Refrigerator Express 40' Steel Reefer "76060" (std O), *17*		85
___	**84118** BAR 40' Steel Reefer "7342" (std O), *17*		85
___	**84119** BN 40' Steel Reefer "70609" (std O), *17*		85
___	**84120** Eastern States ERDX 40' Steel Reefer "10060" (std O), *17*		85
___	**84121** National Car Co. 40' Steel Reefer "2430" (std O), *17*		85
___	**84122** FGE 40' Steel Reefer "41475" (std O), *17*		85
___	**84123** B&M PS-2CD Covered Hopper "5717" (std O), *17*		90
___	**84124** L&N PS-2CD Covered Hopper "37399" (std O), *17*		90
___	**84125** MILW PS-2CD Covered Hopper "98333" (std O), *17*		90
___	**84126** NP PS-2CD Covered Hopper "75675" (std O), *17*		90
___	**84127** AT&SF PS-2CD Covered Hopper "304713" (std O), *17*		90
___	**84128** TLDX Demonstrator PS-2CD Covered Hopper "91" (std O), *17, 19*		90
___	**84129** AT&SF Wide Vision Caboose "999705" (std O), *17*		95
___	**84130** BN Freedom Train Wide Vision Caboose "12618" (std O), *17*		95
___	**84131** BNSF Wide Vision Caboose "12584" (std O), *17*		95
___	**84132** CSX Wide Vision Caboose "903180" (std O), *17*		95
___	**84133** D&H Wide-Vision Caboose "35712," *18*		100
___	**84134** GN Wide-Vision Caboose "X-109," *18*		100
___	**84135** C&O Northeast Caboose "A918" (std O), *17*		90
___	**84137** Conrail Northeast Caboose "18866" (std O), *17*		90
___	**84138** Pere Marquette Northeast Caboose "A909" (std O), *17*		90
___	**84139** WM Northeast Caboose circle herald "1874" (std O), *17*		90
___	**84140** WM Northeast Caboose circus herald "1882" (std O), *17*		90
___	**84141** WM USRA 2-bay Hopper 3-pack #1 (std O), *17*		220
___	**84145** WM USRA 2-bay Hopper 3-pack #2 (std O), *17*		220
___	**84149** Reading USRA 2-bay Hopper 3-pack (std O), *17*		220
___	**84153** B&O 1905 2-bay Hopper 3-pack (std O), *17*		220
___	**84157** Bethlehem Steel 1905 2-bay Hopper 3-pack (std O), *17*		220
___	**84161** Logging Disconnect Stock Car, *17*		40

		Esc	Mint
84163	Logging Disconnect Christmas 4-pack (std O), *17*		160 ___
84165	Logging Disconnect Dinner Train 4-pack (std O), *17, 19*		160 ___
84166	Logging Disconnect, *1-pair, brown (std O), 17, 19*		65 ___
84167	Logging Disconnect, *2-pair, brown (std O), 17*		125 ___
84187	B&O 18" Heavyweight Coach 2-pack #1, *18*		400 ___
84190	B&O 18" Heavyweight Coach 2-pack #2, *18*		400 ___
84193	Reading, Blue Mountain & Northern 18" Heavyweight Coach 2-pack #1, *18*		400 ___
84196	Reading, Blue Mountain & Northern 18" Heavyweight Coach 2-pack #2, *18*		400 ___
84199	MILW 18" Heavyweight Coach 2-pack #1, *18*		400 ___
84202	MILW 18" Heavyweight Coach 2-pack #2, *18*		400 ___
84205	Nickel Plate Road 18" Heavyweight Coach 2-pack #1, *18*		400 ___
84208	Nickel Plate Road 18" Heavyweight Coach 2-pack #2, *18*		400 ___
84208	Smithsonian Boxcar, Southern "1401," *17*		85 ___
84211	TH&B 18" Heavyweight Coach 2-pack #1, *18*		400 ___
84214	TH&B 18" Heavyweight Coach 2-pack #2, *18*		400 ___
84217	Wabash 18" Heavyweight Coach 2-pack #1, *18*		400 ___
84220	Wabash 18" Heavyweight Coach 2-pack #2, *18*		400 ___
84226	American Freedom Train Add-On 2-pack #4, *17*		300 ___
84229	Conrail 21" Theater Inspection Car "9," *17*		340 ___
84230	NS 21" Theater Inspection Car Buena Vista, *17*		340 ___
84231	CSX 21" Theater Inspection Car Alabama, *17*		340 ___
84232	UP 21" Theater Inspection Car Fox River, *17*		340 ___
84237	Cass Scenic RR 3-Truck Shay Locomotive "6," *CC, 17*		1500 ___
84238	Elk River Lumber Co. 3-Truck Shay Locomotive "20," *CC, 17*		1500 ___
84239	WM 3-Truck Shay Locomotive "6," *CC, 17*		1500 ___
84240	West Side Lumber Co. 3-Truck Shay Locomotive "3," *CC, 17*		1500 ___
84248	SP AC-9 2-8-8-4 Locomotive "3800," *CC, 17*		2000 ___
84249	SP AC-9 2-8-8-4 Locomotive "3805," *CC, 17*		2000 ___
84250	SP AC-9 Daylight 2-8-8-4 Locomotive "3811," *CC, 17*		2000 ___
84251	AT&SF 2-8-4 Berkshire Locomotive "4103," *17-18*		450 ___
84252	Nickel Plate Road 2-8-4 Berkshire Locomotive "767," *17-18*		450 ___
84253	Pere Marquette 2-8-4 Berkshire Locomotive "1223," *17-18*		450 ___
84254	IC 2-8-4 Berkshire Locomotive "8006," *17-18*		450 ___
84255	Lionel Lines 2-8-4 Berkshire Locomotive "726," *17-18*		450 ___
84256	AT&SF SD40 Diesel "5006," *CC, 17*		650 ___
84257	AT&SF SD40 Diesel "5018," *CC, 17*		650 ___
84258	UP SD40 Diesel "4057," *CC, 17*		650 ___
84259	UP SD40 Diesel "4062," *CC, 17*		650 ___
84260	CSX SD40 Diesel "4614," *CC, 17*		650 ___
84261	CSX SD40 Diesel "4621," *CC, 17*		650 ___
84262	PRR SD40 Diesel "6041," *CC, 17*		650 ___
84263	PRR SD40 Diesel "6089," *CC, 17*		650 ___
84264	Southern SD40 Diesel "3170," *CC, 17*		650 ___
84265	Southern SD40 Diesel "3200," *CC, 17*		650 ___
84267	SP SD40R Diesel "7372," *CC, 17*		650 ___
84268	WM SD40 Diesel "7547," *CC, 17*		650 ___
84269	WM SD40 Diesel "7549," *CC, 17*		650 ___
84270	B&O EMD Torpedo GP9 Diesel "3414," *CC, 18*		550 ___
84271	B&O EMD Torpedo GP9 Diesel "3419," *CC, 18*		550 ___
84272	C&NW EMD Torpedo GP9 Diesel "1725," *CC, 18*		550 ___
84273	C&NW EMD Torpedo GP9 Diesel "1730," *CC, 18*		550 ___

			Mint
____	84274	MILW EMD Torpedo GP9 Diesel "202," *CC, 18*	550
____	84275	MILW EMD Torpedo GP9 Diesel "208," *CC, 18*	550
____	84276	Nickel Plate Road EMD Torpedo GP9 Diesel "482," *CC, 18*	550
____	84277	Nickel Plate Road EMD Torpedo GP9 Diesel "484," *CC, 18*	550
____	84278	TH&B EMD Torpedo GP9 Diesel "402," *CC, 18*	550
____	84279	TH&B EMD Torpedo GP9 Diesel "403," *CC, 18*	550
____	84280	Wabash EMD Torpedo GP9 Diesel "484," *CC, 18*	550
____	84281	Wabash EMD Torpedo GP9 Diesel "486," *CC, 18*	550
____	84282	BN GE U33C Diesel "5716," *CC, 18*	580
____	84283	BN GE U33C Diesel "5723," *CC, 18*	580
____	84284	D&H GE U33C Diesel "757," *CC, 18*	580
____	84285	D&H GE U33C Diesel "762," *CC, 18*	580
____	84286	Guilford D&H GE U33C Diesel "650," *CC, 18*	580
____	84287	Guilford D&H GE U33C Diesel "654," *CC, 18*	580
____	84288	GN GE U33C Diesel "2530," *CC, 18*	580
____	84289	GN GE U33C Diesel "2541," *CC, 18*	580
____	84290	IC GE U33C Diesel "5052," *CC, 18*	580
____	84291	IC GE U33C Diesel "5054," *CC, 18*	580
____	84292	PC GE U33C Diesel "6547," *CC, 18*	580
____	84293	PC GE U33C Diesel "6561," *CC, 18*	580
____	84294	Sacramento Trolley, *17-18*	100
____	84295	Connecticut Trolley, *17-18*	100
____	84296	SP Salad Bowl Express Diesel Freight Set, *CC, 17*	900
____	84297	Logging Disconnect Steel Tank Car (std O), *17*	40
____	84303	Bucking Feed and Tack, *17*	85
____	84304	CB&Q Gondola with covers, *17*	55
____	84306	Illuminated John Deere Flagpole, *17-18*	60
____	84307	Illuminated Lionel Flagpole with flag, *17-18*	50
____	84308	Gray Half-Covered Bridge, *17*	60
____	84309	PRR Blinking Water Tower, *17-18*	45
____	84310	Modular Train Car Repair Facility, *16-17*	110
____	84312	Alaska RR Gondola with canisters, *17, 19*	55
____	84314	BNSF ACF Covered Hopper "405850," *18*	60
____	84315	Branchline Water Tank Kit, *16-19*	40
____	84317	Passenger Station, *17*	80
____	84318	Illuminated Station Platform, *17-20*	43
____	84327	Santa Fe Operating Billboard, *17*	70
____	84328	Polar Express Steam Passenger Set, LionChief, *17-19*	420
____	84328P	Polar Express Steam Passenger Set, LionChief w/Personalized Tender, *2019-20*	420
____	84330	Witches Brew 1-D Tank Car, *17-18*	70
____	84332	Halloween Boxcar, SpookySounds, *17-18*	80
____	84333	Strasburg RR Gondola with vats, *17, 19*	65
____	84334	Strasburg Half-covered Bridge, *17-18*	60
____	84335	PRR Culvert Gondola "374200," *17, 19*	65
____	84336	UP Log Car, *17*	65
____	84337	MKT Wood-chip Hopper, *17*	65
____	84338	CSX Wood-chip Hopper, *17-18*	65
____	84339	SP Jumping Hobo Boxcar, *17*	80
____	84340	Santa and Snowman Operating Boxcar, *17-18*	90
____	84341	Tell-Tale Reindeer Car, *17*	80
____	84366	PRR Wood-chip Hopper, *17-19*	65
____	84367	Christmas Pylon, *17*	160

		Esc	Mint
84369	NYC Welding Car "X939," *17*		80 ___
84369	L&N Hummingbird 21" Diner w/StationSounds, *18*		330 ___
84370	Polar Express Hopper with silver, *17-18*		70 ___
84371	Mickey's Holiday Hopper with presents, *17-18*		70 ___
84372	Christmas Station Platform, *17-18*		43 ___
84373	Special Trolley Announcement Track, *18-20*		50 ___
84374	Christmas Music Boxcar, *17*		80 ___
84375	Christmas Boxcar, *17*		65 ___
84376	Angela Trotta Thomas Signature Express Aquarium Car, *17-18*		85 ___
84377	Christmas Peppermint 1-D Tank Car, *17-18*		60 ___
84378	Santa's Choice Milk Car with platform, *17-18*		180 ___
84380	Reading & Northern Auxiliary Tender "425-A," *CC, 18*		300 ___
84383	Elevated Oil Tank, *17-18*		95 ___
84388	Gray 10" Girder Bridge, *17-20*		25 ___
84400	BN "Pulling for Freedom" SD60M Diesel "1991," *CC, 17*		650 ___
84401	BN SD60M Diesel "9200," *CC, 17*		650 ___
84402	BN SD60M Diesel "9225," *CC, 17*		650 ___
84403	Soo Line SD60M Diesel "6058," *CC, 17*		650 ___
84404	Soo Line SD60M Diesel "6061," *CC, 17*		650 ___
84405	Conrail SD60M Diesel "5504," *CC, 17*		650 ___
84406	Conrail SD60M Diesel "5510," *CC, 17*		650 ___
84407	CSX SD60M Diesel "8783," *CC, 17*		650 ___
84408	CSX SD60M Diesel "8784," *CC, 17*		650 ___
84409	NS SD60M Diesel "6808," *CC, 17*		650 ___
84410	NS SD60M Diesel "6815," *CC, 17*		650 ___
84411	UP SD60M Diesel "6165," *CC, 17*		650 ___
84412	UP SD60M Diesel "6187," *CC, 17*		650 ___
84413	B&O FA A-A Diesel Set, "814, 815," *17-18*		500 ___
84416	GN FA A-A Diesel Set, "278A, 278B," *17-18*		500 ___
84419	NH FA A-A Diesel Set, "417, 418," *17-18*		500 ___
84422	UP FA A-A Diesel Set, "1616, 1617," *17-18*		500 ___
84433	Polar Express 40' Scale Reefer "122517," *17*		90 ___
84434	NS 30,000-gallon 1-D Tank Car 3-pack (std O), *16*		250 ___
84438	NS 30,000-gallon 1-D Tank Car "362785" (std O), *16*		80 ___
84439	UTLX 30,000-gallon 1-D Tank Car 3-pack (std O), *16*		250 ___
84443	PESX 30,000-gallon 1-D Tank Car 3-pack (std O), *16, 19*		250 ___
84447	TILX 30,000-gallon 1-D Tank Car 3-pack (std O), *16, 19*		250 ___
84451	PRR Flatcar 6-pack, *17*		120 ___
84452	AT&SF Flatcar 6-pack, *17-18*		120 ___
84453	UP Flatcar 6-pack, *17-18*		120 ___
84454	Trailer Train Flatcar 6-pack, *17*		120 ___
84455	Assorted Flatcar 6-pack, *17-18*		120 ___
84456	B&O Gondola 6-pack, *17-18*		120 ___
84457	UP Gondola 6-pack, *17-18*		120 ___
84458	East Assorted Gondola 6-pack, *17*		120 ___
84459	Midwest Assorted Gondola 6-pack, *17*		120 ___
84460	West Assorted Gondola 6-pack, *17-18*		120 ___
84462	2-Rail Conversion Kit, 50-ton Scale Trucks, *16-20*		20 ___
84463	2-Rail Conversion Kit, 70-ton Scale Trucks, *16-20*		20 ___
84465	B&O 2-8-2 Light Mikado Locomotive "4500," *CC , 17*		1300 ___
84466	GTW 2-8-2 Light Mikado Locomotive "3734," *CC, 17*		1300 ___
84467	Maine Central 2-8-2 Light Mikado Locomotive "624," *CC, 17*		1300 ___
84468	NYC 2-8-2 Light Mikado Locomotive "5187," *CC, 17*		1300 ___

		Esc	Mint
___	84469	PRR 2-8-2 Light Mikado Locomotive "9630," *CC*, *17*		1300
___	84470	Southern 2-8-2 Light Mikado Locomotive "4758," *CC*, *17*		1300
___	84471	UP 2-8-2 Light Mikado Locomotive "2537," *CC*, *17*		1300
___	84472	AT&SF 2-8-2 Mikado Locomotive, *Brass Hybrid* "3222," *CC*, *17*		1300
___	84480	John Deere Covered Bridge, *17-18*		70
___	84481	John Deere General Store, *17-18*		85
___	84482	John Deere Gondola with hay bales, *17-18*		75
___	84483	John Deere Grain Vat Car, *17*		75
___	84485	Disney Covered Bridge, *17-18*		70
___	84486	MILW NW2 Diesel Locomotive "1649," *CC*, *16*		500
___	84487	Donald Duck Holiday 1-D Tank Car, *17*		70
___	84489	Polar Express Covered Bridge, *17-18*		70
___	84490	NS First Responders Diesel Freight Set, *LionChief, 17-18*		450
___	84496	Shell Service Station, *17*		150
___	84498	NS Fire Rescue Car, *17-18*		75
___	84499	Mickey Mouse & Friends Industrial Water Tower, *17-20*		100
___	84500	NS Unibody 1-D Tank Car "490112," *17-18*		75
___	84507	New York Central & Hudson River S2 Electric "3207," *CC*, *17*		800
___	84508	NYC S2 Electric "113," *CC*, *17*		800
___	84509	NYC S2 Electric "115," *CC*, *17*		800
___	84510	PC S2 Electric "4710," *CC*, *17*		800
___	84511	NYC "Lightning Stripe" S2 Electric "101," *CC*, *17*		800
___	84512	S2 Electric Scale Tinplate Freight Set, *CC, 17*		1000
___	84525	Uptown Apartment Building, *17*		100
___	84526	Leuzure Marble Co. Warehouse , *17*		110
___	84529	NS Veterans Wide Vision Caboose "6920" (std O), *17-18*		95
___	84530	NS First Responders Wide Vision Caboose "9-1-1" (std O), *17-18*		95
___	84532	Nickel Plate Road 2-8-2 Light Mikado Locomotive "587," *CC*, *17*		1300
___	84538	NS 65' Mill Gondola "195029" (std O), *17*		80
___	84539	NS 65' Mill Gondola "195065" (std O), *17*		80
___	84553	Logging Disconnect Reindeer Train 4-pack A, *17*		160
___	84554	Logging Disconnect Reindeer Train 4-pack B, *17*		160
___	84555	Logging Disconnect Santa Claus Observation (std O), *17*		45
___	84562	BN "Pulling for Freedom" SD60M Diesel "1991," *LionChief, 17*		500
___	84563	BN SD60M Diesel "9215," *LionChief, 17*		500
___	84564	Soo Line SD60M Diesel "6060," *LionChief, 17*		500
___	84565	Conrail SD60M Diesel "5509," *LionChief, 17*		500
___	84566	CSX SD60M Diesel "8757," *LionChief, 17*		500
___	84567	NS SD60M Diesel "6810," *LionChief, 17*		500
___	84568	UP SD60M Diesel "6170," *LionChief, 17*		500
___	84570	First Responders EMT Boxcar, *17-20*		93
___	84571	First Responders Police Boxcar, *17-20*		93
___	84572	First Responders Fire Fighter Boxcar, *17-20*		93
___	84573	Happy Birthday Boxcar, *17*		90
___	84574	Personalized 2017 Merry Christmas Boxcar, *17*		90
___	84575	U.S. Army Boxcar, *17-20*		90
___	84576	U.S. Marine Boxcar, *17-20*		90
___	84577	U.S. Air Force Boxcar, *17-20*		90
___	84578	U.S. Navy Boxcar, *17-20*		90
___	84579	U.S. Coast Guard Boxcar, *17-20*		90
___	84580	From The Home Front Boxcar, blue, *17-20*		90
___	84581	From The Home Front Boxcar, green, *17-20*		90
___	84582	BNSF 65' Mill Gondola "518375" (std O), *17*		80
___	84583	BNSF 65' Mill Gondola "518392" (std O), *17*		80

		Esc	Mint
84584	C&NW 65' Mill Gondola "342045" (std 0), *17*		80 ___
84585	C&NW 65' Mill Gondola "342049" (std 0), *17*		80 ___
84586	CSX 65' Mill Gondola "491616" (std 0), *17*		80 ___
84587	CSX 65' Mill Gondola "491638" (std 0), *17*		80 ___
84590	SP 65' Mill Gondola "365136" (std 0), *17*		80 ___
84591	SP 65' Mill Gondola "365142" (std 0), *17*		80 ___
84592	UP 65' Mill Gondola "96267" (std 0), *17*		80 ___
84593	UP 65' Mill Gondola "96281" (std 0), *17*		80 ___
84599	Bucking Feed & Tack Building, *18-20*		85 ___
84600	Polar Express Combination Car, *18-20*		75 ___
84601	Polar Express Letters to Santa Mail Car, *18-20*		75 ___
84602	Polar Express Disappearing Hobo Car, *18-20*		80 ___
84603	Polar Express Hot Chocolate Car, *18-19*		75 ___
84604	Polar Express Diner, *18-20*		75 ___
84605	Polar Express Baggage Car, *18-20*		75 ___
84605P	Personalized Polar Express Baggage Car, *2019-20*		95 ___
84611	Lionel BlueTooth Radio Tower, *17*		100 ___
84616	Wonder Woman Boxcar, *17*		80 ___
84621	17 National Lionel Train Day Boxcar, *17*		85 ___
84622	D&RGW EMD SD40T-2 Diesel "5401," *CC, 17*		600 ___
84623	D&RGW EMD SD40T-2 Diesel "5405," *CC, 17*		600 ___
84624	KCS EMD SD40T-2 Diesel "6102," *CC, 17*		600 ___
84625	KCS EMD SD40T-2 Diesel "6110," *CC, 17*		600 ___
84626	Lancaster & Chester EMD SD40T-2 Diesel "6002," *CC, 17*		600 ___
84627	GECX EMD SD40T-2 Diesel "8661," *CC, 17*		600 ___
84628	GECX EMD SD40T-2 Diesel "8678," *CC, 17*		600 ___
84629	Ohio Central EMD SD40T-2 Diesel "4026," *CC, 17*		600 ___
84630	Ohio Central EMD SD40T-2 Diesel "4027," *CC, 17*		600 ___
84631	RJ Corman EMD SD40T-2 Diesel "5361," *CC, 17*		600 ___
84632	RJ Corman EMD SD40T-2 Diesel "5409," *CC, 17*		600 ___
84633	SP EMD SD40T-2 Diesel "8532," *CC, 17*		600 ___
84634	SP EMD SD40T-2 Diesel "8548," *CC, 17*		600 ___
84635	UP EMD SD40T-2 Diesel "8593," *CC, 17*		600 ___
84636	UP EMD SD40T-2 Diesel "8715," *CC, 17*		600 ___
84637	Cotton Belt EMD SD40T-2 Diesel "9389," Bicentennial, *CC, 17*		600 ___
84638	ACL EMD E6 A-A Diesel Set "500-501," *CC, 17*		1000 ___
84641	AT&SF EMD E6 A-A Diesel Set "12-13," *CC, 17*		1000 ___
84644	C&NW EMD E6 A-A Diesel Set "5005A-5005B," *CC, 17*		1000 ___
84647	FEC EMD E3 A-A Diesel Set "1001-1002," *CC, 17*		1000 ___
84650	IC EMD E6 A-A Diesel Set "4003-4004," *CC, 17*		1000 ___
84653	KCS EMD E3 A-A Diesel Set "2-3," *CC, 17*		1000 ___
84656	L&N EMD E6 A-A Diesel Set "754-755," *CC, 17*		1000 ___
84659	MILW EMD E6 A-A Diesel Set "15A-15B," *CC, 17*		1000 ___
84662	UP EMD E6 A-A Diesel Set "996-997," *CC, 17*		1000 ___
84666	Battle for Guadalcanal, *17*		85 ___
84667	Battle of the Bulge Boxcar, *17*		85 ___
84668	Silent Service Boxcar, *17*		85 ___
84669	Desert Storm Boxcar, *18, 20*		90 ___
84670	Korean War Boxcar, *18, 20*		85 ___
84671	Vietnam War Boxcar, *18, 20*		85 ___
84672	Memorial Day Boxcar, *18, 20*		90 ___
84674	AT&SF 2-8-2 Mikado Locomotive, Brass Hybrid, Painted, Unlettered, *CC, 17*		1300 ___
84675	AT&SF 2-8-2 Mikado Locomotive, Brass Hybrid, Unpainted, *CC, 17*		1300 ___

____ 84676	Peanuts Hilltop Boxcar, *18*	90
____ 84677	Peanuts Meadow Boxcar, *18*	90
____ 84678	Peanuts Winter Boxcar, *18*	90
____ 84679	AT&SF 4-6-2 Pacific Locomotive "1369," LionChief Plus, *17-18*	450
____ 84680	CNJ 4-6-2 Pacific Locomotive "832," LionChief Plus, *17-18*	450
____ 84681	Alton 4-6-2 Pacific Locomotive "5299," LionChief Plus, *17-18*	450
____ 84682	Southern 4-6-2 Pacific Locomotive "1401," LionChief Plus, *17-18*	450
____ 84683	MILW 4-6-2 Pacific Locomotive "810," LionChief Plus, *17-18*	450
____ 84685	Polar Express Scale 2-8-4 Berkshire Locomotive "1225," CC, *17*	1500
____ 84686	Nickel Plate Road 2-8-4 Berkshire Locomotive "759," CC, *17*	1500
____ 84687	Nickel Plate Road 2-8-4 Berkshire Locomotive "765," CC, *17*	1500
____ 84688	Nickel Plate Road 2-8-4 Berkshire Locomotive "767," CC, *17*	1500
____ 84689	Southern 2-8-4 Berkshire Locomotive "2716," CC, *17*	1500
____ 84690	W&LE 2-8-4 Berkshire Locomotive "6401," CC , *17*	1500
____ 84691	American Railroads 2-8-4 Berkshire Locomotive "759," CC, *17*	1500
____ 84692	RF&P 2-8-4 Berkshire Locomotive "752," CC, *17*	1500
____ 84693	Pere Marquette 2-8-4 Berkshire Locomotive "1225," CC, *17*	1500
____ 84694	Pere Marquette 2-8-4 Berkshire Locomotive "1223," CC, *17*	1500
____ 84695	L&N 2-8-4 Berkshire Locomotive "1992," CC, *17*	1500
____ 84696	D&H Alco RS-3 Diesel "4121," LionChief Plus, *17-18*	350
____ 84697	AT&SF Alco RS-3 Diesel "2099," LionChief Plus, *17-18*	350
____ 84698	Peabody Coal Short Line Alco RS-3 Diesel "101," LionChief Plus, *17-18*	350
____ 84699	B&M Alco RS-3 Diesel "1536," LionChief Plus, *17-18*	350
____ 84700	Hot Wheels Diesel Freight Set, LionChief, *17-19*	400
____ 84705	Hot Wheels 50th Anniversary Auto Rack, *17-18*	85
____ 84706	Hot Wheels 50th Anniversary Auto Loader, *17-18*	90
____ 84707	Hot Wheels 50th Anniversary Flatcar w/Piggyback Trailers, *17-18*	85
____ 84708	Hot Wheels Auto Rack, *18*	85
____ 84709	NH RS-3 Diesel Freight Set, LionChief, *18*	300
____ 84719	AT&SF Super Chief Diesel Passenger Set, LionChief, *18-20*	430
____ 84724	AT&SF Add-on Baggage Car "1386," *18-20*	90
____ 84725	AT&SF Add-on Vista Dome Car "500," *18-20*	95
____ 84726	SP Rising Sun 0-8-0 Steam Freight Set, LionChief, *17-18*	320
____ 84732	BNSF Tier 4 Modern Freight Set, LionChief, *18-20*	400
____ 84737	Construction Railroad Diesel Freight Set, LionChief, *18-19*	350
____ 84747	18 Christmas Boxcar, *18*	65
____ 84748	Christmas Music Boxcar #18, *18*	80
____ 84754	Anheuser-Busch Clydesdale Old-Time Steam Freight Set, LionChief, *18-19*	420
____ 84760	Daisy Duck 1-D Tank Car, *18-20*	75
____ 84761	Chip 'n' Dale Chasing Gondola, *18-20*	80
____ 84762	SP Daylight 1-D Tank Car, *17-19*	60
____ 84763	Disney Villains Ursula Hi-Cube Boxcar, *18, 20*	80
____ 84764	Disney Villains Queen of Hearts Hi-Cube Boxcar, *18, 20*	80
____ 84765	Angela Trotta Thomas Christmas Passenger Car 2-pack, *18, 20*	300
____ 84766	Gondola w/Construction Signs, *18-19*	65
____ 84767	Harry Potter Dementors Coach w/Sound, *18-20*	85
____ 84768	Moe & Joe Lumber Flatcar, *18-19*	90
____ 84769	Wile E. Coyote & Road Runner Ambush Shack, *18-19*	120
____ 84770	Peabody Coal Hopper 6-pack, *18-20*	150
____ 84771	PRR Hopper 6-pack, *18-19*	150
____ 84772	N&W Hopper 6-pack, *18-20*	150
____ 84773	UP Hopper 6-pack, *18-20*	150

		Esc	Mint
84774	NS Hopper 6-pack, *18-20*		150 ___
84775	DM&IR Ore Car 6-pack, *18-19*		150 ___
84776	C&NW Ore Car 6-pack, *18-20*		150 ___
84777	GN Ore Car 6-pack, *18-20*		150 ___
84778	MILW Ore Car 6-pack, *18-19*		150 ___
84779	B&LE Ore Car 6-pack, *18-20*		150 ___
84780	U.S. Caboose, *18*		75 ___
84781	ELX Halloween Caboose, *18-20*		75 ___
84782	Presidential Caboose, *18-20*		75 ___
84784	John Deere Harvest Dump Car, *18-19*		80 ___
84785	Naughty or Nice Ore Car 2-pack, *18*		80 ___
84786	Christmas Essentials Barrel Car, *18-19*		70 ___
84787	Santa Freight Lines Steam Set, LionChief, *18-19*		300 ___
84792	House Under Construction, *18-19*		100 ___
84794	Budweiser Bar & Grille, *18*		90 ___
84795	Deluxe Christmas House, *18, 20*		130 ___
84797	Christmas Industrial Water Tower, *18, 20*		85 ___
84798	Hunting Rabbit Car, *18-19*		85 ___
84799	Marvin the Martian Earth Stomper Flatcar, *18-19*		95 ___
84801	Justice League Boxcar, *17*		85 ___
84802	Gilbson Wine 1-D Tank Car "66719," *17*		75 ___
84803	Tidewater 1-D Tank Car "1367," *17*		75 ___
84804	A.E. Staley 1-D Tank Car "704," *17*		75 ___
84805	Mid-Continent Petroleum 1-D Tank Car "1018," *17*		75 ___
84806	Shell 1-D Tank Car "662," *17*		75 ___
84807	John Deere 1-D Tank Car "236," *17*		75 ___
84810	Polar Express 1-D Tank Car "122518," *17*		75 ___
84811	Polar Express Scale Baggage Car, *17*		200 ___
84812	Polar Express Scale Combine, *17*		200 ___
84813	Polar Express Scale Coach, *17*		200 ___
84814	Polar Express Scale Diner, *17*		200 ___
84815	Polar Express Scale Observation, *17*		200 ___
84816	PRR 1930 Broadway Limited Steam Passenger Set, *CC, 17*		2000 ___
84821	PRR Heavyweight Combine Liberty Hill, *17-18*		200 ___
84822	PRR Heavyweight Sleeper Cent Fawn, *17-18*		200 ___
84823	PRR Heavyweight Sleeper Central Park, *17-18*		200 ___
84824	PRR Heavyweight Sleeper Lafayette Square, *17-18*		200 ___
84825	PRR Heavyweight Diner "4498," *17-18*		200 ___
84826	PRR Heavyweight Observation Colonel Lindbergh, *17-18*		200 ___
84827	PRR Heavyweight Observation Washington Circle, *17-18*		200 ___
84828	BNSF 66' Mill Gondola "518726," w/Graffiti, *17*		80 ___
84829	BNSF 66' Mill Gondola "518770," *17*		80 ___
84830	BNSF 66' Mill Gondola "518795," *17*		80 ___
84831	GNTX Railgon 66' Mill Gondola "290146," w/Graffiti, *17*		80 ___
84832	GNTX Railgon 66' Mill Gondola "290087," *17*		80 ___
84833	GNTX Railgon 66' Mill Gondola "290102," *17*		80 ___
84834	Atlantic & Western 66' Mill Gondola "400704," w/Graffiti, *17*		80 ___
84835	Atlantic & Western 66' Mill Gondola "400664," *17*		80 ___
84836	Atlantic & Western 66' Mill Gondola "400675," *17*		80 ___
84837	Arkansas & Oklahoma 66' Mill Gondola "35018," w/Graffiti, *17*		80 ___
84838	Arkansas & Oklahoma 66' Mill Gondola "35007," *17*		80 ___
84839	Arkansas & Oklahoma 66' Mill Gondola "35055," *17*		80 ___
84840	Steelton & Highspire 66' Mill Gondola "125," w/Graffiti, *17*		80 ___

		Esc	Mint
___	**84841** Steelton & Highspire 66' Mill Gondola "117," *17*		80
___	**84842** Steelton & Highspire 66' Mill Gondola "118," *17*		80
___	**84843** Demonstrator GE AC6000 Diesel "6000," *CC, 17*		650
___	**84844** Demonstrator GE AC6000 Diesel "6001," *CC, 17*		650
___	**84845** Demonstrator GE AC6000 Diesel "6002," *CC, 17*		650
___	**84846** CSX GE AC6000 Diesel "691," *CC, 17*		650
___	**84847** CSX GE AC6000 Diesel "5014," *CC, 17*		650
___	**84848** CSX CSX GE AC6000 Diesel "Diversity 5000," *CC, 17*		650
___	**84849** CSX CSX GE AC6000 Diesel "Diversity 5001," *CC, 17*		650
___	**84850** SP GE AC6000 Diesel "601," *CC, 17*		650
___	**84851** SP GE AC6000 Diesel "602," *CC, 17*		650
___	**84852** UP GE AC6000 Diesel "7566," *CC, 17*		650
___	**84853** UP GE AC6000 Diesel "7579," *CC, 17*		650
___	**84854** TTX Husky Double-Stack Car "56210," w/Trailers, *17*		130
___	**84855** TTX Husky Double-Stack Car "56289," w/Trailers, *17*		130
___	**84856** TTX Husky Double-Stack Car "56368," w/Trailers, *17*		130
___	**84857** TTX Husky Double-Stack Car "56150," w/Trailers, *17*		130
___	**84858** TTX Husky Double-Stack Car "56168," w/Trailers, *17*		130
___	**84859** TTX Husky Double-Stack Car "56174," w/Trailers, *17*		130
___	**84860** BNSF Husky Double-Stack Car "203003," w/Trailers, *17*		130
___	**84861** BNSF Husky Double-Stack Car "203015," w/Trailers, *17*		130
___	**84862** BNSF Husky Double-Stack Car "203032," w/Trailers, *17*		130
___	**84863** ARZC Husky Double-Stack Car "100000," w/Trailers, *17*		130
___	**84864** ARZC Husky Double-Stack Car "100002," w/Trailers, *17*		130
___	**84865** ARZC Husky Double-Stack Car "100005," w/Trailers, *17*		130
___	**84866** Southwind Husky Double-Stack Car "5003," w/Trailers, *17*		130
___	**84867** Southwind Husky Double-Stack Car "5005," w/Trailers, *17*		130
___	**84868** Southwind Husky Double-Stack Car "5008," w/Trailers, *17*		130
___	**84869** Hot Wheels Boxcar, *18*		85
___	**84870** NP 50' Flatcar "65110" w/NPT 40' Trailer, *17*		120
___	**84871** NP 50' Flatcar "65126" w/NPT 40' Trailer, *17*		120
___	**84872** PRR 50' Flatcar "469615" w/PRRZ 40' Trailer, *17*		120
___	**84873** PRR 50' Flatcar "469675" w/PRRZ 40' Trailer, *17*		120
___	**84874** Trailer Train 50' Flatcar "475227" w/SOUZ 40' Trailer, *17*		120
___	**84875** Trailer Train 50' Flatcar "475274" w/SOUZ 40' Trailer, *17*		120
___	**84876** UP 50' Flatcar "53017" w/UPZ 40' Trailer, *17*		120
___	**84877** UP 50' Flatcar "53022" w/UPZ 40' Trailer, *17*		120
___	**84878** Wabash 50' Flatcar "25535" w/WABZ 40' Trailer, *17*		120
___	**84879** Wabash 50' Flatcar "25549" w/WABZ 40' Trailer, *17*		120
___	**84880** D&RGW 50' Flatcar "21032" w/RGMW 40' Trailer, *17*		120
___	**84881** D&RGW 50' Flatcar "21036" w/RGMW 40' Trailer, *17*		120
___	**84882** C&O 40' Trailer 2-pack, *17*		65
___	**84883** GM&O 40' Trailer 2-pack, *17*		65
___	**84884** L&N 40' Trailer 2-pack, *17*		65
___	**84885** SAL 40' Trailer 2-pack, *17*		65
___	**84886** Frisco 40' Trailer 2-pack, *17*		65
___	**84887** WP 40' Trailer 2-pack, *17*		65
___	**84888** PRR X31 Boxcar "78401," w/Circle Keystone, *17*		120
___	**84889** PRR X31 Boxcar "78498," w/Circle Keystone, *17*		80
___	**84890** PRR X31 Boxcar "68408," w/Shadow Keystone, *17*		80
___	**84891** PRR X31 Boxcar "77061," w/Shadow Keystone, *17*		80
___	**84892** PRR X31 Boxcar "76803," w/Plain Keystone, *17*		80
___	**84893** PRR X31 Boxcar "77734," w/Plain Keystone, *17*		80
___	**84894** PRR X31 Boxcar "497310," w/Stores, *17*		80

		Esc	Mint
84895	PRR X31 Boxcar "497329," w/Stores, *17*		80 ___
84896	N&W X31 Boxcar "46146," *17*		80 ___
84897	N&W X31 Boxcar "46340," *17*		80 ___
84898	Personalized Man's Best Friend Boxcar, *18-20*		90 ___
84899	Personalized World's Best Cat Boxcar, *18-20*		90 ___
84904	BNSF Scale Autorack, Orange "965375," *18*		120 ___
84905	BNSF Scale Autorack, Orange "965530," *18*		120 ___
84906	Ferromex Scale Autorack "705473," *18*		120 ___
84907	Ferromex Scale Autorack "953615," *18*		120 ___
84908	Southern Scale Autorack "159162," *18*		120 ___
84909	Southern Scale Autorack "159166," *18*		120 ___
84910	CSX Scale Autorack "156256," *18*		120 ___
84911	CSX Scale Autorack "973924," *18*		120 ___
84912	NS Scale Autorack "983818," *18*		120 ___
84913	NS Scale Autorack "992879," *18*		120 ___
84914	MKT Scale Autorack "254176," *18*		120 ___
84915	MKT Scale Autorack "942194," *18*		120 ___
84916	Union Tank Car Cylindrical Covered Hopper "44072," *18-19*		90 ___
84917	Union Tank Car Cylindrical Covered Hopper "44094," *18-19*		90 ___
84918	Davis Industries Cylindrical Covered Hopper "1002," *18-19*		90 ___
84919	Davis Industries Cylindrical Covered Hopper "1003," *18-19*		90 ___
84920	Conrail Cylindrical Covered Hopper "884244," *18-19*		90 ___
84921	Conrail Cylindrical Covered Hopper "884270," *18-19*		90 ___
84922	CSX Cylindrical Covered Hopper "225370," *18-19*		90 ___
84923	CSX Cylindrical Covered Hopper "225382," *18-19*		90 ___
84924	Wilkes-Barre Mining Cylindrical Covered Hopper "104," *18*		90 ___
84925	Wilkes-Barre Mining Cylindrical Covered Hopper "106," *18*		90 ___
84926	SP Cylindrical Covered Hopper "1002," *18*		90 ___
84927	SP Cylindrical Covered Hopper "1027," *18*		90 ___
84928	John Quincy Adams Presidential Boxcar, *18*		70 ___
84929	James K. Polk Presidential Boxcar, *18*		70 ___
84930	Benjamin Harrison Presidential Boxcar, *18*		70 ___
84934	NYC 4-6-4 Hudson Locomotive "5425," LionChief Plus, *17-18*		450 ___
84935	B&A 4-6-4 Hudson Locomotive "616," LionChief Plus, *17-18*		450 ___
84936	Nickel Plate Road 4-6-4 Hudson Locomotive "170," LionChief Plus, *17-18*		450 ___
84937	GN 4-6-4 Hudson Locomotive "171," LionChief Plus, *17-18*		450 ___
84938	AT&SF EMD GP38 Diesel "3441," LionChief Plus, *17-18*		350 ___
84939	NS First Responders EMD GP38 Diesel "5642," LionChief Plus, *17-18*		350 ___
84940	Seaboard System EMD GP38 Diesel "543," LionChief Plus, *17-18*		350 ___
84941	FEC EMD GP38 Diesel "506," LionChief Plus, *17-18*		350 ___
84942	PRR 4-4-2 Atlantic Locomotive "460," *CC, 17*		800 ___
84943	PRR 4-4-2 Atlantic Locomotive "68," *CC, 17*		800 ___
84944	PRR 4-4-2 Atlantic Locomotive 1163," *CC, 17*		800 ___
84945	PRSL 4-4-2 Atlantic Locomotive "6009," *CC, 17*		800 ___
84946	LIRR 4-4-2 Atlantic Locomotive "1611," *CC, 17*		800 ___
84947	GN 4-4-2 Atlantic Locomotive "1707," *CC, 17*		800 ___
84948	PRR 2-8-0 Consolidation Locomotive "1288," *CC, 18*		750 ___
84949	PRSL 2-8-0 Consolidation Locomotive "8072," *CC, 18*		750 ___
84950	LIRR 2-8-0 Consolidation Locomotive "109," *CC, 18*		750 ___
84951	Bellefonte Central 2-8-0 Consolidation Locomotive "21," *CC, 18*		750 ___
84952	PRR 2-8-0 Consolidation Locomotive "3529," Weathered, *CC, 18*		750 ___
84953	Pennsylvania Coal Hauler Steam Freight Set, *CC, 18*		1100 ___

		Esc	Mint
___ 84964	Angela Trotta Thomas 4-6-4 Hudson Locomotive, LionChief Plus, *18*		450
___ 84965	Rio Grande A5 0-4-0 Locomotive "62," LionChief Plus, *18*		480
___ 84966	NYC A5 0-4-0 Locomotive "1662," LionChief Plus, *18*		480
___ 84967	PRR A5 0-4-0 Locomotive "577," LionChief Plus, *18*		480
___ 84968	UP A5 0-4-0 Locomotive "218," LionChief Plus, *18*		480
___ 84985	LIRR B60 Baggage Car "7715," *17-18*		160
___ 84986	LIRR B60 Baggage Car "7724," *17-18*		160
___ 84987	PRR B60 Baggage Car, Clerestory "7918," *17-18*		160
___ 84988	PRR B60 Baggage Car, Clerestory "7941," *17-18*		160
___ 84989	PRR B60 Baggage Car, Round Roof "7919," *17-18*		160
___ 84990	PRR B60 Baggage Car, Round Roof "7938," *17-18*		160
___ 84991	PRR B60 Baggage Car, Round Roof, Messenger "9352," *17-18*		160
___ 84992	PRR B60 Baggage Car, Round Roof, Messenger "9379," *17-18*		160
___ 84993	PRR B60 Baggage Car, Round Roof, 1960s "9356," *17-18*		160
___ 84994	PRR B60 Baggage Car, Round Roof, 1960s "9384," *17-18*		160
___ 84995	PRSL Baggage Car "5437," *17-18*		160
___ 84996	PRSL B60 Baggage Car "6403," *17-18*		160
___ 84997	LIRR 18" Heavyweight Passenger Coach 2-pack, *#1, 17-18*		400
___ 85000	LIRR 18" Heavyweight Passenger Coach 2-pack, *#2, 17-18*		400
___ 85003	PRSL 18" Heavyweight Passenger Coach 2-pack, *#1, 17-18*		400
___ 85006	PRSL 18" Heavyweight Passenger Coach 2-pack, *#2, 17-18*		400
___ 85009	PRR 18" Heavyweight Passenger Coach 2-pack, *#1, 17-18*		400
___ 85012	PRR 18" Heavyweight Passenger Coach 2-pack, *#2, 17-18*		400
___ 85015	ACL/PRR Champion Passenger Car 4-pack, *17-18*		620
___ 85016	ACL/PRR Champion Passenger Car 2-pack, *17-18*		310
___ 85017	ACL Champion 21" Diner, w/StationSounds, *17-18*		310
___ 85018	ACL EMD SW7 Diesel "648," *CC, 18*		500
___ 85019	BN EMD SW7 Diesel "111," *CC, 18*		500
___ 85020	Conemaugh & Black Lick EMD SW7 Diesel "106," *CC, 18*		500
___ 85021	Chessie System EMD SW7 Diesel "5224," *CC, 18*		500
___ 85022	LV EMD SW7 Diesel "222," *CC, 18*		500
___ 85023	MEC EMD SW7 Diesel "331," *CC, 18*		500
___ 85024	NYC EMD SW7 Diesel "8853," *CC, 18*		500
___ 85025	Frisco EMD SW7 Diesel "303," *CC, 18*		500
___ 85026	Southern EMD SW7 Diesel "1100," *CC, 18*		500
___ 85027	UP EMD SW7 Diesel "1808," *CC, 18*		500
___ 85028	AT&SF EMD SD45 Diesel "5305," *CC, 18*		600
___ 85029	AT&SF EMD SD45 Diesel "5319," *CC, 18*		600
___ 85030	B&P EMD SD45 Diesel "453," *CC, 18*		600
___ 85031	B&P EMD SD45 Diesel "455," *CC, 18*		600
___ 85032	C&NW EMD SD45 Diesel "6485," *CC, 18*		600
___ 85033	C&NW EMD SD45 Diesel "6568," *CC, 18*		600
___ 85034	Montana Rail Link EMD SD45 Diesel "320," *CC, 18*		600
___ 85035	Montana Rail Link EMD SD45 Diesel "331," *CC, 18*		600
___ 85036	MPI EMD SD45 Diesel "9009," *CC, 18*		600
___ 85037	MPI EMD SD45 Diesel "9011," *CC, 18*		600
___ 85038	N&W EMD SD45 Diesel "1776," *CC, 18*		600
___ 85039	N&W EMD SD45 Diesel "1790," *CC, 18*		600
___ 85040	NYS&W EMD SD45 Diesel "3612," *CC, 18*		600
___ 85041	NYS&W EMD SD45 Diesel "3614," *CC, 18*		600
___ 85042	WC EMD SD45 Diesel "6525," *CC, 18*		600
___ 85043	WC EMD SD45 Diesel "6580," *CC, 18*		600
___ 85046	BNSF EMD SD70ACe Diesel "9214," *CC, 18*		600

85047	BNSF EMD SD70ACe Diesel "9287," *CC, 18*		600 ___
85048	CN EMD SD70ACe Diesel "8101," *CC, 18*		600 ___
85049	CN EMD SD70ACe Diesel "8103," *CC, 18*		600 ___
85050	CSX EMD SD70ACe Diesel "4849," *CC, 18*		600 ___
85051	Demonstrator EMD SD70ACe Diesel "1201," *CC, 18*		600 ___
85052	Demonstrator EMD SD70ACe Diesel "1202," *CC, 18*		600 ___
85053	KCS EMD SD70ACe Diesel "4156," *CC, 18*		600 ___
85054	KCS EMD SD70ACe Diesel "4164," *CC, 18*		600 ___
85055	NS EMD SD70ACe Diesel "1030," *CC, 18*		600 ___
85056	NS EMD SD70ACe Diesel "1111," *CC, 18*		600 ___
85057	UP EMD SD70ACe Diesel "8650," *CC, 18*		600 ___
85058	UP EMD SD70ACe Diesel "8665," *CC, 18*		600 ___
85059	MKT EMD NW2 Diesel "7," LionChief Plus, *18*		320 ___
85060	PRR EMD NW2 Diesel "9172," LionChief Plus, *18*		320 ___
85061	Nickel Plate Road EMD NW2 Diesel "13," LionChief Plus, *18*		320 ___
85062	UP EMD NW2 Diesel "1037," LionChief Plus, *18*		320 ___
85063	MILW EMD NW2 Diesel "1649," LionChief Plus, *18*		320 ___
85065	Hot Wheels 50th Anniversary Boxcar, *17-18*		85 ___
85066	TTX Husky Double-Stack Car "56210," w/EOT Device, *17*		150 ___
85067	TTX Husky Double-Stack Car "56180," w/EOT Device, *17*		150 ___
85068	BNSF Husky Double-Stack Car "203054," w/EOT Device, *17*		150 ___
85069	ARZC Husky Double-Stack Car "100008," w/EOT Device, *17*		150 ___
85070	Southwind Husky Double-Stack Car "5009," w/EOT Device, *17*		150 ___
85071	AT&SF Wide-Vision Caboose w/Camera "999718," *18*		125 ___
85072	BN Wide-Vision Caboose w/Camera "12345," *18*		125 ___
85073	Chessie System Wide-Vision Caboose w/Camera "903118," *18*		125 ___
85074	CSX Wide-Vision Caboose w/Camera "903282," *18*		125 ___
85075	Reading Wide-Vision Caboose w/Camera "94116," *18*		125 ___
85076	UP Wide-Vision Caboose w/Camera "13605," *18*		125 ___
85077	NS Wide-Vision Caboose w/Camera "555059," *18*		125 ___
85078	PRR Wide-Vision Caboose w/Camera "477900," *18*		125 ___
85079	DODX Wide-Vision Caboose "902," *18*		100 ___
85080	Montana Rail Link Wide-Vision Caboose "1005," *18*		100 ___
85081	UTLX 30,000-Gallon 1-D Tank Car "212189" w/FreightSounds, *18*		150 ___
85082	GATX 30,000-Gallon 1-D Tank Car "36323" w/FreightSounds, *18*		150 ___
85083	Philadelphia Energy Solutions 30,000-Gallon 1-D Tank Car "0756" w/FreightSounds, *18*		150 ___
85084	TILX 30,000-Gallon 1-D Tank Car "254088" w/FreightSounds, *18*		150 ___
85085	ADM 30,000-Gallon 1-D Tank Car "29248" w/FreightSounds, *18*		150 ___
85086	Cargill 30,000-Gallon 1-D Tank Car "7964" w/FreightSounds, *18*		150 ___
85087	UTLX 30,000-Gallon 1-D Tank Car "212187" w/EOT Device, *18*		150 ___
85088	GATX 30,000-Gallon 1-D Tank Car "36328" w/EOT Device, *18*		120 ___
85089	ADM 30,000-Gallon 1-D Tank Car "29252" w/EOT Device, *18*		120 ___
85090	Cargill 30,000-Gallon 1-D Tank Car "7968" w/EOT Device, *18*		120 ___
85091	ACFX 30,000-Gallon 1-D Tank Car "89990" w/EOT Device, *18*		120 ___
85092	Procor 30,000-Gallon 1-D Tank Car "43579" w/EOT Device, *18*		120 ___
85093	American Potash PS-2 Covered Hopper "31259," *17*		75 ___
85094	American Potash PS-2 Covered Hopper "31275," *17*		75 ___
85095	Bucyrus Erie PS-2 Covered Hopper "1114," *17*		75 ___
85096	Bucyrus Erie PS-2 Covered Hopper "1118," *17*		75 ___
85097	Georgia Marble PS-2 Covered Hopper "31340," *17*		75 ___
85098	Georgia Marble PS-2 Covered Hopper "31341," *17*		75 ___
85099	Ready Mixed Concrete PS-2 Covered Hopper "331," *17*		75 ___
85100	Ready Mixed Concrete PS-2 Covered Hopper "340," *17*		75 ___

		Esc	Mint
_____ 85101	Linde PS-2 Covered Hopper "209," *17*		75
_____ 85102	Linde PS-2 Covered Hopper "211," *17*		75
_____ 85103	U.S. Borax PS-2 Covered Hopper "31064," *17*		75
_____ 85104	U.S. Borax PS-2 Covered Hopper "31066," *17*		75
_____ 85105	Tank Train 2-Pack with EOT Device, #1, *17*		200
_____ 85108	Tank Train 2-Pack with EOT Device, #2, *17*		200
_____ 85111	Tank Train 2-Pack with EOT Device, #3, *17*		200
_____ 85114	GATX Tank Train 2-Pack with EOT Device, *17*		200
_____ 85117	CN Tank Train 2-Pack with EOT Device, *17*		200
_____ 85120	Cibro Tank Train 2-Pack with EOT Device, *17*		200
_____ 85126	Tank Train Car #1, *17*		90
_____ 85127	Tank Train Car #2, *17*		90
_____ 85128	Tank Train Car #3, *17*		90
_____ 85129	Tank Train Car #4, *17*		90
_____ 85130	Tank Train Car #5, *17*		90
_____ 85131	Tank Train Car #6, *17*		90
_____ 85132	Tank Train Car #1, *17*		90
_____ 85133	Tank Train Car #2, *17*		90
_____ 85134	Tank Train Car #3, *17*		90
_____ 85135	Tank Train Car #4, *17*		90
_____ 85136	Tank Train Car #5, *17*		90
_____ 85137	Tank Train Car #6, *17*		90
_____ 85138	Tank Train Car #1, *17*		90
_____ 85139	Tank Train Car #2, *17*		90
_____ 85140	Tank Train Car #3, *17*		90
_____ 85141	Tank Train Car #4, *17*		90
_____ 85142	Tank Train Car #5, *17*		90
_____ 85143	Tank Train Car #6, *17*		90
_____ 85144	GATX Tank Train Car #1, *17*		90
_____ 85145	GATX Tank Train Car #2, *17*		90
_____ 85146	GATX Tank Train Car #3, *17*		90
_____ 85147	GATX Tank Train Car #4, *17*		90
_____ 85148	GATX Tank Train Car #5, *17*		90
_____ 85149	GATX Tank Train Car #6, *17*		90
_____ 85150	CN Tank Train Car #1, *17*		90
_____ 85151	CN Tank Train Car #2, *17*		90
_____ 85152	CN Tank Train Car #3, *17*		90
_____ 85153	CN Tank Train Car #4, *17*		90
_____ 85154	CN Tank Train Car #5, *17*		90
_____ 85155	CN Tank Train Car #6, *17*		90
_____ 85156	Cibro Tank Train Car #1, *17*		90
_____ 85157	Cibro Tank Train Car #2, *17*		90
_____ 85158	Cibro Tank Train Car #3, *17*		90
_____ 85159	Cibro Tank Train Car #4, *17*		90
_____ 85160	Cibro Tank Train Car #5, *17*		90
_____ 85161	Cibro Tank Train Car #6, *17*		90
_____ 85168	Tacoma Rail EMD SD70ACe Diesel "7001," *CC, 18*		600
_____ 85169	Tacoma Rail EMD SD70ACe Diesel "7002," *CC, 18*		600
_____ 85170	Atlanta & West Point USRA 4-6-2 Pacific Locomotive "290," *CC, 18*		1400
_____ 85171	B&O USRA 4-6-2 Pacific Locomotive "5300," *CC, 18*		1400
_____ 85172	Reading & Northern USRA 4-6-2 Pacific Locomotive "425," *CC, 18*		1400
_____ 85173	NP USRA 4-6-2 Pacific Locomotive "2256," *CC, 18*		1400
_____ 85174	Southern USRA 4-6-2 Pacific Locomotive "1372," *CC, 18*		1400
_____ 85175	Halloween USRA 4-6-2 Pacific Locomotive "1031," *CC, 18*		1400

Number	Description	Esc	Mint
85176	C&O USRA 2-6-6-2 Locomotive "1522," *CC, 18*		1600 __
85177	W&LE USRA 2-6-6-2 Locomotive "8007," *CC, 18*		1600 __
85178	B&O USRA 2-6-6-2 Locomotive "7555," *CC, 18*		1600 __
85179	Buffalo, Rochester & Pittsburgh USRA 2-6-6-2 Locomotive "755," *CC, 18*		1600 __
85180	GN USRA 2-6-6-2 Locomotive "1855," *CC, 18*		1600 __
85181	MEC USRA 2-6-6-2 Locomotive "1205," *CC, 18*		1600 __
85182	NYC USRA 2-6-6-2 Locomotive "1400," *CC, 18*		1600 __
85183	SP USRA 2-6-6-2 Locomotive "3932," *CC, 18*		1600 __
85184	WM USRA 2-6-6-2 Locomotive "960," *CC, 18*		1600 __
85185	Renz Hobby Shop, *17*		300 __
85186	AT&SF EMD F3 A-A Diesel Set, *CC, 17*		850 __
85189	AT&SF Powered EMD F3 B Diesel, *CC, 17*		450 __
85190	At&SF SuperBass EMD F3 B Diesel, *CC, 17*		300 __
85191	GN EMD F3 A-A Diesel Set, *CC, 17*		850 __
85194	GN Powered EMD F3 B Diesel, *CC, 17*		450 __
85195	GN SuperBass EMD F3 B Diesel, *CC, 17*		300 __
85196	T&P EMD F7 A-A Diesel Set, *CC, 17*		850 __
85199	T&P Powered EMD F7 B Diesel, *CC, 17*		450 __
85200	T&P SuperBass EMD F3 B Diesel, *CC, 17*		300 __
85201	NYO&W EMD F3 A-A Diesel Set, *CC, 17*		850 __
85204	NYO&W Powered EMD F3 B Diesel, *CC, 17*		450 __
85205	NYO&W SuperBass EMD F3 B Diesel, *CC, 17*		300 __
85206	PRR EMD F7 A-A Diesel Set, *CC, 17*		850 __
85209	PRR Powered EMD F7 B Diesel, *CC, 17*		450 __
85210	PRR SuperBass EMD F7 B Diesel, *CC, 17*		300 __
85211	Reading EMD F3 A-A Diesel Set, *CC, 17*		850 __
85214	Reading Powered EMD F3 B Diesel, *CC, 17*		450 __
85215	ReadingSuperBass EMD F3 B Diesel, *CC, 17*		300 __
85216	Conrail EMD F7 A-A Diesel Set "1792-1730," *CC, 17*		850 __
85219	Conrail Powered EMD F7 B Diesel "3861," *CC, 17*		450 __
85220	Conrail SuperBass EMD F7 B Diesel "3872," *CC, 17*		300 __
85222	CSX Maxi-Stack "85222," *17*		75 __
85223	BNSF Maxi-Stack "237342," *17-18*		75 __
85226	180-Watt PowerHouse Power Supply, 10-amp, *19-20*		150 __
85227	GN Oriental Ltd Heavyweight Baggage/Coach, *17-18*		400 __
85230	GN Oriental Ltd Heavyweight Sleeper/Coach, *17-18*		400 __
85233	GN Oriental Ltd Heavyweight Sleeper/Diner, *17-18*		400 __
85236	GN Oriental Ltd Heavyweight Sleeper/Observation, *17-18*		400 __
85241	Mystery Machine FT Diesel Freight Set, Lionchief, *18-20*		430 __
85246	Anheuser-Busch Vintage Refrigerator Car, *18-20*		80 __
85247	Budweiser Clydesdale Vintage Refrigerator Car, *18-19*		80 __
85248	Budweiser Vintage Refrigerator Car, *18-20*		80 __
85253	End of the Line Express Diesel Freight Set, LionChief, *18-20*		330 __
85258	AT&SF FT Ranger Diesel Freight Set, LionChief, *18*		430 __
85263	Tomb of the Unknown Soldier Walking Brakeman Car, *18*		100 __
85264	Harry Potter Hogwarts Add-on Coach, *18, 20*		75 __
85269	Scooby Doo Sam Witches Café, *18-20*		100 __
85270	Hot Wheels Checkered Flagpole, *18*		60 __
85271	Polar Express Flagpole, *18-20*		60 __
85274	PRR Gla Hopper 3-pack #1, *18*		225 __
85278	PRR Gla Hopper 3-pack #2, *18*		225 __
85282	PRR Coal Goes To War Gla Hopper 3-pack #3, *18*		225 __
85286	Berwind Gla Hopper 3-pack, *18*		225 __

	MODERN 1970-2021	Esc	Mint
___	85290	PRR MOW PRR Gla Hopper 3-pack #4, *18*		225
___	85294	Lionelville Hobby Shop, *18*		300
___	85295	Layout Control System CSM2, *18-20*		110
___	85296	Layout Control System IRV2, *18-20*		100
___	85297	PRR N5 Caboose "477819," *18*		100
___	85298	PRR N5 Caboose "478884," *18*		100
___	85299	Reading & Northern N5 Caboose "477514," *18*		100
___	85300	PRSL N5 Caboose "202," *18*		100
___	85301	RJ Corman N5 Caboose, *18*		100
___	85309	Flight Night Halloween Pylon, *18-19*		150
___	85310	Witches Brew Storage Tank, *18-19*		85
___	85314	Hometown Brewery Kit, *2019*		"70
___	85315	UP EMD SD70ACe Diesel "1943," *CC, 18*		600
___	85316	UP Wide-Vision Caboose, Spirit of Union Pacific "1943," *18*		100
___	85317	UP Spirit of the Union Pacific Boxcar, *18*		85
___	85318	Personalized Happy Birthday Boxcar, *18*		90
___	85319	Personalized 18 Merry Christmas Boxcar, *18*		90
___	85320	Personalized Happy Anniversary Boxcar, *18-19*		90
___	85321	John Deere Flatcar w/Tractor Load, *18*		80
___	85322	Personalized 18 Halloween Boxcar, *18*		90
___	85323	Scooby Doo Boxcar, *18*		85
___	85324	Thomas & Friends Christmas Freight Set, LionChief, *18-20*		200
___	85326	NYC Vision Baggage Car "9152," *18*		330
___	85327	NYC Baggage Car 2-pack #1, *18*		350
___	85330	NYC Baggage Car 2-pack #2, *18*		350
___	85333	NYC Baggage/Combine 2-pack, *18*		400
___	85336	NYC 18" Heavyweight Baggage Car 2-pack, *18*		350
___	85339	SP Scale RPO Passenger Car "5124," *18*		160
___	85340	L&N Scale RPO Passenger Car "1099," *18*		160
___	85341	LIRR Scale RPO Passenger Car "737," *18*		160
___	85342	MILW Scale RPO Passenger Car "2105," *18*		160
___	85343	NYC Scale RPO Passenger Car "4819," *18*		160
___	85344	PRR Scale RPO Passenger Car "5265," *18*		160
___	85345	PRR Scale RPO Passenger Car "5269," *18*		160
___	85346	PC Scale RPO Passenger Car "5267," *18*		160
___	85347	UP Scale RPO Passenger Car "2060," *18*		160
___	85348	MILW 18" Columbian Passenger Car 2-pack #A, *18*		400
___	85351	MILW 18" Columbian Passenger Car 2-pack #B, *18*		400
___	85354	MILW 18" Columbian Passenger Car 2-pack #C, *18*		400
___	85357	MILW 18" Columbian Passenger Car 2-pack #D, *18*		400
___	85360	UP Challenger 21" Passenger Car 4-pack, *18*		700
___	85361	UP Challenger 21" Passenger Car 2-pack, *18*		350
___	85362	UP Challenger 21" Diner w/StationSounds, *18*		330
___	85367	L&N Hummingbird 21" Passenger Car 4-pack, *18*		700
___	85368	L&N Hummingbird 21" Passenger Car 2-pack, *18*		350
___	85370	Reading & Northern 18" Excursion and Business Car 2-pack #A, *18*		400
___	85373	Reading & Northern 18" Excursion and Business Car 2-pack #B, *18*		400
___	85376	Reading & Northern 21" Dome Car w/StationSounds, *18*		350
___	85377	MOW Disconnect Work Car 4-pack, *18*		160
___	85378	PRR Disconnect Work Car 4-pack, *18*		160
___	85379	AT&SF Disconnect Work Car 4-pack, *18*		160
___	85380	UP Disconnect Work Car 4-pack, *18*		160
___	85381	NYC Disconnect Work Car 4-pack, *18*		160
___	85382	D&RGW Disconnect Work Car 4-pack, *18*		160

		Esc	Mint	
85383	Layout Control System IRV2 Sensor Add-on, *18-20*		30	___
85384	Orange 10" Straight FasTrack 4-pack, *18-20*		25	___
85386	Pennsylvania Lines 2-8-0 Consolidation Locomotive "7109," *CC, 18*		750	___
85387	Western Allegheny 2-8-0 Consolidation Locomotive "85," *CC, 18*		750	___
85389	White 10" Straight FasTrack 4-pack, *18-20*		25	___
85390	White O-36 Curve Fastrack 4-pack, *18-20*		25	___
85391	White PEP Activation Track, *18-20*		25	___
85392	White 10" Terminal FasTrack, *18-20*		10	___
85400	Polar Express Skiing Hobo Observation w/Snowy Roof, *2019-20*		90	___
85401	UP LED Flag Boxcar, Yellow and Gray "1862," *18*		120	___
85402	UP LED Flag Boxcar, C&NW Heritage "1995," *18*		120	___
85403	UP LED Flag Boxcar, MKT Heritage "1988," *18*		120	___
85404	UP LED Flag Boxcar, MP Heritage "1982," *18*		120	___
85405	UP LED Flag Boxcar, D&RGW Heritage "1989," *18*		120	___
85406	UP LED Flag Boxcar, SP Heritage "1996," *18*		120	___
85407	UP LED Flag Boxcar, WP Heritage "1983," *18*		120	___
85408	UP LED Flag Boxcar, Spirit of Union Pacific "1943"" *18*		120	___
85409	UP LED Flag Boxcar, Steam Program "4-8-8-4," *18*		120	___
85410	Polar Express Hero Boy's Home, *18-20*		90	___
85411	Pylon with World War II Planes, *18*		145	___
85412	Santa's Sleigh Pylon, *18*		135	___
99000	Keebler Elf Express Steam Freight Set, *99 u*		1188	___
99001	Mickey's Holiday Express Freight Set, *99 u*		180	___
99002	Looney Tunes Square Window Caboose, *99 u*		NRS	___
99006	Keebler Bulkhead Flatcar, *99 u*		NRS	___
99007	Smuckers Fudge 1-D Tank Car, *99 u*		90	___
99008	Mickey's Merry Christmas Boxcar, *99 u*		NRS	___
99009	Mickey's Holiday Express Square Window Caboose, *99 u*		NRS	___
99013	Case Cutlery Tank Car "1889," *00 u*		NRS	___
99014	Case Cutlery Gondola "1889," *00 u*		NRS	___
99015	Case Cutlery Boxcar "1889," *00 u*		NRS	___
99018	Case Cutlery Rolling Stock 3-pack, *00 u*		210	___
6446-25	N&W Covered Quad Hopper, *70 u*	203	290	___
8054/55	Burlington F3 Diesel AA Set, *80*	360	385	___
8251-50	Horn/Whistle Controller, *72-74*	1	2	___
8260/62	Southern Pacific F3 Diesel AA Set, *82*	490	520	___
683617	NYC Empire State Express Martin Van Buren Combine, *2019*		155	___
8365/66	CP F3 Diesel AA Set (SSS), *73*	355	405	___
683618	NYC Empire State Express Franklin Roosevelt Observation, *2019*		155	___
8370/72	NYC F3 Diesel AA Set, *83*	330	435	___
8464/65	D&RGW F3 Diesel AA Set (SSS), *74*	220	325	___
8480/82	Union Pacific F3 Diesel AA Set, *84*	280	365	___
8555/57	Milwaukee Road F3 Diesel AA Set (SSS), *75*	240	315	___
8580/82	Illinois Central F3 Diesel AA Set, *85, 87*	420	485	___
8851/52	New Haven F3 Diesel AA Set, *78 u, 79*	250	430	___
8952/53	PRR F3 Diesel AA Set, *79*	350	500	___
8970/71	PRR F3 Diesel AA Set, *79 u, 80*	330	425	___
16321/22	Sealand TTUX Flatcar Set with trailers, *90*	65	73	___
16345/46	SP TTUX Flatcar Set with trailers, *92*	55	65	___
18117/18	Santa Fe F3 Diesel AA Set "200," *93*	330	410	___
18119/20	UP Alco Diesel AA Set, *94*	200	235	___
18901/02	PRR Alco Diesel AA Set, *88*	110	130	___
18903/04	Amtrak Alco Diesel AA Set, *88-89*	90	130	___
18908/09	NYC Alco Diesel AA Set, *93*	105	115	___

			Esc	Mint
___	**18934/35**	Reading Alco Diesel AA Set, *95*	75	95
___	**30066/67**	C&O Empire Builder Steam Freight Set, *CC, 07-09*		2700
___	**52315/20**	PRR FM Diesel and Caboose, *04 u*		440
___	**6464-500**	Timken Boxcar, orange, *70 u*	241	344
___	**1027390**	Central Pacific 1860s Wood Coach w/RailSounds, 2-pack, *2019*		350
___	**6464-500**	Timken Boxcar, yellow, *70 u*	210	350
___	**6476-135**	LV Hopper "25000" (O27), *70-71 u*	6	11
___	**1823010**	Thomas' Best Buddies LionChief Set: Percy, *2018-19*		200
___	**8552/53/54**	SP Alco Diesel ABA Set, *75-76*	200	245
___	**1823011**	Percy, Sodor Locomotive, LionChief, *2018-19*		120
___	**1823020**	Thomas' Best Buddies LionChief Set: James, *2018-19*		200
___	**1823021**	James, Sodor Locomotive, LionChief, *2018-19*		120
___	**1823030**	Sodor Railway Troublemaker Diesel LionChief Set, *2018-19*		200
___	**1823031**	Diesel, Sodor Locomotive, LionChief, *2018-19*		120
___	**1823040**	Thomas Kinkade Christmas LionChief Steam Freight Set, *18, 20*		400
___	**1823050**	Mickey Mouse Celebration LionChief Steam Freight Set, *2018*		400
___	**1830010**	Polar Express Snowman & Children People Pack, *19-20*		30
___	**1831010**	N&W Brass Hybrid USRA 4-8-2 K2 Locomotive "118," *CC, 2018*		1400
___	**1831020**	N&W Brass Hybrid USRA 4-8-2 K2 Locomotive "123," *CC, 2018*		1400
___	**1831030**	N&W Brass Hybrid USRA 4-8-2 K2 Locomotive "116," *CC, 2018*		1400
___	**1831040**	N&W Brass Hybrid USRA 4-8-2 K2 Locomotive "125," *CC, 2018*		1400
___	**1831050**	N&W Brass Hybrid USRA 4-8-2 K2 Locomotive "9999," *CC, 2018*		1400
___	**1831060**	PRR 4-6-2 Pacific K4 Locomotive w/Long-haul Tender "5453," *CC, 2018*		1300
___	**1904010**	58" x 86" Lionel Train Table, *2019-20*		900
___	**1908080**	Improved CW-80 Transformer, *2019-20*		150
___	**1908010**	Layout Control System CSM2 DZ-2500 Breakout Board, *18, 20*		25
___	**1908010**	DZ-2500 Breakout Board, *2019*		25
___	**1918210**	Anheuser-Busch Malt Tonics Woodside Refrigerator Car, *2019*		80
___	**1922010**	UP Sherman Hill 4-8-8-4 Steam Freight Set, LionChief Plus 2.0, *2019*		1600
___	**1922020**	Nickel Plate Fast Freight 2-8-4 Steam Freight Set, LionChief Plus 2.0, *2019*		800
___	**1922030**	Warren G. Harding Funeral Steam Passenger Train, *CC, 2018*		2000
___	**1922040**	AT&SF Gold Bonnet Streamlined Passenger Set, *CC, 2019*		1000
___	**1922050**	NYC Pacemaker Steam Passenger Set, *CC, 2019*		2000
___	**1922060**	BNSF Diesel Freight Oil Train Set, *CC, 2019*		1000
___	**1922070**	Pennsylvania Limited 2-8-4 Steam Passenger Set, LionChief Plus 2.0, *2019*		800
___	**1922080**	Lionel GE Bi-Polar Electric State Set, *CC, 2019*		1800
___	**1922090**	Erie Mining Diesel Ore Set, *CC, 2019*		900
___	**1923020**	NYC Flyer 0-8-0 Steam Freight Set, LionChief , *2018-19*		350
___	**1923030**	Polar Express 15th Anniversary Steam Passenger Set, LionChief, *2019*		450
___	**1923040**	UP Flyer 0-8-0 Steam Freight Set, LionChief, *19-20*		300
___	**1923050**	NS Tier 4 GE ET44C4 Diesel Freight Set, LionChief, *19-20*		400
___	**1923070**	Blue Comet Steam Passenger Set, LionChief, *19-20*		370
___	**1923080**	Promontory Summit 150th Anniversary Steam Locomotive Set, *2019*		550
___	**1923090**	LV GE U36B Diesel Freight Set, LionChief, *19-20*		330
___	**1923100**	U.S. Steam 0-8-0 Steam Freight Set, LionChief, *19-20*		400
___	**1923110**	UP America Proud GP38 Diesel Freight Set, LionChief, *19-20*		400
___	**1923130**	Polar Express Trolley Set, *2019*		200
___	**1923140**	Disney Christmas Steam Freight Set, LionChief, *19-20*		350
___	**1923150**	Winter Wonderland Steam Freight Set, LionChief, *19-20*		300

| --- | --- | --- | --- |
1925001	FasTrack Screws, 100-pack, *2019-20*		10 __
1926011	CSX 86-foot 4-Door High Cube Boxcar (Boxcar Logo) "181032," *2018*		100 __
1926012	CSX 86-foot 4-Door High Cube Boxcar (Boxcar Logo) "181056," *2018*		100 __
1926013	CSX 86-foot 4-Door High Cube Boxcar (Boxcar Logo w/Graffiti) "181053," *2018*		100 __
1926014	CSX 86-foot 4-Door High Cube Boxcar (C&O bleedthrough) "180455," *2018*		100 __
1926021	DT&I 86-foot 4-Door High Cube Boxcar, Green "26341," *2018*		100 __
1926022	DT&I 86-foot 4-Door High Cube Boxcar, Purple/Pink "26888," *2018*		100 __
1926023	DT&I 86-foot 4-Door High Cube Boxcar, Blue "26443," *2018*		100 __
1926024	DT&I 86-foot 4-Door High Cube Boxcar, Blue w/Graffiti "26834," *2018*		"100 __
1926031	N&W 86-foot 4-Door High Cube Boxcar "355155," *2018*		100 __
1926032	N&W 86-foot 4-Door High Cube Boxcar "355197," *2018*		100 __
1926041	Southern 86-foot 4-Door High Cube Boxcar "42954," *2018*		100 __
1926042	Southern 86-foot 4-Door High Cube Boxcar "42995," *2018*		100 __
1926051	UP 86-foot 4-Door High Cube Boxcar "980421," *2018*		100 __
1926052	UP 86-foot 4-Door High Cube Boxcar "980434," *2018*		100 __
1926053	UP 86-foot 4-Door High Cube Boxcar w/Graffiti "980455," *2018*		100 __
1926061	Wabash 86-foot 4-Door High Cube Boxcar "55023," *2018*		100 __
1926062	Wabash 86-foot 4-Door High Cube Boxcar "55055," *2018*		100 __
1926070	ART Refrigerator Car w/FreightSounds "31823," *2018*		150 __
1926080	FGE Refrigerator Car w/FreightSounds "38947," *2018*		150 __
1926090	GN Refrigerator Car w/FreightSounds "68112," *2018*		150 __
1926100	NYC (MDT) Refrigerator Car w/FreightSounds "19091," *2018*		150 __
1926110	PFE Refrigerator Car w/FreightSounds "5860," *2018*		150 __
1926120	AT&SF Refrigerator Car w/FreightSounds "3526," *2018*		150 __
1926131	PRR Bunk Car "498393," *2018*		100 __
1926132	PRR Bunk Car "498396," *2018*		100 __
1926133	PRR Bunk Car "498398," *2018*		100 __
1926141	AT&SF Bunk Car "196752," *2018*		100 __
1926142	AT&SF Bunk Car "196754," *2018*		100 __
1926143	AT&SF Bunk Car "196459," *2018*		100 __
1926151	NYC Bunk Car "x19075," *2018*		100 __
1926152	NYC Bunk Car "x19076," *2018*		100 __
1926153	NYC Bunk Car "x19078," *2018*		100 __
1926161	D&RGW Bunk Car "x2380," *2018*		100 __
1926162	D&RGW Bunk Car "x2384," *2018*		100 __
1926163	D&RGW Bunk Car "x2387," *2018*		100 __
1926171	UP Bunk Car "906115," *2018*		100 __
1926172	UP Bunk Car "906118," *2018*		100 __
1926173	UP Bunk Car "906121," *2018*		100 __
1926181	MOW Bunk Car "99832," *2018*		100 __
1926182	MOW Bunk Car "99835," *2018*		100 __
1926183	MOW Bunk Car "99837," *2018*		100 __
1926190	PRR Kitchen Car w/Sounds "492774," *2018*		150 __
1926200	AT&SF Kitchen Car w/Sounds "194200," *2018*		150 __
1926210	NYC Kitchen Car w/Sounds "x22483," *2018*		150 __
1926220	D&RGW Kitchen Car w/Sounds "x4013," *2018*		150 __
1926230	UP Kitchen Car w/Sounds "903675," *2018*		150 __
1926240	MOW Kitchen Car w/Sounds "99402," *2018*		150 __
1926250	PRR Tool Car "493551," *2018*		90 __
1926260	AT&SF Tool Car "190455," *2018*		90 __

		Esc	Mint
___ 1926270	NYC Tool Car "x13568," *2018*		90
___ 1926280	D&RGW Tool Car "x4510," *2018*		90
___ 1926290	UP Tool Car "915129," *2018*		90
___ 1926300	MOW Tool Car "99500," *2018*		90
___ 1926311	Chessie 52-foot Coil Gondola "305005," *2018*		90
___ 1926312	Chessie 52-foot Coil Gondola "305012," *2018*		90
___ 1926321	C&SS 52-foot Coil Gondola 3859," *2018*		90
___ 1926322	C&SS 52-foot Coil Gondola "3862," *2018*		90
___ 1926331	DT&I 52-foot Coil Gondola "9326," *2018*		90
___ 1926332	DT&I 52-foot Coil Gondola "9372," *2018*		90
___ 1926341	EJ&E 52-foot Coil Gondola "4144," *2018*		90
___ 1926342	EJ&E 52-foot Coil Gondola "4156," *2018*		90
___ 1926351	P&LE 52-foot Coil Gondola "50062," *2018*		90
___ 1926352	P&LE 52-foot Coil Gondola "50086," *2018*		90
___ 1926361	Union RR 52-foot Coil Gondola "3021," *2018*		90
___ 1926362	Union RR 52-foot Coil Gondola "3163," *2018*		90
___ 1926370	Polar Express 52-foot Coil Gondola "122519" w/Presents, *2018-19*		95
___ 1926381	ACL 50-foot Bulkhead Flatcar "78310," *2019*		100
___ 1926382	ACL 50-foot Bulkhead Flatcar "78348,". *2019*		100
___ 1926391	B&O 50-foot Bulkhead Flatcar "8831," *2019*		100
___ 1926392	B&O 50-foot Bulkhead Flatcar "8844," *2019*		100
___ 1926401	D&RGW 50-foot Bulkhead Flatcar "22392," *2019*		100
___ 1926402	D&RGW 50-foot Bulkhead Flatcar "22420," *2019*		100
___ 1926411	MKT 50-foot Bulkhead Flatcar "13912," *2019*		100
___ 1926421	SAL 50-foot Bulkhead Flatcar "48102," *2019*		100
___ 1926422	SAL 50-foot Bulkhead Flatcar "48124," *2019*		100
___ 1926431	Frisco 50-foot Bulkhead Flatcar "4052," *2019*		100
___ 1926432	Frisco 50-foot Bulkhead Flatcar "4058," *2019*		100
___ 1926441	AT&SF Grand Canyon Line 50-foot Double-Door Boxcar "10206," *2018*		80
___ 1926442	AT&SF Scout 50-foot Double-Door Boxcar "10295," *2018*		80
___ 1926443	AT&SF El Capitan 50-foot Double-Door Boxcar "10350," *2018*		80
___ 1926444	AT&SF Super Chief 50-foot Double-Door Boxcar "10410," *2018*		80
___ 1926445	AT&SF Chief 50-foot Double-Door Boxcar "10456," *2018*		80
___ 1926451	KCS 50-foot Double-Door Boxcar "20825," *2018*		80
___ 1926452	KCS 50-foot Double-Door Boxcar "20856," *2018*		80
___ 1926461	Monon 50-foot Double-Door Boxcar "1423," *2018*		80
___ 1926462	Monon 50-foot Double-Door Boxcar "1426," *2018*		80
___ 1926471	T&P 50-foot Double-Door Boxcar "70707," *2018*		80
___ 1926472	T&P 50-foot Double-Door Boxcar "70735," *2018*		80
___ 1926480	ELX Halloween 50-foot Double-Door Boxcar "103119," *2018*		80
___ 1926491	UP CA-4 Caboose "3830," *2018*		100
___ 1926492	UP CA-4 Caboose "3830," *2018*		100
___ 1926493	UP CA-4 Caboose "3859," *2018*		100
___ 1926501	Bartlett Grain PS-2CD 4427-cu-ft Covered Hopper "5509," *2019*		100
___ 1926502	Bartlett Grain PS-2CD 4427-cu-ft Covered Hopper "5511," *2019*		100
___ 1926511	BN PS-2CD 4427-cu-ft Covered Hopper "439397," *2019*		100
___ 1926512	BN PS-2CD 4427-cu-ft Covered Hopper "450621," *2019*		100
___ 1926521	Cargill PS-2CD 4427-cu-ft Covered Hopper "2819," *2019*		100
___ 1926522	Cargill PS-2CD 4427-cu-ft Covered Hopper "2853," *2019*		100
___ 1926531	Conrail PS-2CD 4427-cu-ft Covered Hopper "886283," *2019*		100
___ 1926532	Conrail PS-2CD 4427-cu-ft Covered Hopper "886304," *2019*		100
___ 1926540	Ely Thomas Logging Cars 2-pack A, *2019*		150
___ 1926550	Ely Thomas Logging Cars 2-pack B, *2019*		150

		Esc	Mint
1926560	Long Bell Logging Cars 2-pack A, *2019*	150	___
1926570	Long Bell Logging Cars 2-pack B, *2019*	150	___
1926580	NY&P Logging Cars 2-pack A, *2019*	150	___
1926590	NY&P Logging Cars 2-pack B, *2019*	150	___
1926600	Unlettered Logging Cars 2-pack A, *2019*	150	___
1926610	Unlettered Logging Cars 2-pack B, *2019*	150	___
1926620	B&O Sentinel PS-1 Boxcar "466024" w/FreightSounds, *2019*	135	___
1926630	GN PS-1 Boxcar "39412" w/FreightSounds, *2019*	135	___
1926640	PRR PS-1 Boxcar "24267" w/FreightSounds, *2019*	135	___
1926650	D&RGW Cookie Box PS-1 Boxcar "60034" w/FreightSounds, *2019*	135	___
1926660	Southern PS-1 Boxcar "330434" w/FreightSounds, *2019*	135	___
1926670	SP Overnight PS-1 Boxcar "97945" w/FreightSounds, *2019*	135	___
1926680	NYS&W PS-1 Boxcar "501" w/FreightSounds, *2019*	135	___
1926690	WP PS-1 Boxcar "19531" w/FreightSounds, *2019*	135	___
1926701	B&M 40-foot Flatcar "33700" w/Sherman Tank Load, *2019*	130	___
1926702	B&M 40-foot Flatcar "33745" w/Sherman Tank Load, *2019*	130	___
1926711	NYC 40-foot Flatcar "496250" w/Sherman Tank Load, *2019*	130	___
1926712	NYC 40-foot Flatcar "496271" w/Sherman Tank Load, *2019*	130	___
1926721	PRR 40-foot Flatcar "925148" w/Sherman Tank Load, *2019*	130	___
1926722	PRR 40-foot Flatcar "925164" w/Sherman Tank Load, *2019*	130	___
1926731	SP 40-foot Flatcar "140014" w/Sherman Tank Load, *2019*	130	___
1926732	SP 40-foot Flatcar "140125" w/Sherman Tank Load, *2019*	130	___
1926741	UP 40-foot Flatcar "51125" w/Sherman Tank Load, *2019*	130	___
1926742	UP 40-foot Flatcar "51196" w/Sherman Tank Load, *2019*	130	___
1926751	US Army 40-foot Flatcar "35351" w/Sherman Tank Load, *2019*	130	___
1926752	US Army 40-foot Flatcar "35359" w/Sherman Tank Load, *2019*	130	___
1926760	CTCX 30,000-gallon 1-D Tank Car 3-pack, *2019*	250	___
1926770	GATX 30,000-gallon 1-D Tank Car 3-pack, *2019*	250	___
1926780	SCMX 30,000-gallon 1-D Tank Car 3-pack, *2019*	250	___
1926790	TILX (Black) 30,000-gallon 1-D Tank Car 3-pack, *2019*	250	___
1926800	TILX (White) 30,000-gallon 1-D Tank Car 3-pack, *2019*	250	___
1926810	VMSX 30,000-gallon 1-D Tank Car 3-pack, *2019*	250	___
1926820	Polar Express 15th Anniversary Boxcar w/FreightSounds, *2019*	145	___
1926830	C&NW NE Caboose "10808," *2019*	100	___
1926840	Conrail (RDG patch) NE Caboose "19730," *2019*	100	___
1926850	D&H NE Caboose "35802," *2019*	100	___
1926860	L&HR NE Caboose "17," *2019*	100	___
1926870	LV NE Caboose "95003," *2019*	100	___
1926880	Halloween (ELX) NE Caboose "1313," *2019*	100	___
1926890	Alaska RR EV Caboose "1086" w/CupolaCam, *2019*	130	___
1926900	C&O EV Caboose "3160" w/CupolaCam, *2019*	130	___
1926910	Conrail EV Caboose "22137" w/CupolaCam, *2019*	130	___
1926920	D&RGW EV Caboose "01510" w/CupolaCam, *2019*	130	___
1926930	Milwaukee Road EV Caboose "992303" w/CupolaCam, *2019*	130	___
1926940	MKT EV Caboose "100" w/CupolaCam, *2019*	130	___
1926950	N&W EV Caboose "555100" w/CupolaCam, *2019*	130	___
1926960	Lionel Lines EV Caboose "6960" w/CupolaCam, *2019*	130	___
1926971	Detroit Salt PS-2CD 4427-cu-ft Covered Hopper "5436," *2019*	100	___
1926972	Detroit Salt PS-2CD 4427-cu-ft Covered Hopper "5446," *2019*	100	___
1926981	Producers Grain PS-2CD 4427-cu-ft Covered Hopper "3926," *2019*	100	___
1926982	Producers Grain PS-2CD 4427-cu-ft Covered Hopper "3940," *2019*	100	___
1927010	AT&SF 21-inch Passenger Car 4-pack, *2019*	700	___
1927020	AT&SF 21-inch Passenger Car 2-pack #1, *2019*	350	___

		Esc	Mint
____ 1927030	AT&SF 21-inch Dome Car "550" w/StationSounds, *2019*		340
____ 1927040	AT&SF 21-inch Passenger Car 2-pack #2, *2019*		350
____ 1927070	Midnight Special 18-inch Passenger Car 2-pack #1, *2018*		400
____ 1927080	Midnight Special 18-inch Passenger Car 2-pack #2, *2018*		400
____ 1927090	Midnight Special 18-inch Passenger Car 2-pack #3, *2018*		400
____ 1927100	Midnight Special Diner "1305," w/StationSounds, *2018*		330
____ 1927110	SP 18-inch Passenger Car 2-pack #1, *2018-19*		400
____ 1927120	SP 18-inch Passenger Car 2-pack #2, *2018-19*		400
____ 1927130	SP 18-inch Passenger Car 2-pack #3, *2018-19*		400
____ 1927140	SP 18-inch Passenger Car 2-pack #4, *2018-19*		400
____ 1927150	NYC Pacemaker 2-car Add-on Set, *2019*		400
____ 1927160	NYC Pacemaker Diner "617" w/StationSounds, *2019*		330
____ 1927170	N&W Cavalier 18-inch Passenger Car 2-pack A, *2019*		400
____ 1927180	N&W Cavalier 18-inch Passenger Car 2-pack B, *2019*		400
____ 1927190	N&W Cavalier 18-inch Diner "1018" w/StationSounds, *2019*		33
____ 1927200	611 Excursion Train NS Coach 4-pack, *2019*		700
____ 1927210	611 Excursion Train Private Car 2-pack A, *2019*		350
____ 1927220	611 Excursion Train Private Car 2-pack B, *2019*		350
____ 1927230	611 Excursion Train Dome Car w/StationSounds, *2019*		340
____ 1927241	611 Excursion Train N&W Tool Car "1407," *2019*		180
____ 1927242	N&W Cavalier Baggage "110," *2019*		180
____ 1927243	N&W Cavalier Baggage "114," *2019*		180
____ 1927251	PC 60-foot Baggage "7533," *2019*		180
____ 1927252	PC 60-foot Baggage "7551," *2019*		180
____ 1927261	SP 60-foot Baggage "6340," *2019*		180
____ 1927262	SP 60-foot Baggage "6344," *2019*		180
____ 1927271	REA 60-foot Baggage "1631," *2019*		180
____ 1927272	REA 60-foot Baggage "1650," *2019*		180
____ 1927281	UP 60-foot Baggage "1830" (Greyhound), *2019*		180
____ 1927282	UP 60-foot Baggage "1841" (Greyhound), *2019*		180
____ 1927283	UP 60-foot Baggage "1830" (Yellow), *2019*		180
____ 1927284	UP 60-foot Baggage "1837" (Yellow), *2019*		180
____ 1927291	ACL 60-foot Baggage "555," *2019*		180
____ 1927292	ACL 60-foot Baggage "559," *2019*		180
____ 1927300	ACL 60-foot Railway Post Office "11," *2019*		180
____ 1927310	N&W Cavalier Railway Post Office "96," *2019*		180
____ 1927320	Southern 60-foot Railway Post Office "39," *2018-19*		160
____ 1927330	AT&SF 60-foot Railway Post Office "65," *2019*		180
____ 1927340	UP 60-foot Railway Post Office "2062," *2019*		180
____ 1927350	UP Excursion 21-inch Passenger Car Expansion Set, *2019*		350
____ 1927351	Polar Express Railway Post Office, White Roof, *2019*		180
____ 1927352	Polar Express Railway Post Office, Black Roof, *2019*		180
____ 1927360	LIRR 21-inch Streamlined Coach 4-pack, *2019*		700
____ 1927370	LIRR 21-inch Streamlined Coach 2-pack, *2019*		350
____ 1927360	UP Challenger 21-inch Passenger Car Expansion Set, *2019*		350
____ 1927380	UP 1860s Wood Coach w/RailSounds, *2-pack, 2019*		350
____ 1927461	Southern 60-foot Baggage "100," *2018-19*		160
____ 1927462	Southern 60-foot Baggage "109," *2018-19*		160
____ 1927470	Southern 18-inch Passenger Car 2-pack #1, *2018-19*		400
____ 1927480	Southern 18-inch Passenger Car 2-pack #2, *2018-19*		400
____ 1927490	Southern 18-inch Passenger Car 2-pack #3, *2018-19*		400
____ 1927500	Southern Diner "3168" w/StationSounds, *2018-19*		330
____ 1927510	MP Sunshine Special 18-inch Passenger Car 2-pack #1, *2018-19*		400

		Mint	
1927520	MP Sunshine Special 18-inch Passenger Car 2-pack #2, *2018-19*	400	___
1927530	MP Sunshine Special 18-inch Passenger Car 2-pack #3, *2018-19*	400	___
1927540	MP Sunshine Special 18-inch Passenger Car 2-pack #1, *2018-19*	330	___
1927550	MP Sunshine Special 60-foot Railway Post Office "45," *2018-19*	160	___
1927560	Defense Special Heavyweight Passenger Car 2-pack A, *2019*	400	___
1927570	Defense Special Heavyweight Passenger Car 2-pack B, *2019*	400	___
1927580	Defense Special Heavyweight Passenger Car 2-pack C, *2019*	400	___
1927590	Defense Special Heavyweight Passenger Car 2-pack D, *2019*	400	___
1927600	611 Excursion Train NS Coach 2-pack, *2019*	350	___
1927610	CP 21-inch Passenger Car 4-pack, *2019*	700	___
1927620	CP 21-inch Passenger Car 2-pack, *2019*	350	___
1927630	Polar Express Hot Chocolate Car w/StationSounds, *2019*	330	___
1927640	Polar Express Abandoned Toy Car, *2019*	200	___
1927650	Polar Express 15th Anniversary Coach, *2019*	200	___
1927660	Pennsylvania Limited Suetonius Coach, *2019*	75	___
1927670	Lionel State Set Add-on 2-pack, *2019*	530	___
1927680	Northern Central 1860s Wood Coach w/RailSounds, 2-pack, *2019*	350	___
1927690	Woodruff Sleeping and Parlor 1860s Wood Coach, 2-pack, *2019*	300	___
1927700	Blue Comet Heavyweight Coach, *19-20*	75	___
1927710	CP 21-inch Diner "550" w/StationSounds, *2019*	330	___
1927730	PRR 1860s Wood Coach w/RailSounds, 2-pack, *2019*	350	___
1928011	BN Auto Rack "159173," *2018-19*	80	___
1928012	BN Auto Rack "159433," *2018-19*	80	___
1928021	Conrail Auto Rack "980139," *2018-19*	80	___
1928022	Conrail Auto Rack "456249," *2018-19*	80	___
1928031	GT Auto Rack "50454," *2018-19*	80	___
1928032	GT Auto Rack "50490," *2018-19*	80	___
1928041	SP Auto Rack "518027," *2018-19*	80	___
1928042	SP Auto Rack "518114," *2018-19*	80	___
1928051	TTX Auto Rack "710866," *2018-19*	80	___
1928052	TTX Auto Rack "710877," *2018-19*	80	___
1928060	Mickey Mouse Celebration Aquarium Car, *2018*	100	___
1928070	NYC Flatcar w/Boat "28070," *2018-19*	70	___
1928080	Hot Wheels Fuel 1-Dome Tank Car, *2018-19*	75	___
1928091	Branch Line Passenger Car 2-pack, *2018-19*	75	___
1928092	James Trucks Wagon Car 2-pack, *2018-19*	75	___
1928093	S.C. Ruffey Wagon Car, *2018-19*	45	___
1928110	BN Hopper 6-pack, *2019*	150	___
1928120	C&NW Hopper 6-pack, *2019*	150	___
1928130	CSX Hopper 6-pack, *19-20*	150	___
1928140	PP&L Hopper 6-pack, *19-20*	150	___
1928150	Reading Lines Hopper 6-pack, *19-20*	150	___
1928160	Bethlehem Steel Ore Car 6-pack, *19-20*	150	___
1928170	CN Ore Car 6-pack, *19-20*	150	___
1928180	Erie Mining Ore Car 6-pack, *2019*	150	___
1928190	PRR Ore Car 6-pack, *19-20*	150	___
1928200	UP Ore Car 6-pack, *19-20*	150	___
1928220	Anheuser-Busch 1890s Woodside Refrigerator Car, *2019*	80	___
1928240	Anheuser-Busch Uni-Body 1-D Tank Car "4271," *2019*	75	___
1928250	Anheuser-Busch Barrel Car "28250," *2019*	80	___
1928260	Miller High Life Woodside Refrigerator Car, *19-20*	80	___
1928270	Coors Golden Beer Woodside Refrigerator Car, *19-20*	80	___
1928280	Hamm's Beer Woodside Refrigerator Car, *2019*	80	___

		Esc	Mint
___	**1928330** Pez Mint Car, *2019*		80
___	**1928340** John Deere Mower Stockcar, *2019*		80
___	**1928350** John Deere Flatcar "28350" w/Piggyback Trailers, *2019*		85
___	**1928360** Scooby-Doo Aquarium Car, *19-20*		100
___	**1928370** Spy Vs. Spy Challenge Boxcar, *2019*		85
___	**1928380** Trick or Treat Boxcar w/HalloweenSounds, *2019*		80
___	**1928390** Undead Gondola, *2019*		70
___	**1928400** Polar Express Hero Boy Walking Brakeman Car, *2019*		100
___	**1928410** Polar Express Reindeer Car, *2019*		80
___	**1928420** Polar Express Searchlight Car, *2019*		70
___	**1928430** Polar Express Barrel Car, *2019*		80
___	**1928440** Sweetest Helper Refrigerator Car, *19-20*		80
___	**1928450** Snowball Fight Animated Gondola, *19-20*		75
___	**1928460** Santa Mobile Rest Stop Flatcar, *19-20*		75
___	**1928470** Santa Freight Lines Christmas Transfer Caboose, *19-20*		70
___	**1928480** Santa Freight Lines Santa Finder Searchlight Car, *19-20*		65
___	**1928490** Christmas Boxcar 2019, *2019*		65
___	**1928500** Christmas Music Boxcar, *2019*		80
___	**1928510** UP Barrel Ramp Car "28510," *19-20*		75
___	**1928520** BNSF Maxi-Stack, *2018-19*		80
___	**1928530** CSX Maxi-Stack, *2018-19*		80
___	**1928540** TTX Maxi-Stack, *2018-19*		80
___	**1928550** NPR Flatcar "1937" w/Trailer, *2019*		70
___	**1928560** Batman & Robin Boxcar, *19-20*		80
___	**1928570** Batman Bat-Signal Searchlight Car, *2019*		70
___	**1928580** Batman The Joker Laughing Gas Missile Car, *19-20*		90
___	**1928590** Happy Birthday Scooby-Doo Sound Car, *2019-20*		85
___	**1928600** Batman Classic Gotham City Villains Boxcar, *19-20*		80
___	**1928610** Chevy Auto Rack "1911," *19-20*		85
___	**1928620** Chevy Flatcar w/Frames, *2019*		75
___	**1928630** Looney Tunes Scent-imental Over You Chasing Gondola, *2019*		80
___	**1928640** Thomas the Tank Engine Boxcar, *2019*		75
___	**1928650** Percy Boxcar, *2019*		75
___	**1928660** James Boxcar, *2019*		75
___	**1928670** Mickey's Wish List Boxcar, *19-20*		70
___	**1928680** UP Uni-Body 1-D Tank Car "8665," *19-20*		70
___	**1928690** Toyota Auto Rack "1937," *2019*		85
___	**1928700** Toyota Flatcar w/Frames, *2019*		75
___	**1929040** Anheuser-Busch Barrel Loader, *2019*		70
___	**1929050** Polar Express Barrel Loader, *2019*		70
___	**1929060** Polar Express Station Platform, *2019*		55
___	**1929070** Winter Wonderland Station Platform, *19-20*		50
___	**1929080** Hot Wheels Crash City Café, *2018-19*		100
___	**1929090** Illuminated Christmas Half-Covered Bridge, *19-20*		70
___	**1929100** Defect Detector, *18, 20*		80
___	**1929110** Halloween House, *2018*		130
___	**1929130** Elf Tug of War Accessory, *2019*		75
___	**1929160** Sir Topham Hatt Gateman, *2019*		120
___	**1929170** Haunted House, *19-20*		250
___	**1929230** Burning House, *2019-20*		120
___	**1929804** Peel and Stick Lights, 4-pack, *2019-20*		10
___	**1929815** Peel and Stick Lights, 15-pack, *2019-20*		28
___	**1929904** Peel and Stick LED Lights, 4-pack, *2019-20*		10
___	**1929915** Peel and Stick LED Lights, 15-pack, *2019-20*		28

MODERN 1970-2021		Esc	Mint
1930010	Coal Load Kit, *2018*	20	___
1930160	Brown Picket Fence, *2019-20*	20	___
1930050	Lumber Load Kit, *2019*	25	___
1930060	Millennial People Pack, *18-20*	30	___
1930070	Trick or Treat Figures, *18-20*	30	___
1930080	Halloween Lawn Figures, *18-20*	25	___
1930120	Mickey Mouse Celebration Billboard, 3-pack, *2018*	20	___
1930130	Thomas & Friends Covered Bridge, *2018-19*	70	___
1930140	Trolley House, *2019*	50	___
1930150	Budweiser Billboard 3-pack, *2019*	25	___
1930170	Green Iron Fence, *2019-20*	20	___
1930180	Benches, 6-pack, *2019-20*	10	___
1930190	Sitting People with Benches, 6-pack, *2019-20*	23	___
1930200	Winter Action Figures, 6-pack, *2019-20*	23	___
1930210	Sled Kids, 3-pack, *2019-20*	23	___
1930220	Sitting People, 6-pack, *2019-20*	23	___
1930230	People on Sleigh Figure Pack, *2019-20*	23	___
1930240	People Waving, 6-pack, *2019-20*	23	___
1930250	People Eating, 6-pack, *2019-20*	23	___
1930260	Prisoners (striped), 6-pack, *2019-20*	23	___
1930270	Travelers, 6-pack, *2019-20*	23	___
1930280	Horses, 4-pack, *2019-20*	23	___
1930290	Cows and Calves (brown), *6-pack, 2019-20*	23	___
1930300	Unpainted Figures, 36-pack, *2019-20*	35	___
1930310	Unpainted Animals, 36-pack, *2019-20*	35	___
1930320	Smoking Tony Lighted Figure, *2019-20*	20	___
1930330	Railroad Worker with Lamp Lighted Figure, *2019-20*	20	___
1930340	Miner with Headlamp Lighted Figure, *2019-20*	20	___
1930350	Man with Flashlight Lighted Figure, *2019-20*	20	___
1930360	Man with Flashing Jackhammer Lighted Figure, *2019-20*	20	___
1930370	Braga House, *2019-20*	75	___
1930380	Fraser House, *2019-20*	75	___
1930390	Harwell House, *2019-20*	75	___
1930400	Olson House Kit, *2019-20*	22	___
1930410	Morris House Kit, *2019-20*	22	___
1930420	Bishop House Kit, *2019-20*	22	___
1930430	Davis House Kit, *2019-20*	22	___
1930440	Church, *2019-20*	86	___
1931060	L&N USRA 4-8-2 Light Mountain Locomotive "404," *CC, 2018*	1300	___
1931070	MP USRA 4-8-2 Light Mountain Locomotive "5307," *CC, 2018*	1300	___
1931080	NC&StL USRA 4-8-2 Light Mountain Locomotive "551," *CC, 2018*	1300	___
1931090	NH USRA 4-8-2 Light Mountain Locomotive "3301," *CC, 2018*	1300	___
1931100	Frisco USRA 4-8-2 Light Mountain Locomotive "1501," *CC, 2018*	1300	___
1931110	Soo Line USRA 4-8-2 Light Mountain Locomotive "4005," *CC, 2018*	1300	___
1931120	Southern USRA 4-8-2 Light Mountain Locomotive "1483," *CC, 2018*	1300	___
1931130	Southern USRA 4-8-2 Light Mountain Locomotive "1495," *CC, 2018*	1300	___
1931140	North Pole Central USRA 4-8-2 Light Mountain Locomotive "1224," *CC, 2018*	1300	___
1931150	SP 4-4-2 Atlantic A-6 Locomotive "3001," *CC, 2018*	800	___
1931160	SP 4-4-2 Atlantic A-6 Locomotive "3000," *CC, 2018*	800	___
1931170	SP 4-4-2 Atlantic A-6 Locomotive "3002," *CC, 2018*	800	___
1931180	UP 4-4-2 Atlantic Locomotive "3304," *CC, 2018*	800	___

		Esc	Mint
MODERN 1970-2021			
___	1931190	C&NW 4-4-2 Atlantic Locomotive "394," *CC, 2018*		800
___	1931200	IC 4-4-2 Atlantic Locomotive "1003," *CC, 2018*		800
___	1931210	Clinchfield 4-6-6-4 Locomotive "675," *CC, 2018*		2,000
___	1931220	D&RGW 4-6-6-4 Locomotive "3800," *CC, 2018*		2,000
___	1931230	D&RGW 4-6-6-4 Locomotive "3805," *CC, 2018*		2,000
___	1931240	UP 4-6-6-4 Challenger Locomotive "3975," *CC, 2018*		2,000
___	1931250	UP 4-6-6-4 Challenger Locomotive "3977," *CC, 2018*		2,000
___	1931260	UP 4-6-6-4 Challenger Locomotive "3985," *CC, 2018*		2,000
___	1931270	UP 4-6-6-4 Challenger Locomotive "3981," *CC, 2018*		2,000
___	1931280	UP 4-6-6-4 Challenger Locomotive "3717," *CC, 2018*		2,000
___	1931290	UP 4-6-6-4 Challenger Locomotive "3949," *CC, 2018*		2,000
___	1931300	Undecorated 4-6-6-4 Challenger Locomotive "9999," *CC, 2018*		2,000
___	1931311	UP Vision Auxiliary Water Tender "907853," *CC, 2018*		500
___	1931312	UP Vision Auxiliary Water Tender "907856," *CC, 2018*		500
___	1931313	UP Vision Auxiliary Water Tender "907857," *CC, 2018*		500
___	1931314	UP Vision Auxiliary Water Tender "809," *CC, 2018*		500
___	1931315	UP Vision Auxiliary Water Tender "814," *CC, 2018*		500
___	1931316	UP Vision Auxiliary Water Tender "903026," *CC, 2018*		500
___	1931320	Clinchfield Vision Auxiliary Water Tender "X675," *CC, 2018*		500
___	1931330	D&RGW Vision Auxiliary Water Tender "3800A," *CC, 2018*		500
___	1931340	N&W 4-8-4 Northern J-Class "600," *CC, 2019*		1500
___	1931350	N&W 4-8-4 Northern J-Class "603," *CC, 2019*		1500
___	1931360	N&W 4-8-4 Northern J-Class "611" (c1982), *CC, 2019*		1500
___	1931370	N&W 4-8-4 Northern J-Class "611" (c2016), *CC, 2019*		1500
___	1931380	American Freedom Train 4-8-4 "611," *CC, 2019*		1500
___	1931390	N&W 4-8-4 Northern J-Class "746," *CC, 2019*		1500
___	1931400	C&O 2-10-4 Texas T1 "3001," *CC, 2019*		1500
___	1931410	C&O 2-10-4 Texas T1 "3039," *CC, 2019*		1500
___	1931420	PRR 2-10-4 Texas J1a "6174," *CC, 2019*		1500
___	1931430	PRR 2-10-4 Texas J1a "6434," *CC, 2019*		1500
___	1931440	PRR 2-10-4 Texas J1a "6500" (artist conception), *CC 2019*		1500
___	1931450	NYC 4-6-4 Hudson J3a "5405," *CC, 2019*		1400
___	1931460	NYC 4-6-4 Hudson J3a "5413," *CC, 2019*		1500
___	1931470	NYC 4-6-4 Hudson J3a "5418," *CC, 2019*		1400
___	1931480	NYC 4-6-4 Hudson J3a "5452," *CC, 2019*		1500
___	1931490	Ely Thomas Two-Truck Shay Locomotive "6," *CC, 2019*		1200
___	1931500	Lima Stone Two-Truck Shay Locomotive "10," *CC, 2019*		1200
___	1931510	Lima Locomotive Works Two-Truck Shay Locomotive "2," *CC, 2019*		1200
___	1931520	Long Bell Two-Truck Shay Locomotive "5," *CC, 2019*		1200
___	1931530	NY&P Two-Truck Shay Locomotive "3," *CC, 2019*		1200
___	1931540	Roaring Camp Two-Truck Shay Locomotive "1," *CC, 2019*		1200
___	1931550	North Pole Woodworks Two-Truck Shay Locomotive "25," *CC, 2019*		1200
___	1931560	Sleepy Hollow Casket, Two-Truck Shay Locomotive "31," *CC, 2019*		1200
___	1931650	Central Pacific 4-4-0 Hybrid Jupiter, (painted), *CC 2019*		1100
___	1931660	UP 4-4-0 Hybrid, "119," (painted), *CC 2019*		1100
___	1931670	Schenectady Locomotive Works 4-4-0 Hybrid, (unpainted), *CC 2019*		1100
___	1931680	Rogers Locomotive Works 4-4-0 Hybrid, (unpainted), *CC 2019*		1100
___	1931690	C&O 2-10-4 Texas T1 "3020," *CC* (weathered), *2019*		1700
___	1931700	PRR 2-10-4 Texas J1a "6481," *CC* (weathered), *2019*		1700
___	1931710	B&LE 2-10-4 Texas "643," *CC, 2019*		1500
___	1931720	CB&Q 2-10-4 Texas "6328," *CC, 2019*		1500
___	1931730	DM&IR 2-10-4 Texas "717," *CC, 2019*		1500
___	1931740	KCS 2-10-4 Texas "905," *CC, 2019*		1500

		Esc	Mint
1931750	D&RGW 2-10-4 Texas "1450," CC, 2019		1500 ___
1931760	Southern 2-10-4 Texas "5300," CC, 2019		1500 ___
1931770	Central Pacific 4-4-0 Hybrid Leviathan, (painted), CC 2019		1100 ___
1931780	Northern Central 4-4-0 Hybrid York, (painted), CC 2019		1100 ___
1931820	PRR 4-4-0 Hybrid, "573," (painted), CC 2019		1100 ___
1932010	AT&SF 2-8-4 Berkshire Locomotive "4101," LionChief Plus 2.0, 19-20		500 ___
1932020	C&O 2-8-4 Berkshire Locomotive "2687," LionChief Plus 2.0, 2019		500 ___
1932030	NPR 2-8-4 Berkshire Locomotive "765," LionChief Plus 2.0, 19-20		500 ___
1932040	Pere Marquette 2-8-4 Berkshire Locomotive "1225," LionChief Plus 2.0, 19-20		500 ___
1932050	Southern 2-8-4 Berkshire, "2716," LionChief Plus 2.0, 2019-20		500 ___
1932080	Disney 2-8-4 Berkshire Locomotive "2019," LionChief Plus 2.0, 19-20		525 ___
1932090	Polar Express 2-8-4 Berkshire Locomotive "1225," LionChief Plus 2.0, 19-20		525 ___
1932100	North Pole Central 2-8-4 Berkshire Locomotive "1224," LionChief Plus 2.0, 19-20		500 ___
1932110	Halloween (ELX) 2-8-4 Berkshire Locomotive "1031," LionChief Plus 2.0, 19-20		500 ___
1932120	GN 2-4-2 Columbia Locomotive "374," LionChief, 2019		200 ___
1932130	PRR 2-4-2 Columbia Locomotive "619" LionChief, 2019		200 ___
1932140	AT&SF 2-4-2 Columbia Locomotive "3452," LionChief, 2019		200 ___
1932150	Southern 2-4-2 Columbia Locomotive "1412," LionChief, 2019		200 ___
1932161	UP 4-8-8-4 Big Boy Locomotive "4012," LionChief Plus 2.0, 2019		1200 ___
1932162	UP 4-8-8-4 Big Boy Locomotive "4014," LionChief Plus 2.0, 2019		1200 ___
1932163	UP 4-8-8-4 Big Boy Locomotive "4017," LionChief Plus 2.0, 2019		1200 ___
1932164	UP 4-8-8-4 Big Boy Locomotive "4018," LionChief Plus 2.0, 2019		1200 ___
1932170	UP 4-8-8-4 Big Boy Locomotive "4000" (Greyhound), LionChief Plus 2.0, 2019		1200 ___
1933011	BN Alco RS-11 Diesel "4186," CC, 2018		500 ___
1933012	BN Alco RS-11 Diesel "4190," CC, 2018		500 ___
1933021	CV Alco RS-11 Diesel "3601," CC, 2018		500 ___
1933022	CV Alco RS-11 Diesel "3611," CC, 2018		500 ___
1933031	Conrail Alco RS-11 Diesel "7640," CC, 2018		500 ___
1933032	Conrail Alco RS-11 Diesel "7651," CC, 2018		500 ___
1933041	Depew, Lancaster & Western Alco RS-11 Diesel "1800," CC, 2018		500 ___
1933042	Depew, Lancaster & Western Alco RS-11 Diesel "1804," CC, 2018		500 ___
1933051	L&N Alco RS-11 Diesel "952," CC, 2018		500 ___
1933052	L&N Alco RS-11 Diesel "955," CC, 2018		500 ___
1933061	SCL Alco RS-11 Diesel "1202," CC, 2018		500 ___
1933062	SCL Alco RS-11 Diesel "1210," CC, 2018		500 ___
1933081	BN EMD SD40-2 Diesel "6702," CC, 2018		550 ___
1933082	BN EMD SD40-2 Diesel "8002," CC, 2018		550 ___
1933083	BN non-powered EMD SD40-2 Diesel "6772," 2018		300 ___
1933091	FEC EMD SD40-2 Diesel "703," CC, 2018		550 ___
1933092	FEC EMD SD40-2 Diesel "713," CC, 2018		550 ___
1933093	FEC non-powered EMD SD40-2 Diesel "714," 2018		300 ___
1933101	FURX EMD SD40-2 Diesel "3012," CC, 2018		550 ___
1933102	FURX EMD SD40-2 Diesel "3021," CC, 2018		550 ___
1933103	FURX non-powered EMD SD40-2 Diesel "3049," 2018		00 ___
1933111	Milwaukee Road Bicentennial EMD SD40-2 Diesel "156," CC, 2018		550 ___
1933112	Milwaukee Road EMD SD40-2 Diesel "190," CC, 2018		550 ___
1933113	Milwaukee Road EMD SD40-2 Diesel "196," CC, 2018		550 ___
1933114	Milwaukee Road non-powered EMD SD40-2 Diesel "197," 2018		300 ___

			Esc	Mint
___	1933121	Soo Line "Bandit" EMD SD40-2 Diesel "6301," *CC, 2018*		550
___	1933122	Soo Line "Bandit" EMD SD40-2 Diesel "6345," *CC, 2018*		550
___	1933123	Soo Line "Bandit" non-powered EMD SD40-2 Diesel "6362," *2018*		300
___	1933131	UP EMD SD40-2 Diesel "3696," *CC, 2018*		550
___	1933132	UP EMD SD40-2 Diesel "3707," *CC, 2018*		550
___	1933133	UP non-powered EMD SD40-2 Diesel "B3641," *2018*		300
___	1933141	W&LE EMD SD40-2 Diesel "6310," *CC, 2018*		550
___	1933142	W&LE EMD SD40-2 Diesel "6311," *CC, 2018*		550
___	1933143	W&LE non-powered EMD SD40-2 Diesel "6347," *2018*		300
___	1933151	W&S EMD SD40-2 Diesel "4001," *CC, 2018*		550
___	1933152	W&S EMD SD40-2 Diesel "4003," *CC, 2018*		550
___	1933153	W&S non-powered EMD SD40-2 Diesel "4005," *2018*		300
___	1933160	AT&SF Alco PA-PA Diesel Set "54-54," *CC, 2018*		1000
___	1933163	AT&SF Alco PB w/SuperBass Sound "54A," *CC, 2018*		500
___	1933170	D&RGW Alco PA-PA Diesel Set "6001-6003," *CC, 2018*		1000
___	1933173	D&RGW Alco PB w/SuperBass Sound "6002," *CC, 2018*		500
___	1933180	NYC Alco PA-PA Diesel Set "4903-4904," *CC, 2018*		1000
___	1933183	NYC Alco PB w/SuperBass Sound "4303," *CC, 2018*		500
___	1933190	PRR Alco PA-PA Diesel Set "5754-5755," *CC, 2018*		1000
___	1933193	PRR Alco PB w/SuperBass Sound "5754B," *CC, 2018*		500
___	1933200	SP Alco PA-PA Diesel Set "6034-6039," *CC, 2018*		1000
___	1933203	SP Alco PB w/SuperBass Sound "5922," *CC, 2018*		500
___	1933210	UP Alco PA-PA Diesel Set "606-607," *CC, 2018*		1000
___	1933213	UP Alco PB w/SuperBass Sound "606B," *CC, 2018*		500
___	1933221	BNSF (ATSF Patch) GE C44-9W Diesel "599," *CC, 2018*		
___	1933222	BNSF (ATSF Patch) GE C44-9W Diesel "662," *CC, 2018*		
___	1933223	BNSF (ATSF Patch) non-powered GE C44-9W Diesel "604," *2018*		500
___	1933231	BNSF GE C44-9W Diesel "703," *CC, 2018*		550
___	1933232	BNSF GE C44-9W Diesel "4173," *CC, 2018*		550
___	1933233	BNSF non-powered GE C44-9W Diesel "5282," *2018*		300
___	1933241	Pilbara Rail GE C44-9W Diesel "7079," *CC, 2018*		550
___	1933242	Pilbara Rail GE C44-9W Diesel "7097," *CC, 2018*		550
___	1933243	Pilbara Rail non-powered GE C44-9W Diesel "7098," *2018*		300
___	1933251	Quebec, North Shore & Labrador GE C44-9W Diesel "405," *CC, 2018*		550
___	1933252	Quebec, North Shore & Labrador GE C44-B141 Diesel "407," *CC, 2018*		550
___	1933253	Quebec, North Shore & Labrador non-powered GE C44-9W Diesel "413," *2018*		300
___	1933261	UP (SP Patch) GE C44-9W Diesel "9615," *CC, 2018*		550
___	1933262	UP (SP Patch) GE C44-9W Diesel "9617," *CC, 2018*		550
___	1933263	UP (SP Patch) non-powered GE C44-9W Diesel "9647," *2018*		300
___	1933271	UP GE C44-9W Diesel w/Cheyenne Service Unit Plaque "9700," *CC, 2018*		550
___	1933272	UP GE C44-9W Diesel "9650," *CC, 2018*		550
___	1933273	UP non-powered GE C44-9W Diesel "9654," *2018*		300
___	1933281	BNSF GE ES44AC Diesel "6411," *CC, 2019*		600
___	1933282	BNSF GE ES44AC Diesel "6425," *CC, 2019*		600
___	1933283	BNSF non-powered GE ES44AC Diesel "6438," *2019*		350
___	1933291	CitiRail GE ES44AC Diesel "1201," *CC, 2019*		600
___	1933292	CitiRail GE ES44AC Diesel "1210," *CC, 2019*		600
___	1933293	CitiRail non-powered GE ES44AC Diesel "1212," *2019*		350
___	1933301	GE Demonstrator ES44AC Diesel "2005," *CC, 2019*		600
___	1933302	GE Demonstrator ES44AC Diesel "2012," *CC, 2019*		600
___	1933310	Iowa Interstate GE ES44AC Diesel "516," *CC, 2019*		600

1933321	UP GE ES44AC Diesel "7964," *CC, 2019*	600	___
1933322	UP GE ES44AC Diesel "8109," *CC, 2019*	600	___
1933323	UP non-powered GE ES44AC Diesel "8140," *2019*	350	___
1933324	UP GE ES44AC Diesel, Fantasy Greyhound scheme, "8044," *CC, 2019*	600	___
1933325	UP GE ES44AC Diesel, Fantasy 49er scheme, "8149," *CC, 2019*	600	___
1933326	UP GE ES44AC Diesel Fantasy "119," *CC, 2019*	600	___
1933327	UP GE ES44AC Diesel Fantasy Jupiter "60," *CC, 2019*	600	___
1933331	Allegheny RR EMD GP35 Diesel "305," *CC, 2019*	500	___
1933332	Allegheny RR EMD GP35 Diesel "306," *CC, 2019*	500	___
1933341	AT&SF EMD GP35 Diesel "2835," *CC, 2019*	500	___
1933342	AT&SF EMD GP35 Diesel "2858," *CC, 2019*	500	___
1933343	AT&SF non-powered EMD GP35 Diesel "2932," *2019*	300	___
1933351	C&NW EMD GP35 Diesel "826," *CC, 2019*	500	___
1933352	C&NW EMD GP35 Diesel "830," *CC, 2019*	500	___
1933353	C&NW non-powered EMD GP35 Diesel "841," *2019*	300	___
1933361	Conrail EMD GP35 Diesel "2398," *CC, 2019*	500	___
1933362	Conrail EMD GP35 Diesel "3630," *CC, 2019*	500	___
1933363	Conrail non-powered EMD GP35 Diesel "3692," *2019*	300	___
1933371	BNSF EMD GP35 Diesel "2570," *CC, 2019*	500	___
1933372	BNSF EMD GP35 Diesel "2615," *CC, 2019*	500	___
1933373	BNSF non-powered EMD GP35 Diesel "2931," *2019*	300	___
1933381	Lycoming Valley EMD GP35 Diesel "5510," *CC, 2019*	500	___
1933382	Lycoming Valley EMD GP35 Diesel "5514," *CC, 2019*	500	___
1933391	PRR EMD GP35 Diesel "2298," *CC, 2019*	500	___
1933392	PRR EMD GP35 Diesel "2333," *CC, 2019*	500	___
1933393	PRR non-powered EMD GP35 Diesel "2356," *2019*	300	___
1933401	RF&P EMD GP35 Diesel "131," *CC, 2019*	500	___
1933402	RF&P EMD GP35 Diesel "134," *CC, 2019*	500	___
1933403	RF&P non-powered EMD GP35 Diesel "138," *2019*	300	___
1933411	Apache RR Alco C-420 Diesel "81," *CC, 2019*	500	___
1933412	Apache RR Alco C-420 Diesel "82," *CC, 2019*	500	___
1933413	Apache RR non-powered Alco C-420 Diesel "84," *2019*	300	___
1933421	D&H Alco C-420 Diesel "404," *CC, 2019*	500	___
1933422	D&H Alco C-420 Diesel "414," *CC, 2019*	500	___
1933423	D&H non-powered Alco C-420 Diesel "204," *2019*	300	___
1933430	D&M Alco C-420 Diesel "976," *CC, 2019*	500	___
1933441	Erie Mining Alco C-420 Diesel "7220," *CC, 2019*	500	___
1933442	Erie Mining non-powered Alco C-420 Diesel "7221," *2019*	300	___
1933451	L&HR Alco C-420 Diesel "21," *CC, 2019*	500	___
1933452	L&HR Alco C-420 Diesel "23," *CC, 2019*	500	___
1933453	L&HR non-powered Alco C-420 Diesel "21," *CC, 2019*	300	___
1933461	LIRR Alco C-420 Diesel "202," *CC, 2019*	500	___
1933462	LIRR Alco C-420 Diesel "218," *CC, 2019*	500	___
1933471	P&N Alco C-420 Diesel "2000," *CC, 2019*	500	___
1933472	P&N Alco C-420 Diesel "2001," *CC, 2019*	500	___
1933480	NYS&W Alco C-420 Diesel "2010," *CC, 2019*	500	___
1933490	Alco Demonstrator FA A-A Diesel Set, *CC, 2019*	900	___
1933498	Alco Demonstrator FB-2 Unit, *CC, 2019*	450	___
1933499	Alco Demonstrator FB-2 Unit w/RailSounds, *2019*	430	___
1933500	C&NW Alco FA A-A Diesel Set, *CC, 2019*	900	___
1933508	C&NW Alco FB-2 Unit, *CC, 2019*	450	___
1933509	C&NW Alco FB-2 Unit w/RailSounds, *2019*	430	___
1933510	CP Alco FA-2 A-A Diesel Set "4082/4083," *CC, 2019*	900	___

		Esc	Mint
___	**1933518** CP Alco FB-2 "4469," *CC, 2019*		450
___	**1933519** CP Alco FB-2 Unit w/RailSounds, *2019*		430
___	**1933520** LV Alco FA A-A Diesel Set, *CC, 2019*		900
___	**1933528** LV Alco FB-2 Unit, *CC, 2019*		450
___	**1933529** LV Alco FB-2 Unit w/RailSounds, *2019*		430
___	**1933530** MP Alco FA A-A Diesel Set, *CC, 2019*		900
___	**1933538** MP Alco FB-2 Unit, *CC, 2019*		450
___	**1933539** MP Alco FB-2 Unit w/RailSounds, *2019*		430
___	**1933540** NYC Alco FA A-A Diesel Set, *CC, 2019*		900
___	**1933548** NYC Alco FB-2 Unit, *CC, 2019*		450
___	**1933549** NYC Alco FB-2 Unit w/RailSounds, *2019*		430
___	**1933550** SP&S Alco FA A-A Diesel Set, *CC, 2019*		
___	**1933558** SP&S Alco FB-2 Unit, *CC, 2019*		
___	**1933559** SP&S Alco FB-2 Unit w/RailSounds, *2019*		
___	**1933561** LIRR Alco FA Cab Car "607," *CC, 2019*		430
___	**1933562** LIRR Alco FA Cab Car "609," *CC, 2019*		430
___	**1933563** LIRR Alco FA Cab Car "608," *CC, 2019*		430
___	**1933564** LIRR Alco FA Cab Car "610," *CC, 2019*		430
___	**1933571** Milwaukee Road GE Bi-Polar Electric "E-1," *CC, 2019*		1300
___	**1933572** Milwaukee Road GE Bi-Polar Electric "E-2," *CC, 2019*		1300
___	**1933573** Milwaukee Road GE Bi-Polar Electric "E-3," *CC, 2019*		1300
___	**1933574** Milwaukee Road GE Bi-Polar Electric "E-4," *CC, 2019*		1300
___	**1933575** Milwaukee Road GE Bi-Polar Electric "E-5," *CC, 2019*		1300
___	**1933580** GN B595, *2019*		1300
___	**1933590** NH GE Bi-Polar Electric "380," *CC, 2019*		1300
___	**1933600** NYC GE Bi-Polar Electric "300," *CC, 2019*		1300
___	**1933610** PRR GE Bi-Polar Electric "4501," *CC, 2019*		1300
___	**1933620** Polar Express GE Bi-Polar Electric "E-25," *CC, 2019*		1300
___	**1933630** NS GE C44-9W Diesel "8520," *CC, 2018*		550
___	**1934011** BNSF GE ET44AC Diesel "3738," LionChief Plus 2.0, *2019*		400
___	**1934012** BNSF GE ET44AC Diesel "3776," LionChief Plus 2.0, *2019*		400
___	**1934021** CSX GE ET44AC Diesel "3277," LionChief Plus 2.0, *2019*		400
___	**1934022** CSX GE ET44AC Diesel "3291," LionChief Plus 2.0, *2019*		400
___	**1934031** NS GE ET44AC Diesel "3600," LionChief Plus 2.0, *2019*		400
___	**1934032** NS GE ET44AC Diesel "3619," LionChief Plus 2.0, *2019*		400
___	**1934041** UP GE ET44AC Diesel "2645," LionChief Plus 2.0, *2019*		400
___	**1934042** UP GE ET44AC Diesel "2727," LionChief Plus 2.0, *2019*		400
___	**1934050** BN Alco RS-3 Diesel "4068," LionChief, *2019*		200
___	**1934060** CNJ Alco RS-3 Diesel "1552," LionChief, *2019*		200
___	**1934070** Delaware-Lackawanna Alco RS-3 Diesel "4103," LionChief, *2019*		200
___	**1934080** UP Alco RS-3 Diesel "1219," LionChief, *2019*		"200
___	**1934090** AT&SF EMD FT Diesel A-A Set "123/124," LionChief Plus 2.0, *2019*		550
___	**1934098** AT&SF EMD FT B Unit, LionChief Plus 2.0, *2019*		300
___	**1934100** GN EMD FT Diesel A-A Set "400/401," LionChief Plus 2.0, *2019*		550
___	**1934108** GN EMD FT B Unit, LionChief Plus 2.0, *2019*		300
___	**1934110** NYC EMD FT Diesel A-A Set "1603/1604," LionChief Plus 2.0, *2019*		550
___	**1934118** NYC EMD FT B Unit, LionChief Plus 2.0, *2019*		300
___	**1934120** Texas Special EMD FT Diesel A-A Set "219/220," LionChief Plus 2.0, *2019*		550
___	**1934128** Texas Special EMD FT B Unit, LionChief Plus 2.0, *2019*		300
___	**1935010** Area 51 Motorized Trackmobile "51," *CC, 2019*		350
___	**1935020** Bethlehem Steel Motorized Trackmobile "12," *CC, 2019*		350
___	**1935030** BN Motorized Trackmobile, *CC, 2019*		350
___	**1935040** Granite Run Quarries Motorized Trackmobile, *CC, 2019*		350

MODERN 1970-2021		Esc	Mint
1935050	Milwaukee Road Motorized Trackmobile, *CC, 2019*		350 ___
1935060	PP&L Motorized Trackmobile "16," *CC, 2019*		350 ___
1935070	AT&SF Motorized Trackmobile "8," *CC, 2019*		350 ___
1935080	SP Motorized Trackmobile "5," *CC, 2019*		350 ___
1935090	WWII U.S. War Bonds Trollery, *2019*		100 ___
1938010	Mickey Mouse Celebration True Original Boxcar, *2018*		85 ___
1938030	Well-Stocked Angela Trotta Thomas Boxcar, *2018*		85 ___
1938040	Jupiter Anniversary Boxcar, *2019*		85 ___
1938050	Southern Ry. 125th Anniversary Boxcar, *2019*		85 ___
1938060	Westinghouse Air Brake 150th Anniversary Boxcar, *2019*		85 ___
1938100	Pez Vintage Boxcar, *2019*		85 ___
1938110	Looney Tunes Duck Dodgers Boxcar, *2019*		90 ___
1938120	Looney Tunes Rabbit Season Boxcar, *2019*		90 ___
1938130	Looney Tunes Road Runner Boxcar, *2019*		90 ___
1938180	Martin Van Buren Presidential Boxcar, *2019*		70 ___
1938190	James Buchanan Presidential Boxcar, *2019*		70 ___
1938200	William McKinley Presidential Boxcar, *2019*		70 ___
1938210	WWII Kiss the Way Goodbye Boxcar, *2019*		85 ___
1938220	WWII Sherman Tank Boxcar, *2019*		85 ___
1938320	Christmas Caboose, *2019-20*		90 ___
1938240	WWII Liberty Ships Boxcar, *2019*		85 ___
1938260	Wings of Angels—Blonde Boxcar, *2019*		90 ___
1938270	Wings of Angels—Redhead Boxcar, *2019*		90 ___
1938280	Wings of Angels—Brunette Boxcar, *2019*		90 ___
1938290	Happy Birthday 2019 Boxcar, *2019*		95 ___
1938300	Merry Christmas 2019 Boxcar, *2019*		90 ___
1938310	Angela Trotta Thomas Christmas Boxcar, *2019*		90 ___
1938340	Happy Birthday Caboose, *2019-20*		90 ___
1938370	UP Anniversary Boxcar "199," *2019*		85 ___
1942170	UP Vision Challenger Boxcar 6-pack #1, *2018*		390 ___
1942180	UP Vision Challenger Boxcar 6-pack #2, *2018*		390 ___
1942190	UP Vision Challenger Boxcar 6-pack #3, *2018*		390 ___
1942200	UP Vision Challenger Boxcar 6-pack #4, *2018*		390 ___
1942210	UP Vision Challenger Express Boxcar 6-pack, *2018*		390 ___
2022010	Granite Run Quarry Steam Freight Set, LionChief Plus 2.0, *2019*		350 ___
2022020	Christmas Candies Steam Freight Set, LionChief Plus 2.0, *2019*		350 ___
2022030	Easter Eggspress Steam Freight Set, LionChief Plus 2.0, *2019*		350 ___
2022040	Manufacturers Railway Alco S-2 Diesel Freight Set, *CC, 2019*		800 ___
2022050	George H.W. Bush Funeral Diesel Passenger Train, *CC, 2019*		1200 ___
2022060	Pennsylvania Fast Freight Electric Freight Set, LionChief Plus 2.0, *2019*		700 ___
2022070	B&M E8 Diesel Passenger Set, *CC, 2020*		800 ___
2022080	Preamble Express Diesel Passenger Set, *CC, 2020*		800 ___
2022090	Polar Express Elf Steam Work Train Set, LionChief, *2020*		450 ___
2022100	Pennsylvania Train Master Diesell Freight Set, *CC, 2020*		900 ___
2022110	Central of New Jersey Red Baron SD40 Diesel Freight Set, *CC, 2020*		850 ___
2022120	Lionel 120th Deluxe LionChief Plus 2.0 F3 Diesel Freight Set, *CC, 2020*		1000 ___
2022130	SP Vision Stock Express Steam Freight Train Set, *CC, 2020*		2500 ___
2022140	North Pole Central Snowflake Limited Steam Freight Set, *CC, 2020*		1000 ___
2023010	Strasburg RR Steam Freight Set, LionChief , *2019-20*		370 ___
2023020	Shark Research & Rescue Diesel Freight Set, LionChief, *2019*		400 ___
2023030	Budweiser Delivery ET44 Diesel Freight Set, LionChief, *2020*		370 ___

	2023040	Disney Frozen 2 Steam Freight Set, LionChief, *2020*		400
	2023050	Area 51 ET44 Diesel Freight Set, LionChief, *2020*		430
	2023070	Lionel Junction North Pole Central Steam Freight Set, LionChief, *2020*		300
	2023080	Christmas Light Express Steam Freight Set, LionChief, *2020*		430
	2023090	Witherslack Hall Steam Passenger Set, LionChief, *2020*		400
	2023100	GE Tier 4 ET44 Diesel Freight Set, LionChief, *2020*		400
	2023110	Toy Story Steam Freight Set, LionChief, *2020*		400
	2023120	Lionel Lines LionChief Steam Freight Set, *2020*		300
	2023130	Star Trek Diesel Freight Set, LionChief, *2020*		450
	2023140	Polar Express Steam Passenger Set, LionChief, *2020*		400
	2023150	Alaska GP38 Diesel Freight Set, LionChief, *2020*		400
	2023160	Baldwin Locomotive Works Steam Freight Set, LionChief, *2020*		400
	2023170	Hogwarts Express Steam Passenger Set, LionChief, *2020*		400
	2025010	Lighted FasTrack 10" Straight, 4-pack, *2020*		60
	2025020	Lighted Fastrack O-36 Curve, 4-pack, *2020*		60
	2025050	Merry Christmas FasTrack Girder Bridge, *2020*		25
	2026010	Side Dump Car 4-pack, *2019*		160
	2026020	Christmas Side Dump Car 4-pack, *2019*		160
	2026030	Easter Eggspress Side Dump Car 4-pack, *2019*		160
	2026040	Ely Thomas Lumber Logging Caboose, "1," *2019*		45
	2026050	Safety First Logging Caboose, "3," *2019*		45
	2026061	AT&SF 40' Plug-Door Refrigerator Car, "14180," *2019*		90
	2026062	AT&SF 40' Plug-Door Refrigerator Car, "14193," *2019*		90
	2026071	BAR 40' Plug-Door Refrigerator Car, "7728," *2019*		90
	2026072	BAR 40' Plug-Door Refrigerator Car, "7777," *2019*		90
	2026081	GB&W 40' Plug-Door Refrigerator Car, "21002," *2019*		90
	2026082	GB&W 40' Plug-Door Refrigerator Car, "21038," *2019*		90
	2026091	PFE 40' Plug-Door Refrigerator Car, "18015," *2019*		90
	2026092	PFE 40' Plug-Door Refrigerator Car, "18118," *2019*		90
	2026101	Reading 40' Plug-Door Refrigerator Car, "272," *2019*		90
	2026102	Reading 40' Plug-Door Refrigerator Car, "278," *2019*		90
	2026111	Therm Ice 40' Plug-Door Refrigerator Car, "8907," *2019*		90
	2026112	Therm Ice 40' Plug-Door Refrigerator Car, "8910," *2019*		90
	2026120	AT&SF PS-1 Boxcar, "17819" w/FreightSounds, *2019*		135
	2026130	DT&I PS-1 Boxcar, "14253" w/FreightSounds, *2019*		135
	2026140	EL PS-1 Boxcar, "74210" w/FreightSounds, *2019*		135
	2026150	GN PS-1 Boxcar, "19038" w/FreightSounds, *2019*		135
	2026160	Illinois Terminal PS-1 Boxcar, "8427" w/FreightSounds, *2019*		135
	2026170	NYC PS-1 Boxcar, "163194" w/FreightSounds, *2019*		135
	2026180	PC PS-1 Boxcar, "253321" w/FreightSounds, *2019*		135
	2026190	UP PS-1 Boxcar, "125404" w/FreightSounds, *2019*		135
	2026200	B&O I-12 BW Caboose, "C2428," *2019*		110
	2026210	B&O I-12 BW Caboose, "C2406," *2019*		110
	2026220	B&O I-12 BW Caboose, "C2822," *2019*		110
	2026230	B&O I-12 BW Caboose, "C2457," *2019*		110
	2026240	Chessie System I-12 BW Caboose, "902440," *2019*		110
	2026250	Polar Express I-12 BW Caboose, "C2425," *2019*		110
	2026260	Anheuser Busch 8,000-Gallon 1-D Tank Car, "4274," *2019*		80
	2026270	Deep Rock 8,000-Gallon 1-D Tank Car, "6516," *2019*		80
	2026280	Everett Distilling 8,000-Gallon 1-D Tank Car, "41," *2019*		80
	2026290	Hercules Powder 8,000-Gallon 1-D Tank Car, "10673," *2019*		80
	2026300	Independence Energy 8,000-Gallon 1-D Tank Car, "1776," *2019*		80

2026310	Sinclair 8,000-Gallon 1-D Tank Car, "13103," *2019*	80	___
2026320	Amtrak Veterans 60' LED Flag Boxcar "70042," *2019*	120	___
2026330	I Love USA 60' LED Flag Boxcar, *2019*	120	___
2026340	KCS 60' LED Flag Boxcar "4006," *2019*	120	___
2026350	NS First Responders 60' LED Flag Boxcar "9-1-1," *2019*	120	___
2026360	NS Veterans 60' LED Flag Boxcar "6920," *2019*	120	___
2026370	UP B167, *2019*	120	___
2026380	UP Transcontinental 60' LED Flag Boxcar "150," *2019*	120	___
2026391	AT&SF 60' Boxcar "37639," *2019*	100	___
2026392	AT&SF 60' Boxcar "37719," *2019*	100	___
2026401	CP 60' Boxcar "205502," *2019*	100	___
2026402	CP 60' Boxcar "205525," *2019*	100	___
2026411	DT&I 60' Boxcar "25525," *2019*	100	___
2026412	DT&I 60' Boxcar "25528," *2019*	100	___
2026421	NYC 60' Boxcar "56451," *2019*	100	___
2026422	NYC 60' Boxcar "56516," *2019*	100	___
2026431	PRR 60' Boxcar "11789," *2019*	100	___
2026432	PRR 60' Boxcar "11813," *2019*	100	___
2026441	PC 60' Boxcar "274570," *2019*	100	___
2026442	PC 60' Boxcar "274584," *2019*	100	___
2026450	Chevrolet 60' Boxcar "26450," *2019*	100	___
2026460	Ford 60' Boxcar "26460," *2019*	100	___
2026470	Area 51 57' Smoking Mechanical Refrigerator Car w/ FreightSounds, *2020*	200	___
2026480	AT&SF 57' Smoking Mechanical Refrigerator Car w/FreightSounds, *2020*	200	___
2026490	BNSF 57' Smoking Mechanical Refrigerator Car w/FreightSounds, *2020*	200	___
2026500	Conrail 57' Smoking Mechanical Refrigerator Car w/FreightSounds, *2020*	200	___
2026510	Halloween Smoking 57' Mechanical Refrigerator Car, *2020*	200	___
2026520	PFE 57' Smoking Mechanical Refrigerator Car w/FreightSounds, *2020*	200	___
2026530	UP 57' Smoking Mechanical Refrigerator Car w/FreightSounds, *2020*	200	___
2026541	AT&SF "Beer Car" Insulated Boxcar "625355," *2020*	100	___
2026542	AT&SF "Beer Car" Insulated Boxcar "625380," *2020*	100	___
2026551	BN "Beer Car" Insulated Boxcar "3069," *2020*	100	___
2026552	BN "Beer Car" Insulated Boxcar "3116," *2020*	100	___
2026561	BNSF "Beer Car" Insulated Boxcar "782403" w/Graffiti, *2020*	110	___
2026562	BNSF "Beer Car" Insulated Boxcar "782425," *2020*	100	___
2026563	BNSF "Beer Car" Insulated Boxcar "782483," *2020*	100	___
2026571	Conrail "Beer Car" Insulated Boxcar "376045," *2020*	100	___
2026572	Conrail "Beer Car" Insulated Boxcar "376142," *2020*	100	___
2026581	Coors "Beer Car" Insulated Boxcar "24," *2020*	100	___
2026582	Coors "Beer Car" Insulated Boxcar "26," *2020*	100	___
2026591	Manufacturers Ry. "Beer Car" Insulated Boxcar "2520," *2020*	100	___
2026592	Manufacturers Ry. "Beer Car" Insulated Boxcar "2540," *2020*	100	___
2026601	SP "Beer Car" Insulated Boxcar "691783" w/Graffiti, *2020*	110	___
2026602	SP "Beer Car" Insulated Boxcar "691729," *2020*	100	___
2026603	SP "Beer Car" Insulated Boxcar "691745," *2020*	100	___
2026611	AT&SF 50' Flatcar "91156" w/20' Trailers, *2020*	120	___
2026612	AT&SF 50' Flatcar "91220" w/20' Trailers, *2020*	120	___
2026621	DT&I 50' Flatcar "911" w/20' Ford Trailers, *2020*	120	___
2026622	DT&I 50' Flatcar "924" w/20' Ford Trailers, *2020*	120	___

			Esc	Mint
____	**2026631**	PRR 50' Flatcar "469469" w/Mason Dixon Trailers, *2020*		120
____	**2026632**	PRR 50' Flatcar "469625" w/Mason Dixon Trailers, *2020*		120
____	**2026641**	Trailer Train 50' Flatcar "475231" w/Hennis Trailers, *2020*		120
____	**2026642**	Trailer Train 50' Flatcar "475293" w/Hennis Trailers, *2020*		120
____	**2026651**	UP 50' Flatcar "53085" w/Merchants Trailers, *2020*		120
____	**2026652**	UP 50' Flatcar "53091" w/Merchants Trailers, *2020*		120
____	**2026661**	North Pole Central 50' Flatcar "2024" w/20' Sled-Ex Trailers, *2020*		120
____	**2026662**	North Pole Central 50' Flatcar "2025" w/20' Sled-Ex Trailers, *2020*		120
____	**2026671**	Polar Express 50' Flatcar "122420" w/20' Trailers, *2020*		125
____	**2026672**	Polar Express 50' Flatcar "122520" w/20' Trailers, *2020*		125
____	**2026680**	Polar Express Elf Work Train, 4-pack, *2020*		200
____	**2026690**	Buffalo, Rochester & Pittsburgh 2-bay Hopper, 3-pack, *2020*		280
____	**2026700**	Blue Coal 2-bay Hopper, 3-pack, *2020*		280
____	**2026710**	NYO&W 2-bay Hopper, 3-pack, *2020*		280
____	**2026720**	Rutland 2-bay Hopper, 3-pack, *2020*		280
____	**2026730**	Waddell Coal 2-bay Hopper, *3-pack, 2020*		280
____	**2026741**	CB&Q Friendship Train PS-1 Boxcar "36262," *2020*		75
____	**2026742**	C&NW Friendship Train PS-1 Boxcar "143576," *2020*		75
____	**2026743**	L&N Friendship Train PS-1 Boxcar "16576," *2020*		75
____	**2026744**	NYC Friendship Train PS-1 Boxcar "161500," *2020*		75
____	**2026745**	SP Friendship Train PS-1 Boxcar "97994," *2020*		75
____	**2026746**	UP Friendship Train PS-1 Boxcar "187989," *2020*		75
____	**2026750**	Chateau Martin Wine Car "132," *2020*		100
____	**2026760**	Cloverland Dairy Milk Car "101," *2020*		100
____	**2026770**	D&RGW Milk Car "1612," *2020*		100
____	**2026780**	Frisco Milk Car "5009," *2020*		100
____	**2026790**	Reid Ice Cream Milk Car "103," *2020*		100
____	**2026800**	Scenic Citrus Milk Car "977," *2020*		100
____	**2026810**	Armour Vision Stockcar 3-pack w/Sound Car, *2020*		400
____	**2026820**	AT&SF Vision Stockcar 3-pack w/Sound Car, *2020*		400
____	**2026830**	CP Vision Stockcar 3-pack w/Sound Car, *2020*		400
____	**2026840**	CB&Q Vision Stockcar 3-pack w/Sound Car, *2020*		400
____	**2026850**	C&NW Vision Stockcar 3-pack w/Sound Car, *2020*		400
____	**2026860**	MKT Vision Stockcar 3-pack w/Sound Car, *2020*		400
____	**2026870**	PRR N5 Caboose "476998," *2020*		100
____	**2026880**	PRR N5 Caboose "477714," *2020*		100
____	**2026890**	PRR N5 Caboose "492418," *2020*		100
____	**2026900**	PC N5 Caboose "22838," *2020*		100
____	**2026910**	Lionel Lines NE Caboose "120," *2020*		115
____	**2026930**	NYC Wood Caboose "19020" w/CupolaCam, *2020*		190
____	**2026940**	NYC Safety Wood Caboose "18906" w/CupolaCam, *2020*		190
____	**2026950**	Ford 2-bay Hopper, 3-pack, *2020*		280
____	**2026960**	AT&SF Vision Refrigerator Car 3-pack, *2020*		350
____	**2026970**	PFE Vision Refrigerator Car 3-pack, *2020*		350
____	**2026980**	MDT Vision Refrigerator Car 3-pack, *2020*		350
____	**2026990**	PRR Vision Refrigerator Car 3-pack, *2020*		350
____	**2027011**	Christmas Disconnect Passenger Car, Baggage, *2019*		45
____	**2027012**	Christmas Disconnect Passenger Car, Coach, *2019*		45
____	**2027013**	Christmas Disconnect Passenger Car, Diner, *2019*		45
____	**2027014**	Christmas Disconnect Passenger Car, Sleeper, *2019*		45
____	**2027015**	Christmas Disconnect Passenger Car, Observation, *2019*		45
____	**2027021**	NYC Disconnect Passenger Car, Baggage, *2019*		45
____	**2027022**	NYC Disconnect Passenger Car, Coach, *2019*		45
____	**2027023**	NYC Disconnect Passenger Car, Diner, *2019*		45

		Esc	Mint
2027024	NYC Disconnect Passenger Car, Sleeper, *2019*		45 ___
2027025	NYC Disconnect Passenger Car, Observation, *2019*		45 ___
2027031	PRR Disconnect Passenger Car, Baggage, *2019*		45 ___
2027032	PRR Disconnect Passenger Car, Coach, *2019*		45 ___
2027033	PRR Disconnect Passenger Car, Diner, *2019*		45 ___
2027034	PRR Disconnect Passenger Car, Sleeper, *2019*		45 ___
2027035	PRR Disconnect Passenger Car, Observation, *2019*		45 ___
2027041	D&RGW Disconnect Passenger Car, Baggage , *2019*		45 ___
2027042	D&RGW Disconnect Passenger Car, Coach, *2019*		45 ___
2027043	D&RGW Disconnect Passenger Car, Diner, *2019*		45 ___
2027044	D&RGW Disconnect Passenger Car, Sleeper, *2019*		45 ___
2027045	D&RGW Disconnect Passenger Car, Observation, *2019*		45 ___
2027051	AT&SF Disconnect Passenger Car, Baggage , *2019*		45 ___
2027052	AT&SF Disconnect Passenger Car, Coach, *2019*		45 ___
2027053	AT&SF Disconnect Passenger Car, Diner, *2019*		45 ___
2027054	AT&SF Disconnect Passenger Car, Sleeper, *2019*		45 ___
2027055	AT&SF Disconnect Passenger Car, Observation, *2019*		45 ___
2027061	SP Disconnect Passenger Car, Baggage, *2019*		45 ___
2027062	SP Disconnect Passenger Car, Coach, *2019*		45 ___
2027063	SP Disconnect Passenger Car, Diner, *2019*		45 ___
2027064	SP Disconnect Passenger Car, Sleeper, *2019*		45 ___
2027065	SP Disconnect Passenger Car, Observation, *2019*		45 ___
2027070	AT&SF California Limited 18" Passenger Car 2-pack, *A, 2019*		400 ___
2027080	AT&SF California Limited 18" Passenger Car 2-pack, *B, 2019*		400 ___
2027090	AT&SF California Limited 18" Passenger Car 2-pack, *C, 2019*		400 ___
2027100	AT&SF California Limited 18" Diner "1406" w/StationSounds, *2019*		330 ___
2027110	AT&SF Shadow Line 18" Passenger Car 2-pack, *2019*		400 ___
2027120	Alaska RR 21" Passenger Car 4-pack, *2019*		720 ___
2027130	Alaska RR 21" Passenger Car 2-pack, *2019*		420 ___
2027140	Alaska RR 21" Diner "400" w/StationSounds, *2019*		330 ___
2027160	Alaska RR VistaVision Camera Dome Car "501," *2019*		330 ___
2027170	UP Challenger 21" Passenger Car Expansion 2-pack, *3, 2019*		360 ___
2027180	NS Executive Train 21" Passenger Car 4-pack, *2019*		770 ___
2027190	NS Executive Train 21" Passenger Car 2-pack, *2019*		360 ___
2027200	NS 21" Diner "Delaware" w/StationSounds, *2019*		340 ___
2027210	Philadelphia & Reading Observation, *2019-20*		85 ___
2027220	Ferdinand Magellan Observation, *2019*		85 ___
2027230	UP Excursion 21" Passenger Car Expansion 2-pack, *3, 2019*		360 ___
2027240	UP Excursion 21" Passenger Car Expansion 2-pack, *4, 2019*		360 ___
2027250	Amtrak VistaVision Dome Car "9463," *2019*		330 ___
2027260	UP Excursion VistaVision Dome Car "Colorado Eagle," *2019*		330 ___
2027270	UP Challenger VistaVision Dome Car "7005," *2019*		330 ___
2027280	Auto-Train VistaVision Dome Car "706," *2019*		330 ___
2027290	PRR VistaVision Dome Car "Catenary View," *2019*		330 ___
2027300	N&W VistaVision Dome Car "1613," *2019*		330 ___
2027310	Southern VistaVision Dome Car "1613," *2019*		330 ___
2027330	Friendship Train 18" Sleeper 2-pack, *2020*		400 ___
2027340	American Freedom Train 18" Passenger Car 2-pack, *1, 2020*		380 ___
2027350	American Freedom Train 18" Passenger Car 2-pack, *2, 2020*		380 ___
2027360	Chessie Steam Special Passenger Car 2-pack, *1, 2020*		450 ___
2027370	Chessie Steam Special Passenger Car 2-pack, *2, 2020*		450 ___
2027380	Chessie Steam Special Passenger Car 2-pack, *3, 2020*		450 ___
2027390	Chessie Steam Special Passenger Car 2-pack, *4, 2020*		450 ___
2027480	Polar Express 18" Hobo Passenger Car w/Snowy Roof, *2020*		220 ___

	2027400	SP Golden State 21" Passenger Car 4-pack, *2020*		730
	2027410	SP Golden State 21" Passenger Car 2-pack, *2020*		360
	2027420	SP Golden State 21" Diner w/StationSounds, *2020*		360
	2027430	Reading 18" Passsenger Car 2-pack, *1, 2020*		380
	2027440	Reading 18" Passsenger Car 2-pack, *2, 2020*		380
	2027450	Reading 18" Passsenger Car 2-pack, *3, 2020*		380
	2027460	B&M 18" Passenger Car 2-pack, *2020*		380
	2027470	Polar Express 18" Hobo Passenger Car w/Black Roof, *2020*		220
	2027490	PRR/AT&SF 21" Passsenger Car 2-pack, *2020*		400
	2027500	PRR/UP 21" Passsenger Car 2-pack, *2020*		400
	2027510	PRR/MP 21" Passsenger Car 2-pack, *2020*		400
	2027520	SP Lark 21" Passenger Car 4-pack, *2020*		730
	2027530	SP Lark 21" Passenger Car 2-pack, *2020*		360
	2027540	SP Lark 21" Diner w/StationSounds , *2020*		460
	2027550	SP Daylight 18" Heavyweight Passenger Car 2-pack, *A, 2020*		400
	2027560	SP Daylight 18" Heavyweight Passenger Car 2-pack, *B, 2020*		400
	2027570	SP Daylight 18" Heavyweight Passenger Car 2-pack, *C, 2020*		400
	2027580	UP 21" Baggage Car "Promontory," *2019*		180
	2027590	SP Penn-Golden State 21" Passenger Car 2-pack, *2020*		360
	2027600	PRR/Frisco 21" Passsenger Car 2-pack, *2020*		400
	2027610	SP Daylight 18" Heavyweight Diner w/StationSounds, *2020*		330
	2027620	Chessie Steam Special Dome Car w/StationSounds, *2020*		400
	2027630	Lionel Lines 21" VistaVision Dome Car "Chesterfield," *2020*		340
	2027640	SP Cities 21" VistaVision Dome Car "3601," *2020*		340
	2027650	SP Daylight VistaVision Dome Car, *2020*		340
	2027660	SP Golden State 21" VistaVision Dome Car, *2020*		340
	2027670	SP Lark 21" VistaVision Dome Car, *2020*		340
	2027680	GN 21" VistaVision Dome Car "1325," *2020*		340
	2027690	Lionel Lines Vision 21" Baggage "Madison," *2020*		350
	2027700	SP Vision Baggage Car, *2020*		350
	2027710	SP Vision Baggage Car "Daylight," *2020*		350
	2027720	SP Vision Baggage Car "Golden State," *2020*		350
	2027730	SP Vision Baggage Car "Lark," *2020*		350
	2027740	REA Vision Baggage Car , *2020*		350
	2027750	Lionel Lines 21" Passenger Car 4-pack, *2020*		730
	2027760	Lionel Lines 21" Diner "Mount Clemens" w/StationSounds , *2020*		330
	2027770	Milwaukee Road 21" VistaVision Dome Car "60," *2020*		340
	2027780	NYC 21" VistaVision Dome Car "Hudson Vista," *2020*		340
	2027790	NS 21" VistaVision Dome Car "50," *2020*		340
	2027800	Polar Express Skiing Hobo Observation w/Black Roof, *2020*		85
	2027810	Great Central Pullman Coach, *2020*		80
	2028010	George H.W. Bush Funeral Mint Car, *2019*		90
	2028020	Shark Aquarium Car "23020," *2019*		100
	2028030	PRR Flatcar w/Trailers "925030," *2019*		85
	2028040	PRR Walking Brakeman Car "24095," *2019*		100
	2028060	Ford Auto Rack "19032020," *2020*		85
	2028090	Finding Nemo Aquarium Car, *2020*		100
	2028100	Inside Out Memory Ball Transport Car, *2020*		90
	2028110	Polar Express Elf Bobbing Car, *2020*		85
	2028120	Polar Express Hot Cocoa Car, *2020*		180
	2028130	Olaf's Personal Flurry 1-D Tank Car, *2020*		80
	2028150	Monster Containment Car, *2020*		80
	2028160	Jack O'Lantern Flatcar, *2020*		80
	2028170	Thomas & Friends Nia Boxcar, *2020*		75

		Esc	Mint
2028180	Thomas & Friends Rebecca Boxcar, *2020*		75 ___
2028190	Thomas & Friends Gordon Boxcar, *2020*		75 ___
2028200	Christmas Boxcar 2020, *2020*		65 ___
2028210	Christmas Music Boxcar 2020, *2020*		80 ___
2028220	Anheuser Busch Brewing Refrigerator Car, *2020*		80 ___
2028230	Enjoy Budweiser Refrigerator Car, *2020*		80 ___
2028240	Anheuser Busch Cold Storage Car, *2020*		90 ___
2028250	Miller High Life Woodside Refrigerator Car, *2020*		80 ___
2028260	Coors Banquet Woodside Refrigerator Car, *2020*		80 ___
2028270	Batman vs. The Joker Duel Car, *2020*		85 ___
2028280	Batman Shark Repellent Unibody 1-D Tank Car, *2020*		75 ___
2028290	Batman Hi-Cube Boxcar, *2020*		80 ___
2028300	Christmas Light Express Boxcar "84746," *2020*		90 ___
2028310	Best of Lionel Milk Car, *2020*		180 ___
2028320	Alien Radioactive Flatcar, *2020*		85 ___
2028340	Angela Trotta Thomas Gondola w/Presents and Trees, *2020*		80 ___
2028350	Angela Trotta Thomas Christmas Boxcar, *2020*		75 ___
2028360	Mickey & Friends Christmas 1-D Tank Car, *2020*		70 ___
2028380	John Deere Flatcar "28380" w/3 Tractors, *2020*		95 ___
2028410	National Lampoon's Christmas Vacation 30th Anniversary Lighted Boxcar, *2020*		90 ___
2028430	Thomas & Friends 75th Birthday Music Car, *2020*		80 ___
2028440	A Christmas Story Leg Lamp Boxcar, *2020*		75 ___
2028450	Angela Trotta Thomas Christmas Hopper, *2020*		65 ___
2028460	Winter Wonderland Wintry Mix 1-D Tank Car, *2020*		80 ___
2028470	Polar Express Present Mint Car, *2020*		90 ___
2028480	Angela Trotta Thomas 120th Anniversary Boxcar, *2020*		75 ___
2028500	Lionel Ale 1-D Tank Car, *2020*		75 ___
2028510	Thomas Kinkade Santa's Special Delivery Boxcar "28510," *2020*		75 ___
2028520	Romulan Ale 1-D Tank Car, *2020*		80 ___
2028530	Tribble Transport Car, *2020*		80 ___
2028540	Captain Kirk Boxcar, *2020*		75 ___
2028550	Captain Picard Boxcar, *2020*		75 ___
2028570	Pizza Planet Aquarium Car, *2020*		100 ___
2029010	85th Anniversary Gateman, *2020*		110 ___
2029020	Bluetooth Speaker Bandstand, *2020*		275 ___
2029030	Next Stop, Santa Passenger Station, *2020*		100 ___
2029040	End of the Line Passenger Station, *2020*		100 ___
2029050	Polar Express Passsenger Station, *2020*		110 ___
2029060	Chuga Chuga Brew Thru Bar, *2020*		90 ___
2029160	J Tower Switch Tower, *2020*		80 ___
2029170	Halloween Freight Station, *2020*		125 ___
2029180	Christmas Operating Freight Station, *2020*		125 ___
2029200	Area 51 Search Tower, *2020*		100 ___
2029210	Santa Tracker Command Tower, *2020*		100 ___
2029220	Roasted Chestnuts Retreat, *2020*		125 ___
2029230	Taco Stand, *2020*		125 ___
2029240	Fake News Stand, *2020*		125 ___
2029250	Strasburg RR Groffs Grove Pep Platform , *2019*		45 ___
2029260	Strasburg RR East Strasburg Station, *2020*		100 ___
2029270	Lionelville Freight Station, *2020*		125 ___
2029280	Area 1 Souvenir Stand, *2020*		125 ___
2030010	Strasburg RR Cherry Hill Station, *2020*		20 ___
2030050	Stars & Stripes Billboard 3-pack, *2019-20*		20 ___

			Esc	Mint
___	2030060	Fun with Puns Billboard 3-pack, *2019*		20
___	2030070	Strasburg RR Billboard 3-pack, *2020*		20
___	2030130	Crossing Shanty, *2020*		20
___	2030140	Polar Express Elf Warming Shack 3 pack, *2020*		60
___	2030150	Polar Express Barrel Shed, *2020*		25
___	2030160	Winter Wonderland Barrel Shed, *2020*		25
___	2030170	Anheuser Busch Barrel Shed, *2020*		25
___	2030180	City Park People 6-pack, *2020*		23
___	2030190	Street People 6-pack, *2020*		23
___	2030200	Walking Figures 6-pack, *2020*		23
___	2030210	City People 6-pack, *2020*		23
___	2030220	Highway Lamp Single 3-pack, *2020*		27
___	2030230	Highway Lamp Double 2-pack, *2020*		27
___	2030240	Construction Signs 5-pack, *2020*		8
___	2030250	Halloween Signs 5-pack, *2020*		8
___	2030260	Christmas Signs 5-pack, *2020*		8
___	2030270	Santa's Elves Houses 3-pack, *2020*		60
___	2031010	B&A 4-6-6T "400," *CC, 2019*		1100
___	2031020	NYC 4-6-6T "1297," *CC, 2019*		1100
___	2031030	CN 4-6-6T "51," *CC, 2019*		1100
___	2031040	CNJ 4-6-6T "231," *CC, 2019*		1100
___	2031050	DL&W 4-6-6T "428," *CC, 2019*		1100
___	2031060	IC 4-6-6T "205," *CC, 2019*		1100
___	2031070	NH 4-6-6T "1850,"*CC, 2019*		1100
___	2031080	US Army Transportation Corps 4-6-6T "1945," *CC, 2019*		1100
___	2031090	B&O 2-8-8-4 EM-1 "7609," *CC, 2019*		1700
___	2031100	B&O 2-8-8-4 EM-1 "7600," *CC, 2019*		1700
___	2031110	D&RGW 2-8-8-4 EM-1 "224," *CC, 2019*		1700
___	2031120	DM&IR 2-8-8-4 EM-1 "220," *CC, 2019*		1700
___	2031130	NP 2-8-8-4 EM-1 "5011," *CC, 2019*		1700
___	2031140	UP 2-8-8-4 EM-1 "4050," *CC, 2019*		1700
___	2031150	WM 2-8-8-4 EM-1 "1213," *CC, 2019*		1700
___	2031160	AT&SF 4-8-4 Northern "3751," *CC, 2019*		1600
___	2031170	AT&SF 4-8-4 Northern "3759," *CC, 2019*		1600
___	2031180	AT&SF 4-8-4 Northern "3757," *CC, 2019*		1600
___	2031190	AT&SF 4-8-4 Northern "3765," *CC, 2019*		1600
___	2031200	ACL 4-8-4S Northern "1800," *CC, 2019*		1600
___	2031210	Rock Island 4-8-4S Northern "5100," *CC, 2019*		1600
___	2031220	D&RGW 4-8-4S Northern "1802," *CC, 2019*		1600
___	2031230	MP 4-8-4S Northern "2202," *CC, 2019*		1600
___	2031240	Frisco 4-8-4S Northern "4500," *CC, 2019*		1600
___	2031250	Frisco 4-8-4S Northern "4524," *CC, 2019*		1600
___	2031261	UP 4-8-8-4 Big Boy "4014," Excursion Version, *CC, 2019*		2200
___	2031262	UP 4-8-8-4 Big Boy "4005," *CC, 2019*		2200
___	2031263	UP 4-8-8-4 Big Boy "4012," Greyhouse, *CC, 2019*		2200
___	2031271	Reading 4-8-4 T1 "2107," *CC, 2020*		1700
___	2031272	Reading 4-8-4 T1 "2111," *CC, 2020*		1700
___	2031281	Reading 4-8-4 T1 Rambles "2100," *CC, 2020*		1700
___	2031282	Reading 4-8-4 T1 Rambles "2101," *CC, 2020*		1700
___	2031290	Reading, Blue Mountain & Northern 4-8-4 T1 "2102," *CC, 2020*		1700
___	2031300	Reading, Blue Mountain & Northern 4-8-4 T1 We The People "2102," *CC, 2020*		1700
___	2031310	Conrail 4-8-4 T1 "2101," *CC, 2020*		1700
___	2031320	American Freedom Train Vision 4-8-4 T1 "1," *CC, 2020*		1700

		Esc	Mint
2031330	PRR B6sb 0-6-0 "525," CC, 2020		700 ___
2031340	PRR B6sb 0-6-0 "660," CC, 2020		700 ___
2031351	PRR B6sb 0-6-0 "711," CC, 2020		700 ___
2031352	PRR B6sb 0-6-0 1644," CC, 2020		700 ___
2031360	AT&SF B6sb 0-6-0 "2101," CC, 2020		700 ___
2031370	Bethlehem Steel B6sb 0-6-0 "1904," CC, 2020		700 ___
2031380	Milwaukee Road B6sb 0-6-0 "1534," CC, 2020		700 ___
2031390	GN B6sb 0-6-0 "90," CC, 2020		700 ___
2031400	Lionel Lines Vision 4-8-4 GS-4 "120," CC, 2020		2000 ___
2031411	SP Vision 4-8-4 GS-1 Brass Hybrid "4470," CC, 2020		2200 ___
2031412	SP Vision 4-8-4 GS-1 Brass Hybrid "4471," CC, 2020		2200 ___
2031421	SP Vision 4-8-4 GS-1 Brass Hybrid "708," CC, 2020		2200 ___
2031422	SP Vision 4-8-4 GS-1 Brass Hybrid "4403," CC, 2020		2200 ___
2031430	Vision 4-8-4 GS-1 Brass Hybrid Pilot "9999," CC, 2020		2200 ___
2031440	SP Vision 4-8-4 GS-2 Black "4410," CC, 2020		2000 ___
2031450	SP Vision 4-8-4 GS-2 Black "4411," CC, 2020		2000 ___
2031460	SP Vision 4-8-4 GS-2 Daylight "4412," CC, 2020		2000 ___
2031470	SP Vision 4-8-4 GS-2 Lark "4414," CC, 2020		2000 ___
2031480	SP Vision 4-8-4 GS-3 Daylight "4416," CC, 2020		2000 ___
2031500	SP Vision 4-8-4 GS-3 Daylight "4423," CC, 2020		2000 ___
2031510	SP Vision 4-8-4 GS-3 Golden State "4428," CC, 2020		2000 ___
2031520	SP Lines Vision 4-8-4 GS-4 Daylight "4449," CC, 2020		2000 ___
2031530	SP Vision 4-8-4 GS-4 Daylight "4449," CC, 2020		2000 ___
2031540	American Freedom Train Vision 4-8-4 GS-4 "4449," CC, 2020		2000 ___
2031550	BNSF Vision 4-8-4 GS-4 "4449," CC, 2020		2000 ___
2031560	SP Vision 4-8-4 GS-4 Daylight "4439," CC, 2020		2000 ___
2031570	SP Lines Vision 4-8-4 GS-5 Daylight "4458," CC, 2020		2000 ___
2031580	SP Lines Vision 4-8-4 GS-5 Daylight "4459," CC, 2020		2000 ___
2031590	SP Lines Vision 4-8-4 GS-6 "4460," CC, 2020		2000 ___
2031600	SP Vision 4-8-4 GS-6 "4462," CC, 2020		2000 ___
2031610	SP Vision 4-8-4 GS-6 "4467," CC, 2020		2000 ___
2031620	WP Vision 4-8-4 GS-6 "481," CC, 2020		2000 ___
2031630	WP Vision 4-8-4 GS-6 "486," CC, 2020		2000 ___
2031640	Chessie Steam Special Vision GS-4 "4449," CC, 2020		2000 ___
2031650	Chessie Steam Special Auxiliary Water Tender w/RailSounds, CC, 2020		350 ___
2031660	Conrail Auxiliary Water Tender w/RailSounds, CC, 2020		350 ___
2031671	Freedom Train 1975 Auxiliary Water Tender w/RailSounds, CC, 2020		350 ___
2031672	Freedom Train 1976 Auxiliary Water Tender w/RailSounds, CC, 2020		350 ___
2031673	American Freedom Train Auxiliary Water Tender "4449" w/ RailSounds, CC, 2020		350 ___
2031680	SP Daylight Auxiliary Water Tender w/RailSounds, CC, 2020		350 ___
2031690	Black Auxiliary Water Tender w/RailSounds, CC, 2020		350 ___
2031700	UP 4-8-8-4 Big Boy "4014" First Run Edition, CC, 2019		2200 ___
2032010	AT&SF 0-6-0T "95" LionChief Plus 2.0, 2019-20		250 ___
2032020	Brooklyn Eastern District Terminal 0-6-0T "15" LionChief Plus 2.0, 2019-20		250 ___
2032030	Bethlehem Steel 0-6-0T "76" LionChief Plus 2.0, 2019-20		250 ___
2032040	D&RGW 0-6-0T "27" LionChief Plus 2.0, 2019-20		250 ___
2032050	PRR 0-6-0T "2295" LionChief Plus 2.0, 2019-20		250 ___
2032100	C&O Lionmaster 2-6-6-6 Allegheny "1601," CC, 2020		1100 ___
2032110	C&O Lionmaster 2-6-6-6 Allegheny "1607," CC, 2020		1100 ___
2032120	C&O Lionmaster 2-6-6-6 Allegheny "1611," CC, 2020		1100 ___

	MODERN 1970-2021	Esc	Mint
___	**2032130** Virginian Lionmaster 2-6-6-6 Allegheny "906," *CC, 2020*		1100
___	**2032200** AT&SF 0-8-0 "729" LionChief, *2020*		220
___	**2032210** GN 0-8-0 "831" LionChief, *2020*		220
___	**2032220** Reading 0-8-0 "1493" LionChief, *2020*		220
___	**2032230** SP 0-8-0 "1849" LionChief, *2020*		220
___	**2033011** B&LE SD38 Diesel "861," *CC, 2019*		600
___	**2033012** B&LE SD38 Diesel "863," *CC, 2019*		600
___	**2033021** Conrail SD38 Diesel "6929," *CC, 2019*		600
___	**2033022** Conrail SD38 Diesel "6957," *CC, 2019*		600
___	**2033031** CSX SD38 Diesel "2461," *CC, 2019*		600
___	**2033032** CSX SD38 Diesel "2463," *CC, 2019*		600
___	**2033041** GTW SD38 Diesel "6252," *CC, 2019*		600
___	**2033042** GTW SD38 Diesel "6254," *CC, 2019*		600
___	**2033051** NS SD38 Diesel "3806," *CC, 2019*		600
___	**2033052** NS SD38 Diesel "3808," *CC, 2019*		600
___	**2033061** Rail Logix SD38 Diesel "2001," *CC, 2019*		600
___	**2033062** Rail Logix SD38 Diesel "2002," *CC, 2019*		600
___	**2033070** AT&SF Alco S-4 Diesel Switcher "1527," *CC, 2019*		500
___	**2033080** EL Alco S-4 Diesel Switcher "513," *CC, 2019*		500
___	**2033090** Ford Alco S-2 Diesel Switcher "10013," *CC, 2019*		500
___	**2033100** Morristown & Erie Alco S-2 Diesel Switcher "14," *CC, 2019*		500
___	**2033110** NYS&W Alco S-2 Diesel Switcher "206," *CC, 2019*		500
___	**2033120** Nickel Plate Road Alco S-4 Diesel Switcher "79," *CC, 2019*		500
___	**2033130** NP Alco S-4 Diesel Switcher "717," *CC, 2019*		500
___	**2033140** Northern Pacific Terminal Alco S-2 Diesel Switcher "40," *CC, 2019*		500
___	**2033150** Portland Terminal Alco S-2 Diesel Switcher "1001," *CC, 2019*		500
___	**2033160** SP Alco S-4 Diesel Switcher "1820," *CC, 2019*		500
___	**2033170** Youngstown Sheet & Tube Alco S-2 Diesel Switcher "1001," *CC, 2019*		500
___	**2033181** CITX SD70M-2 Diesel "140," *CC, 2019*		600
___	**2033182** CITX SD70M-2 Diesel "141," *CC, 2019*		600
___	**2033183** CITX SD70M-2 Diesel "142" unpowered, *2019*		300
___	**2033191** EMD SD70M-2 Diesel "74," *CC, 2019*		600
___	**2033192** EMD SD70M-2 Diesel "75," *CC, 2019*		600
___	**2033193** EMD SD70M-2 Diesel "76" unpowered, *2019*		300
___	**2033201** FEC SD70M-2 Diesel "104," *CC, 2019*		600
___	**2033202** FEC SD70M-2 Diesel "105," *CC, 2019*		600
___	**2033203** FEC SD70M-2 Diesel "106" unpowered, *2019*		300
___	**2033211** NS SD70M-2 Diesel "2717," *CC, 2019*		600
___	**2033212** NS SD70M-2 Diesel "2731," *CC, 2019*		600
___	**2033213** NS SD70M-2 Diesel "2778" unpowered, *2019*		300
___	**2033221** P&W SD70M-2 Diesel "4301," *CC, 2019*		600
___	**2033222** P&W SD70M-2 Diesel "4302," *CC, 2019*		600
___	**2033231** Vermont Ry. SD70M-2 Diesel "431," *CC, 2019*		600
___	**2033232** Vermont Ry. SD70M-2 Diesel "432," *CC, 2019*		600
___	**2033240** Alaska RR F7 A-A set, *CC, 2019*		900
___	**2033248** Alaska RR F7B Diesel "1503," *CC, 2019*		450
___	**2033249** Alaska RR F7B SuperBass Diesel "1517," *CC, 2019*		440
___	**2033250** BN F7 Diesel A-A set, *CC, 2019*		900
___	**2033258** BN F7B Diesel "761," *CC, 2019*		450
___	**2033259** BN F7B SuperBass Diesel "741," *CC, 2019*		440
___	**2033260** CGW F7 Diesel A-A set, *CC, 2019*		900
___	**2033268** CGW F7B Diesel "114-B," *CC, 2019*		450
___	**2033269** CGW F7B SuperBass Diesel "114-0," *CC, 2019*		440

| --- | --- | --- | --- |
2033270	D&RGW F7 Diesel A-A set, *CC, 2019*		900 ___
2033278	D&RGW F7B Diesel "5652," *CC, 2019*		450 ___
2033279	D&RGW F7B SuperBass Diesel "5653," *CC, 2019*		440 ___
2033280	NS F9 Diesel A-A set, *CC, 2019*		900 ___
2033288	NS F7B Diesel "4275," *CC, 2019*		450 ___
2033289	NS F7B SuperBass Diesel "4276," *CC, 2019*		440 ___
2033290	PC F7 Diesel A-A set, *CC, 2019*		900 ___
2033298	PC F7B Diesel "3460," *CC, 2019*		450 ___
2033299	PC F7B SuperBass Diesel "712," *CC, 2019*		440 ___
2033300	Cotton Belt F7 Diesel A-A set, *CC, 2019*		900 ___
2033308	Cotton Belt F7B Diesel "926," *CC, 2019*		450 ___
2033309	Cotton Belt F7B SuperBass Diesel "928," *CC, 2019*		440 ___
2033310	UP SD70ACe Diesel "4141," *CC , 2019*		600 ___
2033319	UP SD70ACe Diesel "4141" unpowered, *2019*		300 ___
2033321	UP SD70AH Diesel "9096," *CC , 2019*		600 ___
2033322	UP SD70AH Diesel "9069," *CC , 2019*		600 ___
2033323	UP SD70AH Diesel "9088," *CC , 2019*		600 ___
2033330	KCS SD70ACe Diesel "4006," *CC , 2019*		600 ___
2033340	Amtrak E8 AA Diesel Set "4316/249," *CC, 2020*		1000 ___
2033350	DL&W E8 AA Diesel Set "810/811," *CC, 2020*		1000 ___
2033360	NYC E8 AA Diesel Set "4038/4041," *CC, 2020*		1000 ___
2033370	PRR E8 AA Diesel Set "5711/5809," *CC, 2020*		1000 ___
2033380	Southern E8 AA Diesel Set "6901/6914," *CC, 2020*		1000 ___
2033390	Frisco E8 AA Diesel Set "2003/2006," *CC, 2020*		1000 ___
2033401	DL&W Train Master Diesel "853," *CC, 2020*		550 ___
2033402	DL&W Train Master Diesel "854," *CC, 2020*		550 ___
2033411	FM Demonstrator Train Master Diesel "TM-3," *CC, 2020*		550 ___
2033412	FM Demonstrator Train Master Diesel "TM-4," *CC, 2020*		550 ___
2033420	PRR Train Master Diesel "8703," *CC, 2020*		550 ___
2033431	Southern Train Master Diesel "6301," *CC, 2020*		550 ___
2033432	Southern Train Master Diesel "6302," *CC, 2020*		550 ___
2033441	SP Train Master Diesel "4800," *CC, 2020*		550 ___
2033442	SP Train Master Diesel "4812," *CC, 2020*		550 ___
2033451	Virginian Train Master Diesel "55," *CC, 2020*		550 ___
2033452	Virginian Train Master Diesel "60," *CC, 2020*		550 ___
2033461	CP SD40 Diesel "740," *CC, 2020*		550 ___
2033462	CP SD40 Diesel "752," *CC, 2020*		550 ___
2033471	CNJ SD40 Diesel "3064," *CC, 2020*		550 ___
2033472	CNJ SD40 Diesel "3069," *CC, 2020*		550 ___
2033481	C&O SD40 Diesel "7452," *CC, 2020*		550 ___
2033482	C&O SD40 Diesel "7464," *CC, 2020*		550 ___
2033490	CSX SD40 Diesel "4617," *CC, 2020*		550 ___
2033501	C&NW SD40 Diesel "867," *CC, 2020*		550 ___
2033502	C&NW SD40 Diesel "876," *CC, 2020*		550 ___
2033520	BNSF GE ES44AC Diesel "5815," *CC, 2020*		550 ___
2033530	CSX GE ES44AC Diesel "3010," *CC, 2020*		550 ___
2033539	CSX GE ES44AC Diesel "3010" unpowered, *2020*		350 ___
2033541	KCS de Mexico GE ES44AC Diesel "4748," *CC, 2020*		550 ___
2033542	KCS de Mexico GE ES44AC Diesel "4762," *CC, 2020*		550 ___
2033549	KCS de Mexico GE ES44AC Diesel "4764" unpowered, *2020*		350 ___
2033551	SVTX GE ES44AC Diesel "1912," *CC, 2020*		550 ___
2033552	SVTX GE ES44AC Diesel "1982," *CC, 2020*		550 ___
2033559	SVTX GE ES44AC Diesel "1986" unpowered, *2020*		350 ___
2033560	UP GE ES44AC Diesel "8003," *CC, 2020*		550 ___

| --- | --- | --- | --- |
___	2033571	Christmas ES44AC Diesel "1224," *CC*, 2020	550
___	2033572	Christmas ES44AC Diesel "1225," *CC*, 2020	550
___	2033590	UP SD70ACe Diesel "8937," *CC*, 2019	600
___	2033600	UP SD70AH Diesel "1111," *CC*, 2019	600
___	2033610	CSX First Responders GE ES44AC Diesel "911," *CC*, 2020	550
___	2033619	CSX First Responders GE ES44AC Diesel "911" unpowered, *2020*	350
___	2033620	CSX Veterans GE ES44AC Diesel "1776," *CC*, 2020	550
___	2033629	CSX Veterans GE ES44AC Diesel "1776" unpowered, *2020*	350
___	2033630	CSX GE ES44AC Diesel "3194," *CC*, 2020	550
___	2033639	CSX GE ES44AC Diesel "3194" unpowered, *2020*	350
___	2034010	PRR GG1 Electric "4935" LionChief Plus 2.0, *2019*	500
___	2034020	PRR GG1 Electric "4877" LionChief Plus 2.0, *2019*	500
___	2034030	PRR GG1 Electric "4872" LionChief Plus 2.0, *2019*	500
___	2034040	PRR GG1 Electric "4890" LionChief Plus 2.0, *2019*	500
___	2034050	PRR GG1 Electric "4916" LionChief Plus 2.0, *2019*	500
___	2034061	Conrail LionMaster SD80MAC Diesel "4100" LionChief Plus 2.0, *2019*	450
___	2034062	Conrail LionMaster SD80MAC Diesel "4102" LionChief Plus 2.0, *2019*	450
___	2034071	CSX LionMaster SD80MAC Diesel "4592" LionChief Plus 2.0, *2019*	450
___	2034072	CSX LionMaster SD80MAC Diesel "4594" LionChief Plus 2.0, *2019*	450
___	2034081	NS LionMaster SD80MAC Diesel "7217" LionChief Plus 2.0, *2019*	450
___	2034082	NS LionMaster SD80MAC Diesel "7219" LionChief Plus 2.0, *2019*	450
___	2034091	UP LionMaster SD90MAC Diesel "8025" LionChief Plus 2.0, *2019*	450
___	2034092	UP LionMaster SD90MAC Diesel, *"8026," LionChief Plus 2.0, 2019*	450
___	2034100	NYC F3 AA Diesel Set "1620/1621" LionChief Plus 2.0, *2020*	700
___	2034110	PRR F3 AA Diesel Set "9542/9542A" LionChief Plus 2.0, *2020*	700
___	2034120	UP F3 AA Diesel Set "1445/1455" LionChief Plus 2.0, *2020*	700
___	2034130	SP F3 AA Diesel Set "6148/6157" LionChief Plus 2.0, *2020*	700
___	2034180	Conrail GP38 Diesel "7670" LionChief, *2020*	220
___	2034190	BN GP38 Diesel "7670" LionChief, *2020*	220
___	2034190	SP Vision 4-8-4 GS-3 LAUPT Special "4426," *CC*, 2020	2000
___	2034200	Chessie System GP38 Diesel "3847" LionChief, *2020*	220
___	2034210	North Pole Central GP38 Diesel "1224" LionChief, *2020*	220
___	2034220	Lightning McQueen GP38 Diesel "95" LionChief, *2020*	220
___	2035010	ELX Trolley, *2020*	100
___	2035020	Fort Collins Trolley, *2020*	100
___	2035030	Toy Story Handcar, *2020*	100
___	2035050	Lionelville Trolley, *2020*	100
___	2038010	B&O 190th Anniversary Boxcar, *2019*	85
___	2038020	D&RGW 150th Anniversary Boxcar, *2019*	85
___	2038030	Casey Jones 120th Anniversary MUSA Boxcar, *2020*	85
___	2038040	BN 50th Anniversary MUSA Boxcar, *2020*	85
___	2038050	George H.W. Bush Boxcar, *2019-20*	80
___	2038060	William Henry Harrison Presidential Boxcar, *2020*	80
___	2038070	James Garfield Presidential Boxcar, *2020*	80
___	2038080	Battlefield Honor—Berlin Wall Boxcar, *2020*	90
___	2038090	Battlefield Honor—Candy Bombers Boxcar, *2020*	90
___	2038110	Angela Trotta Thomas Well Stocked Shelves Boxcar Middle Shelf, *2019*	85
___	2038120	2020 Happy Birthday Boxcar, *2020*	90
___	2038130	Happy Anniversary Boxcar, *2020*	90
___	2038140	2020 Merry Christmas Boxcar, *2020*	90
___	2038150	Foghorn Leghorn Crockett-Doodle Do Boxcar, *2020*	90

		Esc	Mint
2038160	Picnic With Porky Pig Boxcar, *2020*		90 ___
2038170	Robin Hood Daffy Duck Boxcar, *2020*		90 ___
2038200	Wings of Angels—Jessamyne Rose Boxcar, *2020*		90 ___
2038210	Wings of Angels—Ashten Goodenough Boxcar, *2020*		90 ___
2038220	Wings of Angels—Jessie Ray Boxcar, *2020*		90 ___
2043011	BN 50' Boxcar "217552" (std O), *2020*		45 ___
2043012	BN 50' Boxcar "217618" (std O), *2020*		45 ___
2043013	BN 50' Boxcar "217685" (std O), *2020*		45 ___
2043014	BN 50' Boxcar "217741" (std O), *2020*		45 ___
2043021	Golden West 50' Boxcar "767130" (std O), *2020*		45 ___
2043022	Golden West 50' Boxcar "767150" (std O), *2020*		45 ___
2043023	Golden West 50' Boxcar "767167" (std O), *2020*		45 ___
2043024	Golden West 50' Boxcar "767193" (std O), *2020*		45 ___
2043031	KCS 50' Boxcar "117731" (std O), *2020*		45 ___
2043032	KCS 50' Boxcar "117756" (std O), *2020*		45 ___
2043033	KCS 50' Boxcar "117782" (std O), *2020*		45 ___
2043034	KCS 50' Boxcar "117790" (std O), *2020*		45 ___
2043041	Railbox 50' Boxcar "10051" (std O), *2020*		45 ___
2043042	Railbox 50' Boxcar "10189" (std O), *2020*		45 ___
2043043	Railbox 50' Boxcar "10524" (std O), *2020*		45 ___
2043044	Railbox 50' Boxcar "10582" (std O), *2020*		45 ___
2043051	Milwaukee Road Centerbeam Flatcar "6300" (std O), *2020*		45 ___
2043052	Milwaukee Road Centerbeam Flatcar "6318" (std O), *2020*		45 ___
2043053	Milwaukee Road Centerbeam Flatcar "6336" (std O), *2020*		45 ___
2043054	Milwaukee Road Centerbeam Flatcar "6354" (std O), *2020*		45 ___
2043061	Trailer Train Centerbeam Flatcar "83729" (std O), *2020*		45 ___
2043062	Trailer Train Centerbeam Flatcar "83741" (std O), *2020*		45 ___
2043063	Trailer Train Centerbeam Flatcar "83754" (std O), *2020*		45 ___
2043064	Trailer Train Centerbeam Flatcar "83773" (std O), *2020*		45 ___
2043071	UP Centerbeam Flatcar "217015" (std O), *2020*		45 ___
2043072	UP Centerbeam Flatcar "217031" (std O), *2020*		45 ___
2043073	UP Centerbeam Flatcar "217047" (std O), *2020*		45 ___
2043074	UP Centerbeam Flatcar "217063" (std O), *2020*		45 ___
2043081	WP Centerbeam Flatcar "1404" (std O), *2020*		45 ___
2043082	WP Centerbeam Flatcar "1412" (std O), *2020*		45 ___
2043083	WP Centerbeam Flatcar "1420" (std O), *2020*		45 ___
2043084	WP Centerbeam Flatcar "1428" (std O), *2020*		45 ___
2043091	BNSF Bulkhead Flatcar "545475" (std O), *2020*		45 ___
2043092	BNSF Bulkhead Flatcar "545512" (std O), *2020*		45 ___
2043093	BNSF Bulkhead Flatcar "545587" (std O), *2020*		45 ___
2043094	BNSF Bulkhead Flatcar "545628" (std O), *2020*		45 ___
2043101	GN Bulkhead Flatcar "160325" (std O), *2020*		45 ___
2043102	GN Bulkhead Flatcar "160331" (std O), *2020*		45 ___
2043103	GN Bulkhead Flatcar "160350" (std O), *2020*		45 ___
2043104	GN Bulkhead Flatcar "160374" (std O), *2020*		45 ___
2043111	NS Bulkhead Flatcar "118024" (std O), *2020*		45 ___
2043112	NS Bulkhead Flatcar "118033" (std O), *2020*		45 ___
2043113	NS Bulkhead Flatcar "118045" (std O), *2020*		45 ___
2043114	NS Bulkhead Flatcar "118068" (std O), *2020*		45 ___
2043121	Trailer Train Bulkhead Flatcar "81023" (std O), *2020*		45 ___
2043122	Trailer Train Bulkhead Flatcar "81094" (std O), *2020*		45 ___
2043123	Trailer Train Bulkhead Flatcar "81118" (std O), *2020*		45 ___
2043124	Trailer Train Bulkhead Flatcar "81145" (std O), *2020*		45 ___
2043131	Bethlehem Steel Gondola "3131" (std O), *2020*		45 ___

| --- | --- | --- | --- |
___	2043132	Bethlehem Steel Gondola "3145" (std O), *2020*		45
___	2043133	Bethlehem Steel Gondola "3168" (std O), *2020*		45
___	2043134	Bethlehem Steel Gondola "3192" (std O), *2020*		45
___	2043141	Chessie System Gondola "305001" (std O), *2020*		45
___	2043142	Chessie System Gondola "305014" (std O), 2020		
___	2043143	Chessie System Gondola "305036" (std O), *2020*		45
___	2043144	Chessie System Gondola "305055" (std O), *2020*		45
___	2043151	MKT Gondola "14025" (std O), *2020*		45
___	2043152	MKT Gondola "14032" (std O), *2020*		45
___	2043153	MKT Gondola "14041" (std O), *2020*		45
___	2043154	MKT Gondola "14049" (std O), *2020*		45
___	2043161	Reading Gondola "29061" (std O), *2020*		45
___	2043162	Reading Gondola "29086" (std O), *2020*		45
___	2043164	Reading Gondola "29172" (std O), *2020*		45
___	2043170	BN Rotary Gondola 4-pack A, *2020*		280
___	2043180	BN Rotary Gondola 4-pack B, *2020*		280
___	2043190	BN Rotary Gondola 2-pack, *2020*		140
___	2043200	Conrail Rotary Gondola 4-pack A, *2020*		280
___	2043210	Conrail Rotary Gondola 4-pack B, *2020*		280
___	2043220	Conrail Rotary Gondola 2-pack, *2020*		140
___	2043230	CSX Rotary Gondola 4-pack A, *2020*		280
___	2043240	CSX Rotary Gondola 4-pack B, *2020*		280
___	2043250	CSX Rotary Gondola 2-pack, *2020*		140
___	2043260	NS Rotary Gondola 4-pack A, *2020*		280
___	2043270	NS Rotary Gondola 4-pack B, *2020*		280
___	2043280	NS Rotary Gondola 2-pack, *2020*		140
___	2943163	Reading Gondola "29169" (std O), *2020*		45
___	79C95204C	Sears Santa Fe Diesel Freight Set, *71 u*	150	165
___	79C9715C	Sears 4-unit Diesel Freight Set, *75 u*	50	65
___	79C9717C	Sears 7-unit Steam Freight Set, *75 u*	150	165
___	79N95223C	Sears 6-unit Diesel Freight Set, *74 u*	150	165
___	79N9552C	Sears 6-unit Steam Freight Set, *72 u*	150	165
___	79N9553C	Sears 6-unit Diesel Freight Set, *72 u*	150	165
___	79N96178C	Sears 4-unit Steam Freight Set, *74 u*	50	65
___	79N97082C	Sears Steam Freight Set, *70 u*		NRS
___	79N97101C	Sears 5-unit Steam Freight Set, *72 u*	150	165
___	79N98765C	Sears Logging Empire Set, *78 u*	100	115
___	T1428R-RODTS	Tony Stewart NASCAR Steam Freight Set, *12-14*		300
___	T1828RRMMKB	Kyle Busch NASCAR Steam Freight Set, *12-14*		300
___	T2428RRDUJG	Jeff Gordon NASCAR Steam Freight Set, *12-14*		300
___	T4828RRLOJJ	Jimmy Johnson NASCAR Steam Freight Set, *12-14*		300
___	T4828RRLOJJ	Dale Earnhardt Jr. NASCAR Steam Freight Set, *12-14*		300
___	TX328RRG-MDE	Dale Earnhardt NASCAR Steam Freight Set, *12-14*		300
___	UCS	Remote Control Track (O), *70*	4	7
Unnumbered Items				
___		Black Cave Flyer Playmat, *82*		8
___		C&NW Passenger Car Set, *93*	385	460
___		Erie Set (FF 7), *93*	385	460
___		Frisco Set (FF 5), *91*	405	425
___		Jersey Central Set, *86*	345	370
___		Missouri Pacific Set, *95*		390

Nickel Plate Road Set (FF 6), *92*		
N&W Powhatan Arrow Passenger Car Set, *95*		
Pere Marquette Set, *93*		
Union Pacific Set, *94*		
Western Maryland Set (FF 4), *89*		
B&A Hudson and Standard O Car Set, *86 u*	1700	
Toys "R" Us Thunderball Freight Set, *75 u*	NRS	
Cannonball Freight Playmat, *81-82*	8	
Chesapeake & Ohio Set, *95-96*	NRS	
Commando Assault Train Playmat, *83-84*	8	
Favorite Food Freight Set, *81-82*	255	355
The General Set, *77-80*	240	285
L.A.S.E.R. Playmat, *81-82*	8	
New Haven Set, *94-95*	400	
Northern Pacific Set, *90-92*	190	250
Rock Island & Peoria Set, *80-82*	240	315
Rocky Mountain Platform, *83-84*	8	
Spirit of '76 Set, *74-76*	600	720
Station Platform, *83-84*	8	
Baltimore & Ohio Set, *94, 96*	NRS	
D&RGW California Zephyr Set, *92, 93*	900	
Erie-Lackawanna Passenger Car Set, *93, 94*	940	980
GN Empire Builder Set, *92, 93*	620	730
Lionel Lines Madison Car Set, *91, 93*	560	620
New York Central Set, *89, 91*	240	270
Wabash Set (FF 1), *86, 87*	755	905
Amtrak Passenger Car Set, *89, 89 u*	640	770
Burlington Texas Zephyr Set, *80, 80 u*	980	1150
Chessie System Special Set, *80, 86 u*	560	620
Chicago & Alton Limited Set, *81, 86 u*	560	620
Great Northern Set (FARR 3), *81, 81 u*	620	690
Milwaukee Road Set (FF 2), *87, 90 u*	380	405
Santa Fe Set (FARR 1), *79, 79 u*	460	580
Southern Set (FARR 4), *83, 83 u*	620	690
Union Pacific Set (FARR 2), *80, 80 u*	540	580
UP Overland Route Set, *84, 92 u*	770	840
Illinois Central Set, *91-92, 95*	255	285
Pennsylvania Set, *87-90, 95*	240	270
IC City of New Orleans Set, *85, 87, 93*	885	1045
SP Daylight Steam Set, *90, 92, 93*	790	940
Blue Comet Set, *78-80, 87 u*	560	620
Mickey Mouse Express Set, *77-78, 78 u*	1050	1800
Pennsylvania Set (FARR 5), *84-85, 89 u*	600	660
Southern Crescent Limited Set, *77-78, 87 u*	540	650
Joshua Lionel Cowen Set, *80, 80 u, 82*	540	580
NYC 20th Century Limited Set, *83, 83 u, 95*	1000	1200
Southern Pacific Daylight Diesel Set, *82-83, 82-83 u, 90 u*	2150	2300
N&W Powhatan Arrow Set, *81, 81 u, 82 u, 91 u*	1450	1700
Santa Fe Super Chief Set, *91, 91 u, 92 u, 93, 95*	1400	1700
Pennsylvania Set, *79-80, 79-80 u, 81 u, 83 u*	1200	1350
Lionel Lines Set, *82-84 u, 86, 86-87 u, 94-95*	530	620
Mint Set, *79 u, 80-83, 84 u, 86 u, 87, 91 u, 93*	940	1073

Section 4
LIONEL CORPORATION TINPLATE

		Retail
____ 11-1001	No. 400E Locomotive, black, brass trim (std)	900
____ 11-1002	No. 400E Locomotive, gray, nickel trim (std)	900
____ 11-1003	No. 400E Locomotive, gray, brass trim (std)	900
____ 11-1005	No. 390 Locomotive, green	600
____ 11-1006	No. 400E Locomotive, crackele black, brass trim	900
____ 11-1008	No. 400E Lionel Lines Locomotive	900
____ 11-1009	No. 400E Locomotive, blue, brass trim	900
____ 11-1010	No. 385E Locomotive (std)	700
____ 11-1012	No. 1835E Locomotive, black, nickel trim	700
____ 11-1013	AF No. 4694 Warrior Passenger Set	1400
____ 11-1014	AF No. 4694 Iron Monarch Passenger Set	1250
____ 11-1015	No. 392E Locomotive, black, brass trim	800
____ 11-1016	No. 392E Locomotive, gray, nickel trim	800
____ 11-1017	No. 400E Locomotive, blue, nickel trim (std)	900
____ 11-1018	No. 7 Lionel Locomotive (std)	900
____ 11-1019	No. 6 Pennsylvania Locomotive (std)	900
____ 11-1020	American Flyer No. 4696 Locomotive	1000
____ 11-1021	No. 400E Presidential Locomotive (std)	1000
____ 11-1022	No. 400E Red Comet Locomotive (std)	1000
____ 11-1023	No. 400E Locomotive, blue, brass trim (std)	900
____ 11-1024	No. 400E Locomotive, black, brass trim (std)	900
____ 11-1025	No. 400E Lionel Lines Locomotive (std)	900
____ 11-1026	No. 400E Locomotive, pink (std)	1000
____ 11-1027	No. 400E Locomotive, state green (std)	1000
____ 11-1028	No. 400E Locomotive, black, brass trim (std)	1000
____ 11-1029	No. 6 NYC Locomotive (std)	900
____ 11-1030	No. 6 General Locomotive (std)	900
____ 11-1031	No. 6 Texas Locomotive (std)	950
____ 11-1038	No. 6 B&O Locomotive (std)	900
____ 11-1039	No. 6 Long Island Locomotive (std)	900
____ 11-1040	No. 6 Strasburg Locomotive (std)	900
____ 11-1041	No. 6 PRR Locomotive (std)	900
____ 11-1042	Great Northern Steam Locomotive (std)	1000
____ 11-1043	Lehigh Valley Steam Locomotive (std)	1000
____ 11-1045	PRR Steam Locomotive (std)	1000
____ 11-2003	No. 8E Electric Locomotive, olive green (std)	500
____ 11-2004	No. 8E Electric Locomotive, dark olive green (std)	500
____ 11-2005	No. 8E Electric Locomotive, orange (std)	500
____ 11-2006	No. 8E Electric Locomotive, red/cream (std)	500
____ 11-2007	American Flyer Presidential Passenger Set (std)	1800
____ 11-2008	AF No. 4689 Presidential Locomotive, blue (std)	800
____ 11-2009	Big Brute Electric Engine, zinc chromate	1500
____ 11-2010	Big Brute Electric Engine, green	1500

Lionel Corporation Tinplate		Retail	
11-2015	Super 381 Electric Engine, state green (std)	1300	___
11-2016	Super 381 MILW Electric Engine (std)	1300	___
11-2017	No. 408E Electric Locomotive (std)	900	___
11-2018	No. 408E Electric Locomotive, Mojave	900	___
11-2019	No. 408E Electric Locomotive, pink	900	___
11-2020	No. 9 Electric Locomotive, green	600	___
11-2021	No. 9 Electric Locomotive, orange	600	___
11-2022	No. 9 Electric Locomotive, gray, nickel trim	600	___
11-2023	No. 9 Electric Locomotive, dark green	600	___
11-2024	No. 8 Trolley (std)	530	___
11-2025	No. 9 Trolley (std)	650	___
11-2026	No. 8 Christmas Trolley (std)	570	___
11-2027	No. 381E Electric Locomotive, blue (std)	900	___
11-2028	No. 381E Electric Locomotive, brown (std)	900	___
11-2029	No. 381E Great Northern Electric Locomotive (std)	900	___
11-2031	No. 4689 President's Locomotive, red (std)	900	___
11-2033	Big Brute Electric Locomotive, brown (std)	1600	___
11-2034	Big Brute Electric Locomotive, orange (std)	1600	___
11-2038	Super 381 MILW Electric Locomotive (std)	1300	___
11-2039	Super 381 PRR Electric Locomotive (std)	1300	___
11-2040	Super 381 Electric Locomotive, two-tone brown (std)	1300	___
11-2041	Super 381 New Haven Electric Locomotive (std)	1300	___
11-5001	No. 384 Locomotive Passenger Set, black, brass trim	600	___
11-5002	No. 384 Locomotive Christmas Freight Set (std)	600	___
11-5003	No. 384 Locomotive LV Passenger Set (std)	600	___
11-5004	No. 384 Locomotive NYC Freight Set	600	___
11-5006	No. 384E Locomotive Girl's Passenger Set	600	___
11-5007	No. 386 Freight Set (std)	600	___
11-5008	No. 340E Coal Freight Set (std)	600	___
11-5009	No. 342E Baby State Passenger Set (std)	600	___
11-5010	No. 384E Blue Comet Passenger Set (std)	600	___
11-5011	No. 386 Christmas Freight Set (std)	600	___
11-5012	No. 342E Passenger Set (std)	600	___
11-5013	No. 318E Christmas Freight Set (std)	600	___
11-5014	No. 384E PRR Steam Passenger Set (std)	600	___
11-5501	No. 263E Steam Christmas Freight Set	600	___
11-5502	No. 263E Steam B&O Freight Set	600	___
11-5505	No. 249E Christmas Steam Passenger Set	500	___
11-5506	No. 299 Freight Set	450	___
11-5507	No. 269E Distant Control Freight Set	500	___
11-5508	Celebration Passenger Set	480	___
11-5509	No. 269E Christmas Distant Control Freight Set	500	___
11-5510	No. 269E Distant Control Freight Set	500	___
11-6001	No. 263E Locomotive, black, brass trim	430	___
11-6002	No. 263E Locomotive, blue	430	___
11-6003	No. 277W Remote Control Work Train	680	___

	Lionel Corporation Tinplate	Retail
___	11-6004 Blue Comet Distant Control Passenger Set	650
___	11-6005 No. 275W Distant Control Freight Set	600
___	11-6006 UP Streamliner Passenger Set, silver	800
___	11-6007 UP Streamliner Passenger Set, yellow	800
___	11-6008 No. 249E Steam Passenger Set, black, brass trim	600
___	11-6009 No. 249E Steam Passenger Set, blue	600
___	11-6010 No. 249E Steam Passenger Set, gray, nickel trim	600
___	11-6012 No. 260E Locomotive, black, brass trim	430
___	11-6013 No. 255E Locomotive, gray, nickel trim	430
___	11-6014 No. 255E Lionel Lines Locomotive	430
___	11-6015 No. 279E Distant Control Passenger Set	750
___	11-6016 No. 295E Distant Control Passenger Set	750
___	11-6017 Hiawatha Distance Control Streamliner Set	900
___	11-6018 Hiawatha Passenger Train Set	900
___	11-6019 Hiawatha Distance Control Freight Set	900
___	11-6020 UP City of Denver Passenger Set, green	590
___	11-6021 UP City of Denver Passenger Set, yellow/brown	700
___	11-6022 No. 262E Locomotive, black, brass trim	300
___	11-6023 No. 262E Locomotive, black, nickel trim	300
___	11-6024 No. 260E Locomotive, black, brass trim	450
___	11-6025 No. 214 Armored Motor Car Set	400
___	11-6028 No. 256 Electric Locomotive, orange	450
___	11-6029 No. 214 Armored Motor Car Set	400
___	11-6030 No. 295E Distant Control Passenger Set	750
___	11-6031 No. 279E NYC Distance Control Passenger Set	700
___	11-6033 No. 265E Commodore Vanderbilt Locomotive	430
___	11-6036 No. 263E Baby Blue Comet Locomotive	460
___	11-6037 Girls Freight Set	830
___	11-6038 No. 284E Distant Control Freight Set	700
___	11-6039 No. 616 Flying Yankee Passenger Set, black/chrome	590
___	11-6040 No. 616 Flying Yankee Passenger Set, red/chrome	590
___	11-6041 No. 616 Flying Yankee Passenger Set, green/chrome	590
___	11-6046 No. 279E Distant Control Passenger Set	700
___	11-6047 No. 264 Red Comet Locomotive	460
___	11-6048 No. 263E Baby Blue Comet Locomotive, brass trim	500
___	11-6050 No. 256 New Haven Electric Locomotive	500
___	11-6051 No. 256 Great Northern Electric Locomotive	500
___	11-6052 No. 263E Locomotive, black, nickel trim	500
___	11-6053 No. 263E Chessie Locomotive	500
___	11-6054 No. 263E Southern Locomotive	500
___	11-6055 Boys Freight Set	900
___	11-6056 No. 261E LL Locomotive and Tender	350
___	11-6057 No. 216E Locomotive and Tender	350
___	11-6061 No. 256 MILW Electric Locomotive	500
___	11-6062 No. 256 PRR Electric Locomotive	500
___	11-30004 No. 213 Cattle Car, cream/maroon (std)	130

Lionel Corporation Tinplate		Retail
11-30005	No. 213 Cattle Car, terra-cotta/green (std)	130
11-30006	No. 214 Boxcar, cream/orange (std)	130
11-30007	No. 214 Boxcar, yellow/brown (std)	130
11-30008	No. 214R Refrigerator Car, white/blue (std)	130
11-30009	No. 215 Tank Car, silver, nickel trim (std)	130
11-30010	No. 215 Tank Car, green, brass trim (std)	130
11-30011	No. 215 Tank Car, white (std)	130
11-30012	No. 216 Hopper Car, red (std)	130
11-30013	No. 217 Caboose, orange/maroon (std)	140
11-30014	No. 217 Caboose, red (std)	160
11-30015	No. 513 Cattle Car, green/orange, brass trim (std)	100
11-30016	No. 514 Boxcar, cream/orange (std)	100
11-30017	No. 514R Refrigerator Car, ivory/peacock, brass trim (std)	100
11-30018	No. 515 Tank Car, terra-cotta, brass trim (std)	100
11-30019	No. 516 Hopper Car, red, brass trim (std)	120
11-30020	No. 517 Caboose, pea green/red (std)	120
11-30021	No. 212 Gondola, maroon (std)	110
11-30022	No. 212 Gondola, pea green (std)	110
11-30023	No. 513 Cattle Car, cream/maroon, nickel trim (std)	100
11-30024	No. 514R Refrigerator Car, white/blue, nickel trim (std)	100
11-30025	No. 515 Tank Car, silver, nickel trim (std)	100
11-30026	No. 516 Hopper Car, red, nickel trim (std)	100
11-30027	No. 517 Caboose, red, nickel trim (std)	120
11-30028	No. 520 Floodlight Car, green, nickel trim (std)	130
11-30029	No. 520 Floodlight Car, terra-cotta, brass trim (std)	130
11-30030	No. 514R Christmas Refrigerator Car, (std)	100
11-30031	No. 514 Christmas Boxcar (std)	100
11-30032	No. 515 MTH/Lionel Tank Car (std)	100
11-30033	No. 211 Flatcar, black, brass trim, with wood (std)	120
11-30034	No. 211 Flatcar, black, nickel trim, with wood (std)	120
11-30035	No. 218 Dump Car, Mojave, nickel trim (std)	140
11-30036	No. 218 Dump Car, Mojave, brass trim (std)	140
11-30037	No. 219 Crane Car, white (std)	200
11-30038	No. 219 Crane Car, yellow, nickel trim (std)	200
11-30039	No. 219 Crane Car, yellow (std)	380
11-30042	No. 514 Boxcar, red/black (std)	100
11-30043	No. 512 Gondola, peacock, brass trim (std)	80
11-30044	No. 512 Gondola, green, nickel trim (std)	80
11-30045	No. 514 Boxcar, yellow/brown (std)	100
11-30046	No. 511 Flatcar, black, brass trim, with wood (std)	100
11-30047	No. 511 Flatcar, black, nickel trim, with wood (std)	100
11-30048	No. 216 Hopper Car, dark green (std)	130
11-30050	No. 219 Crane Car, white, brass trim (std)	380
11-30051	No. 514R NYC Refrigerator Car (std)	100
11-30055	No. 212 Gondola, gray (std)	110
11-30056	No. 213 Cattle Car, Mojave/maroon (std)	130

	Lionel Corporation Tinplate	Retail
___	**11-30057** No. 213 Cattle Car, terra-cotta/maroon (std)	130
___	**11-30058** No. 214 Boxcar, terra-cotta/black, brass trim (std)	130
___	**11-30059** No. 214R Refrigerator Car, white/peacock, brass trim (std)	130
___	**11-30060** No. 214R Refrigerator Car, ivory/peacock, brass trim (std)	130
___	**11-30061** No. 215 Tank Car, silver, brass trim (std)	130
___	**11-30062** No. 215 Tank Car, silver, nickel trim (std)	130
___	**11-30063** No. 217 Caboose, olive green (std)	140
___	**11-30064** No. 217 Lionel Lines Caboose (std)	140
___	**11-30065** No. 217 Caboose, pea green/red (std)	140
___	**11-30066** No. 217 Caboose, red/peacock (std)	160
___	**11-30067** No. 218 Dump Car, gray (std)	140
___	**11-30068** No. 218 Dump Car, pea green (std)	140
___	**11-30069** No. 218 Dump Car, peacock (std)	140
___	**11-30070** No. 219 Crane Car, peacock/dark green (std)	200
___	**11-30071** No. 219 Lionel Lines Crane Car (std)	380
___	**11-30072** No. 220 Floodlight Car, green, nickel trim (std)	140
___	**11-30073** No. 220 Floodlight Car, terra-cotta, brass trim (std)	140
___	**11-30074** No. 513 Cattle Car, orange/pea green (std)	100
___	**11-30075** No. 514 Christmas Boxcar (std)	100
___	**11-30076** No. 514R Refrigerator Car, ivory/blue (std)	100
___	**11-30077** No. 515 Tank Car, cream (std)	100
___	**11-30078** No. 515 Tank Car, ivory (std)	100
___	**11-30079** No. 515 Tank Car, orange (std)	100
___	**11-30080** No. 516 Christmas Hopper Car (std)	120
___	**11-30081** No. 516 Hopper Car, red (std)	120
___	**11-30082** No. 517 Caboose, red/black (std)	120
___	**11-30083** No. 520 Floodlight Car, green, nickel trim (std)	130
___	**11-30087** No. 516 Hopper Car, red, brass trim (std)	100
___	**11-30088** AF 4018 Automobile Car, white/blue	150
___	**11-30089** AF 4020 Stock Car, blue	150
___	**11-30090** AF 4006 Hopper Car, red	150
___	**11-30091** AF 4017 Sand Car, green	150
___	**11-30092** AF 4010 Tank Car, cream/blue	150
___	**11-30093** AF 4022 Machine Car, orange	110
___	**11-30094** AF 4021 Caboose, red	160
___	**11-30095** AF 4018 Automobile Car, orange/maroon	130
___	**11-30096** AF 4022 Machine Car, blue	110
___	**11-30097** AF 4022 Machine Car, orange/green	110
___	**11-30098** AF 4010 Tank Car, blue	130
___	**11-30099** AF 4017 Sand Car, maroon	130
___	**11-30100** AF 4006 Hopper Car, green	130
___	**11-30101** AF 4020 Stock Car, cream/maroon	130
___	**11-30102** AF 4021 Caboose, red/maroon	140
___	**11-30103** AF 4021 Caboose, cream/red	140
___	**11-30104** No. 215 Tank Car (std)	130
___	**11-30105** No. 214R Refrigerator Car (std)	130

Lionel Corporation Tinplate		Retail
11-30107	No. 214R Altoona 36 Lager Refrigerator Car (std)	130 ___
11-30108	No. 214R Budweiser Refrigerator Car (std)	140 ___
11-30109	No. 214R Burp-oh Beer Refrigerator Car (std)	130 ___
11-30110	No. 214R Hood's Dairy Refrigerator Car (std)	130 ___
11-30111	No. 214R Old Reading Refrigerator Car (std)	130 ___
11-30112	No. 214R Palisades Park Refrigerator Car (std)	130 ___
11-30113	No. 214 Circus Boxcar (std)	130 ___
11-30114	No. 214 M&M's Christmas Boxcar (std)	140 ___
11-30115	No. 215 Budweiser Tank Car (std)	140 ___
11-30116	No. 215 Freedomland Tank Car (std)	130 ___
11-30117	No. 215 Gulf Tank Car (std)	130 ___
11-30118	No. 215 Tropicana Tank Car (std)	130 ___
11-30119	No. 513 UP Cattle Car (std)	100 ___
11-30120	No. 513 WM Cattle Car (std)	100 ___
11-30121	No. 514 B&O Boxcar (std)	100 ___
11-30122	No. 514 State of Maine Boxcar (std)	120 ___
11-30123	No. 514R PFE Refrigerator Car (std)	100 ___
11-30124	No. 514R Tropicana Refrigerator Car (std)	120 ___
11-30125	No. 515 Anheuser Busch Tank Car (std)	110 ___
11-30126	No. 515 Hooker Chemicals Tank Car (std)	100 ___
11-30127	No. 516 Blue Coal Hopper Car (std)	100 ___
11-30128	No. 516 Waddell Coal Hopper Car (std)	120 ___
11-30129	No. 517 Pennsylvania Caboose (std)	120 ___
11-30130	No. 517 Santa Fe Caboose (std)	140 ___
11-30131	No. 215 Lionel Lines Tank Car (std)	130 ___
11-30134	No. 515 Christmas Tank Car (std)	100 ___
11-30136	No. 214 Christmas Boxcar (std)	150 ___
11-30137	No. 214 UP Boxcar (std)	150 ___
11-30138	No. 214R Horlacher's Brewing Refrigerator Car (std)	150 ___
11-30139	No. 214R Coors Refrigerator Car (std)	140 ___
11-30140	No. 215 Keystone Gasoline Tank Car (std)	150 ___
11-30141	No. 215 Texaco Tank Car (std)	150 ___
11-30142	No. 216 Peabody Hopper Car (std)	130 ___
11-30143	No. 216 Pennsylvania Power & Light Hopper Car (std)	130 ___
11-30144	No. 213 Cattle Car (std)	130 ___
11-30146	No. 217 Jersey Central Caboose (std)	140 ___
11-30147	No. 214 Jersey Central Boxcar (std)	130 ___
11-30148	No. 214 U.S. Army Boxcar (std)	130 ___
11-30149	No. 215 MTH/Lionel Tank Car	130 ___
11-30150	No. 212 Lionel Lines Gondola (std)	130 ___
11-30151	No. 212 Circus Gondola (std)	130 ___
11-30152	No. 212 NYC Gondola (std)	130 ___
11-30153	No. 214 MKT Boxcar (std)	150 ___
11-30154	No. 214 NYC Boxcar (std)	150 ___
11-30155	No. 215 C&O Tank Car (std)	150 ___
11-30156	No. 215 Shell Tank Car (std)	150 ___

	Lionel Corporation Tinplate	Retail
____	**11-30157** No. 216 Hopper Car, red, brass trim (std)	150
____	**11-30158** No. 216 LV Hopper Car (std)	150
____	**11-30159** No. 217 Pennsylvania Caboose (std)	160
____	**11-30160** No. 219 B&O Crane Car (std)	220
____	**11-30161** No. 219 Crane Car, ivory/red (std)	400
____	**11-30162** No. 219 Lionel Lines Crane Car (std)	220
____	**11-30163** No. 219 Crane Car, red/silver (std)	400
____	**11-30164** No. 514R Christmas Refrigerator Car (std)	120
____	**11-30168** No. 515 PRR Tank Car (std)	120
____	**11-30169** No. 515 Texaco Tank Car (std)	120
____	**11-30170** No. 515 Esso Tank Car (std)	120
____	**11-30180** No. 219 Crane Car, black/cream (std)	220
____	**11-30182** No. 217 NYC Illuminated Caboose (std)	160
____	**11-30185** No. 212 Gondola, pea green (std)	150
____	**11-30193** No. 514R Altoona Brewing Refrigerator Car (std)	120
____	**11-30194** No. 514R PFE Refrigerator Car (std)	120
____	**11-30195** No. 514R REA Refrigerator Car (std)	120
____	**11-30196** No. 514R Robin Hood Beer Refrigerator Car (std)	120
____	**11-30197** No. 514 UP Boxcar (std)	120
____	**11-30198** No. 514 Santa Fe Boxcar (std)	120
____	**11-30199** No. 514 PRR Boxcar (std)	120
____	**11-30200** No. 514 B&O Boxcar (std)	120
____	**11-30201** No. 215-3 Shell 3-D Tank Car (std)	150
____	**11-30202** No. 215-3 Mazda Lamps 3-D Tank Car (std)	150
____	**11-30203** No. 215-3 Celanese Chemicals 3-D Tank Car (std)	150
____	**11-30204** No. 215-3 Clark Oil 3-D Tank Car (std)	150
____	**11-30205** No. 215-2 Sterling Fuels 2-D Tank Car (std)	150
____	**11-30206** No. 215-2 Philadelphia Quartz 2-D Tank Car (std)	150
____	**11-30207** No. 215-2 Cook's Paints 2-D Tank Car (std)	150
____	**11-30208** No. 215-2 Hercules 2-D Tank Car (std)	150
____	**11-30209** No. 216-1 PRR Covered Hopper (std)	150
____	**11-30210** No. 216-1 P&LE Covered Hopper (std)	150
____	**11-30211** No. 216-1 Jack Frost Covered Hopper (std)	150
____	**11-30212** No. 216-1 GE Lamps Covered Hopper (std)	150
____	**11-30213** No. 212-1 PRR Covered Gondola Car (std)	150
____	**11-30214** No. 212-1 Covered Gondola Car (std)	150
____	**11-30215** No. 212-1 NYC Covered Gondola Car (std)	150
____	**11-30216** No. 212-1 GN Covered Gondola Car (std)	150
____	**11-30217** No. 211 Flatcar with wheel load (std)	150
____	**11-30218** No. 211 Altoona Shops Flatcar with wheel load (std)	150
____	**11-30219** No. 211 Baldwin Flatcar with wheel load (std)	150
____	**11-30220** No. 211 Lima Flatcar with wheel load (std)	150
____	**11-30221** No. 217-1 Chessie Bay Window Caboose (std)	160
____	**11-30222** No. 217-1 UP Bay Window Caboose (std)	160
____	**11-30223** No. 217-1 NYC Bay Window Caboose (std)	160
____	**11-30224** No. 217-1 Long Island Bay Window Caboose (std)	160

Lionel Corporation Tinplate		Retail	
11-30225	PRR Automobile Car (std)	150	___
11-30227	Shell Tank Car (std)	150	___
11-30230	Waddell Coal Hopper (std)	150	___
11-30232	PRR Caboose (std)	160	___
11-40001	Presidential Passenger Set, blue (std)	1200	___
11-40002	No. 339 Pullman Car, green (std)	150	___
11-40003	No. 332 Mail/Baggage Car, green (std)	150	___
11-40004	No. 332 LV Ithaca Baggage Car	150	___
11-40005	No. 339 LV Easton Passenger Coach	150	___
11-40007	300 Series 3-Car Passenger Set, blue/silver (std)	400	___
11-40009	3-Car State Passenger Set, green (std)	1200	___
11-40010	Pennsylvania State Baggage Car, green (std)	400	___
11-40011	Illinois State Coach, green (std)	400	___
11-40012	Solarium State Car, green (std)	400	___
11-40013	MILW 3-Car State Passenger Set (std)	1200	___
11-40014	MILW State Baggage Car (std)	400	___
11-40015	MILW State Passenger Coach (std)	400	___
11-40016	MILW Solarium State Car (std)	400	___
11-40017	3-Car Showroom Passenger Set, green (std)	1500	___
11-40018	Showroom Passenger Coach, green (std)	500	___
11-40019	3-Car Showroom Passenger Set, zinc chromate (std)	1500	___
11-40020	Showroom Passenger Coach, zinc chromate (std)	500	___
11-40021	3-Car Blue Comet Passenger Set (std)	1100	___
11-40022	No. 432 Olbers Blue Comet Baggage Car (std)	380	___
11-40023	No. 419 Tuttle Blue Comet Passenger Coach (std)	380	___
11-40024	No. 4343 Diner Car	180	___
11-40025	339 Series Passenger Car, pink	130	___
11-40026	332 Series Baggage Car, pink	130	___
11-40027	309 Series 3-Car State Passenger Set, brown (std)	1200	___
11-40028	Pennsylvania State Baggage Car, brown (std)	400	___
11-40029	Illinois State Passenger Coach, brown (std)	400	___
11-40030	Solarium State Car, brown (std)	400	___
11-40031	State 3-Car Passenger Set, blue (std)	1200	___
11-40032	Pennsylvania State Baggage Car, blue (std)	400	___
11-40033	Illinois State Passenger Coach, blue (std)	400	___
11-40034	Solarium State Car, blue (std)	400	___
11-40035	309 Series 3-Car Passenger Set, blue (std)	400	___
11-40036	309 Series 3-Car Passenger Set, green (std)	400	___
11-40037	309 Series 3-Car Passenger Set, red (std)	400	___
11-40038	No. 309 Passenger Coach (std)	140	___
11-40039	No. 310 Baggage Car (std)	140	___
11-40040	3-Car Blue Comet Passenger Set, nickel trim (std)	1100	___
11-40041	No. 432 Blue Comet Baggage Car, nickel trim (std)	380	___
11-40042	No. 423 Blue Comet Passenger Coach, nickel trim (std)	380	___
11-40043	3-Car Stephen Girard Set, brass trim	600	___
11-40044	No. 4427 Stephen Girard Baggage Car, brass trim	200	___

	Lionel Corporation Tinplate	Retail
___	**11-40045** No. 427 Stephen Girard Passenger Coach, brass trim	200
___	**11-40046** 3-Car Stephen Girard Set, nickel trim	600
___	**11-40047** No. 4427 Stephen Girard Baggage Car, nickel trim	200
___	**11-40048** No. 427 Stephen Girard Passenger Coach, nickel trim	200
___	**11-40049** No. 418 3-Car Passenger Set, green, brass trim (std)	600
___	**11-40050** No. 418 Diner, green, brass trim (std)	200
___	**11-40051** No. 418 3-Car Passenger Set, orange, brass trim (std)	600
___	**11-40052** No. 418 Diner, orange brass trim (std)	200
___	**11-40053** No. 418 3-Car Passenger Set, Mojave, brass trim (std)	600
___	**11-40054** No. 418 Diner, Mojave, brass trim (std)	200
___	**11-40055** No. 418 3-Car Passenger Set, pink, brass trim (std)	600
___	**11-40056** No. 418 Diner, pink, brass trim (std)	200
___	**11-40057** Lionel 3-Car Pullman Passenger Set (std)	700
___	**11-40058** Pennsylvania 3-Car Pullman Passenger Set (std)	700
___	**11-40059** No. 332 Baggage Car (std)	140
___	**11-40060** No. 339 Passenger Coach (std)	140
___	**11-40061** Great Northern State 3-Car Passenger Set (std)	1200
___	**11-40062** Great Northern State Baggage Car (std)	430
___	**11-40063** Great Northern State Passenger Coach (std)	430
___	**11-40064** Great Northern State Solarium Car (std)	430
___	**11-40065** Presidential 3-Car Passenger Set (std)	1200
___	**11-40066** Presidential Baggage Car (std)	430
___	**11-40067** Presidential Passenger Coach (std)	430
___	**11-40068** Red Comet 3-Car Passenger Set (std)	1140
___	**11-40069** Red Comet Baggage Car (std)	400
___	**11-40070** Red Comet Passenger Coach (std)	400
___	**11-40072** President's Passenger Set, red (std)	1300
___	**11-40073** No. 310 Baggage Car (std)	140
___	**11-40074** No. 309 Passenger Coach (std)	140
___	**11-40076** Green Comet 3-Car Passenger Set (std)	1140
___	**11-40077** NYC 3-Car Passenger Set, brown (std)	700
___	**11-40078** General 3-Car Pullman Passenger Set (std)	700
___	**11-40079** Green Comet Baggage Car (std)	400
___	**11-40080** Green Comet Passenger Coach (std)	400
___	**11-40081** Showroom 3-Car Passenger Set, brown (std)	1600
___	**11-40082** Showroom Passenger Coach, brown (std)	540
___	**11-40083** Showroom 3-Car Passenger Set, orange (std)	1600
___	**11-40084** Showroom Passenger Coach, orange (std)	540
___	**11-40095** 3-car B&O Pullman Passenger Set (std)	700
___	**11-40096** 3-car Long Island Pullman Passenger Set (std)	700
___	**11-40097** 3-car Strasburg Pullman Passenger Set (std)	700
___	**11-40098** 3-car PRR Pullman Passenger Set (std)	700
___	**11-40099** 3-car MILW State Passenger Set (std)	1200
___	**11-40100** MILW State Solarium Car (std)	400
___	**11-40101** MILW State Passenger Coach (std)	400
___	**11-40102** MILW State Baggage Car (std)	400

Lionel Corporation Tinplate		Retail	
11-40103	3-car PRR State Passenger Set (std)	1200	___
11-40104	PRR State Solarium Car (std)	400	___
11-40105	PRR State Passenger Coach (std)	400	___
11-40106	PRR State Baggage Car (std)	400	___
11-40107	3-car State Passenger Set, two-tone brown (std)	1200	___
11-40108	State Solarium Car, two-tone brown (std)	400	___
11-40109	State Passenger Coach, two-tone brown (std)	400	___
11-40110	State Baggage Car, two-tone brown (std)	400	___
11-40111	3-car Great Northern Presidential Set (std)	1200	___
11-40112	Great Northern Presidential Diner (std)	400	___
11-40113	3-car Lehigh Valley Presidential Set (std)	1200	___
11-40114	Lehigh Valley Presidential Diner (std)	400	___
11-40115	3-car New Haven State Passenger Set (std)	1200	___
11-40116	New Haven State Solarium Car (std)	400	___
11-40117	New Haven State Passenger Coach (std)	400	___
11-40118	New Haven State Baggage Car (std)	400	___
11-60033	No. 607 Christmas Coach Passenger	90	___
11-70002	No. 2814 Boxcar, cream/orange	80	___
11-70003	No. 2814R Refrigerator Car, white/brown	80	___
11-70004	No. 2814R Christmas Refrigerator Car	80	___
11-70005	No. 2814R Refrigerator Car, Ivory/peacock	80	___
11-70006	No. 2815 Tank Car, silver	90	___
11-70007	No. 2815 Tank Car, orange, nickel trim	80	___
11-70008	No. 2817 Caboose, red/green	90	___
11-70009	No. 2815 Christmas Tank Car	80	___
11-70010	No. 2813 Cattle Car, cream/maroon	80	___
11-70011	No. 2812 Gondola, apple green	80	___
11-70012	No. 2811 Flatcar, silver	70	___
11-70013	No. 2816 Hopper Car, red	90	___
11-70014	No. 2816 Hopper Car, olive green	80	___
11-70015	No. 2820 Floodlight Car, terra-cotta	90	___
11-70016	No. 2815 Sunoco Tank Car	80	___
11-70017	No. 2810 Crane Car, terra-cotta/maroon	180	___
11-70018	No. 2811 Flatcar, maroon	70	___
11-70019	No. 2814R MTH/Lionel Refrigerator Car	90	___
11-70024	No. 2814 Christmas Boxcar	80	___
11-70025	No. 2814 Boxcar, cream/orange	80	___
11-70026	No. 2814 Boxcar, orange/brown	80	___
11-70027	No. 2814 Boxcar, white brown	80	___
11-70028	No. 2816 Christmas Hopper Car	80	___
11-70029	No. 2817 Caboose, red/brown	90	___
11-70030	No. 2812 Gondola, dark orange	70	___
11-70031	No. 813 Cattle Car, brown	80	___
11-70032	No. 2816 Hopper Car, black	80	___
11-70033	No. 2820 Floodlight Car, light green	90	___
11-70034	No. 2814R Refrigerator Car, white/brown	80	___

Lionel Corporation Tinplate	Retail
___ **11-70035** No. 2651 Flatcar, green	60
___ **11-70036** No. 2652 Gondola, red	60
___ **11-70037** No. 2653 Hopper Car, black	60
___ **11-70038** No. 2654 Shell Tank Car, yellow	60
___ **11-70039** No. 2655 Boxcar, yellow/brown	60
___ **11-70040** No. 2656 Cattle Car, red/brown	60
___ **11-70041** No. 2657 Caboose, red/maroon	60
___ **11-70042** No. 659 Dump Car, green	60
___ **11-70043** No. 659 Dump Car, orange	60
___ **11-70045** No. 2814 Boxcar, yellow/brown	90
___ **11-70046** No. 2817 Caboose, red	100
___ **11-70047** No. 2814 Christmas Boxcar	80
___ **11-70048** No. 2815 Christmas Tank Car	90
___ **11-70049** No. 2814R Refrigerator Car, silver frame	90
___ **11-70050** No. 2814R Refrigerator Car, black frame	80
___ **11-70051** No. 2817 Caboose, red/maroon	90
___ **11-70052** No. 2654 Shell Tank Car, gray	60
___ **11-70053** No. 2654 Shell Tank Car, black	60
___ **11-70054** No. 2653 Hopper Car, green	60
___ **11-70055** No. 2653 Hopper Car, red	60
___ **11-70056** No. 2655 Boxcar, yellow/maroon	60
___ **11-70057** No. 2655 Boxcar, yellow/brown	60
___ **11-70058** No. 2656 Cattle Car, gray/red	60
___ **11-70059** No. 2656 Cattle Car, burnt orange	60
___ **11-70060** No. 659 Dump Car, blue	60
___ **11-70061** No. 900 Ammunition Car, gray	60
___ **11-70064** No. 2814R Hoods Dairy Refrigerator Car	80
___ **11-70065** No. 2814R Isaly's Refrigerator Car	80
___ **11-70066** No. 2814R Sheffield Farms Refrigerator Car	90
___ **11-70067** No. 2814R Palisades Park Refrigerator Car	80
___ **11-70068** No. 2654 UP Tank Car, yellow	60
___ **11-70069** No. 2654 M&M's Tank Car	70
___ **11-70070** No. 2654 Baker's Chocolate Tank Car	60
___ **11-70071** No. 2654 Budweiser Tank Car	70
___ **11-70072** No. 2655 Delaware & Hudson Boxcar	60
___ **11-70073** No. 2655 Railbox Boxcar	60
___ **11-70074** M&M's Christmas Boxcar	70
___ **11-70076** No. 2654 LL Tank Car, orange/blue	70
___ **11-70078** No. 900 Ammunition Car, green	60
___ **11-70079** No. 2820 LL Floodlight Car, black/orange	120
___ **11-70080** No. 2820 U.S. Army Air Corps Floodlight Car	120
___ **11-70081** No. 2810 Crane Car, yellow/red	180
___ **11-70082** No. 2810 Crane Car, white/red	180
___ **11-70083** No. 2660 Crane Car, cream/red	100
___ **11-70084** No. 2660 Crane Car, terra-cotta/maroon	100
___ **11-70085** No. 2660 Crane Car, yellow/red	100

Lionel Corporation Tinplate		Retail	
11-70086	No. 2660 Crane Car, peacock/dark green	100	
11-70087	No. 2813 LL Cattle Car, cream/tuscan	90	
11-70088	No. 2813 LL Cattle Car, terra cotta/pea green	90	
11-70089	No. 2810 B&O Crane Car	180	
11-70091	No. 2815 LL Tank Car, cream, orange/blue	80	
11-70092	No. 2810 Crane Car, blue	180	
11-70095	No. 2820 LL Floodlight Car, black/peacock	120	
11-70096	No. 2814 Southern Boxcar	90	
11-70097	No. 2814 Chessie Boxcar	90	
11-70098	No. 2814 Blue Comet Boxcar, nickel trim	90	
11-70098	No. 2814 Blue Comet Boxcar, brass trim	90	
11-70102	No. 2654 Mobilgas Tank Car	70	
11-70103	No. 2654 Esso Tank Car	70	
11-70104	No. 2653 Blue Coal Hopper	70	
11-70105	No. 2653 Peabody Hopper	70	
11-70106	No. 2655 Altoona Brewing Boxcar	70	
11-70107	No. 2655 Hood's Grade A Milk Boxcar	70	
11-70108	No. 2655 LL Boxcar	70	
11-70109	No. 2657 LL Caboose, green/red	70	
11-70110	No. 2657 LL Caboose, orange/red	70	
11-70113	No. 2814 PRR Boxcar	90	
11-70114	No. 2814 ATSF Grand Canyon Boxcar	90	
11-70115	No. 2814 Long Island Boxcar	90	
11-70116	No. 2814 Alaska Boxcar	90	
11-70117	No. 2814R M. K. Goetz Brewing Refrigerator Car	90	
11-70118	No. 2814R Gerber Refrigerator Car	90	
11-70119	No. 2814R Roberts & Oake Meats Refrigerator Car	90	
11-70120	No. 2814R Sullivan's Packing Refrigerator Car	90	
11-70121	No. 2816 Western Maryland Coal Car	90	
11-70122	No. 2816 P&LE Coal Car	90	
11-70123	No. 2816 Waddell Mining Coal Car	90	
11-70124	No. 2816 Blue Coal Car	90	
11-70125	No. 2815 Clark Oil Tank Car	90	
11-70126	No. 2815 Celanese Chemicals Tank Car	90	
11-70127	No. 2815 Shell Tank Car	90	
11-70128	No. 2815 Cook's Paints Tank Car	90	
11-70129	No. 2817 C&O Caboose	100	
11-70130	No. 2817 Long Island Caboose	100	
11-70131	No. 2817 Southern Caboose	100	
11-70132	No. 2817 Jersey Central Caboose	100	
11-70133	No. 2814R Gerber Refrigerator Car	90	
11-70144	No. 2815 Shell Tank Car	90	
11-70154	No. 2814 ATSF Grand Canyon Boxcar	90	
11-80001	2600 Series 4-Car Blue Comet Passenger Set	430	
11-80002	UP Articulated Baggage Car, silver	150	
11-80003	UP Articulated Baggage Car, yellow	150	

Lionel Corporation Tinplate		Retail
___ 11-80004	UP Articulated Coach, silver	150
___ 11-80005	UP Articulated Coach, yellow	150
___ 11-80006	No. 2613 Series Pullman Coach, blue	110
___ 11-80007	2600 Series 3-Car Passenger Set, red	300
___ 11-80008	2600 Series 3-Car Passenger Set, green	300
___ 11-80009	Milwaukee Road Articulated Baggage Car	150
___ 11-80010	Milwaukee Road Articulated Coach	150
___ 11-80011	Articulated Streamliner Baggage Car	150
___ 11-80012	Articulated Streamliner Coach	150
___ 11-80013	No. 2613 Series Pullman Coach, red	100
___ 11-80014	No. 2613 Series Pullman Coach, green	100
___ 11-80015	No. 605 Christmas Baggage Car	90
___ 11-80016	710 Series 3-Car Passenger Set, blue	350
___ 11-80017	No. 710 Series Baggage Car, blue	120
___ 11-80018	No. 710 Series Passenger Coach, blue	120
___ 11-80019	710 Series 3-Car Passenger Set, orange	350
___ 11-80020	No. 710 Series Baggage Car, orange	120
___ 11-80021	No. 710 Series Passenger Coach, orange	120
___ 11-80022	710 Series 3-Car Passenger Set, red	350
___ 11-80023	No. 710 Series Baggage Car, red	120
___ 11-80024	No. 710 Series Passenger Coach, red	120
___ 11-80025	No. 1695 3-Car Passenger Set, blue/silver	350
___ 11-80026	No. 1685 Passenger Car, blue/silver	120
___ 11-80027	1695 Series 3-Car Passenger Set, red/maroon	380
___ 11-80028	No. 1695 Passenger Coach, red/maroon	130
___ 11-80029	City of Denver Coach, yellow/green	110
___ 11-80030	City of Denver Coach, green	110
___ 11-80031	No. 605 Baggage Car	90
___ 11-80032	No. 607 Passenger Coach	90
___ 11-80034	No. 2613 NYC Pullman Car, LCCA 2012 Convention	100
___ 11-80036	No. 605 Red Comet Baggage Car	90
___ 11-80039	600 Series 3-Car Red Comet Passenger Set	270
___ 11-80040	2600 Series 4-Car Blue Comet Passenger Set, brass trim	430
___ 11-80041	No. 2613 Pullman Coach, brass trim	110
___ 11-80042	Flying Yankee Chrome Coach	110
___ 11-80047	710 Series 3-Car NH Passenger Set	400
___ 11-80048	710 Series 3-Car GN Passenger Set	400
___ 11-80049	2600 Series 4-Car Chessie Passenger Set	430
___ 11-80050	2600 Series 4-Car Southern Passenger Set	430
___ 11-80051	No. 2613 Chessie Pullman Coach	110
___ 11-80052	No. 2613 Southern Pullman Coach	110
___ 11-80053	No. 710 NH Baggage Car	140
___ 11-80054	No. 710 NH Passenger Coach	140
___ 11-80055	No. 710 GN Baggage Car	140
___ 11-80056	No. 710 GN Passenger Coach	140
___ 11-80059	710 Series 3-car MILW Passenger Set	400

Lionel Corporation Tinplate		Retail	
11-80060	No. 713 MILW Baggage Car	140	___
11-80061	No. 710 MILW Passenger Coach	140	___
11-80062	710 Series 3-car PRR Passenger Set	400	___
11-80063	No. 713 PRR Baggage Car	140	___
11-80064	No. 710 PRR Passenger Coach	140	___
11-90001	No. 300 Hellgate Bridge, green/cream	500	___
11-90002	No. 300 Hellgate Bridge, silver/white	500	___
11-90003	No. 092 Signal Tower, cream/red	70	___
11-90006	No. 437 Switch Tower	280	___
11-90007	No. 155 Freight Shed	330	___
11-90008	No. 116 Passenger Station	400	___
11-90009	No. 438 Signal Tower	150	___
11-90010	No. 192 Villa Set	200	___
11-90011	No. 191 Villa	70	___
11-90012	No. 54 Street Lamp Set, green	45	___
11-90013	No. 54 Street Lamp Set, red	45	___
11-90014	No. 56 Gas Lamp Set, green	35	___
11-90015	No. 56 Gas Lamp Set, maroon	35	___
11-90016	No. 57 Corner Lamp Set, black	40	___
11-90017	No. 57 Corner Lamp Set, red	35	___
11-90018	No. 58 Lamp Set, single arc, cream	35	___
11-90019	No. 58 Lamp Set, single arc, dark green	35	___
11-90020	No. 59 Gooseneck Lamp Set, black	40	___
11-90021	No. 59 Gooseneck Lamp Set, maroon	40	___
11-90022	No. 1184 Bungalow (std)	200	___
11-90023	No. 1184 Bungalow (std)	200	___
11-90024	No. 1189 Villa (std)	300	___
11-90025	No. 1191 Villa (std)	300	___
11-90026	No. 165 Magnetic Crane	300	___
11-90027	No. 441 Weighing Station (std)	380	___
11-90028	No. 69 Operating Warning Bell	50	___
11-90029	No. 78 Automatic Control Signal (std)	70	___
11-90030	No. 79 Flashing Railroad Signal	70	___
11-90031	No. 80 Operating Semaphore	70	___
11-90032	No. 63 Lamp Post Set, aluminum	50	___
11-90033	No. 87 Railroad Crossing Signal	50	___
11-90034	No. 92 Floodlight Tower Set	160	___
11-90035	No. 94 High Tension Tower Set	150	___
11-90036	No. Automatic Block Signal (std)	70	___
11-90037	No. 163 Freight Accessory Set, green cart	100	___
11-90038	No. 163 Freight Accessory Set, orange cart	100	___
11-90039	No. 208 Tools and Chest, dark gray	80	___
11-90040	No. 208 Tools and Chest, silver	80	___
11-90041	No. 550 Miniature Figures	100	___
11-90042	No. 64 Lamp Post Set, light green	30	___
11-90043	No. 85 Race Car Set	700	___

Lionel Corporation Tinplate		Retail
____ 11-90044	Straight Race Car Track Section	20
____ 11-90045	Inside Curve Race Car Track Section	20
____ 11-90046	Outside Curve Race Car Track Section	20
____ 11-90047	No. 55 Airplane & No. 49 Airport Set with mat	800
____ 11-90048	No. 49 Airport Mat	60
____ 11-90049	No. 90 Flagpole	50
____ 11-90050	No. 205 Merchandise Containers, 3 pieces (std)	130
____ 11-90052	No. 442 Diner	160
____ 11-90053	No. 43 Runabout Boat, red/white	450
____ 11-90054	No. 44 Speed Boat	450
____ 11-90055	No. 71 Telegraph Post Set, gray/red	80
____ 11-90056	Teardrop Lamp Set, pea green	20
____ 11-90057	No. 46 Crossing Gate	40
____ 11-90058	Small Oil Drum Set	20
____ 11-90060	No. 115 Passenger Station, beige/pea green	300
____ 11-90061	No. 115 Passenger Station, cream, orange/blue	300
____ 11-90062	No. 134 Lionel City Station with stop	330
____ 11-90063	No. 444 Roundhouse Section	500
____ 11-90064	No. 200 Turntable, red/black	200
____ 11-90065	No. 89 Flagpole, blue base (std)	50
____ 11-90066	No. 89 Flagpole, white base (std)	50
____ 11-90067	No. 89 American Flag Pole, white base (std)	50
____ 11-90068	Operating Industrial Crane	350
____ 11-90069	Operating Industrial Crane, TCA 2010 Convention	350
____ 11-90070	No. 552 Diner, orange/blue	200
____ 11-90071	No. 552 Diner, white/blue	200
____ 11-90072	No. 911 Country Estate, cream/red	140
____ 11-90073	No. 911 Country Estate, red/green	140
____ 11-90074	No. 912 Suburban Home, ivory/peacock	140
____ 11-90075	No. 912 Suburban Home, mustard/green	140
____ 11-90076	No. 913 Landscaped Bungalow, white/maroon	110
____ 11-90077	No. 913 Landscaped Bungalow, light green/peacock	110
____ 11-90078	AF No. 2050 Old Glory Flag Pole	100
____ 11-90079	No. 43 Runabout Boat, orange/blue	400
____ 11-90084	No. 57 Lamp Post Set, Lionel & American Flyer Aves.	40
____ 11-90085	No. 57 Lamp Post Set, orange, 21st St. & Fifth Ave.	40
____ 11-90086	AF No. 2013 Corner Lamp Set, yellow	40
____ 11-90089	No. 436 Power Station, cream	150
____ 11-90090	No. 436 Power Station, terra-cotta	150
____ 11-90094	No. 438 Signal Tower	160
____ 11-90095	No. 116 Passenger Station	400
____ 11-90096	No. 1184 Bungalow, gray/green	200
____ 11-90097	No. 1184 Bungalow, white/maroon	200
____ 11-90098	No. 1189 Villa (std)	300
____ 11-90099	No. 1191 Villa (std)	300
____ 11-90100	No. 442 Diner	160

Lionel Corporation Tinplate		Retail	
11-90101	No. 54 Lamp Post Set, pea green	45	___
11-90102	No. 54 Lamp Post Set, state brown	45	___
11-90103	No. 58 Lamp Post Set, peacock	35	___
11-90104	No. 58 Lamp Post Set, orange	35	___
11-90105	No. 59 Lamp Post Set, dark green	40	___
11-90106	No. 59 Lamp Post Set, light green	40	___
11-90107	No. 92 Floodlight Tower Set	170	___
11-90108	No. 79 Flashing Signal	70	___
11-90109	No. 69 Warning Signal	50	___
11-90110	No. 94 High Tension Tower Set	170	___
11-90111	No. 57 Corner Lamp Set, orange, Lionel	40	___
11-90112	No. 57 Corner Lamp Set, blue, Lionel	40	___
11-90113	No. 57 Corner Lamp Set, blue/yellow	40	___
11-90114	No. 152 Operating Crossing Gate	40	___
11-90115	No. 153 Operating Block Signal	40	___
11-90116	No. 154 Highway Flashing Signal	40	___
11-90117	No. 437 Switch Signal Tower, cream/orange	300	___
11-90118	No. 437 Switch Signal Tower, terra-cotta/green	300	___
11-90119	AF No. 4230 Roadside Flashing Signal	100	___
11-90120	No. 200 Turntable, gray/green	200	___
11-90121	No. 200 Turntable, orange/blue	200	___
11-90122	No. 437 Switch Tower	280	___
11-90123	No. 98 Coal Bunker	180	___
11-99030	No. 25 Illuminated Track Bumpers (std)	60	___

Section 5
CLUB CARS AND SPECIAL PRODUCTION

			Esc	Mint
Artrain				
___	9486	GTW "I Love Michigan" Boxcar, *87*	155	305
___	17885	1-D Tank Car, *90*	35	65
___	17891	GTW 20th Anniversary Boxcar, *91*	40	75
___	19425	CSX Flatcar with "Art in Celebration" trailer, *96*	40	80
___	52013	Norfolk Southern Flatcar with trailer, *92*	115	230
___	52024	Conrail Auto Carrier, *93*	45	90
___	52049	BN Gondola with coil covers, *94*	30	55
___	52097	Chessie System Reefer, *95*	20	35
___	52140	Union Pacific Bunk Car, *97*	20	35
___	52165	SP Caboose "6256," *98*	30	60
___	52197	Santa Fe GP38 Diesel, *99*	125	245
___	52227	"Artistry in Space" Boxcar, *00*	40	75
___	52255	30th Anniversary Flatcar with billboard, *01*	50	100
___	52283	Paint Vat Car, *02*	30	60
___	52331	Flatcar with "America's Railways" trailer, *03*	75	150
___	52349	Hometown Art Museum Hopper, purple, *04*	20	35
___	52350	"Native Views" 3-bay Hopper, *04*	35	65
___	52411	"35 Years" 1-D Tank Car, *06*	20	35
Carnegie Science Center				
___	25085	Miniature Railroad & Village Boxcar, *09*	25	50
___	26750	Great Miniature Railroad & Village Boxcar, *99*	40	80
___	36202	Great Miniature Railroad 80th Anniversary Boxcar, *00*	55	110
___	36234	Great Miniature Railroad & Village Boxcar, *01*	25	50
___	52277	Carnegie Science Center 10th Anniversary Boxcar, *02*	30	60
___	52332	Miniature Railroad & Village Boxcar, *03*	30	60
___	52362	Miniature Railroad & Village 50th Anniversary Boxcar, *04*	25	50
___	52399	MRR&V Express Boxcar, *05*	25	50
___	52432	Miniature Railroad & Village Boxcar, *06*	25	50
___	52510	Miniature Railroad & Village Caboose, *08*	25	50
Chicagoland Railroad Club				
___	52081	C&NW Boxcar "6464-555," *96*	35	70
___	52101	BN Maxi-Stack Flatcar "64287" with containers, *97*	40	80
___	52102	SF Extended Vision Caboose, red roof, *96*	40	75
___	52103	SF Extended Vision Caboose, black roof, *96*	40	75
___	52120	Shedd Aquarium Car "3435-557," *98*	50	100
___	52148	REA/Santa Fe Operating Boxcar, *99*	35	70
___	52170	SP Operating Boxcar "52170-561," *99*	35	65
___	52171	UP Operating Boxcar "52171-561," *99*	35	65
___	52178	Burlington Operating Boxcar "52178-559," *00*	35	70
___	52179	ACL Operating Boxcar "52179-560," *00*	40	75
___	52215	C&NW 3-bay Cylindrical Hopper, *01*	30	60

CLUB CARS AND SPECIAL PRODUCTION		Esc	Mint	
52216	C&NW Cylindrical Hopper, 02	30	60	___
52223	REA/Santa Fe Centennial Operating Boxcar, 00	35	65	___
52251	PRR Express Car, green, 01	35	65	___
52259	MP GP20 Diesel, traditional, 01	125	250	___
52292	PRR Express Car, tuscan red, 02	25	50	___
52327	City of Los Angeles Express Car, 04	35	65	___
52328	City of New Haven Express Car, 04	30	55	___
52363	City of New Orleans Express Car, 04	30	55	___
52364	City of New York Express Car, 04	35	65	___
52388	Great Northern Tool Car, 06	25	50	___
52389	Great Northern Crew Car, 06	25	50	___
52390	Great Northern Welding Caboose, 06	40	80	___
52391	Great Northern Racing Crew Car, 06	25	50	___
52426	City of San Francisco Express Car, 07	30	55	___
52427	Rock Island Rocket Express Car, 07	30	55	___
52475	Western Pacific UP Heritage Boxcar, 07	30	60	___

Classic Toy Trains

52126	MILW Boxcar "21027" with CTT Logo, 97	25	50	

Dept. 56

16270	Heritage Village Boxcar "9796," 96	30	55	___
52096	Snow Village Boxcar "9756," 95	45	85	___
52139	Square Window Caboose "6256," 97	35	70	___
52157	Holly Brothers 3-D Tank Car, 98	45	85	___
52175	4-6-4 Hudson Locomotive, CC, 99	175	350	___
52199	4-bay Hopper "6756," 00	30	55	___
52254	"Happy Holidays" Gondola, 01	20	35	___

Eastwood Automobilia

16275	Radio Flyer Boxcar "16275," 96	25	50	___
16757	Johnny Lightning Auto Carrier "3435," 96	45	90	___
16985	Flatcar with 2 Ford vans, 97	25	50	___
52044	Vat Car, 95	15	30	___
52083	PRR Flatcar "21697" with tanker, 95	20	40	___
52130	Flatcar with Hot Wheels tanker, 97	30	60	___
16275	Radio Flyer Boxcar "16275," 96	25	50	___
16757	Johnny Lightning Auto Carrier "3435," 96	45	90	___
16985	Flatcar with 2 Ford vans, 97	25	50	___
52044	Vat Car, 95	15	30	___
52083	PRR Flatcar "21697" with tanker, 95	20	40	___
52130	Flatcar with Hot Wheels tanker, 97	30	60	___

Gadsden-Pacific Division Toy Train Operating Museum

17872	Anaconda Ore Car, 88	35	70	___
17878	Magma Ore Car, 89	30	55	___
17881	Phelps Dodge Ore Car, 90	20	40	___
17886	Cyprus Ore Car, 91	15	30	___

	CLUB CARS AND SPECIAL PRODUCTION	Esc	Mint
____	**19961** Inspiration Consolidated Copper Ore Car, *92*	15	30
____	**52011** Tucson, Cornelia & Gila Bend Ore Car, *93*	15	30
____	**52027** Pinto Valley Mine Ore Car, *94*	15	30
____	**52071** Copper Basin Railway Ore Car, *95*	15	30
____	**52089** SMARRCO Ore Car, *96*	10	25
____	**52124** El Paso & Southwestern Ore Car, *97*	20	40
____	**52164** SP Ore Car, *98*	20	35
____	**52177** Arizona Southern Ore Car, *99*	20	35
____	**52213** BHP Copper Ore Car, *00*	15	30
____	**52248** Tombstone & Western Ore Car, *01*	20	40
____	**52279** Dragoon & Northern Ore Car, *02*	25	50
____	**52307** Twin Buttes Ore Car, *03*	20	35
____	**52358** AJO & Southwestern Ore Car, *04*	25	45
____	**52386** Ray & Gila Bend Ore Car, *05*	24	45
____	**52421** Calabasas, Tuscon & Northwestern Ore Car, *06*	25	45
____	**52473** Mascot & Western Ore Car, *07*	45	90
____	**52524** Tucson, Globe & Northern Ore Car, *08*	20	40
____	**52558** Port of Tucson Ore Car, *09*	25	45
____	**52579** Rosemont Copper Ore Car, *10*	20	40
____	**52588** ASARCO Ore Car, *11*	20	40
____	**58234** ASARCO Haden Smelter Ore Car, *15*		45
____	**58262** Union Pacific Ore Car, *16*		45
____	**58513** Freeport-McMoRan Ore Car, *12*	20	40
____	**58557** San Pedro & Southwestern Ore Car, *13*	20	40
____	**58583** Arizona Eastern Ore Car, *14*	20	40

Houston Tinplate Operators Society

		Esc	Mint
____	**8900** Sam Houston Mint Car, *00*	60	120
____	**8901** Miracle Petroleum 1-D Tank Car, *01*	50	100
____	**8902** USS Houston Submarine Car, *02*	50	100
____	**8903** Railway Express Boxcar, *03*	50	100
____	**8904** Lone Star Bay Window Caboose, *04*	50	100
____	**8999** Lone Star Aquarium Car, mermaid or trout, *99*	50	100

Inland Empire Train Collectors Association

		Esc	Mint
____	**1979** Boxcar, *79*	5	15
____	**1980** SP-type Caboose, *80*	5	15
____	**1981** Quad Hopper, *81*	5	15
____	**1982** 3-D Tank Car, *82*	5	15
____	**1983** Reefer, *83*	5	15
____	**1986** Bunk Car, *86*	5	15
____	**7518** Carson City Mint Car, *84*	25	45

Lionel Central Operating Lines

		Esc	Mint
____	**1981** Boxcar, *81*	10	25
____	**1986** Work Caboose, shell only, *86*	5	15
____	**5724** Pennsylvania Bunk Car, *84*	20	40

CLUB CARS AND SPECIAL PRODUCTION		Esc	Mint	
6508	Canadian Pacific Crane Car, 83	20	40	___
6907	NYC Wood-sided Caboose, 97	25	50	___
9184	Erie Bay Window Caboose, 82	10	20	___
9475	D&H "I Love NY" Boxcar, 85	20	35	___
16342	CSX Gondola with coil covers, 92	10	20	___
17221	NYC Boxcar, 95	15	30	___

Lionel Collectors Club of America

LCCA National Convention Cars

		Esc	Mint	
6112	Commonwealth Edison Quad Hopper with coal, 83	40	80	___
6323	Virginia Chemicals 1-D Tank Car, 86	35	65	___
6567	Illinois Central Gulf Crane Car "100408," 85	35	65	___
7403	LNAC Boxcar, 84	10	25	___
9118	Corning Covered Quad Hopper, 74	45	90	___
9155	Monsanto 1-D Tank Car, 75	25	45	___
9159UP	UP Reefer, 10	50	100	___
9212	Seaboard Coast Line Flatcar with trailers, 76	15	30	___
9259	Southern Bay Window Caboose, 77	15	40	___
9358	"Sands of Iowa" Covered Quad Hopper, 80	20	35	___
9435	Central of Georgia Boxcar, 81	15	30	___
9460	D&TS Automobile Boxcar, 82	20	35	___
9701	Baltimore & Ohio Automobile Boxcar, 72	85	170	___
9727	TA&G Boxcar, 73	70	135	___
9728	Union Pacific Stock Car, 78	10	25	___
9733	Airco Boxcar with tank car body, 79	25	50	___
17870	East Camden & Highland Boxcar (std 0), 87	20	35	___
17873	Ashland Oil 3-D Tank Car, 88	35	70	___
17876	Columbia, Newberry & Laurens Boxcar (std 0), 89	20	40	___
17880	D&RGW Wood-sided Caboose (std 0), 90	30	55	___
17887	Conrail Flatcar with Armstrong Tile trailer (std 0), 91	25	50	___
17888	Conrail Flatcar with Ford trailer (std 0), 91	40	80	___
17892	Conrail Flatcar with Armstrong and Ford Trailers (std 0), 91	70	140	___
17899	NASA Tank Car "190" (std 0), 92	25	50	___
27019	Imco PS-2 Covered Hopper, 09	25	50	___
52023	D&TS 2-bay ACF Hopper "2601" (std 0), 93	20	40	___
52038	Southern Hopper "360794" with coal (std 0), 94	25	45	___
52074	Iowa Beef Packers Reefer "197095" (std 0), 95	15	30	___
52090	Pere Marquette DD Boxcar "71996" (std 0), 96	25	50	___
52110	CStPM&O Boxcar "71997" (std 0), 97	25	50	___
52151	Amtrak Baggage Boxcar "71998" (std 0), 98	35	65	___
52176	Fort Worth & Denver Boxcar "8277" (std 0), 99	30	55	___
52195	Double-stack Car with 2 containers, 00	50	100	___
52244	Louisville & Nashville Horse Car "2001," 01	25	50	___
52266	PRR "Coal Goes To War" Hopper "707025," 02	45	85	___
52267	PRR "Coal Goes To War" Hopper "707026," 02	45	90	___
52299	Las Vegas Mint Car, 03	40	80	___

	CLUB CARS AND SPECIAL PRODUCTION	Esc	Mint
___	52343 MILW Milk Car, orange, 04	80	160
___	52344 MILW Milk Car, blue, 04	105	205
___	52393 MKT Speeder, yellow, nonpowered, 05	10	20
___	52394 Frisco Speeder, red, powered, 05	10	25
___	52395 Frisco Flatcar, silver, 05	10	25
___	52396 Frisco Flatcar with 2 speeders, 05	65	125
___	52412 UP Auxiliary Power Car, 06	30	55
___	52455 C&NW/UP Tank Car, 07	55	110
___	52491 PS-2 Covered Hopper 2-pack, 08	70	140
___	52507 NYC Water Tower, 08	45	85
___	52514 ATSF Mint Car with Gold, 09	140	275
___	52543 BNSF Mechanical Reefer, 09	70	140
___	52559 UP Cylindrical Hopper, 10	50	100
___	52562 D&RGW Uranium Transport Mint Car, 10	115	230
___	58254 Providence & Worcester Flatcar, 15	50	130
___	58271 MP Maxi-Stack Container Car with containers, 16		100
___	58509 Norfolk Southern Camouflage PS-1 Boxcar, 12	50	95
___	58560 Southern Tennessean Boxcar, 13	45	90
___	58576 Monon Operating Boxcar, 14	65	125
___	58599 UP Cylindrical Hopper, 11	55	150
___	72511 Alamo Mint Car, 11	75	150
___	75511 Federal Reserve Mint Car, 11	100	200

LCCA Meet Specials

		Esc	Mint
___	1130 Tender, 76	5	15
___	6014-900 Frisco Boxcar (027), 75	15	30
___	6483 Jersey Central SP-type Caboose, 82	15	30
___	9016 Chessie System Hopper (027), 79	10	20
___	9036 Mobilgas 1-D Tank Car (027), 78	10	20
___	9142 Republic Steel Gondola, green or blue, with canisters, 77	10	25

Other LCCA Production

		Esc	Mint
___	4001 RJ Corman Boxcar, 99	40	80
___	4002 RJ Corman Boxcar, 99	20	40
___	6464-2002 Maddox Retirement Boxcar, 02	50	100
___	8068 Rock Island GP20 Diesel, 80	60	120
___	9739 D&RGW Boxcar, 78	10	25
___	9771 Norfolk & Western Boxcar, 77	15	30
___	14154 Water Tower with LCCA plaque, 04	45	90
___	17174 Great Northern 3-bay Hopper, 03	10	25
___	17234 Port Huron & Detroit Boxcar, 00	25	45
___	17377 American Railway Express Reefer "302," 06	25	50
___	17412 Gondola, blue, 02	15	30
___	17895 LCCA Tractor, 91	10	20
___	17896 Lancaster Lines Tractor, 91	15	30
___	18090 D&RGW 4-6-2 Locomotive and Tender, 90	155	305
___	18483 C&O Ballast Tamper, 07	40	75

CLUB CARS AND SPECIAL PRODUCTION	Esc	Mint	
18490	UP Ballast Tamper, yellow, 06	65	125	
19998	"Seasons Greetings" Boxcar, 03	20	40	
26023	Flatcar with bulldozer, 04	30	55	
26024	Flatcar with scraper, 04	35	65	
26049	Speedboat Willie Flatcar with boat, 05	25	45	
26132	UP 1-D Tank Car, 06	15	30	
26780	Operating Giraffe Car, green or pink, 05	35	70	
26791	UP Chase Gondola, red, 03	15	30	
26791	Rio Grande Chase Gondola, black, 06	15	30	
26795	Mrs. O'Leary's Dairy Farm Stock Car, 07	50	100	
26834	"La Cosa Nostra Railway" Operating Ice Car, 07	40	75	
29232	Lenny the Lion Hi-Cube, signed by Lenny Dean, 98	35	65	
52025	Madison Hardware Tractor and Trailer, 93	10	20	
52039	"Track 29" Bumper, 94	10	25	
52055	SOVEX Tractor and Trailer, 94	10	20	
52056	Southern Tractor and Trailer, 94	15	25	
52091	Lenox Tractor and Trailer, 95	5	15	
52092	Iowa Interstate Tractor and Trailer, 95	10	20	
52100	Grand Rapids Station Platform, 98	10	25	
52107	On-track Pickup, orange, 96	25	50	
52108	On-track Van, blue, 96	20	35	
52131	Beechcraft Airplane, blue, 97	10	25	
52138	Beechcraft Airplane, orange, 97	10	25	
52152	Ben Franklin and Liberty Bell Reefer, 98	60	120	
52153	6414 Auto Set, 4-pack, 98	35	70	
52206	SD40 Diesel and Extended Vision Caboose, 00	325	650	
52257	"Season's Greetings" Gondola, 01	20	35	
52273	Flatcar with submarine, 02	110	220	
52300	Halloween General Train, 04	180	360	
52348	Halloween General Sheriff and Outlaw Car, 04	60	115	
52405	Halloween General Add-on Cars, 06	80	160	
52406	Halloween General Cannon, 08	70	135	
52423	New Haven Alco Diesel Passenger Set, 09	255	510	
52468	Postwar "2434" Passenger Coach, 09	40	75	
52469	Postwar "2432" Passenger Coach, 09	40	75	
52528	Burlington Alco Diesel Passenger Set, 09	150	340	
52540	Passenger Shelter, 09	10	25	
52581	Texas Special Milk Car, 10	55	110	
52582	Gondola with dinosaurs, 12	25	45	
58217	B&M Smoking Caboose, 15		105	
58224	Walking Brakeman Car, 15		100	
58249	Holiday Boxcar, 15	20	80	
58251	Maine Central Flatcar with trailers, 15		100	
58272	MKT Maxi-Stack Container Car with containers, 16		100	
58526	Texas Special Cow and Calf SW9 Switchers, 14		375	
58532	Lou Caponi Blue Coal Train, 14	100	200	

	CLUB CARS AND SPECIAL PRODUCTION	Esc	Mint
___	**58549** Texas Special Diamonds Mint Car, *14*	40	75
___	**58561** Southern Pelican Boxcar, *13*	35	70
___	**58584** 45th Anniversary Auto Rack Loader, *14*	60	120

Lionel Operating Train Society

LOTS National Convention Cars

		Esc	Mint
___	**303** Stauffer Chemical 1-D Tank Car, *85*	105	210
___	**3764** Kahn's Brine Tank Reefer, *81*	45	85
___	**6111** L&N Covered Quad Hopper, *83*	20	40
___	**6211** C&O Gondola with canisters, *86*	45	90
___	**9414** Cotton Belt Boxcar, *80*	30	55
___	**16812** Grand Trunk 2-bay ACF Hopper (std O), *96*	30	60
___	**16813** Pennsylvania Power & Light Hopper (std O), *97*	40	80
___	**17874** Milwaukee Road Log Dump Car "59629," *88*	75	150
___	**17875** Port Huron & Detroit Boxcar "1289," *89*	25	50
___	**17882** B&O DD Boxcar "298011" with ETD, *90*	35	65
___	**17890** CSX Auto Carrier "151161," *91*	40	80
___	**18890** Union Pacific RS3 Diesel "8805," *89*	75	145
___	**19960** Western Pacific Boxcar "1952" (std O), *92*	35	65
___	**38356** Dow Chemical 3-D Tank Car, *87*	65	125
___	**52014** BN TTUX Flatcar Set with N&W trailers, *93*	105	205
___	**52041** BN TTUX Flatcar Set with Conrail trailers, *94*	45	85
___	**52067** Burlington Operating Ice Car "50240," *95*	30	60
___	**52135** ATSF Reefer "22739," *98*	30	55
___	**52162** Gulf Mobile & Ohio DD Boxcar "24580," *99*	35	65
___	**52196** CP Maxi-Stack Flatcar "524115" with 2 containers, *00*	50	95
___	**52234** WM Well Car with transformer, *01*	30	60
___	**52261** Schlitz Beer Reefer "92132," *02*	30	60
___	**52281** PRR Operating Boxcar, *03*	30	55
___	**52342** Southern Stock Car, sound, *04*	30	55
___	**52346** D&H PS-2 Cement Hopper, *06*	35	65
___	**52347** SF SD80 MAC Diesel, TMCC, *04*	175	350
___	**52380/81** Virginian Coal Hopper, *05*	25	50
___	**52382** SF Extended View Caboose, *05*	165	325
___	**52425** SP&S Boxcar (std O), *07*	45	90
___	**52474** NYC Evans Auto Loader with 4 Studebakers, *08*	40	80
___	**52550** NC&StL Dixieland Boxcar, *09*	40	75
___	**52566** NH State of Maine Boxcar, *10*	30	60
___	**52580** Robin Hood Beer Double-sheathed Boxcar, *11*	40	80
___	**58223** Chicago Great Western Flatcar with Edelweiss Beer Trailers, *15*		75
___	**58508** Genesee Beer & Ale Double-sheathed Boxcar, *11* 35		70
___	**58553** UP Maxi-Stack Car with WP feather containers, *13* 40		75
___	**58575** H. J. Heinz Double-sheathed Boxcar, *14*	35	70
___	**80948** Michigan Central Boxcar, *82*	115	230
___	**83862** Cradle of Liberty Boxcar, *16*		75
___	**83863** Santa Fe Warbonnet Tank Car, *16*		75

CLUB CARS AND SPECIAL PRODUCTION		Esc	Mint	
83872/3	D&RGW 2-car Ore Car Set, 17		110	___
121315	Pennsylvania Hi-Cube Boxcar, 84	175	345	___

LOTS Meet Specials

52413	Saratoga Brewery Reefer, 06	30	60	___
52456	Alpenrose Dairy Milk Car, 07	50	95	___
52506	Studebaker Automobile Parts Boxcar, 08	40	75	___
52552	Radioactive Waste Removal Car, 09	45	85	___
58236	Tucker Automobile Parts Boxcar, 15		75	___

Other LOTS Production

1233	Seattle & North Coast Hi-Cube Boxcar, 86	350	450	___
52042	BN TTUX Flatcar "637500C" with CN trailer, 94	30	60	___
52048	Canadian National Tractor and Trailer "197993," 94	20	35	___
52129	Lighted Billboard with Angela Trotta Thomas art, 97	15	30	___
52217	LOTS/LCCA 2000 Convention Billboard, 00	5	10	___
52260	National Aquarium in Baltimore Car, 01	55	110	___
52280	"More Precious than Gold" Mint Car, 02	45	90	___
52309	Patriotic Tank Car, 03	35	70	___
52359	Silver Anniversary Ore Car "1979," 04	20	40	___
52360	Silver Anniversary Ore Car "2004," 04	20	40	___
52419	Touring Layout Aquarium Car, 05	45	90	___
52477	Santa Fe Warbonnet Boxcar, 07	40	75	___
52523	Santa Fe Flatcar with trailer and tractor, 08	45	90	___
52553	Tennessee Aquarium Car, 09	35	65	___
52567	Santa Fe ACF 2-bay Hopper, 10	30	60	___
52590	Santa Fe Warbonnet Mint Car, 11	40	75	___
58228	Burlington Zephyr Double-sheathed Boxcar, 15		75	___
58535	Santa Fe ACF Transparent Boxcar, 12	40	75	___
58566	Virginia & Truckee Carson City Mint Car, 13	35	70	___
58593	Porter Locomotive Parts Boxcar, 14		70	___
58594/5	Santa Fe Crane and Work Caboose, 14		135	___

Lionel Century Club

14532	PRR Sharknose Diesel AA Set, LCC II, 00	350	690	___
18053	2-8-4 Berkshire Locomotive "726," 97	360	705	___
18057	6-8-6 PRR S2 Steam Turbine Locomotive "671," 98	290	570	___
18058	4-6-4 Hudson Locomotive "773," 97	375	735	___
18068	Tender for PRR Steam Turbine Locomotive "773," 99	105	210	___
18135	NYC F3 Diesel AA Set, 99	325	650	___
18178	NYC F3 Diesel B Unit, 99	115	230	___
18314	PRR GG1 Electric "2332," 97	280	560	___
18340	FM Train Master Set, LCC II, 00	450	900	___
24510	PRR Sharknose Diesel B Unit, LCC II, 00	100	200	___
28069	NYC 4-8-6 Niagara Locomotive "6024," CC, LCC II, 00	460	920	___
29173	Empire State Express Passenger Car 4-pack, LCC II, 02	175	350	___
29178	Empire State Express Passenger Car 2-pack, LCC II, 02	90	175	___

	CLUB CARS AND SPECIAL PRODUCTION	Esc	Mint
___	**29181** Empire State Express Diner, LCC II, *02*	95	190
___	**29204** Boxcar "1900-2000," *96*	165	330
___	**29226** Berkshire Boxcar, *97*	75	145
___	**29227** GG1 Boxcar, *98*	30	55
___	**29228** PRR Turbine Boxcar "671," *99*	30	60
___	**29248** F3 Boxcar "2333," *99*	35	65
___	**31716** Niagara Milk Train Set, LCC II, *00*	150	300
___	**31726** PRR Sharknose Coal Train Set, LCC II, *00*	90	180
___	**31731** Train Master Freight Train Set, LCC II, *00*	90	180
___	**38000** NYC 4-6-4 Hudson Empire State Locomotive, LCC II, *02*	495	990
___	**39201** Hudson Boxcar "773," *00*	30	60
___	**39215** Niagara Boxcar, LCC II, *01*	25	50
___	**39217** Boxcar, LCC II, *00*	30	60
___	**39218** Gold Boxcar, LCC II, *00*	45	85
___	**39237** M-10000 Boxcar, LCC II, *00*	35	70
___	**39246** PRR Sharknose Boxcar, LCC II, *00*	30	55
___	**39265** Fairbanks-Morse Train Master Boxcar, LCC II, *00*	30	60
___	**39266** Empire State Boxcar, LCC II, *00*	20	40
___	**51007** UP M-10000 4-car Passenger Set, LCC II, *00*	485	970
___	**51249** UP Overland Route Sleeper Car, LCC II, *02*	60	120

Lionel Railroader Club

		Esc	Mint
___	**780** Boxcar, *82*	35	65
___	**781** Flatcar with trailers, *83*	25	50
___	**782** 1-D Tank Car, *85*	25	45
___	**784** Covered Quad Hopper, *84*	30	60
___	**11183** Lincoln Funeral Train	400	800
___	**11319** PRR Tuscan K4 Locomotive, CC	450	900
___	**11320** PRR Tuscan K4 Locomotive	375	750
___	**12875** Tractor and Trailer, *94*	10	20
___	**12921** Illuminated Station Platform, *95*	10	20
___	**14274** Water Tower, *07*	10	20
___	**15034** 50th Anniversary Mail Car, *10*	25	50
___	**15035** Holiday Boxcar, *10*	25	50
___	**16800** Ore Car, yellow, *86*	35	70
___	**16801** Bunk Car, blue, *88*	20	35
___	**16802** Tool Car, *89*	25	35
___	**16803** Searchlight Car, *90*	10	25
___	**16804** Bay Window Caboose, *91*	15	30
___	**16839** Covered Bridge, *11*	25	50
___	**18680** 4-6-4 Hudson Locomotive, *00*	150	300
___	**18684** 4-6-2 Pacific Locomotive, *99*	110	220
___	**18818** GP38-2 Diesel, *92*	100	115
___	**19399** Christmas Boxcar, *13*	30	60
___	**19437** Flatcar with trailer, *97*	30	55
___	**19473** Operating Log Dump Car "3351," *99*	20	40

CLUB CARS AND SPECIAL PRODUCTION		Esc	Mint	
19685	Western Union Dining Car, 02	20	40	___
19695	Western Union 1-D Tank Car, 03	10	20	___
19774	Porthole Caboose, 99	25	50	___
19775	Stock Car, 99	25	50	___
19924	Boxcar, 93	10	20	___
19930	Quad Hopper with coal, 94	10	20	___
19935	1-D Tank Car, 95	10	25	___
19940	Vat Car, 96	15	30	___
19953	6464 Boxcar, 97	20	35	___
19965	Aquarium Car "3435," 99	30	55	___
19966	Gondola "9820" (std O), 98	15	30	___
19978	Gold Membership Boxcar, 99	25	45	___
19991	Gold Membership Boxcar, 00	35	65	___
19992	Western Union Tool Car "3550," 00	25	50	___
19993	Gold Membership Boxcar, 01	35	65	___
19994	Western Union Passenger Car "1307," 01	30	60	___
19995	25th Anniversary Boxcar (std O), 01	25	50	___
24217	Animated Billboard, 08	15	30	___
25073	Holiday Boxcar, 09	20	50	___
25631	Lincoln Train Passenger Car 2-pack	150	300	___
25635	Red Passenger Car 3-pack, 12	210	420	___
25635	Red Arrow Diner, 12	70	140	___
26089	Western Union Gondola with handcar, 05	35	65	___
26165	Western Union Reefer, 04	15	30	___
26382	Flatcar with tractor and tanker, 08	30	60	___
26413	Commemorative 4-bay Hopper, 08	35	70	___
26636	"6830" 50th Anniversary Flatcar with submarine, 11	30	55	___
26637	"6640" 50th Anniversary USMC Missile Launching Car, 11	35	65	___
27940	"6469" Liquified Gas Tank Car, 13	25	50	___
27943	"6416" Boat Loader, 13	25	50	___
27944	"3413" Mercury Capsule Launch Car, 13	30	60	___
27945	"6460-60" LV Covered Quad Hopper, 13	30	55	___
28062	4-6-4 Hudson Locomotive, 00	575	1150	___
28571	GP9 Diesel, CC, 07	125	250	___
28665	Western Union 2-8-4 Berkshire Locomotive "665," 05	90	175	___
29200	Lionel Boxcar "9700," 96	20	40	___
29313	"3409" 50th Anniversary Helicopter Car, 11	35	70	___
29657	"6413" 50th Anniversary Mercury Capsule Car, 12	30	55	___
29658	"6465" 50th Anniversary Cities Service 2-D Car, 12	25	50	___
29931	Holiday Boxcar, 05	10	25	___
29939	30th Anniversary Boxcar, 06	25	50	___
29941	Holiday Boxcar, 06	10	25	___
29946	Holiday Boxcar, 07	20	35	___
29947	Commemorative Boxcar, 07	15	30	___
29957	Holiday Boxcar, 08	25	50	___
29977	Holiday Boxcar, 11	30	60	___

	CLUB CARS AND SPECIAL PRODUCTION	Esc	Mint
____ 36521	Western Union Searchlight Caboose, 05	15	30
____ 36769	4th of July Lighted Boxcar, 03	35	70
____ 37968	Clock Tower with wreath, 11	25	45
____ 39249	Holiday Boxcar, 03	15	30
____ 39264	Holiday Boxcar, 04	25	50
____ 39352	"6445" 50th Anniversary Fort Knox Mint Car, 12	35	70
____ 39353	50th Anniversary Santa Fe Boxcar, 11	30	55
____ 39496	"6475" 50th Anniversary Vat Car, 10	30	60
____ 58613	Holiday Boxcar, 14	30	90
____ 58632	1955 Maintenance of Way Truck, 13	85	165
____ 81116	Polar Express Operating Billboard, 14	30	60
____ 81117	Polar Express Flatcar with silver bell, 14	25	45

Lionel Railroad Club Milwaukee

		Esc	Mint
____ 52116	MILW Flatcar "194797," black, with tractor and trailer, 97	40	75
____ 52163	CMStP&P "Hiawatha" DD Automobile Boxcar, 98	30	60
____ 52180	MILW Flatcar "194799," tuscan, with trailer, 99	40	75
____ 52228	CMStP&P 1-D Water Tank Car "908309," 00	25	50
____ 52229	MILW 1-D Diesel Fuel Tank Car "907797," 00	25	50
____ 52230	1-D Tank Car 2-pack, 00	70	140
____ 52246	CMStP&P "Olympian" Boxcar "194701," 01	35	65
____ 52265	MILW/Zoological Society Aquarium Car "4701," orange, 02	30	55
____ 52278	MILW/Zoological Society Aquarium Car "4702," blue, 03	50	95
____ 52297	MILW Reefer "194703," yellow, 03	35	65
____ 52298	MILW Flatcar "194704" with orange trailer, 04	60	115
____ 52337	MILW/Zoological Society Motorized Aquarium Car, 04	45	90
____ 52368	MILW Flatcar "472004," black, 05	35	65
____ 52369	MILW Trailer Train Auto Carrier "194705," 05	45	85
____ 52370	CMStP&P Milk Car "364," tan, 05	40	80
____ 52387	CMStP&P Flatcar "194706," gray, 06	25	50
____ 52400	MILW PS-2 2-bay Hopper "99607," orange, 06	45	85
____ 52401	MILW PS-2 2-bay Hopper "98809," yellow, 06	35	65
____ 52402	CMStP&P URTX Operating Ice Car "4706," 06	45	85
____ 52428	CMStP&P 0-4-0 Switcher and Caboose Set, 60th Anniversary, 06	140	275
____ 52429	CMStP&P 0-4-0 Switcher, 06	100	200
____ 52430	CMStP&P Offset Cupola Caboose, 06	35	70
____ 52458	MILW Stock Car "102721" (std O), 07	35	65
____ 52466	CMStP&P Stock Car "105254" (std O), 07	35	65
____ 52551	MILW "Big M" DD Boxcar "200947," yellow, 09	30	60
____ 52572	MILW Reiman Aquarium Car, 11	40	75
____ 52599	MILW 2-bay ACF Hopper, 12	30	60
____ 58263	Breast Cancer Awareness Boxcar, 16		80
____ 58563	CMStP&P Round-Roof Boxcar, 13	35	70
____ 58591	MILW Flatcar with auto frames, 14	30	60

Long Island Toy Train Locomotive Engineers

		Esc	Mint	
58520	Entenmann's Vat Car, 12	35	65	___
58556	Flatcar with U.S. Navy airplane, 13	35	70	___
58562	Entenmann's Quad Hopper, 14	40	75	___

Nassau Lionel Operating Engineers

		Esc	Mint	
8389	Long Island Boxcar, 89	50	100	___
8390	Long Island Covered Quad Hopper, 90	50	100	___
8391A	Long Island Bunk Car, 91	45	90	___
8391B	Long Island Tool Car, 91	45	90	___
8392	Long Island 1-D Tank Car, 92	55	105	___
52007	Long Island RS3 Diesel "1552," 93	125	250	___
52019	Long Island Boxcar, 93	35	65	___
52020	Long Island Bay Window Caboose, 93	50	95	___
52026	Long Island Flatcar "8394" with Grumman trailer, 94	235	465	___
52061	Long Island Stern's Pickle Products Vat Car "8395," 95	100	200	___
52072	Grumman Tractor, 94	40	75	___
52076	Long Island Observation Car "8396," 96	175	350	___
52112	Long Island Ronkonkoma Vista Dome Car "9783," 97	150	300	___
52122	Meenan Oil 1-D Tank Car "8397" (std O), 97	30	60	___
52123	Long Island Hicksville Diner Car "9883," 98	150	300	___
52144	Long Island Flatcar with Grumman van, 99	50	95	___
52145	Long Island Jamaica Passenger Coach, 99	150	300	___
52145	Long Island Penn Station Passenger Coach, 99	150	300	___
52166	Long Island Flatcar "8398" with Grumman trailer, 98	40	75	___
52174	REA Baggage Car "0083," 00		400	___
52186	Grucci Fireworks Boxcar, 00	35	70	___
52209	World's Fair Sleeper/Roomette Car "0183," 01		170	___
52232	Central RR of Long Island Boxcar, 01	30	60	___
52235	World's Fair Vista Dome Car "0283," 02		NRS	___
52256	New York & Atlantic Boxcar "8302," 02	30	60	___
52263	World's Fair Combination Car "0383," 02		NRS	___
52296	Long Island Flatcar with Republic tanker, 03	40	80	___
52329	New York & Atlantic Caboose, 04	40	80	___
52341	Long Island Flatcar with Pan Am trailer, 05	45	85	___
52365	Long Island Flatcar with Lilco transformer, 04	70	135	___
52420	Long Island 80th Anniversary Boxcar, 06	25	45	___
52480	Long Island Flatcar with pipes, 08	25	50	___
52489	Long Island Flatcar with P.C. Richard & Son trailer, 07	35	65	___
52555	Martha Clara Vineyards Vat Car, 09	30	60	___
52568	Flatcar with NY Islanders refrigerated trailer, 10	30	60	___
52586	Flatcar with Cradle of Aviation Museum trailer, 11	25	50	___
52592	Petland Discounts Aquarium Car, 11	35	70	___
58212	Cross Harbor Round-roof Boxcar, 15		65	___
58240	LIRR GLa Hopper, black, 16		80	___

	CLUB CARS AND SPECIAL PRODUCTION	Esc	Mint
58240	LIRR GLa Hopper, tuscan, *16*		80
58266	Nathan's 100th Anniversary Reefer, *16*		65
58500	Nassau County Firefighters Museum Tank Car, *12*	30	55
58567	Nathan's Famous Reefer "83131," *13*	40	75
58568	Nathan's Famous Reefer "83132," *13*	40	75
___ 58573	Long Island PS1 Boxcar "8312," *14*		80
___ 58581	Long Island Double-sheathed Boxcar, *14*		65
___	LIRR PS-2CD Scale Hopper, *17*		70

Railroad Museum of Long Island

___ 52416	RMLI 15th Anniversary LIRR Boxcar, *05*	85	170
___ 52433	Atlantis Marine World Aquarium Car, *06*	75	145
___ 52453	North Fork Bank Mint Car, *07*	45	90
___ 52497	LIRR Flatcar with Entenmann's trailer and tractor, *08*	55	110
___ 52498	Boeing Fairchild Container Car, *10*	40	75
___ 52548	RMLI "Celebrating 175 Years of Railroading" Boxcar, *09*	45	90
___ 52557	Entenmann's Operating Boxcar, *10*	45	90
___ 52570	Riverhead Building Supply Boxcar, *11*	30	60
___ 52571	Riverhead Visitor's Center Boxcar, *11*	30	60
___ 52577	King Kullen Boxcar, *11*	30	60
___ 52595	J. P. Holland Submarine Car, *12*	30	60
___ 58227	World's Fair Crew Car, *15*		75
___ 58259	Steam Up LIRR 39 Boxcar, *16*		85
___ 58521	Wonder Bread PS-2 Covered Hopper, *12*	30	60
___ 58551	Flatcar with White Castle refrigerated trailer, *13*	30	60
___ 58554	RCA Operating Radar Car, *13*	30	60
___ 58555	Flatcar with produce trailers, *15*		75
___ 58579	World's Fair Exhibit Car, *14*		80
___ 58580	World's Fair Tool Car, *15*		60

St. Louis Lionel Railroad Club

___ 52099	MP Flatcar with St. Louis trailer, *96*	35	65
___ 52104	St. Louis tractor and trailer, *96*	10	20
___ 52117	Wabash Flatcar with REA tractor and trailer, *97*	35	65
___ 52136A	Christmas Tractor and Trailer, *97*		NRS
___ 52136B	Frisco Tractor and Trailer, *98*		NRS
___ 52147	Frisco Campbell TOFC Flatcar, *98*	40	75
___ 52150	Frisco Campbell TOFC Flatcar, *98*	65	130
___ 52167	ATSF Flatcar "831999" with Navajo trailer, *99*	40	75
___ 52190	IC Flatcar with trailers, *00*	40	80
___ 52222	Cotton Belt Flatcar with SP tractor and trailer, *01*	25	50
___ 52224A	SP Flatcar with Navajo tractor and trailer, *01*	10	25
___ 52224B	SP Flatcar with service tractor and trailer, *01*	10	25
___ 52258	UP Flatcar with UP tractor and trailer, *02*	30	55
___ 52290	UP Flatcar with tractor trailer, *03*	40	75
___ 52336	U.S. Army Flatcar with tanker truck, *04*	65	125

CLUB CARS AND SPECIAL PRODUCTION		Esc	Mint	
52371	NYC Flatcar with Fire Company tanker truck, 05	70	145	
52392	PRR Flatcar with Hood's Milk tanker truck, 06	50	100	
52440	U.S.M.C. Flatcar with tractor and trailer, 07	70	135	
52490	Silver Special Flatcar with USA tractor and trailer, 08	50	100	
52513	Frisco Flatcar with U.S.A.F. trailer, 09	60	120	

Train Collectors Association

TCA National Convention Cars

511	St. Louis Baggage Car, 81	20	40	
2671-1968	TCA Tender, shell only, 68	30	55	___
5734	REA Reefer, 85	25	50	
6315	Pittsburgh 1-D Tank Car, 72	30	60	___
6436-1969	Open Quad Hopper, red, 69	40		___
6464-1965	Pittsburgh Boxcar, blue, 65	125	210	___
6464-1967	WP Convention Boxcar, 67	434	560	___
6464-1970	Chicago Boxcar, 70	45	85	___
6464-1971	Disneyland Boxcar, 71	210	240	___
6517-1966	Bay Window Caboose, 66	150	250	___
6926	New Orleans Extended Vision Caboose, 86	20	40	___
7205	Denver Combination Car, 82	25	50	___
7206	Louisville Passenger Car, 83	30	55	___
7212	Pittsburgh Passenger Car, 84	25	50	___
7812	Houston Stock Car, 77	10	25	
8476	4-6-4 Locomotive "5484," 85	155	310	
9123	Dearborn 3-tier Auto Carrier, 73	20	35	
9319	"Silver Jubilee" Mint Car, 79	65	130	
9544	Chicago Observation Car, 80	25	50	
9611	Boston Hi-Cube Boxcar, 78	10	25	___
9774	Orlando "Southern Belle" Boxcar, 75	15	35	___
9779	Philadelphia Boxcar "9700-1976," 76	20	35	___
9864	Seattle Reefer, 74	25	50	___
11737	TCA 40th Anniversary F3 Diesel ABA Set, 93	265	530	___
17879	Valley Forge Dining Car, 89	30	60	___
17883	New Georgia Passenger Car, 90	35	65	___
17898	Wabash Reefer "21596," 92	25	45	___
19211	Vermont Railway Flatcars (2) with 4 trailers, 08	80	160	___
52008	Bucyrus Erie Crane Car, 93	25	50	___
52035	Yorkrail GP9 Diesel "1750," shell only, 94	30	55	___
52036	TCA 40th Anniversary Bay Window Caboose, 94	20	40	___
52037	Yorkrail GP9 Diesel "1754," 94	75	150	___
52062	Skytop Observation Car, 95	180	360	___
52085	Full Vista Dome Car, 96	60	115	___
52106	City of Phoenix Diner, 97	50	100	___
52142	Massachusetts Central Maxi-Stack Flatcar "5100-01," 98	60	120	___
52143	City of Providence Passenger Car, 98	70	140	___
52146	Ocean Spray Reefer, 98	120	235	___

			Esc	Mint
CLUB CARS AND SPECIAL PRODUCTION				
___	52155	City of San Francisco Baggage Car, 99	70	140
___	52191	City of Grand Rapids Aluminum Passenger Car, 00	70	135
___	52210	Rico Station, 00	15	30
___	52220	City of Chattanooga Vista Dome Car, 01	70	140
___	52221	Norfolk Southern Boxcar, 01	25	50
___	52274	City of Los Angeles Railway Post Office Car, 03	35	80
___	52237	Lionel Gondola, yellow, 01	55	110
___	52238	Lionel Gondola, red, 01	55	110
___	52239	Lionel Gondola, silver, 01	55	110
___	52240	Lionel Gondola 3-pack, 01	55	110
___	52241	Lionel Gondola, black, 02	5	15
___	52242	Lionel Gondola, blue, 02	20	35
___	52250	City of Chicago Combination Car, 02	65	130
___	52272	Lionel Gondola, gold, 02	40	80
___	52276	California Gold Mint Car, 03	35	65
___	52333	Harmony Dairy Milk Car, 04	45	90
___	52338	Lionel 50th Anniversary Mint Car, 04	40	75
___	52339	50th Anniversary Convention Banquet Car with coin, 04	180	360
___	52340	Train Order Building, 04	45	90
___	52373	Montana Rail Link 2-car Set, 05	45	90
___	52374	Montana Rail Link 2-bay Hopper, 05	25	50
___	52375	Montana Rail Link Flatcar with pulp-wood logs, 05	25	50
___	52376	GN Reefer, 05	30	60
___	52403	T&P Stock Car (std O), 06	40	75
___	52414	Flatcar with 3 snowmobiles, 07	40	80
___	52481	Ben & Jerry's Reefer, 08	50	95
___	52500	ATSF Grand Canyon Reefer, 09	30	60
___	52508	Celebrate America Mint Car, 09	50	95
___	58216	NYC Merchants Despatch Reefer, 15		90
___	58258	Made in the USA Boxcar, 16		80
___	58544	St. Louis Reefer, 13	45	85
___	58547	Cotton Belt Blue Streak Merchandise Boxcar, 13	35	75
___	58571	Bethlehem Steel PS-1 Boxcar, 14	40	80
___	58572	Reading Philadelphia Mint Car, 14	40	80

TCA Museum-Related and Other Cars

			Esc	Mint
___	1018-1979	Mortgage Burning Hi-Cube Boxcar, 79	20	35
___	5731	L&N Reefer, 90	50	95
___	7780	TCA Museum Boxcar, 80	10	25
___	7781	Hafner Boxcar, 81	10	25
___	7782	Carlisle & Finch Boxcar, 82	10	25
___	7783	Ives Boxcar, 83	10	25
___	7784	Voltamp Boxcar, 84	10	25
___	7785	Hoge Boxcar, 85	10	25
___	9771	Norfolk & Western Boxcar, 77	15	30
___	16811	Rutland Boxcar "5477096," 96	20	35

CLUB CARS AND SPECIAL PRODUCTION		Esc	Mint	
52045	Pennsylvania Dutch Milk Car "61052," 94	45	90	__
52051	Baltimore & Ohio Sentinel Boxcar "6464095," 95	20	40	__
52052	TCA 40th Anniversary Boxcar, 94	45	90	__
52063	NYC Pacemaker Boxcar "6464125," 95	175	345	__
52064	Missouri Pacific Boxcar "6464150," 95	185	370	__
52065	Pennsylvania Dutch Grain Operating Boxcar "9208," 96	50	100	__
52118	Rio Grande Boxcar "5477097," 97	30	55	__
52119	TCA Museum 20th Anniversary Boxcar, 97	35	70	__
52128	Pennsylvania Dutch Pretzels Boxcar, 99	40	80	__
52172	L&N "Share the Freedom" Boxcar "5477099," 99	25	55	__
52198	Frisco Boxcar "5477000," 00	25	45	__
52215	Museum Work Train Gondola with pipes, 03	30	55	__
52226	Angela Trotta Thomas Boxcar "2000," 01	50	100	__
52243	Museum Work Train 1-D Tank Car, 01	25	50	__
52271	Museum Work Train Flatcar with wheel load, 02	10	20	__
52289	National Toy Train Museum 25th Anniversary Bullion Car, 02	40	75	__
52295	National Toy Train Museum Gondola with pipes, 03	5	15	__
52310	Museum Work Train Boxcar, 04	30	55	__
52311	50th Anniversary Golden Express Freight Set, 04	200	450	__
52321	SP Trainmaster Locomotive, 04	175	345	__
52372	Museum Work Train Baggage Car, 05	35	70	__
52408	N&W Caboose, 06	30	55	__
52409	Museum Work Train Idler Caboose, 06	35	70	__
52437	Museum Work Train Crane Car, 07	40	80	__

TCA Bicentennial Special Set

		Esc	Mint	
1973	Bicentennial Observation Car, 76	25	50	__
1974	Bicentennial Passenger Car, 76	25	50	__
1975	Bicentennial Passenger Car, 76	25	50	__
1976	Bicentennial U36B Diesel, 76	85	165	__

Atlantic Division

		Esc	Mint	
1980	Atlantic Division Flatcar with trailers, 80	20	35	__
6101	Burlington Northern Covered Quad Hopper, 82	20	35	__
9186	Conrail N5c Caboose, 79	15	30	__
9193	Budweiser Vat Car, 84	55	110	__
9466	Wanamaker Boxcar, 83	70	135	__
9788	Lehigh Valley Boxcar, 78	10	25	__
58598	Philly Pretzel Factory Boxcar, 14		40	__
	Wawa Hoagiefest Boxcar, 17		70	__

Desert Division

		Esc	Mint	
52088	Desert Division 25th Anniversary On-track Step Van, 96	60	120	__
52105	Superstition Mountain Operating Gondola "61997," 97	40	80	__
52442	Verde Canyon Boxcar, 07	30	55	__
52443	Grand Canyon Boxcar, 07	30	55	__
58222	Los Alamos Mint Car, 16		80	__

	CLUB CARS AND SPECIAL PRODUCTION	Esc	Mint
___	**58226** Cumbres & Toltec Boxcar, *16*		80
___	Fred Harvey Boxcar, *17*		80

Dixie Division

		Esc	Mint
___	**27007/87** Dixie Division 20th Anniversary PS-1 Boxcar, *06*	40	80
___	**52127** Dixie Division 10th Anniversary Southern 3-bay Hopper, *98*	35	70

Eastern Division

		Esc	Mint
___	**52059** Clinchfield Quad Hopper "16413" with coal, *94*	55	110
___	**9783** B&O Time-Saver Boxcar, *77*	15	30

Fort Pitt Division

		Esc	Mint
___	**1984-30X** Heinz Ketchup Boxcar, *84*	250	500

Great Lakes Division

		Esc	Mint
___	**1983** Churchill Downs Boxcar, *83*	100	200
___	**1983** Churchill Downs Reefer, *83*	125	250
___	**9740** Chessie System Boxcar, *76*	10	25

Great Lakes Division: Detroit-Toledo Chapter

		Esc	Mint
___	**8957** Burlington Northern GP20 Diesel, *80*	115	230
___	**8958** Burlington Northern GP20 Diesel Dummy Unit, *80*	75	150
___	**9119** Detroit & Mackinac Covered Quad Hopper, *77*	10	20
___	**9272** New Haven Bay Window Caboose, *79*	10	20
___	**9401** Great Northern Boxcar, *78*	10	25
___	**9730** CP Rail Boxcar, *76*	10	25
___	**52000** Detroit-Toledo Division Flatcar with trailer, *92*	45	85

Great Lakes Division: Three Rivers Chapter

		Esc	Mint
___	**9113** Norfolk & Western Quad Hopper, *76*	15	30

Great Lakes Division: Western Michigan Chapter

		Esc	Mint
___	**9730** CP Rail Boxcar, *74*	10	25

Lake & Pines Division

		Esc	Mint
___	**52018** 3-M Boxcar, *93*	225	450

Lone Star Division

		Esc	Mint
___	**7522** New Orleans Mint Car with coin, *86*	210	420
___	**52093** Lone Star Division Boxcar "6464696," *96*	15	30
___	**52585** Texas Special Mint Car, *11*	35	65
___	**58512** SP Daylight Mint Car, *12*	35	65
___	**58552** Texas Special Mint Car with silver bars, *12*	35	65

Lone Star Division: North Texas Chapter

		Esc	Mint
___	**9739** D&RGW Boxcar, *76*	10	20

METCA

		Esc	Mint
___	**10** Jersey Central F3 A Unit, shell only, *71*	10	25
___	**9272** New Haven Bay Window Caboose, *79*	10	25
___	**9754** New York Central Pacemaker Boxcar, *76*	15	30

CLUB CARS AND SPECIAL PRODUCTION		Esc	Mint	
52485	New York Central Mint Car with copper load, 08	60	120	
52486	Pennsylvania Mint Car, green, 09	65	125	
52487	Pennsylvania Mint Car, tuscan, 09	65	125	
52488	NYC Lightning Stripe Mint Car, 10	30	60	
52574	Fort Knox 50th Anniversary Mint Car, 11	50	100	
52583	B&O Capitol Dome Mint Car, 11	50	100	
52596	LIRR Mint Car, 12	50	100	
58033	Jersey Central Boxcar, 16		80	
58174	Lehigh Valley Map Boxcar, 16		80	
58280	REA Christmas Boxcar, 16		80	
58523	Blue Comet Mint Car, 13	35	70	
58243	Entenmann's Gondola with load, 15		70	
58285	Brookside Milk Reefer, 17		85	
58286	Riverside Milk Reefer, 17		85	
58534	Jersey Central Mint Car, 13	35	70	
58569	Erie Lackawanna Mint Car, 14	35	70	

Midwest Division

		Esc	Mint	
4	C&NW F3 Diesel A Unit, shell only, 77	40	80	
5	Midwest Division Covered Quad Hopper, 78	25	45	
1287	C&NW Reefer, 84		NRS	
7600	Frisco "Spirit of '76" N5c Caboose "00003," 76	20	40	
9872	PFE Reefer "00006," 79	205	410	

Midwest Division: Museum Express

		Esc	Mint	
9264	ICG Covered Quad Hopper, 78	10	25	
9289	C&NW N5c Caboose, 80	25	45	
9785	Conrail Boxcar, 77	20	35	
9786	C&NW Boxcar, 79	10	20	

NETCA

		Esc	Mint	
1203	Boston & Maine NW2 Diesel, shell only, 72	35	65	
5710	Canadian Pacific Reefer, 82	25	45	
5716	Vermont Central Reefer, 83	15	30	
6124	Delaware & Hudson Covered Quad Hopper, 84	15	30	
8051	Hood's Milk Boxcar, 86	40	75	
9181	Boston & Maine N5c Caboose, 77	20	35	
9400	Conrail Boxcar, tuscan or blue, 78	10	25	
9415	Providence & Worcester Boxcar, 79	20	35	
9423	NYNH&H Boxcar, 80	15	30	
9445	Vermont Northern Boxcar, 81	20	40	
9753	Maine Central Boxcar, 75	20	35	
9768	Boston & Maine Boxcar, 76	20	40	
9785	Conrail Boxcar, 78	10	25	
16911	B&M Flatcar with trailer, 95	75	150	
22677	B&M Baked Beans Boxcar, 10	25	45	
52001	B&M Quad Hopper with coal, 92	40	75	

	CLUB CARS AND SPECIAL PRODUCTION	Esc	Mint
___	**52016** B&M Gondola with coil covers, *93*	35	65
___	**52043** L.L. Bean Boxcar, *94*	105	210
___	**52080** B&M Flatcar "91095" with trailer, *95*	110	215
___	**52111** Ben & Jerry's Flatcar with trailer, *96*	160	315
___	**52212** Berkshire Brewing Reefer, *00*	80	155
___	**52236** Moxie Boxcar, *01*	80	160
___	**52270** Jenney Manufacturing Tank Car, *02*	75	150
___	**52306** NH Flatcar with New England Transportation trailer, *03*	75	150
___	**52352** Poland Spring Boxcar, *04*	65	130
___	**52379** CP Rail with W.B. Mason trailer, *05*	40	75
___	**52383** Fisk Tire Boxcar, *05*	55	110
___	**52397** D&H Flatcar with Vermont Railway trailer, *06*	45	90
___	**52418** Indian Motocycle Boxcar, *06*	95	190
___	**52434** New England Central Flatcar with Cabot's trailer, *07*	50	95
___	**52448** Oilzum Tanker 2-car Set, *08*	55	105
___	**52457** Cape Cod Potato Chip Boxcar, *07*	50	95
___	**52484A** Cabot's Reefer, *08*	125	250
___	**52484B** Bay State Beer Reefer, *09*	45	90
___	**52589** B&M Flatcar with Howard Johnson trailer, *11*	50	100
___	**58221** G. Fox & Co. Boxcar, *15*		60
___	**58522** Grafton & Upton Flatcar with Spag's trailer, *12*	45	90
___	Warwick Ice Cream Reefer, *17*		100

Ozark Division: Gateway Chapter

		Esc	Mint
___	**5700** Oppenheimer Reefer, *81*	55	110
___	**9068** Reading Bobber Caboose, *76*	10	20
___	**9601** Illinois Central Gulf Hi-Cube Boxcar, *77*	10	20
___	**9767** Railbox Boxcar, *78*	10	20
___	**52003** "Meet Me In St. Louis" Flatcar with trailer, *92*	260	520

Pacific Northwest Division

		Esc	Mint
___	**52077** Great Northern Hi-Cube Boxcar "9695," *95*	230	460

Rocky Mountain Division

		Esc	Mint
___	**1971-1976** Rocky Mountain Division Reefer, *76*	40	75

Sacramento Sierra Chapter

		Esc	Mint
___	**6401** Virginian Bay Window Caboose, *84*	20	35
___	**9301** U.S. Mail Operating Boxcar, *76*	20	40
___	**9414** Cotton Belt Boxcar, *80*	20	35
___	**9427** Bay Line Boxcar, *81*	15	30
___	**9444** Louisiana Midland Boxcar, *82*	20	35
___	**9452** Western Pacific Boxcar, *83*	20	35
___	**9705** D&RGW Boxcar, *75*	20	40
___	**9723** Western Pacific Boxcar, *73*	15	30
___	**9726** Erie-Lackawanna Boxcar, *79*	10	25
___	**9730** CP Rail Boxcar, *77*	15	30

CLUB CARS AND SPECIAL PRODUCTION		Esc	Mint	
9785	Conrail Boxcar, 78	10	20	___

Southern Division

1976	FEC F3 Diesel ABA, shells only, 76	140	275	___
1986	Southern Division Bunk Car, 86	15	30	___
6111	L&N Covered Quad Hopper, 83	10	20	___
9287	Southern N5c Caboose, 77	10	20	___
9352	Trailer Train Flatcar with circus trailers, 80	30	55	___
9403	Seaboard Coast Line Boxcar, 78	10	20	___
9405	Chattahoochie Boxcar, 79	10	20	___
9443	Florida East Coast Boxcar, 81	10	25	___
9471	ACL Boxcar, 84	10	25	___
9482	Norfolk & Southern Boxcar, 85	10	25	___
16606	Southern Searchlight Car, 88	10	25	___
19942	Southern Division 30th Anniversary Boxcar, 96	10	20	___

Western Division

52275	Western Pacific Boxcar, 03	55	105	___

Toy Train Operating Society

TTOS National Convention Cars

1984	Sacramento Northern Boxcar, 84	45	85	___
1985	Snowbird Covered Quad Hopper, 85	30	55	___
6017	SP-type Caboose, blue, 68	125	210	___
6017	SP-type Caboose, brown, 69	200	300	___
6057	SP-type Caboose, orange, 69	125	210	___
6076	Santa Fe Hopper (O27), 70	45	85	___
6167-1967	Hopper, olive drab with gold lettering, 67	45	85	___
6257	SP-type Caboose, red, 69	125	210	___
6476-1	LV Hopper, gray, 69	40	75	___
6582	Portland Flatcar with wood, 86	30	55	___
9326	Burlington Northern Bay Window Caboose, 82	10	25	___
9347	Niagara Falls 3-D Tank Car, 79	25	45	___
9355	Delaware & Hudson Bay Window Caboose, 82	25	50	___
9361	C&NW Bay Window Caboose, 82	30	55	___
9382	Florida East Coast Bay Window Caboose, 82	35	70	___
9512	Summerdale Junction Passenger Car, 74	30	55	___
9520	Phoenix Combination Car, 75	20	35	___
9526	Snowbird Observation Car, 76	25	50	___
9535	Columbus Baggage Car, 77	35	50	___
9678	Hollywood Hi-Cube Boxcar, 78	15	30	___
9868	Oklahoma City Reefer, 80	25	45	___
9883	Phoenix Reefer, 83	25	50	___
17871	NYC Flatcar "81487" with Kodak and Xerox trailers, 87	110	215	___
17877	MKT 1-D Tank Car "3739469," 89	35	70	___
17884	Columbus & Dayton Terminal Boxcar (std O), 90	20	40	___

			Esc	Mint
CLUB CARS AND SPECIAL PRODUCTION				
____	17889	SP Flatcar "15791" (std O) with trailer, *91*	35	65
____	19963	Union Equity 3-bay ACF Hopper "86892" (std O), *92*	20	40
____	52010	Weyerhaeuser DD Boxcar "838593" (std O), *93*	20	40
____	52029	Ford 1-D Tank Car "12" (027), *94*	20	40
____	52030	Ford Gondola "4023," *94*	15	30
____	52031	Ford Hopper "1458" (027), *94*	20	35
____	52057	Western Pacific Boxcar "64641995," *95*	25	50
____	52087	New Mexico Central Boxcar "64641996," *96*	30	55
____	52114	NYC Flatcar with Gleason and SASIB trailers, *97*	30	60
____	52149	Conrail Flatcar with Blum coal shovel, *98*	30	60
____	52192	SP Crane and Gondola Set, *00*	40	75
____	52193	SP Gondola "6060," *00*	25	50
____	52194	SP Crane Car "7111," *00*	20	35
____	52231	British Columbia 1-D Tank Car, *01*	10	25
____	52253	San Pedro Boxcar, *02*	20	35
____	52288	D&RGW Cookie Boxcar, *03*	10	20
____	52293	D&RGW 1-D Tank Car, *03*	20	40
____	52351	BNSF Icicle Reefer with ETD, *04*	30	60
____	52378	Las Vegas & Tonopah Boxcar, *05*	35	70
____	52410	SP Flatcar with 2 trailers, *06*	35	70
____	52441	Pennsylvania Operating Hopper, *07*	30	60
____	52445	Pennsylvania Boxcar, *07*	35	70
____	52545	Erie "6464" Boxcar, *09*	25	50
____	58257	50th Anniversary Mint Car, *16*		65
____	58333	Sierra Railroad Sierra Beer Boxcar, *13*	35	70
____	58535	Smokey Bear Gondola, *15*		55
TTOS Division Cars				
____	52009	Sacramento Valley Division WP Boxcar, *93*	25	45
____	52040	Wolverine Division GTW Flatcar with tractor and trailer, *94*	25	50
____	52058	Central California Division Santa Fe Boxcar, *95*	20	40
____	52086	Canadian Division Pacific Great Eastern Boxcar, *96*	25	50
____	52113	Northeastern Division Genesee & Wyoming 3-bay Hopper, *97*	20	35
____	52264	New Mexico Division Durango & Silverton Operating Hopper, *02*	30	55
Other TTOS Production				
____	1983	Phoenix 3-D Tank Car, *83*	50	100
____	17894	Southern Pacific Tractor, *91*	10	20
____	27148	BNSF "4427" PS2 Hopper, *06*	25	50
____	52021	Weyerhaeuser Tractor and Trailer, *93*	15	30
____	52022	Union Pacific Boxcar, *93*	200	400
____	52032	Ford 1-D Tank Car (027) with Kughn inscription, *94*	50	95
____	52046	ACL Boxcar "16247," *94*	55	110
____	52053	Carail Boxcar, *94*	30	55
____	52068	Toy Train Parade Contadina Boxcar "16245," *94*	30	55
____	52078	Southern Pacific SD9 Diesel "5366," *96*	120	235

CLUB CARS AND SPECIAL PRODUCTION		Esc	Mint	
52079	Southern Pacific Bay Window Caboose, *96*	30	55	___
52084	Union Pacific I-Beam Flatcar "16380" with load, *95*	80	155	___
52384	Transparent Damage Control Boxcar, *03*	35	70	___
52451	Pennsylvania "X2454" Boxcar, *07*	90	175	___
52505	Forest Service/Smokey Bear Flatcar with airplane, *08*	25	45	___
52525	SP "X6454" Boxcar, *08*	25	50	___
52526	SP "X6454" Boxcar, *08*	45	90	___
52547	C&NW Reefer, *09*	30	50	___

TTOS Southwestern Division

		Esc	Mint	
19962	Southern Pacific 3-bay ACF Hopper "496035" (std O), *92*	35	65	___
52047	Cotton Belt Wood-sided Caboose (std O), smoke, *93–94*	35	70	___
52073	Pacific Fruit Express Reefer "459402" (std O), *95*	30	65	___
52098	National Bureau of Standards Boxcar (std O), *96*	20	45	___
52121	Mobilgas Tank Car "238" (std O), *97*	40	75	___
52154	Pacific Fruit Express Reefer "459403" (std O), *98*	25	55	___
52205	SP Overnight Merchandise Service Boxcar 5-pack, *00*	95	185	___
52287	Operating MX Missile Car, *02*	30	55	___
52385	Ward Kimball Boxcar, *05*	30	55	___
52431	Operating MX Missile Car, *06*	30	60	___
52476	Life Savers Tank Car, *07*	45	85	___
52515	Life Savers Wild Cherry Tank Car, *08*	40	75	___
52565	Life Savers Pep O Mint Tank Car, *09*	30	60	___
52569	Life Savers Butter Rum Tank Car, *10*	30	60	___
52591	Life Savers Wint O Green Tank Car, *11*	30	60	___
58208	Life Savers Peppermint Tank Car, *14*	30	60	___
58548	Life Savers Bay Window Caboose, *13*	40	80	___

Virginia Train Collectors

		Esc	Mint	
7679	Boxcar, *79*	5	15	___
7681	N5c Caboose, *81*	10	25	___
7682	Covered Quad Hopper, *82*	10	25	___
7683	Virginia Fruit Express Reefer, *83*	10	25	___
7684	Vitraco 3-D Tank Car, *84*	10	25	___
7685	Boxcar, *85*	10	25	___
7686	GP7 Diesel, *86*	50	100	___
7692-1	Baggage Car (O27), *92*	25	45	___
7692-2	Combination Car (O27), *92*	25	45	___
7692-3	Dining Car (O27), *92*	25	45	___
7692-4	Passenger Car (O27), *92*	25	45	___
7692-5	Vista Dome Car (O27), *92*	25	45	___
7692-6	Passenger Car (O27), *92*	25	45	___
7692-7	Observation Car (O27), *92*	25	45	___
7696	20th Anniversary Station, *96*	35	65	___
52060	Tender "7694" with whistle, *94*	35	70	___

Section 6
BOXES 1970–2021

			Good P-5	Exc P-7
____	020	90-Degree Crossover, *45-61*	3	8
____	020X	45-Degree Crossover	3	8
____	022	Switch Controller	2	5
____	022	Remote Control Switches, pair (with both inserts)	5	18
____	022	Remote Control Switches, pair (yellow, with both inserts)	6	15
____	022A	Remote Control Switches, pair (with both inserts)	9	21
____	25	Bumper	2	7
____	26	Bumper	2	5
____	30	Water Tower	12	35
____	35	Boulevard Lamp	4	13
____	36	Operating Car Remote Control Set	5	13
____	37	Uncoupling Track Set	2	6
____	38	Operating Water Tower	22	69
____	40	Hookup Wire, 8 reels (dealer box)	33	118
____	41	U.S. Army Switcher	20	45
____	42	Manual Switches	3	10
____	42	Picatinny Arsenal Switcher	27	73
____	44	U.S. Army Mobile Launcher	23	73
____	44	U.S. Army Mobile Launcher (with orange sleeve)	38	135
____	45	U.S. Marines Mobile Launcher	39	87
____	45/45N	Automatic Gateman	5	18
____	48	Super O Insulated Straight Track, *6 pieces (dealer box)*	15	47
____	49	Super O Insulated Curved Track, *6 pieces (dealer box)*	15	41
____	50	Section Gang Car (early classic)	11	34
____	50	Section Gang Car (brown corrugated)	5	17
____	50	Section Gang Car (orange picture)	16	37
____	51	Navy Yard Switcher	23	67
____	52	Fire Car	31	74
____	53	Rio Grande Snowplow	35	85
____	54	Ballast Tamper	17	42
____	55	PRR Tie-Jector Car	17	39
____	56	Lamp Post	6	17
____	56	M&StL Mine Transport	43	148
____	57	AEC Switcher	71	261
____	58	Lamp Post	10	25
____	58	Great Northern Rotary Snow Blower	72	186
____	59	Minuteman Switcher	80	280
____	60	Lionelville Rapid Transit Trolley (classic)	11	43
____	60	Lionelville Rapid Transit Trolley (brown corrugated)	14	34
____	64	Highway Lamp Post	12	45
____	65	Handcar	29	131
____	68	Executive Inspection Car	22	69
____	69	Maintenance Car	23	77

BOXES		Good P-5	Exc P-7	
70	Yard Light	4	12	___
71	Lamp Post	4	11	___
75	Goose Neck Lamps	3	14	___
76	Boulevard Street Lamps	5	25	___
76	Boulevard Street Lamps (Hillside Checkerboard)	13	59	___
89	Flagpole	7	32	___
91	Circuit Breaker	8	27	___
92	Circuit Breaker		10	___
93	Water Tower	15	35	___
97	Coal Elevator	26	54	___
108	Trestle Set (overstamped)	10	33	___
110	Graduated Trestle Set	1	5	___
111	Elevated Trestle Set	4	13	___
112	Remote Control Switches, pair (Super O)	7	18	___
112LH	Remote Control Super O Switch, left-hand	6	17	___
112RH	Remote Control Super O Switch, right-hand	6	17	___
114	Newsstand with horn	7	27	___
115	Passenger Station (113-1, Star Corp. stamped on box)	41	134	___
118	Newsstand with whistle	7	28	___
122	Lamp Assortment	22	90	___
123	Lamp Assortment	19	92	___
123-60	Replacement Lamp Assortment	5	55	___
125	Whistle Shack	4	19	___
128	Animated Newsstand	12	31	___
130	60-degree Crossing (Super O)	2	7	___
132	Passenger Station	12	29	___
133	Passenger Station	10	22	___
138	Water Tower	12	38	___
140	Automatic Banjo Signal (classic)	4	12	___
142	Manual Switches, pair (Super O)	5	12	___
145	Automatic Gateman (brown corrugated)	6	20	___
145	Automatic Gateman (cellophane), 66	11	45	___
148	Dwarf Trackside Signal	5	21	___
150	Telegraph Pole Set	5	16	___
151	Automatic Semaphore	3	12	___
151	Automatic Semaphore (narrower box, earlier postwar)	12	28	___
151	Automatic Semaphore (blister pack enclosure)	20	75	___
152	Automatic Crossing Gate	3	11	___
153	Automatic Block Control Signal	6	14	___
154	Automatic Highway Signal (cellophane)	5	20	___
154	Automatic Highway Signal (all other boxes)	3	9	___
155	Blinking Light Signal	9	34	___
156	Station Platform	13	38	___
157	Station Platform	7	22	___
160	Unloading Bin	20	100	___
161	Mail Pickup Set (with liner)	12	39	___

	BOXES	Good P-5	Exc P-7
___ 163	Single Target Block Signal (white box)	20	58
___ 164	Log Loader	21	55
___ 167	Whistle Controller	2	6
___ 175	Rocket Launcher	20	64
___ 175-50	Rocket, separate sale	58	152
___ 175-50	Dealer Display Box, 6 rockets	75	447
___ 182	Magnetic Crane	21	67
___ 192	Operating Control Tower	35	120
___ 193	Industrial Water Tower	13	43
___ 195	Floodlight Tower	6	21
___ 195	Floodlight Tower (cellophane)	9	38
___ 195-75	Floodlight Extension, 8-bulb (classic)	6	36
___ 195-75	Floodlight Extension, 8-bulb (white box)	6	55
___ 197	Rotating Radar Antenna	10	45
___ 197-15	Separate Sale Radar Head	29	90
___ 199	Microwave Relay Tower	6	45
___ 202	UP Alco Diesel A Unit	11	45
___ 204	Santa Fe Alco AA Set (master carton)	85	215
___ 204	Santa Fe Alco AA Set (P and T boxes)	20	115
___ 204P	Santa Fe A Unit	17	44
___ 204T	Santa Fe Diesel Dummy A Unit	19	42
___ 208	Santa Fe Alco AA Set (master carton)	47	250
___ 208	Santa Fe Alco AA Set (P and T boxes)	21	100
___ 208P	Santa Fe Alco A Unit	18	78
___ 208T	Santa Fe Alco Dummy A Unit	34	76
___ 209	New Haven Alco AA Set (master carton)	104	369
___ 209	New Haven Alco AA Set (P and T boxes)	93	298
___ 209P	New Haven Alco A Unit	20	87
___ 209T	New Haven Diesel Dummy A Unit	45	135
___ 210	Texas Special Alco AA Set (P and T boxes)	12	92
___ 210P	Texas Special Alco A Unit	9	33
___ 210T	Texas Special Alco Dummy A Unit	19	44
___ 211	Texas Special Alco AA Set (P and T boxes)	29	111
___ 211P	Texas Special Alco A Unit (brown corrugated)	20	55
___ 212P	USMC Alco Diesel A Unit	42	83
___ 212T	USMC Diesel Dummy A Unit	183	535
___ 214	Plate Girder Bridge (classic)	3	10
___ 214	Plate Girder Bridge (Hillside orange picture)	9	28
___ 216	Burlington Alco Diesel A Unit	30	97
___ 217	B&M Alco AB Set (C and P boxes)	45	132
___ 217C	B&M Alco B Unit	15	50
___ 217P	B&M Alco A Unit	18	51
___ 217-16	Sleeve for 217 and 218 outer boxes	42	85
___ 218	Santa Fe Alco AA Set (master carton)	26	104
___ 218C	Santa Fe Alco Diesel B Unit	20	76
___ 218P	Santa Fe Alco Diesel A Unit	18	67

BOXES		Good P-5	Exc P-7	
218T	Santa Fe Diesel Dummy A Unit	18	68	___
220	Santa Fe Alco AA Set (P and T boxes)	17	93	___
220T	Santa Fe Alco Dummy A Unit	20	100	___
221	2-6-4 Locomotive	19	68	___
221T	Tender	10	36	___
221W	Whistling Tender	14	45	___
223P	Santa Fe Alco A Unit	15	86	___
224	2-6-2 Locomotive	17	137	___
224	U.S. Navy Alco AB Set (C and P boxes)	26	134	___
224P	U.S. Navy Alco A unit	43	193	___
225	C & O Alco Diesel A Unit	12	57	___
226	B&M Alco Diesel AB Set (C and P boxes)	24	100	___
226C	B&M Alco Diesel B Unit	13	30	___
226P	B&M Alco Diesel A Unit	9	44	___
228P	CN Alco Diesel A Unit	20	74	___
229C	M&StL Alco B Unit	14	44	___
229P	M&StL Alco A Unit (brown corrugated)	8	42	___
230P	C&O Alco A Unit	14	59	___
231P	Rock Island Alco A Unit	12	50	___
233	2-4-2 Scout Locomotive	15	35	___
234W	Whistle Tender	12	33	___
235	2-4-2 Scout Locomotive	26	126	___
236	2-4-2 Scout Locomotive	10	40	___
237	2-4-2 Scout Locomotive	10	37	___
239	2-4-2 Scout Locomotive	18	39	___
238	Engine and Tender Master Carton	15	34	___
243	2-4-2 Scout Locomotive	11	34	___
243W	Tender	5	27	___
244T	Tender (overstamped 1625T box)	23	79	___
245	2-4-2 Scout Locomotive	15	50	___
246	2-4-2 Scout Locomotive	13	37	___
247	2-4-2 Scout Locomotive	14	37	___
247T	Tender	7	31	___
248	2-4-2 Scout Locomotive	11	40	___
249	2-4-2 Scout Locomotive	17	44	___
250	2-4-2 Scout Locomotive	10	30	___
250T	Tender	8	24	___
252	Crossing Gate	3	9	___
253	Block Control Signal	5	11	___
256	Illuminated Freight Station	20	43	___
257	Freight Station with diesel horn	9	33	___
260	Bumper (Hagerstown checkerboard)	5	14	___
260	Bumper (all other boxes)	2	4	___
262	Highway Crossing Gate	4	26	___
264	Operating Forklift Platform	22	61	___
282	Portal Gantry Crane	44	113	___

BOXES		Good P-5	Exc P-7
___ 299	Code Transmitter Beacon Set	10	54
___ 308	Railroad Sign Set	2	11
___ 309	Yard Sign Set	3	12
___ 310	Billboard Set	2	7
___ 313	Bascule Bridge	30	133
___ 314	Scale Model Girder Bridge	5	18
___ 315	Illuminated Trestle Bridge	24	88
___ 316	Trestle Bridge	7	28
___ 317	Trestle Bridge	9	27
___ 321	Trestle Bridge	5	14
___ 321-100	Trestle Bridge	7	20
___ 332	Arch-Under Trestle Bridge	5	16
___ 334	Operating Dispatching Board	10	49
___ 342	Culvert Loader	36	87
___ 345	Culvert Unloader	25	98
___ 348	Manual Culvert Unloader	21	60
___ 350	Engine Transfer Table	16	58
___ 350-50	Transfer Table Extension	15	57
___ 352	Ice Depot	23	69
___ 353	Trackside Control Signal	3	14
___ 356	Operating Freight Station	8	37
___ 356-35	Baggage Trucks Set	12	41
___ 362	Barrel Loader	11	27
___ 362-78	Wooden Barrels	1	7
___ 364	Conveyor Lumber Loader	10	26
___ 365	Dispatching Station	15	38
___ 375	Turntable	26	76
___ 394	Rotary Beacon	7	24
___ 394-37	Rotating Beacon Cap	2	6
___ 395	Floodlight Tower	8	27
___ 397	Operating Coal Loader	8	41
___ 397	Operating Coal Loader (separate label on box)	10	43
___ 400	B&O Passenger Rail Diesel Car	21	57
___ 404	B&O Baggage-Mail Rail Diesel Car	32	84
___ 410	Billboard Blinker	3	15
___ 413	Countdown Control Panel	6	18
___ 415	Diesel Fueling Station	15	42
___ 419	Heliport Control Tower	28	130
___ 443	Missile Launching Platform	12	40
___ 445	Switch Tower	11	24
___ 448	Missile Firing Range Set	13	68
___ 450	Operating Signal Bridge	5	18
___ 452	Overhead Gantry Signal	11	51
___ 455	Operating Oil Derrick	17	71
___ 456	Coal Ramp	16	41
___ 460	Piggyback Transportation Set	16	52

BOXES		Good P-5	Exc P-7	
460-150	Two Trailers	71	224	___
461	Platform with truck and trailer	11	42	___
462	Derrick Platform Set	45	161	___
464	Lumber Mill	9	38	___
465	Sound Dispatching Station	11	33	___
470	Missile Launching Platform	5	33	___
494	Rotary Beacon (classic)	6	24	___
497	Coaling Station	19	49	___
600	MKT NW2 Switcher	26	77	___
601	Seaboard NW2 Switcher	25	81	___
602	Seaboard NW2 Switcher	34	78	___
610	Erie NW2 Switcher	15	95	___
611	Jersey Central NW2 Switcher (overstamped 621 box)	50	112	___
613	UP NW2 Switcher	26	93	___
614	Alaska NW2 Switcher	37	129	___
616	Santa Fe NW2 Switcher	23	103	___
617	Santa Fe NW2 Switcher	30	114	___
621	Jersey Central NW2 Switcher	24	64	___
622	Santa Fe NW2 Switcher	35	117	___
623	Santa Fe NW2 Switcher	19	63	___
624	C&O NW2 Switcher	32	87	___
625	LV GE 44-ton Switcher	74	319	___
626	B&O GE 44-ton Switcher	41	148	___
628	Northern Pacific GE 44-ton Switcher	20	95	___
629	Burlington GE 44-ton Switcher	37	181	___
637	2-6-4 Locomotive	14	55	___
637LTS	2-6-4 Locomotive and Tender (master carton)	40	210	___
646	4-6-4 Locomotive	23	76	___
665	4-6-4 Locomotive	19	55	___
665LTS	4-6-4 Locomotive and Tender (master carton)	45	280	___
671	6-8-6 Steam Turbine Locomotive	29	88	___
671R	6-8-6 Steam Turbine Locomotive	38	124	___
671W	Whistle Tender	14	52	___
671-75	Smoke Lamp, 12 volt	2	7	___
675	2-6-2 Locomotive (classic), *47, 49*	19	53	___
675	2-6-2 Locomotive (brown corrugated), *52*	34	60	___
681	6-8-6 Steam Turbine Locomotive	28	92	___
681LTS	6-8-6 Steam Turbine Locomotive and Tender (master carton)	150	525	___
682	6-8-6 Steam Turbine Locomotive	48	161	___
682LTS	6-8-6 Steam Turbine Locomotive and Tender (master carton)	400	850	___
685	4-6-4 Hudson Locomotive	25	66	___
685LTS	4-6-4 Hudson Locomotive and Tender (master carton)	185	475	___
726	2-8-4 Berkshire Locomotive, *46*	65	162	___
726	2-8-4 Berkshire Locomotive (after 1946)	39	100	___
726RR	2-8-4 Berkshire Locomotive	27	63	___
736	2-8-4 Berkshire Locomotive, *50*	33	91	___

BOXES		Good P-5	Exc P-7
____ 736	2-8-4 Berkshire Locomotive	33	72
____ 736X	2-8-4 Berkshire Locomotive	33	107
____ 736LTS	2-8-4 Berkshire Locomotive and Tender (master carton)	63	231
____ 736W	Pennsylvania Tender	17	69
____ 746	N&W 4-8-4 Locomotive	57	181
____ 746LTS	N&W 4-8-4 Locomotive and Tender (master carton)	170	460
____ 746W	N&W Whistle Tender	35	114
____ 746WX	N&W Whistle Tender, long stripe	50	147
____ 760	Curved Track	10	26
____ 773	4-6-4 Hudson Locomotive, *50*	96	300
____ 773	4-6-4 Hudson Locomotive, *64, 66*	86	173
____ 773LTS	4-6-4 Hudson Locomotive and Tender (master carton), *50*	118	561
____ 773LTS	4-6-4 Hudson and Whistle Tender (master carton), *64, 66*	86	300
____ 773W	NYC Tender	20	80
____ 810	Milwaukee Road Freight Set	75	500
____ 920-2	Tunnel Portals	6	20
____ 927	Lubricating Kit	2	8
____ 928	Maintenance and Lubricating Kit	5	25
____ 943	Ammo Dump	3	10
____ 951	Farm Set	13	43
____ 952	Figure Set	11	35
____ 953	Figure Set	14	42
____ 957	Farm Building and Animal Set	20	48
____ 959	Barn Set	18	46
____ 960	Barnyard Set	10	58
____ 963	Frontier Set	15	55
____ 965	Farm Set	15	50
____ 966	Firehouse Set	15	50
____ 969	Construction Set	9	40
____ 970	Ticket Booth	11	53
____ 972	Landscape Tree Assortment	10	35
____ 981	Freight Yard Set	11	36
____ 983	Farm Set	15	46
____ 984	Railroad Set	10	53
____ 986	Farm Set	21	94
____ 987	Town Set		185
____ 1000W	Steam Freight Set	40	95
____ 1001	Diesel Freight Set	20	65
____ 1001	2-4-2 Scout Locomotive	8	40
____ 1001T	Tender	6	20
____ 1002	Gondola	4	10
____ X1004	PRR Baby Ruth Boxcar	4	12
____ 1005	Sunoco 1-D Tank Car	4	11
____ 1007	LL SP-type Caboose	4	10
____ 1009	Manumatic Track Section	7	21
____ 1019	Remote Control Track Set (027)	5	9

BOXES		Good P-5	Exc P-7	
1024	Manual Switches	3	6	___
1025	Illuminated Bumper (027)	2	6	___
1032	Transformer, 75 watts	2	7	___
1033	Transformer, 90 watts	4	15	___
1034	Transformer, 75 watts	2	12	___
1041	Transformer, 50 watts	3	11	___
1041	Transformer, 60 watts	5	16	___
1043	Transformer, 50 watts	4	13	___
1043-500	Transformer, 50 watts, ivory	25	77	___
1044	Transformer, 90 watts	5	14	___
1045	Operating Watchman	6	34	___
1047	Operating Switchman	31	93	___
1060	2-4-2 Locomotive (brown corrugated)	23	102	___
1107	Steam Freight Set	15	46	___
1109	Steam Freight Set	13	40	___
1110	2-4-2 Locomotive	5	26	___
1112	Scout Set	8	25	___
1113	Scout Set	13	40	___
1117	Scout Steam Freight Set	14	35	___
1119	Scout Set	12	45	___
1120	2-4-2 Scout Locomotive	5	18	___
1121	027 Remote Control Switches, pair	3	12	___
1121LH	027 Remote Control Switch, left-hand	2	8	___
1121RH	027 Remote Control Switch, right-hand	2	10	___
1122	027 Remote Control Switches, pair	3	13	___
1130	2-4-2 Locomotive	8	26	___
1130T	Tender (classic)	5	19	___
1130T	Tender (orange perforated)	18	41	___
1130T-500	Tender, pink, from Girls Set	46	182	___
1232	Transformer, 75 watts, made for export	4	14	___
1407B	Steam Switcher Work Set	45	310	___
1417WS	Steam Work Train Set	28	145	___
1423W	Steam Freight Set	22	120	___
1425B	Steam Switcher Freight Set	65	245	___
1427WS	Steam Freight Set	10	35	___
1429WS	Steam Freight Set	34	150	___
1431	Steam Freight Set	15	75	___
1432W	027 Steam Passenger Set	60	282	___
1433W	Steam Freight Set	14	37	___
1435WS	Steam Freight Set	10	35	___
1447WS	Turbine Locomotive Set	29	143	___
1451WS	027 Steam Freight Set	26	110	___
1453WS	027 Steam Freight Set	23	66	___
1455WS	Steam Freight Set	26	73	___
1457B	Santa Fe Freight Set (marked 1457), *49*	52	149	___
1457B	Santa Fe Freight Set, *50*	51	152	___

BOXES		Good P-5	Exc P-7
___ **1459WS**	Steam Freight Set	35	85
___ **1463WS**	Steam Freight Set	33	97
___ **1464W**	Union Pacific Diesel Passenger Set	161	494
___ **1465**	Steam Freight Set	28	76
___ **1467W**	Union Pacific Freight Set	48	118
___ **1469WS**	Steam Freight Set	27	73
___ **1471**	Steam Freight Set	25	70
___ **1471WS**	Steam Freight Set	23	62
___ **1473WS**	Steam Freight Set	29	77
___ **1475WS**	Steam Freight Set	14	93
___ **1479WS**	Steam Freight Set	33	156
___ **1481WS**	Steam Freight Set	28	80
___ **1483WS**	Steam Freight Set	37	99
___ **1485WS**	Steam Freight Set	23	58
___ **1500**	Steam Freight Set	13	52
___ **1502WS**	Steam Freight Set	166	467
___ **1503WS**	Steam Freight Set	34	71
___ **1505WS**	Steam Freight Set	33	98
___ **1507WS**	Steam Freight Set	32	92
___ **1511S**	Steam Freight Set	22	55
___ **1513S**	Steam Freight Set	35	108
___ **1515WS**	Steam Freight Set	35	93
___ **1517W**	Texas Special Freight Set	49	171
___ **1519WS**	Steam Freight Set	51	170
___ **1520W**	Texas Special Passenger Set	170	667
___ **1521WS**	Steam Work Train Set	76	224
___ **1523**	Diesel Freight Set	48	198
___ **1525**	Diesel Freight Set	30	68
___ **1527**	O27 Steam Work Train Set	57	175
___ **1529**	Pennsylvania Diesel Freight Set	71	213
___ **1531W**	Diesel Freight Set	36	103
___ **1533WS**	Steam Freight Set	27	65
___ **1534W**	Burlington Diesel Passenger Set	200	424
___ **1535W**	Diesel Freight Set	90	250
___ **1536W**	Diesel Passenger Set	75	422
___ **1537WS**	Steam Freight Set	20	58
___ **1538WS**	Hudson Passenger Set	157	638
___ **1539W**	Santa Fe Diesel Freight Set	116	218
___ **1542**	Electric Freight Set	13	46
___ **1543**	Lehigh Valley Freight Set	14	38
___ **1547S**	Steam Freight Set	19	45
___ **1549**	Steam Work Train Set	32	85
___ **1551W**	Diesel Freight Set	10	49
___ **1552W**	Diesel Passenger Set	65	278
___ **1553W**	Diesel Freight Set	28	72
___ **1555WS**	O27 Steam Freight Set	25	61

BOXES		Good P-5	Exc P-7	
1557	Diesel Freight Set	28	79	___
1559W	MILW Diesel Freight Set	35	90	___
1562W	Burlington GP7 Diesel Passenger Set	37	159	___
1569	UP Diesel Freight Set	19	64	___
1571	LV Diesel Freight Set	26	61	___
1573	Steam Freight Set	27	65	___
1575	Diesel Freight Set	27	64	___
1577S	Steam Freight Set	32	75	___
1578S	Steam Passenger Set	154	461	___
1581	Jersey Central Mixed Set	32	77	___
1583WS	Steam Freight Set	28	63	___
1585W	Diesel Freight Set	27	70	___
1586	Diesel Passenger Set	33	100	___
1587S	Girls Train Set	481	1181	___
1589WS	027 Steam Freight Set	38	125	___
1590	Steam Freight Set	24	60	___
1591	USMC Military Set	130	634	___
1593	UP Diesel Work Train Set	35	100	___
1599W	Texas Special Freight Set	35	106	___
1600	Diesel Passenger Set	165	537	___
1601W	Wabash GP7 Diesel Set	51	239	___
1603WS	Steam Freight Set	40	95	___
1605W	Santa Fe Diesel Freight Set	51	164	___
1607WS	Steam Work Train Set	19	47	___
1608W	New Haven Passenger Set	138	528	___
1609W	Steam Freight Set	33	80	___
1611	027 Alaska Diesel Freight Set	72	206	___
1612	027 General Set	40	135	___
1613S	Steam Freight Set	33	93	___
1615	B&M Diesel Freight Set	28	70	___
1615	0-4-0 Locomotive	21	56	___
1615LTS	0-4-0 Locomotive and Tender (master carton)	34	102	___
1615T	Tender	10	64	___
1617S	Steam Work Train	63	140	___
1619W	Santa Fe Diesel Freight Set	46	108	___
1621WS	027 Steam Freight Set (brown corrugated)	75	232	___
1621WS	027 Steam Freight Set (suitcase)	38	105	___
1623W	NP Diesel Freight Set	58	165	___
1625	0-4-0 Locomotive	32	116	___
1625T	Tender	33	113	___
1625WS	Steam Freight Set	40	133	___
1626W	Santa Fe Diesel Passenger Set		123	___
1627S	Stream Freight Set	20	45	___
1629WS	C&O Diesel Freight Set	20	85	___
1631WS	027 Steam Freight Set	27	76	___
1633	U.S. Navy Diesel Freight Set	100	363	___

BOXES		Good P-5	Exc P-7
___ 1637	Santa Fe Diesel Freight Set	23	58
___ 1639WS	Steam Freight Set	16	38
___ 1640-100	Presidential Kit	20	70
___ 1643	C&O Diesel Freight Set	20	55
___ 1647	U.S. Marines Military Set	40	113
___ 1648	Steam Freight Set	12	41
___ 1649	Santa Fe Diesel Freight Set	24	63
___ 1650	Steam Military Set	44	97
___ 1651	Passenger Train Set	42	178
___ 1654	2-4-2 Locomotive	14	37
___ 1654W	Whistle Tender	14	23
___ 1655	2-4-2 Locomotive	18	40
___ 1656	0-4-0 Locomotive	26	107
___ 1656LTS	4-4-0 Locomotive and Tender (master carton)	50	225
___ 1665	0-4-0 Locomotive	35	150
___ 1666	2-6-2 Locomotive	15	45
___ 1682T	Tender	5	21
___ 1800	General Gift Pack	20	112
___ 1809	Western Gift Pack	12	60
___ 1862	4-4-0 Civil War General Locomotive	27	82
___ 1862T	Tender	15	54
___ 1865	Western & Atlantic Coach	10	43
___ 1866	Western & Atlantic Mail-Baggage Car	10	43
___ 1872	4-4-0 Civil War General Locomotive	40	100
___ 1872LTS	4-4-0 Locomotive and Tender (master carton)	115	400
___ 1872T	Tender	19	57
___ 1875	Western & Atlantic Coach	38	168
___ 1875W	Western & Atlantic Coach, whistle	18	116
___ 1876	Western & Atlantic Baggage Car	21	81
___ 1877	Flatcar with fence and horses	15	44
___ 2001	Track Make-up Kit (027)	800	2000
___ 2002	Track Make-up Kit (027)	700	1400
___ 2016	2-6-4 Locomotive	9	30
___ 2018	2-6-4 Locomotive	12	30
___ 2018-14	Sleeve for Outer Box	6	20
___ 2020	6-8-6 Steam Turbine Locomotive	17	73
___ 2020W	Tender	11	52
___ 2023	Union Pacific Alco AA Set (master carton), *50*	37	91
___ 2023	Union Pacific Alco AA Set (master carton), *51*	30	90
___ 2025	2-6-2 or 2-6-4 Locomotive	15	57
___ 2026	2-6-2 or 2-6-4 Locomotive	19	65
___ 2028	Pennsylvania GP7 Diesel	25	141
___ 2029	2-6-4 Locomotive	12	47
___ 2031	Rock Island Alco AA Set (master carton), *52*	65	165
___ 2032	Erie Alco AA Set (master carton)	53	88
___ 2033	Uinion Pacific Alco AA Set (master carton)	36	91

BOXES		Good P-5	Exc P-7	
2034	2-4-2 Scout Locomotive	12	47	___
2035	2-6-4 Locomotive	18	73	___
2036	2-6-4 Locomotive	14	58	___
2036LTS	2-6-4 Locomotive and Tender (master carton)	450	1424	___
2037	2-6-4 Locomotive (brown corrugated)	11	35	___
2037-500	2-6-4 Locomotive, pink, from Girls Set	72	259	___
2046	4-6-4 Locomotive	29	77	___
2046LTS	4-6-4 Locomotive and Tender (master carton)	90	302	___
2046T	Lionel Lines Tender, for export	24	74	___
2046W	Lionel Lines Tender (early classic, with liner)	20	66	___
2046W	Lionel Lines Tender (marked 2046)	21	67	___
2046W	Pennsylvania Tender	29	93	___
2046W-50	Pennsylvania Tender	13	55	___
2055	4-6-4 Locomotive	21	70	___
2055LTS	4-6-4 Locomotive and Tender (master carton)	57	242	___
2056	4-6-4 Locomotive	19	49	___
2065	4-6-4 Locomotive	19	49	___
2103W	Steam Freight Set	25	90	___
2105WS	Steam Freight Set	48	115	___
2113WS	Steam Freight Set	41	194	___
2120WS	Steam Passenger Set	100	565	___
2121WS	Steam Freight Set	35	188	___
2124W	GG1 Passenger Set	147	1112	___
2126WS	Steam Turbine Passenger Set	67	537	___
2129WS	Steam Freight Set	113	600	___
2136WS	Steam Passenger Set	38	149	___
2139W	GG1 Freight Set	233	787	___
2140WS	Steam Turbine Passenger Set	60	816	___
2141WS	Steam Turbine Freight Set	35	189	___
2146W	Berkshire Passenger Set	75	499	___
2147WS	Steam Freight Set	54	140	___
2148WS	Hudson Passenger Set	324	1522	___
2149	Santa Fe Diesel Freight Set	78	315	___
2151W	F3 Freight Set	82	280	___
2153WS	Steam Freight Set	60	175	___
2155WS	Berkshire Freight Set	50	244	___
2159W	GG1 Freight Set	107	545	___
2161W	Santa Fe Twin Diesel Freight Set	45	162	___
2163WS	Steam Freight Set	45	160	___
2165WS	Steam Freight Set	50	150	___
2167WS	Steam Freight Set	42	159	___
2171W	NYC Diesel Freight Set	35	128	___
2173WS	Steam Freight Set	54	163	___
2175W	Santa Fe Diesel Freight Set	53	174	___
2177WS	Steam Freight Set	21	72	___
2179WS	Steam Freight Set	27	75	___

BOXES		Good P-5	Exc P-7
____ 2183WS	Steam Freight Set	37	90
____ 2185W	NYC Diesel Freight Set	40	105
____ 2187WS	Steam Freight Set	24	68
____ 2190W	Santa Fe Diesel Passenger Set	39	182
____ 2191W	Santa Fe Diesel Freight Set	43	164
____ 2193W	NYC Diesel Freight Set	44	116
____ 2201WS	Steam Freight Set	51	129
____ 2203WS	Steam Freight Set	59	244
____ 2205WS	Steam Freight Set	30	93
____ 2207W	Santa Fe Diesel Freight Set	37	151
____ 2209W	NYC Diesel Freight Set	41	122
____ 2211WS	Steam Freight Set	29	86
____ 2213WS	Steam Freight Set	33	98
____ 2217WS	Steam Turbine Freight Set	65	206
____ 2219W	Diesel Freight Set	94	314
____ 2221WS	Steam Freight Set	36	129
____ 2222WS	Hudson Passenger Set	123	675
____ 2223W	Lackawanna FM Freight Set	132	370
____ 2225T	Tender	20	88
____ 2225WS	Steam Freight Set	45	170
____ 2226W	Tender	33	100
____ 2226WX	Lionel Lines Tender	40	105
____ 2227W	Santa Fe Diesel Freight Set	72	230
____ 2229W	NYC Diesel Freight Set	34	125
____ 2231W	Southern Diesel Freight Set	75	288
____ 2234W	Santa Fe Passenger Set	77	345
____ 2235W	Milwaukee Road Diesel Freight Set	53	157
____ 2237WS	Steam Freight Set	48	155
____ 2239W	Illinois Central Freight Set	151	486
____ 2240	Wabash F3 AB Set (C and P boxes)	60	293
____ 2240	Wabash F3 AB Set (master carton)	107	718
____ 2240C	Wabash F3 B Unit	40	166
____ 2240P	Wabash F3 A Unit	30	94
____ 2241WS	Steam Freight Set	20	68
____ 2242	New Haven F3 AB Set (C and P boxes)	109	600
____ 2242	New Haven F3 AB Set (master carton)	300	940
____ 2242C	New Haven F3 B Unit	80	328
____ 2242P	New Haven F3 A Unit	117	302
____ 2243	Santa Fe F3 AB Set (C and P boxes)	30	99
____ 2243	Santa Fe F3 AB Set (master carton)	38	143
____ 2243C	Santa Fe F3 B Unit	27	87
____ 2243P	Santa Fe F3 A Unit	28	85
____ 2243W	Diesel Freight Set	33	115
____ 2244W	Wabash Passenger Set	204	760
____ 2245	Texas Special F3 AB Set (C and P boxes)	54	288
____ 2245	Texas Special F3 AB Set (master carton)	300	800

BOXES		Good P-5	Exc P-7	
2245C	Texas Special F3 B Unit	35	144	___
2245P	Texas Special F3 A Unit	26	94	___
2247W	Wabash F3 Diesel Freight Set	80	280	___
2251W	Diesel Freight Set	40	170	___
2254W	Pennsylvania GG1 Passenger Set, 55	225	1129	___
2255W	Diesel Work Train Set	35	140	___
2257	SP-type Caboose	4	16	___
2257WS	Steam Freight Set	29	126	___
2259W	New Haven Electric Freight Set	39	168	___
2261WS	Steam Freight Set	30	90	___
2263W	New Haven Freight Set	43	204	___
2265WS	Steam Freight Set	26	104	___
2267W	Diesel Freight Set	56	220	___
2269W	B&O Diesel Freight Set	132	649	___
2270W	Jersey Central Passenger Set	321	1142	___
2271W	Pennsylvania GG1 Freight Set	44	385	___
2273W	Milwaukee Road Diesel Freight Set	93	743	___
2274W	Pennsylvania Passenger Set	208	759	___
2275W	Wabash GP7 Freight Set	53	130	___
2276W	Budd Passenger Set	60	328	___
2277WS	Work Train Set	28	170	___
2279W	NH Electric Freight Set	68	127	___
2283W	Steam Freight Set	25	125	___
2289WS	Berkshire Super O Freight Set	76	196	___
2291W	Rio Grande Diesel Freight Set	129	441	___
2292WS	Steam Passenger Set	119	781	___
2293W	Pennsylvania GG1 Freight Set	163	796	___
2295WS	N&W Steam Freight Set	169	703	___
2296W	Canadian Pacific Passenger Set	393	1657	___
2297WS	N&W Steam Freight Set	109	570	___
2321	Lackawanna FM Train Master Diesel	41	115	___
2322	Virginian FM Train Master Diesel	33	118	___
2328	Burlington GP7 Diesel	34	103	___
2329	Virginian Electric Locomotive	78	227	___
2330	Pennsylvania GG1 Electric Locomotive	71	258	___
2331	Virginian FM Train Master Diesel	32	150	___
2332	Pennsylvania GG1 Electric Locomotive	36	109	___
2332-275	Pennsylvania GG1 Electric Locomotive	64	201	___
2333	NYC F3 AA Set (master carton)	47	146	___
2333	NYC F3 AA Set (P and T boxes)	39	179	___
2333P	NYC F3 A Unit (brown corrugated)	25	99	___
2333	Santa Fe F3 AA Set (master carton)	62	152	___
2333	Santa Fe F3 AA Set (P and T boxes)	33	101	___
2333T	Santa Fe F3 Dummy A Unit	27	82	___
2333P	Santa Fe F3 A Unit	17	109	___
2337	Wabash GP7 Diesel, 58	28	158	___

BOXES		Good P-5	Exc P-7
____ 2338	MILW GP7 Diesel (classic)	28	109
____ 2338	MILW GP7 Diesel (brown corrugated)	17	61
____ 2338X	MILW GP7 Diesel (brown corrugated marked 2338X)	30	96
____ 2339	Wabash GP7 Diesel, *57*	27	126
____ 2340-10	Pennsylvania GG1 Electric, tuscan	73	205
____ 2340-25	Pennsylvania GG1 Electric, green, gold stripes	36	127
____ 2341	Jersey Central FM Train Master Diesel	167	703
____ 2343	Santa Fe F3 AA Set (master carton)	40	137
____ 2343	Santa Fe F3 AA Set (P and T boxes)	38	133
____ 2343C	Santa Fe F3 B Unit	29	103
____ 2343P	Santa Fe F3 A Unit	22	55
____ 2343T	Santa Fe F3 Dummy Unit	27	86
____ 2344	NYC F3 AA Set (master carton)	83	480
____ 2344	NYC F3 AA Set (P and T boxes)	63	210
____ 2344C	NYC F3 B Unit	45	125
____ 2344P	NYC F3 A Unit	169	143
____ 2344T	NYC F3 Dummy Unit	33	184
____ 2345	Western Pacific F3 AA Set (master carton)	175	557
____ 2345	Western Pacific F3 AA Set (P and T boxes, brown corrugated)	50	311
____ 2345P	Western Pacific F3 A Unit	40	160
____ 2345T	Western Pacific F3 Dummy A Unit	92	278
____ 2346	B&M GP9 Diesel	30	127
____ 2347	C&O GP9 Diesel	450	1350
____ 2348	M&StL GP9 Diesel	36	144
____ 2349	Northern Pacific GP9 Diesel	65	185
____ 2349-12	Sleeve for 2349 and 2359 outer boxes	21	96
____ 2350	New Haven EP-5 Electric Locomotive	33	95
____ 2351	Milwaukee Road EP-5 Electric Locomotive	46	136
____ 2352	Pennsylvania EP-5 Electric Locomotive	50	195
____ 2353	Santa Fe F3 AA Set (master carton)	72	211
____ 2353	Santa Fe F3 AA Set (P and T boxes)	40	132
____ 2353P	Santa Fe F3 A Unit (brown corrugated)	30	55
____ 2353T	Santa Fe F3 Dummy Unit	29	100
____ 2354	NYC F3 AA Set (master carton)	42	248
____ 2354P	NYC F3 A Unit (brown corrugated)	44	102
____ 2354T	NYC F3 Dummy Unit	35	134
____ 2355	Western Pacific F3 AA Set (master carton)	113	352
____ 2355	Western Pacific F3 AA Set (P and T boxes)	60	293
____ 2355P	Western Pacific F3 A Unit	45	156
____ 2355T	Western Pacific F3 Dummy A Unit	43	162
____ 2356	Southern F3 AA Set (master carton)	75	431
____ 2356C	Southern F3 B Unit	43	215
____ 2356P	Southern F3 A Unit	40	107
____ 2356T	Southern F3 Dummy Unit	71	302
____ 2357	SP-type Caboose	7	18
____ 2358	Great Northern EP-5 Electric Locomotive	77	209

BOXES		Good P-5	Exc P-7	
2359	Boston & Maine GP9 Diesel	28	95	___
2360-10	Pennsylvania GG1 Electric Locomotive, tuscan	122	286	___
2360-25	Pennsylvania GG1 Electric Locomotive, green	46	209	___
2363	Illinois Central F3 AB Set (master carton)	154	598	___
2363	Illinois Central F3 AB Set (C and P boxes)	94	430	___
2363C	Illinois Central F3 B Unit	68	191	___
2363P	Illinois Central F3 A Unit	33	119	___
2365	C&O GP7 Diesel	25	81	___
2367	Wabash F3 AB Diesel Set Master Carton	45	89	___
2367C	Wabash F3 B Unit	37	265	___
2367P	Wabash F3 A Unit	40	139	___
2368	B&O F3 AB Set (master carton)	200	830	___
2368C	B&O F3 B Unit	71	262	___
2368P	B&O F3 A Unit	35	200	___
2373	CP F3 AA Set (P and T boxes)	183	470	___
2373P	CP F3 A Unit	63	241	___
2373T	CP F3 Dummy A Unit	68	238	___
2378	Milwaukee Road F3 AB Set (master carton)	165	851	___
2378C	Milwaukee Road F3 B Unit	101	265	___
2378P	Milwaukee Road F3 A Unit	60	214	___
2379C	Rio Grande F3 B Unit	52	224	___
2379P	Rio Grande F3 A Unit	49	159	___
2383	Santa Fe F3 AA Units (master carton)	55	204	___
2383P	Santa Fe F3 A Unit	27	90	___
2383T	Santa Fe F3 Dummy Unit	36	97	___
2400	Maplewood Pullman Car	19	77	___
2401	Hillside Observation Car	17	78	___
2402	Chatham Pullman Car	19	79	___
2403B	Tender with bell	19	94	___
2404	Santa Fe Vista Dome Car	15	48	___
2405	Santa Fe Pullman Car	14	47	___
2406	Santa Fe Observation Car	15	46	___
2408	Santa Fe Vista Dome Car	12	44	___
2409	Santa Fe Pullman Car	12	45	___
2410	Santa Fe Observation Car	11	48	___
2411	Lionel Lines Flatcar	8	40	___
2412	Santa Fe Vista Dome Car	16	53	___
2414	Santa Fe Pullman Car	13	47	___
2416	Santa Fe Observation Car (orange perforated)	17	69	___
2416	Santa Fe Observation Car (orange picture)	15	49	___
2419	DL&W Work Caboose	12	37	___
2420	DL&W Work Caboose with searchlight	19	53	___
2421	Maplewood Pullman Car	12	40	___
2422	Chatham Pullman Car	11	38	___
2423	Hillside Observation Car	13	43	___
2426W	Hudson Tender (early classic)	83	301	___

BOXES		Good P-5	Exc P-7
___ 2426W	Hudson Tender (middle classic)	72	217
___ 2429	Livingston Pullman Car	20	65
___ 2430	Pullman Car, blue	14	41
___ 2431	Observation Car, blue	14	42
___ 2432	Clifton Vista Dome Car	13	39
___ 2434	Newark Pullman Car	14	37
___ 2435	Elizabeth Pullman Car	20	52
___ 2436	Mooseheart Observation Car	14	36
___ 2436	Mooseheart Observation Car (classic)	12	34
___ 2440	Pullman Car, green	9	33
___ 2441	Observation Car, green	9	33
___ 2442	Pullman Car, brown	9	41
___ 2442	Clifton Vista Dome Car	18	52
___ 2443	Observation Car, brown	10	44
___ 2444	Newark Pullman Car	15	48
___ 2445	Elizabeth Pullman Car	25	100
___ 2446	Summit Observation Car	15	46
___ 2452	Pennsylvania Gondola	8	24
___ 2452X	Pennsylvania Gondola	5	15
___ X2454	Pennsylvania Boxcar (marked Box Car)	12	34
___ X2454	Pennsylvania Boxcar (marked Merchandise Car)	23	71
___ 2456	Lehigh Valley Hopper	5	39
___ 2457	Pennsylvania N5-type Caboose	6	36
___ 2458	Pennsylvania Automobile Boxcar	14	39
___ 2460	Bucyrus Erie Crane Car (box with toy logo)	16	56
___ 2460	Bucyrus Erie Crane Car (box without toy logo)	22	119
___ 2461	Transformer Car	17	48
___ 2465	Sunoco 2-D Tank Car	4	13
___ 2466T	Tender	5	26
___ 2466W	Tender	12	40
___ 2466WX	Tender	15	49
___ 2472	PRR N5-type Caboose	4	15
___ 2481	Plainfield Pullman Car	40	170
___ 2482	Westfield Pullman Car	41	165
___ 2483	Livingston Observation Car	46	169
___ 2501W	M&StL Diesel Freight Set	41	249
___ 2502W	Budd RDC Set	112	205
___ 2503WS	Super O Steam Freight Set	27	70
___ 2505W	Super O Electric Freight Set	74	273
___ 2507W	New Haven Diesel Freight Set	51	405
___ 2509WS	Super O Steam Freight Set	51	299
___ 2511W	Pennsylvania Electric Work Set	47	250
___ 2513W	Virginian Rectifier Set	67	307
___ 2515WS	Super O Steam Freight Set	93	405
___ 2517W	Rio Grande Diesel Freight Set	65	193
___ 2518W	Pennsylvania Electric Passenger Set	142	731

BOXES		Good P-5	Exc P-7	
2519W	Virginian Train Master Super O Freight Set	39	399	___
2521	President McKinley Observation Car	27	82	___
2521WS	Super O Steam Freight Set	40	218	___
2522	President Harrison Vista Dome Car	28	88	___
2523	President Garfield Pullman Car	29	84	___
2523W	Santa Fe Super O Freight Set	35	257	___
2525WS	Super O Steam Work Train Set	152	562	___
2526W	Santa Fe Passenger Set	33	583	___
2527	Missile Launcher Set, yellow	37	101	___
2528WS	Super O General Set	38	162	___
2530	REA Baggage Car	35	105	___
2530	REA Baggage Car (orange perforated)	100	337	___
2531	Silver Dawn Observation Car	22	60	___
2531WS	Super O Steam Freight Set	38	109	___
2532	Silver Range Vista Dome Car	25	57	___
2533	Silver Cloud Pullman Car	23	63	___
2533W	Super O GN Electric Freight Set	98	455	___
2534	Silver Bluff Pullman Car	23	60	___
2535WS	Steam Freight Set	45	169	___
2537W	New Haven Freight Set	42	304	___
2541	Alexander Hamilton Observation Car	27	74	___
2541W	Santa Fe Super O Freight Set	129	583	___
2542	Betsy Ross Vista Dome Car	24	78	___
2543	William Penn Pullman Car	27	80	___
2543WS	Berkshire Freight Set	92	383	___
2544	Molly Pitcher Pullman Car	28	82	___
2544W	Santa Fe Passenger Set	92	835	___
2545WS	Super O Military Set	93	783	___
2547WS	Super O Steam Freight Set	35	104	___
2549W	Super O Military Set	33	191	___
2550	B&O Baggage-Mail Rail Diesel Car	45	173	___
2551	Banff Park Observation Car	32	130	___
2551W	GN Electric Set	120	662	___
2552	Skyline 500 Vista Dome Car	39	119	___
2553	Blair Manor Pullman Car	64	171	___
2553WS	Berkshire Freight Set	65	289	___
2554	Craig Manor Pullman Car	65	169	___
2555	Sunoco 1-D Tank Car	10	46	___
2555	Sunoco 1-D Tank Car (overstamped 2755 box)	22	72	___
2559	B&O Passenger Rail Diesel Car	42	128	___
2560	Lionel Lines Crane Car	21	64	___
2561	Vista Valley Observation Car	38	125	___
2561	Vista Valley Observation Car (orange perforated)	65	174	___
2562	Regal Pass Observation Car	38	125	___
2562	Regal Pass Observation Car (orange perforated)	57	174	___
2563	Indian Falls Pullman Car	42	140	___

	BOXES		Good P-5	Exc P-7
___	2570	Super O Santa Fe Work Train Set	43	230
___	2572	Boston & Maine Military Set	35	145
___	2574	Santa Fe Military Set	70	270
___	2625	Irvington Pullman Car	33	115
___	2627	Madison Pullman Car	28	105
___	2628	Manhattan Pullman Car	29	104
___	2671T	Pennsylvania Tender, for export	19	59
___	2671W	Pennsylvania Tender	24	72
___	2671WX	Lionel Lines Tender	27	71
___	2755	Sunoco 1-D Tank Car	14	61
___	2758	PRR Automobile Boxcar	9	34
___	2855	Sunoco 1-D Tank Car	32	129
___	3330	Flatcar with submarine kit	18	82
___	3330-100	Operating Submarine Kit, separate sale	41	163
___	3349	Turbo Missile Launch Car	7	50
___	3356	Operating Horse Car and Corral Set (classic)	19	61
___	3356	Operating Horse Car and Corral Set (orange picture)	23	88
___	3356-2	Horse Car	71	512
___	3356-100	Black Horses (classic)	4	17
___	3356-100	Black Horses (white box)	9	24
___	3356-150	Horse Car Corral	68	639
___	3357	Hydraulic Maintenance Car	11	33
___	3357-27	Trestle Components for Cop and Hobo Car	9	27
___	3359	Lionel Lines Twin-bin Coal Dump Car	14	44
___	3360	Operating Burro Crane	21	64
___	3361	Operating Log Dump Car	5	22
___	3361X	Operating Log Dump Car	7	26
___	3362	Helium Tank Unloading Car	15	39
___	3362/3364	Operating Unloading Car (Hagerstown checkerboard)	20	50
___	3364	Log Unloading Car	10	31
___	3366	Circus Car Corral Set	36	142
___	3366-100	White Horses	11	38
___	3370	W&A Outlaw Car	11	38
___	3376	Bronx Zoo Car	13	44
___	3376-160	Bronx Zoo Car, green	17	53
___	3410	Helicopter Car	17	60
___	3413	Mercury Capsule Car	18	75
___	3419	Helicopter Car	18	49
___	3424	Wabash Operating Boxcar	23	57
___	3424-75	Low Bridge Signal (marked 3424-75, or overstamped on 3424-100 box)	82	247
___	3424-100	Low Bridge Signal	4	18
___	3428	U.S. Mail Operating Boxcar	11	54
___	3434	Poultry Dispatch Car	33	66
___	3435	Traveling Aquarium Car	36	104
___	3444	Erie Operating Gondola	11	30
___	3451	Operating Log Dump Car	11	32

BOXES		Good P-5	Exc P-7	
3454	PRR Operating Merchandise Car	32	109	___
3456	N&W Operating Hopper	14	43	___
3459	LL Operating Coal Dump Car (no toymaker logo)	21	84	___
3459	LL Operating Coal Dump Car (toymaker logo)	16	68	___
3461	LL Operating Log Car	9	27	___
3461X	Automatic Lumber Car	16	44	___
3461-25	Lionel Lines Operating Log Car, green	14	60	___
3462	Automatic Milk Car	11	38	___
3462-70	Milk Cans	2	10	___
3464	NYC Operating Boxcar	5	17	___
3464	Santa Fe Operating Boxcar	5	12	___
3469	LL Operating Coal Dump Car	13	38	___
3469X	LL Operating Coal Dump Car	8	23	___
3470	Target Launching Car	16	38	___
3472	Automatic Milk Car	16	38	___
3474	Western Pacific Operating Boxcar	12	50	___
3482	Automatic Milk Car	18	70	___
3484	Pennsylvania Operating Boxcar	13	30	___
3484-25	ATSF Operating Boxcar	9	35	___
3494	NYC Operating Boxcar	18	43	___
3494-150	Missouri Pacific Operating Boxcar	15	46	___
3494-275	State of Maine Operating Boxcar	17	49	___
3494-550	Monon Operating Boxcar	46	194	___
3494-625	Soo Operating Boxcar	54	189	___
3509	Satellite Launching Car	16	62	___
3512	Fireman and Ladder Car	17	64	___
3519	Satellite Launching Car	16	42	___
3520	Searchlight Car	11	32	___
3530	GM Generator Car	18	68	___
3530-50	Searchlight with pole and base, separate sale	44	92	___
3535	Security Car with searchlight	14	59	___
3540	Operating Radar Car	27	68	___
3545	Operating TV Monitor Car	21	84	___
3559	Operating Coal Dump Car	14	39	___
3562-1	ATSF Operating Barrel Car	27	100	___
3562-25	ATSF Operating Barrel Car, gray	17	54	___
3562-50	ATSF Operating Barrel Car, yellow	17	48	___
3562-75	ATSF Operating Barrel Car, orange	24	53	___
3619	Helicopter Reconnaissance Car	12	53	___
3620	Searchlight Car with insert	23	65	___
3650	Extension Searchlight Car	11	39	___
3656	Operating Cattle Car	16	44	___
3656	Stockyard with cattle (set box with car box)	16	56	___
3656-9	Cattle (marked 3656 on 4 sides, unnumbered tuck flaps)	6	17	___
3656-9	Cattle (marked 3656 on 4 sides, 3656-44 on 1 tuck flap)	3	10	___
3656-9	Cattle (marked 3656-34 on 4 sides, 3656-44 on 1 tuck flap)	3	9	___

BOXES		Good P-5	Exc P-7
___ 3656-9	Cattle (marked 3656 on 4 sides, 3656-44 on 1 tuck flap, OPS markings)	8	19
___ 3656-9	Cattle (unnumbered sides, marked 3656-44 on 1 tuck flap)	8	19
___ 3656-9	Cattle (unnumbered sides, marked 3656-34 on 1 tuck flap)	10	28
___ 3656-150	Corral Platform, separate sale	140	657
___ 3662	Automatic Milk Car (classic), *55*	17	48
___ 3662	Automatic Milk Car (orange picture), *64*	19	66
___ 3662	Automatic Milk Car (white box), *66*	20	72
___ 3665	Minuteman Operating Car	21	48
___ 3672	Bosco Operating Milk Car	52	170
___ 3820	USMC Operating Submarine Car	23	67
___ 3830	Operating Submarine Car	17	47
___ 3854	Automatic Merchandise Car	73	635
___ 3927	Lionel Lines Track Cleaning Car	12	29
___ 4109WS	Electronic Control Set	90	485
___ 4357	SP-type Caboose, electronic	30	103
___ 4452	PRR Gondola, electronic	26	97
___ 4454	Baby Ruth PRR Boxcar, electronic	26	109
___ 4457	PRR N5-type Caboose, tintype, electronic	23	89
___ 4671W	Tender	43	139
___ 5160	Viewing Stand	12	52
___ 5459	LL Coal Dump Car, electronic	23	143
___ 6001T	Tender	3	10
___ 6002	NYC Gondola	2	7
___ 6004	Baby Ruth PRR Boxcar	3	11
___ 6007	Lionel Lines SP-type Caboose	2	8
___ 6009	Remote Control Uncoupling Track	2	9
___ 6012	Gondola	3	10
___ 6014	Boxcar	3	12
___ 6014-60	Frisco Boxcar, white (middle classic)	8	18
___ 6014-60	Frisco Boxcar, white	5	16
___ 6014-85	Bosco or Frisco Boxcar, orange (classic)	7	23
___ 6014-85	Boxcar (Hagerstown production)		19
___ 6014-100	Airex Boxcar, red	8	24
___ 6014-100	Airex Boxcar, red (orange perforated)	12	35
___ 6014-150	Wix Boxcar	37	181
___ 6014-335	Frisco Boxcar	6	23
___ 6014-410	Frisco Boxcar	15	66
___ 6015	Sunoco 1-D Tank Car	4	14
___ 6017	Lionel Lines SP-type Caboose	2	8
___ 6017-1	Caboose	10	29
___ 6017-50	U.S. Marine Corps SP-type Caboose (box marked 6017-60)	16	66
___ 6017-60	USMC Caboose	5	18
___ 6017-85	Lionel Lines SP-type Caboose, gray	8	32
___ 6017-100	B&M SP-type Caboose	16	52
___ 6017-185	ATSF SP-type Caboose	5	19
___ 6017-200	U.S. Navy SP-type Caboose	32	125

BOXES		Good P-5	Exc P-7	
6017-235	ATSF SP-type Caboose	9	29	___
6019	Remote Control Track	2	5	___
6020W	Tender	8	37	___
6024	Nabisco Shredded Wheat Boxcar	5	27	___
6024-60	RCA Whirlpool Boxcar	15	64	___
6025	Gulf 1-D Tank Car (classic)	6	17	___
6025-60	Gulf 1-D Tank Car	5	28	___
6025-60	Gulf 1-D Tank Car (classic, overstamped 6024 box)	8	40	___
6025-85	Gulf 1-D Tank Car (classic)	6	37	___
6026T	Lionel Lines Tender	8	23	___
6026W	Lionel Lines Tender (classic or picture)	11	37	___
6027	Alaska SP-type Caboose	50	231	___
6029	Remote Control Uncoupling Track (classic)	2	9	___
6029	Remote Control Uncoupling Track (orange picture)	3	15	___
6032	Short Gondola	3	12	___
6034	Boxcar (Hagerstown production)	2	9	___
X6034	Baby Ruth PRR Boxcar	2	11	___
6035	Sunoco 1-D Tank Car	4	13	___
6037	Lionel Lines SP-type Caboose	2	9	___
6050	Lionel Savings Bank Boxcar	6	27	___
6050-110	Swift Boxcar	7	27	___
6057	Lionel Lines SP-type Caboose	6	40	___
6059	M&StL SP-type Caboose	7	21	___
6059-50	M&StL SP-type Caboose (Hagerstown checkerboard)	8	25	___
6062	NYC Gondola	6	21	___
6066T	Tender	9	20	___
6110	2-4-2 Locomotive	4	23	___
6111-75	Flatcar with logs	11	62	___
6111-110	Flatcar	18	62	___
6112-1	Canister Car	10	35	___
6112-25	Canister Set	10	34	___
6112-85	Short Gondola (marked "Canister Car")	5	24	___
6112-135	Short Gondola (marked "Canister Car")	7	33	___
6119	DL&W Work Caboose, red	5	21	___
6119-25	DL&W Work Caboose, orange	8	30	___
6119-50	DL&W Work Caboose, brown	10	34	___
6119-75	DL&W Work Caboose	9	37	___
6119-100	DL&W Work Caboose (classic)	9	36	___
6119-100	DL&W Work Caboose (picture, perforated, or window)	22	63	___
6121	Flatcar with pipes	13	49	___
6121-60	Flatcar with pipes	14	69	___
6121-85	Flatcar with pipes (classic)	15	63	___
6130	ATSF Work Caboose (cellophane)	11	44	___
6130	ATSF Work Caboose (Hagerstown checkerboard)	13	47	___
6130	ATSF Work Caboose (all other boxes)	5	24	___
6149	Remote Control Uncoupling Track, *64, 69*	3	7	___

BOXES		Good P-5	Exc P-7
___ 6151	Flatcar with patrol truck	11	43
___ 6162-60	Alaska Gondola	28	142
___ 6162-110	NYC Gondola, blue (orange picture)	10	36
___ 6162-110	NYC Gondola, red, separate sale (orange picture with label)	21	82
___ 6167-85	Union Pacific SP-type Caboose	19	66
___ 6175	Flatcar with rocket	8	37
___ 6220	Santa Fe NW2 Switcher	23	100
___ 6250	Seaboard NW2 Switcher	31	126
___ 6257	SP-type Caboose	4	10
___ 6257X	SP-type Caboose	13	37
___ 6257-25	SP-type Caboose	3	13
___ 6257-50	SP-type Caboose	5	13
___ 6262	Flatcar with wheel load	8	30
___ 6264	Flatcar with lumber, separate sale	48	139
___ 6311	Flatcar with pipes	11	53
___ 6315	Gulf 1-D Chemical Tank Car (classic)	14	49
___ 6315	Gulf 1-D Chemical Tank Car (Hagerstown checkerboard)	22	52
___ 6315-60	Gulf 1-D Chemical Tank Car (orange picture)	8	34
___ 6342	NYC Gondola	22	161
___ 6343	Barrel Ramp Car	11	37
___ 6346	Alcoa Quad Hopper	13	39
___ 6356	NYC Stock Car	10	28
___ 6357	SP-type Caboose (classic)	6	20
___ 6357	Caboose (orange perforated)	8	20
___ 6357	SP-type Caboose (orange perforated, overstamped)	18	67
___ 6357-50	ATSF SP-type Caboose	163	498
___ 6361	Timber Transport Car	14	41
___ 6361	Timber Transport Car (Hagerstown checkerboard)	19	62
___ 6362	Truck Car	12	41
___ 6376	LL Circus Stock Car	11	41
___ 6401	Flatcar, gray	24	98
___ 6403B	Tender with bell	23	72
___ 6405	Flatcar with piggyback van	6	33
___ 6407	Flatcar with rocket	97	317
___ 6411	Flatcar with logs	5	22
___ 6413	Mercury Capsule Carrying Car	21	58
___ 6414	Evans Auto Loader (classic)	24	62
___ 6414	Evans Auto Loader (orange picture)	27	84
___ 6414	Evans Auto Loader (orange picture, overstamped 6416 box)	32	104
___ 6414	Evans Auto Loader (orange perforated), *59*	19	86
___ 6414	Evans Auto Loader (cellophane), *66*	23	110
___ 6414-25	Four Automobiles, separate sale	140	484
___ 6414-85	Evans Auto Loader (orange picture)	143	438
___ 6415	Sunoco 3-D Tank Car (classic)	10	25
___ 6415	Sunoco 3-D Tank Car (orange picture)	12	37
___ 6415	Sunoco 3-D Tank Car (cellophane)	22	71

BOXES		Good P-5	Exc P-7	
6415	Sunoco 3-D Tank Car (Hillside checkerboard)	19	42	
6415	Sunoco 3-D Tank Car (orange picture with label)	40	102	
6416	Boat Transport Car	36	121	
6417	PRR N5c Porthole Caboose	4	19	
6417-1	PRR N5c Porthole Caboose, without New York Zone	8	37	
6417-25	Lionel Lines N5c Porthole Caboose	7	27	
6417-50	Lehigh Valley N5c Porthole Caboose	23	78	
6418	Machinery Car	19	59	
6419	DL&W Work Caboose	13	32	
6419-25	DL&W Work Caboose	7	27	
6419-50	DL&W Work Caboose	10	37	
6419-100	N&W Work Caboose	38	66	
6420	DL&W Work Caboose with searchlight	14	41	
6424	Twin Auto Flatcar	14	41	
6424-60	Twin Auto Flatcar	16	36	
6424-85	Twin Auto Flatcar	13	66	
6424-110	Twin Auto Flatcar	22	80	
6425	Gulf 3-D Tank Car	10	32	
6427	Lionel Lines N5c Porthole Caboose	9	22	
6427-60	Virginian N5c Porthole Caboose	68	238	
6427-500	PRR N5c Porthole Caboose, sky blue, from Girls Set	46	158	
6428	U.S. Mail Boxcar	13	49	
6429	DL&W Work Caboose	33	147	
6430	Flatcar with trailers	12	45	
6431	Flatcar with vans and tractor (cellophane), *66*	55	168	
6434	Poultry Dispatch Stock Car	17	44	
6436	Lehigh Valley Open Quad Hopper, black	9	28	
6436-25	Lehigh Valley Open Quad Hopper, maroon	8	31	
6436-110	Lehigh Valley Open Quad Hopper, red	10	30	
6436-500	Lehigh Valley Open Quad Hopper, lilac, from Girls Set	51	179	
6436-1969	TCA Hopper (Hagerstown checkered)	14	43	
6437	PRR N5c Porthole Caboose	9	22	
6440	Flatcar with vans	13	38	
6440	Green Pullman Car	10	39	
6441	Green Observation Car	10	38	
6442	Brown Pullman Car	10	40	
6443	Brown Observation Car	10	41	
6445	Fort Knox Gold Reserve Car	16	47	
6446	N&W Covered Quad Hopper	10	37	
6446	N&W Covered Quad Hopper (orange picture)	15	71	
6446-25	N&W Covered Quad Hopper	12	34	
6446-60	Lehigh Valley Covered Quad Hopper	73	380	
6447	PRR N5c Porthole Caboose	49	248	
6448	Exploding Target Range Boxcar	10	35	
6452	Pennsylvania Gondola	3	14	
X6454	Santa Fe, NYC, or Baby Ruth Boxcar	6	30	

BOXES		Good P-5	Exc P-7
___ X6454	PRR Boxcar	6	25
___ X6454	PRR Boxcar (classic, overstamped 3464 box)	8	35
___ X6454	SP Boxcar	7	23
___ X6454	Erie Boxcar	7	28
___ 6456	Lehigh Valley Short Hopper	4	17
___ 6456-25	LV Short Hopper (25 rubber-stamped on end flaps)	10	33
___ 6456-75	Lehigh Valley Short Hopper	32	133
___ 6457	SP-type Caboose	5	15
___ 6460	Bucyrus Erie Crane Car	14	48
___ 6460-25	Bucyrus Erie Crane Car, red cab	16	51
___ 6461	Transformer Car	9	34
___ 6462	NYC Gondola, black	4	11
___ 6462-25	NYC Gondola, green	6	19
___ 6462-75	NYC Gondola, red	4	17
___ 6462-100	NYC Gondola, red		40
___ 6462-125	NYC Gondola, red plastic	5	20
___ 6462-500	NYC Gondola, pink, from Girls Set	41	127
___ 6463	Rocket Fuel 2-D Tank Car	11	36
___ 6464-1	Western Pacific Boxcar	10	42
___ 6464-25	Great Northern Boxcar	19	49
___ 6464-50	M&StL Boxcar	14	43
___ 6464-50	M&StL Boxcar (overstamped with S and Silver)	16	48
___ 6464-75	Rock Island Boxcar	13	48
___ 6464-100	Western Pacific Boxcar	25	89
___ 6464-125	NYC Pacemaker Boxcar	21	90
___ 6464-150	Missouri Pacific Boxcar	16	67
___ 6464-175	Rock Island Boxcar	12	54
___ 6464-175	Rock Island Boxcar (overstamped with S and Silver)	20	75
___ 6464-200	Pennsylvania Boxcar	12	95
___ 6464-200	Pennsylvania Boxcar (Hagerstown checkerboard)	18	53
___ 6464-225	SP Boxcar	13	51
___ 6464-250	Western Pacific Boxcar (orange picture with label)	44	138
___ 6464-250	Western Pacific Blue Feather Boxcar (classic for 6464-100), *54*	97	457
___ 6464-250	Western Pacific Boxcar (cellophane)	24	91
___ 6464-275	State of Maine Boxcar	19	64
___ 6464-300	Rutland Boxcar, *55*	22	85
___ 6464-325	B&O Sentinel Boxcar	62	192
___ 6464-350	MKT Boxcar	34	132
___ 6464-375	Central of Georgia Boxcar	16	60
___ 6464-400	B&O Time-Saver Boxcar	13	37
___ 6464-425	New Haven Boxcar (classic)	10	41
___ 6464-425	New Haven Boxcar (Hagerstown)	16	42
___ 6464-450	Great Northern Boxcar	13	51
___ 6464-450	Great Northern Boxcar (cellophane)	18	60
___ 6464-475	B&M Boxcar (classic)	11	40
___ 6464-475	B&M Boxcar (orange picture)	24	99

BOXES		Good P-5	Exc P-7	
6464-500	Timken Boxcar	19	69	___
6464-510	NYC Pacemaker Boxcar	81	301	___
6464-515	MKT Boxcar	75	276	___
6464-525	M&StL Boxcar	10	41	___
6464-650	D&RGW Boxcar (cellophane)	15	61	___
6464-700	Santa Fe Boxcar	17	54	___
6464-725	New Haven Boxcar (orange picture, 735 on box)	14	33	___
6464-725	New Haven Boxcar (Hagerstown checkerboard)	20	62	___
6464-825	Alaska Boxcar	45	176	___
6464-900	NYC Boxcar	9	40	___
6465	Gulf 2-D Tank Car, black (classic)	4	14	___
6465	Sunoco 2-D Tank Car (classic, overstamped 2465 box)	5	20	___
6465	Sunoco 2-D Tank Car (classic, overstamped 6555 box)	6	21	___
6465	Sunoco 2-D Tank Car (orange picture, 6464-900 label)	11	45	___
6465-60	Gulf 2-D Tank Car (classic)	5	21	___
6465-60	Sunoco 2-D Tank Car (classic)	3	14	___
6465-85	Lionel Lines 2-D Tank Car (orange perforated)	27	80	___
6465-110	Cities Service 2-D Tank Car (orange perforated)	16	55	___
6465-160	Lionel Lines Tank Car (orange picture)	41	135	___
6466T	Lionel Lines Tender	9	19	___
6466W	Lionel Lines Tender (with liner)	15	42	___
6466WX	Lionel Lines Tender (with liner)	18	46	___
6467	Miscellaneous Car	14	42	___
6468	B&O Auto Boxcar, tuscan (marked X)	38	184	___
6468	B&O Auto Boxcar, *blue*	10	29	___
6468-25	NH Auto Boxcar	15	37	___
6469	Liquified Gas Tank Car	21	76	___
6470	Explosives Boxcar	11	33	___
6472	Refrigerator Car	6	22	___
6473	Horse Transport Car	9	31	___
6473	Horse Transport Car (end flaps half white, half orange)	25	90	___
6475	Pickles Vat Car (orange picture)	19	65	___
6476	Lehigh Valley Short Hopper	6	20	___
6476	Lehigh Valley Short Hopper (orange perforated)	13	40	___
6476-85	Lehigh Valley Short Hopper	15	52	___
6476-135	Lehigh Valley Short Hopper	8	27	___
6476-160	Lehigh Valley Short Hopper (Hagerstown checkerboard)	10	32	___
6477	Miscellaneous Car with pipes	11	47	___
6482	Refrigerator Car	8	36	___
6500	Flatcar with Bonanza airplane	105	280	___
6501	Flatcar with jet boat	34	87	___
6511	Flatcar with pipes	10	28	___
6512	Cherry Picker Car	13	45	___
6517	Lionel Lines Bay Window Caboose	13	42	___
6517-60	Bay Window Caboose (TCA)	30	110	___
6517-75	Erie Bay Window Caboose	58	271	___

BOXES		Good P-5	Exc P-7
____ 6518	Transformer Car	21	55
____ 6519	Allis-Chalmers Flatcar (classic)	21	72
____ 6519	Allis-Chalmers Flatcar (orange perforated)	33	106
____ 6520	(A) Searchlight Car 2 City	15	48
____ 6530	Firefighting Instruction Car	16	59
____ 6536	M&StL Open Quad Hopper	19	84
____ 6544	Missile Firing Car	22	104
____ 6555	Sunoco 1-D Tank Car	13	30
____ 6556	MKT Stock Car	47	186
____ 6557	SP-type Smoking Caboose	25	103
____ 6560	Bucyrus Erie Crane Car (Hagerstown checkerboard)	16	62
____ 6560	Bucyrus Erie Crane Car (all other boxes)	11	39
____ 6560-25	Bucyrus Erie Crane Car, 8-wheel (with liner)	15	59
____ 6561	Cable Car, 2 reels	10	42
____ 6562-1	NYC Gondola, gray	6	20
____ 6562-25	NYC Gondola, red	5	17
____ 6562-50	NYC Gondola, black	6	18
____ 6572	REA Reefer (classic)	15	47
____ 6572	REA Reefer (orange picture)	15	44
____ 6636	Alaska Open Quad Hopper	16	54
____ 6646	Lionel Lines Stock Car	6	22
____ 6650	IRBM Rocket Launcher	10	33
____ 6654W	Whistle Tender	10	24
____ 6657	Rio Grande SP-type Caboose	26	80
____ 6660	Boom Car	13	48
____ 6670	Derrick Car	15	55
____ 6672	Santa Fe Refrigerator Car	13	35
____ 6736	Detroit & Mackinac Open Quad Hopper	16	52
____ 6800	Flatcar with airplane (classic)	19	57
____ 6800	Flatcar with airplane (orange perforated)	17	68
____ 6800-60	Airplane, separate sale	84	186
____ 6801	Flatcar with brown and white boat	13	40
____ 6801-50	Flatcar with yellow and white boat	10	46
____ 6801-60	Boat, separate sale	28	93
____ 6801-75	Flatcar with blue and white boat	11	47
____ 6802	Flatcar with girders (late classic)	8	29
____ 6802	Flatcar with girders (orange perforated)	18	50
____ 6803	Flatcar with USMC tank and sound truck	35	105
____ 6804	Flatcar with USMC trucks	31	98
____ 6805	Atomic Energy Disposal Flatcar	20	115
____ 6806	Flatcar with USMC trucks	34	98
____ 6807	Flatcar with boat	25	87
____ 6808	Flatcar with military units	31	93
____ 6809	Flatcar with USMC trucks	33	101
____ 6810	Flatcar with trailer	7	33
____ 6812	Track Maintenance Car	17	57

BOXES		Good P-5	Exc P-7	
6814	Rescue Caboose	21	65	___
6816	Flatcar with Allis-Chalmers bulldozer	46	165	___
6816-100	Allis-Chalmers bulldozer	125	433	___
6817	Flatcar with Allis-Chalmers motor scraper	47	193	___
6818	Flatcar with transformer	8	30	___
6819	Flatcar with helicopter	11	60	___
6820	Aerial Missile Transport Car with helicopter	64	239	___
6821	Flatcar with crates	6	30	___
6822	Searchlight Car	10	29	___
6823	Flatcar with IRBM missiles	18	65	___
6825	Flatcar with arch trestle bridge	7	26	___
6826	Flatcar with Christmas trees	25	69	___
6827	Flatcar with Harnischfeger power shovel	28	104	___
6827-100	Harnischfeger Power Shovel	39	80	___
6828	Flatcar with Harnischfeger crane (cellophane, no crane kit box)	30	87	___
6828	Flatcar with Harnischfeger crane (orange picture, no crane kit box)	18	70	___
6828	Harnischfeger Crane Kit, used with flatcar	14	68	___
6828-100	Harnischfeger Crane, separate sale	47	153	___
6830	Flatcar with submarine	21	57	___
6844	Missile Carrying Car	18	89	___
11001	Steam Freight Set (advance catalog 1962)	9	27	___
11011	Diesel Freight Set	30	85	___
11201	Steam Freight Set	20	65	___
11212	Diesel Freight Set	38	98	___
11222	O27 Steam Freight Set	20	58	___
11232	NH Diesel Freight Set	20	65	___
11242	Steam Freight Set	30	70	___
11268	Military Set	35	105	___
11278	Steam Freight Set	22	55	___
11288	Steam Freight Set	38	100	___
11321	Diesel Freight Set	17	34	___
11331	Steam Freight Set	14	40	___
11341	Diesel Freight Set	10	26	___
11375	O27 Steam Freight Set	15	55	___
11415	Steam Freight Set (advance catalog 1963)	17	60	___
11420	Steam Freight Set	10	30	___
11430	Steam Freight Set	20	65	___
11440	Diesel Freight Set	17	65	___
11450	Steam Freight Set	22	62	___
11460	Steam Freight Set	12	30	___
11490	Santa Fe Passenger Set	43	117	___
11500	Steam Freight Set	30	105	___
11520	Steam Freight Set	39	91	___
11540	Steam Freight Set	13	33	___
11550	Steam Freight Set	18	55	___
11560	Texas Special Set	15	42	___

BOXES		Good P-5	Exc P-7
___ 11590	Santa Fe Passenger Set	28	100
___ 11710	Steam Freight Set	30	95
___ 11750	Steam Freight Set	18	52
___ 12710	Steam Freight Set	37	142
___ 12730	Santa Fe Diesel Freight Set	60	174
___ 12760	Berkshire Freight Set	150	400
___ 12780	Santa Fe Passenger Set	193	611
___ 12800	B&M Diesel Freight Set	27	75
___ 12800X	B&M Diesel Freight Set	60	190
___ 12820	Virginian Train Master Freight Set	86	315
___ 12840	Steam Freight Set	44	198
___ 12850	Diesel Freight Set	38	173
___ 13008	Super O Introductory Set	20	66
___ 13018	Santa Fe Space-age Military Set	212	744
___ 13028	Super O Space Set	108	305
___ 13048	Super O Steam Freight Set	60	158
___ 13058	Santa Fe Space-age Military Set	130	400
___ 13088	Santa Fe Passenger Set	288	867
___ 13098	Steam Freight Set	79	275
___ 13108	Santa Fe Space Set	60	168
___ 13118	Berkshire Freight Set	73	288
___ 13128	Santa Fe Space-age Military Set	205	650
___ 13150	Hudson Freight Set	296	900
___ A	Transformer, 90 watts	5	13
___ CTC	Master Carton		167
___ CO-1	Track Clips, *100*	5	15
___ ECU-1	Electronic Control Unit	32	150
___ KW	Transformer, 190 watts	7	20
___ KW	Transformer, 190 watts (yellow)	5	19
___ LTC	Lockon	1	5
___ LW	Transformer, 125 watts	5	13
___ R	Transformer, 110 watts	5	13
___ RCS	Remote Control Track	3	12
___ RW	Transformer, 110 watts	5	18
___ S	Transformer, 80 watts	5	28
___ SW	Transformer, 130 watts	6	16
___ TW	Transformer, 175 watts	3	13
___ UCS	Remote Control Track (O)	2	6
___ UTC	Lockon	6	11
___ VW	Transformer, 150 watts	6	18
___ Z	Transformer, 250 watts	25	83
___ ZW	Transformer, 250 Watts	10	17
___ ZW	Transformer, 275 watts (classic)	12	28
___ ZW	Transformer, 275 watts (orange, with inserts)	10	34
___ ZW	Transformer, 275 watts (yellow, with inserts)	13	32

NOTES

		Good	Exc
___ 463W	Steam Freight Set (224, 2466W, 2458, 2452, 2555, 2457), *45*		793
___ 1000W	027 Steam Freight Set (2016, 6026W, 6014, 6012, 6017), *55*		320
___ 1001	027 Diesel Freight Set (610, 6012, 6014, 6017), *55*		250
___ 1105	027 Diesel Freight Set (1055, 6042, 6044, 6045, 6047), *59*		
___ 1107	027 Diesel Freight Set (1055, 6042, 6044, 6047), *60*		
___ 1111	027 Scout Freight Set (1001, 1001T, 1002, 1005, 1007), *48*		225
___ 1112	027 Scout Freight Set (1001 or 1101, 1001T, 1002, 1004, 1005, 1007), *48*	10	250
___ 1113	027 Scout Freight Set (1120, 1001T, 1002, 1005, 1007), *50*		115
___ 1115	027 Scout Freight Set (1110, 1001T, 1002, 1005, 1007), *49*		162
___ 1117	027 Scout Freight Set (1110, 1001T, 1002, 1005, 1004,1007), *49*		170
___ 1119	027 Freight Scout Set (1110, 1001T, 1002, 1004, 1007), *51-52*		160
___ 1123	027 Steam Freight Set (1060, 1060T, 6042, 6406, 6067), *60-62*		49
___ 1400	027 Steam Passenger Set (221, 221T, two 2430, 2431), *46*		777
___ 1400W	027 Steam Passenger Set (221, 221W, two 2430 2431), *46*		720
___ 1401	027 Steam Freight Set (1654, 1654T, 2452X, 2465, 2472), *46*		120
___ 1401W	027 Steam Freight Set (1654, 1654W, 2452X, 2465, 2472), *46*		220
___ 1402	027 Steam Passenger Set(1666, 2466T, two 2440, 2441), *46*		550
___ 1402W	027 Steam Passenger Set (1666, 2466W, two 2440, 2441), *46*		550
___ 1403	027 Steam Freight Set (221, 221T, 2411, 2465, 2472), *46*		400
___ 1403W	027 Steam Freight Set (221, 221W, 2411, 2465, 2472), *46*		500
___ 1405	027 Steam Freight Set (1666, 2466T, 2452X, 2465, 2472), *46*		145
___ 1405W	027 Steam Freight Set (1666, 2466W, 2452X, 2465, 2472), *46*		280
___ 1407B	027 Steam Switcher Set (1665, 2403B, 2560, 2452X, 2419), *46*		1933
___ 1409	027 Steam Freight Set (1666, 2466T, 3559, 2465, 3454, 2472), *46*		425
___ 1409W	027 Steam Freight Set (1666, 2466W, 3559, 2465, 3454, 2472), *46*		435
___ 1411W	027 Steam Freight Set (1666, 2466WX, 2452X, 2465, 2454, 2472), *46*		250
___ 1413WS	027 Steam Freight Set (2020, 2466WX, 2452X, 2465, 2454, 2472), *46*		350
___ 1415WS	027 Steam Freight Set (2020, 2020W, 3459, 3454, 2465, 2472), *46*		530
___ 1417WS	027 Steam Work Train Set (2020, 2020W, 2465, 3451, 2560, 2419), *46*		720
___ 1419WS	027 Steam Freight Set (2020, 2020W, 3459, 2452X, 2560, 2419, 97), *46*		880
___ 1421WS	027 Steam Freight Set (2020, 2020W, 3451, 2465, 3454, 2472, 164), *46*		1100
___ 1423W	027 Steam Freight Set (1655, 6654W, 6452, 6465, 6257), *48-49*		239
___ 1425B	027 Steam Switcher Freight Set (1656, 2403B, 6456, 6465, 6257X), *48*		825
___ 1425B	027 Steam Switcher Freight Set (1656, 6403B, 6456, 6465, 6257), *49*		825
___ 1426WS	027 Steam Passenger Set (2026, 6466WX, two 6440, 6441), *48-49*		471
___ 1427WS	027 Steam Freight Set (2026, 6466WX, 6454, 6465, 6257), *48*		302

SETS		Good	Exc
1429WS	027 Steam Freight Set (2026, 6466WX, 3451, 6454, 6465, 6257), *48*		282 ___
1430WS	027 Steam Passenger Set (2025, 6466WX, 2400, 2401, 2402), *48-49*		894 ___
1431	027 Steam Freight Set (1654, 1654T, 2452X, 2465, 2472), *47*		235 ___
1431W	027 Steam Freight Set (1654, 1654W, 2452X, 2465, 2472), *47*		175 ___
1432	027 Steam Passenger Set (221, 221T, two 2430, 2431), *47*		850 ___
1432W	027 Steam Passenger Set (221, 221W, two 2430 2431), *47*		795 ___
1433	027 Steam Freight Set (221, 221T, 2411, 2465, 2457), *47*		560 ___
1433W	027 Steam Freight Set (221, 221 W, 2411, 2465, 2457), *47*		375 ___
1434WS	027 Steam Passenger Set (2025, 2466WX, two 2440, 2441), *47*		555 ___
1435WS	027 Steam Freight Set (2025, 2466WX, 2452X, 2454, 2457), *47*		240 ___
1437WS	027 Steam Freight Set (2025, 2466WX, 2452X, 2465, 2454, 2472), *47*		608 ___
1439WS	027 Steam Freight Set (2025, 2466WX, 3559, 2465, 3454, 2457), *47*		470 ___
1441WS	027 Steam Work Train Set (2020, 2020W, 2560, 2461, 3451, 2419), *47*		1225 ___
1443WS	027 Steam Freight Set (2020, 2020W, 3459, 3462, 2465, 2457), *47*		400 ___
1445WS	027 Steam Freight Set (2025, 6466WX, 6454, 3559, 6465, 6357), *48*		325 ___
1447WS	027 Steam Work Train Set (2020, 6020W, 3451, 2461, 2460, 6419), *48*		460 ___
1447WS	027 Steam Work Train Set (2020, 6020W, 6461, 3461, 2460, 6419), *49*		475 ___
1449WS	027 Steam Freight Set (2020, 6020W, 3462, 3459, 6411, 6465, 6357), *48*		430 ___
1451WS	027 Steam Freight Set (2026, 6466WX, 6462, 3464, 6257), *49*		296 ___
1453WS	027 Steam Freight Set (2026, 6466WX, 3464, 6465, 3461, 6357), *49*		386 ___
1455WS	027 Steam Freight Set (2025, 6466WX, 6462, 6465, 3472, 6357), *49*		335 ___
1457B	027 Diesel Freight Set (6220, 3464, 6462, 6520, 6419), *49-50*		710 ___
1459WS	027 Steam Freight Set (2020, 6020W, 6411, 3656, 6465, 3469, 6357), *49*		1090 ___
1461S	027 Steam Freight Set (6110, 6001T, 6002, 6004, 6007), *50*		175 ___
1463W	027 Steam Freight Set (2036, 6466W, 6462, 6465, 6257), *50*		230 ___
1463WS	027 Freight Set (2026, 6466W, 6462, 6465, 6257), *51*		269 ___
1464W	027 UP Diesel Passenger Set (2023 AA, 2481, 2482, 2483), *50*		2041 ___
1464W	027 UP Passenger Set (2023 AA, 2421, 2422, 2423), *51*		895 ___
1464W	027 UP Passenger Set (2033 AA, 2421, 2422, 2423), *52-53*		795 ___
1465	027 Steam Freight Set (2034, 6066T, 6032, 6035, 6037), *52*		264 ___
1467W	027 UP Diesel Freight Set (2023 AA, 6656, 6465, 6456, 6357), *50-51*		572 ___
1467W	027 Erie Diesel Freight Set (2032 AA, 6656, 6456, 6465, 6357), *52-53*		805 ___
1469WS	027 Steam Freight Set (2035, 6466W, 6462, 6465, 6456, 6257), *50-51*		313 ___
1471WS	027 Steam Freight Set (2035, 6466W, 3469, 6465, 6454, 3461, 6357), *50-51*		450 ___
1473WS	027 Steam Freight Set (2046, 2046W, 3464, 6465, 6520, 6357), *50*		560 ___
1475WS	027 Steam Freight Set (2046, 2046W, 3656, 3461, 6472, 3469, 6419), *50*		615 ___
1477S	027 Steam Freight Set (2026, 6466T, 6012, 6014, 6017), *51-52*		288 ___

SETS		Good	Exc
1479WS	027 Steam Freight Set (2056, 2046W, 6462, 6465, 6456, 6257), *52*		348
1481WS	027 Steam Freight Set (2035, 6466W, 3464, 3472, 6465, 6462, 6357), *51*		510
1483WS	027 Steam Freight Set (2056, 2046W, 3472, 6462, 6465, 3474, 6357), *52*		1010
1484WS	027 Steam Passenger Set (2056, 2046W, 2421, 2422, 2423, 2429), *52*		1150
1485WS	027 Steam Freight Set (2025, 6466W, 6462, 6465, 6257), *52*		270
1500	027 Steam Freight Set (1130, 6066T, 6032, 6034, 6037), *53*		190
1500	027 Steam Freight Set (1130, 1130T, 6032, 6034, 6037), *54*		133
1501S	027 Steam Freight Set (2026, 6066T, 6032, 6035, 6037), *53*		250
1502WS	027 Steam Passenger Set (2055, 2046W, 2421, 2422, 2423), *53*		750
1503WS	027 Steam Freight Set (2055, 6026W, 6462, 6465, 6456, 6257), *53-54*		597
1505WS	027 Steam Freight Set (2046, 2046W, 6462, 6464-1, 6415, 6357)		430
1507WS	027 Steam Freight Set, *53* (2046, 2046W, 6415, 6462, 3472, 6468, 6357), *53*		450
1509WS	027 Steam Freight Set (2046, 2046W, 6456, 3520, 3469, 6460, 6419), *53*		500
1511S	027 Steam Freight Set (2037, 6066T, 6032, 3474, 6035, 6037), *53*		250
1513S	027 Steam Freight Set (2037, 6026T, 6012, 6014, 6015, 6017), *54-55*		311
1515WS	027 Steam Freight Set (2065, 2046W, 6462, 6415, 6464-25, 6456-25, 6357), *54*		434
1516WS	027 Passenger Set (2065, 2046W, 2434, 2432, 2436), *54*		650
1517W	027 Diesel Freight Set (2245P/C AB, 6464-225, 6561, 6462-25, 6427), *54*		1250
1519WS	027 Steam Freight Set (2065, 6026W, 6356, 6462-75, 3482, 3461-25, 6427), *54*		615
1520W	027 Texas Special Passenger Set (2245P/C AB, 2432, 2435, 2436), *54*		1700
1521WS	027 Steam Work Train Set (2065, 2046W, 3620, 6561, 6460, 3562, 6419), *54*		758
1523	027 Diesel Work Train Set (6250, 6511, 6456-25, 6460-25, 6419-25), *54*		615
1525	027 Diesel Freight Set (600, 6111, 6014, 6017), *55*		245
1527	027 Steam Work Train Set (1615, 1615T, 6462-125, 6560, 6119), *55*		388
1529	027 PRR Diesel Freight Set (2028, 6311, 6436, 6257), *55*		660
1531W	027 Diesel Freight Set (2328, 6462-125, 6465, 6456 or 6456-25, 6257), *55*		637
1533WS	027 Steam Freight Set (2055, 6026W, 3562-50, 6436, 6465, 6357), *55*		465
1534W	027 Diesel Passenger Set (2328, 2432, 2434, 2436), *55*		1000
1535W	027 Diesel Freight Set (2243P/2243C AB, 6462-125, 6436, 6464-50 or 6468X, 6257), *55*		1650
1536W	027 Texas Special Passenger Set (2245P/C AB, two 2432, 2436), *55*		1800
1537WS	027 Steam Freight Set (2065, 6026W, 3469, 6464-275, 3562-50, 6357), *55*		508
1538WS	027 Steam Passenger Set (2065, 2046W, 2432, 2434, 2435, 2436), *55*		900

SETS		Good	Exc
1539W	027 Santa Fe Diesel Freight Set (2243P/C AB, 3620, 6446, 6561, 6560, 6419), *55*		850 ___
1541WS	027 Steam Freight Set (2065, 2046W, 3482, 6415, 3461-25, 3494-1, 6427), *55*		600 ___
1542	027 Electric Freight Set (520, 6014, 6012, 6017), *56*		218 ___
1543	027 Diesel Freight Set (627, 6121, 6112, 6017), *56*		236 ___
1545	027 Diesel Freight Set (628, 6424, 6014, 6025, 6257), *56*		265 ___
1547S	027 Steam Freight Set (2018, 6026T, 6121, 6112, 6014, 6257), *56*		198 ___
1549	027 Steam Work Train Set (1615, 1615T, 6262, 6560, 6119-25), *56*		980 ___
1551W	027 Diesel Freight Set (621, 6362, 6425, 6562-25, 6257), *56*		566 ___
1552	027 Diesel Passenger Set (629, 2432, 2434, 2436), *56*		840 ___
1553W	027 MILW Diesel Freight Set (2338, 6430, 6462-125, 6464-425, 6346, 6257), *56*		608 ___
1555WS	027 Steam Freight Set (2018, 6026W, 3361, 6464-400, 6462-125, 6257), *56*		280 ___
1557W	027 Diesel Work Train Set (621, 6436, 6511, 3620, 6560, 6119-25), *56*		445 ___
1559W	027 MILW Diesel Freight Set (2338, 6414, 3562-50, 6362, 3494-275, 6357), *56*		800 ___
1561WS	027 Steam Freight Set (2065, 6026W, 3424, 6262, 6562-25, 6430, 6257), *56*		733 ___
1562W	027 Diesel Passenger Set (2328, two 2442, 2444, 2446), *56*		2178 ___
1563W	027 Wabash Diesel Freight Set (2240P/C AB, 6467, 3562-50, 6414, 3620, 6357), *56*		1570 ___
1565WS	027 Steam Freight Set (2065, 6026W, 3662, 3650, 6414, 6346, 6357), *56*		535 ___
1567W	027 Santa Fe Diesel Freight Set (2243P/C AB, 3356, 3424, 6430, 6672, 6357), *56*		1200 ___
1569	027 UP Diesel Freight Set (202, 6014, 6111, 6112, 6017), *57*		220 ___
1571	027 LV Diesel Freight Set (625, 6424, 6476, 6121, 6112, 6017), *57*		400 ___
1573	027 Steam Freight Set (250, 250T, 6112, 6025, 6476, 6464-425, 6017), *57*		195 ___
1575	027 MP Diesel Freight Set (205P/T AA, 6121, 6112, 6111, 6560-25, 6119-100), *57*		320 ___
1577S	027 Steam Freight Set (2018, 1130T, 6014, 6121, 6464-475, 6111, 6112, 6017), *57*		235 ___
1578S	027 Steam Passenger Set (2018, 1130T, 2432, 2434, 2436), *57*		555 ___
1579S	027 Steam Freight Set (2037, 1130T, 6476, 6121, 6468-25, 6111, 6112, 6025, 6017), *57*		260 ___
1581	027 Jersey Central Diesel Freight Set (611, 6464-650, 6424, 6024, 6025, 6476, 6560-25, 6119-100), *57*		495 ___
1583WS	027 Steam Freight Set (2037, 6026W, 6482, 6112, 6646, 6121, 6476, 6017), *57*		260 ___
1585W	027 Seaboard Diesel Freight Set (602, 6014, 6111, 6464-525, 6025, 6121, 6112, 6476, 6024, 6017), *57*		493
1586	027 Santa Fe Diesel Passenger Set (204P/T AA, two 2432, 2436), *57*		670 ___

SETS		Good	Exc
___ **1587S**	O27 Steam Freight Set (Girls Set) (2037-500, 1130T-500, 6462-500, 6464-515, 6436-500, 6464-510, 6427-500), *57-58*		3731 _
___ **1589WS**	O27 Steam Freight Set (2037, 6026W, 6424, 6464-450, 6025, 6024, 6111, 6112, 6017), *57*		500 _
___ **1590**	O27 Steam Freight Set (249, 250T, 6014, 6151, 6112, 6017), *58*		384 _
___ **1591**	O27 Military Set (212, 6803, 6809, 6807, 6017-50), 58		2260 _
___ **1593**	O27 UP Diesel Work Set (613, 6476, 6818, 6660, 6112, 6119-100), *58*		590 _
___ **1595**	O27 Military Set (1625, 1625T, 6804, 6806, 6808, 6017-85), *58*		2050 _
___ **1597S**	O27 Steam Freight Set (2018, 1130T, 6014, 6818, 6476, 6025, 6112, 6017), *58*		355 _
___ **1599**	O27 Texas Special Freight Set (210P/T AA, 6801, 6014, 6424, 6112, 6465, 6017), *58*		430 _
___ **1600**	O27 Burlington Diesel Passenger Set (216, 6572, 2432, 2436), *58*		750 _
___ **1601W**	O27 Wabash Diesel Freight Set (2337, 6800, 6464-425, 6801, 6810, 6017), *58*		766 _
___ **1603WS**	O27 Steam Freight Set (2037, 6026W, 6424, 6014, 6818, 6112, 6017), *58*		340 _
___ **1605W**	O27 Santa Fe Diesel Freight Set (208P/T AA, 6800, 6464-425, 6801, 6477, 6802, 6017), *58*		1015 _
___ **1607WS**	O27 Steam Work Train Set (2037, 6026W, 6465, 6818, 6464-425, 6660, 6112, 6119-100), *58*		500 _
___ **1608W**	O27 NH Diesel Passenger Set (209P/T AA, two 2432, 2434, 2436), *58*		1865 _
___ **1609**	O27 Steam Freight Set (246, 1130T, 6162-25, 6476, 6057), *59-60*		135 _
___ **1611**	O27 Alaska Diesel Freight Set (614, 6825, 6162-60, 6465, 6027), *59*		487 _
___ **1612**	O27 General Set (1862, 1862T, 1866, 1865), *59-60*		368 _
___ **1613S**	O27 B&O Steam Freight Set (247, 247T, 6826, 6819, 6821, 6017), *59*		345 _
___ **1615**	O27 B&M Diesel Freight Set (217P/C AB, 6800, 6464-475, 6812, 6825, 6017-100), *59*		520 _
___ **1617S**	O27 Steam Work Train Set (2018, 1130T, 6816, 6536, 6812, 6670, 6119-100), *59*		800 _
___ **1619W**	O27 Santa Fe Diesel Freight Set (218P/T AA, 6819, 6802, 6801, 6519, 6017-185), *59*		450 _
___ **1621WS**	O27 Steam Freight Set (2037, 6026W, 6825, 6519, 6062, 6464-475, 6017), *59*		520 _
___ **1623W**	O27 NP Diesel Freight Set (2349, 3512, 3435, 6424, 6062, 6017), *59*		1600 _
___ **1625WS**	O27 Steam Freight Set (2037, 6026W, 6636, 3512, 6470, 6650, 6017), *59*		563 _
___ **1626W**	O27 Santa Fe Diesel Passenger Set (208P/T AA, 3428, two 2412, 2416), *59*		875 _
___ **1627S**	O27 Steam Freight Set (244, 244T, 6062, 6825, 6017), *60*		190 _
___ **1629**	O27 C&O Diesel Freight Set (225, 6650, 6470, 6819, 6219), *60*		345 _
___ **1631WS**	O27 Steam Freight Set (243, 243W, 6519, 6812, 6465, 6017), *60*		275 _
___ **1633**	O27 U.S. Navy Diesel Freight Set (224P/C AB, 6544, 6830, 6820, 6017-200), *60*		1240 _
___ **1635WS**	O27 Steam Freight Set (2037, 6026W or 243W, 6361, 6826, 6636, 6821, 6017), *60*		400 _

SETS		Good	Exc
1637W	027 Santa Fe Diesel Freight Set (218P/T AA, 6475, 6175, 6464-475, 6801 or 6424-110, 6017-185), *60*		560 ___
1639WS	027 Steam Freight Set (2037, 6026W or 243W, 6816, 6817, 6812, 6530, 6560, 6119-100), *60*		1250 ___
1640W	027 Santa Fe Diesel Passenger Set (218P/T AA, 3428, two 2412, 2416, 1640-100), *60*		750 ___
1641	027 Steam Freight Set (246, 244T, 3362, 6162, 6057), *61*		175 ___
1642	027 Steam Freight Set (244, 1130T, 3376, 6405, 6119), *61*		225 ___
1643	027 C&O Diesel Freight Set (230, 3509, 6050, 6175, 6058), *61*		328 ___
1644	027 General Set (1862, 1862T, 3370, 1866, 1865), *61*		425 ___
1645	027 Diesel Freight Set (229, 3410, 6465-110, 6825, 6059), *61*		250 ___
1646	027 Steam Freight Set (233, 233W, 6162, 6343, 6476, 6017), *61*		325 ___
1647	027 U.S. Marines Military Set (45, 3665, 3519, 6830, 6448, 6814), *61*		1055 ___
1648	027 Steam Freight Set (2037, 233W, 6062, 6465-110, 6519, 6476, 6017), *61*		366 ___
1649	027 Santa Fe Diesel Freight Set (218P/C AB, 6343, 6445, 6475, 6405, 6017), *61*		538 ___
1650	027 Steam Military Set (2037, 233W, 6544, 6470, 3330, 3419, 6017), *61*		537 ___
1651	027 Santa Fe Diesel Passenger Set, *61* (218P/T or 220T AA, two 2412, 2414, 2416)		671 ___
1800	General Gift Pack, *59-60* (1862, 1862T, 1865, 1866, 1877, storybook)		437 ___
1805	027 Military Set (Land-Sea and Air Gift Pack), *60* (45, 3429, 3820, 6640, 6824)		1795 ___
1809	Western Gift Pack (244, 1130T, 3370, 3376, 1877, 6017), *61*		300 ___
1810	Space Age Gift Pack (231, 3665, 3519, 3820, 6017), *61*		1165 ___
2100	Steam Passenger Set (224, 2466T, two 2442, 2443), *46*		550 ___
2100W	Steam Passenger Set (224, 2466W, two 2442, 2443), *46*		640 ___
2101	Steam Freight Set (224, 2466T, 2555, 2452, 2457), *46*		350 ___
2101W	Steam Freight Set (224, 2466W, 2555, 2452, 2457), *46*		395 ___
2103W	Steam Freight Set (224, 2466W, 2458, 3559, 2555, 2457), *46*		467 ___
2105WS	Steam Freight Set (671, 2466W, 2555, 2454, 2457), *46*		464 ___
2110WS	Steam Passenger Set (671, 2466W, three 2625), *46*		1875 ___
2111WS	Steam Freight Set (671, 2466W, 3459, 2411, 2460, 2420), *46*		895 ___
2113WS	Steam Freight Set (726, 2426W, 2855, 3854, 2857), *46*		2093 ___
2114WS	Steam Passenger Set (726, 2426W, three 2625), *46*		2500 ___
2115WS	Steam Work Train Set (726, 2426W, 2458, 3451, 2460, 2420), *46*		1325 ___
2120S	Steam Passenger Set (675, 2466T, two 2442, 2443), *47*		500 ___
2120WS	Steam Passenger Set (675, 2466WX, two 2442, 2443), *47*		500 ___
2121S	Steam Freight Set (675, 2466T, 2555, 2452, 2457), *47*		400 ___
2121WS	Steam Freight Set (675, 2466WX, 2555, 2452, 2457), *47*		405 ___
2123WS	Steam Freight Set (675, 2466WX, 2458, 3559, 2555, 2457), *47*		450 ___

SETS		Good	Exc
___ 2124W	PRR Electric Passenger Set (2332 GG-1 green, 2625 Irvington, 2625 Madison, 2625 Manhattan), *47*		3200
___ 2125WS	Steam Freight Set (671, 671W, 2411, 2454, 2452, 2457), *47*		550
___ 2126WS	Steam Passenger Set, *47* (671, 671W, 2625 Irvington, 2625 Madison, 2625 Manhattan)		1950
___ 2127WS	Steam Work Train Set (671, 671W, 3459, 2461, 2460, 2420), *47*		670
___ 2129WS	Steam Freight Set (726, 2426W, 3854, 2411, 2855, 2457), *47*		2250
___ 2131WS	Steam Work Train Set (726, 2426W, 3462, 3451, 2460, 2420), *47*		1200
___ 2133W	Diesel Freight Set (2333P/T AA, 2458, 3459, 2555, 2357), *48*		1350
___ 2135WS	Steam Freight Set (675, 2466WX, 2456, 2411, 2357), *48*		403
___ 2135WS	Steam Freight Set (675, 6466WX, 6456, 6411, 6457), *49*		559
___ 2136WS	Steam Passenger Set (675, 2466WX, two 2442, 2443), *48*		660
___ 2136WS	Steam Passenger Set (675, 6466WX, two 6442, 6443), *49*		802
___ 2137WS	Steam Freight Set (675, 2466WX, 2458, 3459, 2456, 2357), *48*		720
___ 2139W	PRR Electric Freight Set (2332, 6456, 3464, 3461, 6457), *49*		1360
___ 2139W	PRR Electric Freight Set (2332, 2458, 3451, 2456, 2357), *48*		1425
___ 2140WS	Steam Passenger Set (671, 2671W, 2400, 2401, 2402), *48-49*		1600
___ 2141WS	Steam Freight Set (671, 2671W, 3451, 3462, 2456, 2357), *48*		388
___ 2143WS	Steam Work Train Set (671, 2671W, 3459, 2461, 2460, 2420), *48*		795
___ 2144W	PRR Electric Passenger Set (2332, 2625, 2627, 2628), *48-49*		2065
___ 2145WS	Steam Freight Set (726, 2426W, 3462, 2411, 2460, 2357), *48*		815
___ 2146WS	Steam Passenger Set (726, 2426W, 2625, 2627, 2628), *48-49*		2000
___ 2147WS	Steam Freight Set (675, 6466WX, 3472, 6465, 3469, 6457), *49*		388
___ 2148WS	Hudson Passenger Set (773, 2426W, 2625, 2627, 2628), *50*		5550
___ 2149B	Diesel Work Train Set (622, 6520, 3469, 2460, 6419), *49*		690
___ 2150WS	Steam Passenger Set (681, 2671W, 2421, 2422, 2423), *50*		1000
___ 2151W	Diesel Freight Set, *49* (2333P/T AA, 3464, 6555, 3469, 6520, 6457)		1078
___ 2153WS	Steam Work Train Set, *49* (671, 2671W, 3469, 6520, 2460, 6419)		1010
___ 2155WS	Steam Freight Set (726, 2426W, 6411, 3656, 2460, 6457), *49*		998
___ 2159W	Electric Freight Set (2330, 3464, 6462, 3461, 6456, 6457), *50*		3000
___ 2161W	Santa Fe Diesel Freight Set (2343P/T AA, 3469, 3464, 3461, 6520, 6457), *50*		1520
___ 2163WS	Steam Freight Set (736, 2671WX, 6472, 6462, 6555, 6457), *50*		550
___ 2163WS	Steam Freight Set (736, 2671WX, 6472, 6462, 6465, 6457), *51*		644
___ 2165WS	Steam Freight Set (736, 2671WX, 3472, 6456, 3461, 6457), *50*		705
___ 2167WS	Steam Freight Set (681, 2671W, 6462, 3464, 6457), *50-51*		618
___ 2169WS	Hudson Freight Set (773, 2426W, 3656, 6456, 3469, 6411, 6457), *50*		2810
___ 2171W	NYC Diesel Freight Set (2344P/T AA, 3469, 3464, 3461, 6520, 6457), *50*		1100
___ 2173WS	Steam Freight Set (681, 2671W, 3472, 6555, 3469, 6457), *50*		595
___ 2173WS	Steam Freight Set (681, 2671W, 3472, 6465, 3469, 6457), *51*		523

SETS		Good	Exc
2175W	Santa Fe Diesel Freight Set (2343P/T AA, 6456, 3464, 6555, 6462, 6457), *50*	244	897 ___
2175W	Santa Fe Diesel Freight Set (2343 AA, 6456, 3464, 6465, 6462, 6457), *51*	163	935 ___
2177WS	Steam Freight Set (675, 2046W, 6462, 6465, 6457), *52*		309 ___
2179WS	Steam Freight Set (671, 2046WX, 3464, 6465, 6462, 6457), *52*		508 ___
2183WS	Steam Freight Set (726, 2046W, 3464, 6462, 6465, 6457), *52*		900 ___
2185W	NYC Diesel Freight Set (2344P/T AA, 6456, 3464, 6555, 6462, 6457), *50*		960 ___
2185W	NYC Diesel Freight Set (2344 AA, 6456, 3464, 6465, 6462, 6457), *51*		1018 ___
2187WS	Steam Freight Set (671, 2046WX, 6462, 3472, 3469, 6456, 6457), *52*		650 ___
2189WS	Steam Freight Set (726, 2046W, 3520, 3656, 6462, 3461, 6457), *52*		580 ___
2190W	Santa Fe Diesel Passenger Set (2343P/T AA, 2531, 2532, 2533, 2534), *52*		1900 ___
2190W	Santa Fe Diesel Passenger Set (2353P/T AA, 2531, 2533, 2532, 2534), *53*		1900 ___
2191W	Santa Fe Diesel Freight Set (2343P/C/T ABA, 6462, 6656, 6456, 6457), *52*		1355 ___
2193W	NYC Diesel Freight Set (2344P/C/T ABA, 6462, 6656, 6456, 6457), *52*		1040 ___
2201WS	Steam Freight Set (685, 6026W, 6462, 6464-50, 6465, 6357), *53*		478 ___
2203WS	Steam Freight Set (681, 2046WX, 6415, 3520, 6464-25, 6417), *53*		637 ___
2205WS	Steam Freight Set (736, 2046W, 3484, 6415, 6468, 6456, 6417), *53*		586 ___
2207W	Santa Fe Diesel Freight Set (2353P/C/T ABA, 6462, 3484, 6415, 6417), *53*		910 ___
2209W	NYC Diesel Freight Set (2354P/C/T ABA, 6462, 3484, 6415, 6417), *53*		1650 ___
2211WS	Steam Freight Set (681, 2046WX, 3656, 6464-75, 3461, 6417), *53*		740 ___
2213WS	Steam Freight Set (736, 2046W, 3461, 3520, 3469, 6460, 6419), *53*		697 ___
2217WS	Steam Freight Set (682, 2046WX, 6464-175, 3562-25, 6356, 6417), *54*		850 ___
2219W	Diesel Freight Set (2321, 6456-25, 6464-50, 6462-25, 6415, 6417), *54*		1535 ___
2221WS	Steam Freight Set (646, 2046W, 6468, 3620, 3469, 6456-25, 6417-25), *54*		500 ___
2222WS	Steam Passenger Set (646, 2046W, 2530, 2531, 2532), *54*		1800 ___
2223W	Diesel Freight Set (2321, 6464-100, 3461-25, 3482, 6462-125, 6417-50), *54*		3063 ___
2225WS	Steam Work Train Set (736, 2046W, 3461-25, 3562 or 3562-25, 3620, 6460, 6419), *54*		1020 ___
2227W	Santa Fe Diesel Freight Set (2353P/T AA, 3562-25, 6356, 6456-75, 6468, 6417-25), *54*		1725 ___
2229W	NYC Freight Set (2354P/T AA, 3562-25, 6356, 6456-75, 6468, 6417-25), *54*		1300 ___
2231W	Southern Diesel Freight Set (2356P/C/T ABA, 6511, 6561, 3482, 6415, 6417-25), *54*		3048 ___
2234W	Santa Fe Diesel Passenger Set (2353P/T AA, 2530, 2531, 2532, 2533), *54*		932 ___

SETS		Good	Exc
____ 2235W	MILW Diesel Freight Set (2338, 6436-25, 6362, 6560, 6419), *55*		733
____ 2237WS	Steam Freight Set (665, 6026W, 3562-50, 6464-275, 6415, 6417), *55*		393
____ 2239W	Illinois Central Diesel Freight Set (2363P/C AB, 6672, 6464-125, 6414, 6517), *55*		1700
____ 2241WS	Steam Freight Set (646, 2046W, 3359, 6446, 3620, 6417), *55*		615
____ 2243W	Diesel Freight Set (2321, 3662, 6511, 6462-125, 6464-300, 6417), *55*		1375
2244W	Wabash Diesel Passenger Set (2367P/C AB, 2530, 2531, 2533), *55*		3650
2245WS	Steam Freight Set (682, 2046WX, 3562-25, 6436-25, 6561, 6560, 6419), *55*		1150
2247W	Wabash Diesel Freight Set (2367P/C AB, 6462-125, 3662, 6464-150, 3361, 6517), *55*		2348
____ 2249WS	Steam Freight Set (736, 2046W, 6464-275, 6414, 3359, 3562-50, 6517), *55*		784
____ 2251W	Diesel Freight Set (2331, 6464-275, 3562-50, 6414, 3359, 6517), *55*		2000
____ 2253W	PRR Electric Freight Set (2340-25, 3361, 6464-300, 3620, 6414, 6417), *55*		2700
____ 2254W	PRR Electric Passenger Set (2340, 2541, 2542, 2543, 2544), *55*		5500
____ 2255W	Diesel Work Train Set (601, 3424, 6362, 6560, 6119-25), *56*		843
____ 2257WS	Steam Freight Set (665, 2046W, 3361, 6346, 6467, 6462-125, 6427), *56*		500
____ 2259W	NH Electric Freight Set (2350, 6464-425, 6430, 3650, 6511, 6427), *56*		775
____ 2261WS	Steam Freight Set (646, 2046W, 3562-50, 6414, 6436-25, 6376, 6417), *56*		570
____ 2263W	NH Electric Freight Set (2350, 3359, 6468-25, 6414, 3662, 6517), *56*		1000
____ 2265WS	Steam Freight Set (736, 2046W, 3620, 3424, 6430, 6467, 6517), *56*		560
____ 2267W	Diesel Freight Set (2331, 3562-50, 3359, 3361, 6560, 6419-50), *56*		2150
____ 2269W	B&O Diesel Freight Set (2368P/C AB, 3356, 6518, 6315, 3361, 6517), *56*		3200
____ 2270W	Jersey Central Diesel Passenger Set (2341, 2531, 2532, 2533), *56*		5730
____ 2271W	PRR Electric Freight Set (2360-25, 3424, 3662, 6414, 6418, 6417), *56*		2200
____ 2273W	MILW Diesel Freight Set (2378P/C AB, 342, 6342, 3562-50, 3662, 3359, 6517), *56*		3500
____ 2274W	PRR Electric Passenger Set (2360, 2541, 2542, 2543, 2544), *56*		2650
____ 2275W	Wabash Diesel Freight Set (2339, 3444, 6464-475, 6425, 6427), *57*		793
____ 2276W	Budd RDC Set (404, two 2559), *57*		2035
____ 2277WS	Steam Work Train Set (665, 2046W, 6446-25, 3650, 6560-25, 6119-75), *57*		585
____ 2279W	NH Electric Freight Set (2350, 3424, 6464-425, 6424, 6477, 6427), *57*		890
____ 2281W	Santa Fe Diesel Freight Set (2243P/C AB, 6464-150, 3361, 3562-75, 6560-25, 6119-75), *57*		1050
____ 2283WS	Steam Freight Set (646, 2046W, 3424, 3361, 6464-525, 6562-50, 6357), *57*		750
____ 2285W	Diesel Freight Set (2331, 6418, 6414, 6425, 3662, 6517), *57*		2000

SETS		Good	Exc
2287W	MILW Electric Freight Set (2351, 342, 6342, 6464-500, 3650, 6315, 6427), *57*	2000	___
2289WS	Super O Steam Freight Set (736, 2046W, 3359, 3494-275, 3361, 6430, 6427); *57*	1113	___
2291W	Super O Rio Grande Diesel Freight Set (2379P/C AB, 3562-75, 3530, 3444, 6464-525, 6657), *57*	2135	___
2292WS	Super O Steam Passenger Set (646, 2046W, 2530, 2531, 2532, 2533), *57*	2000	___
2293W	Super O PRR Electric Freight Set (2360, 3662, 3650, 6414, 6518, 6417), *57*	2400	___
2295WS	Super O Steam Freight Set (746, 746W, 342, 6342, 3530, 3361, 6560-25, 6419-100), *57*	2290	___
2296W	Super O CP Diesel Passenger Set (2373P/T AA, 2551, 2552, 2553, 2554), *57*	4275	___
2297WS	Super O Steam Freight Set (746, 746W, 264, 6264, 3356, 3662, 345, 6342, 6517), *57*	2300	___
2501W	Super O Diesel Work Train Set (2348, 6464-525, 6802, 6560-25, 6119-100), *58*	680	___
2502W	Super O Budd RDC Set (400, 2550, 2559), *58*	2000	___
2503WS	Super O Steam Freight Set (665, 2046W, 3361, 6434, 6801, 6536, 6357), *58*	580	___
2505W	Super O Electric Freight Set (2329, 6805, 6519, 6800, 6464-500, 6357), *58*	1400	___
2507W	Super O Diesel Freight Set (2242P/C AB, 3444, 6464-425, 6424, 6468-25, 6357), *58*	2000	___
2509WS	Super O Steam Freight Set (665, 2046W, 6414, 3650, 6464-475, 6805, 6357), *58*	927	___
2511W	Super O Electric Work Set (2352, 3562-75, 3424, 3361, 6560-25, 6119-100), *58*	1100	___
2513W	Super O Electric Freight Set (2329, 6556, 6425, 6414, 6434, 3359, 6427-60), *58*	3000	___
2515WS	Super O Steam Freight Set (646, 2046W, 3662, 6424, 3444, 6800, 6427), *58*	892	___
2517W	Super O Rio Grande Diesel Freight Set (2379P/C AB, 6519, 6805, 6434, 6800, 6657), *58*	2550	___
2518W	Super O PRR Electric Passenger Set (2352, 2531, 2533, 2534), *58*	1850	___
2519W	Super O Diesel Freight Set (2331, 6434, 3530, 6801, 6414, 6464-275, 6557), *58*	1900	___
2521WS	Super O Steam Freight Set (746, 746W, 6805, 3361, 6430, 3356, 6424, 6557), *58*	1828	___
2523W	Super O Santa Fe Diesel Freight Set (2383P/T AA, 264, 6264, 6434, 6800, 3662, 6517), *58*	1300	___
2525WS	Super O Steam Work Train Set (746, 746W, 342, 345, 6519, 6518, 6560-25, 6419-100), *58*	2300	___
2526W	Super O Santa Fe Diesel Passenger Set (2383P/T AA, 2530, 2531, two 2532), *58*	1775	___
2527	Super O Missile Launcher Set (44, 3419, 6844, 6823, 6814, 943), *59-60*	755	___

SETS		Good	Exc
____ 2528WS	Super O General Set (1872, 1872T, 1877, 1876, 1875W), *59-61*		635
____ 2529W	Super Electric Work Train Set (2329, 3512, 6819, 6812, 6560, 6119-25 or 6119-100), *59*		1300
____ 2531WS	Super O Steam Freight Set (637, 2046W, 3435, 6817, 6636, 6825, 6119-100), *59*		888
____ 2533W	Super O GN Electric Freight Set (2358, 6650, 6414, 3444, 6470, 6357), *59*		1910
____ 2535WS	Super O Steam Freight Set (665, 2046W, 3434, 6823, 3672, 6812, 6357), *59*		840
____ 2537W	Super O NH Diesel Freight Set (2242P/C AB, 3435, 3650, 6464-275, 6819, 6427), *59*		2500
____ 2539WS	Super O Steam Freight Set (665, 2046W, 3361, 6464-825, 3512, 6812, 6357, 464), *59*		1015
____ 2541W	Super O Santa Fe Diesel Freight Set (2383P/T AA, 3356, 3512, 6519, 6816, 6427), *59*		2400
____ 2543WS	Super O Steam Freight Set (736, 2046W, 264, 6264, 3435, 6823, 6434, 6812, 6557), *59*		1590
____ 2544W	Super O Santa Fe Diesel Passenger Set (2383P/T AA, 2530, 2561, 2562, 2563), *59-60*		1860
____ 2545WS	Super O Military Set (746, 746W, 175, 6175, 6470, 3419, 6650, 3540, 6517), *59*		3000
____ 2547WS	Super O Steam Freight Set (637, 2046W, 3330, 6475, 6361, 6357), *60*		575
____ 2549W	Super O Military Set (2349, 3540, 6470, 6819, 6650, 3535), *60*		1160
____ 2551W	Super O GN Electric Freight Set (2358, 6828, 3512, 6827, 6736, 6812, 6427), *60*		2300
____ 2553WS	Super O Steam Freight Set (736, 2046W, 3830, 3435, 3419, 3672, 6357), *60*		1615
____ 2555W	Super O Santa Fe Freight Set with matching HO Set (2383P/T AA, 3434, 3366, 6414, 6464-900, 6357-50), *60*		10000
____ 2570	Super O Santa Fe Work Train Set (616, 6822, 6828, 6812, 6736, 6130), *61*		800
____ 2571	Super O Steam Freight Set (637, 736W, 3419, 6445, 6361, 6119-100), *61*		520
____ 2572	Super O B&M Diesel Freight Set (2359, 6544, 3830, 6448, 3519, 3535), *61*		813
____ 2573	Super O Steam Freight Set (736, 736W, 3545, 6416, 6475, 6440, 6357), *61*		1400
____ 2574	Super O Santa Fe Diesel Freight Set (2383P/T AA, 3665, 3419, 3830, 448, 6448, 6437), *61*		1500
____ 2575	Super O PRR Electric Freight Set (2360, 6530, 6828, 6464-900, 6827, 6736, 6560, 6437), *61*		2500
____ 2576	Super O Santa Fe Diesel Passenger Set (2383P/T AA, 2561, two 2562, 2563), *61*		3030
____ 4109WS	Electronic Control Set (671R, 4424W, 4452, 4454, 5459, 4457), *46*		1493
____ 4110WS	Electronic Control Set (671R, 4671W, 4452, 4454, 5459, 4357, 151, 97), *48-49*		2500
____ 11011	O27 Diesel Freight Set (222, 3510, 6076, 6120), *62*		286

SETS		Good	Exc
11201	027 Steam Freight Set (242, 1060T, 6042-75, 6502, 6047), *62*		125 ___
11212	027 Santa Fe Diesel Freight Set (633, 3349, 6825, 6057), *62*		375 ___
11222	027 Steam Freight Set (236, 1050T, 3357, 6343, 6119-100), *62*		243 ___
11232	027 NH Diesel Freight Set (232, 3410, 6062, 6413, 6057-50), *62*		535 ___
11242	027 Steam Freight Set (233, 233W, 6465-100, 6476, 6162, 6017), *62*		192 ___
11252	027 Texas Special Space Set 211P/T AA, 3509, 6448, 3349, 6463, 6057), *62*		500 ___
11268	027 C&O Diesel Freight Set (2365, 3619, 3470, 3349, 6501, 6017), *62*		1425 ___
11278	027 Steam Freight Set (2037, 233W, 6473, 6162, 6050-110, 6825, 6017), *62*		260 ___
11288	027 Space Set (229P/C AB, 3413, 6512, 6413, 6463, 6059), *62*		1215 ___
11298	027 Steam Freight Set (2037, 233W, 6544, 3419, 6448, 3330, 6017), *62*		500 ___
11308	027 Santa Fe Diesel Passenger Set (218P/T AA, two 2412, 2414, 2416), *62*		730 ___
11311	027 Steam Freight Set (1062, 1061T, 6409-25, 6076-100, 6167-25), *63*		113 ___
11321	027 Rio Grande Diesel Freight Set (221, 3309, 6076-75, 6042-75, 6167-50), *63*		350 ___
11331	027 Steam Freight Set (242, 1060T, 6473, 6476-25, 6142, 6059-50), *63*		100 ___
11341	027 Santa Fe Diesel Freight Set (634, 3410, 6407, 6014-325, 6463, 6059-50), *63*		950 ___
11351	027 Steam Freight Set (237, 1060T, 6050-100, 6465-150, 6408, 6162, 6119-110), *63*		190 ___
11361	027 Texas Special Space Set (211P/T AA, 3665-100, 3413-150, 6470, 6413, 6257-100), *63*		750 ___
11375	027 Steam Freight Set (238, 234W, 6822-50, 6465-150, 6414-150, 6476-75, 6162, 6257-100), *63*		700 ___
11385	027 Santa Fe Space Set (223P/218C AB, 3619-100, 3470-100, 3349-100, 3830-75, 6407, 6257-100 or 6017-235), *63*		2000 ___
11395	027 Steam Freight Set (2037, 233W or 234W, 6464-725, 6469-50, 6536, 6440-50, 6560-50, 6119-100), *63*		600 ___
11405	027 Santa Fe Diesel Passenger Set (218P/T AA, two 2412, 2414, 2416), *63*		750 ___
11420	027 Steam Freight Set (1061, 1061T, 6042-250, 6167-25), *64*		200 ___
11430	027 Steam Freight (1062, 1061T, 6176, 6142, 6167-125), *64*		151 ___
11440	027 Rio Grande Diesel Freight Set (221, 3309, 6176-50, 6142-125, 6167-100), *64*		215 ___
11450	027 Steam Freight Set (242, 1060T, 6473, 6142-75, 6176-50, 6059-50), *64*		195 ___
11460	027 Steam Freight Set (238, 234W, 6014-335, 6465-150, 6142-100, 6176-75, 6119-100), *64*		150 ___
11470	027 Steam Freight Set (237, 1060T, 6014-335, 6465-150, 6142-100, 6176-75, 6119-100), *64*		189 ___
11480	027 Diesel Freight Set (213P/T AA, 6473, 6176-50, 6142-150, 6014-335, 6257-100 or 6059), *64*		619 ___

SETS		Good	Exc
___ **11490**	027 Diesel Passenger Set (212P/T AA, 2404, 2405, 2406), *64-65*		360
___ **11500**	027 Steam Freight Set (2029, 234W, 6465-150, 6402-50, 6176-75, 6014-335, 6257-100 or 6059), *64*		438
___ **11500**	027 Steam Freight Set (2029, 234W, 6465-150, 6402-50, 6076, 6014-335, 6257-100 or 6059), *65*		275
___ **11500**	027 Steam Freight Set (2029, 234W, 6465-150, 6402-50, 6176-75, 6014-335, 6059), *66*		275
___ **11510**	027 Steam Freight Set (2029, 1060T, 6465-150, 6402-50, 6176-75, 6014-335, 6257-100 or 6059), *64*		300
___ **11520**	027 Steam Freight Set (242, 1062T, 6176, 3362/64, 6142, 6059), *65-66*		165
___ **11530**	027 Santa Fe Diesel Freight (634, 6014, 6142, 6402, 6130), *65-66*		296
___ **11540**	027 Steam Freight Set (239, 242T, 6473, 6465, 6176, 6119-100), *65-66*		180
___ **11550**	027 Steam Freight Set (239, 234W, 6473, 6465, 6176, 6119), *65-66*		189
___ **11560**	027 Texas Special Freight Set (211P/T AA, 6473, 6076, 6142, 6465, 6059), *65-66*		355
___ **11590**	027 Santa Fe Diesel Passenger Set (212P/T AA, 2408, 2409, 2410), *66*		646
___ **11600**	027 Steam Freight Set (2029, 234W, 6014, 6476, 6315, 6560, 6130), *68*		1280
___ **11710**	027 Steam Freight Set (1061, 1061T or 1062T, 6402, 6142, 6059), *69*		178
___ **11720**	Diesel Freight Set (2024, 6142, 6402, 6176, 6057), *69*		240
___ **11730**	027 UP Diesel Freight Set (645, 6402, 6014-85, 6176, 6142, 6167-85), *69*		800
___ **11740**	027 RI Diesel Freight Set (2041P/T AA, 6315, 6142, 6014-410, 6476, 6057), *69*		310
___ **11750**	027 Steam Freight Set (2029, 234T, 6014-85, 6476, 6473, 6315, 6130), *69*		360
___ **11760**	027 Steam Freight Set (2029, 234W, 6014-410, 6315, 6476, 3376, 6119), *69*		355
___ **12502**	Prairie-Rider Gift Pack (1862, 1862T, 3376, 1877 or 6473, 1866, 1865), *62*		600
___ **12512**	Enforcer Gift Pack (45, 3413, 3619, 3470, 3349, 6017), *62*		1100
___ **12700**	Steam Freight Set (736, 736W, 6464-725, 6162-100, 6414-75, 6476-125, 6437, no transformer), *64*		1000
___ **12710**	Steam Freight Set (736, 736W, 6464-725, 6162-100, 6414-75, 6476-125, 6437, LW transformer), *64-66*		1175
___ **12720**	Santa Fe Diesel Freight Set (2383P/T AA, 6464-725, 6162-100, 6414-75, 6476-125, 6437, no transformer), *64*		1500
___ **12730**	Santa Fe Diesel Freight Set (2383P/T AA, 6464-725, 6162-100, 6414-75, 6476-125, 6437, LW transformer), *64-66*		985
___ **12740**	Santa Fe Diesel Freight Set (2383P/T AA, 3662, 6361, 6436-110, 6315-60, 6464-525, 6822, 6437), *64*		1500
___ **12760**	Steam Freight Set (736, 736W, 3662, 6361, 6436-110, 6315-60, 6464-525, 6822, 6437), *64*		1100
___ **12780**	Santa Fe Diesel Passenger (2383P/T AA, 2521, 2522, two 2523), *64-66*		1855

SETS		Good	Exc
12800	B&M Diesel Freight Set (2346, 6428, 6436, 6464-475, 6415, 6017-100), *65-66*		574 ___
12820	Diesel Freight Set (2322, 3662, 6822, 6361, 6464-725, 6436, 6315, 6437), *65*		1525 ___
12840	Steam Freight Set (665, 736W, 6464-375, 6464-450, 6431, 6415, 6437), *66*		925 ___
12850	Diesel Freight Set, *66* (2322, 3662, 6822, 6361, 6464-725, 6436, 6315, 6437)		1700 ___
13008	Super O Steam Freight Set (637, 736W, 3349, 6448, 6501, 6119-100), *62*		500 ___
13018	Super O Santa Fe Diesel Freight Set (616, 6500, 6650, 3519, 6448, 6017-235), *62*		1200 ___
13028	Super O Space Set (2359, 3665, 3349, 3820, 3470, 6017-100), *62*		1000 ___
13036	Super O General Set (1872, 1872T, 6445, 3370, 1876, 1875W), *62*		980 ___
13048	Super O Steam Freight Set (736, 736W, 6822, 6414, 3362, 6440, 6437), *62*		720 ___
13058	Super O Space Set (2383P/T AA, 3619, 3413, 6512, 470, 6470, 6437), *62*		1600 ___
13068	Super O PRR Electric Freight Set (2360, 6464-725, 6828, 6416, 6827, 6530, 6475, 6437), *62*		3200 ___
13078	Super O PRR Electric Passenger Set (2360, 2521, two 2522, 2523), *62*		3500 ___
13088	Super O Santa Fe Diesel Passenger Set (2383P/T AA, 2521, two 2522, 2523), *62*		2500 ___
13098	Super O Steam Freight Set (637, 736W, 6469, 6464-900, 6414, 6446, 6447), *63*		2000 ___
13108	Super O Santa Fe Space Set (617, 3665, 3419, 6448, 3830, 3470, 6119-100), *63*		1000 ___
13118	Super O Steam Freight Set (736, 736W, 6446-60, 6827, 3362, 6315-60, 6560, 6429), *63*		1500 ___
13128	Super O Santa Fe Space Set (2383P/T AA, 3619, 3413, 6512, 448, 6448, 64337), *63*		1750 ___
13138	Super O PRR Electric Freight Set (2360, 6464-725, 6828, 6416, 6827, 6315-60, 6436-110, 6437), *63*		3800 ___
13148	Super O Santa Fe Diesel Passenger Set (2383P/T AA, 2521, 2522, two 2523), *63*		2500 ___
13150	Super O Hudson Steam Freight Set (773, 736W or 773W, 3434, 6361, 3662, 6415, 3356, 6436-110, 6437), *64*		2500 ___

ABBREVIATIONS

Descriptions

AAR	Association of American Railroads (truck type)
AEC	Atomic Energy Commission
AF	American Flyer
CC	Command Control
DD	Double-door
EMD	Electro-Motive Division
ETD	End-of-train device
FARR	Famous American Railroad Series
FF	Fallen Flag Series
FM	Fairbanks-Morse
GE	General Electric
LL	Lionel Lines
MOW	Maintenance-of-way
MU	Multiple unit (commuter cars)
O	Lionel gauge (1¼" between outside rails)
OO	Lionel gauge (¾" between outside rails)
PFE	Pacific Fruit Express
REA	Railway Express Agency
SSS	Service Station Special
std	Standard gauge (2 1/8" between outside rails)
std O	Standard O (scale length and dimension)
TMCC	TrainMaster Command Control
USMC	United States Marine Corps
1-D	One dome
2-D	Two dome
3-D	Three dome

Railroad names

ACL	Atlantic Coast Line	LV	Lehigh Valley
ATSF	Atchison, Topeka & Santa Fe	MEC	Maine Central
B&A	Boston & Albany	MILW	Milwaukee Road
BAR	Bangor & Aroostook	MKT	Missouri-Kansas-Texas (Katy)
B&LE	Bessemer & Lake Erie	MNS	Minnesota, Northfield &
B&M	Boston & Maine		Southern
BN	Burlington Northern	MP	Missouri Pacific
BNSF	Burlington Northern Santa Fe	M&StL	Minneapolis & St. Louis
B&O	Baltimore & Ohio	NdeM	Nacionales de Mexico
CB&Q	Chicago, Burlington & Quincy		Railway
CMStP&P	Chicago, Milwaukee, St. Paul	NH	New Haven
	& Pacific (Milwaukee Road)	NKP	Nickel Plate Road
CN	Canadian National	NOT&M	New Orleans, Texas & Mexico
CGW	Chicago Great Western	NP	Northern Pacific
CNJ	Central of New Jersey	NS	Norfolk Southern
C&NW	Chicago & North Western	N&W	Norfolk & Western
C&O	Chesapeake & Ohio	NWP	Northwestern Pacific
CP	Canadian Pacific	NYC	New York Central
CRI&P	Chicago, Rock Island &	NYO&W	New York, Ontario & Western
	Pacific (Rock Island)	NYNH&H	New York, New Haven &
C&S	Colorado Southern		Hartford (New Haven)
CUVA	Cuyahoga Valley Railway	OSL	Oregon Short Line
D&H	Delaware & Hudson	P&LE	Pittsburgh & Lake Erie
D&RGW	Denver & Rio Grande Western	PC	Penn Central
DT&I	Detroit, Toledo & Ironton	PRR	Pennsylvania Railroad
DM&IR	Duluth, Missabe & Iron	PMKY	Pittsburgh, McKeesport &
	Range		Youghiogheny
Erie-Lack.	Erie-Lackawanna	PTM	ST Rail System
FEC	Florida East Coast	RFP	Richmond, Fredericksburg &
FWD	Fort Worth & Denver		Potomac
FY&P	Franklin & Pittsylvania	SF	Santa Fe
GM&O	Gulf, Mobile & Ohio	SLSF	St. Louis-San Francisco
GN	Great Northern		(Frisco)
GN&W	Genesee & Wyoming	SP	Southern Pacific
GTW	Grand Trunk Western	SSW	St. Louis Southwestern
IC	Illinois Central		(Cotton Belt)
ICG	Illinois Central Gulf	T&P	Texas & Pacific
IGN	International-Great Northern	TP&W	Toledo, Peoria & Western
KCS	Kansas City Southern	UP	Union Pacific
L&N	Louisville & Nashville	WM	Western Maryland
LNE	Lehigh New England	WP	Western Pacific

NOTES

NOTES

Build Your Toy Train Library

Collectible Lionel Classics

In his new book, *Collectible Lionel Classics*, toy train expert, Roger Carp, provides detailed information on 100 popular postwar Lionel locomotives (steam, diesel, and electric), motorized units, rolling stock, and accessories. Whether you're an experienced collector or new to the hobby, this invaluable guide will be your go-to resource for historical information, product features, and buying tips. The book includes 100 color photos and an in-depth introduction of each product category.

10-8806 •$25.99

American Flyer Pocket Price Guide 1946-2021

Back with its 32nd edition, the *American Flyer Pocket Price Guide 1946-2021* is a customer favorite! This top-selling reference guide provides current market values for American Flyer S gauge trains and accessories manufactured by A.C. Gilbert and Lionel, as well as trains from contemporary manufacturers like American Models and MTH.

10-8621 •$15.99

Buy now from your local hobby shop!
Shop at
KalmbachHobbyStore.com

Kalmbach Media

P38226